W9-APU-110

MMPI–2

MMPI–2 A Practitioner's Guide

Edited by **James N. Butcher**

American Psychological Association
Washington, DC

Published by
American Psychological Association
750 First Street, NE
Washington, DC 20002
www.apa.org

To order
APA Order Department
P.O. Box 92984
Washington, DC 20090-2984
Tel: (800) 374-2721; Direct: (202) 336-5510
Fax: (202) 336-5502; TDD/TTY: (202) 336-6123
Online: www.apa.org/books/
E-mail: order@apa.org

In the U.K., Europe, Africa, and the Middle East, copies may be ordered from
American Psychological Association
3 Henrietta Street
Covent Garden, London
WC2E 8LU England

Typeset in Goudy by Shepherd, Inc., Dubuque, IA

Printer: Data Reproductions, Ann Arbor, MI
Cover Designer: Anne Masters, Washington, DC
Project Manager: Shepherd, Inc., Dubuque, IA

Library of Congress Cataloging-in-Publication Data

MMPI-2 : a practitioner's guide / edited by James N. Butcher.— 1st ed.
p. cm.
Includes bibliographical references and index.
1. Minnesota Multiphasic Personality Inventory. I. Butcher, James Neal, 1933–
II. American Psychological Association.
RC473.M5M65 2005
155.2'83—dc22

2005005198

British Library Cataloguing-in-Publication Data
A CIP record is available from the British Library.

Printed in the United States of America
First Edition

CONTENTS

CONTRIBUTORS

Paul A. Arbisi, University of Minnesota, Minneapolis VA Medical Center
Mera M. Atlis, University of California, San Francisco
Jason R. Bacchiochi, University of Toronto Centre for Addiction and Mental Health, Toronto, Ontario, Canada
R. Michael Bagby, University of Toronto Centre for Addiction and Mental Health, Toronto, Ontario, Canada
Alison S. Bury, University of Toronto Centre for Addiction and Mental Health, Toronto, Ontario, Canada
James N. Butcher, University of Minnesota, Minneapolis
Brenton Crowhurst, Rockyview General Hospital, Calgary, Alberta, Canada
Michael Cullen, University of Minnesota, Minneapolis
Jan J. L. Derksen, Radboud University Nijmegen, Nijmegen, the Netherlands; Free University of Brussels, Belgium
Stephen E. Finn, Center for Therapeutic Assessment, Austin, TX
Maria Garrido, University of Rhode Island, Kingston
Carlton S. Gass, VA Medical Center, Miami, FL
John R. Graham, Kent State University, Kent, OH
Roger L. Greene, Pacific Graduate School of Psychology, Palo Alto, CA
Jungwon Hahn, Merrimack College, North Andover, MA
Allan R. Harkness, University of Tulsa, Tulsa, OK
Jan H. Kamphuis, University of Amsterdam, Amsterdam, the Netherlands
Kelly Klump, Michigan State University, East Lansing
Marylee Losardo, VA Medical Center, Bedford, MA
Margarita B. Marshall, University of Toronto Centre for Addiction and Mental Health, Toronto, Ontario, Canada
John L. McNulty, University of Tulsa, Tulsa, OK

Edwin I. Megargee, Florida State University, Tallahassee
Kathryn B. Miller, University of Minnesota, Minneapolis
Lesley S. Miller, University of Toronto Centre for Addiction and Mental Health, Toronto, Ontario, Canada
Sonia Coelho Mosch, Park Nicollet Clinic/Methodist Hospital, St. Louis Park, Minnesota
Elahe Nezami, Institute for Health Promotion and Disease Prevention Research, Los Angeles, CA
David S. Nichols, Portland, OR
Deniz S. Ones, University of Minnesota, Minneapolis
Walter E. Penk, Texas A&M University, College Station; Harvard Medical School, Cambridge, MA
Julia N. Perry, Minneapolis Veterans Affairs Medical Center, Minneapolis, MN
Jill Rierdan, University of Massachusetts at Boston
Ralph Robinowitz, Dallas, Texas
Steven V. Rouse, Pepperdine University, Malibu, CA
Richard J. Seime, Mayo Clinic, Mayo Clinic College of Medicine, Rochester, MN
Jeanne Tsai, Stanford University, Stanford, CA
Roberto Velasquez, San Diego State University, San Diego, CA
Nathan C. Weed, Central Michigan University, Mount Pleasant
Kevin R. Young, Central Michigan University, Mount Pleasant

PREFACE

My career in psychology has spanned 44 years of research and practical applications with the MMPI/MMPI–2. This has been an enjoyable passage in which I have had the opportunity to work with many researchers and practitioners—MMPI–2ers around the world (sometimes referred to as the "Mult-cult") in different professional contexts. I have had the opportunity to be involved in many collaborative projects on the MMPI that addressed MMPI issues and applications; but the present project—the development of *MMPI–2: A Practitioner's Guide*—has been especially rewarding for me. When I retired from the Department of Psychology at the University of Minnesota in 2003, I found myself with both the time to undertake an extensive project and some unfinished ideas for a project that I have wanted to do for some time—an advanced interpretive guide for the MMPI–2.

The MMPI–2 and its predecessor, the MMPI, have been the most widely used and researched personality assessment instruments, with a research base of over 15,000 published books and articles exploring their various applications. The rich database increases by over 200 articles and books a year. Since the MMPI–2, the revised form of the MMPI, was published in 1989, a number of new scales have been added as interpretive tools; the validity scales have been widely explored to examine their utility; and the clinical and content scales have been further validated to provide objective information in a variety of clinical settings. In addition to the research clarifying the scales making up the test, there has been an expansion of the practical interpretive base for the instrument through a number of introductory level interpretive textbooks that have been made available.

MMPI–2: A Practitioner's Guide was developed to provide clinicians and graduate students in applied psychology with an advanced interpretive textbook that incorporates useful research and applied strategies to aid in test interpretation. The book contains an introductory chapter and 18 chapters that provide comprehensive examinations of MMPI–2 use in diverse applications of personality assessment. Each specialized chapter surveys the research and interpretation tactics that are specific to the setting involved. The contributing authors for each topic have included the following:

- *Survey of relevant research:* The contribution includes a discussion of the research base supporting the special application.
- *Summary of interpretation nuances:* The contributors have incorporated specific considerations that pertain to the application being addressed in the chapter.
- *Highlighted features:* Each chapter features a highlighted exhibit that presents material and provides interpretive guides to help readers obtain a perspective on specific interpretive strategies. These special sections summarize topics of particular interest to the area and focus on interpretive strategies that are particularly valuable to the clinician.
- *Case studies:* The majority of chapters also contain clinical case examples to illustrate the interpretive process. These cases bring interpretive hypotheses to life by illustrating the interpretive points being made in the chapter.

I believe that the various contributions in this volume will add considerably to the teaching of MMPI–2 interpretation.

This book could never have been undertaken without the strong support and encouragement of a number of people. I would like to thank the countless practitioners who attended the MMPI–2 Workshop and Symposium Series that I conducted for 38 years and who provided me with many fruitful questions that broadened my interest in exploring approaches of the MMPI. I am also pleased to acknowledge the support that the chapter contributors to this volume have provided. In the initial phases of this book project, I sought the most productive and historically active MMPI–2 researchers–clinicians on the current scene; each one provided unique "know how" in the project, provided important suggestions about the coverage of the book, and managed the difficult task effectively and with a watchful eye to deadlines.

The enthusiasm and suggestions of several people in the Books Department at the American Psychological Association were central to whatever success this book might enjoy. I want to single out for special praise and appreciation several people who made this book project possible, particularly Gary VandenBos and Susan Reynolds, who provided very strong support along the way and some useful practical guidance in the early development of this project, and Emily Leonard and Jennifer Macomber, who provided substantial editorial expertise and insightful and timely recommendations. I also would like to thank my secretary, Betty Kiminki, for her capable assistance with the reference compendium.

Finally, I would again like to acknowledge and express my appreciation to my family who always support my writing endeavors even though they no doubt take away from family activities at times: my wife Carolyn Williams, my son Janus Dale, my two daughters Sherry and Holly Butcher, and four grandchildren Nick and Neal Younghans and Ben and Sarah Butcher.

I

PERSPECTIVES ON MMPI–2 INTERPRETATION

1

PATHWAYS TO MMPI–2 USE: A PRACTITIONER'S GUIDE TO TEST USAGE IN DIVERSE SETTINGS

JAMES N. BUTCHER

Almost 65 years ago, the Minnesota Multiphasic Personality Inventory (MMPI) was introduced by Hathaway and McKinley (1940) as a means of understanding the psychological problems of patients in psychiatric and medical settings. The test was an instant success and, within a decade of its publication, became one of the most widely used personality assessment instruments. With the MMPI revision in the 1980s, the test—now MMPI–2 for adults and MMPI–A for adolescents—remains the most widely used clinical instrument in personality assessment. More than 14,000 books and articles have been published on the MMPI and MMPI–2 instruments (Butcher, Atlis, & Hahn, 2003), and a number of current textbooks are devoted to introducing the MMPI–2 to students and practitioners interested in updating their base of information (Butcher, 2005; Butcher & Williams, 2000; Friedman, Lewak, Nichols, & Webb, 2001; Graham, 2000; Greene, 2000; Nichols, 2001).

MMPI–2: A Practitioner's Guide was conceived as a compendium of original contributions focusing upon new developments and applications in the MMPI–2 that can serve as a more advanced text in the field than has been heretofore available. The invited contributions provide a comprehensive survey of recent, relevant empirical research along with effective clinical interpretation strategies in a wide variety of applications. The contributors to this volume are a distinguished team of both academic and applied psychologists with established expertise in assessment research and practical contributions to test interpretation. Contributors were selected because of their past scholarship with the test and their ongoing work with the MMPI–2 in real-world applications. Each contributing author was asked to develop a comprehensive chapter covering topics for which that author had broad experience in using the test in particular settings.

The chapters cover a number of theoretical issues defining the application or problem area under review. The content of each chapter details circumstances or issues that apply to the interpretation of the MMPI–2 in the chapter's particular context. An overview of current relevant research underlying the specific application is provided along with established guidelines for administration and interpretation that apply in the test application. Contributors have been encouraged to highlight important differences from "standard" interpretation and to incorporate, where possible, relevant case material to illustrate the test application.

SCOPE OF THE VOLUME

The overall plan for this book is to provide the reader with a panoramic view of MMPI–2–based assessment strategies and to cover a broad range of applications and settings. The book is divided into four general sections: Part I provides a number of theoretical chapters that give the reader a perspective on MMPI–2 interpretation strategies and new measures. This review begins with an exploration of research strategies that have evolved as the MMPI–2 research base has expanded and addresses the need to assess invalidating conditions. Part II deals with personality and therapeutic assessment, including several new scales that are used in personality assessment. Part III of the volume contains chapters designed to provide insights into interpretation of the test in a broad range of settings. Finally, Part IV deals with several important topics that are central to broad MMPI–2 use. Three chapters address special considerations in using the MMPI–2, including computer applications, cross-cultural applications, and use of the test with Hispanic clients.

The chapters included in this volume are described more specifically and the rationale for their inclusion in *MMPI–2: A Practitioner's Guide* clearly noted in the following sections.

Part I: Perspectives on MMPI–2 Interpretation

Part I of the book consists of general chapters that present issues or factors that are important to understanding the operation and interpretation of the MMPI–2 variables across the different clinical applications that are covered in later sections of the book. Chapter 2 authors Butcher, Graham, Kamphuis, and Rouse describe the use of the MMPI–2 in personality and clinical research and highlight ways in which research impacts clinical practice. These authors have detailed basic research methods involving the MMPI/MMPI–2 (Butcher & Graham, 1994; Butcher, Graham, & Ben-Porath, 1995). What place does a chapter on research design and methods of investigation using personality questionnaires have in a volume that is essentially devoted to practical application of the MMPI–2 in a broad range of settings? This chapter addresses the research base and methodological considerations in conducting research on the MMPI–2 with an eye toward helping the practitioner incorporate the latest research findings into practical applications.

Michael Bagby, a long-standing contributor to the research literature on the assessment of malingering, was invited to develop this important topic in chapter 3, "Assessing Underreporting and Overreporting Response Styles on the MMPI–2" (e.g., Bagby, Buis, & Nicholson, 1995; Bagby, Nicholson, et al., 1997). The assessment of protocol validity is perhaps one of the most essential tasks facing the MMPI–2 interpreter in the process of interpreting a protocol. In addition to his work on the MMPI–2, Bagby has conducted substantial research on other personality measures and addresses the relative effectiveness of the MMPI–2 validity indicators compared with other measures. This chapter by Bagby, Marshall, Bury, Bacchiochi, and Miller is a must-read for practitioners and for students to gain a familiarity with this critical aspect of MMPI–2 interpretation.

Part II: Applications for the MMPI–2 in Assessment and Therapy

Many scales and clinical code types yield personality information. The MMPI–2 Personality Psychopathology Five (PSY–5) scales can provide a convenient overview of personality for the practitioner. Chapter 4 authors Harkness and McNulty provide an introduction to the PSY–5, including interpretation, along with information on how such personality information may be relevant to the formation of an alliance with the patient, likely problem vulnerabilities, and the implications of personality for treatment planning.

Chapter 5 author Jan Derksen from the University of Nijmegen is both an academic psychologist and a trained psychoanalyst. Derksen provides his perspective on using the MMPI–2 to assess clients with personality disorders. His work in the area of personality disorders (Derksen, Maffei, &

Groen, 1999) has been extensive from both a clinical and a research perspective.

Chapter 6 is devoted to another important assessment task that practitioners find themselves addressing in several settings (e.g., mental health facilities and personal injury litigation, to name just two), namely, whether the client is experiencing posttraumatic stress disorder (PTSD) symptoms. The MMPI–2 literature on PTSD is abundant (Keane, Weathers, & Kaloupek, 1992; Litz et al., 1991; Penk, Drebing, & Schutt, 2002). Much of the MMPI–2 literature emerged from the study of PTSD symptoms among combat veterans; however, the variables and interpretation strategies emerging from this assessment situation have been carried over into assessment of traumatic psychological reactions in civilian populations as well (Penk et al., 2002). In this chapter, Walter Penk and his colleagues (Jill Rierdan, Marylee Losardo, and Ralph Robinowitz) have provided an up-to-date survey of this topic and illustrated the application of the MMPI–2 for assessing PTSD.

Because of the importance of the topic of psychological assessment in treatment planning in all clinical settings and the extent of research available in the area of intervention (Butcher, Rouse, & Perry, 2000; Chisholm, Crowther, & Ben-Porath, 1997), two chapters in the book are devoted to the use of the MMPI–2 in treatment planning. In chapter 7, an overview of treatment planning with the MMPI–2 is provided by Julia Perry, Kathyrn Miller, and Kelly Klump—all clinical psychologists who have written about the topic and have extensive experience with a broad range of clients. Next, in chapter 8, Steve Finn and Jan Kamphuis describe the effective treatment strategy of using the MMPI–2 to bring about behavior change through the mechanism of therapeutic feedback, a procedure that is being widely used today (Finn & Martin, 1997; Finn & Tonsager, 1992). Steve Finn is a pioneer in the important technique of therapeutic assessment. These authors provide an empirical rationale for using this treatment strategy with mental health clients and illustrate its use in the clinical setting.

Part III: Applications of the MMPI–2 Across Diverse Populations

Part III of the book is devoted to exploring the use of the MMPI–2 in wide-ranging test applications. Test interpretation strategies across varied settings are illustrated to provide readers with a perspective on both the resiliency of the MMPI–2 scales in assessing clients and the need to consider specifically altered tactics in understanding clients from a broad range of symptoms and problems. The test's adaptability at addressing personality and psychological problems in a number of settings can be seen from its uses in mental health settings such as outpatient and inpatient psychiatric facilities and drug and alcohol treatment programs. Similarities and differences in use can also be noted in applying the test in different venues. In health care settings, the presenting problems, personality styles, referral issues, and purposes of the testing would be different, for example, in conducting neuropsychological evaluations to explore symptomatic behavior among individuals with head injury than those factors would be in assessing personality factors in clients with chronic pain patterns. Still other factors could be involved in screening applicants for highly responsible jobs such as airline pilot or police officer.

In chapter 9, David Nichols and Brenton Crowhurst address the use of the MMPI–2 in the inpatient mental health setting—one of the settings for which the MMPI was originally developed in the 1940s. No MMPI–2 expert working in the field today is better qualified to address assessment in inpatient mental health settings than David Nichols; he has devoted much of his career to psychological evaluations at the Dammasch State Hospital in Wilsonville, Oregon. In addition to his extensive clinical assessment work, Nichols has contributed substantially to the research and theoretical literature on the MMPI and the MMPI–2 in his career and has written an introductory textbook in test interpretation (Nichols, 2001).

The use of the MMPI–2 in outpatient mental health settings, one of the most widespread applications of the MMPI–2, is addressed by Roger Greene in chapter 10. Outpatient mental health settings make up a broad conglomeration of facilities—from community mental health centers that serve large urban populations to small independent private practice offices staffed only by an independent practitioner. However, MMPI–2 interpretation of outpatients follows well-established principles as described by Roger Greene. Having written a widely used text in the field, Greene is well qualified to undertake the exploration and summary of the factors pertinent to outpatient mental health patient assessment (Greene, 2000). He has an extensive background in research and clinical practice in outpatient settings and has broad experience supervising students in this application.

Another MMPI-based test application that dates back to the beginnings of the MMPI in the early 1940s is its use in medical or health care settings (Schiele, Baker, & Hathaway, 1943; Schiele & Brozek, 1948). One of the original intended uses of the MMPI was for the assessment of patients being seen in medical settings as a means of understanding the mental health problems that so often are part of medical syndromes. As is shown in chapter 11 by Paul Arbisi of the Minneapolis Veteran's Administration Hospital and Richard Seime from Mayo Clinic in Rochester, the test has been used with a large variety of medical problems and for an equally varied number of clinical tasks, from assessment of chronic pain to the study of psychological factors in heart disease.

The MMPI and the MMPI–2 have a long tradition of use in neuropsychology. Extensive research has been devoted to the evaluation of behavior that can be associated with neurological disorders such as epilepsy, head and spinal injury, and others (Gass, 1996b, 2000; Nelson, 1995). In chapter 12, Carlton Gass—who has been a frequent contributor to the research literature on MMPI–2 in neuropsychological assessment—provides a summary of the use of the MMPI–2 in a neuropsychological test battery and provides an illustration of its use.

In discussions of the use of the MMPI–2 in correctional settings, the name Megargee comes to the forefront because of his extensive and unique contributions to the field. Edwin (Ned) Megargee has contributed particularly to the assessment of felons throughout his career in psychology by developing a classification strategy that uses the individual's self-reported MMPI responses as a basis for viewing his or her psychological adjustment and problems (Megargee, 1995). In chapter 13, Megargee provides a current view of his system of classification for felons and includes a practical example of how the system works.

Another area of MMPI and MMPI–2 research that has provided a rich database for patient assessment is the topic of assessing alcohol and drug abusing clients with the MMPI–2. In chapter 14, Kevin Young and Nathan Weed discuss the application of the MMPI–2 in assessing clients with drug and alcohol problems. Nathan Weed was instrumental in the original development of the two alcohol–drug abuse scales, the Addiction Potential Scale (APS) and the Abuse Acknowledgment Scale (AAS; Weed, Butcher, McKenna, & Ben-Porath, 1992).

The original MMPI was developed by Hathaway and McKinley (1940) to aid in the evaluation and diagnosis of patients in psychiatric and medical settings; however, very early in its history, it came to be used in the evaluation of job applicants. Much of the early work centered on evaluation of military personnel during the Second World War. Use of the test for evaluation expanded following the war with applications in screening of airline pilots, police and fire department personnel, seminary applicants, and people in educational training settings. Over the decades since its origin, it has become widely used as a means of evaluating psychological adjustment in personnel settings. When the MMPI was updated in the 1980s, some items were modified and some dropped, in part, because of their objectionability in personnel settings. Rouse and Butcher (1995) surveyed personnel uses of the MMPI and the MMPI–2, finding more than 450 articles on the topic. Chapter 15, by James Butcher, Deniz Ones, and Michael Cullen, is devoted to the evaluation of clients in personnel settings, provides general perspectives on personnel assessment, and addresses more specifically the use of the MMPI–2 in these settings. As with the other applied chapters in the book, this chapter illustrates the use of the MMPI–2 in interpretation.

One of the expanding applications of the MMPI–2 in forensic psychology is taken up in chapter 16, "Use of the MMPI–2 in Personal Injury and Disability Evaluations." The author of this chapter, Paul Arbisi, is well known for his study of the MMPI–2's effectiveness in assessing malingering and for his development (with Yossef Ben-Porath) of the Infrequency–Psychopathology (*Fp*) scale (Arbisi & Ben-Porath, 1995, 1997). Arbisi has been involved in developing interpretation strategies in work compensation cases for several years and has established himself in the role of teaching MMPI–2 interpretation in personal injury litigation cases with the MMPI–2 Workshops. In this chapter, he provides a solid background for employing the test in this application and includes case material that illustrates the effectiveness of the instrument in clarifying the expression of mental health symptoms in the litigation process.

Part IV: Special Considerations in MMPI–2 Interpretation

Several chapters are included in the final section of the book to address topics of relevance to test interpretation that cross settings or specific applications. These topics have broad relevance for MMPI–2 test use and require attention by practitioners because they provide unique information pertinent to practical use of the test. In the first chapter of this section, the use of psychological assessment with the assistance of computer technology is addressed. Computer-based assessment and the use of computer technology in the interpretation of psychological tests have been widely explored in contemporary psychology (Butcher, Berah, et al., 1998; Finger & Ones, 1999; Fowler, 1969, 1987; Shores & Carstairs, 1998). In chapter 17 of this book, "Computer-Based Assessment With the MMPI–2," authors Mera Atlis, Jungwon Hahn, and James Butcher survey the past history of computerized assessment with the MMPI–2, discuss several current issues with respect to computer-based assessment, and provide specific relevant considerations for practitioners in using computers in their practice.

The United States has a very diverse population comprised of numerous subcultural groups and different native languages, for which the MMPI–2 has been adapted. In addition, the test has been widely adapted for many languages and cultures around the world. The last two chapters in this book focus on ethnic and cultural factors that warrant consideration in MMPI–2 interpretation. Chapter 18 addresses factors to consider in the interpretation of Hispanic MMPI–2 results, because people of Hispanic origin make up one of the largest ethnic groups in the country, and people of Latino descent have been widely studied with the MMPI–2 (Cabiya et al., 2000; Velasquez, Ayala, & Mendoza, 1998). The chapter was written by Maria Garrido and Roberto Velasquez, two academic psychologists who have broad clinical experience as well as a substantial history of teaching others about the adaptation of MMPI–2 test interpretation strategies to Latino populations (Velasquez, Maness, & Anderson, 2002).

Chapter 19, the final chapter of the book, addresses more broadly cross-cultural applications of the MMPI–2, including international adaptations. The MMPI and the MMPI–2 have been widely adapted into other languages and cultures (Butcher, 1996b; Butcher, Berah, et al., 1998; Butcher, Derksen, Sloore, & Sirigatti, 2003). The authors of chapter 19, James Butcher, Sonia Coelho Mosch, Jeanne Tsai, and Elahe Nezami, provide an overview of the process of adaptation of the MMPI–2 into other languages and cultures and include a discussion of factors related to interpreting profiles from clients with differing cultural experience.

THE RESTRUCTURED CLINICAL SCALES

During the first 40 years of its use, the original MMPI underwent a proliferation of scale development—in fact, there were about as many scales on the test as there were items (see Dahlstrom, Welsh, & Dahlstrom, 1975). Most of these scales had limited clinical applications or were redundant, and most did not survive the "utility criteria" that were used by the Restandardization Committee to be carried over into the MMPI–2 when the test was revised in 1989 (Butcher, Dahlstrom, Graham, Tellegen, & Kaemmer, 1989). Additional MMPI–2 scales have been developed since the test was revised; and some new validity measures (e.g., Variable Response Inconsistency [VRIN], True Response Inconsistency [TRIN], Back Infrequency [*F(B)*], Infrequency–Psychopathology [*Fp*], and Superlative Self-Presentation [S]) and clinical symptom measures—such as the content scales and addiction measures ACK (Alcohol Admission Scale) and PRO (Proclivity)—have come to be widely used. The PSY–5 scales, addressing personality dimensions represented in the test (see chap. 4), have taken their place in clinical use and research along with the traditional clinical scales.

One new set of measures, the Restructured Clinical Scales (RC Scales; Tellegen et al., 2003), is considered by the scale authors to have potential as a means of clarifying the interpretation of the clinical scales in a psychometrically sophisticated way. The use of the RC Scales is mentioned in some chapters of this volume, but the scales are not covered in a separate chapter, in large part, because insufficient information has been available to support their use. They are briefly introduced here so that readers who are unfamiliar with them can have a working knowledge of their operation when they are encountered in later chapters.

The extent to which these new scales will find a place in clinical research and interpretation is yet to be determined. The RC Scales were developed to try and capture the meanings of the original clinical scales while at the same time eliminating two problems thought to impact the original clinical scales: item overlap among the clinical scales and the strong relationship of some of the clinical scales to an underlying factor referred to as "demoralization." It was thought that by removing these "problems" from the clinical scales, the remaining core constructs would be better (i.e., have more discriminant validity) than the original clinical scales published by Hathaway and McKinley (1943). (See chap. 2 by authors Butcher, Graham, Kamphuis, and Rouse for a description of scale development procedures along with possible criteria with which to appraise new measures developed for the MMPI–2.)

The RC Scales were designed by Tellegen et al. (2003) to refine the clinical interpretation of the traditional clinical scales by identifying and removing the "demoralization" markers in the scales and restructuring the scales to build measures that addressed the core construct of each scale without the influence of the general maladjustment items. These efforts were viewed as a means of improving both the convergent and discriminant validity of the clinical scales. The scale authors recommended that the RC Scales be viewed as supplemental measures and not be considered as replacements for the original clinical scales.

The RC Scales were developed in several stages. Initially, the authors developed a "demoralization scale" in order to capture the general maladjustment dimension that they considered to impact the existing clinical scales. These problem items were then removed from the clinical scales. By eliminating these "demoralization" items from the traditional clinical scales, the authors thought that their impact on the scale's operation would be reduced. For some scales, items other than demoralization content were also eliminated such as the correction items on Scale 2. It is not clear in some cases why items were eliminated from the core dimension—for example, on some scales only a small number (e.g., seven) remained from the original clinical scale items. The reduced numbers of items on the clinical scales were then considered to be "seed" clusters for the next phase in the development—broadening the item makeup by including items from the full MMPI–2 item pool by determining which items were correlated with the "seed" constructs. The authors next conducted both internal and external validity analyses to further explore the psychometric functioning of the resulting RC Scales. The scales include the following: RCd (Demoralization), RC1 (Somatic Complaints), RC2 (Low Positive Emotions), RC3 (Cynicism), RC4 (Antisocial Behavior), RC6 (Ideas of Persecution), RC7 (Dysfunctional Negative Emotions), RC8 (Aberrant Experiences), and RC9 (Hypomanic Activity).

What do the RC Scales measure? Within the MMPI–2, what concepts are they related to and different from? How do they compare with the traditional clinical scales? What are their relationships (either positive or negative) with other widely used MMPI–2 scales, such as the MMPI–2 content scales?

Tellegen and his colleagues provided initial analyses of the RC Scales' internal validity and predictive validity using a group of mental health outpatients (Graham, Ben-Porath, & McNulty, 1999) and two inpatient samples (Arbisi, Ben-Porath, & McNulty, 2003a). The only published study available, the test manual (Tellegen et al., 2003) reported that the RC Scales have a comparable degree of association to external behavioral correlates to the traditional clinical scales. The monograph describing the development of the RC Scales did not include information on the relationships of the RC Scales to other widely used MMPI–2 measures such as the MMPI–2 content scales and supplemental scales or the new PSY–5 scales. Moreover, no information was published on the use of the RC Scales in samples other than severely disturbed psychiatric patients such as medical patients, job applicants, or forensic cases, with which the test is widely used.

The correlational psychometric procedures used in the development resulted in measures that are highly similar or redundant to the MMPI–2 content scales and PSY–5 scales. The extent to which the RC Scales operate like the MMPI–2 content scales has yet to be determined. However, an examination of the content overlap between the RC Scales and other MMPI–2 measures shows more overlap between the RC3 scale and the content scale Cynicism (CYN; 80% of the items are in common) than is shown with the parent scale *Hy* (Hysteria). Future research analyses on the relationships with other widely used MMPI–2 measures must be provided so that their value in the interpretation process can be fully understood. If the RC Scales turn out to operate in a manner similar to the MMPI–2 content scales, then their utility is likely to be more limited in, for example, medical or forensic settings in which the obvious item content (being generally transparent) can be consciously manipulated by persons wishing to present a picture of extremely virtuous personal qualities. Defensive profiles generally produce low-ranging content scale scores (Butcher, Graham, Williams, & Ben-Porath, 1990).

Another important characteristic of the RC Scales that is likely to affect their scale utility in some settings involves what has been referred to by Nichols (in press) as "construct drift." Some RC Scales (particularly RC3) bear little resemblance to the original clinical scale and do not address problems that the original clinical scales assess in forensic evaluations; in fact, there is a negative correlation between RC3 and its parent scale—*Hy* (−.42; Tellegen et al., 2003)—suggesting that the RC3 scale is *not* measuring characteristics that are traditionally assessed by the *Hy* scale. (For current views of the complex nature of high *Hy* scorers and the personality characteristics of hysteroid adjustment along with physical symptom expression, see Butcher, 2005; Graham, 2000; Greene, 2000; Nichols, 2001.) Instead, the RC3 scale appears to be a redundant measure of cynicism as assessed by the CYN scale. The *Hy* scale is one of the most frequent high points in medical and forensic (personal injury) applications. For example, Butcher, Atlis, and Hahn (2003) researched base rates on several large clinical samples; they found that 10.47% of men in a large medical population have *Hy* as their highest peak score and 26.37% of the sample have a 1–3 two-point code. In addition, in a sample of personal injury litigants, 17.2% of the cases had elevated and well-defined high-point *Hy* scores and 18.9% of the sample had well-defined 1–3 profiles (Butcher, 1997a). Therefore, the RC3 scale's "drift" away from the core constructs of the high *Hy* scorer will likely make this measure irrelevant in addressing problems in personal injury and medical evaluations. From an examination of the item contents in the RC Scale item domains, it appears that the traditional *Hy* scale constructs are not included.

The extent to which these seemingly "unrelated" modified measures, such as RC3, can add to the interpretation of the original MMPI clinical scales needs to be determined by further research, particularly with diverse settings such as medical and forensic populations. In medical settings, the profile high points for the RC Scales will likely be quite noncongruent with the original scale elevations. For a patient who has a high *Hy* score on the *Hy* scale (or a code type with *Hy* as a member), the RC3 is not likely to be prominent and is not likely to be a factor in the interpretive process. No research on the use of the RC Scales in medical or forensic settings is available; thus, their use in these evaluations is questionable.

How will these measures fare in future MMPI–2 applications? Only time and substantial amounts of additional data will tell. One can hypothesize, for example, based on the low to negative relationship between the RC Scale and the original clinical scale, that they will not add much, if anything, in some settings such as medical or forensic (personal injury) applications.

SUMMARY

In summary, the contributions in this book provide diverse perspectives on the theoretical and practical issues in interpreting the MMPI–2 test across the spectrum of applied settings in psychology. The various contributions explore the widely used scales and interpretive strategies for the MMPI–2 test in a variety of applications. The contributors have provided insights into effective test interpretation strategies for a number of applied settings and have offered practical guidelines for approaching profiles in these contexts. Finally, the contributors have illustrated characteristic interpretive strategies that apply for each setting.

2

EVALUATING MMPI–2 RESEARCH: CONSIDERATIONS FOR PRACTITIONERS

JAMES N. BUTCHER, JOHN R. GRAHAM,
JAN H. KAMPHUIS, AND STEVEN V. ROUSE

Personality questionnaires are among the most versatile and effective methods for gaining a psychological understanding of people and for obtaining a perspective on symptomatic patterns of those experiencing mental health problems. Over the past century, personality questionnaires have been widely used to study in a cost-effective manner a broad range of problems that patients have. The methodology in personality questionnaire research has evolved substantially since early personality questionnaires were first explored (Galton, 1885; Woodworth, 1920). Of the various self-report measures that have been published in psychology, none has been subjected to more empirical scrutiny and systematic research than the MMPI and its successors, MMPI–2 and MMPI–A (Butcher, Atlis, & Hahn, 2003; Butcher & Rouse, 1996). This chapter is devoted to an exploration of important factors in evaluating research with the MMPI–2 and an examination of the effectiveness of methods of accumulating valuable information on the test that can guide clinical practice.

What place does a chapter on research design and methods of investigation using personality questionnaires have in a volume that is essentially devoted to practical application of the MMPI–2 in a broad range of settings? The primary goal of this chapter is to explore methodological factors in conducting research on the MMPI–2 to provide the researcher and practitioner with the tools for appraising MMPI–2-based research.

RATIONALE FOR MMPI–2 RESEARCH: IMPORTANCE OF BUILDING RESEARCH ON PAST ADVANCES AND MISTAKES

One of the primary strengths of the MMPI–2 derives from the immense body of research that has accumulated in the six decades since its development. More than 14,000 articles and books have been published on the MMPI, the MMPI–2, and the MMPI–A on topics ranging from the use of these tests in medical settings, occupational settings, and forensic settings to pure research on the psychometric qualities of the MMPI scales (Butcher, Atlis, et al., 2003). In fact, with more than 250 publications in a typical year, the MMPI–2 and the MMPI–A are the most frequently researched personality inventories available to be used in clinical practice. Obviously, not all research is good research; one of the goals of this chapter is to highlight some of the key methodological issues that can differentiate the stronger studies from the weaker studies.

The fact that the MMPI–2 is so widely researched is highly important for practicing clinicians. Because the ethics code of the American Psychological Association (APA, 2002) places responsibility on the psychologist for ensuring that he or she is using psychological tests in a manner that is consistent with published research on its usefulness, the psychologist must select an assessment battery composed of tests that can be interpreted on the basis of well-documented guidelines. By basing their interpretive comments on the results of empirical research, clinicians can be more confident in their use of the test.

MMPI users have a long history of allowing their use of the instrument to be guided by empirical research rather than being guided by subjective impressions or idiosyncratic interpretive strategies. After Meehl (1954) provided compelling evidence that actuarial personality descriptions (based on statistical decision-making algorithms) were more accurate than personality descriptions formed on the basis of intuitive clinical judgment, he called for the development of a “cookbook” (Meehl, 1956), an empirically based guide that would allow test users to generate hypotheses about test takers on the basis of established correlates and statistical evidence. Two large-scale cookbooks of this type were published during the following decade (Gilberstadt & Duker, 1965; Marks & Seeman, 1963), each of which identified several distinct patterns of elevated scores and provided clinical correlates of those profile patterns. This paved the way for an early computerized MMPI interpretive program (Pearson & Swenson, 1967), which generated reports based on empirically observed correlates of elevated scales and combinations of elevated scales. Today, clinicians who use the MMPI–2 have access to a wide range of resources (Butcher, 2005a; Butcher & Williams, 2000; Craig, 1999; Friedman, Lewak, Nichols, & Webb, 2001; Graham, 2000; Greene, 2000; Groth-Marnat, 2003; Nichols, 2001) that provide interpretive guidelines for MMPI–2 scales, supported by a large body of empirical research. Because of its strong empirical foundation, the MMPI–2 is widely used in many applied fields of psychology; in forensic psychology, for example, the primary exception to the acceptance of the MMPI–2 is when the psychologist uses the test in a way that is not supported by empirical literature (Otto, 2002).

In light of the long-standing use of empirically based research in understanding scores on the MMPI–2, clinicians should be extremely skeptical of research articles that purport to offer new interpretive strategies. This is especially true when those strategies are idiosyncratic approaches that stand in distinct opposition to an empirically based use of the test. An example of this ill-advised approach can be seen in a recent critique of the MMPI–2 in which Senior and Douglas (2001b) argued that an unconventional approach should be used in interpreting the MMPI–2 in forensic settings. Their rationale, the "paucity of studies examining the forensic role of the MMPI–2" (p. 203), suggests that these authors might not have performed a sufficient literature search. In fact, Butcher, Atlis, et al. (2003) located 184 different empirical sources that specifically address the use of the MMPI–2 in forensic settings. However, even if Senior and Douglas were correct regarding the extensiveness of the literature base, the critique seems to reflect some basic misunderstandings about the MMPI–2 and the method by which interpretive hypotheses are formed. For example, the argument that "MMPI–2 interpretive cookbooks . . . are inadequate substitutes for empirical accuracy" (p. 203) is inconsistent with the principle of interpretive cookbooks; indeed, these empirical collections of research results epitomize the empirical approach. In addition, these authors appeared to be working under the assumption that clinicians have been encouraged to accept on blind faith all of the correlates of elevated scores as true for each individual test taker who receives an elevated score. This is not the case. In fact, the computerized Minnesota Report for the MMPI–2 (Butcher, 2005b) includes a cautionary reminder of the probabilistic nature of these correlates: "The MMPI–2 interpretation can serve as a useful source of hypotheses about clients. . . . The personality description, inferences, and recommendations contained herein should be verified by other sources of clinical information because individual clients may not fully match the prototype." The alternative approach proposed by Senior and Douglas was to rationally evaluate the self-report of individual test takers on a scale-by-scale basis or even an item-by-item basis. However, this encourages the clinician to rely on the type of idiosyncratic, unempirical approach that is in danger of being rejected in forensic settings (Otto, 2002).

The following sections of this article are structured by presenting topics as they typically appear in published empirical articles. The sections include discussions of the issues and strategies in research grouped under the following section titles: Methods and Procedures, Results, and Discussion and Conclusions.

METHODS AND PROCEDURES

In this section, we address several important factors with respect to the manner in which research studies are constructed. We first review the factors that are important to selecting a study population and several situations in sample selection that can influence or limit the generalizability of the results. Then we examine problems that can result from using nonstandard administration procedures to collect data. Finally, we examine factors involved in developing new scales for the MMPI–2 .

Considerations for Developing or Evaluating Basic Research Samples

When a researcher collects a sample of participants for a study, his or her ultimate concern is not whether the observable trends are true for the sample but whether these observations can be generalized to a larger population. For example, Gilmore, Lash, Foster, and Blosser (2001) observed that the MMPI–2 TRT (Negative Treatment Indicators) scale effectively differentiated between substance abusers who completed treatment and those who either withdrew from treatment or showed lower levels of motivation and compliance. However, their concern was focused not just on the individuals who comprised the sample but on whether these observations could be generalized to the broader population of adults seeking substance abuse treatment. A careful examination of the sample used in a study allows us to determine how confident we can be in generalizing findings from the sample onto the broader population. Two important aspects of a sample should be examined: the representativeness of the sample and the size of the sample.

Representativeness

The first issue to consider is whether or not the sample is likely to be representative of the population or at least representative enough for the purposes of the study. An example of the importance of a representative sample can be seen in the 1947 movie *Magic Town*. In this film, Jimmy

Stewart plays an unsuccessful pollster who stumbles across the midwestern town of Grandview, a town that statistically matches the demographics of the American population and whose opinions perfectly represent the population's opinions; rather than polling large segments of the American population, he can get a clear assessment of the general attitudes from this one town's residents. Although such a premise might make for an interesting fictional movie, it is very unlikely that a researcher would ever be able to stumble across a "magic sample" that responds to the MMPI–2 in a manner that perfectly represents the way the American population would respond to that test. For this reason, critical readers of research articles should be particularly wary of studies that use "convenience samples" (i.e., samples that were selected because they were easily accessible); such samples weaken our confidence in generalizing findings to a broader population.

However, some misunderstandings are common in regard to a sample's representativeness. First, some people assume that a sample must be randomly selected in order to be representative; occasionally, people criticize research because the sample was not created by randomly selecting a large number of people from the general population. However, this criticism may reflect a misunderstanding of the principle of representativeness. It is true that random selection is one method of obtaining a sample that is likely to be representative of the population, but this is not the only approach. For example, the individuals in the MMPI–2 normative sample (Butcher, Dahlstrom, Graham, Tellegen, & Kaemmer, 1989) were recruited not through a random sampling of the entire U.S. population but rather through a systematic effort intended to recruit individuals that reflected the demographics of the population. A representative sample is important for research; this does not imply that it needs to be a randomly selected sample.

Second, the need for a representative sample does not imply that it needs to be representative of the U.S. population. Instead, it needs to represent the population to which the generalizations will be made. One would not argue that Gilmore et al.'s (2001) sample represented the entire U.S. population; however, it would be possible to create a compelling argument that this sample represented the population of adults seeking substance abuse treatment. Oftentimes a researcher is not trying to create generalizations that will apply to all individuals but is instead trying to generalize about a specific subset of individuals, and it is important to consider whether or not the research sample used is representative of that subset.

This relates to an issue described by Stanovich (2004) as the "College Sophomore Problem"; because a large number of studies are based on research with college students (and typically those enrolled in introductory psychology classes), we may question the generalizability of their findings. Stanovich argued that readers of psychological research should be aware of this issue and take it seriously but that this issue in itself does not invalidate research. After all, many psychological processes (such as the functioning of the visual system) are so basic that the demographics of the subject sample have little bearing on the generalizability of the findings. Even when student participant research is focused on higher-level psychological processes (as is usually the case with MMPI–2 research), Stanovich argued, we should not assume that the results are wrong; they may be simply incomplete. In other words, the responses given by a sample of college students may be very informative but we should be wary of generalizations made on the basis of these samples without supporting evidence from replication studies.

Sample Size

The second issue to consider is the size of the sample, and there are two potential problems that might be encountered. The most obvious concern arises when a sample is too small; in such cases, results may not be statistically significant simply because the power of the study was too low. Cohen (1988) proposed that prior to collecting data, researchers should determine how large a sample would be needed to reach a power level of .80; at a power level of .80, there is an 80% chance for one's expected results to be statistically significant. However, Cohen also recognized that there would be instances in which a higher or lower power level would be appropriate. In the past, journal articles often did not formally address power or a researcher's rationale in selecting a sample size. However, contemporary researchers are urged to provide this information (Wilkinson & The Task Force on Statistical Inference, 1999). When power information has not been provided, it is important for the reader to critically examine the results of the research; when the results of a study include some significant and some insignificant findings, it is important to question whether the insignificance might have been due to a sample that was simply too small to detect a real relationship between the variables being studied.

Although a sample needs to be large enough to obtain statistically significant results, a second problem can occur when a sample is extremely large. In such cases, results may be statistically significant simply because of the sheer size of the sample, even when the results are not particularly meaningful. Imagine, for example, that the mean score on the MMPI–2 Depression scale was 49.9 for a sample of 50,000 right-handed individuals but was 50.1 for a sample of 50,000 left-handed individuals. Although this may reach a level of statistical significance, the practical importance of such a difference in scores is negligible. An effect size (d), however, allows readers of a research report to determine whether the results are strong enough to have practical significance (Cohen, 1988; Rosenthal, Rosnow, & Rubin, 2000). For example, according to Cohen, an effect size of .20 may be statistically significant but carries only a "small" level of practical significance, whereas a "large" effect size ($d = .80$) would represent a statistical finding strong enough to have substantial real-world implications; in the fictional situation just described, the effect size of the difference between right- and left-handed individuals would be less than .01, indicating that such a difference in scores was essentially meaningless. Because statistically significant results do not always have practically significant implications, the APA has urged researchers to report effect sizes ever since the fourth edition of the publication manual (APA, 1994) and has strengthened this mandate in the current fifth edition (APA, 2001). Despite this urging, this information is not available in many articles; as a result, critical readers of research should be cautious when statistically significant findings are presented without indication of the effect size.

The importance of both of these issues can be seen, for example, in the work of Lewis, Simcox, and Berry (2002) on the utility of the MMPI–2 Validity Scales for identifying individuals who feign psychiatric symptoms in pretrial psychiatric evaluations. On the Back Infrequency scale [*F(B)*], the mean score of 31 "honest" individuals was 63.3, while the mean score of 24 "feigners" was 116.8. Not only was the resulting *t* value statistically significant at a level of $p < .01$, but the effect size was 3.6, substantially larger than the level at which Cohen (1988) considered an effect size to be "large." A power analysis would reveal that this sample size would not have been large enough to detect this difference if the effect size had not been so large. In fact, with a sample of this size, a "moderate" effect size of about .50 would only be statistically significant approximately 60% of the time. However, because previous research had found the *F(B)* scale to be very effective in identifying malingerers, large effect sizes could be expected, so a sample of this size proved to be very appropriate.

Controlling for Demographic Differences Between Groups

In conducting or evaluating MMPI–2 research, the issue of demographic differences between groups whose MMPI–2 scores are compared is important. Traditionally, psychological researchers have been taught that it is important to ensure that groups (e.g., substance abusers versus general psychiatric patients) that are compared on relevant variables (e.g., MacAndrew Alcoholism Scale—Revised [MAC–R] scores) are not different on other variables (e.g., age or education) that could affect the results. This is typically accomplished by matching the comparison groups on as many relevant demographic variables as possible.

However, such matching on demographic variables may not always be appropriate. Butcher, Graham, and Ben-Porath (1995) recommended that matching groups of individuals on variables other than the one of primary interest makes sense only if differences between the groups on these other variables can be assumed to be because of sampling procedures and that, in fact, the populations from which the samples are drawn are not different on these variables. Thus, if researchers are confident that populations of interest (e.g., substance abusers versus general psychiatric patients) are equivalent on a variable such as educational level, even if samples from these two populations differ on educational level, matching the groups for education would be appropriate. However, if there is evidence that the populations of interest actually differ on a variable such as education, then matching the groups on this variable could mask important relationships or differences and results could probably not be generalized to all members of the comparison groups. The best rule of thumb is probably that unless data are available suggesting that differences between groups on variables such as educational level are because of sampling procedures and do not represent actual differences in the populations from which the samples were chosen, groups should not be matched on these variables.

Studying Ethnic Differences on the MMPI–2

Because the developmental and normative groups for the original MMPI were quite homogeneous in terms of ethnic backgrounds (i.e., almost all were Caucasians), there has been considerable concern that using the MMPI/MMPI–2 with members of ethnic minority groups may not be appropriate because the test may discriminate against such individuals by portraying them as more psychopathological than they really are. Early studies reporting that average scores of some ethnic minority groups were higher than Caucasian groups for some MMPI scales added to concerns about possible test bias.

Many studies have reported mean scores for African American, Latino, Asian American, Native American, and other ethnic minority groups. Generally, the findings have suggested small differences between minority and majority groups on some MMPI/MMPI–2 scales. Differences have been smaller when groups have been matched for socioeconomic status. Hall, Bansal, and Lopez (1999) conducted a meta-analysis of 50 comparative MMPI/MMPI–2 studies of African American males and females and Latino American and European American males. Because of the small number of published studies, Latino–Anglo and Asian American–European American comparisons were not included in the meta-analysis. Hall et al. concluded that the MMPI and MMPI–2 do not unfairly portray people of African American or Latino descent as psychopathological.

Although studies comparing mean scores of groups of ethnic minority and majority individuals are somewhat informative, they do not really address the validity of MMPI–2 scales in assessing minority test takers. Differences in mean scores between groups do not necessarily indicate that MMPI–2 scales are differentially valid for members of the groups, just as equivalent means scores for groups do not mean that scales are equally valid for the groups. As Pritchard and Rosenblatt (1980) and Timbrook and Graham (1994) have suggested, the most meaningful studies in this area are ones that examine the relative ability of MMPI–2 scales to predict conceptually relevant extratest characteristics of members of minority and majority groups.

Timbrook and Graham (1994) demonstrated this methodology using data from the MMPI–2 normative sample. MMPI–2 scores of African American and Caucasian subjects were used to predict ratings—completed by their spouses—of conceptually relevant characteristics. Results suggested that, although there were some mean MMPI–2 scale differences between African American and Caucasian individuals, MMPI–2 scales were equally valid in predicting conceptually relevant characteristics of individuals in the two groups. Two more recent studies have been reported that provide further support for the effectiveness of the MMPI–2 with minorities. Arbisi, Ben-Porath, and McNulty (2002) used a similar methodology to that of Timbrook and Graham with samples of African American and Caucasian psychiatric inpatients and reported comparable validity of MMPI–2 scales for these two groups of patients. Greene, Robin, Albaugh, Caldwell, and Goldman (2003) reported that the correlates for MMPI–2 scales applied well to a sample of substance abusing American Indian subjects.

In summary, although studies reporting mean scores for ethnic minority and majority groups are of some value, the appropriateness of using the MMPI–2 (or other psychological tests) with members of ethnic minority groups is most adequately determined by comparing the extent to which test scores predict conceptually relevant extratest variables for the groups.

Another important consideration in this kind of research has to do with how participants are categorized into groups. Care should be taken to describe just how groups were formed. For example, not all Black persons should be considered to be African American. The heterogeneity of ethnic minority groups must also be considered. For example, grouping Mexican American, Cuban American, and Puerto Rican subjects together under the rubric *Hispanic* may obscure important differences among these subgroups. Because there are data suggesting that personality test scores of members of ethnic minority groups are most different from those of the majority group for minority group individuals who are less acculturated into the majority culture, it is important to consider acculturation when studying the relative validity of MMPI–2 scores for minority and majority group members (Okazaki & Sue, 2000).

Issues Concerning the Administration of the MMPI–2

It is essential for investigators to follow standardized test administration procedures if the study is going to provide results comparable to the results of previous research and allow others to replicate the findings. Several considerations related to procedures in administering the MMPI–2 are discussed in this section. Research studies that deviate substantially from standard test administration procedures can produce undesired or questionable results. Deviations from standard practice include such conditions as: uncontrolled test administration procedures, using altered or nonstandard forms of the MMPI–2, administration of shortened versions of the test, administration of MMPI–2 scales out of context, and using poorly translated forms of the test. In evaluating MMPI–2 research, ensure that the investigators have followed standard procedures for administering and processing the test.

The Importance of Standard Administration of the MMPI–2

One of the guiding principles underlying the use of standardized tests is that they be administered in a prescribed and consistent manner. Carefully described methods and procedures must be followed in administering a test so that future investigators can replicate the study. It is also important to ensure that the conditions under which the test is being completed are similar for all individuals and that they are comparable to the administration procedures used to develop the test norms. The administration of the MMPI–2 can be relatively straightforward in that the instructions printed on the booklet are easy to follow. Yet, because of the relative simplicity in the test administration procedures, the possibility exists for wide deviation from standard instructions, which can result in procedures that invalidate the test.

Controlled Versus Uncontrolled Administration

Careful monitoring of the test administration is important to obtain comparable results. It is not appropriate, in most situations, to allow research participants to self-administer the MMPI–2 by taking the instrument home with them or to mail test materials to them to self-administer. In uncontrolled administrations, the researcher cannot be assured that the person actually completed the test or took the task seriously. It is important in administering the test *not* to provide additional instructions such as defining words. It is also important to avoid reading the items to the person; if an oral administration is necessary because of vision problems or low reading level, then the audio version of the test should be administered.

Full Form Versus Shortened Versions

Much research has been devoted to the question of whether short forms of the MMPI–2 (see Butcher & Hostetler, 1990; Dahlstrom, 1980; Greene, 1982; Lachar, 1979) can be used in lieu of the long form. A short form of the test should be distinguished from the "abbreviated MMPI" in which all of the items in scales of interest are administered but not all possible MMPI–2 scales are available. For example, administering the first 370 items on MMPI–2 or the first 350 items on MMPI–A allows the researcher to fully score the original validity scales (*L* [Lie], *F* [Infrequency], and *K* [Correction]) and clinical scales, but the newer validity scales (*F(B)*, VRIN [Variable Response Inconsistency], TRIN [True Response Inconsistency], and *S* [Superlative Self-Presentation]), content scales, and most supplementary scales cannot be scored from the abbreviated version. Short forms, on the other hand (such as in the recently published study by Dahlstrom & Archer, 2000), provide clearly inadequate estimates of the full-scale scores. Research has shown that MMPI short forms cannot be used for clinical prediction because the resulting profiles are not sufficiently close to full-form profiles (Butcher & Hostetler, 1990). Caution should also be exercised when evaluating the results of computer-adaptive or tailored MMPI–2 scores. (See chap. 17 by Atlis, Hahn, and Butcher for a fuller discussion of adaptive testing.) Although the adaptive version of the MMPI–2 can provide a time-efficient administration and accuracy with respect to the highest one or two scale scores, it does not provide full profile information.

Administering Individual Scales Extracted From the Full Form

Interpretation problems can occur if the items for a particular scale are extracted from the full form and administered separately—that is, administered out of the context of the full test item pool. The two scales in which this procedure has been most widely used are the Post-Traumatic Stress Disorder (PTSD) Scale and the MAC–R. Several problems can result from scoring a scale with items that have been administered separately from the other items in the MMPI–2. One problem that can result when the item administration context is changed is that the task in responding to the items is altered. Including only similar items on a brief scale (most often with highly transparent or obvious content) can markedly change the stimuli and the task that clients are being asked to undertake. This "altered mind-set" in responding to the items has not been widely studied—and the norms may not apply in this situation. Research has shown inconsistent results as to whether the altered scale would produce a different response attitude from that which would have been obtained if all of the items had been administered. For example, Megargee (1979) reported that a correlation of only .55 was obtained when an extracted version of the Overcontrolled Hostility (O–H) scale was compared with the full form of the MMPI administered on the same day. However, MacAndrew (1979) reported that scores on the MacAndrew Alcoholism Scale produced results that were similar when administered independently or in the context of the entire MMPI.

Another limitation of using extracted scales noted by Butcher et al. (1995) is that the researcher is not able to examine the performance of the scale in the context of other MMPI–2 measures, which usually provide valuable information in the evaluation of a scale's performance. For example, if only the items contained on a particular scale are administered, then the validity scales cannot be used to eliminate invalid records and a weaker data set may result because of the likely inclusion of invalid profiles. In general, scales should not be administered out of context unless equivalence can be demonstrated.

Quality of Translated Versions of the MMPI–2

As with the original MMPI, the MMPI–2 and the MMPI–A have been found to have considerable generalizability when translated and adapted to other languages and cultures (Butcher, 1996a, 2004; see chap. 19 of this volume). In developing a test translation, it is crucial to ensure that the items are translated in such a way as to have both linguistic and psychological equivalence (Sperber, Devellis, & Boehlecke, 1994). Effective test translation procedures have been developed for the MMPI–2 (Butcher & Han, 1996; Butcher & Pancheri, 1976) as follows: (a) Careful item translation typically uses multiple bilinguals to obtain an initial rendering of the item pool; (b) back translation of the translated items is typically completed to determine the equivalence of the item translations; and (c) once an acceptable version of the instrument is obtained, researchers commonly conduct a bilingual test–retest study to determine if bilingual subjects produce the same pattern of scores in both languages. In bilingual test–retest studies, individuals who have lived in both cultures for 5 years or more and are fluent in both languages are administered the instrument in both languages. The two test results are then evaluated statistically (analogous to a test–retest study) by examining differences in mean scores, scale intercorrelations, and factor analyses. Once a careful translation is completed, then further research to develop appropriate in-country norms and external validity research need to be considered.

The use of poor translations can have a negative impact on the test's utility and acceptability in the target country (Butcher, 2004). A number of negative consequences can occur if a poorly translated and adapted version of a test is introduced in a new country. One consequence is that the test results may not be valid in clinical applications and may provide misleading results about patients. Another consequence is that poorly translated tests may actually attain wide use simply because psychologists in the target country are in great need of usable assessment devices. Over time, the tests' flaws emerge and people become discouraged that the translated tests are not effective and they gain a negative reputation. This situation has occurred in several countries with the original MMPI, and later (more effective) translations had an uphill struggle for acceptance because of the earlier ill-fated effort.

Strategies for Evaluating New Scales

When new scales are developed for the MMPI–2, the scale developers are encouraged to provide sufficient information about their psychometric properties to allow other researchers and practitioners to evaluate their "place" in the existing network of MMPI–2 measures. That is, scale developers should provide information as to how new measures compare with existing scales including such characteristics as: overlap with existing scales, intercorrelation with existing measures, and evidence that the scale or scales add incrementally to the existing and widely used measures. Butcher and Williams (2000) pointed out that a new scale should be used because it performs a particular assessment better or more efficiently than other scales or provides valuable information not accessible through another assessment approach. Butcher and Williams provide the following guidelines for researchers and practitioners for appraising the value and suitability of proposed new measures:

- *The construct on which the scale is based needs to be well defined.* The variable in question should not simply be the result of interesting group differences in convenience samples. The construct should be related to personality or symptomatic variables in a clearly important way. The dimension or set of characteristics should be a personality variable and not nonpersonality factors such as abilities, intellectual qualities, and so forth.
- *The item pool is relevant for the construct being assessed.* The MMPI–2 item pool has limitations. It is not possible, for example, to develop a scale measuring language ability or successful performance as a tightrope walker in the circus because the test was designed for assessing mental health problems. Scale developers should ascertain whether the item content of the MMPI–2 is relevant to the question studied.
- *The research design should include sufficient samples to allow for cross-validation.* This is most necessary for empirically derived scales to eliminate items that would be selected on the basis of chance or specific sample characteristics. The sample sizes for both the developmental and the cross-validated samples should be sufficient to provide stable test scores and to reduce error.
- *The scale needs to have appropriate statistical properties.* The scale should have high internal consistency (Osburn, 2000) if the

scale is desirable as a measure of a single dimension. It is valuable for a scale to have a meaningful factor structure particularly if it is multifaceted or made up of several discrete content groups regardless of the scale development approach used. The scale's factor structure should be reported. If the proposed measure is an empirical scale, it is not required that the scale possess high internal consistency. However, it should possess other relevant psychometric properties, such as test–retest reliability.

- *All scales, even those developed by rational or internal consistency methods, should have demonstrable validities.* It is important for any scale to measure what it is supposed to assess, regardless of the method of scale construction. That is, all personality measures should predict, describe, or detect the psychological characteristics they purport to measure.
- *Test applications need to be explored and demonstrated.* Does the scale possess sensitivity and specificity in predicting the quality it is supposed to assess? How well the scale classifies relevant cases should be reported.
- *Construct validity for the scale should be reported.* Correlations between the proposed scale and other, well-established MMPI–2 measures need to be described. For example, it may be useful in describing the interscale relationships to report intercorrelations between the proposed scale and other well-established dimensions of the MMPI such as major factor dimensions, A and R, to establish the new scale's independence. It is also useful to provide a table of item–scale overlap with existing MMPI–2 scales (see Butcher, Arbisi, Atlis, & McNulty, 2003). This allows users to compare the new measures with existing ones.

RESULTS

This section is directed toward defining MMPI–2 scale attributes and presenting results in a balanced and meaningful way. Several data-processing decisions that are important to the presentation of MMPI–2 findings are described: establishing exclusion validation criteria for research studies, using well-defined codes, and incorporating non-*K* scores in the analysis.

Establishing Exclusion Validation Criteria for Research Studies

For MMPI–2 scores to convey meaningful information in either clinical assessments or research studies, we must have confidence that the scores are from valid protocols. Can we be relatively sure that the test takers approached the MMPI–2 in the manner intended? Standard MMPI–2 instructions call for the test takers to read each item, consider the content of the item, and respond *true* or *false* to the item as it applies to them. One of the positive features of the MMPI–2 is that it has well-researched scales for assessing test validity. These scales should be used to identify and exclude invalid protocols from research samples prior to any data analysis.

Nichols, Greene, and Schmolck (1989) identified two kinds of deviant responding that should be considered. *Content nonresponsiveness* or *inconsistent responding* occurs when test takers respond inconsistently to test items or omit large numbers of items. *Content-responsive faking* occurs when test takers consider the content of items but do not respond to them in an honest, candid manner. Both kinds of deviant responding should be considered in MMPI–2 research.

Inconsistent responding can be identified using the Variable Response Inconsistency (VRIN) scale, which is useful in detecting random responding, and the TRIN scale, which is useful in detecting tendencies to answer MMPI–2 items *true* or *false* without consideration of their content. The Cannot Say (?) measure is simply the number of MMPI–2 items omitted or answered both *true* and *false*.

Content-responsive faking can take the form of overreporting (i.e., faking bad) or underreporting (i.e., faking good). The (*F*), *F(B)*, and Infrequency–Psychopathology (*Fp*) scales all have demonstrated ability to identify overreporting on the MMPI–2. The *L*, *K*, and *S* scales are effective measures of underreporting.

Butcher et al. (1995) suggested criteria for excluding invalid protocols from MMPI–2 research samples. They indicated that protocols should be excluded from data analysis if any of the following criteria are met: more than 30 omitted items (Cannot Say); VRIN score greater than 80T; TRIN raw score greater than 12 or less than 6; *F* raw score greater than 30; *L* score greater than 80T; *K* score greater than 80T; or *S* score greater than 80T. Although Butcher et al. did not suggest criteria for the *F(B)* or *Fp* scales, examination of recommendations in the MMPI–2 manual (Butcher et al., 2001) indicates that *F(B)* or *Fp* T scores greater than 100 indicate invalid responding.

Different criteria should be used to exclude invalid protocols when the purpose of the study is to examine the accuracy with which MMPI–2 validity scales can identify fake-good or fake-bad protocols. Because measures of content responsive faking (*F*, *F(B)*, *Fp*, *L*, *K*, and *S*) typically are used as predictor variables in such studies, these scales obviously should not also be used to exclude participants. In faking studies, only content-nonresponsive invalidity (as assessed by CNS, VRIN, and TRIN) should be used as a basis for excluding protocols.

In addition to applying appropriate criteria for invalid responding to exclude protocols from research studies, authors should state clearly how many protocols were eliminated on the basis of each criterion as well as the total number of protocols eliminated. If possible, it is helpful to compare the included and excluded participants on demographic and mental status variables to ensure that participants remaining in the analyses are similar to those who were excluded.

Choosing Reliable Classification Variables: Importance of Using Well-Defined Scales or Code Types

The primary purpose of many MMPI–2 studies is to identify extratest correlates for MMPI–2 scales and configurations of scales. Many of these studies have been correlational in nature. Scores for a group of participants on a specific MMPI–2 scale (e.g., Scale 1, Hypochondriasis) are correlated with extratest measures (e.g., therapist ratings of symptoms) for participants. Such studies typically report numerous correlations between MMPI–2 scales and extratest measures. Often a Bonferroni-type correction is applied to adjust alpha levels to take into account the number of correlations that were calculated.

Early in the history of the original MMPI, the importance of considering configurations of scales was emphasized. The notion is that persons grouped together on the basis of more than one MMPI–2 scale will be more like each other than persons grouped together based on elevated scores on a single scale and that more specific correlates can be identified for configurations of scales than for individual scales. Typically, research participants are grouped together on the basis of having a particular clinical scale (e.g., Scale 1, Hypochondriasis) higher than any other clinical scale. These have been referred to as "high-point" codes. In addition, some studies have grouped participants together on the basis of the two or three highest clinical scales (i.e., 2-point or 3-point codes).

Early MMPI research did not take into account how much more elevated scales in the code type were than other scales in the profile. For example, a protocol with a T score of 80 on Scale 2, a T score of 75 on Scale 7, and a T score of 74 on Scale 8 would have been classified as a 2–7 two-point code. This approach does not consider that the MMPI–2 scales are not perfectly reliable and that a difference of one T-score point between Scale 7 and Scale 8 (in the preceding example) is probably not a meaningful difference. This person could just as well have considered a 2–8-code type.

Butcher et al. (1995) emphasized the importance of taking code-type definition into account. *Definition* simply refers to the difference in T-score points between the lowest scale in a code type and the next highest scale in the profile. Based on the typical reliability of MMPI–2 scales, it is recommended that only code types with at least 5 T-score points of definition be used in clinical interpretation and research. This increases the likelihood that the scales in the code type are meaningfully different from other scales in the profile. McNulty, Ben-Porath, and Graham (1998) demonstrated empirically that defined code types yield stronger and more narrowly focused correlates than corresponding code types that have not been defined.

Use of Non-*K* and *K* Corrected Profiles

The *K* weights used in the *K* correction (Meehl & Hathaway, 1946) were derived empirically to improve the discrimination of cases in a psychiatric setting by correcting the profile to detect psychopathology (adding points to defensive records). The five scales were thought to be improved by adding a portion of *K* to five scales: *Hy* (Hysteria), Pd (Psychopathic Deviate), *Pt* (Psychasthenia), *Sc* (Schizophrenia), and *Ma* (Hypomania). The *K* scale has been shown to be effective at detecting defensive responses and problem denial (Butcher & Williams, 2000; Graham, 2000; Greene, 2000); however, the *K* weights have been questioned as an effective means of correcting for this response style (Archer, Fontaine, & McCrae, 1998; Sines, Baucom, & Gruba, 1979) and because of psychometric problems this correction can have. For example, researchers need to be aware that using *K*-corrected scores in research introduces artificial covariance among scales and can create significant problems for studies such as those involving factor analyses. In an empirical effort to improve the *K* correction, Weed (1993) attempted to derive other possible weightings of *K* in order to increase the discriminative power of the correction for defensive profiles; however, no other weightings were found to actually improve the discriminations.

For several years, researchers have been encouraged to incorporate non-*K* corrected scores into their MMPI validity studies to examine further the relative effectiveness of the two approaches in predicting behavior and to build a strong database for empirically based interpretation for the non-*K* corrected scores (Butcher et al., 1995; Butcher & Tellegen, 1978). However, this recommendation has generally been ineffective, and research to date has not yet produced a comfortable base of interpretive information for solid reliance on non-*K* corrected scores (Wooten, 1984). Research has demonstrated that there are no differences between *K* corrected and non-*K* corrected scores when external criteria (such as therapists' ratings) are used to verify their accuracy (Barthlow, Graham, Ben-Porath, Tellegen, & McNulty, 2002). However, other reports have concluded otherwise (Detrick, Chibnall, & Rosso, 2001).

In evaluating the *K* versus non-*K* profiles in the research literature, the practitioner should be aware of the following two factors:

- In cases when the *K* scale elevation exceeds a T of 70, one can never be assured that the person has cooperated with the evaluation. Therefore, not relying on the clinical measures for defensive profiles seems the most prudent strategy.

- The interpreter also needs to be aware that in some cases when *K* is elevated, some of the clinical scale elevations (e.g., on *K* corrected scales such as *Sc* or *Pt*) can be accounted for by the elevation on *K* alone. That is, the person may have actually endorsed few (or none) of the other items contained on the scale.

Retesting Under Altered Instructions of People Who Invalidated Their Tests Because of Defensiveness

There is considerable evidence to indicate that in some settings, such as employment or child custody evaluations, many people invalidate their tests in an effort to make a positive impression because they are extremely defensive. However, if people are informed in advance that the test has a means of detecting defensive responding and they are encouraged to be more honest in their response to the items, then they tend to produce more valid results. Several studies have shown that when people who have invalidated the MMPI–2 in these situations are given an opportunity to retake the test (after being informed that they have invalidated their initial testing as a result of defensiveness), many produce more valid and usable test results (Butcher, Morfitt, Rouse, & Holden, 1997; Fink & Butcher, 1972). The retest procedure has been used effectively in a number of personnel contexts. Butcher et al. (1997) found that on retesting under altered instructions, about two thirds of job applicants with invalid profiles produced valid results when the test was readministered with instructions to be less defensive. Usually about 16% of the retest cases then produced clinically significant results in the readministration. Cigrang and Staal (2001) and Gucker and McNulty (2004) reported similar results when they replicated the study with altered instructions. (See the discussion in chap. 15 of this volume.)

Is it possible, then, to simply use altered instructions in the initial assessment in order to obtain fewer defensive, invalid records? Some research has shown that administering the test under altered instructions in this setting does lower defensiveness (Butcher, Atlis, & Fang, 2000); however, the use of altered instructions in the initial testing would represent a deviation from standard practice that would not be defensible in the event of litigation.

Issues of Validity, Reliability, and Utility: Research Variables and Power of Results

Why should the clinician care about the psychometric properties on new MMPI–2 scales? Are the reported indices not mere technical matters, of interest only to the scientific community and irrelevant to the practitioner? Most test users realize that validity estimates (e.g., convergent and discriminant correlations) and reliability estimates (e.g., test–retest correlations, standard error of measurement) on instruments are of real, practical utility to any clinical practice. Validity speaks to the question of whether a score meaningfully relates to the construct one is trying to assess. For example, does a scale putatively measuring malingering not in fact measure rare physical complaints in most health settings? (See Greve and Bianchini's Fake-Bad Scale [FBS] in Arbisi & Butcher, 2004a.) Reliability speaks to the confidence you can invest in the replicability and accuracy of the score. Reliability coefficients tell you how much you can trust the value you just obtained for a given client on a given measure. It is reflected in the standard error of measurement, and it guides, for instance, the MMPI–2 interpretation rule of using well-defined code types.

Although most test users are cognizant of the importance of these indices of psychometric quality, another equally important domain in appreciating the clinical applicability of measures is often overlooked: the hit rates, the base rates, and their interplay (Meehl & Rosen, 1955). A few examples of good and bad research and some common mistakes can orient you to these issues so that you can make informed decisions. Being sensitive to the effects of base rates on hit rates helps invest appropriate confidence (or lack thereof) in published research findings.

Hit Rates

The interpretation of the MMPI–2 heavily relies on *cutoff scores*, critical scores beyond which clinical attention is warranted. For example, on the clinical scales, a score greater than 65 is thought to be indicative of clinically significant problems or dysfunction. As a result of the MMPI–2 uniform T distribution across clinical (and content) scales, a score of 65 indicates that less than 8% of individuals from the normative sample achieved a score of that magnitude or higher.

Cutoffs, however, are imperfect heuristic rules. Sometimes a score of greater than 65 is obtained by a "normal" person (false positive); conversely, a person scoring below 65 may be experiencing significant problems (false negative). To index the quality of test-related decisions, several indexes have been proposed (so-called *hit rate* indexes). Traditionally, the utility of self-report tests is evaluated by their sensitivity and specificity indexes. *Sensitivity* is the probability that an individual who has the condition will be identified as such by the test ($A/A + C$; see Table 2.1). *Specificity* is the probability that an individual who does *not* have the condition will not be identified as such by the test ($D/B + D$). More loosely, how well does the test pick up on true positives versus true negatives? The denominators of these probability concepts consist of the known positives (sensitivity) versus known negatives (specificity); sensitivity is the proportion (hence, probability) of true positives the test detects, specificity the proportion of true negatives the test detects.

TABLE 2.1
2 × 2 Contingency Table

Test result	Disorder present? Yes	No	Row total
Test value > cutoff	*A*	*B*	*A* + *B*
Test value < cutoff	*C*	*D*	*C* + *D*
Column total	*A* + *C*	*B* + *D*	*A* + *B* + *C* + *D* = *N*

Note. Formulas: base rate = (*A* + *C*/*N*); sensitivity = (*A*/*A* + *C*); specificity = (*D*/*B* + *D*); positive predictive power = (*A*/*A* + *B*); negative predictive power = (*D*/*C* + *D*).

Faulty classificatory decisions fall into two categories: One may incorrectly assign a diagnosis to a person who does not have the disorder (false positive), or one may fail to detect a disorder that is in fact present (false negative). In any given practice, one type of mistake may be much more important than the other, depending on the aim of classification. For example, if you were involved in preliminary drug *screening*, you would likely prefer tests that minimize the number of false negatives—that is, that are "inclusive" and have high sensitivity. On the other hand, in the more final states of *determination* of whether this person used a particular illegal drug, you would be looking for tests that minimize false positives (given the severity of the adverse consequences) and have high specificity. You have to ask yourself, "What hit rates am I trying to maximize?" Do you care more about sensitivity or specificity or, alternatively, about avoiding false negatives or avoiding false positives? Do you wish to screen or rule in? The asymmetry of the weight attached to the types of mistakes reflects the so-called relative (dis)utility you attribute to these outcomes.

In clinical practice, one usually knows the individual's test score and wants to evaluate the score's accuracy in determining the presence of a particular condition. This information can be derived from a different set of hit rates, the indexes of positive and negative predictive power. *Positive predictive power* (PPP, or A/A + B) is the probability that when the test indicates that the person has the disorder, it is in fact true; its complement, *negative predictive power* (NPP, or *D*/*C* + *D*), reflects the probability that when the test indicates that the patient does not have the disorder, this is actually true. Ideally, the researcher presents tables exhibiting these indexes for various specific cutoff scores, thus allowing the clinician to make an informed decision, fitting with his or her aims.

A couple of MMPI–2/MMPI–A examples may illustrate these points. High scores on the Alcohol Admission Scale (ACK) are meaningful as predictors of alcohol abuse, as few false positives are obtained. On the other hand, low scores are not particularly informative, as high numbers of false negatives are likely. In other words, the scale is high in PPP but lacks NPP. Conversely, it has been established that adolescents who score in the elevated range on Scale 4 of the MMPI–A have more reports of abuse in their files. Suppose a clinician would defend in court the idea that his client was abused as a child, citing evidence of a high score on Scale 4. Would this stand? No, because the clinician failed to pay attention to false negatives and false positives. Scale 4 is low on PPP but may have reasonable NPP. Again, this may or may not be consistent with the profile of hit rates you are looking for in your clinical practice. When the cell counts in both *A* and *D* increase relative to the cell counts in *B* and C, the phi coefficient of association between the test prediction and the "state of nature" increases.

Base Rates

In evaluating the utility of test indexes for your own practice, note that some of these hit ratios are quite sensitive to base rate effects (Kamphuis & Finn, 2002; Streiner, 2003). *Base rates* can be defined as the percentage of individuals who have the condition of interest in a specified sample or, in the contingency table, as (*A* + C/*N*). When the base rate in your clinical practice, the so-called "local" base rate, is notably different from the base rate operative in the research that underlies the reported indexes, you cannot expect to achieve similar proportions of correct decisions. Base rates affect the PPP and NPP hit rates for different cutoff points, specifically the distribution of true and false positives and negatives. It is reflected in the MMPI–2/MMPI–A interpretation books in contingent statements like "in inpatient settings, a score of 75 means . . ." and so on. Recently, Greve and Bianchini (Arbisi & Butcher, 2004a) discussed the so-called "somatic malingering" scale, the Lees-Haley Fake-Bad Scale. The proposed cutoff score was optimal for the base rate observed in their study: about 50%. In most settings, malingering is considerably less prevalent and the number of false positives one is likely to obtain by simply adopting the Greve and Bianchini cutoff score may be prohibitively large. This may be an example of research where insufficient attention has been paid to the importance of base rate effects.

A more positive relevant example may be found in the MMPI–2 *Fp* scale for psychiatric malingering (Arbisi & Ben-Porath, 1995). A conservative cutoff of T > 100 is recommended to help identify malingering. Lower cutoff scores have been shown to (marginally) increase the test's NPP but, inevitably, at the cost of lower PPP. To his credit, Arbisi (Arbisi & Ben-Porath, 1995) has provided sufficient detail on the hit rates under various scenarios (i.e., base rates and cutoffs) for test consumers to make informed decisions.

Discrepant Base Rates and Cutoffs

What can you do when your base rate is significantly discrepant? You may consider altering the cutoff score, especially if the test developers have documented hit rates for multiple cutoffs. Suppose you have a setting heavily involved in child custody cases. Decisions based on the customary cutoffs for "defensiveness" may well show that "defensiveness" is ubiquitous: Everybody is trying to "look good" (or at least not "bad"). This phenomenon is inherent to this setting: It would be highly unusual for individuals looking to adopt a child to emphasize their (normal) shortcomings and problem areas. The standard cutoff then results in too many false positives, and a higher, more conservative cutoff is warranted for noteworthy levels of defensiveness. This may not be immediately intuitive, until one realizes that a higher cutoff score is nothing more than imposing some extra conditions for meeting the "positive" status.

DISCUSSION AND CONCLUSIONS

Objectively interpreted questionnaires are among the most effective methods for evaluating personality. The MMPI–2 is the most widely used instrument for personality evaluation, in part because it possesses an expanding array of empirical research to support its use. It is important for consumers of psychological research to be assured that the research used to guide clinical practice is of the highest quality. This article provides researchers and practitioners with an overview of pertinent methodological considerations for conducting objective personality research and evaluating MMPI–2 studies to ensure that dependable new information can be effectively incorporated into clinical decision making. A number of key considerations for appraising the conclusions of empirical research are highlighted in Exhibit 2.1.

General Considerations for Appraising the Discussion and Conclusions Sections of Empirical Articles

Some of the research and opinion articles that find their way into published sources do not enhance practical application but can actually mislead practitioners. It is important for practitioners to evaluate fully new publications to determine whether the results and conclusions can be trusted to become integrated into the clinical assessment process. Unfortunately, for many readers, it is tempting to rely only on the titles or abstracts (as a time-saving strategy in one's busy schedule) to develop conclusions rather than appraising the results and conclusions of the full paper. A cursory review of published findings can be problematic in that some articles have titles that are misleading and abstracts that do not convey the essential thrust of the study or the accuracy of the results. For example, as noted ear-

EXHIBIT 2.1

Highlight: Important Considerations in Evaluating MMPI–2-Based Research

- Evaluate the extent to which the investigators have framed the study appropriately in the context of existing literature for the problem being investigated.
- Be wary of article titles; they can be misleading and off the mark from what the research findings actually are.
- Carefully appraise new measures or proposed interpretive strategies that promise new and different ways of evaluating MMPI–2 responses. Novel is not always better.
- Carefully examine the samples on which the study is based (particularly samples of convenience) because they may not permit generalization of findings beyond the study itself.
- In matching groups for comparisons in research, a good rule of thumb to follow is that matching is not necessary unless existing data show differences between groups (e.g., education level).
- Ensure that the samples on which the study is based are appropriate to the problem being assessed.
- Research, to date, has not shown that the MMPI–2 unfairly portrays minority clients.
- Tests should be administered in a standard, controlled manner to match standards followed in the development of the MMPI–2 norms.
- Validity indices should be used to eliminate invalid records and to eliminate noncredible participants from the research sample.
- New scales should be examined against existing MMPI–2 measures to determine where (or if) the scale provides new information or if it is simply an alternate form of other published scales.
- When the goal of the research is to describe scale or code type correlates, then the use of well-defined scores (i.e., that are at least 5 T-score points higher than the next scale) is recommended to ensure reliable findings.
- Evaluate whether *K* or non-*K* corrected scores have been incorporated in the study and whether documentation on their effectiveness has been noted.
- When cutoff scores are used or when recommendations about prediction made, evaluate the predictive power—examine specificity and sensitivity.
- Not all reported "significant results" are useful. Examine effect sizes of results to determine if the reported effects are practical to address. Effect sizes for a comparison allow the researcher to determine whether the results are strong enough to have practical significance.
- Assess the degree of similarity between your local clinical practice and the published research sample, both in terms of the selection of patients and in terms of the base rate of the phenomenon of interest.
- Look for cross-validated results, because single sample hit rates are optimized for that sample only.
- Decide which hit rates are most important to you: overall accuracy (i.e., total number of correct decisions) or avoiding false negatives (e.g., screening, looking for maximally sensitive measures) or false positives (e.g., looking for maximal specificity)?
- Adjust the cutoff score if there is major discrepancy between your local base rate and the research base rate, provided you have sufficient information to do so.

lier, some articles that start off with the words "Validity of . . ." may actually report evidence of invalidity.

Another characteristic of empirical articles that can mislead readers occurs when authors provide only a partial or skimpy review of past relevant research rather than a thorough exploration of the extensive network of past research. The existing research literature needs to be tied into the results of the study to ensure that spurious findings are not given more weight than they deserve. The conclusions from the study need to be consistent with the existing literature or clearly supplant them. Implications of the findings should be noted in the article.

In the discussion of the results, authors should reiterate the size and makeup of the sample so that readers can determine the extent to which the results can generalize to other populations and whether the results would likely be representative of the population or at least representative enough for the purposes of the study. Any demographic or ethnic differences on MMPI–2 scores should be interpreted in the context of existing literature.

In discussing the results, authors should weigh and evaluate the impact that the application of various exclusion criteria based on invalidity indices might have had on the findings and describe how such exclusions could have influenced the results. If research comparisons excluded participants, it may be valuable to report how these excluded participants differed from non-excluded participants, for example, whether there were any demographic or mental status variables associated with the exclusion status.

When discussing the meaning and utility of a new scale, authors should examine the psychometric characteristics and predictive efficiency and not simply rely on the scale name or author's intent in developing the scale. Examining the availability of validity research—the pattern of external relationships or external correlates—is crucial in evaluating the potential utility of a new measure. Also valuable is examining the relationship between the new scale and the existing MMPI–2 scales in order to understand the new scale's place in the network of available MMPI–2 measures. Traditionally, determining the relationships between the new measure and the MMPI–2 factors *A* and *R* has been of value in gaining a further understanding of the scale's functioning.

The discussion section should also provide an explanation of the significant and useful results in the study by comparing the present findings with research findings reported in related studies. The effect sizes of results should be examined to determine if the reported effects are practical. Effect sizes for a comparison allow the researcher to determine whether the results are strong enough to have practical significance.

3

ASSESSING UNDERREPORTING AND OVERREPORTING RESPONSE STYLES ON THE MMPI–2

R. MICHAEL BAGBY, MARGARITA B. MARSHALL, ALISON S. BURY, JASON R. BACCHIOCHI, AND LESLEY S. MILLER

The MMPI–2 (Butcher, Graham, et al., 2001) is the measure most commonly used to assess personality and psychopathology in a variety of assessment contexts (Camara, Nathan, & Puente, 2000; Greene, 2000). Although there are many attributes of this instrument that contribute to its frequent and wide-ranging use, perhaps one of its greatest strengths, distinguishing it from other instruments, is the inclusion of a number of extensively examined and well-validated scales to detect response bias. Indeed, since its inception, the MMPI and its revision, the MMPI–2, have included validity scales to detect the underreporting (i.e., fake-good responding) and overreporting (i.e., fake-bad responding). It is widely accepted that test takers may be motivated for a variety of reasons not to respond honestly or in a straightforward manner to items on instruments measuring psychopathology. Such responding, of course, directly affects scores on the content and clinical scales, which comprise the interpretative meaning of test results.

Detecting such responding, therefore, is an important part of the assessment process.

Fake-good response style has the effect of lowering content and clinical scales; in many assessment contexts, respondents may be consciously or unconsciously motivated by personal goals to underreport symptoms of psychopathology. For example, disputing parents undergoing child custody and access evaluation may not report emotional problems they experience; and job applicants, in an effort "to put their best foot forward," may present themselves in an overly favorable light. Prisoners seeking parole or early release may exaggerate overall level of adjustment and may fail to admit to behavioral problems they possess; and psychiatric inpatients may attempt to disclaim the presence of lingering psychopathological symptoms in order to secure release from the hospital.

Fake-bad response style has the effect of elevating content and clinical scales. Fake-bad responses, in contrast to fake-good responses, are typically intentional and engaged with the full awareness of the respondent, although there are some instances in which individuals may be unconsciously motivated to fabricate and exaggerate psychiatric symptoms (e.g., factitious disorder and conversion disorder). Overreporting may also occur in a number of contexts. Personal injury litigants or combat veterans may exaggerate the extent of psychological trauma they have experienced in order to maximize their chances of receiving financial compensation for disability claims. Individuals genuinely experiencing psychopathology may exaggerate their symptoms as a "cry for help." Criminal litigants may claim the presence of psychopathological symptoms that they do not in fact possess in order to plead insanity as a way of avoiding criminal charges, prolonged imprisonment, or even the death penalty.

Given that underreporting and overreporting response styles have the potential to invalidate MMPI–2 protocols and that such responding likely occurs in a variety of important assessment contexts, the assessment and accurate detection of response biases are critical aspects of MMPI–2 interpretation. The purpose of this chapter is to present an overview of the more widely used MMPI–2 validity scales and indexes used to detect underreporting and overreporting responding; review the empirical literature addressing the validity of these scales and indexes; discuss some interpretational issues; and, where applicable, highlight emerging themes in recent research that have direct bearing on clinical applicability.

In general, the empirical review centers around three core areas: clinical utility, classification accuracy, and incremental validity. Because examining individual validity scale elevations is perhaps the most commonly used method to determine profile validity, we evaluate clinical utility in terms of mean group differences between those identified as underreporting or overreporting and those not so identified. Classification accuracy is determined by examining the capacity of validity scales to detect accurately underreporting and overreporting, and we rely mostly on the overall correct classification rate. In this discussion, we use scale incremental validity to refer to whether the nonstandard validity scales (i.e., those not included in the test publisher's scoring system) add a statistically significant incremental increase in the predictive capacity of the standard validity scales (i.e., those that are part of the test publisher's scoring system) in the detection of response dissimulation (see Butcher, Graham, & Ben-Porath, 1995). The general principle here is that if existing nonstandard scales or newly developed scales cannot consistently outperform standard validity scales, then there is no compelling reason to implement them in the clinical setting.

Two meta-analytic reviews have been published recently, one addressing underreporting (Baer & Miller, 2002) and the other examining overreporting (Rogers, Sewell, Martin, & Vitacco, 2003). In the spirit of brevity, we rely heavily on these excellent reports in our summary examination of the validity scales; but we also review articles published subsequent to these reviews. We present underreporting and overreporting in separate sections and begin each section with definitions and descriptions of selected validity scales and indexes.

UNDERREPORTING RESPONSE BIAS

The MMPI–2 includes a number of scales that assess the underreporting of psychopathology, including the standard validity scales *L* (Lie), *K* (Correction), and *S* (Superlative Self-Presentation). A number of "nonstandard" scales also exist. The most well-known and widely used scales include the Edwards Social Desirability (Esd) scale (Edwards, 1957) and the Wiggins Social Desirability (Wsd) scale (Wiggins, 1959). More recently developed scales are the Other Deception (Od) scale (Nichols & Greene, 1991) and the Positive Mental Health (PMH4) scale (Nichols, 1991). A number of indexes also exist that are used to assess underreporting. These indexes typically use multiple scales in combination with one another. Several other nonstandard scales and indexes of underreporting exist but are not widely known and are rarely used; therefore, we do not review them here. Interested readers are referred to Baer and colleagues (Baer, Wetter, & Berry, 1992; Baer & Miller, 2002), who provide an excellent summary of these infrequently used scales and indexes.

Before proceeding to the description of the underreporting scales, it is important to recognize that although many investigators and clinicians assume and treat underreporting as a unidimensional construct, results and interpretation from factor analytic investigation of underreporting scales suggest the presence of at least two independent components variously labeled but invariably measuring two constructs—self-deception (SD) and positive impression management (PIM; Bagby & Marshall, 2004; Damarin & Messick, 1965, as cited in Paulhus, 1984; Paulhus, 1984, 1986, 2002; Meehl & Hathaway, 1946; Sackeim & Gur, 1978; Strong, Greene, Hoppe, & Olesen, 1999; Strong, Greene, & Kordinak, 2002; Wiggins, 1959, 1964). *Self-deception* has been broadly defined as a dispositional tendency to think of oneself in a favorable light, whereas *positive impression management* refers to the deliberate attempt to distort one's responses in order to create a favorable impression with others (Barrick & Mount, 1996, p. 262). Different MMPI–2 underreporting scales have separate and unique associations with these two components. To the extent to which the data support such designation, we indicate in our description of each scale whether it measures SD or PIM responding.

Many clinicians and research investigators use the terms *socially desirable responding, defensive responding, positive impression management,* and *faking-good* interchangeably in the context of discussing underreporting and the MMPI–2. In this chapter, we use the term *underreporting* to represent the act of responding, whether intentional or unintentional. Socially desirable responding refers most broadly to the motivation that underlies the underreporting act, whether intentional or unintentional. The terms faking-good and positive impression management are broadly conceptualized as intentional efforts to underreport, as manifest, for example, in studies instructing participants to "fake-good." The term defensive responding is more complex than faking-good and positive impression management and seems to encompass self-deception and impression management.

Scale Descriptions

As discussed earlier, the standard validity scales (i.e., *L*, *K*, and *S*) are widely used and part of the test publisher's scoring system. In contrast, the nonstandard validity scales are not part of the test publisher's scoring system and, as such, are not typically used in clinical practice. A brief description of the standard validity scales and the better-known nonstandard scales and indexes are provided in Table 3.1. More detailed descriptions of these can be found in Butcher and Williams (2000); Friedman, Lewak, Nichols, and Webb (2001); Graham (2000); Greene (2000); and Nichols (2001). Chapter 15 in this volume provides some case illustrations of how some of these validity scales have been used in an applied context (personnel selection).

Lie (L) *Scale (Hathaway & McKinley, 1940)*

The *L* scale was developed using a rational scale construction methodology to detect the deliberate and overt acknowledgment of uncommon virtues. Paulhus (1986) described *L* as a measure of other deception, and, as noted by Nichols (2001), it is positively correlated with

TABLE 3.1
Summary of Description of Underreporting Scales and Indexes

Scale/index	Number of items	Description	Style of responding
Standard			
L	15	Obvious, infrequent virtues	PIM
K	30	Subtle adjustment, defensiveness	SD
S	50	More socially desirable than *K*	SD
Nonstandard			
Esd	39	Absence of psychological symptoms	SD
Od	33	Deliberate positive impression management	PIM
PMH4	34	Good psychological adjustment	SD
Tt	26	Absence of less common psychological symptoms	Unclear
Wsd	40	Subtle, heterogeneous item content	PIM
Indexes			
L + K	—	Obvious, infrequent virtues and subtle adjustment, defensiveness	
L + K – F	—	Obvious, infrequent virtues and subtle adjustment, defensiveness minus endorsement of psychopathology	
O–S	—	Endorsement of obvious items versus subtle items	

the Positive Malingering (Mp) scale (later updated and renamed the Other Deception [Od] scale; see subsequent discussion and Table 3.1), which was specifically designed to address this construct. The *L* scale consists of 15 items that represent pervasive but relatively trivial faults that most people would admit (Nichols, 2001). As such, high scores on *L* are interpreted as an unsophisticated attempt to deny small shortcomings (Butcher, Graham, et al., 2001). The *L* scale consistently loads on the impression management factor (Bagby & Marshall, 2004).

Correction (K) Scale (Meehl & Hathaway, 1946)

In developing the *K* scale, Meehl and Hathaway (1946) attempted to reduce the number of false negatives produced by the MMPI scoring (i.e., indicating no evidence of psychopathology when it exists); the scale was constructed selecting only those items that distinguished persons exhibiting significant psychopathology and whose overall profiles were within the normal range of scores from individuals not exhibiting psychopathology who produced elevated profiles (Nichols, 2001). As such, the 30-item *K* scale is recognized as a more subtle measure of impression management than the *L* scale (Butcher, Graham, et al., 2001; Nichols, 2001). High *K* scores indicate denial of negative and unstable emotionality, interpersonal difficulties, cynicism and mistrust, introversion, and other adjustment problems (Nichols, 2001). According to Paulhus (1986), the *K* scale is primarily an index of self-deception. In the factor analytic investigation of Bagby and Marshall (2004), the *K* scale loaded clearly on the self-deception factor. However, Nichols has suggested that *K* also demonstrates susceptibility to other deception or impression management.

Superlative Self-Presentation (S) *Scale (Butcher & Han, 1995)*

The 50 items selected for the *S* scale discriminated a large sample of airline pilot applicants, presumed and verified to be responding in a highly defensive manner, from the MMPI–2 normative sample. High *S* scores reflect the denial of misanthropic attitudes, suspicion of others, irritability, hypersensitivity, anxiety, internal conflict, or dissonance. In addition, such scores indicate that respondents assert benevolent beliefs regarding others, personal contentment, mild-mannered and self-controlled character, and adherence to conventional values (Nichols, 2001). *S* scores are highly correlated with *K* scores but are more evenly distributed across the entire pool of items (Butcher, Graham, et al., 2001). As with *K*, the *S* scale primarily assesses self-deceptive responding; even so, it is also susceptible to the effects of impression management, although it loads exclusively on the self-deceptive factor (Bagby & Marshall, 2004).

Underreporting Case Study. Dr. Joseph Smith, a psychiatrist, was referred for a psychological assessment by his regulatory college in order to clarify the following: (a) whether Dr. Smith presented with a mental condition; if so, (b) to clarify the effects of the mental condition or disorder on Dr. Smith in terms of his ability to exercise judgment, make decisions, accurately perceive events, or interact with others; and (c) to clarify whether the effects of the condition posed any possible risk of harm to his patients.

Dr. Smith's professional competence came into question following a complaint to the college by the parents of one of Dr. Smith's son's classmates. The parents alleged that Dr. Smith had presented with increasingly bizarre and inappropriate behavior whenever in their company, such as at their sons' joint soccer games. The parents also alleged that Dr. Smith had been verbally abusive toward their son in an unprovoked manner and that Dr. Smith had confided in them that he was experiencing a great deal of stress and had jokingly stated that he felt he was "cracking up."

During the clinical interview, when queried regarding the parents' complaints against him, Dr. Smith indicated that he, indeed, had been under a great deal of strain at work, but he denied any impairment in his functioning because of stress. He admitted that he had responded in an excessively harsh manner to their son regarding his actions during a game, but he denied problems related to impulsivity or aggressive outbursts.

Review of his medical file revealed that Dr. Smith presented with a history of recurrent unipolar depression that reportedly had been in remission for the prior 3 years. During prior major depressive episodes, Dr. Smith had discontinued working for up to 3 months at a time and had presented with suicidal ideation without intent. He presented with no history of suicide attempts or self-harm behavior. He denied current symptoms of psychopathology during the clinical interview.

Behavioral observations revealed a man in his late 40s who was neatly dressed in a suit and tie, was well groomed, and presented in a pleasant, polite, and professional manner. His responses during the interview appeared to be straightforward and consistent. His affect was euthymic and stable during the interview with no gross abnormalities in speech, thought content, thought processes, or motor coordination.

The results of the MMPI–2 indicated that the number of items left uncompleted was within acceptable limits. In addition, review of his VRIN and TRIN scores suggested that he attended appropriately to test items and responded in a consistent manner to items with similar content. The degree to which response styles may have affected or distorted the report of symptoms on the MMPI–2 was also assessed. Review of Dr. Smith's Infrequency [*F*], Back Infrequency [*F(B)*], and Infrequency–Psychopathology [*Fp*] scores revealed no elevations that would indicate overreporting of psychopathology. In terms of defensive responding, no significant elevation was seen on the *L* (52T) scale, while significant elevations were seen on the *K* (74T) and *S* (70T) scales. This pattern of elevations was strongly suggestive of underreporting of psychopathology and was more suggestive of self-deception than of deliberate attempts at impression management.

In addition to providing information regarding test-taking response styles, scores on the MMPI–2 validity scales also provide information regarding personality characteristics of the test taker. Dr. Smith's MMPI–2 validity scale scores were consistent with those of individuals who try to maintain a facade of adequacy and control while admitting to no personal problems or weaknesses. His scores suggested a person who exhibits a serious lack of personal insight and understanding into his own behavior. Persons with validity scale scores in this range may be seriously disturbed psychologically but are reluctant to look at the source of their problems or difficulties.

Regardless of the nature of the motivation (i.e., intentional versus unintentional) underlying Dr. Smith's defensive response style during the assessment, the presence or absence of a psychiatric disturbance could not be inferred based on evidence of defensive responding. As such, diagnostic impressions and conclusions regarding Dr. Smith's mental state were based on a detailed file review and behavioral observations made over the course of the assessment.

Edwards' Social Desirability (Esd) Scale (Edwards, 1957)

The Esd is a 39-item scale that was developed based on the unanimous judgments of 10 raters regarding the socially desirable direction of responses. This methodology resulted in a final pool of items with high scores reflecting the absence of any type of psychopathological symptoms, as well as social ease. This scale also loads on the self-deceptive factor.

Positive Malingering (Mp) Scale (Cofer, Chance, & Judson, 1949)

The 33 items of the original Mp scale distinguished college students explicitly instructed to engage in positive impression management from students responding honestly and students instructed to overreport but for which the item endorsement frequency did not differ across the honest and fake-bad groups (Friedman et al., 2001). High Mp scores reflect the denial of common flaws that are underreported by individuals who are deliberately responding in a socially desirable manner. The MMPI–2 version of the Mp scale includes only 26 items.

Other Deception (Od) Scale (Nichols & Greene, 1991)

The Od scale is composed of 33 items and is a revised version of the Mp scale (Cofer et al., 1949), which distinguished college students explicitly instructed to engage in positive impression management but was insensitive to overreporting. Nichols and Greene (1991) explicitly designed the Od scale to reflect the impression management factor within Paulhus's (1984, 1986) model of social desirability. High Od scores reflect the denial of even minor negative traits, and factor analytic investigations have this scale loading clearly on the impression management factor.

Positive Mental Health (PMH4) Scale (Nichols, 1991)

The PMH4 scale consists of 34 items that were designed as a general measure of mental health and that appear on a minimum of 4 of the 28 supplementary scales that were designed to measure desirable traits. High PMH4 scores represent the endorsement of a variety of positive traits associated with good psychological adjustment. This scale loads on the self-deception factor.

Test-Taking (Tt) Defensiveness Scale (Hanley, 1957)

The 26 items selected for inclusion on the Tt scale were those for which a group of judges unanimously agreed on the socially desirable response but for which only half of the normative group endorsed in the socially desirable direction. This scale loads equally on both the self-deceptive and impression management factors.

Wiggins's Social Desirability (Wsd) Scale (Wiggins, 1959)

The Wsd scale consists of 40 items that discriminate research participants (college students) responding in a socially desirable manner from those responding under standard instructions. High scores on Wsd are associated with a deliberate attempt to manage positive impressions and suggest the assertion of a wide variety of positive traits that are cumulatively unrealistic. This scale loads on the impression management factor.

Gough's Dissimulation Index (F–K; *Gough, 1950)*

Gough (1950) proposed that examining the discrepancy between the *F* and *K* scales could provide an indication of faking-good or faking-bad; thus, the *F–K* index provides an estimate of underreporting (measured by *K*) relative to overreporting (measured by *F*) and can be used to assess for both response styles by subtracting the raw *K* score from the raw *F* score. Research suggests, however, that this scale is less effective at discriminating underreporting, which is indicated by negative values, from overreporting, which is indicated by positive values (Friedman et al., 2001; Nichols, 2001). According to Graham (2000), research supporting the use of *F–K* to identify faking-good is limited; thus, the routine use of the scale is not recommended.

L + K *Index (Cofer et al., 1949)*

This index is calculated by adding the raw *L* score to the raw *K* score. Conceptually, the *L* + *K* scale provides an estimate of the tendency to deliberately exaggerate socially desirable attributes as well as more subtle attempts to deny psychopathology. Baer et al. (1992) concluded that it is no better than *L* or *K* alone.

L + K – F *Index (Lanyon & Lutz, 1984)*

This scale represents the relative degree of deliberate and subtler tendencies to underreporting versus overreporting and is calculated by subtracting the raw *F* score from the sum of the *L* and *K* scores. Baer et al. (1992) concluded that it is no better than *L* or *K* alone.

Obvious–Subtle Index (O–S *Index; Wiener, 1948)*

This bidirectional index, derived by subtracting the summed total of the Wiener–Harmon subtle items from the summed total of the

Wiener–Harmon obvious items, represents the relative endorsement of the Obvious versus the Subtle scales. Greene (2000) has proposed that subtle items lack face validity, making it more difficult to fake on these items. Thus, a large negative discrepancy between the endorsement of obvious and subtle items, respectively, would be suggestive of symptom overreporting. Graham (2000) did not recommend the use of this index, because the endorsement of subtle items may be confounded with nay-saying response biases. Moreover, criticisms of the lack of criterion validity of the subtle items for psychopathology have challenged seriously whether the subtle items add anything to the index; rather, lower scores on the obvious content items probably carry most, if not all, of the predictive weight (see also the description of the O–S index in the description of fake-bad scales).

Utility of the MMPI–2 Indexes of Underreporting

Group Differences

When individuals underreport on the MMPI–2, scores on the validity scales designed to detect underreporting are increased. Deliberate underreporting typically results in scores above 65T on the standard validity scales *L*, *K*, and *S* (Butcher & Williams, 2000; Graham, 2000). A common method of examining the validity of underreporting scales, therefore, is to compare mean scale scores between groups responding "honestly" compared with those "faking-good." As noted by Baer and Miller (2002), three research designs have been used to examine the properties of the MMPI–2 underreporting validity scales and indexes: the analog, the differential prevalence, and the known groups designs. Most research has focused on comparing MMPI–2 protocols completed under standard instruction conditions by respondents who have little or no motivation to underreport to those of analog research participants instructed to underreport or fake-good (i.e., the analog research design). Fewer studies have used the differential prevalence design, in which a set of protocols from a group of respondents suspected of underreporting is compared to that of an honestly responding sample. No studies examining underreporting have used the known groups design, in which scores on a measure or scale from a group of respondents who are independently identified as underreporting are analyzed for evidence of response dissimulation.

In total, group differences on the MMPI–2 validity scale scores produced by respondents in contexts in which underreporting is experimentally manipulated, suspected, or known versus those in which respondents are not similarly motivated have been examined in at least 20 published studies (see Table 3.2). Almost all of these investigations used an analog research design. A recent meta-analysis covering most of these studies (Baer & Miller, 2002) reported that in general, the motivation to fake-good

TABLE 3.2
Summary of Studies Examining the Underreporting Validity Scales of the MMPI–2

Study	Group differences	Classification accuracy	Incremental validity	Other
Archer, Handel, & Couvadelli (2004)	*	*	*	
Austin (1992)	*			
Baer & Sekirnjak (1997)	*		*	
Baer, Wetter, & Berry (1995)	*		*	
Baer, Wetter, Nichols, Greene, & Berry (1995)	*		*	
Bagby, Buis, & Nicholson (1995)	*		*	
Bagby & Marshall (2004)	*		*	
Bagby, Nicholson, Buis, Radovanovic, & Fidler (1999)				
Bagby, Rogers, & Buis (1994)	*			
Bagby, Rogers, Buis, & Kalemba (1994)	*			
Bagby, Rogers, Nicholson, Buis, Seeman, & Rector (1997)	*		*	
Bannatyne, Gacono, & Greene (1999)				*
Bathurst, Gottfried, & Gottfried (1997)				
Brems & Harris (1996)	*			
Brophy (2003)				*
Butcher (1994a)	*			
Butcher, Atlis, & Fang (2000)	*			
Butcher, Morfitt, Rouse, & Holden (1997)	*			
Cassisi & Workman (1992)	*			
Cigrang & Staal (2001)	*			
Graham, Watts, & Timbrook (1991)	*	*		
Lim & Butcher (1996)	*	*		
Nicholson, Mouton, Bagby, Buis, Peterson, & Buigas (1997)				*
Posthuma & Harper (1998)	*			
Shores & Carstairs (1998)	*			
Strong, Greene, Hoppe, Johnston, & Olesen (1999)				
Strong, Greene, & Kordinak (2002)				*
Timbrook, Graham, Keiller, & Watts (1993)			*	*

is associated with higher scores on both the standard and nonstandard validity scales of the MMPI–2. Baer and Miller (2002) reported that among the standard validity scales, *S* was associated with the mean largest effect size (Cohen's $d = 1.51$). Among the nonstandard validity scales, Wsd was associated with the largest mean effect sizes (Cohen's $d = 1.56$; Baer & Miller, 2002).

Three studies published subsequent to the Baer and Miller (2002) meta-analysis reported mean group differences in scores on the MMPI–2 underreporting validity scales. Consistent with the existing literature, Archer, Handel, and Couvadelli (2004) reported that *L*, *K*, and *S* successfully discriminated protocols completed by psychiatric inpatients classified as responding defensively versus nondefensively both in a combined sample and in separate samples of men and women. Cohen's *d* effect sizes ranged from moderate to large for all three scales. In the defensive responding group, on average, *L* scores were half of a standard deviation higher, *K* scores were three fourths of a standard deviation higher, and *S* scores were nearly a full standard deviation higher than the scores in the nondefensive group (Archer et al., 2004). Brophy (2003) reported that $L + K$ and $L + K - F$ indexes extracted from a subsample of protocols from the MMPI–2 normative sample thought to simulate underreporting ranged from 70T to 73T. On average, these simulated scores were about two standard deviations higher than those for the overall normative sample.

Using a large sample of honest protocols, Bagby and Marshall (2004) factor analyzed scores from the standard MMPI–2 validity scales (i.e., the *L*, *K*, and *S* scales), as well as several nonstandard validity scales including the Esd, Od, PMH4, and Wsd scales. Consistent with the results of previous studies (Paulhus, 1984; Nichols & Greene, 1988, as cited in Nichols & Greene, 1997), a two-factor model emerged with scores on the *L*, Od, and Wsd scales loading on one factor corresponding to the impression management component of socially desirable responding, whereas scores on the *K*, *S*, Esd, and PMH4 scales loaded onto a second factor corresponding to the self-deception component of socially desirable responding.

Scores on the standard MMPI–2 underreporting validity scales—the Esd, the Od, the PMH4, and the Wsd—and the factor component scales representing PIM and SD of individuals completing the MMPI–2 as part of pre-employment selection screening or as family custody litigation assessment (i.e., differential prevalence group samples) were then compared with those of parallel analog samples instructed to fake-good. The overall pattern of differences for the individual MMPI–2 underreporting validity scales indicated that deliberate attempts to fake-good in the analog sample were associated with significant elevations on the scales measuring positive impression management (i.e., *L*, Od, and Wsd) compared with the responses of analog participants given standard instructions. In contrast, individuals in the differential prevalence group samples demonstrated elevations on the scales measuring self-deception (i.e., the *K*, *S*, Esd, and PMH4 scales) compared with the analog participants responding honestly.

Furthermore, this same pattern of results was even more striking when the factor component scale scores measuring PIM and SD responding of the differential prevalence and analog samples were compared. The analog sample participants receiving fake-good instruction scored, on average, 1.51 standard deviations higher on the PIM factor component scale than did the analog participants receiving standard instructions (versus 0.55 for the SD factor component scale scores). Meanwhile, the differential prevalence groups scored, on average, 1.02 standard deviations higher on the SD factor component scale compared with the analog sample participants receiving standard instructions (versus 0.47 for the PIM factor component scale scores). Finally, the differential prevalence group sample scored, on average, 0.42 standard deviations higher on the SD factor component score but 1.19 standard deviations lower on the PIM factor component score compared with the analog sample participants receiving fake-good instructions. This pattern of results suggests that the MMPI–2 underreporting validity scales are differentially linked to specific assessment contexts. These results also highlight the fact that the practice of developing and validating validity scales based on analog research designs and samples may not produce findings that can be generalized to real-world contexts. For the clinician, this means that elevations of the MMPI–2 underreporting validity scales related to self-deception in the absence of similar elevations on the validity scales related to positive impression management may not necessarily be indicative of deliberate attempts to underreport.

There is some evidence from three additional investigations that coaching respondents about the MMPI–2 underreporting validity scales is associated with more moderate elevations on the standard validity scales. Specifically, these studies have examined the effects of providing information about the presence of validity scales to individuals who produce invalid MMPI–2 protocols (Butcher, Atlis, & Fang, 2000; Butcher, Morfitt, Rouse, & Holden, 1997; Cigrang & Staal, 2001). Butcher et al. (1997) as well as Cigrang and Staal (2001) reported that instructing job applicants who produced invalid MMPI–2 profiles about the presence of validity scales resulted in lower scores on *L*, *K*, and *S*. Although this result seems to generalize to student samples, the mean group differences in *L*, *K*, and *S* scores are not significant (Butcher, Atlis, et al., 2000).

Classification Accuracy

In general, faking-good appears to be more difficult to detect than faking-bad, as evidenced by the fact that classification rates for the fake-good validity scales are typically lower than those for the indexes of over-reporting (Graham, 2000). Across both analog and differential prevalence designs, Baer and Miller (2002) found that studies examining the classification accuracy of the MMPI–2 validity scales consistently support the Wsd scale as the most accurate indicator of underreporting and as the scale most resistant to the effects of coaching. The Wsd scale is associated with the highest mean levels of specificity and positive predictive power, regardless of whether research participants in analog designs responding to instructions to fake-good are coached about the presence of validity scales or not (Baer & Miller, 2002). The Wsd scale is also associated with the highest mean sensitivity and negative predictive power in classifying participants as honest versus fake-good responders when participants responding to fake-good instructions are coached about the presence of validity scales (Baer & Miller, 2002). When such participants are not coached about the presence of validity scales, *S* is associated with the highest level of sensitivity and negative predictive power; Esd is associated with equally high sensitivity in such contexts (Baer & Miller, 2002). Overall, classification accuracy appears to decrease when participants are coached about the presence of validity scales (Baer & Miller, 2002).

Receiver operating characteristics analysis has also been used to evaluate the discriminant validity of the MMPI–2 underreporting validity scales. Nicholson et al. (1997) reported that the *S* scale was most sensitive to differences between students instructed to fake-good from students responding to standard instructions with no motivation to underreport. In addition, *S* and the *O–S* index were associated with significantly more discriminant power than both *K* and *F–K*; there were significant differences between *S* and the *O–S* index, indicating the discriminant ability of these scales.

Incremental Validity

The relative utility of the nonstandard validity scales over and above the standard validity scales remains uncertain. Although some studies have demonstrated incremental validity for the nonstandard scales (Baer, Wetter, Nichols, Greene, & Berry, 1995; Baer & Sekirnjak, 1997; Bagby, Buis, & Nicholson, 1995; Bagby, Rogers, Nicholson, Buis, Seeman, & Rector, 1997), Baer and Miller (2002) noted that only two studies showed attendant improvements in classification accuracy. Furthermore, support for the incremental validity of specific nonstandard scales is inconsistent. Overall, there is limited evidence that Esd, Mp, Od, *O–S*, and Wsd may have incremental validity over *L* and *K*, and replication using differential prevalence and known-groups designs is needed to verify these results. In addition, three of these studies (Baer et al., 1995; Baer & Sekirnjak, 1997; Bagby et al., 1997) were published when the *S* scale was still considered a nonstandard validity scale; as such, previous results may not hold if *L*, *K*, and *S* are considered together. Although the *S* scale items are most similar to those of the *K* scale, Nichols (2001) pointed out that the items included on *S* are less subtle than those of *K*, suggesting that *S* may account for some additional variance in underreporting responding that is not measured by *K* or *L* alone. Indeed, Archer et al. (2004) demonstrated that the *S* scale did account for a significant amount of additional variance in predicting defensive versus nondefensive responding in a psychiatric sample.

Taxometric Analysis of Socially Desirable Responding

Perhaps some of the most interesting work with enormous potential to enhance the applied utility of the MMPI–2 underreporting validity scales is the work of Strong and Greene and their colleagues (Strong, Greene, Hoppe, Johnston, & Oleson, 1999; Strong, Greene, & Kordinak, 2002) who have used taxometric procedures to examine the structure of self-deception and impression management responding. Results from these investigations have indicated that impression management responding is best conceptualized as a taxonomic category, with distinct and identifiable boundaries; in contrast, self-deceptive responding was represented best as a dimensional construct (Strong et al., 1999, 2002). These results suggest base rate estimates of impression management, and the classification rates for validity scales measuring this response style can be developed in the absence of a separate external criterion, which in turn permits the production of cut scores that are valid, reliably accurate, and probably applicable across a range of populations (Strong et al., 2002). Application of taxometric analyses to some of the individual validity scales from the MMPI–2 clearly identified as assessing impression management to derive cut scores would be extremely useful, as they could be used to identify those respondents who intentionally sought to create a favorable impression.

On the other hand, self-deceptive responding as a dimensional construct is conceptually more complex and its dimensional status is consistent with the idea of a "systematic error" component, suggesting that it cannot be easily extracted from valid trait variance associated with this construct. Elevations on validity scales measuring SD should, therefore, not be interpreted as necessarily invalidating the protocol, but instead should be interpreted as part of the overall profile. In contrast, although PIM may also have valid relations with personality traits, its discreteness can be clearly defined and measured; elevations of PIM–related scales would therefore indicate that the profile is clearly invalid because of an intentional effort to dissemble. Of course, much of this is speculative at this point, and more research is needed in this area. However, from an applied research perspective, separating PIM from SD has the potential to provide the clinician with a more nuanced interpretation of the test taker's motivation.

ASSESSING OVERREPORTING WITH THE MMPI–2

The terms faking-bad, malingering, and overreporting are often used interchangeably in the context of discussing overreporting and the MMPI–2. In this chapter, we connote overreporting to represent both intentional and unintentional responding. Fake-bad responding refers to intentional efforts to overreport, as manifest, for example, in studies instructing participants to fake-bad. As with the MMPI–2 underreporting scales, there are both standard and nonstandard validity scales designed to detect overreporting on the MMPI–2 and fake-bad indexes. As with the underreporting validity scales, a myriad of overreporting validity scales have been developed. In this chapter, we limit our review to those used most frequently or gaining recent prominence, whether deserved or not. Brief descriptions of the family of *F* scales—*F*, *F(B)*, and *Fp*—and the nonstandard validity scales and indexes are provided in Table 3.3. Chapter 16 in this volume provides case illustrations about how some of these validity scales have been used in an applied context (disability evaluations).

Scale Description

Infrequency (F) *Scale (Meehl & Hathaway, 1946)*

The *F* scale was originally designed to assess deviant or atypical ways of responding by identifying items that were endorsed rarely by the MMPI normative sample (i.e., less than 10%). The *F* scale items reflect a wide range of psychiatric symptoms, including bizarre sensations, psychotic symptoms, atypical beliefs, and unlikely self-descriptions (Dahlstrom, Welsh, & Dahlstrom, 1972). The logic underlying the scale was that it would be relatively unlikely that such a wide range of symptoms would characterize any specific disorder. As such, most bona fide psychiatric patients endorse only a small subset of items related to symptoms of their disorder. A high *F* scale score reflects endorsement of a combination of diverse and unusual problems that rarely occur together in bona fide psychopathology. High *F* scale scores may be a result of random responding, severe distress or psychopathology, overendorsement of symptoms related to

TABLE 3.3
Summary Description of Overreporting Scales and Indexes

Scale/Index	Number of items	Description
Standard		
F	60	Rare symptoms of psychopathology
F(B)	40	Rare symptoms of psychopathology from second half of MMPI–2
Fp	27	Rare symptoms of psychopathology but not symptom severity
Nonstandard		
Ds	58	Stereotypes about symptoms of neurosis
Ds–R	32	Stereotypes about symptoms of neurosis
D–S	27	Items have face but no predictive validity
FBS	43	Faking by personal injury claimants
F–ptsd	32	Rare symptoms of PTSD
Ob		Endorsement of obvious symptoms of psychopathology
Md		Symptoms associated with feigned depression
Indexes		
F–K		Underreporting relative to overreporting
O–S index	253	Endorsement of obvious items versus subtle items

a "cry for help," or "faking-bad" (i.e., symptom exaggeration or malingering). The *F* scale on the MMPI–2 is largely intact, with only four items being dropped from the original MMPI version; the current version is thus comprised of 60 items.

Back Infrequency [F(B)] *Scale (Butcher, Graham, et al., 2001)*

This scale was developed for the MMPI–2 to complement the *F* scale, drawing 40 items from the back half of the MMPI–2. Like the F scale, elevated scores on *F(B)* may reflect random responding, acute psychosis, or overreporting of symptoms. In contrast to the *F* scale, which reflects strange and atypical behavior and symptoms, *F(B)* items reflect suicidal ideation, hopelessness, and problems with relations.

Infrequency–Psychopathology (Fp) *Scale (Arbisi & Ben-Porath, 1995)*

Increased scores on *F* and *F(B)* can be elevated by malingering or severe psychopathology (Graham, 2000; Greene, 2000). Thus, individuals who are experiencing severe distress often obtain highly elevated scores on *F* and *F(B)* that are difficult to differentiate from faking-bad. *Fp* was developed by Arbisi and Ben-Porath (1995) to disentangle these two potential contributors to such scale elevation. In particular, *Fp* was designed to be less reflective of severity of psychopathology and general maladjustment than *F* and *F(B)*. As such, elevations on *Fp* should be more directly attributable to malingering and not severe psychopathology. The 27 items were selected on the basis of being rarely endorsed (i.e., less than 20% of the time) by both the MMPI–2 normative sample and psychiatric inpatients. The item content is diverse, including psychotic symptoms, very unusual habits, highly amoral attitudes, and identity confusion. This scale is best used in combination with *F* and is well validated (Arbisi & Ben-Porath, 1995, 1997, 1998). Recent criticism suggests that the *Fp* scale is confounded with fake-good responding as it includes four items from the *L* scale (Gass & Luis, 2001a). Empirical studies indicate, however, that almost all of the *Fp* items, including those also residing on the *L* scale, contribute to identifying malingering (Strong, Greene, & Schinka, 2000) and that excluding the *L* scale items actually decreases the capacity of *Fp* to detect malingering (Arbisi, Ben-Porath, & McNulty, 2003b).

Malingering Case Study. Ms. Anna P. was referred for a psychological assessment by her insurance company in order to clarify *Diagnostic and Statistical Manual of Mental Disorders* (4th ed., *DSM–IV*; American Psychiatric Association, 1994) diagnoses, level of impairment, and ability to return to work. She was a 48-year-old married woman with a university level education, who had been employed as an administrative assistant in a large advertising agency for 5 years prior to taking a disability leave 4 years before because of chronic neck and back pain and depression. She had not returned to work since that time. She described an onset of significant back and neck pain 4 years ago in the absence of an accident or injury. Multiple physical examinations with a variety of specialists revealed no organic abnormalities that would account for her complaints of pain. She sought psychiatric treatment 3 years before because of additional complaints of mood problems and was diagnosed with unipolar depression as well as chronic pain. Despite numerous psychiatric and pain interventions, Ms. P. demonstrated no improvement in her mood or pain symptoms or level of functioning.

At the time of the assessment, Ms. P. reported spending the majority of her time in a sedentary position at home watching television. She stated that she rarely socialized and found it difficult to do almost anything around the house, including any household chores. She stated that she often found it difficult even to follow a television program or film because of pain and concentration difficulties.

Behavioral observations revealed a woman who was neatly dressed and well groomed, presenting in a polite, resigned, and fatigued manner. Her affect remained dysphoric throughout the interview. Her speech was normal in pace and volume. No gross abnormalities in thought content, thought processes, or motor coordination were observed. She moved somewhat slowly and demonstrated frequent pain behaviors such as grimacing, wincing, or holding a hand to her back. She tended to respond in an acquiescent or suggestible manner to interview questions regarding psychopathology; in other words, she tended to endorse an unusually wide range and severe degree of psychopathology during the structured clinical interview.

The results of the MMPI–2 indicated that the number of items left uncompleted was within acceptable limits. Review of her VRIN (Variable Response Inconsistency) and TRIN (True Response Inconsistency) scores suggested appropriate attention to item content and consistent responding to items with similar content. The degree to which response styles may have affected or distorted the report of symptoms on the MMPI–2 was also assessed. Significant elevations were seen on the *F* (120T), *F(B)* (120T), and *Fp* (113T) scales, indicating significant overreporting of psychopathology. This combination of elevations, particularly that seen on the *Fp* scale, is strongly suggestive of malingering of psychopathology. This pattern of overendorsing of psychopathology was reflected in Ms. P.'s Personality Assessment Inventory (PAI) results, which showed a significant elevation on the Negative Impression Management (NIM) scale (88T).

Although a diagnosis of malingering indicates the presence of significant or gross exaggeration of symptoms, such a diagnosis does not preclude the presence of genuine underlying psychopathology. Ms. P.'s tendency to exaggerate or overendorse psychopathology during the assessment precluded clarification of any possible underlying, bona fide psychopathology. As such, further investigation of potential diagnoses of pain disorder and major depressive disorder was recommended on conclusion of the assessment.

Gough Dissimulation Index (F–K; *Gough, 1950)*

As described previously, this index represents the tendency to underreport psychopathology or minimize psychological disturbance versus the tendency to overreport psychopathology or exaggerate psychological disturbance. According to Graham (2000), whenever *F* raw scores exceed *K* raw scores, faking-bad is a consideration. Larger (positive valence) discrepancies suggest an overreporting response style but may also reflect confusion, distress, or severity of psychopathology.

Gough Dissimulation Scales (Ds *and* Ds–R; *Gough, 1954)*

The Dissimulation (*Ds*) scale was developed to identify individuals who were simulating or exaggerating symptoms of neurosis. The scale was constructed by using 74 MMPI items that mental health professionals judged to be indicative of psychopathology but that were not typically endorsed by psychiatric patients. *Ds* items are thought to reflect stereotypes about neuroticism, such as nonspecific fears, inability to share with others, and social avoidance (Greene, 2000). The *Ds* scale was revised to a shorter, 40-item version called Dissimulation—Revised (*Ds*–R; Greene, 2000). The analogous scales for the MMPI–2—*Ds*2 and *Ds*–R2—used the MMPI–2 items that were retained from MMPI scales, which numbered 58 and 34, respectively.

*Obvious–Subtle Index (*O–S *Index; Greene, 1991)*

As described previously, the O–*S* index represents the ratio of endorsement of "subtle" versus "obvious" items and is thought to represent the relative presence of faking-good or faking-bad. The subtle items, which reside on a number of clinical scales, have no face validity and are the direct consequence of the empirical keying item selection strategy employed by the MMPI test developers. The obvious items have high face validity, that is, they were judged to be easily identifiable as indicating emotional disturbance (Wiener, 1948); thus, individuals motivated to exaggerate psychopathology would be expected to endorse these items more frequently than the subtle items. Consequently, a large positive discrepancy between the endorsement of obvious and subtle items, respectively, is thought to be suggestive of symptom overreporting. This index used to be available as part of the test publisher's interpretative report. However, the subtle items have no criterion validity for bona fide psychopathology, and it is the obvious items that carry the predictive weight in this index (Bagby, Rogers, & Buis, 1994; Bagby, Rogers, Nicholson, et al., 1997; Sivec, Lynn, & Garske, 1994; Timbrook, Graham, Keiller, & Watts, 1993).

A little known but potentially promising variant of the Wiener (1948) subtle items is the Deceptive–Subtle (*D–S*) scale developed by Dannenbaum and Lanyon (1993). In contrast to the Wiener subtle items, which ostensibly have predictive but not face validity, the *D–S* items have face validity but no predictive validity. Thus, potential malingers would actually score lower on this scale compared to psychiatric patients and a nonclinical sample (see Bagby, Buis, & Nicholson, 1995; Bagby, Nicholson, & Buis, 1998).

Obvious (Ob) *Scale (Wiener, 1948)*

The total of the obvious items has been suggested as an alternative to the O–*S* index based on studies that suggest that they account for most of its predictive power.

Utility of the MMPI–2 Overreporting Scales and Indexes

Group Differences

When normal individuals attempt to simulate serious psychopathology on the MMPI or MMPI–2, they tend to overendorse deviant items (Graham, 2000). The result is to produce scores on validity scales and indexes that are much higher than those of seriously disturbed patients. Similarly, Rogers, Sewell, and Ustad (1995) found that psychiatric patients instructed to fake-bad or exaggerate symptoms had profiles that resembled nonpsychiatric simulators. A fake-bad profile on the MMPI–2 typically shows an elevation on the validity scales and indexes *F*, *F(B)*, and *Fp* (usually 100T for all three scales; Graham, 2000). In contrast, acutely psychotic patients produce *F* scale scores in the range of 70T to 90T.

A meta-analysis of 73 studies of overreporting on the MMPI–2 (Rogers, Sewell, Martin, & Vitacco, 2003; see Table 3.4) indicated that the validity scales and indexes are quite effective in distinguishing research participants instructed to fake-bad from nonclinical participants completing the MMPI–2 under standard instructions (M Cohen's d = 2.49). Overall, and among the standard overreporting validity scales, the largest effect size for this comparison was associated with the *F* scale (M Cohen's d = 4.05), consistent with the results of an earlier meta-analysis of 15 studies of overreporting on the MMPI–2 (Rogers et al., 2003; Rogers, Sewell, & Salekin, 1994). Among the nonstandard validity scales and indexes alone, the Ob was associated with the highest mean effect size (M Cohen's d = 3.57; Rogers et al., 2003) for this comparison.

The MMPI–2 validity scales and indexes are also effective at distinguishing research participants instructed to fake a psychiatric disorder from bona fide psychiatric patients completing the MMPI–2 under standard instructions (M Cohen's d = 1.51), with the highest mean Cohen's d associated with the *F* scale (d = 2.21; Rogers et al., 2003). As before, the highest mean Cohen's d among the nonstandard overreporting validity scales and indexes for this comparison was associated with Ob (d = 2.03; Rogers et al., 2003). Studies published subsequently to the meta-analysis of Rogers et al. (2003) report similar results (Frueh et al., 2003; Larrabee, 2003a, 2003b; Steffan, Clopton, & Morgan, 2003). However, several other studies suggest that *Fp* may be more sensitive in such comparisons. For example, Blanchard, McGrath, Pogge, and Khadivi (2003) reported that *Fp* was associated with largest effect size among the standard scales, and *F–K* among the nonstandard scales, when comparing students instructed to overreport and bona fide inpatients. Bury and Bagby (2002) compared bona fide workplace injury insurance claimants with PTSD with students instructed to complete the MMPI–2 once under standard instructions and a second time under instructions to fake PTSD who received no coaching, coaching about the symptoms of PTSD, coaching about the presence of validity scales, or combined coaching (i.e., symptom coaching and validity scale coaching). The largest mean effect size across the comparisons of faking students versus bona fide PTSD claimants among the standard MMPI–2 overreporting validity scales was associated with the *Fp* scale, whereas the largest mean effect size among the nonstandard MMPI–2 overreporting validity scales

TABLE 3.4
Summary of Studies Examining the Overreporting Validity Scales of the MMPI–2

Study	Group differences	Classification accuracy	Incremental validity	Other
Alexy & Webb (1999)				
Arbisi & Ben-Porath (1995)	*		*	
Arbisi & Ben-Porath (1997)	*			
Arbisi & Ben-Porath (1998)	*	*	*	
Arbisi, Ben-Porath, & McNulty (2003b)	*	*	*	
Archer, Handel, Greene, Baer, & Elkins (2001)	*	*		
Austin (1992)	*			
Bagby, Buis, & Nicholson (1995)	*		*	
Bagby, Nicholson, Bacchiochi, Ryder, & Bury (2002)	*		*	
Bagby, Nicholson, & Buis (1998)	*	*	*	
Bagby, Rogers, & Buis (1994)	*	*		
Bagby, Rogers, Buis, & Kalemba (1994)	*	*		
Bagby, Rogers, Buis, et al.(1997)	*		*	
Bagby, Rogers, Nicholson, et al. (1997)	*		*	
Baldrachi, Hilsenroth, Arsenault, Sloan, & Walter (1999)	*			
Bathurst, Gottfried, & Gottfried (1997)				
Ben-Porath, Butcher, & Graham (1991)	*			
Berry et al. (1996)	*	*		
Berry et al. (2001)	*	*		
Berry, Wetter, Baer, Youngjohn, et al. (1995)	*			
Blanchard et al. (2003)	*	*		
Bowler, Hartney, & Ngo (1998)	*			
Brems & Harris (1996)	*			
Bury & Bagby (2002)	*	*	*	
Butcher, Arbisi, Atlis, & McNulty (2003)		*		*
Cassisi & Workman (1992)	*	*		
Cramer (1995)	*			
Cumella, Wall, & Kerr-Almeida (2000)				
Elhai, Gold, Frueh, & Gold (2000)	*	*		*
Elhai, Gold, Sellers, & Dorfman (2001)	*	*	*	*

TABLE 3.4
(Continued)

Study	Group differences	Classification accuracy	Incremental validity	Other
Elhai, Ruggiero, Frueh, Beckham, Gold, & Feldman (2002)	*	*	*	*
Fox, Gerson, & Lees-Haley (1995)		*		*
Franklin, Repasky, Thompson, Shelton, & Uddo (2002)	*			
Franklin, Repasky, Thompson, Shelton, & Uddo (2003)	*			
Frueh et al. (2003)	*			
Frueh, Smith, & Barker (1996)	*			
Gandolfo (1995)				*
Graham, Watts, & Timbrook (1991)	*	*		
Greiffenstein, Baker, Gola, Donders, & Miller (2002)	*	*		
Greiffenstein, Gola, & Baker (1995)	*	*		*
Heinze & Purisch (2001)	*	*		*
Hoffman, Scott, Emick, & Adams (1999)	*			
Iverson, Franzen, & Hammond (1995)	*	*		
Kirz, Drescher, Klein, Gusman, & Schwartz (2001)	*			
Klonsky & Bertelson (2000)				
Ladd (1998)	*			
Lamb, Berry, Wetter, & Baer (1994)	*			
Larrabee (2003a)	*			
Larrabee (2003b)	*	*	*	
Lees-Haley (1991)	*			*
Lees-Haley (1992)		*		
Lees-Haley (1997)				
LePage & Mogge (2001)				
Lewis, Simcox, & Berry (2002)	*	*		
Lim & Butcher (1996)	*	*		
Linbald (1994)	*			
Meyers, Millis, & Volkert (2002)	*	*		*
Mittenberg, Tremont, & Rayls (1996)				*
Morrell & Rubin (2001)	*			
Nicholson et al. (1997)				*
Pensa, Dorfman, Gold, & Schneider (1996)	*	*		
Posthuma & Harper (1998)	*			
Rogers, Bagby, & Chakraborty (1993)	*	*		

(continued)

TABLE 3.4
(Continued)

Study	Group differences	Classification accuracy	Incremental validity	Other
Rogers, Sewell, & Ustad (1995)	*	*		
Rothke et al. (2000)		*		
Senior & Douglas (2001a)		*		
Shores & Carstairs (1998)	*	*		
Siegel (1996)				
Sivec, Hilsenroth, & Lynn (1995)	*	*		
Sivec, Lynn, & Garske (1994)	*	*	*	
Steffan, Clopton, & Morgan (2003)	*	*	*	
Storm & Graham (2000)	*	*		
Strong, Greene, & Schinka (2000)				*
Stukenberg, Brady, & Klinetob (2000)				
Timbrook, Graham, Keiller, & Watts (1993)	*			
Tsushima & Tsushima (2001)	*			
Viglione et al. (2001)	*			
Walters & Clopton (2000)	*	*		
Welburn et al. (2003)	*			
Wetter, Baer, Berry, & Reynolds (1994)	*			
Wetter, Baer, Berry, Robinson, & Sumpter (1993)	*	*		
Wetter, Baer, Berry, Smith, & Larsen (1992)	*			
Wetter & Deitsch (1996)	*			
Wong, Lerner-Poppen, & Durham (1998)	*	*		*
Youngjohn, Davis, & Wolf (1997)	*			

and indexes was associated with the *Ds2* scale. Frueh et al. (2003) reported that *F* and *F–K* were associated with higher effect sizes than *Fp* when comparing compensation-seeking versus non-compensation-seeking veterans with PTSD. Larrabee (2003b) found that among the standard scales, *F* and *F(B)* were equally effective in discriminating compensation-seeking litigant malingering neurocognitive dysfunction from nonlitigating bona fide closed head injury. Finally, Steffan et al. (2003) compared students instructed to feign depression who were either uncoached or coached about the presence of validity scales on the MMPI–2 with students who were self-reporting depressive symptoms. Steffan et al. (2003) reported that in the comparison of coached feigners versus depressed students, the largest effect sizes were associated with *F(B)* among the family of *F* scales, and *F–K* for nonstandard scales. In contrast, when the uncoached feigners were compared with the depressed students, the largest effect sizes were associated with *F* among the standard scales, and the *Ds2* among the nonstandard scales.

Overall then, these results suggest that the validity scales and indexes on the MMPI–2, particularly the *F* scale, are generally effective at detecting faking by nonclinical samples (e.g., college students or community adults). The findings of analog studies (i.e., studies in which normal individuals are asked to simulate a disorder) appear to generalize, in so far as the validity scales and indexes are also effective in detecting faking in real-world samples. For example, the *F* scale readily distinguishes prison inmates responding honestly and those instructed to fake-bad (Iverson, Franzen, & Hammond, 1995) and psychiatric patients responding honestly from those instructed to fake-bad (Arbisi & Ben-Porath, 1998; Berry et al., 1996; Rogers et al., 1995).

Classification Accuracy

As noted earlier, classification accuracy is typically higher for the fake-bad validity scales and indexes in detecting of overreporting than for underreporting validity scales and indexes in detecting faking-good. Among the family of *F* scales, Rogers et al. (2003) reported in a recent meta-analysis that the *F* scale was associated with the highest mean overall correct classification (OCC) rate (M OCC = .86). Among the nonstandard scales, the *O–S* index was associated with the highest mean OCC rate (M OCC = .85; Rogers et al., 2003), although it is important to emphasize that it is likely that the sum of obvious items was carrying the predictive load. Classification rates are lower when the comparison group comprises psychiatric patients, reflecting the fact that psychiatric samples have higher elevations on the validity and clinical scales, with a resultant decrease in separation between groups. However, classification accuracy remains acceptable (Rogers et al., 2003). Three recent studies have reported results that are inconsistent with those of the meta-analysis by Rogers et al. Arbisi et al. (2003b) found that *Fp* demonstrated the highest OCC rate in distinguishing veteran psychiatric inpatients responding under standard instructions from those instructed to fake-bad. Blanchard et al. (2003) reported that *Fp* (OCC = .99) and *F–K* (OCC = .97), among the standard and nonstandard scales, respectively, were most accurate in classifying students instructed versus overreport from bona fide inpatients. Finally, Bury and Bagby (2002) found that OCC rates were highest for *F(B)* (M OCC = .77), among the standard scales, and *Ds2* (M OCC = .79), among the nonstandard scales, for classifying students faking PTSD who were uncoached, coached about PTSD symptoms, or coached about the presence of validity scales versus bona fide PTSD claimants. Classification accuracy was higher among the standard scales using *Fp* (OCC = .75) when distinguishing students who were coached about both PTSD symptoms and validity scales; as in the previous comparisons, *Ds*2 (OCC = .75) was associated with the highest OCC rate among the nonstandard scales.

Receiver operating characteristics analysis has also been used to evaluate the discriminant ability of the MMPI–2 underreporting validity scales and indexes. Nicholson et al. (1997) reported that *F* and *F–K* were most sensitive to differences between students instructed to fake-bad and forensic psychiatric patients and general psychiatric patients. Significance testing of the area under the curve associated with various overreporting validity scales and indexes confirmed that *F* and *F–K* were associated with significantly more discriminant power than *Ds*–R2, *Fp*, *F(B)*, and *O–S* in the comparison of students instructed to fake-bad and forensic psychiatric patients. Nicholson et al. reported similar results for the comparison of students faking-bad with general psychiatric patients; specifically, *F*, *F–K*, and *Fp* were associated with significantly more discriminant power than the remaining overreporting validity indexes.

Incremental Validity

The relative utility of the nonstandard overreporting validity scales and indexes over and above the standard overreporting validity scales remains uncertain, as very few studies have examined this issue. Despite this, some studies have demonstrated incremental validity for the nonstandard scales and indexes (Bagby et al., 1995; Bury & Bagby, 2002; Sivec et al., 1994), although there is currently not enough data to suggest that these measures consistently add clinically meaningful information beyond the family of *F* scales. For example, Bury and Bagby (2002) demonstrated incremental validity for *Ds*2 and Ob over the family of *F* scales in distinguishing uncoached students faking PTSD versus bona fide claimants and students faking PTSD who were coached about both PTSD symptoms and the presence of validity scales versus bona fide PTSD claimants. At the same time, however, the family of *F* scales adds incrementally to both *Ds*2 and Ob. Likewise, *Ds*2 and *F–K* add incrementally to prediction of symptom coached students versus bona fide claimants; but, in reverse, the family of *F* scales added incrementally to both *Ds*2 and *F–K*. Similarly, the *D–S* scale, which on its own is a significant predictor of malingering, is unable to add any significant predictive variance to the family of *F* scales. Overall, there is only limited evidence to suggest that nonstandard validity scales and indexes add incremental validity in the predictions of fake-bad responding to the family of *F* scales.

Future incremental validity studies that compare the standard validity scales with nonstandard scales and indexes must use the standard validity in the manner that is recommended in the test publisher's manual. It is recommended, for example, that the family of *F* scales be used in combination to detect the presence of fake-bad responding. To this end, analyses comparing the incremental predictive capacity of nonstandard validity scales should remove predictive variance of the family of *F* scales in combination or as a "block" and then examine the remaining variance with the nonstandard scales (see, e.g., Bury & Bagby, 2002).

Taxonometric Analysis of Fake-Bad Responding

Strong et al. (2000) applied taxonometric procedures to the *F* and *Fp* scales, which revealed that overreporting was a taxon and, therefore, were able to generate cut reliable and scores for detecting faking-bad for these scales. Consistent with the development strategies of these scales, fewer *F* scale items survived consistency tests than did *Fp* items, suggesting that *Fp*, in comparison with *F*, is a purer measure of malingering than *F*. The *F* scale contains some items maximally sensitive to severe psychopathology, whereas other items are sensitive to malingering. *Fp*, in contrast, is composed mostly of items sensitive to malingering. These findings support the clinical use of these scales sequentially, screening first with *F* and then confirming or disconfirming the presence of malingering with scores from *Fp*.

Effects of Coaching

A growing body of evidence suggests that the clinical utility of the validity scales and their capacity to discriminate between malingerers and bona fide psychiatric patients are not as accurate when test takers are coached about the operating characteristics of the MMPI–2 validity scales (Bury & Bagby, 2002; Lamb, Berry, Wetter, & Baer, 1994; Rogers, Bagby, & Chakraborty, 1993; Storm & Graham, 2000). Storm and Graham (2000) found that knowledge about validity scales significantly reduced the accuracy of the *F* scale in classifying fake-bad profiles. Rogers et al. (1993) found that knowledge about the validity scales enabled most fakers to escape detection on the *F* scale when faking schizophrenia, as compared to only one third (approximately) of fakers who did not have this knowledge. Coaching on the validity scales may allow simulators to produce clinical profiles in the range of psychiatric patients without significantly elevating validity scales and indexes (Berry, Wetter, & Baer, 1995). Rogers et al. (1993) also found that knowledge about the validity scales was more effective for escaping detection than knowledge about symptoms or knowledge about both symptoms and the validity scales. Bury and Bagby reported a similar pattern of results in a study examining feigned PTSD, although the classification rates were not significantly altered relative to the uncoached condition. In sum, it is clear that respondents' knowledge of the operating characteristics of the MMPI–2 clearly enhances the capacity to feign.

EXHIBIT 3.1

Highlight: Interpretation of the MMPI–2 Validity Scales and Indexes

- Test takers may be motivated for a variety of reasons not to respond honestly or in a straightforward manner to items on instruments measuring psychopathology.
- The MMPI–2 has included validity scales to detect the underreporting (i.e., fake-good responding) and overreporting (i.e., fake-bad responding).
- In many assessment contexts, respondents may be consciously or unconsciously motivated by personal goals to underreport symptoms of psychopathology. For example, disputing parents undergoing child custody and access evaluation may not report emotional problems they experience, and job applicants, in an effort "to put their best foot forward," may present themselves in an overly favorable light.
- In this chapter, we connote underreporting to represent both intentional and unintentional responding. Fake-good is conceptualized as an intentional effort to underreport, as manifest, for example, in studies instructing participants to fake-good.
- In a number of contexts, overreporting of symptoms may occur. For example, personal injury litigants or combat veterans may exaggerate the extent of psychological trauma they experience in order to maximize their chances of receiving financial compensation.
- Individuals genuinely experiencing psychopathology may exaggerate their symptoms as a "cry for help."
- The motivation to overreport, in contrast to underreporting, is typically intentional and engaged with the full awareness of the respondent.
- Given that underreporting and overreporting response styles have the potential to invalidate MMPI–2 protocols and that such responding likely occurs in a variety of important assessment contexts, the assessment and accurate detection of response biases are critical aspects of MMPI–2 interpretation.
- Fake-good response style has the effect of lowering content and clinical scales.
- Deliberate underreporting typically results in scores above 65T on the standard validity scales *L, K,* and *S*.
- Meta-analyses have indicated that the validity scales and indexes are reasonably effective in distinguishing research participants instructed to fake-good from nonclinical participants completing the MMPI–2 under standard instructions.
- Overall, these results suggest that *S* is the most sensitive standard validity scale for detecting the effects of underreporting among groups of participants deliberately instructed to fake-good.
- Support for the incremental validity of specific nonstandard scales and indexes designed to detect underreporting (additional validity scale measures that are not incorporated in standard MMPI–2 scoring) is inconsistent. The extent to which scales such as Esd, Mp, Od, *O–S,* and Wsd improve interpretations beyond *L, K,* and *S* needs to be determined.
- Results and interpretation from factor analytic investigation of underreporting scales suggest the presence of at least two independent components variously labeled but invariably measuring two constructs—self-deception (SD) and positive impression management (PIM).
- Different validity scales are differentially sensitive to these two response styles.
- Recent taxonometric investigations have indicated that impression management responding is best conceptualized as a taxonomic category, with distinct and identifiable boundaries; in contrast, self-deceptive responding is represented best as a dimensional construct.
- In general, faking-good appears to be more difficult to detect than faking-bad, as evidenced by the fact that classification rates for the fake-good validity scales are typically lower than those for the indexes of overreporting.

EXHIBIT 3.1
(Continued)

- Fake-bad response style has the effect of elevating content and clinical scales.
- Deliberate overreporting typically results in scores above 100T on the standard validity scales *F, F(B),* and *Fp.*
- Meta-analyses have indicated that the validity scales and indexes are quite effective in distinguishing research participants instructed to fake-bad from nonclinical participants completing the MMPI–2 under standard instructions.
- Overall, these results suggest that the validity scales and indexes on the MMPI–2, particularly the *F* scale, are generally effective at detecting overreporting by nonclinical samples (e.g., college students or community adults).
- The relative utility of the nonstandard overreporting validity scales and indexes over and above the standard overreporting validity scales remains uncertain. The extent to which scales such as *F–K, Ds*2, and *Ob* improve interpretations beyond *F, F(B),* and *Fp* needs to be examined further.
- There is some evidence in the research literature that coaching respondents about the MMPI–2 validity scales is associated with more moderate elevations on the standard validity scales. Specific scales designed to be impervious to the effects of coaching have been developed.
- A number of supplementary validity scales designed to detect overreporting of specific disorders (e.g., PTSD, depression) or in specific contexts (e.g., litigation) have been developed. Further validation of these scales is necessary. Taxonometric investigations of overreporting indicate that this type of response bias is best conceptualized as a taxonomic category.

Partly in response to the concern that validity scale coaching enhances one's capacity to fake successfully, coupled with the fact that coaching in applied contexts probably occurs (Wetter & Corrigan, 1995; Youngjohn, 1995; Youngjohn, Lees-Haley, & Binder, 1999), Bacchiochi and Bagby (2005) have developed an MMPI–2 Malingering Discriminant Function index (M–DFI) that has so far proven to be impervious to the effects of coaching, at least as compared with the family of *F* scales and nonstandard fake-bad validity scales. Following in part the procedure used by Rogers and colleagues to develop the Rogers Discriminant Function scale (Rogers, Sewell, Morey, & Ustad, 1996) for the Personality Assessment Inventory (Morey, 1991), the 17 clinical, content, and content component scales were submitted to discriminant function analysis to extract those scales that were able to maximally distinguish a sample of bona fide psychiatric patients (n = 383) from research participants who had been instructed to fake-bad and who had received validity scale coaching (n = 377). In the derivation sample, 85% of the validity coached feigners and 85% of the bona fide psychiatric patients were correctly classified. In the replication sample, the same function correctly identified 83% of the 157 feigners and 85% of the bona fide psychiatric patients. This sum raw score was transformed into a T score. In a subsequent hierarchical logistic regression, the M–DFI outperformed the family of *F* scales and was able to add significant incremental validity to the family of *F* scales in distinguishing bona fide patients from validity scale coached feigners. More important, whereas the family of *F* scales showed diminution in predictive power in the validity coached condition, the M–DFI showed no such reduction. More validation research is needed for this scale. (See Exhibit 3.1 for a discussion of interpretive strategies for the validity scales.)

Disorder- or Situation-Specific Malingering Scales

Recently, some investigators attempted to develop malingering scales designed to detect the feigning of specific disorders. Elhai et al. (2002) developed the Infrequency–Post-Traumatic Stress Disorder (*F–ptsd*) scale to detect feigned posttraumatic stress disorder (PTSD), and Steffan et al. (2003) designed the Malingered Depression (Md) scale to detect feigned depression. In a similar vein, Lees-Haley and colleagues (Lees-Haley, 1992; Lees-Haley, English, & Glenn, 1991) developed the Fake-Bad Scale (FBS), which was designed to detect the feigning of conditions most likely to emerge in personal injury cases, including depression, PTSD, somatic complaints, and neurocognitive dysfunction associated with closed head injury. At present, the *F–ptsd* and the Md scales have not been extensively examined and the use of them in the clinical context seems premature, although the development, rational, and preliminary validation data for the *F–ptsd* make this scale promising.

The FBS has been more extensively examined. In a comprehensive study that included nearly 20,000 MMPI–2 protocols from a variety of samples, including general medical patients, chronic pain patients, and personal injury litigants, Butcher, Arbisi, Atlis, and McNulty (2003) reported that the standard cut scale for the FBS classified nearly 40% of the individuals in some samples as malingering, a remarkably inflated figure compared to base rates reported in other studies. The FBS also correlated more highly with MMPI–2 clinical and content scales than it did with the validity scales, prompting Butcher et al. (2003) to conclude that the FBS most likely measures general maladjustment.

Bury and Bagby (2002) reported the FBS to be a poor predictor of PTSD, as it was systematically removed as a nonsignificant contributor in four logistic regression equations designed to discriminate feigned PTSD from bona fide PTSD. Tsushima and Tsushima (2001) reported that the FBS was significantly higher in personal injury litigants compared to patients not involved in litigation, whereas the family of *F* scales showed no such differences. However, the personal injury litigants also scored significantly higher than those patients not involved in litigation on seven of the nine clinical scales (Mf [Masculinity–Femininity] not included as a clinical scale) and did not correlate highly with the other validity scales. Although Tsushima and Tsushima suggested that these data support the validity of the FBS in personal injury cases, a more accurate interpretation of these data, at least in the opinion of the writers of this chapter, is that it supports the contention that this scale does not measure malingering but, rather, bona fide symptom severity. Larrabee (1998, 2003a, 2003b) has reported that the FBS is associated with the largest mean difference effect size among the standard and nonstandard validity scales in distinguishing compensation-seeking litigant malingering neurocognitive dysfunction from nonlitigating bona fide closed head injury patients. Thus, with this sample, the FBS appears promising; however, these findings need independent replication with alternative samples. Based on the results from this study and other empirical investigations (e.g., Bury & Bagby, 2002), Arbisi (see chap. 16, this volume) recommended that the FBS *not* be used in disability evaluations. The assessor should be aware that it is highly probable that the FBS will classify an inordinate number of disability claimants with bona fide health and psychiatric problems as malingerers.

CONCLUSIONS

Overall, the scales and indexes on the MMPI–2 are mostly effective in discriminating fake-good and fake-bad responding from honest responding. Coaching about the presence of validity scales or the operating characteristics of them makes it more difficult to detect a feigned protocol. The development of additional validity scales impervious to coaching is needed. With respect to underreporting, clinicians and researchers alike should be aware that there are distinct response styles—SD and PIM. Different validity scales are differentially sensitive to these two response styles. Several nonstandard validity scales and indexes look promising, producing excellent classifications, accuracy, and large effect sizes, and should be considered as potential candidates for inclusion among the standard scales. Insufficient empirical evidence exists at present, however, to suggest that these scales add incrementally to the standard validity scales.

II

APPLICATIONS FOR THE MMPI–2 IN ASSESSMENT AND THERAPY

4

AN OVERVIEW OF PERSONALITY: THE MMPI–2 PERSONALITY PSYCHOPATHOLOGY FIVE (PSY–5) SCALES

ALLAN R. HARKNESS AND JOHN L. MCNULTY

In this chapter, we introduce the practitioner to an MMPI–2 tool for personality assessment: the Personality Psychopathology Five (PSY–5) scales (Harkness, McNulty, & Ben-Porath, 1995; Harkness, McNulty, Ben-Porath, & Graham, 2002). The PSY–5 scales tap broad personality traits that influence normal functioning and color clinical problems. The PSY–5 scales provide the MMPI–2 user with "one-stop shopping" for an overview of personality traits. The primary focus of this chapter is to show how PSY–5 scores provide ideas for therapy. For good therapy, we want to promote strong and healthy treatment alliances. We want to maximize the possibility of successful outcomes while minimizing pain, discomfort, and negative effects. We want to enable treatment compliance and motivate energetic patient efforts to succeed. Personality information can help clinicians do all of this. For each significant PSY–5 scale result, we suggest how to structure the alliance, we alert the clinician to potential patient vulnerabilities and life patterns, and we offer ideas on reasonable therapeutic goals.

Although most of this chapter is about applying the PSY–5 to therapy, we do provide a brief introduction to the development and psychometric properties of the MMPI–2 PSY–5 scales. PSY–5 users, in addition to being competent in the use of the MMPI–2, should at minimum have read the PSY–5 test report published by the University of Minnesota Press (Harkness et al., 2002).

A BRIEF ACCOUNT OF PSY–5 SCALE DEVELOPMENT

The PSY–5 scales were constructed in three steps. In the first step, *constructs*—elaborated psychological descriptions—of five personality traits were developed. In the second step, MMPI–2 scales were developed to measure each of the five constructs. In the third step, the construct validity of the MMPI–2 PSY–5 scales was examined.

Step 1: Developing the Five Constructs

Harkness (1990, 1992) studied personality dimensions that could describe both personality psychopathology and normal personality. Harkness applied psychophysical scaling methods to personality disorder criteria and to normal personality trait descriptors. The purpose of these studies was to gain an understanding of both the multidimensional descriptor space and the tight clusters of markers that lay within it. The individual diagnostic criteria of personality disorders (then the *Diagnostic and Statistical Manual of Mental Disorders* [*DSM–III–R;* American Psychiatric Association, 1987]), Cleckley's (1982) psychopathy markers, and the markers of both ends of the 11 primary factors of Tellegen's (1982) Multidimensional Personality Questionnaire (MPQ) were the stimuli in this research. Participants from voluntary services in a Veterans' Administration (VA) Medical Center and student volunteers created personal groupings of these stimuli. Stimuli that were often grouped together have high psychological similarity—and a short psychological distance between them. Stimuli that were rarely grouped together are not regarded as similar: they have large psychological distances between them.

Quantitative analyses of psychological distances between these stimuli (not test item correlations!) gave rise to the PSY–5 constructs. Harkness (1992), using all of the stimuli we have listed, found 60 dense clusters of markers that comprised two groups of fundamental topics: 39 fundamental topics within personality disorder diagnostic criteria and 26 fundamental topics in normal personality functioning (5 of 65 overlap so completely that they were fused to form a total of 60 topics). The 39 fundamental topics in personality disorder criteria showed clear convergence with symptom clusters found by Clark (1990) and oblique factors found by Livesley, Jackson, and Schroeder (1989).

To gain an overview of personality, Harkness and McNulty (1994) sought broad dimensions that could provide relatively global descriptions of personality. We obtained distance matrices on the 60 fundamental topics of personality from 201 subjects. Harkness and McNulty (1994) found that by extracting five latent roots from the summary distance matrix and rotating to approach simple structure, coherent global dimensions emerged. The authors clearly linked these dimensions to the existing personality literature and interpreted them as (a) Aggressiveness; (b) Psychoticism versus good reality contact; (c) a dimension that fit well with Tellegen's (1982) construct of Constraint (see also Watson & Clark, 1993) and Zuckerman's (1994) concept of Sensation Seeking; (d) Negative Emotionality–Neuroticism (Tellegen, 1982, 1985; Watson & Clark, 1984); and (e) a dimension of hedonic capacity, energy, and social engagement (Meehl, 1975, 1987; Tellegen, 1982, 1985) called Positive Emotionality–Extroversion. Constraint was subsequently reversed and renamed *Disconstraint*. Positive Emotionality–Extroversion was subsequently reversed and renamed *Introversion–Low Positive Emotionality*. Note that no MMPI or MMPI–2 items or item responses were involved in the development of the PSY–5 constructs.

Step 2: Development of MMPI–2 PSY–5 Scales

The PSY–5 scale construction was guided by the *quantified communication* perspective (a perspective described extensively in the volume edited by Angleitner & Wiggins, 1985; Harkness, McNulty, et al., 1995). *Communication* stresses selecting items that promote clear and direct communication with the test taker. Obvious, easy-to-understand items are seen as the workhorses pulling the validity coefficients (see, e.g., Childs, Dahlstrom, Kemp, & Panter, 2000; Duff, 1965; Holden & Jackson, 1979). *Quantifying* reflects the application of psychometrics so that the test taker's item responses are scored, aggregated with other appropriate item responses, and interpreted relative to norms. Quantification allows the extraction of different kinds of information than can be obtained from communication that has not been quantified. For example, norms allow the patient's scored test responses to be interpreted relative to known comparison groups. The perspective of quantified communication simply asserts that there is nothing more mystical about questionnaire assessment than it being clear communication that can be accurately quantified.

Harkness, McNulty, et al. (1995) developed Replicated Rational Selection (RRS) to pick MMPI–2 items to measure each of the PSY–5 constructs. As its name implies, RRS identifies test items about which many independent item selectors agree. Independent selectors must agree that an item asks about a specified construct before it is picked to measure that construct. RRS is a method for developing scales that are consistent with the objectives of quantified communication. Each item selector was trained to understand facets of the PSY–5 constructs and asked to examine all 567 MMPI–2 items. Items selected by over 51% of the judges as clearly reflecting a PSY–5 facet were included in a trial scale to measure that construct. Next, the items in the five trial scales were reviewed to ensure that they could be properly keyed, were not projective in nature (a projective aggressiveness item, for example, would ask the respondent whether people *in general* are aggressive), and were relevant to only one construct. Items failing this review were eliminated.

The performance of the trial scale items was analyzed with data from a large college sample (n = 2,928) and three clinical samples (psychiatric setting with more chronic patients, n = 328; psychiatric setting more acute patients, n = 156, and a chemical dependency sample, n = 1,196). Items were eliminated if they showed weak or reversed corrected item-total correlations with their parent trial scale. Also eliminated were items that correlated more strongly with one of the other trial scales than with the items' parent scales. These analyses were conducted on all four samples and resulted in the final item composition of the PSY–5 scales. Internal consistencies were shown to be higher in clinical samples that afford more true score variance. The PSY–5 scales have no item overlap: If an item is scored on one PSY–5 scale, it is scored on no other. This absence of item overlap avoids the risk of inadvertently reinterpreting the same item variance over and over—a very real risk when generating an overview of personality from an ad hoc collection of scales.

The PSY–5 scales' psychometric properties, calculated from the MMPI–2 normative sample, were published in Harkness et al. (2002) and are summarized here. Internal consistency estimates (coefficient alphas) ranged from .65 to .84. One-week stability coefficients calculated from the MMPI–2 normative retest sample ranged from .78 to .88 (combined gender). The PSY–5 scales are distinctive, having mean absolute intercorrelations of .27 for men and .23 for women. The intercorrelations range in magnitude from .03 to .53 in men and from .06 to .50 in women.

Step 3: Construct Validation

Research on the construct validity of the PSY–5 scales has addressed three major topics. The first topic is *structural validity*. To have structural validity, items that we score as scales should work together as factorially identifiable teams. Structural validity is in fact a prerequisite for the construct validity of the PSY–5 scales. Bagby, Ryder, Ben-Dat, Bacchiochi, and

Parker (2002) confirmed the factor structure of the PSY–5 scales in both clinical and nonclinical samples.

Second, the relations between the PSY–5 scales and several other individual differences measures have been established in the research papers cited here: relations with Tellegen's MPQ (Harkness, McNulty, et al., 1995; McNulty, Harkness, & Ben-Porath, 1998); the NEO Personality Inventory (NEO PI; Trull, Useda, Costa, & McCrae, 1995) and NEO PI—Revised (NEO PI–R; Egger, De Mey, Derksen, & van der Staak, 2003; McNulty, Harkness, et al., 1998); and the Zuckerman–Kuhlman Personality Questionnaire (McNulty, Harkness, et al., 1998). All of the studies evidenced the expected pattern of convergent and discriminant validity. Harkness, Spiro, Butcher, and Ben-Porath (1995) found that in the Boston VA normative sample, there were strong and appropriate convergent correlations between PSY–5 scores and 16PF scores obtained 24 to 26 years earlier. This study supported both construct validity and the temporal stability expected of personality trait measures.

Third, researchers have explored the relations between the PSY–5 scales and relevant personality characteristics, diagnoses, and behavior. PSY–5 Aggressiveness predicted Buss and Perry's (1992) Aggression Questionnaire scores, evidencing incremental validity over the NEO PI–R domain scales (Sharpe & Desai, 2001). Psychoticism has been related to psychotic symptoms (Harkness, McNulty, Finger, Arbisi, & Ben-Porath, 1999; McNulty, Harkness, & Wright, 1994). Disconstraint was related to alcohol consumption (Harkness, Spiro, Butcher, & Ben-Porath, 1995) and substance abuse (Rouse, Butcher, & Miller, 1999) and facilitated discrimination between major depression and bipolar depressed patients (Bagby, Buis, Nicholson, Parikh, & Bacchiochi, 1999) and psychotic and Bipolar-I disorder patients (Egger, Delsing, & De Mey, 2000). Depressed patients have elevated Negative Emotionality–Neuroticism and Introversion–Low Positive Emotionality scores relative to nondepressed patients (McNulty et al., 1994), and Negative Emotionality–Neuroticism is related to problems resulting from chronic alcohol abuse (Harkness, Spiro, et al., 1995). Vendrig, Derksen, and De Mey (2000) found relations between Introversion–Low Positive Emotionality and treatment outcome for chronic back pain patients. Convergent and discriminant relations between the PSY–5 scales and personality disorder symptoms were found for the self-report Structured Clinical Interview for *DSM–III–R*—Revised (SCID–II; McNulty, Ben-Porath, & Watt, 1997), the Personality Diagnostic Questionnaire—Revised (Trull et al., 1995), and the Structured Interview for *DSM–III–R* Personality—Revised (Trull et al., 1995). In a forensic sample, Petroskey, Ben-Porath, and Stafford (2003) found construct appropriate relations between the PSY–5 scales for both pre- and postincarceration behaviors.

PSY–5 ADMINISTRATION AND SCORING

The MMPI–2 items that make up the PSY–5 scales should never be administered by themselves; the PSY–5 are not stand-alone scales. They should only be scored following a standardized administration of the full MMPI–2. The overview of personality provided by the PSY–5 should be integrated with and interpreted in the light of other MMPI–2 information. The MMPI–2 clinical scales, content scales, and other supplementary scales provide checks on the personality hypotheses generated by the PSY–5. Because the PSY–5 scales were constructed to foster clear communication, the meaning of each PSY–5 item should be obvious to the test taker. Therefore, a careful assessment of the patient's test-taking approach is a critical first step in interpreting PSY–5 scores. MMPI–2 results should be interpreted in the context of all available information: the full clinical picture, history, observation, other testing, and verified external source material.

There are a number of sources for obtaining PSY–5 scores. MMPI–2 PSY–5 scores can be found on the Pearson Extended Score Report and the Micro Test Q output, and are interpreted in Butcher's *Minnesota Report* (Butcher, 1990a). Not all of these score sources identify the PSY–5 as a group. Some may simply report individual scale scores. For those with clerical aptitude, hand scoring keys are available from Pearson Assessments.

THE BASICS OF PSY–5 INTERPRETATION

Seven PSY–5 results are interpreted. High scores (Uniform T scores of 65 or more) on all of the PSY–5 scales are interpreted. In addition, low scores (Uniform T scores of 40 or less) on two of the scales are interpreted. Low Disconstraint is interpreted as indicating a Constrained personality. Low Introversion–Low Positive Emotionality is interpreted as indicating an Extroverted–High Positive Emotionality personality. In this section, we describe the interpretation given to those five high scores and two low scores. Descriptions are shown in Exhibits 4.1 through 4.5.

High Aggressiveness (AGGR)

High PSY–5 AGGR suggests that the primitive tool of aggression may be used by the patient to achieve his or her ends. Persons high on PSY–5 AGGR (Uniform T scores of 65 or more) may take pleasure in intimidating others. PSY–5 AGGR differs from aggression used as a defense. Interpersonally, those high in PSY–5 AGGR seek to dominate and control others. (See Exhibit 4.1.)

EXHIBIT 4.1
Highlight: Interpretation of High Aggressiveness Scores

Descriptors for high Aggressiveness scale scores ($T \geq 65$)
- Uses aggression to achieve his or her ends
- May take pleasure in intimidating others
- Seeks to dominate and control others
- May have aggressive or antisocial tendencies
- May have history of being physically abusive

EXHIBIT 4.2
Highlight: Interpretation of High Psychoticism Scores

Descriptors for high Psychoticism scale scores ($T \geq 65$)
- May have unusual beliefs
- May have unusual sensory and perceptual experiences
- May have unrealistic expectations of harm from others
- May have delusions of reference
- Thinking may be disorganized, tangential, circumstantial, disoriented
- May be frankly psychotic

High Psychoticism (PSYC)

High PSY–5 PSYC (Uniform T scores of 65 or more) suggests disconnection from reality. High PSYC patients may have unusual beliefs that are not shared in their community. They may have unusual sensory and perceptual experiences. High PSYC patients may have unrealistic expectations of harm from others. An elevated PSY–5 PSYC score does not specify what accounts for the disconnection from reality. A wide variety of causal processes can culminate in the equifinal result of psychoticism. (See Exhibit 4.2.)

High Disconstraint (DISC)

Persons with high scores on PSY–5 DISC (Uniform T scores of 65 or more) tend to be more risk taking, impulsive, and less traditional. They have a slight tendency to prefer romantic partners who have the same features. Construct validity research has shown appropriate convergence with Tellegen's (1982) Constraint scale (negative correlation) and with Zuckerman's (1994) Sensation Seeking scale (positive correlation). Harkness (2002) suggested that high DISC individuals may not easily create mental models of the future that contain negative emotional cues. In a large outpatient sample (Graham, Ben-Porath, & McNulty, 1999), high DISC

EXHIBIT 4.3
Highlight: Interpretation of High and Low Disconstraint Scores

Descriptors for high Disconstraint scale scores (T ≥ 65)
- Risk taking and impulsive
- Uses alcohol or other substances
- Prefers partners who are disconstrained
- Easily bored
- May be less traditional

Descriptors for low Disconstraint scale scores (T ≤ 40)
- Values self-control and planning
- Greater boredom tolerance
- Not a risk taker
- Tends to be traditional, values "following the rules"
- Prefers partners who are also constrained

scores are associated with a history of alcohol, cocaine, and marijuana abuse in both men and women (the PSY–5 analyses are reported in Harkness et al., 2002).

Low Disconstraint, a Constrained Personality

Low scores on DISC (Uniform T scores of 40 or less) suggest a Constrained personality pattern. Constrained personality is characterized by reduced risk taking, greater valuing of self-control and planning, and greater boredom tolerance. The person tends to value traditionalism, tends to accept the mainstream values of the culture, tends to be more of a rule follower, and tends to respect rule following in others. There is some evidence of assortative mating, of preferring partners who are also traditional, planful, and self-controlled. (See Exhibit 4.3.)

High Negative Emotionality–Neuroticism (NEGE)

Persons with high NEGE screen all incoming information for potential problems, and they have a low threshold for detecting danger. They are prone to guilt and worry, and they are self-critical. They can be masters of imagining worst-case scenarios. Outpatients with high NEGE scores tend to be anxious and depressed. (See Exhibit 4.4.)

Elevated Introversion–Low Positive Emotionality (INTR)

Elevated INTR scores are indicative of low capacity to experience positive emotions. As an effect of lowered behavioral engagement, there is

EXHIBIT 4.4
Highlight: Interpretation of High Negative Emotionality–Neuroticism Scores

Descriptors for high Negative Emotionality–Neuroticism scale scores (T ≥ 65)

- Prone to guilt and worry
- Are self-critical
- Imagine worst-case scenarios
- Have low thresholds for detecting danger
- Anxious
- Depressed
- May have somatic complaints

little interest in social interaction. Although a primary label for the scale is Introversion, Tellegen (1982, 1985) and Watson and Clark (1997) argued that the core feature is the low capacity for positive emotions. In a large outpatient sample (Graham et al., 1999), patients with elevated INTR scores were rated by their therapists as having low achievement orientation and as being anxious, depressed, introverted, and pessimistic.

Low Introversion: The Extroverted–High Positive Emotionality Personality

Low INTR scores (Uniform T scores of 40 or less) suggest an Extroverted–High Positive Emotionality pattern. Low INTR scores suggest a good capacity to experience pleasure and joy, to be more interested in social interaction, and to have energy and engagement in life. Extremely low scores may suggest hypomanic features. (See Exhibit 4.5.)

Having covered the basic interpretation of PSY–5 scores, we next discuss one application of PSY–5 scores: providing ideas for planning and conducting therapy.

PSY–5 IDEAS FOR THERAPEUTIC INTERVENTION

In this section, we provide ideas for therapy for patients with each interpretable PSY–5 finding. We present ideas that are supported by PSY–5 construct validity research, that is, the ideas presented in this section are fully consistent with the empirical literature on the PSY–5 constructs. However, the specific ideas—for example, on how to structure an alliance with a high AGGR patient—have not yet been empirically validated. Empirical validation would entail clinical trials comparing therapy designed to be a good match for the patient against therapy chosen to be a poor match for the patient. Clearly, there are moral and ethical problems with true clinical trials.

EXHIBIT 4.5
Highlight: Interpretation of High and Low Introversion–Low Positive Emotionality Scores

Descriptors for High Introversion–Low Positive Emotionality scale scores (T ≥ 65)
- Low capacity to experience positive emotions
- Little interest in social interaction
- Low achievement motivation
- Introverted
- May be dysthymic or depressed
- Pessimistic
- May complain of somatic difficulties

Descriptors for Low Introversion–High Positive Emotionality scale scores (T ≤ 40)
- Good capacity to experience pleasure and joy
- Interested in social interaction
- Have energy and engagement in life
- Extremely low scores may suggest hypomanic features
- Extroverted

For each of the seven interpretable PSY–5 findings, we provide specific ideas on (a) alliance, acceptance, and compliance; (b) problem vulnerabilities and life patterns; and (c) personality-informed treatment goals. Before linking each of these topics to specific PSY–5 findings, we review them.

Alliance, Acceptance, and Compliance

Psychological interventions are always delivered within the context of a relationship, the relationship formed between patient and clinician. The quality of this relationship and the capacity of this relationship to promote effort for change on the part of the patient form the core of the therapeutic alliance. Safran and Muran (2000), in a volume pulling together alliance theory, research, and technique instruction, opened with the following: "After approximately a half century of psychotherapy research, one of the most consistent findings is that the quality of the alliance is the most robust predictor of treatment success. This finding has been evident across a wide range of treatment modalities . . ." (p. 1).

Alliance theory has generally not been informed by modern personality individual differences research. Instead, different therapeutic approaches seem to be built around an "ideal patient." For example, dynamically based therapies, as derivatives of psychoanalysis, have technical features ideally suited to the neurotic Viennese burgher of the 19th century. The ideal patient for the alliance should be on time, be frightened or disgusted by sexual matters, be curious about his or her mind, and be generally tense and worried. The ideal patient should be traditional and rule following. The patient must not be susceptible to boredom, because he or she will need to sit quietly and talk for hours without much seeming to happen. The ideal patient has some suffering that motivates compliance. The ideal patient should be able to form a working alliance with a well-trained and motivated dynamic therapist.

The ideal patient in behavior therapy is a person with enough executive function to, in effect, carry around his or her very own Skinner box. The ideal patient understands and agrees to the goals proposed by the therapist. He or she is already motivated to behave (without being reduced to 90% ad lib feeding weight!). The ideal patient attends to and abides by the consequences highlighted by the therapist.

Early in our training as therapists, we discover that ideal patients are rare. The personality individual differences perspective offers clinicians a fresh and powerful alternative to the "ideal patient" approach to forming an alliance. For each of the interpretable five high scores and two low scores of the PSY–5, we present a tailored approach to forming the alliance.

Problem Vulnerabilities and Life Patterns

The PSY–5 scales are personality trait scales. PSY–5 results may suggest a tendency to experience negative emotions, a tendency to take more physical risks, or a tendency to experience unusual perceptions. McCrae (1993) made an extremely important distinction between such "basic tendencies" (the personality traits) and "characteristic adaptations," which he defined as "the concrete habits, attitudes, roles, relationships, and goals that result from the interaction of basic tendencies with the shaping forces of the social environment" (p. 584). The traits may make our patients vulnerable, using McCrae's terms, to particular habits, destructive attitudes, recurring relationship problems, and problematic goals that fit with—but are not the same as—their personality traits. In this section and the next, a cardinal distinction for the therapist is that the traits are not the same thing as the characteristic adaptations. A person who tends to easily become anxious (the trait) could fashion many alternative adaptations that avoid or temporarily reduce anxiety: social withdrawal, exercise, smoking, drinking, self-help reading, and so on. A basic clinical principle is that traits tend to be resistant to change but characteristic adaptations may be less resistant to change.

Information on problems that tend to develop in the lives of patients can be found by examining the correlates of PSY–5 scales found in a large-scale outpatient sample collected by Graham et al. (1999). At the time their study was published, the authors did not examine the correlates of the PSY–5 scales. However, the PSY–5 test report (Harkness et al., 2002) details specific correlates of each of the PSY–5 scales based on 410 outpatient men and 610 outpatient women with valid MMPI–2 profiles. In the sections that follow, we provide the clinician with a summary of issues, problems, and patterns that may be important in the lives of patients with interpretable PSY–5 scores.

Personality-Informed Treatment Goals

Realistic, obtainable goals promote confidence in the profession and meet our ethical standards by conveying reality to potential consumers. Not even 20 years "on the couch" turns a high NEGE Woody Allen character into a low NEGE person. Harkness and Lilienfeld (1997) noted that a major contribution of personality individual differences science is to guide the development of realistic treatment goals. Drawing on McCrae's (1993) distinction, it is not realistic to expect radical change in personality traits. Rather, it is reasonable to help the patient find new characteristic adaptations—new adaptations that also fit the patient's traits—that are less destructive and that offer greater potential for constructive growth and human relatedness.

The individual differences perspective leads naturally to expectations that are different from those of the classic pathology perspective. The typical disease or disorder formulation carries hidden within it the implicit assumption that an external, foreign condition has come upon an otherwise perfect person of ideal health. This disease formulation kindles hope of potential "cure," of restoration to some platonic ideal of health. Often, however, the proper formulation is an individual differences formulation that substitutes Darwin and Galton for Plato. In this formulation, there is no perfect health; instead, to be human is to be a natural experiment in individual differences. One must learn to live well with oneself. Realistic goals based on good science can prevent patient and therapist alike from laboring with false expectations and setting up failure.

Personality-Based Treatment Ideas for High AGGR Patients

Alliance, Acceptance, and Compliance

A high AGGR score suggests that the patient will attempt to dominate and control the therapist. It is useful to simply predict this to the patient. By predicting domination tactics, the therapist equalizes the relationship. If the patient subsequently attempts to control and dominate, this only demonstrates the therapist's expertise. The therapist can also contain and sublimate the patient's need for control within the therapy by identifying options and giving choices to the patient. Consciously attempting to share control with the patient advances another goal: the therapist can contain any countertransferential revenge-based impulses to control and dominate the patient.

High AGGR patients may be highly competitive and may continually seek to best others. Early "politically correct" confrontations in which cooperativeness is seen as morally superior to competitiveness may threaten the alliance. The patient's response may be to see the therapist as naïve—not street smart—and as attempting to attack the patient from a moral high ground. To establish a working alliance, insight and sensitivity to the patient's worldview are essential. Finding the right balance between validating the patient and advocating change is a constant clinical challenge (Linehan, 1997).

Problem Vulnerabilities and Life Patterns

Legal problems are a major vulnerability. If the patient is entangled in criminal or civil litigation, the true purpose of clinical work, from the patient's perspective, may be to obtain beneficial psychological opinions or recommendations to influence the legal proceeding. Legal motivations may subvert clinical goals, cause the development of pseudoalliance, and promote dishonest communication.

High AGGR may result in the patient having few friends, weakened family relationships, and a social network that responds from fear rather than from love or respect. In school and at work, aggressiveness is rightly seen as a primitive and ineffective method of social influence. Therefore, high AGGR patients are often educational and vocational underachievers. The patient's aggressiveness tends to trigger avoidance behavior in others. The patient may also overinterpret hostile intentions on the part of others. Because the patient upsets or angers others, he or she tends to see other people in an upset, frustrated, or counterhostile state. The patient does not tend to see others at their best. This perceptual sampling bias falsely validates a cynical view of humanity.

Personality-Informed Treatment Goals

Realistic goals can be built around increasing the patient's awareness of the costs of aggression. Although aggression may work as a social influence strategy in the short term, it incurs the costs we have already noted: being feared rather than loved or respected and having legal problems, educational and vocational underachievement, and social isolation. If accounts of recent aggression are presented in the session for clinical work, the therapist can acknowledge the effectiveness of aggressiveness before a thoroughgoing analysis of costs. The therapist can then go on to teach the psychology of effective interpersonal influence and to teach skills from management, attitude change, influence, and leadership literatures so that the patient has alternatives to aggression. Tony Soprano meets Abraham Maslow.

Thus, reasonable goals for therapy can be structured around the patient first developing a heightened awareness (automatic appraisal) of the costs of using an aggressive strategy. Then, the therapist can treat the patient for having a skills deficit in appropriate strategies of interpersonal influence. The explicit teaching of psychologically effective but nonaggressive modes of interpersonal influence thus becomes part of the treatment plan. If a quality alliance has been established and work on the aforementioned modest goals has moved ahead, then consideration of more ambitious goals, such as increasing egalitarianism or consideration of cooperativeness and competitive frameworks, could be attempted.

Personality-Based Treatment Ideas or High PSYC Patients

Alliance, Acceptance, and Compliance

The therapist should appreciate the adaptations that the patient has achieved under extraordinarily challenging conditions. High PSYC patients must manage social interaction even though they do not see the world in the same way as others see it. The ability to trust one's own senses and perceptions, something most of us take for granted, may elude them. High PSYC patients may be seen by others as being bizarre, pitiable, or mad. The therapist should attend to and highlight the level of function and degree of social adaptation that has been achieved. Honoring this achievement is a basis for a working alliance.

A patient with a high score on PSYC has acknowledged that his or her thinking and perception are unusual; the patient is ready to discuss psychoticism. Therapist fears about the malignancy of psychotic features can lead him or her to avoid the topic. Therapist failure to address the central role of psychoticism in the life of the patient may weaken the alliance.

Problem Vulnerabilities and Life Patterns

Social isolation is a major risk in high PSYC. Other people may seem to be hard to predict and "not worth the trouble." One's own intentions may be frequently misunderstood by others. The net effect is the increase, over time, of the perceived costs of human interaction. Less salient are the costs of social avoidance, the loss of support and resources. The patient may also develop dependencies on others because of the educational, legal, and vocational sequellae of psychoticism.

Personality-Informed Treatment Goals

Providing skills in emotion recognition, reality checking, and separating fact from opinion—all of these can be beneficial. Misunderstanding and miscommunication are the enemies of good social functioning. Teaching frequent checks on communication—such as by the therapist reflecting patient communications and asking the patient what he or she got out of a communication—can be valuable. The therapist can help the patient make good decisions about communicating with others about unusual thinking. Therapy and appropriate referral for conditions underlying psychotic phenomena are of course major therapeutic issues.

Personality-Based Treatment Ideas for High DISC Patients

Alliance, Acceptance, and Compliance

The first moments of modern ethical practice entail extensive consent procedures and warnings. A disconstrained patient may interpret these procedures as being excessively cautious or as being indicative of a "cover yourself" attitude. Framing such tasks as universally mandated so that they are taken seriously but do not impair the first impressions of the therapeutic relationship may be helpful.

An alliance can be built upon expertise: Offer the patient a real understanding of the disconstrained personality. Avoid acting like a high school principal—an authoritarian stance will be repugnant to the patient. Offer choices and flexibility. Remember that novelty and spontaneity will be attractive to the patient; predictability and sameness will drive the patient away. Be prepared to hear of less traditional choices, greater risk taking than you may tolerate, and less awareness of long-term consequences. Build your relationship around the goal of helping the person to live with a disconstrained personality, not around shaming the patient into constraint.

Problem Vulnerabilities and Life Patterns

The high DISC patient's shorter time horizon and more venturesome risk assessments create vulnerabilities to alcohol and drug abuse, sexually transmitted diseases, unplanned pregnancy, sexual assault, legal problems, and accidental injury. The concentration on short-term satisfaction to the detriment of one's long-term condition can also be reflected in the financial health of the patient: problems with credit card debt, no savings, and lack of preparation for later life.

The school environment is designed around constrained children, and many high DISC patients suffered in school. They experienced it as a relentless, boring ritual. Teachers often find high DISC students to be problems: they are easily bored, seeking activity and sensation. Such a child might have excelled in a hunter–gatherer culture; however, long days in a city school are a terrible fit to such a child's personality. The result can be educational underachievement. This may cascade into vocational underachievement and further predispose the patient to financial problems.

Personality does not tend to influence mate choice, except for this dimension. High DISC patients may be attracted to other high DISC people. They may have experienced the recurring pattern of excited attraction to a new spontaneous, exciting, and unpredictable other, only to find that these very features work against the longevity of the dyad. The preference for matching on DISC can also exacerbate alcohol or drug problems. If there is a mismatch in DISC within a couple, alcohol or drugs may produce a temporary boost in DISC in the more constrained partner, offering temporary matching on DISC. The phenomenon is nicely illustrated in the film *Who's Afraid of Virginia Woolf?* The already disconstrained and drunk Martha (Elizabeth Taylor) is shown in the opening scenes to be disgusted by her constrained husband George (Richard Burton). Over the course of an evening, George begins to drink, becoming more disconstrained and aggressive. As he shows more DISC and AGGR features, Martha shows fewer expressions of disgust toward him. Self-medication to manage one's level of DISC and the role of DISC in the patient's relationships should be explored.

Personality-Informed Treatment Goals

A reasonable goal is to help a high DISC patient learn to live with a high DISC personality. This means helping the patient find safer, more constructive adaptations that fit with the patient's need for novelty, excitement, and risk taking. There are currently no known interventions for turning high DISC people into low DISC people, and the therapeutic goals should reflect that reality. The therapist should help the patient see how seemingly disparate problems flow in a coherent manner from high DISC: Relationship, alcohol and drug, medical, and financial problems may all share the themes of venturesome risk assessment, short time horizon, boredom susceptibility, and a nontraditional orientation. A personality-based case conceptualization can help the patient understand the underlying disposition and the links to disparate facts in the life pattern. The patient can begin to appreciate the difference between the high DISC "basic tendency" and the particular characteristic adaptations he or she has developed. For therapy, this has clear advantages over a pathological diagnostic formulation.

Personality-Based Treatment Ideas for Low DISC (Constrained) Patients

Alliance, Acceptance, and Compliance

Constrained, low DISC patients may be most comfortable with therapy that gives clear structure. Constrained patients may respond better with specific goals; with an active therapist providing guidance, direction, and advice; and with clear sets of rules and consequences. In effect, you are offering a knowable tradition to a person who yearns to be traditional. "Homework" helps structure therapeutic work outside the session.

Problem Vulnerabilities and Life Patterns

Although it would seem natural to suspect that Constrained, low DISC patients are vulnerable to obsessive–compulsive personality disorder, we know of no strong evidence making this link. We have observed a few highly constrained patients who have unusual bodily preoccupations (though not limited to bowel concerns à la Freud). DISC, versus Constraint, is the only personality variable correlated with romantic choice, and there is some evidence that traditional people prefer traditional partners. In the large outpatient sample we have described, members of a subset of Constrained patients were rated by their therapists as being overly compliant and moralistic. They were also rated as showing some classic "internalizer" features: being more overwhelmed, sad, and more liable to feel like a failure. They were rated as being less antisocial, less self-indulgent, less assertive, and less prone to sexual preoccupations than other patients in this sample. More research on the clinical presentation of Constrained personalities is clearly needed.

Personality-Informed Treatment Goals

Status on DISC versus Constraint tends to be stable. Thus, reasonable clinical goals entail helping the patient find constructive adaptations for a Constrained personality.

Personality-Based Treatment Ideas for High NEGE Patients

Alliance, Acceptance, and Compliance

The high NEGE is the neurotic patient around whom many of the technical features of classic psychoanalysis were designed. However, some of the features of the classic psychoanalytic alliance may promote dependence on the therapist and disconnection from family. Classic analysis promotes the development of transference neurosis in which the patient's anxiety comes to be focused on the therapist: "Does the therapist truly care about me? Does she or he think about me between sessions?" Classic technique fosters such transference neuroses by premeditated lack of feedback from the therapist and by selective reinforcement of verbal productions that support its development. Classic technique very effectively builds the causal attribution that *the therapist is the central figure in the emotional life of the patient*. Although this undoubtedly provides the therapist with leverage, we consider this to be a step in the wrong direction.

Instead, we recommend (a) that the patient be educated about his or her readiness to experience anxiety and (b) that the patient should be encouraged to regard the relationship with the therapist as simply providing more examples of how the patient is constantly screening for signals of danger. Suppose a therapist casually remarks to a patient that her suit is well tailored. The patient may wonder whether the therapist is saying "You are fat and in need of disguise" or "I am noticing your body and will destroy the therapy." We recommend that such worries not be advanced as evidence that the therapist is the center of the patient's emotional life. Instead, we recommend that such worries be used compassionately as examples of how the patient processes all information. Rather than accepting suffering because it motivates, we recommend acting directly to reduce anxiety because it interferes with information processing.

Problem Vulnerabilities and Life Patterns

The patient's acute sensitivity to the anxiety signal predisposes him or her to all forms of aversive conditioning. Avoidance can become a strong mode of behavior. This can be particularly destructive when it blocks constructive, problem-solving behavior.

The patient is vulnerable to developing habits that provide short-term relief from anxiety. Examples include drinking, smoking, sedative or tranquilizer abuse, anxiolytic eating, and excessive sleeping. High NEGE patients with good imaginations may naturally distract themselves by immersion in fiction, television, and sports. All of this distracts from constructive problem solving.

Personality-Informed Treatment Goals

An implicit goal of both dynamic and cognitive therapies seems to be to change the patient from anxious to nonanxious. We know of no evidence indicating that personality change is possible on such a grand scale. If a person learns to identify the anxious aspect of automatic appraisals, we believe it is a false promise to suggest that such awareness will eventuate in the thoughts no longer occurring someday. A goal supported by real outcomes is that the patient can learn to identify and deal with those automatic appraisals. He or she can also learn to select new adaptations to the experience of anxiety. However, the implicit promise of turning a high NEGE patient into a low NEGE former patient has not been demonstrated to be a realistic goal for psychological therapy.

Personality-Based Treatment Ideas for High INTR Patients

Alliance, Acceptance, and Compliance

Therapists like to be effective, and they like to be appreciated by their patients. The appreciation of patients is often registered in the facial expressions of positive emotion. High INTR patients tend to frustrate therapists' needs for appreciation. High INTR patients simply have less positive emotion to express. Therapist observations do not trigger in a high INTR patient the usual facial markers of interest. Therapist jokes seem to fall flat. Astute therapeutic observations cause no discernible reaction. If the high INTR personality is not understood, then the therapist may experience disappointment or upset with such patients. In the worst case of therapeutic narcissism, a therapist may experience unexplained rage at the difficult patient who fails to appreciate the brilliance of the therapist!

A good alliance always begins with a decision by the therapist not to use the patient to meet his or her needs. In the case of high INTR patients, therapists must understand that these patients are not to be used as positive feedback machines. Further, a good alliance should be founded on an understanding that a low level of positive emotionality does not mean that a person is psychologically simple or that the patient's life is impoverished.

Therapies differ in the extent to which they call on the patient to speak, to improvise, and to interact socially. High INTR patients are less talkative. This can be misinterpreted as "not working" or "repressed." Therapies with heavy demands for these activities may be painful for the high INTR patient, causing early dropout.

Problem Vulnerabilities and Life Patterns

Tellegen (1985) suggested that low positive emotionality plays a central role in depression. Meehl (1975) discussed the implications of low hedonic capacity for social interaction: without the cushioning effect of positive emotional experience, social experiences come to be regarded over time as more and more negative. With low positive emotionality comes low reinforceability. Because progress in life and therapy must be self-motivated, high INTR patients are handicapped at the source.

All of the discussion to this point has been of congenital INTR. However, it bears mention that chronic abuse of dopamine agonists—such as cocaine or amphetamine—can produce a reduction of intrinsic pleasure capacity, and, certainly, interuse time periods are characterized by anhedonia. Late onset low positive emotionality in persons with a history of risk factors for cocaine or amphetamine abuse should trigger assessment of this possibility.

Personality-Informed Treatment Goals

Meehl (1975) suggested the possibility of "secondary guilt." This is the guilt that persons low in hedonic capacity experience because they do not feel what others seem to feel about social interaction. Meehl suggested a program of helping patients feel more comfortable being who they are. This is a model for all therapy based on individual differences:

Start with an understanding of the person, and help that person to understand, appreciate, and accept him- or herself. Such patients may benefit from an understanding of the impact that their lack of expressed positive emotion has on broader social interactions. One of our students noted that workers at a local juvenile detention facility have a tendency to "get in the face" of low positive emotionality juveniles. When spoken to, the high INTR juvenile does not react much, so the worker misattributes this to disrespect and escalates until the incarcerated juvenile does react.

Personality-Based Treatment Ideas for Low INTR Patients

Alliance, Acceptance, and Compliance

Miller (1991) noted the possibility of false alliance in the extroverted patients. Such patients are verbally productive, and they want to interact with the therapist. They give plenty of positive facial expressions to the therapist: They are a strong source of positive reinforcement to the therapist. These factors can lead the therapist to overestimate progress.

Extroverted, high positive emotionality patients tend to enjoy talking, they like being the center of attention, and they can be rather dramatic. Therapy that allows the patient to participate in these activities is attractive to the extroverted patient.

Problem Vulnerabilities and Life Patterns

These patients can be strongly engaged, motivated, and attracted by the right stimuli. Thus, the patient may begin many projects while finishing few. Important duties may be neglected in favor of opportunities to interact socially (a major problem for extroverted college students living away from home for the first time). It may be difficult to recognize the downside to a strong capacity to experience positive emotion and to enjoy social interactions. However, in combination with other factors, such as a potentiating peer group and drug or alcohol availability, an extroverted, high positive emotionality personality can amplify life's problems.

Personality-Informed Treatment Goals

The goal is to help the patient understand the possibilities afforded by his or her personality. Such a patient has the advantages of energy, strong potential for positive reinforcement, and the interest in developing a base of social support. These represent many strengths to work with. The main goal is to help the patient to find constructive adaptations that are still consonant with social interest and strong behavioral engagement.

THE CASE OF CYNTHIA G.

Cynthia G.[1] is a 22-year-old woman who reluctantly participated in an outpatient unit intake interview at the insistence of her mother. Cynthia's mother was a successful businesswoman, and Cynthia's four older siblings had pursued successful careers in government and business. Cynthia clearly stood out in the family as not following in the footsteps of her older siblings. During the interview, Cynthia did not volunteer much information, and significant portions of the following were obtained from her mother. Although Cynthia had achieved average grades during her freshman year in college, her next year was disastrous. Her attendance dropped dramatically, and she repeatedly broke campus rules. Cynthia's college career ended at a party. Police were summoned to the party based on reports of gunfire. As the police attempted to break up the party, Cynthia G. became argumentative. She confronted an officer, the altercation escalated, and Cynthia slapped the officer. At this point, she was placed in custody and charged with resisting arrest. She was subsequently expelled from school.

Although she acknowledged some drinking and marijuana use, she did not see her behavior as problematic. She felt that her professors had been rigid and demanding. She claimed that the professors' insistence on attendance had led to failing grades that did not reflect her true knowledge of the courses. She claimed that her poor attendance had been provoked by boring lectures. Cynthia argued against the premise that she should have been attending class: She claimed that by simply reading the assignments she should have been able to gain all the required knowledge. She did not wish to be seen at the clinic, but school expulsion had necessitated moving in with her mother so she had to do as her mother wished.

MMPI–2 Results With the PSY–5 Overview of Personality

Cynthia G.'s MMPI–2 validity scale results are shown in Figure 4.1. Her VRIN (Variable Response Inconsistency) and TRIN (True Response Inconsistency) scores indicate that she responded with appropriate consistency to the content of the items. She produced an elevation on the Lie (*L*) scale (T = 66), suggesting that she tends to present herself in a favorable light. Although the score was not high enough to warrant invalidating the profile, *L* suggests that other scores may underestimate major personality characteristics and problematic symptoms and behaviors, particularly for scales that rely on honest, straightforward responding. Butcher (1990) suggested that persons with *L* scale scores at this level see themselves as rigidly virtuous and perfectionistic. They also tend to see little need to discuss their problems or change their behavior, which clearly characterizes Cynthia.

[1]The authors thank Jim Butcher for providing the clinical data for the case of Cynthia G.

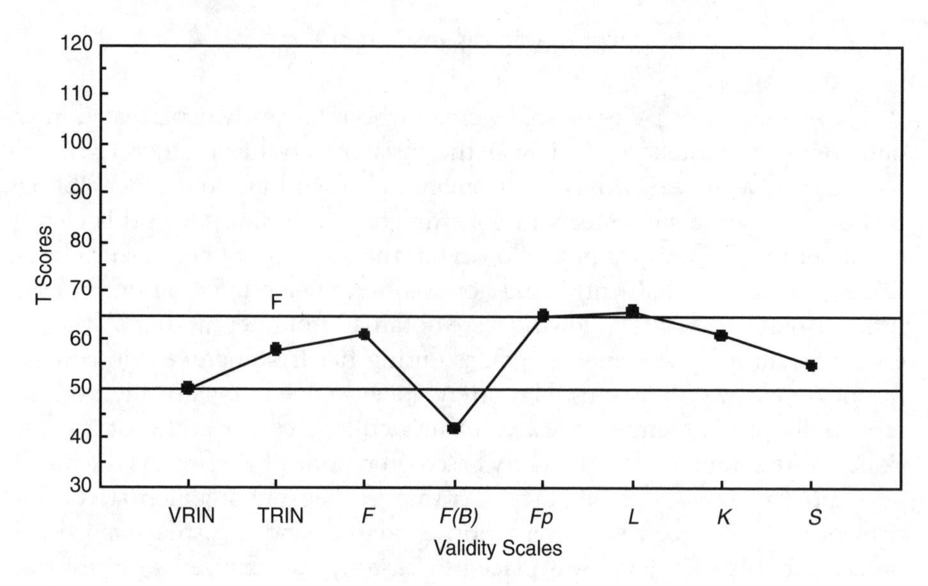

Figure 4.1. MMPI–2 validity scale profile for Cynthia G.

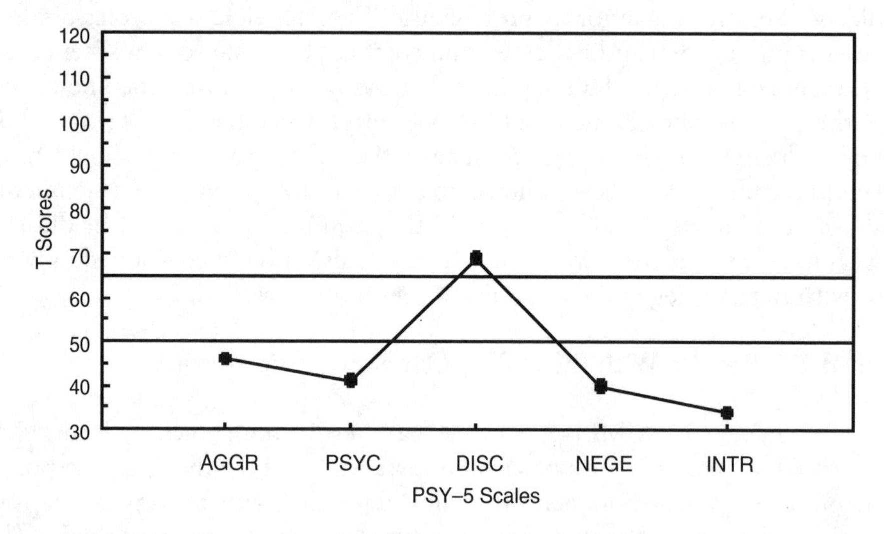

Figure 4.2. MMPI–2 PSY–5 profile for Cynthia G.

Cynthia G.'s PSY–5 profile is shown in Figure 4.2. The profile suggests disconstrained extroversion. This personality overview suggests that Cynthia may tend to be more risk taking, impulsive, and less traditional than others. She is easily bored. Being less rule oriented, it is likely that she would bristle against authority. This is a general property of the disconstrained personality that played out the night Cynthia slapped a police officer, ending her college career. She may prefer romantic partners who are also disconstrained. The revelers at the party visited by police raise the possibility that she prefers disconstrained friends. Harkness (2002) suggested that high DISC individuals may not easily create mental models of the future that contain negative emotional cues; Cynthia's focus is on the here and now. As noted in the earlier discussion, high DISC scorers in the large outpatient sample tended to have histories of alcohol, cocaine, and marijuana abuse. This merits careful exploration in Cynthia's case.

Cynthia's low INTR scores suggest an Extroverted–High Positive Emotionality pattern. Cynthia probably has a good capacity to experience pleasure and joy. She may be very attracted to social interaction and have energy and engagement in life. She should be carefully evaluated for hypomanic features.

How can an alliance be formed with Cynthia? She dislikes being told what to do, she does not enjoy routine and regimentation, she prefers novelty, and she is susceptible to drug and alcohol problems. She is not an ideal patient for therapies from either the dynamic tradition or the behavioral tradition. We next examine how a classic approach could generate a negative treatment outcome with Cynthia.

A Poor Alliance With Cynthia G.

A traditional pathology-oriented alliance would have understood Cynthia as being character disordered, offering her the prediction of a bad prognosis and giving her the ultimatum that she must change or leave the office. The goal, as imagined by the clinician, is that Cynthia could change from being a disconstrained person to becoming a "better" person, a constrained person. An implicit component in this fantasy is that the reason it has not yet happened is that Cynthia has simply not "hit bottom" or tried hard enough. Using the standard approach, the therapist will remind her of how she has gotten into trouble and point out how she is continuing to do it. The end of the pitch is that she must change or see her life fail. The position of the therapist is that of critic and judge. It is a position of power and authority. When the alliance is offered on these terms, Cynthia will probably be repulsed on many levels. In such an alliance, Cynthia will tend to see the therapist as an agent of her mother, of the traditional. Cynthia has little motivation to enter into a collaborative relationship under these conditions. It is interesting to note that in the intake interview Cynthia offered less information to the interviewing psychologist than she did when responding to the MMPI–2. This suggests that an impaired alliance may have been developing in the first hour.

An Alliance Based on the PSY–5 Personality Overview

The first thing that should be offered to Cynthia is expertise. The clinician should be able to articulate a deep understanding of the preferences, habits, values, vulnerabilities, and life patterns of disconstrained and extroverted personalities. The alliance can be constructed around the psychologist's special knowledge of how school systems tend to promote strong boredom, to be highly structured and regimented, and to lack the novelty and risk taking that makes life enjoyable. Cynthia could begin to understand her reaction to her professors' lectures in terms of legitimate individual differences that characterize her. The therapist could explain the special vulnerability she has for drug and alcohol usage: being drawn into a social circle of disconstrained others, she has a strong focus on the enjoyment of pleasure, a time horizon emphasizing the present, and so on. Building an alliance on special expertise, the therapist can offer Cynthia a new way of seeing the patterns in her life.

In an optimal alliance, the clinician has new adaptations to offer the patient. The clinician should offer patterns, habits, and vocations that would allow the patient to become a happy, constructive, high achieving, law-abiding and well-adapted *disconstrained extrovert*. Note that this goal is the polar opposite of the goal of the poor alliance.

How Does Cynthia G.'s PSY–5 Interpretation Fit With Other MMPI–2 Findings?

The overview of personality offered by the PSY–5 and the ideas it offers for structuring the alliance, understanding vulnerabilities, and setting goals accord well with other MMPI–2 findings, as shown in Figure 4.3.

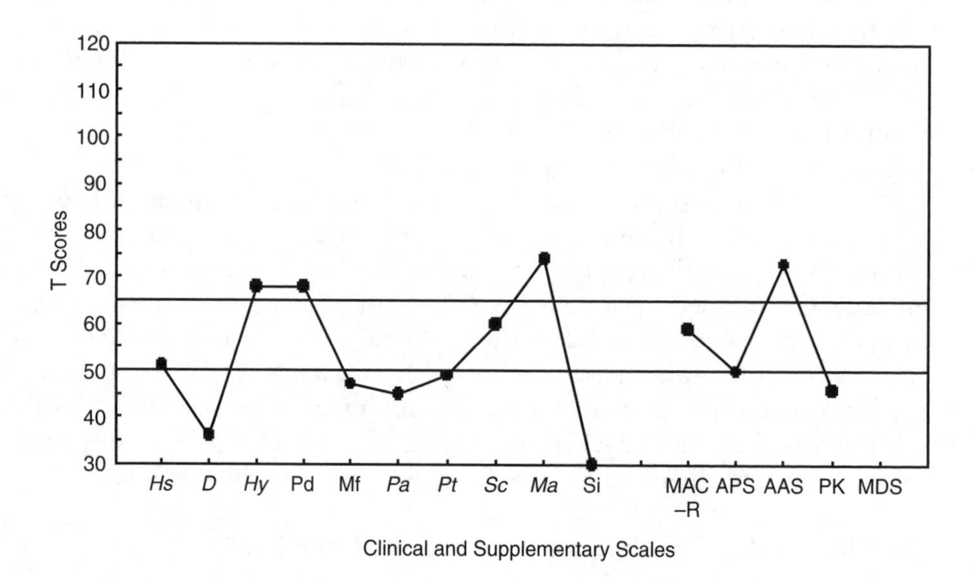

Figure 4.3. MMPI–2 clinical and supplementary scales profile for Cynthia G.

Clinical scales 3 (T = 68), 4 (T = 68), and 9 (T = 74) are elevated, as well as the Addiction Acknowledgment Scale (AAS) supplementary scale (T = 73). In addition, her Scale 0 was quite low (T = 30). This combination of scores is associated with acting out, impulsive behavior. Persons with such scores have little regard for social standards and values and frequently get into trouble with authorities. They are narcissistic, self-indulgent, and easily bored and often act without considering the potential consequences. Furthermore, when in trouble, they refuse to take responsibility for their behavior. Although they may be uninhibited socially and may create a good first impression, persons with these scale elevations may have superficial relations with others and seem incapable of forming deep emotional ties. Substance abuse is typically associated with these scale elevations, which Cynthia G. readily acknowledged with her AAS scale score. Her low score on Scale 0 is classically interpreted as suggesting a person who is sociable and extroverted. All of these classic inferences are consistent with the PSY–5 overview of personality.

One classic inference departs from the PSY–5 picture of personality. The scale elevation on Scale 3, in conjunction with Scale 4, suggests chronic intense anger and aggressive impulses that cannot be expressed appropriately. The PSY–5 picture does not suggest that offensive or instrumental aggressiveness is a core feature of the patient (AGGR Uniform T score is less than 50). The PSY–5 would suggest that the patient becomes rebellious when confronted with authority (more reactive than offensive aggression). Further clinical exploration would be needed to sort out these alternative formulations.

SUMMARY

The PSY–5 scales provide MMPI–2 users with "one-stop shopping" for an overview of major personality individual differences. The scales are constructed to enhance quantified communication. The PSY–5 scales have no item overlap and low intercorrelations. PSY–5 construct validity research was described. For each significant PSY–5 result, we offered ideas for structuring the alliance, noted potential vulnerabilities and life patterns, and suggested reasonable therapeutic goals. These ideas flow from the construct validity research on the PSY–5 and the connection it provides to the larger literature on personality individual differences.

5

THE CONTRIBUTION OF THE MMPI–2 TO THE DIAGNOSIS OF PERSONALITY DISORDERS

JAN J. L. DERKSEN

In the fourth edition text revision of the *Diagnostic and Statistical Manual of Mental Disorders* (*DSM–IV–TR*; American Psychiatric Association [APA], 2000), a *personality disorder* is defined as an enduring pattern of inner experience and behavior that deviates markedly from the expectations of the individual's culture, is pervasive and inflexible, has an onset in adolescence or early adulthood, is stable over time, and leads to distress or impairment. Since the introduction of the separate axis in the *DSM–III* in 1980 (APA, 1980), research has accumulated; and, over time, it has become more and more clear that classification of the 10 personality disorders listed in the *DSM* cannot be differentiated based upon empirical criteria (Derksen, 1995; Derksen, Maffei, & Groen, 1999). The categories, based upon diagnostics in medicine, rely on clear boundaries; and researchers have become aware of the fact that the matter of delineation is extremely difficult. Clinicians as a group tend to support the option of dimensions in which a personality can differ between being slightly and severely dependent, obsessive, or narcissistic. The next version of the *DSM*

(*DSM–V*) will probably no longer present a separate Axis II, but it is unclear what will be presented. Besides classifying personality disorders by means of the *DSM*, clinical psychologists worldwide tend to use psychological tests to verify their diagnoses and to collect information that can guide treatment of the more difficult patients. A self-report technique like the MMPI–2 is easy to administer and delivers a wealth of information that can be used to clarify personality-based problems.

The MMPI–2 is a psychological assessment tool that uses the method of client self-report, which is a major strength of this tool that can greatly contribute to the study of psychological and psychosomatic symptoms and complaints. Stated differently, the MMPI–2 can help map patterns of more or less disturbed personality traits and behavioral styles for different individuals.

Agreement or disagreement with 567 items produces scores for some 50 scales and subscales; some of these scales can then be used to identify a personality disorder or, when this has been accomplished, reveal further details in connection with the disorder. The inventory, developed in the 1940s, was not intended for the diagnosis of personality disorders, but rather was intended simply to identify larger and related groups of symptoms and syndromes such as depression, anxiety, schizophrenia, and paranoia. The many scales and code types (i.e., combinations of elevated clinical scales) have been studied extensively and are widely used by psychologists in clinical practice. This has led to the use of a unique instrument—by the clinical psychologist, in particular—and a completely unique manner of diagnosis in conjunction with other diagnostic techniques. With respect to the MMPI–2 and the diagnosis of personality disorders, different relations and associated questions can exist:

- Which scales and combinations of scales can contribute to the diagnosis of a *DSM* personality disorder?
- How do different personality disorders manifest themselves in terms of the MMPI–2?
- Which scales reveal a more or less pathological style of behavior with clinical relevance but no direct implication of a *DSM* personality disorder?
- What research has contributed to the development of the dimensional scales of the MMPI–2 for the measurement of personality pathology?
- What role can the MMPI–2 play in the extensive (i.e., structural; Derksen, 2002, 2004) psychodiagnostic assessment of a complicated personality disorder?

This chapter begins with the aforementioned questions and ends with a promising clinical approach.

THE MMPI AND THE *DSM*

The MMPI stems from the time when classificatory diagnostics, such as that practiced today with the aid of the *DSM*, were not very characteristic of clinical practice. The empirical tradition of psychological diagnostics set in motion by the MMPI is unique and independent of the clinical psychiatric diagnostics based upon the *DSM*. The first version of the *DSM* classification system appeared in 1952 when the MMPI was more than 10 years old. With the appearance of the fourth edition of the *DSM* in 1994 (APA, 1994), a 300% increase occurred in the number of diagnostic labels—from 106 to 365; and the number of manual pages increased from 128 to 900 (Houts, 2002). While personality disorders were addressed to some extent in 1952, they only received expanded attention and became the object of wide empirical study when placed on a separate *DSM* axis (Axis II) in 1980. With the aid of the MMPI, vulnerabilities in the personalities of patients had already been identified long before that date. The *DSM*, with its categorization of all possible psychological disorders, comes from the tradition of psychiatric practice interested in biological explanations. In contrast, the MMPI and its revision, the MMPI–2 (Butcher, Graham, et al., 2001), come from a clinical psychological tradition emphasizing patient self-report to guide the process of psychological understanding, diagnosis, and determination of the feasibility of treatment.

A psychological diagnosis typically includes not only a *DSM* classification but also much more (Derksen, 2004). During the histories of both the MMPI and the *DSM*, different attempts have been made to actually connect these qualitatively and inherently different methods of classification and diagnosis. Most recently, Blais, Hilsenroth, Castlebury, Fowler, and Baity (2001) tried to predict *DSM–IV* (APA, 2000) cluster B personality disorders on the basis of MMPI–2 scores and thus validate the two systems with respect to each other. This endeavor obviously proved somewhat unsuccessful, in part because of the differing methods and assumptions. The MMPI is a psychological test that measures along dimensions and is therefore not the same as a classification system based on supposedly clearly distinct syndromes. The *DSM* has the pretense of providing a complete overview summary of disorders; however, the aim of the MMPI is much more modest—simply to generate test external correlates or descriptors with clinically relevant knowledge using clearly reliable and valid scales.

In a similar effort, Morey (Morey, Waugh, & Blashfield, 1985) attempted to discern the *DSM–III* personality disorders within the existing pool of MMPI items and construct scales to measure such disorders using the MMPI (APA, 1980, 1987). Unfortunately, this research has not proved very productive for two reasons. First, such an enterprise is pretty much doomed to fail from the beginning because the two traditions rely upon completely different methods of diagnosis, are based on different conceptualizations of psychopathology and psychodiagnostics, and have not been constructed with an eye to being combined or producing information on the same level. The *DSM* does not provide a meaningful criterion for the validity of the MMPI–2; and, vice versa, the MMPI–2 does not provide a meaningful criterion for the validity of the *DSM*. Somwaru and Ben-Porath (1995a) have attempted to develop a set of personality disorder scales using the MMPI–2 items. However, these scales have not been researched sufficiently enough at this point to provide meaningful interpretations. Should one want to map the *DSM* personality disorders using the method of self-report, then creating a separate instrument with relevant items constructed specifically for this purpose seems most natural. Such instruments exist in abundance, with the Millon Clinical Multiaxial Inventory—III (MCMI–III from Millon, Davis, and Millon (1997) as perhaps the best-known approach.

A second problem with attempts to connect the MMPI and the *DSM* relates to the clinical relevance of doing this. One question is, can attempts to establish a *DSM* classification on the basis of a questionnaire method really help us with the process of psychological diagnosis? Most of the *DSM* classifications can be made by the clinician in clinical contact with a patient. In addition, a convincing relation between most *DSM* classifications and choice of treatment is largely lacking; thus, psychological diagnosis is meant to fill this gap. All of this considered together thus suggests that psychological diagnosis using the MMPI–2—among other things—only becomes meaningful *after* a provisional *DSM* classification is made, which is a point to which I return later.

Yet another area in which the MMPI and the *DSM* have been connected is in studies of a particular *DSM* personality disorder using the MMPI. The borderline and antisocial personality disorders have been frequently studied in such a manner. Characteristic MMPI profiles for various groups of *DSM* personality disorders, for example, have been generated. In Figure 5.1, the average MMPI–2 profile is presented for 119 Dutch delinquents who can also be characterized as having a *DSM* antisocial personality disorder (Derksen, De Mey, Sloore, & Hellenbosch, 2004). In another study reported by Graham (2000), Scale 4 is the highest in this case. In contrast, borderline personality disordered patients are typically characterized by a so-called "floating profile" or heightened scores predominantly on scales *F* (Infrequency), 2, 4, 6, 7, and 8 (Dragt & Derksen, 1994; Trull, 1991). Thus, for 46 Belgian borderline patients (17 men and 29 women), the average profile presented in Figure 5.2 was encountered (Knapen, 2002). However, for a second sample of 62 Belgian borderline patients (14 men and 48 women), the average profile is presented in Figure 5.3 (Aerts, 2001). Other *DSM* personality disorders besides the borderline are often

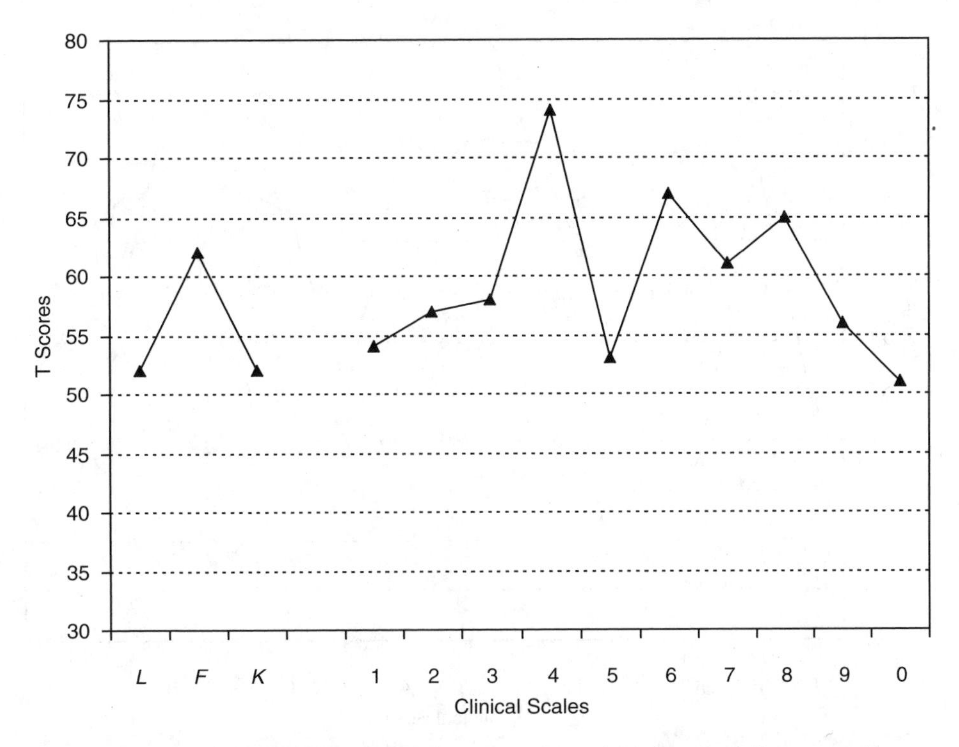

Figure 5.1. Average MMPI–2 profile for 107 male and 12 female delinquents. From *MMPI–2: Handleiding voor afname, scoring en interpertatie* [MMPI–2: Manual for test taking, scoring, and interpretation], by J. Derksen, H. De Mey, H. Sloore, and G. Hellenbosch, 2004, Nijmegen, the Netherlands: PEN Test Publishers.

associated with elevated scores on the clinical scales of the MMPI–2 but not as high as those for the patient with a borderline personality disorder. Scale 4 can thus be seen to play a major role in the antisocial and borderline personality disorders, as well as in a number of other personality disorders, and is therefore considered in greater detail in the next section.

SCALE 4

Green (1991), Butcher (1999a), Graham (2000), and Nichols (2001) have all presented a large number of diagnostic hypotheses for elevated Scale 4 scores, many of which relate to particular characteristics of a personality disorder. Numerous studies have shown that elevated MMPI–2 Scale 4 scores play a role in people diagnosed with a general personality disorder. Scale 4, or the earlier psychopathic deviation scale, was originally developed on the basis of people referred to psychiatry to clarify why they

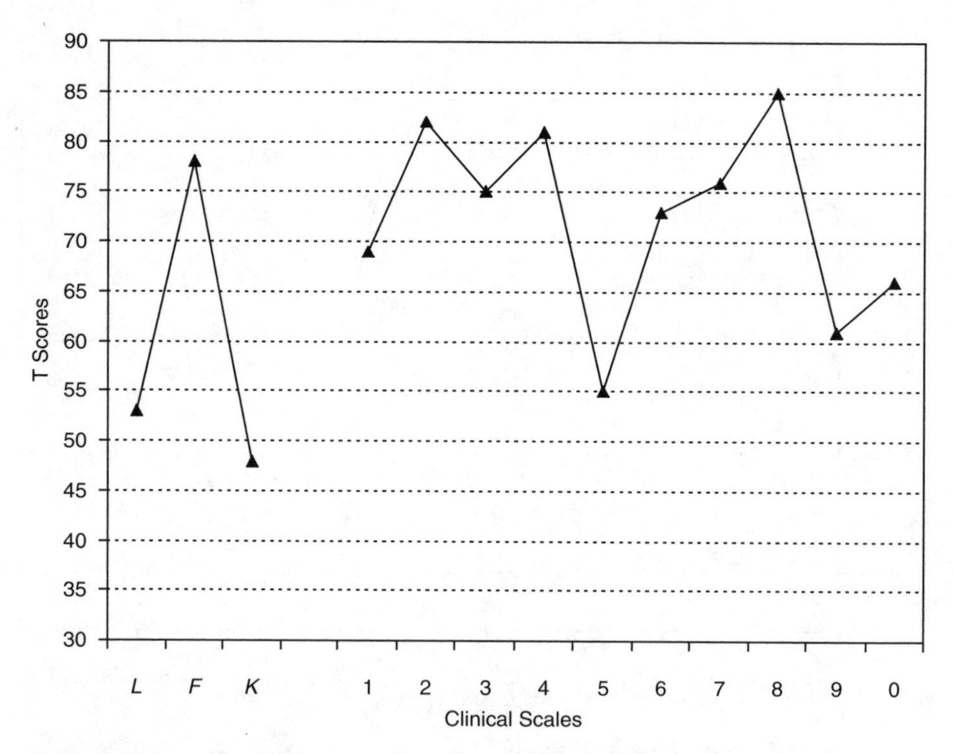

Figure 5.2. Average MMPI–2 profile for 46 Belgian borderline patients. From *Borderline persoonlijkheidsstoornis: Onderzoek naar MMPI–profielen* [Borderline personality disorder: Investigation of MMPI profiles], by I. Aerts, 2001, Brussels, Belgium: Vrije Universiteit, Sfdeling Klinische Psychologie.

were continually in trouble with the law. The difficulties of these individuals were not found to relate to cultural disadvantage; they were all of normal intelligence, and they were all relatively free of serious neurotic or psychotic disorders. Some of the items directly address the tendency to have problems at school or with the law; other items address an absence of concern for the majority of social and moral rules of behavior, the presence of family problems, or the absence of satisfaction with one's existence. Suggested interpretations for Scale 4 include:

- T values of 75 or higher reflect poor adaptation to social circumstances and intimate relations, diffuse experience of one's own identity and/or social identity, antisocial behavior, and problems with the law.
- T values of 65 to 74 reflect rebellion toward authority, possible problems with the law, family problems, underachievement, poor employment history, impulsiveness, poor judgment, impatience, hostility, feelings of boredom, emptiness, and gloominess.

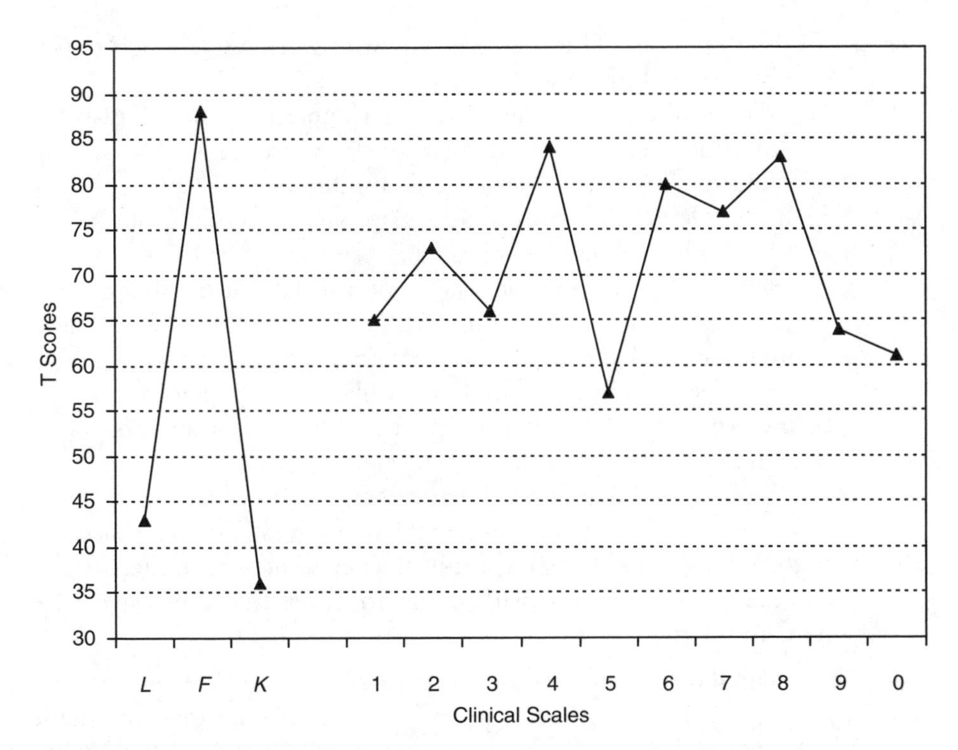

Figure 5.3. Average MMPI–2 profile for 62 Belgian borderline patients. From *Typerende antwoordpatronen van borderline patiânten op de MMPI–2* [Typical response patterns of borderline patients on the MMPI–2], by S. Knapen, 2002, Brussels, Belgium: Vrije Universiteit, Afdeling Klinische Psychologie.

- T values of 55 to 64 reflect unconventional, immature, and egocentric behavior; superficial relations; extravert and energetic traits.

The item content making up this scale is diverse and interesting. Scale 4 has five Harris–Lingoes subscales associated with it:

- Pd1 contains content related to family discord. High scorers on this subscale describe their present family or family of origin as having a shortage of affection, understanding, and support. Such individuals are under the impression that their family is or was critical and that they were never allowed sufficient freedom and independence.
- Pd2 deals with problems with authority. High scorers on this subscale have an aversion to the norms and values of their parents or society in general, they have strong opinions with regard to what is right and what is wrong, and they speak up

for their opinions. They may also admit to getting into trouble at school or with the law.

- Pd3 contains items dealing with social imperturbability. This subscale includes items that relate to feeling comfortable in and familiar with social situations, holding strong opinions with regard to many things, and vigorously defending one's opinions. This subscale has only six items and can therefore never produce a T value of 65 or more, which means that it has little to contribute to our understanding of Scale 4.
- Pd4 contains items related to alienation. High scorers on this subscale feel mostly alienated and isolated. They appear to believe that other people do not understand them and that they must endure a great deal during their lives.
- Pd5 assesses self-alienation. High scorers describe themselves as unhappy and uncomfortable with themselves. They do not find daily life interesting or pleasant. They sometimes indicate feelings of regret or guilt with regard to things that they have done in the past.

The original diagnostic classification associated with Scale 4 (i.e., psychopathic deviate) has not been exclusively confirmed in subsequent research. People with psychopathic personalities and antisocial personality disorders are not the only people found to produce elevated Scale 4 scores (see Figure 5.3, derived from Derksen et al., 2004). Elevated Scale 4 scores are also obtained frequently for people with other types of personality disorders and for those people who do not meet the *DSM* criteria for a personality disorder but who suffer from one or more symptom disorders. Subtypes of borderline patients have also been found to not stand out with regard to impulsive behavior but nevertheless score high on Scale 4. Subsequent inspection of the Harris–Lingoes subscales associated with Scale 4 for these individuals shows that their vulnerabilities revolve around feelings of alienation. Such individuals are further characterized by diffuse identity problems and feelings of depersonalization and derealization. Thus, Scale 4 is, in my view, a maladaptation scale with a clinically significant elevation indicating that the individual is poorly adapted to the environment with respect to his or her behavior (e.g., problems with authority, antisocial behavior, acting out) or emotions. In the latter case, however, the conflict with the environment may not be behaviorally manifest. In sum, an elevated Scale 4 score generally means weak adaptation to the social environment—sometimes as a result of behavior problems, sometimes as a result of emotional alienation, and sometimes as a result of both. Empirical support for this assumption has been provided by Lilienfeld (1999), who found that Pd2 or problems with authority significantly contribute to the validity of the prediction of both global psychopathology and antisocial behavior.

SCALE 7

The next MMPI scale used to measure problematic personality characteristics is Scale 7, named the Psychasthenia scale. This scale was originally constructed to assess patients who obsessively worry, perform compulsive rituals, and/or suffer from exaggerated anxieties. Rather than using the original term *psychasthenia*, the term that is used now is *obsessive–compulsive personality disorder*. Some of the items pertain to uncontrollable or obsessive thoughts, feelings of anxiety, and doubts with respect to one's own capacities. Feelings of unhappiness, physical complaints, and concentration difficulties are also represented within this scale, which has no subscales. This scale is interpreted as follows:

- T values of 75 or higher suggest a high degree of psychological stress (e.g., anxiety, fear, tension, depression), intrusive thoughts, concentration difficulties, fear of going crazy, and obsession–compulsion.
- T values of 65 to 74 indicate moderate anxiety and depression, fatigue, exhaustion, problems sleeping, and feelings of guilt.
- T values of 55 to 64 indicate anxiety, tension, discomfort, insecurity, lack of self-confidence, indecisiveness, shyness, and introversion.

When a profile is characterized by only an elevated Scale 7 score (or a so-called Spike 7), it generally refers to a person who "lives in his or her head" and who has difficulty talking "by means of the belly" (reflecting emotions in talk). Such individuals get caught up in cognitive control exercises; they cannot or dare not listen to what they feel or to their deeper wishes, desires, or drives. They are constantly in doubt and worried as a reaction to stress instead of experiencing the emotions that the stress elicits in them. Instead of Descartes' "cogito ergo sum," the variant "cogito ergo non sum" holds for such individuals, that is, you only exist when you dare to feel and experience.

SCALE 0

The Si scale is also a valuable tool for assessing personality disorders. While scales 4 and 7 have been found to be quite stable, the test–retest values for Scale 0, formerly the Social Introversion scale, have proven even more stable, maintaining a high correlation over long periods of time. This scale was constructed later than the other scales and was initially based on a sample of students scoring at the extremes for social introversion and extraversion. Only females were used for the original development of the scale, but the use of the scale has been expanded to include males. The MMPI–2 includes 69 items for this scale. One group of items concerns participation from a social perspective; the other group concerns general neurotic maladjustment and self-depreciation.

- T values of 75 or higher represent extreme withdrawal, insecurity, and indecisiveness.
- T values of 65 to 74 represent introversion, emotional overcontrol, passivity, and an orientation toward conventional adaptation.
- T values of 55 to 64 represent shyness; timidity; and absence of self-confidence, reliability, and dependence.
- T values lower than 45 represent extraversion, sociability, and friendliness.

Using item factor analyses, Hostetler, Ben-Porath, Butcher, and Graham (1989) developed the following set of subscales:

- Si1 contains items related to shyness. High scorers report feelings of shame in the presence of other people, shyness, discomfort in the presence of others, and discomfort in new situations.
- Si2 contains items related to social avoidance. High scorers dislike crowds and avoid group activities or masses. They also report avoidance of contact with others.
- Si3 contains items related to alienation from oneself and others. High scorers describe themselves as ridden with feelings of low self-esteem and little self-confidence. Such individuals can be very critical of themselves, doubt their own capacity to judge, and feel unqualified to take their destiny into their own hands. They also report feelings of nervousness, anxiety, indecision, and distrust of others.

BEHAVIORAL STYLES

As noted earlier, the *DSM* categorizes disease entities and the MMPI–2 measures dimensions. With the 10 personality disorders of the *DSM*, not all problematic traits are exhibited. The MMPI–2 offers several dimensions named *behavior styles*, which can be clinically useful.

Scale 0 does not address severe psychopathology like the other clinical scales do (with the exception of Scale 5); rather, it addresses personality characteristics and behavioral styles that depend on other elevations or depressions in the profile to actually say something about the vulnerabilities of the individual in question. An elevated Scale 0 score in combination with a depressed Scale 9 score, for example, indicates a behavioral

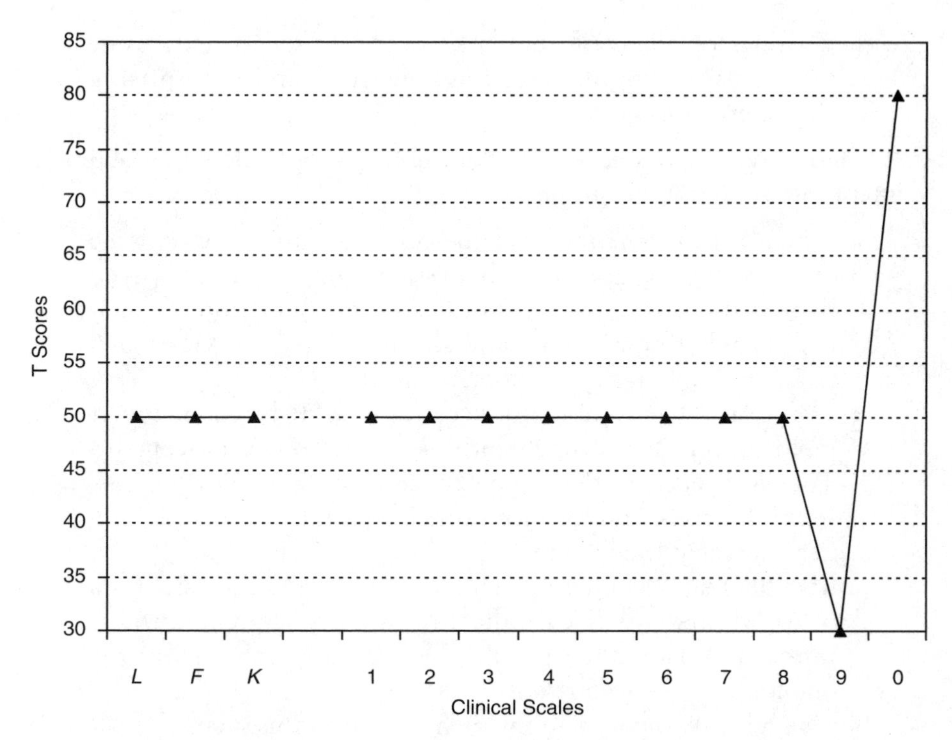

Figure 5.4. Simulated profile illustrating the Behavior Style A personality type.

style that I have termed—for MMPI–2 profile training purposes—*Behavior Style* A (see Figure 5.4). I next present the most important diagnostic hypotheses with respect to Scale 9—the former Hypomania scale—for illustrative purposes.

The construction of Scale 9 was based on patients in an early phase of a manic episode constituting part of a manic-depressive disorder. Those patients who were completely psychotic could not be tested using the standard MMPI questionnaire because of their hyperactive behavior. Some of the items pertain to aspects of hypomania disorders (e.g., activity level, state of excitement, delusions of grandeur). Other items concern relations to family and members of the family, moral values and attitudes, and bodily concerns. The scale is fairly fragmented.

- T values of 75 or higher suggest manic symptoms, excessive and aimless activities, hallucinations, delusions of grandeur, confusion, and "flight of ideas."
- T values of 65 to 74 indicate excessive energy, lack of direction, conceptual disorganization, unrealistic self-appreciation, low frustration tolerance, and impulsivity.

- T values of 55 to 64 indicate energetic, social, extravert, rebellious, excitement-seeking, creative, and enterprising characteristics.

Harris and Lingoes developed four subscales for Scale 9 to group their content into similar item clusters:

- Ma1 relates to amorality. High scorers on this scale describe other people as egoistic, dishonest, and opportunistic. Given these perceptions, they feel justified in their adoption of a similar attitude toward those around them. They can vicariously enjoy the exploitation of others.
- Ma2 relates to psychomotor acceleration. High scorers report rapid speech, fast thought processes, and quick movement. They feel tense, restless, and excited. They are quickly bored, search for risks, and long for excitement and danger as a manner to combat the boredom.
- Ma3 summarizes imperturbability. These people deny any form of social anxiety. They indicate that they feel comfortable interacting with other people. They do not worry about the opinions, values, or attitudes of others.
- Ma4 relates to ego inflation. High scorers on this subscale evaluate their possibilities and their own value unrealistically. They are annoyed by the demands that others impose on them.

Returning to the personality style referred to as Behavior Style A and depicted in Figure 5.4, it can be hypothesized that this profile concerns individuals who feel anxious and shy in social situations, withdraw from social contacts and situations, feel quickly anxious, and avoid attention to themselves. This characterization stems from my clinical experience with patients requesting guidance for social phobic complaints. The individuals in question were found to feel completely in their element when working alone, performing precision work, and trying to limit the time needed to be in contact with their social environment. Of obvious importance in each case was just how the various clinical scales turned out. When Scale 2 was elevated, for example, a measure of gloominess, depression, or negative self-perception was added to the picture. When Scale 8 was also elevated, this meant that the avoidant characteristics revealed by Scale 0 were stronger and could possibly turn into schizoid or schizotypal characteristics.

In Figure 5.5, the opposite of the profile described in the preceding discussion is depicted. These people are—in the words of James Butcher (personal communication, 2002)—people who "go by the lights." They practice no self-observation or self-evaluation whatsoever, and introspection is not their hobby. They are oriented toward the outside world, that is, they are stimulus oriented. They fill up their existence from the outside and

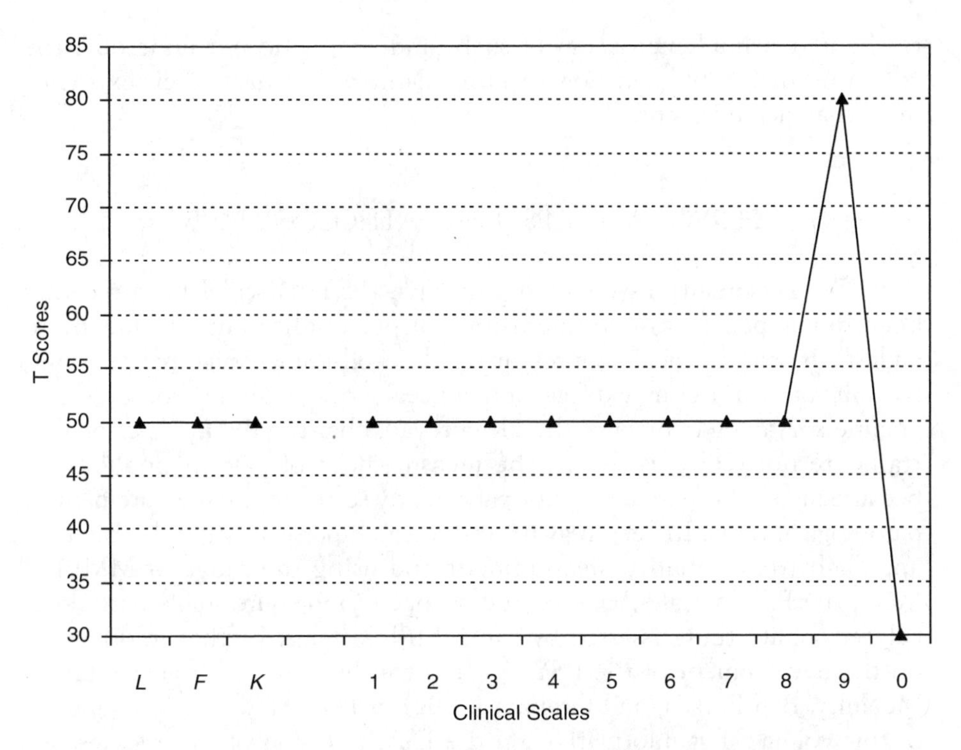

Figure 5.5 Simulated profile illustrating the Behavior Style B personality type.

do not submit to reflection, introspection, or any other form of self-aware behavior. They are fast, impulsive, restless, in search of sensation, and have little eye for how others feel in their presence. I sometimes compare such individuals to disc jockeys, now considered as having Behavior Style B, who constantly talk through the music and apparently cannot keep their mouths shut. Such egocentrism and impulsivity can be exacerbated by elevated Scale 4 scores. People who have an elevated Scale 6 as well may be described as extraordinarily difficult to "reach." A professional helping relationship is difficult to establish with such individuals. For both of the profiles presented in Figure 5.4 and Figure 5.5, it is certainly the case that clear consequences for the interpretation of the results can be drawn on the basis of the extreme configurations. It may be useful, for example, to start with the interpretation of the clinical scales starting with this configuration and, on the basis of these two (0–9 and 9–0), give the remainder of the profile significance.

Finally, and with respect to the description of behavioral styles here, a few additional comments can be made with regard to Scale 5. Elevations between 60 and 70 among young males—who are, in my experience, often students—reveal goodwilled, talkative, and sensitive but otherwise very passive men. They are often creative, make numerous plans but rarely get to the actual implementation of such, and simply do not undertake the action needed to fit their flow of ideas. Fantasy dominates their existence more than achievement.

PERSONALITY PSYCHOPATHOLOGY FIVE

The Personality Psychopathology Five (PSY–5) scales have recently been developed to assess dimensions of personality and are meant to address the pathological counterpart to the well-known Big Five personality traits of neuroticism, extraversion, agreeableness, conscientiousness, and openness. Among clinicians, the idea prevails that the Big Five personality traits are not really useful for the measurement of patient populations because many of the items are not particularly suited to the measurement of pathological traits. In keeping with the research perspective of the Big Five approach to personality measurement and using the range of MMPI–2 items, the PSY–5 scales have been developed to measure stable pathological personality traits assessed by the MMPI–2 items. Further information on the development of the PSY–5 scales can be obtained from Harkness, McNulty, Ben-Porath, and Graham (2002) or from Harkness in chapter 4 of this volume. For information on the Dutch version of these scales, see Vendrig, Derksen, and De Mey (2000) or Egger, De Mey, Derksen, and van der Staak (2003). The PSY–5 scales offer the clinician a quick overview of "naturally occurring" individual differences in personality and also provide information on which themes play an important role in the life of the respondent. The PSY–5 scales include the following constructs:

- AGGR: Aggressivity
- PSYC: Psychoticism
- DISC: Disconstraint
- NEGE: Negative Emotionality–Neuroticism
- INTR: Introversion–Low Positive Emotionality

The PSY–5 scales are not intended to be used as "stand-alone" scales. They are, rather, part of the complete administration of the MMPI–2; thus, interpretation should occur only within the context of the entire MMPI–2. In the following section, a few brief guidelines for the interpretation of the PSY–5 scales are presented in addition to some of the established correlates for the scales. To date, the PSY–5 scales have been used in empirical research to address questions that are more theoretical than clinical. The clinical contribution of the PSY–5 to the interpretation of clinical profiles has yet to become crystallized. The present correlations are based on a study by Graham, Ben-Porath, and McNulty (1999), who examined valid MMPI–2 protocols for 1,020 respondents with the following information also available:

- intake–background information;
- results of SCL–90–R (Symptom Checklist—Revised); and
- ratings of therapists.

Aggressivity

The construct Aggressivity (AGGR) points to predominantly offensive and instrumental aggression. High scorers (T > 65) like to intimidate others and may use aggression as a means of obtaining a goal. (Incidentally, reactive aggression is not measured here.) Interpersonally, there is a connection to such notions as dominance and hate. Research shows high scorers to have an increased probability of (physically) violent behavior. Correlations also exist with violence in the home situation (among men) and arrest (among women). High-scoring women are externally oriented. Low scores are not interpreted.

PSY–5 AGGR correlates significantly with intake information showing active and physically violent behavior among both men and women. Among men, a high AGGR score correlates with a history of violence within the relationship. A strong correlation with the SCL–90–R Hostility scale was found for men ($r = .41$) along with a moderate but significant correlation for women ($r = .19$). The general pattern of correlations for AGGR suggests convergence with external variables measuring aggression, hostility, and dominance.

Psychoticism

The construct Psychoticism (PSYC) measures a certain degree of disconnection from reality. Opinions not shared by others, atypical feelings, and strange perceptions point to such a disconnection. This scale also includes estrangement and an unrealistic expectation of hurt. High scorers have an increased probability of delusions or an unusual, disorganized, and disoriented manner of thinking. Among clinical respondents, one can speak more frequently of psychosis, loose associations, hallucinations, and "flight of ideas." In the case of elevated PSY–5 PSYC scores, the following are also seen: few friends, lower levels of functioning, depression, and low achievement orientation. Anxiety is also often detected among men and hallucinations among women. Low scores on the scale are not interpreted. The PSY–5 PSYC scale thus correlates predominantly with indicators of psychotic or paranoid phenomena.

Disconstraint

The construct of Disconstraint (DISC) is not an easy one to translate. The construct has to do with a tendency toward (physically) risky behavior, impulsivity, and "not being tied" to traditional "limitations" (i.e., moral norms and values). One can speak of behavioral disinhibition, and a certain amount of overlap with sensation seeking exists. High scorers tend to take risks, are impulsive, and are less traditional. They have a slight tendency to search for partners with the same tendencies. They are bored by routine. Research shows correlations with arrest and substance abuse among both men and women. Therapists tend to characterize such high scorers as aggressive and antisocial. Low scorers present an image of considerable (greater than average) self-control, little risk seeking, low impulsivity, and easy conformance to rules. They are also found to frequently choose similarly scoring partners.

Substance use and abuse strongly correlate with high PSY–5 DISC scale scores. The theme of impulsivity is thus discernible here, and a correlation with PSY–5 AGGR also exists.

Negative Emotionality–Neuroticism

The most important characteristics of the PSY–5 NEGE scale are as follows: a focus on problematic features—aspects of incoming information—stimuli, worry, self-critique, feelings of guilt, and anticipation of "the worst case scenario." High scorers report more frequent physical complaints, pessimism, and low achievement motivation. Low scores are not interpreted.

Clinical signs and indicators of anxiety, depression, and negative affect strongly correlate with NEGE scale scores. This holds for somatization, interpersonal sensitivity, and worry as well. In general, both internal and external cues relating to danger are perceived quickly and anticipated upon.

Introversion–Low Positive Emotionality

Respondents who score high on the PSY–5 INTR scale often find it difficult to be positively engaged and to enjoy life. Such individuals are not hedonistic. Therapists more frequently characterize high scorers as pessimistic, depressive, introverted, and somatizing. Low scorers ($T < 40$), in contrast, can be characterized as people who easily enjoy things and are social, energetic, and rarely depressed or dysthymic. Extremely low INTR scores are obtained by hypomanic respondents.

Indicators of depression correlate high with INTR. In addition, indicators of insecurity, anxiety, and somatization correlate high with INTR.

THE ROLE OF THE MMPI–2 IN THE PSYCHOLOGICAL DIAGNOSTIC PROCESS

The question now is, how can the MMPI–2 best serve the psychological diagnostic process? (See Exhibit 5.1 for an overview.) Instead of the

EXHIBIT 5.1
Highlight: Factors in the Assessment of Personality Problems of Mental Health Clients

- The original MMPI was not constructed as a measure of *DSM* personality disorders. It was originally developed to assess symptoms of mental disorders years before the current *DSM* system was developed.
- The MMPI–2 item pool was developed for a broad range of mental health and health problems and not specifically for assessing *DSM* personality disorder. Therefore, clinical diagnosis of personality disorder is not a preferred use of the test.
- A number of scales (e.g., the Pd scale and the Antisocial Personality scale) can contribute to the assessment of personality disorder, although diagnosis is not the primary consideration.
- Some specific personality disorder scales for the MMPI–2 have been developed, but research to this point has not provided a network of interpretive information.
- A great deal of research on personality disorders is available on the original MMPI and MMPI–2. Mean MMPI–2 profiles of the various types of personality disorders contribute only in a small way to clinical practice.
- Several new measures, such as the PSY–5 scales, provide pertinent information for the assessment of personality disorders.
- After the *DSM* classification of personality disorders emerged in the 1980s, the revised version of the MMPI (MMPI–2) was found to contribute to the understanding of personality disorders, particularly with respect to assessment of treatment resistance.
- The MMPI–2 is very helpful in specifying relevant dimensions of personality factors with a personality disorder such as dependence, narcissism, passive aggression, and paranoid traits.
- MMPI–2 profiles of patients with a personality disorder may indicate the possibility of treatment resistance. However, the creative clinical psychologist uses the warnings produced by the profile as opportunities.
- The MMPI–2 and the MMPI–A can be particularly valuable in the assessment of difficult-to-treat patients and should be included in pretreatment evaluation.

diagnosis of a personality disorder with the aid of the MMPI–2, inspection of the profile for a patient already diagnosed with a (clinically) severe personality disorder (most likely by means of the *DSM–IV* [APA, 1994]) may help guide decisions regarding the treatment to be undertaken. Speaking clinically, the MMPI–2 is a test that can help shape the psychological treatment of a patient. Note that not every patient requires examination beyond intake with the help of psychological tests. The need for additional testing clearly depends on the nature of the disorder or disorders, the manner in which the problems began (insidious or acute), and the question of whether yet another personality disorder plays a role in addition to symptom disorders (for an explication of such criteria, see Derksen, 2004). Psychological assessment with the aid of—among other tools—the MMPI–2 may certainly be useful when the contact during the intake indicates that a severe personality disorder is playing a role. As a rule, this disorder meets the criteria for one or more of the *DSM* Axis II disorders. In addition to examination with the aid of the MMPI–2, then, the administration of other frequently used psychological tests may also be called for: for example, the Wechsler Adult Intelligence Scale—Third Edition (WAIS–III) supplemented, if needed, with neuropsychological examination and such projective techniques as the Rorschach or the TAT. These tests supplement the *DSM* categories with dimensional data. These diagnostic hypotheses help connect the *DSM* category with the treatment approach. The following discussion primarily addresses the MMPI–2.

One fact based on my experience with the MMPI–2 is that the test points primarily to aspects of the patient's personality that can stand in the way of successful treatment. Consider, in this light, the presence of elevated scores in scales 4 and 9 but also elevated scores in scales 3, 6, and 8. The hypotheses that research has produced in connection with these scales will not make the average therapist very optimistic. Alternatively, the attitude of the therapist in such cases may be "forewarned is forearmed"; that is, in light of such known stumbling blocks, the clinician can try to think up a strategy to remove or avoid them. An example is the case of a 28-year-old man who was beginning his third relationship after two failed marriages with children and therefore sought counseling. The man related that he was worried about his manner of reacting to intimate relationships and that he wanted psychological treatment to gain insight into his blind spots. He produced a Spike 4 on the MMPI–2, which means that only Scale 4 is found to be significantly elevated with a score of 80. Such a profile presents the hypothesis that the person in question is predisposed to blame others in relationships, experiences little suffering, and shows a tendency to act out in the face of critique or stress. In short, the chances were great that this man would give up therapy after a few sessions and argue that the psychologist had little to contribute. Indeed, further inquiry showed that the man's new girlfriend was the motivation behind the request for help.

Using the MMPI–2 results, the patient was provided feedback of two important points: first, that the psychologist certainly took his request for help seriously; second, that the MMPI–2 suggested that his request for help should not be taken too seriously—that is, his motivation for treatment was doubtful. This situation was discussed openly with the patient; the psychologist and patient then agreed that if the man started to devalue the treatment or the psychologist he was to meet with the psychologist and talk about this *before* further devaluation of the situation or simply staying away. The patient, psychologist, and test triangle can lead to interesting interactions and possible resolution to the resistance.

The specific MMPI scale configurations for patients with a severe personality disorder are of most interest. For a person with an antisocial personality disorder and Scale 4 scores as the highest but no other elevations above 65, for example, very few additional diagnostic hypotheses are provided by the MMPI–2 (see Figure 5.1). The situation changes when the Antisocial Practices (ASP) content scale and the PSY–5 scales are not elevated. The Harris–Lingoes subscales can then be of use, and the problem can be seen to possibly lie in a diffuse identity and not primarily in acting out behavior. When the Scale 2 score is higher than the Scale 4 score and the Scale 7 score is also elevated significantly, psychological treatment has better chances of success. In starting treatment, a good idea may be not to try to influence the feelings of depression, but rather to consider the feelings a help in treatment in the sense that the patient stays more and longer motivated to change. The content scales will also indicate this with characteristic elevations for depression and complaints of anxiety. Little or no elevations on the content scales are typically expected for people with an antisocial personality disorder (except for ANG [Anger] or CYN [Cynicism]). But when such elevations are present, things become more interesting and more opportunities for psychological guidance are provided.

The situation is the same for the borderline patient. A diagnosis of borderline personality disorder as described by the *DSM* is frequently assigned, which leads to a large and very heterogeneous group of patients. In this light, the *DSM* has lost its specificity and provides only a very feeble

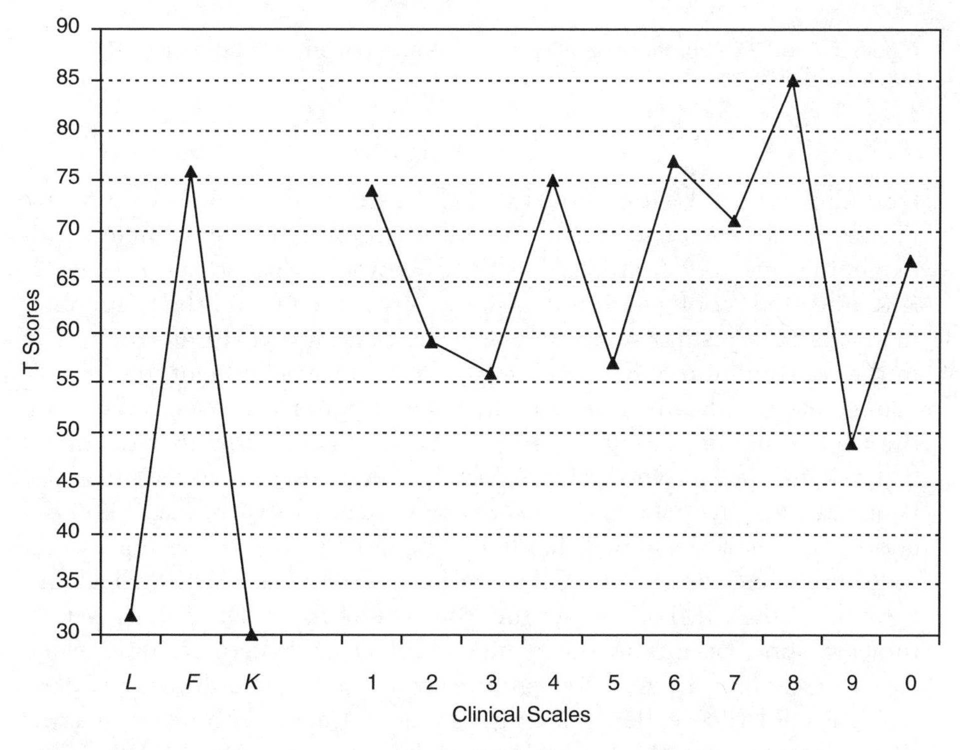

Figure 5.6. MMPI–2 profile of a 30-year-old female patient with borderline personality disorder.

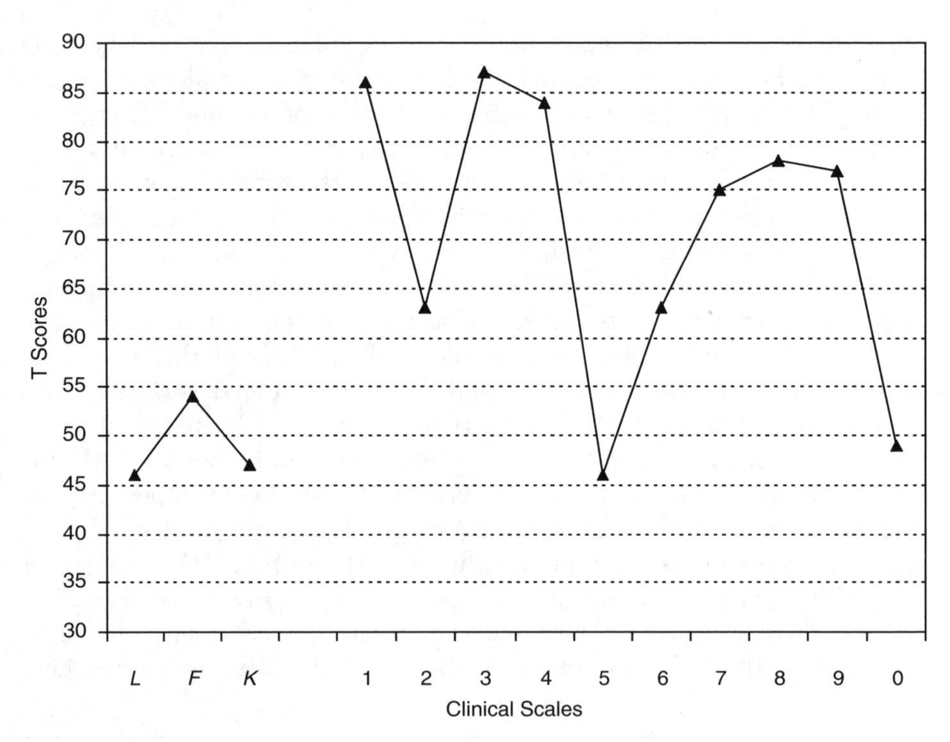

Figure 5.7. MMPI–2 profile of a 37-year-old female patient with borderline personality disorder.

treatment start. Using the MMPI–2 as depicted in Figure 5.6 and Figure 5.7, however, two female borderline patients with very different vulnerabilities may be identified. For the 30-year-old patient, the *L* (Lie), *F*, *K* (Correction) configuration indicates a "cry for help" and the schizophrenia scale indicates just how vulnerable she is. Schizotypal traits are visible in the configuration of 8, 9, and 0. For the 37-year-old patient, the *L, F, K* configuration indicates primarily a stabilized pattern. Her conversion on the main scales of 1, 2, and 3 and the Scale 4 score show that treatment will be difficult. Her vulnerability, which scales 8 and 9 make visible, may be masked by physical complaints. Starting treatment with a light antipsychotic medication may help borderline patients who produce high scores on 6 and 8. Keep an eye on PSY–5 scale aggressivity also. Repeated administration of the MMPI–2 shows the influence of the drug. In our practice, the borderline patients are completely informed of this policy and they are curious regarding the new test profiles they will produce. Inpatients diagnosed as borderline patients often get group treatment without considering their specific vulnerabilities as displayed by means of the MMPI–2. For instance, an elevation of Scale 6 above 80 is not exceptional. In these

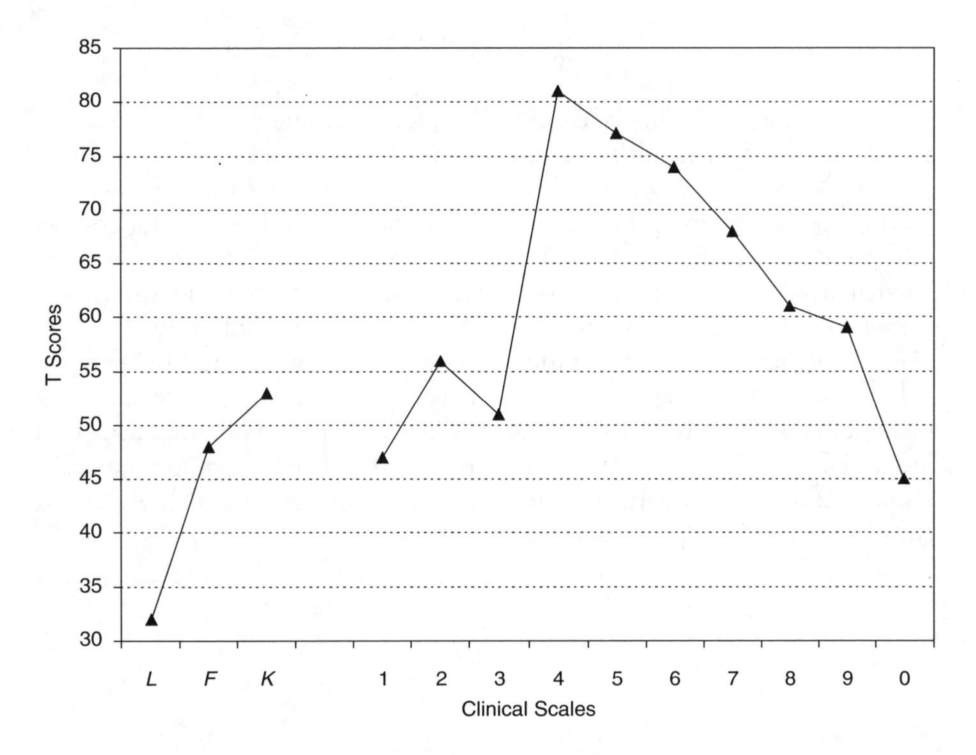

Figure 5.8. Profile of a lawyer who committed suicide.

patients, group treatment is problematic because of their continuously actively defending feeling hurt. They have to put so much energy into neutralizing their vulnerabilities presented by means of the high 6 that not enough energy is left for profiting from the group process.

In closing, I present the profile of a patient about whom I was consulted after his death due to suicide. The 36-year-old lawyer had sought and received help from a number of different agencies. The health provider's report did not seem to have a grip on the man or his problems. The patient was assumed to be a person with a narcissistic personality disorder with only limited suffering or complaints. Shortly before the patient's suicide, the MMPI–2 had been administered in an attempt to gain still greater insight into his personality and complaints. (Obviously, it would have been better to do this earlier in the process.) The MMPI–2 profile for the patient in question is depicted in Figure 5.8. As is common in cases of suicide, he did not suffer from depression; but the combination of elevated scores in scales 4 and 5 presented a possible hypothesis of a parafilia. Subsequent inquiry in the earlier treatment and contact with the former therapist showed that this possibility was never discussed in depth with the patient. Therefore, it is possible that in the end he simply expected no adequate help and gave up.

CONCLUSION

Note that the utility of the MMPI–2 for the clinical user lies predominantly in the further differentiation of the psychological diagnosis of patients with a severe personality disorder and bridging the gap to treatment. The categories of the *DSM* can be supplied with different dimensions via the MMPI–2 and the MMPI–A, and various hypotheses regarding the particular vulnerabilities of a patient can then be generated. Obviously, this use of the questionnaire method in such a manner should be further substantiated with additional empirical research along these lines. In theoretical and research endeavors, the MMPI stimulates the practitioner to think of patients with personality disorders as patients with vulnerabilities that are distributed along several dimensions (i.e., dependency, paranoia, narcissism, obsessiveness, schizotypy, impulsiveness, and acting out). Assessing these dimensions helps to establish treatment phases.

6

THE MMPI–2 AND ASSESSMENT OF POSTTRAUMATIC STRESS DISORDER (PTSD)

WALTER E. PENK, JILL RIERDAN, MARYLEE LOSARDO, AND RALPH ROBINOWITZ

Posttraumatic stress disorder (PTSD) first appeared in the *Diagnostic and Statistical Manual of Mental Disorders* (3rd ed., American Psychiatric Association [APA], 1980), and PTSD criteria continue to be revised (i.e., *DSM–IV–TR*; APA, 2000). Because PTSD criteria are evolving from many clinical studies, practitioners need to stay current for the latest reformulation of the diagnostic criteria (e.g., *DSM–IV–TR*), the latest psychometrically validated assessment techniques (e.g., Weathers & Keane, 1999; Keane, Weathers, & Foa, 2000), and the latest clinical guidelines for treatment and rehabilitation (e.g., Ursano et al., 2004).

The authors wish to express their deep appreciation to Judith Bradley, Maura Herlihy, and Jeffrey Lovelace at the Edith Nourse Rogers Memorial Veterans Hospital, Bedford, Massachusetts, for their valuable assistance in the preparation of this chapter. Special thanks is given to staff of the New Braunfels, Texas, Public Library.

Six classes of diagnostic indicators are to be assessed to determine PTSD:

- Criterion A: Experience of traumatic event(s) with cognitive–affective response of helplessness and horror;
- Criterion B: Intrusive images and memories (e.g., nightmares, flashbacks, distress over reminders of trauma);
- Criterion C: Coping by avoidance (e.g., inability to recall the trauma, feelings of detachment, restricted range of affect, blunted emotions);
- Criterion D: Physiological arousal (e.g., sleeplessness, irritability, hypervigilance);
- Criterion E: One-month duration of criteria B, C, and D (to distinguish acute, transient, statistically normative post-traumatic stress reactions from atypically stable stress symptoms); and
- Criterion F: Occupational–social dysfunction.

The MMPI–2 is well suited for classifying PTSD in terms of a diagnosable syndrome and individual classes of diagnostic indicators. However, since neither the MMPI–2 nor any other single assessment technique has as yet achieved 100% accuracy in classifying PTSD, our recommendation is to administer the MMPI–2 in a multimethod approach to assessment (e.g., Wilson & Keane, 1997). Such a multimethod approach should include several reliable and valid instruments, such as (a) structured interviews, wherein direct, face-valid questions yield self-reports of the presence–absence of specific PTSD symptom classes; (b) independent assessment and verification of trauma exposure if possible; and (c) psychometrically validated tests with items that are not face-valid, such as the MMPI–2 with its PTSD scales.

The MMPI–2's PTSD scales (e.g., Pk [Keane PTSD] scale of Keane, Malloy, & Fairbank, 1984; the Ps [Schlenger PTSD] scale of Schlenger & Kulka, 1989) were empirically derived and validated with criterion group distinction methods (i.e., comparing groups with/without *DSM*-derived diagnoses of PTSD) that identified MMPI items uniquely associated with PTSD-diagnosed groups but not with non-PTSD groups. MMPI–2 PTSD scales may thus be less vulnerable to "faking" and false memories than interviews and other face-valid assessment instruments, because MMPI PTSD scale items do not refer directly to trauma and test takers therefore may be less able to engage in impression management as they respond to particular items that they infer are critical for diagnosis.

In developing the thesis that the MMPI–2 is a valuable tool within a multimethod approach for diagnosing and assessing PTSD, we consider the following issues:

1. Characteristics of PTSD as a unique event-related disorder,
2. Threats to accuracy in assessing PTSD,

3. Advantages of the MMPI–2 for assessing PTSD,
4. Disadvantages and limitations of the MMPI–2 for assessing PTSD,
5. Practice guidelines for using the MMPI–2 and other tests in a multimethod approach to assessing *DSM*-defined PTSD,
6. Supplementation of MMPI–2 scales when assessing PTSD in the context of diagnostic comorbidities,
7. Complex versus simple PTSD,
8. Treatment implications for PTSD derived from the MMPI–2, and
9. New directions for MMPI–2 PTSD research.

CHARACTERISTICS OF PTSD AS A UNIQUE EVENT-RELATED DISORDER

Posttraumatic stress disorder is unique among mental disorders (see PTSD, 309.81; *DSM–IV–TR* [APA, 2000]). This uniqueness derives from several facts. First, PTSD is a disorder directly attributable to a specific event or events (i.e., traumas). As an explicitly event-related disorder—as are only a few other *DSM–IV–TR* (APA, 2000) disorders, such as acute stress disorder and the adjustment disorders—PTSD first requires validation of the traumatic event that constitutes its initial diagnostic criterion.

Second, while it is necessary to validate trauma in order to diagnose PTSD, it is not sufficient. Some traumatized individuals never meet the full set of criteria for PTSD classification. The National Comorbidity Survey (Kessler, Sonnega, Bromet, Hughes, & Nelson, 1995) estimates that, whereas 60.7% of men and 51.2% of women experience at least one trauma during their lifetimes, PTSD prevalence rates average but 8% among adults (*DSM–IV–TR*; APA, 2000, p. 466), a figure that also characterizes prevalence rates for the 34.2% of men and 24.9% of women who, according to the National Comorbidity Survey, report experiencing two or more traumas during their lifetimes. The question of why some traumatized individuals go on to develop PTSD while others do not is a question requiring continued research, along with a corollary question of why some trauma experiences are more likely to conduce to PTSD than are other properly defined and validated trauma experiences.

Third, although trauma does not inevitably conduce to PTSD, the prevalence rate of 8% is indeed high. Compare this to the prevalence rate of 1% for schizophrenia in point-in-time surveys. Consider as well that the 8% prevalence figure equals around 20 million citizens in the United States with its population of 290 million.

Fourth, although PTSD may not always emerge following trauma, other disorders—instead of, as well as in addition to, PTSD—may appear as sequelae to trauma (Keane & Kaloupek, 1997). Depression, substance abuse, and other anxiety disorders are frequently found to accompany exposure to trauma. For example, Galea et al. (2002) reported increases in depression and substance abuse, as well as PTSD, among Manhattan residents after the 9/11 terrorist attacks.

Fifth, wide individual differences in recovery rates from diagnosable PTSD are reported. See, for example, the Vietnam Experiences Study from the Centers for Disease Control (1988), cited in Davidson and Fairbank (1993), reporting high but different current and lifetime prevalence rates than found in the Kulka et al. (1990) National Vietnam Veterans Readjustment Study (NVVRS) results.

Sixth, PTSD is a disorder that may develop among persons at any age and at any stage in personal maturation, with and without other preexisting mental disorders. Since trauma may be experienced by the very young and the very old and among individuals at levels of maturation from the least mature to the most advanced, an exceptionally wide range of individuals may meet PTSD criteria. This calls attention to developmental differences in symptom presentation and assessment and to the need for different interventions in treatment and rehabilitation that are specifically tailored to such individual differences (e. g., Denny, Robinowitz, & Penk, 1987; Penk et al., 1989). Preparatory to MMPI–2 interpretation, for example, this fact implies that it may be less important to search for one code type or a typical MMPI–2 profile for classifying PTSD (where *code type* and *MMPI–2 profile* refer to configurational analysis by clinical and content scales, e.g., Butcher, 2000a) than it is to understand how PTSD is expressed within each MMPI–2 clinical profile that emerges.

Seventh, PTSD may be "faked" by those never traumatized, as well as by those who have experienced trauma but have not developed sufficient symptoms for diagnosis (e.g., Elhai & Frueh, 2001). As a consequence, clinicians must verify accuracy of PTSD diagnoses by using reliable and valid assessment techniques in a multimethod approach and independent corroboration of self-reported occurrences of trauma.

Eighth, as already noted, PTSD is comparatively new, first appearing only 25 years ago in the *DSM–III* (APA, 1980) as an independent diagnostic category. Accordingly, criteria and measures for diagnosing the disorder are likely to continue to change as studies yield more information validating PTSD.

These eight facts—cumulating to the unique status of PTSD in the nomenclature—challenge clinicians in the process of achieving an accurate and valid classification of PTSD.

THREATS TO ACCURACY IN ASSESSING PTSD

Threats to accuracy in assessing PTSD emerge from the characteristics of PTSD as a unique, event-related disorder. Because the defining and diagnostic criteria for PTSD continue to evolve, accurate assessment is threatened, first, by the extent that practitioners fail to use the most currently reliable and valid measures of PTSD.

A second threat is when clinicians fail to confirm trauma exposure and rely on inference from symptom presentation, thereby conflating Diagnostic Indicator Class A (Experience of Trauma) and classes B–D (Reexperiencing, Avoidance, and Hyperarousal).

Another threat to accurate assessment occurs when trauma exposure and PTSD are overlooked for patients who have, concurrently, other conspicuous disorders. For example, among schizophrenic patients, Brady, Rierdan, Penk, Meschede, and Losardo (2003) found no mention of trauma in patient records and no PTSD diagnoses despite interview results that patients were, typically, multiply traumatized. In fact, it is important to note that many individuals are multiply traumatized and that PTSD may ensue from one trauma but not another. Accordingly, assessment instruments must link PTSD symptoms in Diagnostic Indicator classes B–D with the trauma(s) criteria for Class A (Blake et al., 1990, 1995).

A third threat—the opposite of underreporting PTSD in patients with other diagnoses—is failing to assess for other disorders among individuals already diagnosed with PTSD. A fourth threat is reliance on assessment as a onetime clinical intervention. Given (a) that PTSD symptoms show phasic variation, (b) that onset of PTSD symptoms may be delayed after trauma exposure, and (c) that recovery rates show wide individual differences, assessment needs to occur over time. In so doing, attention to onset and remission of other disorders must occur or valid assessment of PTSD is likely to be threatened.

Valid assessment of PTSD—more than assessment of many other disorders—is threatened if attention is not paid to developmental variables, the age and developmental stage of the individual at assessment and the age and developmental stage of the individual when traumatized. Such considerations are necessary to distinguish Simple and Complex PTSD in the context of personality disorders.

Finally, valid assessment is threatened because reports of trauma and PTSD symptoms may be faked. Though rates are unknown, Elhai and Frueh (2001) estimate that malingering occurs in at least 7% of individuals in outpatient settings and up to 20% of individuals in veteran populations.

ADVANTAGES OF THE MMPI–2 FOR ASSESSING PTSD

Fortunately, the MMPI–2 is a comprehensive instrument, well suited to overcome many threats to valid assessment of PTSD. The instrument is objective and standardized, and its scales for PTSD and other disorders have been psychometrically derived using the "classic" criterion-group-distinction methods for test reliability and validation. Also, scales are not face-valid and, as such, are less vulnerable to faking.

Unlike most instruments designed to classify PTSD, no MMPI item asks respondents to self-report and to judge whether or not they meet criteria for PTSD or other disorders. MMPI–2 PTSD scales, in contrast to diagnostic interviews, never present as statements to be answered "True" or "False," "I have been traumatized," or "I have frequent flashbacks about a trauma I experienced," or "I have nightmares about a trauma I endured." Rather, MMPI–2 PTSD scales have been empirically derived by statistically identifying items that differentiate between groups meeting and not meeting PTSD diagnostic criteria and by then forming scales tested for reliability and validity. As a consequence, the MMPI–2, with its objective validity indicators, has psychometrically sound protections against malingering, "faking," symptom exaggeration or denial, disorganization, confusion, and random responding, and thus differs from other tests assessing PTSD that lack such safeguards to "faking."

F (Infrequency) and *F(B)* (Back Infrequency) scales register atypicality in responding. The *K* (Correction) scale measures the extent to which an individual may be denying symptoms. Ratios of *F* to *K* document fake-good and fake-bad approaches to test taking. VRIN (Variable Response Inconsistency) and TRIN (True Response Inconsistency) inform clinicians about the consistency with which individuals respond to MMPI–2 items. It is essential for clinicians to document a variety of response styles such as these, using reliable and valid scales as found in the MMPI–2, given the vulnerability of interviews and tests to exaggeration, denial, and distraction.

Understanding such response biases will assist clinicians in many instances, because a referral to rule out or rule in PTSD may be to search for evidence that compensation and benefits indeed are warranted, or to establish a basis for product liabilities litigation, or to establish a defense in criminal and civil cases (e.g., Lees-Haley, 1997). MMPI–2 validity scales are likely to assist in determining accuracy in reporting symptoms following trauma, enhancing clinicians' personal observations and intuition as to whether or not the client is speaking the truth.

In addition to the advantage of the MMPI–2 in terms of built-in safeguards against response sets, it also has been shown to be valid across many different potential populations of traumatized individuals. Studies demonstrate that the MMPI–2 is clinically accurate in correctly identifying PTSD among civilians as well as among combat veterans, when PTSD is comorbid with other disorders as well as when it is occurring alone, and among people from cultures other than that of the United States and with native languages other than English. (For reviews in this volume, see chap. 18 by Garrido and Velasquez and chap. 19 by Butcher, Mosch, Tsai, and Nezami.)

The MMPI–2, having been translated into more than 30 different languages, can be used to assess trauma in many different cultures (Butcher, 2000a, 2000c).

The MMPI–2 carries the additional advantage of consisting of scales standardized and normed according to uniform scores. Because MMPI–2 scales have been uniformily normed to a common metric (Tellegen & Ben-Porath, 2000), a person's score on a PTSD scale can be compared for degree of disorder with scores on other scales. Because the MMPI–2 consists of many scales uniformly normed and derived from a common pool of items administered to the same large sample, the use of the MMPI–2 is preferable to the practice found in many PTSD research and clinical studies in which many different scales are "stitched together" to form a test battery without regard for their development in disparate populations, the influence of different items and scales on each other, and the absence of an algorithm for reconciling scores from disparate tests that lack uniformity in standardization and norming.

This psychometrically dubious practice of combining disparate scales to form an assessment battery also invalidates any arguments that the 567 items of the MMPI–2 take too much time. Weathers and Keane (1999), reviewing psychological assessment of traumatized adults, described batteries for assessing PTSD, the shortest lasting around 3 hours and the longest up to 12 hours. Average time to complete the MMPI–2 is around one hour and 30 minutes, with the test taker working alone. The yield, available immediately at test completion, is scores for hundreds of scales, automated reports based on decision rules and validated conclusions (see chap. 17 in this volume by Atlis, Hahn, and Butcher). Training to administer the MMPI–2 is minimal, and costs are negligible.

DISADVANTAGES AND LIMITATIONS OF THE MMPI–2 FOR ASSESSING PTSD

The MMPI–2 contains scales to identify the presence or absence of syndromal PTSD (Keane et al., 1984; Schlenger & Kulka, 1989). Moreover, MMPI–2 code typing yields configurations that may be clinically useful in deciding whether persons meet criteria for *DSM*–defined PTSD. But neither the PTSD scales nor code typing have been found to exceed 90% accuracy. This 10% error rate in PTSD classification for MMPI–2 scales or code types (e.g., Wise, 1996), though comparable in accuracy to classifying PTSD with structured clinical interviews and checklists, necessitates using a multimethod approach in assessing PTSD (Keane, Wolfe, & Taylor, 1987; Kulka et al., 1991).

Another limitation is that the MMPI–2 does not ask for information about specific trauma and therefore does not yield data about

Criterion A—the traumatic event. Moreover, the MMPI–2 does not as yet contain scales for the symptom-related diagnostic indicator classes (i.e., Intrusion, Avoidance, Hyperarousal). It follows, therefore, that the MMPI–2 does not link PTSD symptoms to trauma, though desirable for designing and tracking the effectiveness of trauma-focused therapies.

Finally, the MMPI–2 validity scales—identified earlier as one of the strengths of the instrument—may be less than optimally sensitive for some traumatized individuals. Some patients with PTSD present elevated *F* scales; this pattern—suggestive of symptom exaggeration and raising the question of profile invalidity—may in fact reflect the extreme intrusion symptoms and disorganization associated with PTSD. (See Arbisi & Ben-Porath, 2000, and the new *Fp* (Infrequency–Psychopathology) scale to reduce confusion by extreme psychopathology.)

PRACTICE GUIDELINES FOR USING THE MMPI–2 AND OTHER TESTS IN A MULTIMETHOD APPROACH TO ASSESSING *DSM*-DEFINED PTSD

Based on our experiences in delivering clinical services and conducting research, we recommend seven steps for using the MMPI–2 to assess PTSD within the context of a multimethod approach (see Weathers & Keane, 1999; compare Scenario 1, Brief Clinical Assessment, and Scenario 2, Comprehensive Clinical Assessment).

Step 1: Administer the MMPI–2 (Butcher, Dahlstrom, Graham, Tellegen, & Kaemmer, 1989)

In settings answering clinical referrals, we suggest routinely administering the MMPI–2 as the first step in any intake process once it has been determined that the client is able to conform with the request to answer the items. Administering the MMPI–2 before proceeding further into the recommended clinical interviewing may reduce the influence of "leading the client" that occurs when PTSD–specific questions are asked directly. MMPI–2 responses, once completed, can be submitted for scoring and for an automated report (see chap. 17 in this volume by Atlis, Hahn, and Butcher). We recommend further that clinicians defer examining MMPI-2 findings until after all other assessments have been completed.

Step 2: Administer a Trauma Checklist (Criterion A)

As already noted, PTSD Criterion A cannot be identified by the MMPI–2. Consequently, clinicians must use other checklists and structured interviews to determine whether a person has indeed met the first essential criterion for diagnosing PTSD—Criterion A: exposure to "extreme traumatic stressors" with an associated cognitive–affective experience involving "intense fear, helplessness, or horror." This may involve a two-stage process, because not all event *exposure* checklists inquire as to the *experience* of the event.

We recommend administering the Life Events Checklist (LEC) from the Clinician-Administered PTSD Scale (CAPS; Blake et al., 1990, 1995). The LEC lists examples of trauma. Supplemented by the Evaluation of Lifetime Stressors (ELS; Krinsley, 1996), clinicians can learn each person's subjective responses to trauma in terms of perceived life threat and degree of personal injury, can discern numbers of traumas, and can differentiate traumas that are interpersonal versus acts of nature. Measures of trauma exposure and experience are only recently being devised according to psychometric principles, with clinicians being encouraged by findings from research that suggest that clinicians and clients alike need to examine the traumatic event in greater detail than originally thought.

Administering a second checklist or interview certainly is in keeping with the clinician's responsibility to use several methods to verify the experience of trauma(s). Clinicians may choose from several reliable and valid instruments to assess trauma(s) of specific types among at-risk populations who have survived such life-threatening events as rape, automobile accidents, combat, political torture, weather-related disasters, attempted murder and other crimes, industrial accidents, and workplace violence (e.g., Lerner, 1996).

Experience of trauma should be independently corroborated. Kulka et al. (1990) give a Best Practice model of how to verify self-reported combat trauma from sources other than subjects' statements, so necessary in our "False Memory Syndrome" era. Also, MMPI–2 validity scores may add information about test-taking response sets, possibly helping clinicians discern whether self-reports are likely to be distorted by inaccuracies, inconsistencies, exaggerations, or minimizations.

Step 3: Assess PTSD Symptoms in Diagnostic Indicator Classes B (Intrusion), C (Avoidance), and D (Hyperarousal)

After administering the MMPI–2 (Step 1) and interviewing about trauma(s) and reactions to life-threatening events (Step 2, Criterion A), one then interviews and administers tests to identify the other diagnostic indicator classes (Intrusion, Avoidance, Hyperarousal). The MMPI–2 has no scales measuring the extent to which the person who has experienced trauma meets criteria for the other indicator classes comprising PTSD. We recommend a clinician-administered interview and a self-report instrument to classify these classes of PTSD indicators.

The CAPS (Blake et al., 1990) is reliable, with high test–retest and internal consistency correlations, and its validities are thoroughly tested and well regarded. The CAPS yields continuous measures of syndromal PTSD and of the three primary symptom classes (criteria B, C, and D), with exceptionally high degrees of diagnostic specificity and sensitivity. In addition, we recommend the Mississippi Scale for Combat-Related PTSD (Keane, Caddell, & Taylor, 1988) or the Civilian Trauma version of the same instrument, should the client not be a veteran. Both are self-report instruments and, like the CAPS, yield both a total score that serves as a basis for categorizing PTSD as present or absent and scores for specific criteria (see Norris & Riad, 1997, for other self-report instruments). Both the CAPS and the Mississippi, but not the MMPI–2, permit the clinician to link PTSD symptoms to specific traumatic events. And both the CAPS and the Mississippi, but not the MMPI–2, permit clinicians to examine changes from retesting within specific classes of PTSD symptoms.

Administering the MMPI–2, the CAPS, and the Mississippi carries out a multimethod approach in PTSD assessment: it yields perspectives from criterion-group-distinction-derived scales (i.e., Pk and Ps), clinician observation (CAPS), and client self-report (i.e., Mississippi). Accuracy in classifying PTSD and confidence about findings increase when concurrences occur among three different measures. (See Kulka et al., 1991, for strategies to resolve differences from several instruments.)

Step 4: Administer Instruments Assessing Other Diagnoses: The Problem of Comorbidity

It is now a well-established fact that PTSD rarely occurs alone (e.g., Penk et al., 1989; Weathers & Keane, 1999). The MMPI–2 can be helpful in placing PTSD in the context of comorbidity as two questions are assessed simultaneously: (a) Does a traumatized person likely warrant a diagnosis of PTSD? (b) Does the person simultaneously warrant a diagnosis (or diagnoses) of other, concurrent disorders? The MMPI–2 is not called *multiphasic* without good reason: It permits comparing degrees of different kinds of co-occurring mental disorders (and underlying dimensions of these disorders), normed with uniform scales.

One finding that is common across studies when group profiles are presented is that PTSD, in the context of other, concurrent disorders, drives up or *elevates* the T scores of clinical and content scales. However, the usual MMPI–2 clinical profile remains much the same (e.g., Kulka & Schlenger, 1986; Penk et al., 1989; Talbert et al., 1994; Weyermann, Norris, & Hyer, 1996). What this consistent finding means in practice is that comorbidity complicates the treatment of PTSD, which needs to be both more intensive and extensive, for example, when depression, schizophrenia, or substance abuse is comorbid.

The MMPI–2 cannot answer all questions concerning PTSD. Differentiating symptoms (e.g., anhedonia and suicidality) attributable to trauma from symptoms attributable to other preexisting or later developing disorders is difficult. Also, the MMPI–2 cannot determine which among co-occurring disorders came first. In cases for which such distinctions must be operationalized, we favor the Structured Clinical Interview for *DSM–III–R* (SCID; Spitzer, Williams, Gibbon, & First, 1990), an instrument that requires special training to arrive at reliable and valid diagnoses. With the SCID, the clinician can compare MMPI–2 results with interview findings and thereby discern the time course of the development of symptoms and disorders. The SCID can help distinguish whether a person meets criteria for current versus lifetime PTSD; and, as part of the multimethod approach, the SCID helps reduce error in diagnosing PTSD in the context of comorbidity.

Verifying PTSD and other diagnoses by adding the SCID and comparing its results with those of the MMPI–2 will greatly assist the treatment planning process, one dimension of which is to discern whether to intervene with the "uncovering" or "stormy" methods of trauma-focused, insight-oriented, psychodynamic therapy or the "covering over" or "quieting down" methods of mild debriefing, pharmacotherapies, and support (Foa, Keane, & Friedman, 2000).

Step 5: Administer Test to Distinguish Simple and Complex PTSD

Earlier, we cited evidence that one fourth of U.S. citizens report having experienced more than one trauma. A subset of such multiply traumatized individuals evidences a *complex* form of PTSD associated with prolonged, repeated, and early trauma (Herman, 1992; Van der Kolk et al., 1996); in contrast, *simple* PTSD (that is, *DSM*–defined PTSD) is more typically associated with single or adult-onset trauma. The hallmarks of complex PTSD are dissociation, somatization, and affect dysregulation, as well as interferences in characterological development (e.g., Ford, 1999; Ide & Paez, 2000). Preliminary analyses of studies in progress demonstrate that, as in the case of comorbidities, survivors of extreme and multiple traumas attain highly elevated MMPI–2 profiles. We recommend that the Structured Interview for Disorders of Extreme Stress (SIDES; Pelcovitz et al., 1996) be administered when more complicated cases of PTSD are encountered, as indexed by atypically elevated MMPI–2 profiles or SCID interview reports of early, prolonged, or extreme trauma.

Step 6: Administer Tests Assessing Resiliency

The literature is growing demonstrating, in the spirit of a "Positive Psychology," what some call *posttraumatic growth* (e.g., Tedeschi, Park, & Calhoun, 1998). This line of investigation is indebted to studies by researchers such as Aldwin, Levenson, and Spiro (1994), who found that exposure to trauma may have long-range positive as well as negative effects (see also Schnurr, Rosenberg, & Friedman, 1993). Clinicians need to explore with clients the possibilities of both positive and negative life changes attributable to trauma exposure. Clinicians and clients both must be open to the possibility that clients have abilities to cope successfully so that trauma exposure need not inevitably conduce to disorder and may even be so well integrated as to promote development. Not every person traumatized develops PTSD. Assessment may be approached in a manner that leads to discovery of how it is that some clients do not develop PTSD and others do. Treatment must start with the assumption that traumatized persons will recover, improving in their level of distress and functioning. Inventories and instruments that may be helpful in assessing negative and positive life changes following traumatic experiences are, for example, the 21-item, five-factor Post-Traumatic Growth Inventory (Tedeschi & Calhoun, 1996) and the 50-item Stress-Related Growth Scale (Park, Cohen, & Murch, 1996).

Step 7: Integrating MMPI–2 Findings With Multiple Methods

The final step in assessing PTSD is to integrate MMPI–2 findings with results from other tests. Such integration begins with deciding whether the MMPI–2 results can be accepted as valid. Finding *F* and *F(B)* scale scores higher than 120T may lead a clinician to conclude that symptom presentation is invalid because the client did not fully comprehend or idiosyncratically misunderstood MMPI–2 items. *F* scale scores traditionally run higher in PTSD samples, however; and if, in the clinician's opinion, responses in personal interviews (and in, for example, the SCID, recommended in Step 4 in an assessment process) seem coherent, MMPI–2 profiles with *F* scores between 90T and 120T may still be interpretable. Before reaching such a conclusion, the *Fp* scale should be examined; as noted earlier, this new validity indicator (Arbisi & Ben-Porath, 2000) aids the clinician in distinguishing among profiles with high *F* score elevations as a result of random responding and faking versus significant distress and/or severe psychopathology. If the *Fp* scale is less than T score 100, VRIN is less than T score 80 (no random responding), and TRIN is less than T score 100 (i.e., elevations are not likely to be because of acquiescence and nay-saying), MMPI–2 profiles with highly elevated *F* scales may be interpreted as validly reflecting psychopathology rather than as always invalid.

After confirming the validity of the MMPI–2 protocol, the next step is to determine PTSD status according to the MMPI–2 Pk or Ps scales. The 46-item Pk scale (Keane et al., 1984) accurately identifies PTSD in the range of 90% among groups who are combat veterans (e.g., Lyons & Keane, 1992; Lyons & Wheeler-Cox, 1999) but is mildly less accurate (by several percentage points) the more that assessment clients diverge from the original validation sample of treatment-seeking male combat veterans with a single diagnosis of simple PTSD (e.g., Gaston, Brunet, Koszycki, & Bradwejn, 1996; Munley, Bains, Bloem, & Busby, 1995; Perrin, Van Hasselt, Basilio, & Hersen, 1996; Scotti, Sturges, & Lyons, 1996). Though debate persists in locating a "cutoff" score differentiating PTSD and no PTSD, convention has it that scores higher than raw score 30 will accurately classify most PTSD cases.

The second MMPI–2 PTSD identifier, the Ps scale (Schlenger & Kulka, 1989), was developed among non-treatment-seeking Vietnam veterans. The Ps scale has 60 items, overlapping Pk with 46 items and containing 17 unique items. The Ps "cutoff" scores to classify the presence of PTSD are a raw score of 23 or more for males and 26 or more for females. Ps and Pk correlate highly (e.g., 0.92 in Lyons & Wheeler-Cox, 1999). Both may well be calculated with an understanding that Ps may be more accurate when assessing PTSD in non-treatment-seeking or civilian clients (e.g., Kirz, Drescher, Klein, Gusman, & Schwartz, 2001).

Note that just as we have not believed that there is an "addictive personality" (Penk, 1981), we also do not believe that there is one "traumatized personality" or one "MMPI trauma profile," despite efforts to identify an "MMPI trauma profile." Some clinicians and researchers are suggesting that MMPI–2 profile configurations with elevations on scales *F*, 8, and 2 indicate the presence of PTSD (e.g., Wilson & Walker, 1990). Surveys completed to date provide, at best, mild to modest support that one kind of MMPI–2 profile is characteristic of persons who have been traumatized (e.g., Wise, 1996). Whereas the high-point *F*–2–8 configuration is frequently found among samples of Vietnam combat veterans (e.g., Elhai, Forbes, Craemer, McHugh, & Frueh, 2003; Munley et al., 1995; Schlenger & Kulka, 1989; Vanderploeg, Sison, & Hickling, 1987), as well as for survivors of civilian trauma (Gaston et al., 1996), sexual assaults (Kirz et al., 2001), and childhood abuse (Goldwater & Duffy, 1990), a somewhat different group MMPI–2 profile is found among traumatized patients in pain treatment clinics (e.g., Beckham et al., 1997), among survivors of domestic violence (Morrell & Rubin, 2001), and among personal injury plaintiffs (Lees-Haley, 1997). Several MMPI profile types emerge from cluster analyses, and these are not always the *F*–2–8 code type (e.g., Sutker, Allain, &

Motsinger, 1988, among World War II POWs tested later in life; Follette, Naugle, & Follette, 1997, in a study of adult females with child sexual abuse histories).

Finally, code types are seen to vary dramatically when samples are first coded on highest elevated scales on a case-by-case basis (rather than computing a group mean for the sample), and this may be all the more true when comorbidity is considered. From our work in progress, we analyzed frequencies of two-point MMPI–2 codes for 115 patients with two comorbid diagnoses, one of which was current PTSD. We found 23 different two-point code types represented, with only 15 of 115 cases showing the 2–8/8–2 MMPI–2 profile thought to be most prevalent among patients with PTSD. The 6–8/8–6 profile was more frequently found in our sample (26 of 115 cases) than the 2–8/8–2. At the same time, 2% of a comparison sample of comorbid patients without PTSD obtained the 2–8/8–2 profile and 16% obtained the 6–8/8–6 profile.

A variety of MMPI profiles, then, can be found among people with MMPI–2 Pk scores above the cutoff, suggesting that PTSD can occur among different personality types, that people with PTSD vary in their styles of coping—some overcompensating for their symptoms, others undercompensating—and that treatment interventions should be tailored to each individual's unique MMPI–2 profile (e.g., Butcher, 2000a).

That is, once it has been established that a client meets criteria on an MMPI–2 PTSD scale (e.g., obtains a raw score of 30 on Pk), it is recommended that the client meet criteria for diagnosis on at least one of two other reliable and valid instruments that are administered. For the CAPS, this means evidence that the client persistently reexperiences one of the five types of intrusive memories, at least three of seven forms of avoidance, and at least two kinds of increased arousal associated with the trauma. For the Mississippi, this means the client receives a raw score of 130 or higher on the ratings of 17 *DSM–IV* (APA, 1994) symptoms.

Given a putative classification of PTSD on the basis of the MMPI–2 and at least one other instrument, trauma exposure needs to be independently corroborated. If trauma exposure is early, extreme, or prolonged, the presence of complex PTSD needs to be assessed; and, if MMPI–2 scales are atypically elevated, the presence of comorbid disorders or complex PTSD also needs to be determined. To the extent that comorbidity is *not* present, some degree of resiliency can be assumed. This should be detailed in appropriate testing. At this point, the clinician can proceed to evaluate PTSD using traditional methods of interpretation available elsewhere in this volume or in other guidelines (e.g., Butcher, 2000a, 2000c; Butcher & Williams, 2000; Graham, 1993; Greene, 2000), remembering always the uniqueness, as well as the comparability, of each individual's profile.

CASE STUDY: ASSESSING AND TREATING PTSD GUIDED BY MMPI–2

A recently discharged male combat veteran was referred for sleep disturbances and nightmares about events experienced while fighting in Afghanistan. The referring primary care physician had ruled out medical complications as accounting for symptoms. The veteran agreed to be assessed across four, 1-hour sessions at the rate of two sessions per week. He was wondering whether he should apply for benefits, given his recent combat experiences. He denied threats to others or self and denied alcohol and drug abuse.

Session 1 was spent getting acquainted, completing routine intake forms, and administering the MMPI–2. In Session 2, the CAPS, the LEC, the Mississippi, and the Post-Traumatic Growth Inventory were given. This testing was guided in part by the veteran's willingness to bring photos of himself while on duty in Afghanistan to help the examiner get a better understanding of where he served his military experiences. Exposure to trauma was confirmed by information available in Veterans' Administration (VA) files. Session 3 consisted of interviewing with the SCID including the PTSD module, and Session 4 involved developing—interactively—a treatment plan.

MMPI–2 findings (from Session 1) were examined after the structured interviews were completed (Session 3). MMPI–2 T score findings were as follows: MMPI–2 validity scale T scores: Lie (*L*), 48; Infrequency (*F*), 84; Correction (*K*), 48. MMPI–2 Clinical scale T scores: Hypochondriasis (*Hs*, 1), 73; Depression (*D*, 2), 80; Hysteria (*Hy*, 3), 70; Psychopathic Deviate (Pd, 4), 75; Masculinity–Femininity (Mf, 5), 53; Paranoia, (*Pa*, 6), 79; Psychasthenia (*Pt*, 7), 83; Schizophrenia (*Sc*, 8), 81; Mania (*Ma*, 9), 58; Social Introversion (Si, 0), 71. MMPI–2 Content scale T scores were: Health Concerns, 75; Depression, 80; Family Problems, 67; Antisocial Practices, 61; Anger, 80; Cynicism, 75; Anxiety, 77; Obsessiveness, 68; Fears, 70; Bizarre Mentation, 64; Low Self-Esteem, 71; Type A Personality, 62; Social Discomfort, 74; Work Interference, 76; Negative Treatment Indicators, 75.

The Pk score was 34, meeting criteria for PTSD in the context of documented trauma. LEC results indicated moderate exposure to combat over an 8-month period. Responses to the CAPS and the Mississippi (score of 145 is above the suggested cutoff of 130) confirmed that the veteran met criteria for PTSD on three of three instruments. He met *DSM* criteria by reporting at least one Criterion B intrusion symptom (i.e., recurrent, distressing memories and dreams of actual events); more than three Criterion C avoidance symptoms (i.e., not watching films on violence, avoiding situations that might arouse his anger, avoiding people with whom he thought he might get into an argument, doing less and less as a way of controlling feelings and hoping not to feel his emotions); and at least two Criterion D hyperarousal symptoms (i.e., difficulty staying asleep, irritability and outbursts of anger, and uncontrollable startle responses—especially while driving in traffic).

CAPS responses linked PTSD symptoms to actual combat events in Afghanistan. The most life-threatening event that he reported was witnessing a military vehicle hit a mine and explode, killing a friend, hurting others, and injuring himself by shrapnel and fire. He rated these events as horrifying him, shattering his sense of everyday safety, and leaving him for the next several months with an unrelenting fear that he might be killed at any moment no matter how apparently secure the areas were in which he was assigned, no matter how much combat gear he had, and no matter how many fellow soldiers he was with. He constantly struggled with feelings that he no longer had control over circumstances by which he could save himself from death.

His nightmares contained fragments of feeling that he was reliving actual life-threatening events he had encountered in combat. Content, in part, was about his helplessness in not being able to save his friend or to help those who were injured, as well as not being able to protect himself. He reported that sometimes during the day, when awake, he was bothered by thoughts that he could not put out of his mind, thoughts about actual experiences when he was frightened. He noticed that such thoughts intensified while driving in heavy traffic. Such thoughts, though at times vague, were accompanied by difficulties breathing, sweating, fearing that he was trapped, and increasing anger and dread that something terrible was going to happen. He also acknowledged at times being short-tempered with his children and needing to get out of the house for fear that he would lose control.

During the interviews, he described his marriage as happy and satisfying and said it was good to be back with his wife and his three young children after a year away. His only major disappointment was that his employer did not take him back into his original job, offering only a position at the same pay but with less responsibility and less status. He expressed considerable anger over the job change, blaming the federal government for not protecting his job while his National Guard unit was called up and he was sent away in the service of his country.

Although he was quite angry and still grieving, he did nevertheless make some positive responses to the Post-Traumatic Growth Inventory; that is, he wanted to improve his social relationships and not avoid people. He felt his war experiences had taught him to rely more on himself, and he felt confident that he could do a job with more responsibility and, therefore, better pay. He also thought his combat experience deepened his love and respect for his wife and children, although he still found himself holding his feelings in check on many occasions, especially when, suddenly, he felt a surge of anger. He said he had started back to attending church with his family. He concluded that, after being away from his work, it was perhaps time to see if he could learn new work skills so that he could get a better job. He had learned that he could not remain passive about his career and that he needed more schooling to get ahead. He was unhappy about the bleak job market, again expressing anger toward the government for high unemployment and underemployment.

The veteran was struggling with one unexpected feeling, and he had not as yet decided how he could deal with it; that is, despite the dangers of having dealt daily with death and dying, he felt that he had helped to do something very important in Afghanistan. He felt very proud of what he had done. Now that he was back, he missed his deep feelings of having a sense of mission and his sense of pride. His current work simply no longer seemed all that important in contrast to what he had done in Afghanistan. (He was now working for an accounting firm at a low level at modest pay, expecting to be replaced by new computer software.)

His MMPI–2 profile registered well many of the areas of his difficulties in making the transition from his role in combat to his role as a civilian; it was an MMPI–2 profile within the standards of validity for proceeding with an interpretation regarding psychopathology and treatment recommendations. Some of his unusual thinking came through in the elevated *F* score (84T); but, considering only moderately elevated scores on Clinical Scale 8, Schizophrenia (81T), along with a lower Bizarre Mentation score (64T), his "atypicality" was more likely to be situational, more a result of his recent return from a combat zone than of any persisting cognitive disorganization and decompensation. Such a conclusion is further buttressed by his not meeting either lifetime nor current schizophrenia criteria on the SCID. Scores on the Clinical Scale 2, Depression (80T), and the Content scale, Depression (80T), highlighted his difficulty in taking action to complete processing his grief over his losses, underscored further by low energy as registered by Scale 9, Mania (56T). Anxiety was well entrenched, with Scale 7, Psychasthenia (83T), with meeting PTSD criteria on the Pk scale, as well as by a score of 70T on the Content scale, Fears. His Anger (80T) and Cynicism (75T) were well above normal, and coupled with Paranoia (75T), argued against a recommendation for insight-oriented treatment. The conclusion—buttressed by elevated scores on Negative Treatment Indicators (75T) and Work Interference (74T)—was that he was not ready to establish a working alliance with a therapist.

In Session 4, the veteran was told that his pattern of test and interview responses were in keeping with those who, exposed to trauma, were at risk for PTSD and perhaps other disorders. His life was complicated by his continuing to keenly feel his losses of friends and his loss of a sense of mission in his work. He was directed—and he agreed—to continue meeting with his physicians about his health concerns (see Clinical scale of 1, Hypochondriasis, at 73T and Hysteria at 70T); and he was presented a "menu" of treatments and treatment providers to whom he could be referred in a large metropolitan area with considerable resources for veterans—cognitive–behavioral therapies, pharmacotherapy, eye movement desensitization, reprocessing, group therapy, and vocational rehabilitation.

In keeping with MMPI–2 results about treatment readiness, he rejected referrals to all of these treatment resources except that related to work; he agreed to meet with the medical center's vocational rehabilitation staff for career development and career counseling and for linking with the regional benefits officer to explore federal and state educational benefits. Simultaneously, and in keeping with his sense of personal competence and unwillingness to trust others, he was asked to embark on a self-help course—learning more about his PTSD symptoms by reading Raymond B. Flannery's (1992) *Post-Traumatic Stress Disorder: A Victim's Guide to Healing and Recovery*. In this context, he agreed to meet for several more sessions in which we discussed what he had learned from his readings and what health-promoting actions he was taking to change his eating and exercise habits. He agreed—for it made good sense to him as a bookkeeper—to keep a daily diary in which he documented behaviors that he would like to see changed (e.g., sleeplessness, nightmares, shutting down his feelings, being depressed, getting angry and anxious when driving). Together we wrote a plan based on homework assignments in the Flannery book that would help him address his disturbing memories, and we detailed the steps by which he could carry out recommendations of taking accounting and computer courses while he continued his current job.

At present, he continues on target with his educational plan and is connected with the Veterans Administration to support upward mobility in job training. His sleep has improved, nightmares are less frequent, depressing thoughts are fewer, his anger and irritation have started to subside, and he is definitely more optimistic about his ability to change his work conditions once he completes his coursework in accounting. He has also recently spoken with a veteran of the First Gulf War about joining a time-limited, closed group therapy experience led by a clinical psychology intern working under supervision in a VA community-based outpatient clinic. He says that he has some thoughts about his war experiences that he is now beginning to feel that it is safe to talk about, especially with those who may have experienced some of the same kinds of events that he had survived.

TREATMENT IMPLICATIONS FOR PTSD DERIVED FROM THE MMPI–2

The good news about PTSD is that it is a treatable disorder. The bad news is that we do not always know when and how best to treat it. To make matters more complicated, clients with PTSD use avoidance as a salient coping mechanism (Penk, Peck, Robinowitz, Bell, & Little, 1988), that is, they tend to avoid therapies that discuss trauma.

Practice guidelines have been developed through consensus panels and have been recently published (Foa et al., 2000). This compendium presents reviews of the empirically based outcome research and rates effectiveness of PTSD treatments, weighting treatment outcome studies; those based on randomized clinical trials are given higher weights (Level A) than case studies (Level C) and naturalistic outcome studies without controlled comparison groups (Level B). Treatment guidelines are presented for such interventions as: psychological debriefing, cognitive–behavioral therapies, pharmacotherapy, eye movement desensitization and reprocessing, group therapy, psychodynamic therapy, inpatient treatment, psychosocial rehabilitation techniques, hypnosis, marital/family therapy, and creative therapies.

Although the authors of these guidelines recommend when a person should be referred to one or more of these therapies, randomized clinical trials comparing the efficacy of different treatments are scant; and, moreover, there is little empirical basis for recommendations in terms of best client–therapy matches. Progress needs to be made in PTSD treatment, as has been made for treatment of depression, toward relative efficacy of different treatments in general and in interaction with particular sets of client characteristics, with inclusion and exclusion criteria as well as contraindications for type of intervention.

Nonetheless, many clinicians find MMPI–2 results beneficial in treatment planning (see Butcher's [1990b] summary of basic principles for treatment planning). Group therapies probably are suitable when PTSD is found in 4–9 MMPI–2 profiles. Insight therapies and trauma-focused therapies perhaps are not suitable when PTSD is found in 6–8/8–6 profiles or in 8–9/9–8 profiles. Some forms of cognitive–behavioral therapies—cognitive restructuring, coping skills training, and relaxation training—are likely to be appropriate when PTSD is found in MMPI–2 profiles where scales 1, 2, and 3 are elevated and pain is implicated as a major co-occurring component of PTSD symptoms (Otis, Keane, & Kerns, 2003). PTSD in 2–7/7–2 two-point code types seem to benefit from C cognitive–behavioral therapies such as Beck-type approaches (Craighead, Hart, Craighead, & Ilard, 2002).

Pharmacotherapies, particularly the SSRI class of drugs, may possibly be useful in most PTSD cases, independent of MMPI–2 code type. When schizophrenia or bipolar disorder is comorbid with PTSD, pharmacotherapy may be a treatment of choice before treatment for PTSD can effectively proceed.

Currently, psychological debriefing is coming under critical review (McNally, Bryant, & Ehlers, 2003). Litz (2004) and colleagues have completed a landmark review on early interventions, summarizing specific

EXHIBIT 6.1
Highlight: Use of the MMPI–2 in the Assessment of PTSD

- A key recommendation is to use a multimethod approach to assessment, administering several different reliable and valid instruments in a battery.
- The MMPI–2 is well suited to be a significant part of the overall strategy and tactics that clinicians can use in assessing PTSD.
- It is important to integrate MMPI–2 findings with results from other tests.
- Preparatory to MMPI–2 interpretation, it is important to understand how PTSD is expressed within each MMPI–2 clinical profile on a case-by-case basis.
- The MMPI–2, then, contains many scales for classifying PTSD and many other disorders, such as substance abuse, without ever identifying to the test taker the symptoms of such disorders.
- Research has shown that the MMPI–2 is clinically accurate in correctly identifying PTSD not just for combat veterans but for civilians as well, and not just for PTSD alone but also when PTSD occurs along with other disorders.
- Some clients will exaggerate their symptoms for a variety of reasons. Clinicians must verify their classification of PTSD by standardized and objective methods, including use of the validity scales of the MMPI–2.
- Perhaps the most important advantage of using the MMPI–2 in a battery of assessment procedures rests in its so-called "validity" scales.
- In addition to traditional MMPI–2 clinical scales and content scales, there have been two PTSD scales that have been empirically derived by statistically discriminating patients who were experiencing PTSD from other patients (the Pk scale and the Ps scale).
- Other scales, such as the substance abuse scales, can be helpful in examining the problems of individuals with PTSD.
- Among the disadvantages in using the MMPI–2 in assessment of PTSD is the fact that the test does not yield data about exposure to and experience of trauma—Criterion A for diagnosis of PTSD.
- Another disadvantage is that the MMPI–2 does not as yet contain scales for determining the presence of any of the other specific symptom classes that are required for a diagnosis of PTSD.

treatments proven effective in a wide array of traumas—from the professional response to the terrorist attacks of 9/11 to emergency interventions for relief workers, survivors of automobile accidents, and military personnel returning from peacekeeping duties and war zones (see Exhibit 6.1).

NEW DIRECTIONS FOR MMPI–2 PTSD RESEARCH

As the long list of references from peer-reviewed journals shows, a considerable amount of PTSD research has already been done with the MMPI–2. More needs to be done, however, with future research more likely to emerge from scale development (e.g., Butcher, 2000a) than from studies of existing scales, although studies of the latter sort—documenting differences in MMPI–2 scores depending on whether PTSD occurs singly or comorbidly with a variety of disparate disorders and discovering MMPI differences between people with simple versus complex PTSD—may need to be undertaken to provide the empirical rationale for further scale development.

Using the criterion-group-distinction method, MMPI–2 scales need to be empirically derived for (a) PTSD criteria B, C, and D; (b) complex PTSD as distinguished from simple PTSD; (c) prediction of resiliency and recovery; (d) detection of malingerers and reports of "false memories"; (e) distinguishing acute stress disorder (ASD) from PTSD; (f) differentiating lifetime from current PTSD; (g) predicting treatment effectiveness and client–therapy "Match"; and (h) predicting who among traumatized individuals will or will not develop PTSD or other disorders.

Even though MMPI–2 items were not written to detect PTSD, this deficiency has now proven to be an advantage. The MMPI–2 is as accurate in identifying PTSD as are other tests made up of face-valid items, and the MMPI is less subject to impression management by clients than are other interviews, checklists, and inventories.

Having contributed much already to empirically validating PTSD as a disorder, the MMPI–2 can do even more. What is needed now is not to keep testing the same scales from 65 years of MMPI and MMPI–2 research but to develop new scales using the criterion-group-distinction method for improving classification, treatment, and rehabilitation of PTSD. With the rise of violence in the workplace, terrorists bringing violence to civilians, combat veterans returning home from war zones in Afghanistan and Iraq, hundreds of thousands surviving natural disasters such as the tsunami of 2004 in the Indian Ocean—all these events create the need for building a stronger MMPI–2 with each passing day (Penk, Drebing, & Schutt, 2002).

7

TREATMENT PLANNING WITH THE MMPI–2

JULIA N. PERRY, KATHRYN B. MILLER, AND KELLY KLUMP

Psychological treatment planning is a concept that has gained considerable momentum in recent years. It encompasses both general and specific efforts to structure the intervention process and thereby make it more conducive to achieving desired treatment outcomes. In this chapter, we discuss using the MMPI–2 in creating and implementing treatment plans. We present both theoretical and practical information regarding interpretive strategies. We also discuss how some of the new directions being pursued in MMPI–2 research may relate to the treatment planning process.

TREATMENT PLANNING METHODS

Treatment planning is a concept that has been characterized in a number of different ways. Makover's (1992) definition is particularly useful. He has described the construct as "an organized conceptual effort to design a program *outlining in advance* the specific steps by which the therapist will help the patient recover from his or her presenting dysfunctional state" (p. 338). This definition highlights the critical step of strategizing the treatment steps prior to initiating any action with the patient. Makover further has noted that "effective and appropriate treatment planning is a central and persistent challenge for practitioners of psychotherapy" (p. 337).

A range of avenues can be pursued in planning psychological interventions. Numerous theoretical schemes have been proposed for coordinating how such strategies might unfold, including multimodal therapy (Lazarus, 1981, 1989), systematic treatment planning (Beutler & Harwood, 1995), and hierarchical treatment planning (Makover, 1992). These models all involve having the patient and therapist agree, in advance, on what generally will occur during treatment and what the goals of the course of treatment will be. They also all stress the importance of undertaking a high-quality assessment prior to initiating treatment.

Another broad approach to treatment planning involves using objective assessment as the foundation for subsequent efforts. Beutler, Goodrich, Fisher, and Williams (1999) are among the theorists who have highlighted the usefulness of empirically based assessment procedures for strategizing psychological interventions. As Beutler and his colleagues note, objective assessment procedures can help clinicians by providing valuable information regarding patients' functional impairment, subjective distress, readiness for change, problem complexity, resistance tendencies, social support, and coping styles.

Historically, some treatment planning instruments have been specific to certain diagnostic categories or groups of problems, such as the Recovery Attitude and Treatment Evaluator—Questionnaire I (Smith, Hoffman, & Nederhoed, 1995), which is intended for use among patients with substance use problems. Other instruments, such as the Butcher Treatment Planning Inventory (BTPI; Butcher, 1998b), have been created for the purposes of engaging in treatment planning with individuals who possess a range of mental health concerns. Both of these instruments were created with treatment planning in mind. However, this is not always the case. The MMPI–2 was not created expressly for treatment planning, but it has been demonstrated to be a valuable resource for this purpose. Research (e.g., Butcher, Rouse, & Perry, 2000) has supported the appropriateness of deriving clinical hypotheses to be tested throughout a subsequent course of treatment on the basis of MMPI–2 findings.

It is not possible to understand fully the usefulness of objective assessment for treatment planning efforts without paying attention to treatment outcomes. Lambert and Lambert (1999) have highlighted a number of issues relevant to this topic, including the clinical versus statistical significance of treatment gains and the importance of understanding the cost-effectiveness of care. Newman, Ciarlo, and Carpenter (1999) have recommended a set of guidelines for developing, selecting, and using measures of treatment progress and outcome. Chief among these are the instrument's relevance to the target population, its psychometric strength, and its overall usefulness in clinical service.

Different approaches to outcome assessment can be adopted. Clinicians might employ a strategy that examines data collectively, such as through combining MMPI–2 profile data for a group of patients in order to look for trends. This approach enables clinicians to examine whether any change has occurred, how much change has occurred, for what particular subset of patients change has occurred, and whether the change was sustained (Newman & Tejeda, 1999).

Clinicians may also choose to examine patients on an individual basis, using as their data clinical case notes, a tally of observable behaviors, or scores from standardized instruments measured against norms (Newman & Dakof, 1999). In this case, treatment planning efforts can truly be tailored to the individual. Clinicians who continually gather data on their patients would be able to monitor changes (or a lack thereof) in the individual patients' mental health status. This step would allow clinicians to design and select treatment strategies at the outset of treatment and to determine whether and how they might need to adjust their approaches during treatment to best suit the circumstances at hand. It is noteworthy that, when it comes to determining the clinical relevance of observed changes, Newman and Dakof (1999) report that the difference between a clinically significant outcome and a nonsignificant one is best delineated by empirical norms, such as would be available through examining MMPI–2 data both before and after treatment.

MMPI–2 AND TREATMENT PLANNING

The history and characteristics of the MMPI–2 make it an appealing personality measure to use in treatment planning. It is commonly accepted that the MMPI–2 is the most frequently administered objective personality measure; therefore, there are a multitude of research studies and clinical data on its efficacy. The MMPI–2 is composed of 567 true-or-false items that assess a variety of areas, including mental health status, personality related variables, and interpersonal functioning. It can be administered to individuals representing a wide variety of educational and professional backgrounds. It can also be administered to a broad range of mental health patients, including those who are culturally diverse and those who are actively psychotic. These characteristics highlight why the MMPI–2 is used in such a wide variety of settings, from inpatient psychiatric units to outpatient mental health clinics to industrial and organizational settings.

The MMPI–2 scales provide a wide range of information that is useful in treatment planning. Methods of interpreting the validity, clinical, content, and supplementary scales for that purpose are outlined in the following sections.

The Validity Scales

The MMPI–2 validity scales give the test interpreter information regarding patients' present clinical situation, how well they have cooperated with the assessment process, and how amenable they may be to treatment. In interpreting scores on these scales, the clinician must consider both the individual scale scores and the configuration of scores. We first review information regarding the individual scales.

Cannot Say (?)

The Cannot Say score is a useful indicator of the patient's cooperativeness with the psychological evaluation. Patients presenting voluntarily for treatment would be expected to approach the test in an open and honest manner and therefore not omit many items. Butcher (1990b) cautions that patients who omit 8 to 10 responses within the first 370 questions (from which the clinical scales and validity indicators are scored) are being more evasive than would be expected. Patients with 11 to 19 omissions likely have considerable difficulty in discussing personal problems, and patients with 20 or more omissions are likely to be resistant early in therapy (Butcher, 1990b). Graham (2000) recommends interpreting with caution protocols with more than 10 omitted items and further advises paying attention to the scales on which the omitted items occur. From a treatment planning perspective, that information could provide the clinician with an indication of the specific areas in which the patient might demonstrate resistance to psychological interventions.

Lie (L) *Scale*

Individuals with elevated *L* scale scores are presenting as being overly virtuous. Therapeutic concerns related to this presentation include premature treatment termination, denial of a need to change behavior, rigidity, and problems with honest and direct communication. Individuals with elevated *L* scores often do not see a need to discuss their problems or difficulties with anyone (Butcher, 1990b; Graham, 2000).

Infrequency Scales: F, F(B), *and* Fp

The *F* (Infrequency) scale is used in psychological treatment planning to assess the level of psychological distress that the patient is experiencing. *F* scale elevations between 60 and 79 are typical for individuals seeking psychological treatment. *F* scale scores between 80 and 90 suggest that the person is very distressed, is confused, and may be experiencing multiple psychological symptoms; and immediate intervention may be indicated. *F* elevations above 91 in an outpatient assessment are considered to indicate an invalid and uninterpretable profile (Butcher, 1990b; Graham, 2000).

The *F(B)* (Back Infrequency) scale performs the same function as the *F* scale in measuring the endorsement of aberrant items, but it does so for the latter portion of the MMPI–2. The *Fp* (Infrequency–Psychopathology) scale measures the endorsement of problems that are uncommon even among psychiatric inpatients. Both of these are relatively new scales, and limited research data are available regarding their usefulness specifically for treatment planning purposes.

Correction (K) *Scale*

The *K* scale can be used as an indicator of treatment readiness, because it assesses an individual's willingness to disclose personal information. When the *K* score is in the lower ranges (i.e., below 40–45), an openness to emotional expression is indicated. In its upper ranges (i.e., above T = 70), the *K* score suggests a reluctance to identify and discuss emotional issues. Interpretations of the *K* scale should be considered in conjunction with information about socioeconomic status and education level, because individuals from higher socioeconomic classes generally score higher than those from lower socioeconomic brackets on the *K* scale (Butcher, 1990b; Graham, 2000).

Other Validity Indicators

The MMPI–2's other validity indicators include two response inconsistency scales: variable response inconsistency (VRIN) and true response inconsistency (TRIN). Both of these scales provide further assistance to clinicians in understanding how patients report their level of functioning. As such, they have the potential to inform treatment planning, though specific research-based guidelines and recommendations regarding doing so have yet to be established. More generally, these validity indicators' ability to identify individuals who report their symptoms inaccurately can make them useful for identifying people who may not be engaged in the assessment process and therefore may not become engaged in the treatment process (Greene & Clopton, 1999).

Validity Scales Score Configuration

The configuration of the validity scales scores frequently provides more information about treatment readiness than the individual scales. A few prominent configurations are reviewed in the following paragraphs.

The Reluctant or Defensive Patient

This validity pattern of "naïve" defensiveness is characterized by relatively high elevations on *L* or *K* (i.e., scores above 60) and low or no elevation on *F* (i.e., a score below 60). If both *L* and *K* are over 60 and *L* is higher than *K*, the person is considered to be presenting as being overly virtuous and moralistic. Such individuals frequently report that they are psychologically well adjusted, and they deny the need to discuss problems. Thus, individuals with this validity pattern tend to be difficult to engage in the therapeutic process. Profiles with a low *F* score and an elevated *K* score that is higher than the score on *L* suggest individuals who are less moralistic and virtuous than those already described but who are also quite difficult to engage in therapy. Individuals with this configuration often view themselves favorably and are hesitant to reveal their weaknesses (Butcher, 1990b).

The Exaggerating Patient

High elevations on the *F* scale and lower-level elevations on *L* and *K* have been referred to as indicating a "plea for help" pattern. Within the context of this configuration, the problems being presented on the MMPI–2 tend to be nonspecific and to involve several life areas. Consequently, patients with this validity score pattern may have difficulty in focusing on specific problem areas during their treatment sessions (Butcher, 1990b).

The Open and Direct Patient

A problem-oriented approach is reflected in an MMPI–2 profile with a moderate elevation on the *F* scale in conjunction with lower *L* and *K* scores. Patients producing this configuration are relatively easy to engage in psychological treatment and are inclined to discuss their problems with others (Butcher, 1990b).

Underreporting Symptoms (Faking-Good)

A challenge of assessment is to determine how accurately individuals are presenting themselves. Treatment-seeking individuals would not necessarily be expected to minimize their symptoms, yet the desire for impression management could be so strong for some people that they distort or minimize their problems in responding to the inventory items. Several scales on the MMPI–2 are designed to detect deliberate attempts to present oneself in an unrealistically positive manner. As already noted, the *L* and *K* scales have historically been the most valuable in assessing the tendency to underreport symptoms. However, recent research has pointed to two supplementary scales, the Superlative Self-Presentation (*S*) scale and the Wiggins Social Desirability (Wsd) scale, that appear to improve the detection of underreporting (Butcher & Han, 2000). *S* scale scores equal to or greater than 65 reflect individuals who are representing themselves as being better adjusted and as having fewer psychological problems and moral flaws than the average person. The higher the *S* scale score, the greater the person's tendency to minimize problems. These two supplemental scales augment the usefulness of the validity scales regarding an individual's approach to the test and his or her comfort in revealing problems, which are likely to be valuable considerations in treatment planning.

Overreporting Symptoms (Faking-Bad)

Treatment-seeking individuals could be motivated to overreport their symptoms or problems rather than underreport them. The MMPI–2 is also designed to detect exaggeration or attempts at faking-bad. The *F* scale was developed to measure the frequency and severity of the individual's psychological problems. However, it can be difficult to discriminate between those outpatients who are accurately reporting extensive psychopathology and those who are exaggerating their symptoms, supporting the usefulness of *Fp*. The scale was developed on inpatient hospital samples for the purposes of making the distinction between a genuinely high level of reported problems and an exaggeration presentation. There is no set cutoff for *Fp* scores, but the higher they are, the more likely it is that the individual is faking-bad or exaggerating his or her illness (Arbisi & Ben-Porath, 2000).

Openness to Treatment and the MMPI–2 Clinical Scales

The MMPI–2 clinical scales can also provide valuable information regarding treatment openness and readiness, particularly when they are interpreted in conjunction with the validity scales already described.

Scale 1: Hypochondriasis (Hs)

Individuals whose highest scale elevation is on *Hs* typically do not view their problems as psychological in origin; they report numerous somatic complaints and ascribe physical explanations to their symptoms. They typically have low motivation for behavioral change. Noncompliance with treatment and early treatment termination are potential problems among patients with elevations on this scale (Butcher, 1990b; Graham, 2000).

Scale 2: Depression (D)

Individuals with their peak score on the *D* scale are typically experiencing a great deal of psychological distress and therefore are usually motivated for change. A positive response to therapy and a favorable treatment outcome are expected. Several studies support the finding that elevations on the *D* scale are associated with greater length of time in therapy (e.g., Chisholm, Crowther, & Ben-Porath, 2000).

Scale 3: Hysteria (Hy)

Individuals with high *Hy* scores usually do not seek psychological help for their problems. These individuals typically possess therapy-interfering characteristics such as defensiveness, naïveté, and low psychological mindedness. They tend to minimize their personal weaknesses, and they are often unmotivated for change (Butcher, 1990b; Graham, 2000).

Scale 4: Psychopathic Deviate (Pd)

Individuals with elevations on Pd rarely initiate treatment themselves; it is more typical that a spouse, another family member, or the court insists that they seek treatment. People with Pd elevations typically externalize their problems and fail to see a need to change their own behavior. Interpersonally, they are challenging in therapy because they tend to be manipulative, disrespectful, deceptive, and exploitive. Those who exhibit many antisocial behaviors tend to terminate treatment earlier than those who do not engage in such practices (Chisholm et al., 2000).

Scale 5: Masculinity–Femininity (Mf)

The Mf scale can be useful in treatment planning because it is indicative of a person's progressiveness and openness toward different perspectives. Interpretations of this scale should be based on the gender of the individual and the degree of scale elevation (Butcher, 1990b).

Among men:

- $T \leq 45$: Probably poor therapy candidates. Such individuals typically lack psychological insight and are uninterested in treatment or in discussing their problems.
- $T = 65–70$: These individuals possess characteristics, such as sensitivity and insightfulness, that are likely to be beneficial to the therapeutic process.
- $T \geq 75$: Likely to be very passive in relationships. Difficulties with expressing anger and narcissism may interfere with the therapeutic relationship.

Among women:

- $T \leq 40$: Extremely passive, which may be problematic for therapy. These individuals may have long-standing patterns of self-defeating behavior that are resistant to change.

- T ≥ 70: Tend to be aggressive, dominant, rebellious, and cynical in their interactions with others. Difficulties with expressing emotions and a lack of insight are expected. Pure "talk therapy" may not be appropriate.

Scale 6: Paranoia (Pa)

Patients with high *Pa* scores are not viewed as good candidates for psychological treatment because of their tendency to blame others for their problems and because of their lack of trust in relationships. They tend to be argumentative, resentful, and cynical. Early termination is common; in fact, patients with elevations on *Pa* may not return after their first therapy visit (Butcher, 1990b).

Scale 7: Psychasthenia (Pt)

Patients with high *Pt* scores are typically motivated for therapy because of their high level of distress. They are also more likely to remain in therapy, making slow but steady progress. Patients with extremely high elevations on this scale (i.e., T > 90) struggle with obsessiveness and rigidity that may interfere with implementing behavioral change (Butcher, 1990b).

Scale 8: Schizophrenia (Sc)

The degree of elevation on the *Sc* scale is indicative of the severity and chronicity of the individual's problems. Extreme elevations suggest the presence of thought problems and unconventional behavior (Butcher, 1990b).

- T = 65–75: Suggestive of a problematic, chaotic lifestyle. Interpersonal difficulties and distrust may interfere with the establishment of rapport. Psychological treatment may be compromised by odd beliefs, such as a preoccupation with the occult or superstitious beliefs. Lengthy therapy is usually indicated, but prognosis for therapy is poor.
- T ≥ 76: Suggestive of the presence of severe confusion and disorganization. Hospitalization and medication may be required, and purely verbal psychotherapy may not be appropriate until bizarre thought processes are stabilized.

Scale 9: Mania (Ma)

Both individuals with high scores on *Ma* and those with low scores on *Ma* can experience problems in therapy (Butcher, 1990b).

- T < 45: Patients with low scores are expected to struggle in therapy because they are overwhelmed by feelings of depression, hopelessness, and worthlessness.

- T = 46–69: Individuals with scores in this range typically do not seek psychological treatment. They report feeling self-assured and having minimal problems.
- T ≥ 70: Patients scoring in this range tend to be challenging because they are very distractible and uncooperative. They typically do not consider therapy necessary and are therefore likely to miss sessions and to terminate therapy prematurely.

Scale 0: Social Introversion–Extroversion (Si)

The Si scale is very useful because it assesses the individual's level of interpersonal functioning. The score indicates the individual's ease in forming social relationships, which is likely to predict how the therapeutic relationship is approached (Butcher, 1990b; Graham, 2000).

- T < 45: Individuals whose scores fall in this range are extroverted and comfortable in establishing relationships. They may be poor therapy candidates, however, because they are not distressed or motivated to change.
- T = 60–69: These scores reflect difficulty in forming relationships. Patients who score in this range report being shy and having difficulty expressing their feelings. If they are willing to engage in it, group therapy is likely to be helpful in promoting improved interpersonal functioning.
- T ≥ 70: These scores suggest extreme discomfort and inhibition in relationships. Patients' cautious, distrustful approach to relationships is likely to be long-standing and may not be amenable to change in therapy.

MMPI–2 Content Scales

The MMPI–2 content scales are designed to identify specific problems that the individual is experiencing. The Negative Treatment Indicators scale and the Negative Work Attitudes scale are often regarded as helpful scales to consider relative to treatment planning.

Negative Treatment Indicators (TRT)

The TRT scale was designed to assess a patient's cooperativeness toward treatment and belief that he or she can change (Graham, 2000), which is likely to be prognostic. For instance, Clark (2000) found that pretreatment elevations on TRT predicted greater posttreatment dysfunction in men with chronic pain. Greene and Clopton (1999) have provided some general guidelines regarding treatment planning issues for TRT scores in excess of 64. They advise considering elevated TRT scores as suggestive of such issues as lack of motivation, feeling unable to help oneself, disliking going to the doctor and talking about personal problems with others, and preferring drugs or medicine over psychotherapy. However, it should be noted that the data are limited with regard to TRT's ability to predict therapy outcome. For example, a study by Butcher, Rouse, and Perry (2000) did not find a significant correlation between scores on TRT (or on any other clinical or content scale) and therapist-generated descriptors predicting poor therapy prognosis.

Negative Work Attitudes (WRK)

The WRK scale was developed to assess work attitudes or habits. High scorers indicate that their problems interfere with their ability to be successful at work. They tend to struggle in initiating projects, and they may become easily frustrated or overwhelmed (Graham, 2000). This pattern of behavior is likely to make a negative impact on the therapeutic process as well.

Treatment Resistance

Patients' overall resistance to intervention is a critical consideration with treatment planning. Resistance can affect treatment from the outset of the course of therapy (perhaps even preventing individuals from participating in it at all), and it can also alter the course of therapy that is already under way. In other words, it may influence whether and when treatment will be undertaken as well as how it will proceed. Research has related treatment resistance to a large number of demographic variables and factors, typically with the caveat that it is not the variables, per se, on which clinicians should focus but rather the associated patient expectations regarding how helpful or useful psychological treatment will be (Norcross & Beutler, 1997). It is beneficial to bear in mind that treatment resistance can be statelike or traitlike in nature and that instruments such as the MMPI–2 are thought to be most helpful for evaluating resistance in the latter instance (e.g., Beutler et al., 1991). Many of the MMPI–2 scales provide important information about potential treatment resistance issues, as previously indicated in this chapter (see Perry, 2002, for further discussion of this topic).

Benefits for the Therapist of Using the MMPI–2

The breadth of information that the MMPI–2 assesses is of decided benefit to the therapist in treatment planning. The reality of initial interviews in today's economy is that they are time-constrained, limiting the scope of problems that they can address. The MMPI–2 greatly augments the amount of information that can be made available within a given period of time. The instrument identifies attitudes and personality characteristics that may be clinically significant for therapy but that may not be apparent during initial interactions. It also adds dimension to the presenting problems. For example, if someone presents as depressed during the initial interview, scores on the MMPI–2 clinical and content scales could objectively corroborate that impression. They could also indicate comorbid problems and provide additional evidence regarding specific personality characteristics. An individual with a 2–7 code type on the MMPI–2 may come across in an interview in roughly the same way as someone with a 2–8 code type. However, the two individuals are unlikely to behave similarly during treatment and the problems with which they struggle are likely to be quite different. It is valuable for the treatment provider to have an understanding of such factors from the outset of therapy in order to be more effective in tailoring treatment to the individual and in anticipating potential problems.

The MMPI–2 can also assist the therapist in choosing the best treatment modality for the individual. In particular, the extensive information provided about interpersonal functioning can help guide treatment recommendations. For example, if a person is presenting with chemical dependency problems, the MMPI–2 can be helpful in determining whether individual or group therapy might be preferable. A person who scores high on the MMPI–2 Si and *Pa* scales would probably not be as strong a candidate for group therapy as someone who scores low on those scales. Similarly, a person who presents with high scores on the *K*, *Hy*, *D*, and *Hs* scales would probably not be a strong candidate for insight-oriented therapy; a short-term, cognitive–behavioral intervention for depression would likely be indicated instead. Using the MMPI–2 in conjunction with a clinical interview increases the likelihood that the most appropriate treatment for the individual will be identified and implemented.

In addition, the MMPI–2 is a useful resource for treatment providers to use in communicating with insurance companies about the treatment plan, the treatment course, and discharge-related matters. With the advent of managed health care systems and their emphasis on short-term, empirically validated treatments, the MMPI–2 provides a means by which the treatment provider can operationalize and justify treatment decisions and requests. The severity of the problems suggested by the MMPI–2 profile can provide objective evidence for treatment requests, such as hospitalization or additional therapy sessions. The MMPI–2 can also be used, over the course of therapy and during the discharge process, to measure symptom reduction and improvement in functioning. Repeated administrations of the MMPI–2 allow the treatment provider (and the insurance company) to monitor a patient's progress and continually evaluate the appropriateness of the chosen treatment modality and plan for the patient.

Finn (1996b) emphasizes the importance of giving feedback to the patient about his or her MMPI–2 profile. This process is useful for the therapist because individuals respond differentially to the information, and their responses are informative. Individuals who are receptive to and accepting of MMPI–2 feedback, whether it is regarding qualities that they have already ascribed to themselves or characteristics they had not previously self-identified, are likely to respond to the therapeutic process in the same manner. On the other hand, if the patient is hostile and rejecting of the MMPI–2 interpretation, it might affect the therapist's evaluation of that patient's treatment readiness. An MMPI–2 feedback session provides the therapist with a unique sample of the patient's behavior, which is likely to be relevant for therapy but which would not be available merely from a standard interview or initial assessment.

Using computerized and computer-based assessment reports can be especially advantageous to clinicians who administer the MMPI–2 to their patients as well, particularly because of the time savings associated with them. However, it is typically recommended (e.g., Butcher, 2002b) that such reports not be considered in isolation and that the findings be combined with data from other sources. The same caution applies when computerized report data are employed for the purposes of treatment planning. For example, the hypotheses generated by a Minnesota Report can be used to stimulate discussions regarding treatment orientation, strategies, and foci in a manner akin to what would occur if those hypotheses were generated by a clinician trained in MMPI–2 interpretation. Nevertheless, the amount and accuracy of different test interpretation services can vary (Eyde, Kowal, & Fishburne, 1991), and it is important to be aware of that fact when making treatment decisions on the basis of computer-generated reports. Clinicians especially need to guard against allowing overly nonspecific Barnum-type statements (O'Dell, 1972) to have too much weight when treatment process decisions are being made (Butcher, 2002b; Butcher, Perry, & Atlis, 2000).

Benefits for the Patient of Using the MMPI–2

From the patient's perspective, there are several other ways in which the MMPI–2 can be beneficial to treatment planning, particularly when it comes to providing the patient with feedback about the results. A primary way in which the MMPI–2 interpretation may be helpful is in identifying problem areas that the patient has not directly specified. For patients who are receptive to feedback, the MMPI–2 can facilitate the addition of important problem areas to their treatment plans. For example, a person who presents for treatment with "anxiety" as his or her primary complaint may decide, after hearing the MMPI–2 interpretation, that the coexisting discomfort in interpersonal relationships exacerbates the anxiety and therefore should be included in the treatment plan as well.

A second goal of MMPI–2 feedback is to begin building rapport and solidifying the therapeutic alliance (Finn, 1996b). The MMPI–2 can be a useful tool for therapists to communicate their understanding of patients' problems and the distress that they cause. Patients who perceive their therapists as empathic and understanding are likely to be more motivated to initiate therapy and to have trust in the therapeutic process. Since early termination of treatment is a prominent problem in mental health care settings, any factor that reduces the potential for dropout is beneficial for both patient and therapist.

Finally, MMPI–2 feedback can help to build and solidify the therapeutic relationship through reinforcing the credibility of the therapist. The therapist's ability to accurately describe subtle aspects of the patient's personality is likely to increase the patient's faith in the treatment provider and the treatment process.

Treatment planning is most effective when it is a collaborative process between therapist and patient. In that respect, it is important that both parties have comprehensively reviewed the problems identified by the instrument and have agreed on a course of action. The MMPI–2 allows the patient and therapist to identify all such problem areas, to be collaborative in determining their relative importance, and to start building the therapeutic alliance, which will be the ultimate foundation for change.

Assessment and Treatment Planning With Culturally Diverse Patients

A distinct advantage of the MMPI–2 over other objective personality measures is the availability of translations of the instrument into more than 30 different languages. The MMPI–2 has been administered all over the world, and researchers and clinicians have taken great care to establish accurate translations that have been normed on native populations. Multiple translators independently translate the instrument items, and then the independent translations are compared and synthesized into one translation. The translated version is then translated from the new language back into English. After that, both the original instrument and the translation are administered to bilingual individuals in order to measure test–retest reliability. Finally, the test is administered in the new language and the scores obtained are compared to North American standardized norms. If the cultural norms obtained do not match the North American standardized norms, then new, within-culture norms are developed (Butcher, Derksen, Sloore, & Sirigatti, 2003). This careful translation process ensures that the MMPI–2 is culturally relevant, regardless of the language in which it is being administered.

A therapist should be conservative and culturally sensitive when interpreting the MMPI–2 profile of someone from a different culture. In particular, the cultural context of symptoms needs to be taken into consideration. There are certain syndromes found in other cultures that may present like a "mental illness" on the MMPI–2 but that are considered culturally normative within a given context. For example, patients of Hispanic and American Indian descent may attribute psychological symptoms to evil spirits or evil forces (Paniagua, 1998). Among many European cultures, attributions such as these would likely be considered psychotic because of differing mores and standards. It is important to consult with other individuals within the patient's culture, such as family members, in order to understand how normative or unusual an individual's beliefs are. Culturally relevant information should be obtained and incorporated into an MMPI–2 interpretation before a patient feedback session is conducted or an assessment report is written. When it is difficult to discern exactly what the patient is experiencing, a conservative approach to MMPI–2 interpretation is recommended.

A significant challenge in working with culturally diverse patients is bridging cultural and communication barriers. The patient may approach the treatment situation feeling unsure about whether the treatment provider is able to understand or to help him or her. Administering an MMPI–2 in the patient's native language is likely to increase trust in the treatment providers and in the treatment process. It communicates to the patient that the treatment provider understands that there are cultural factors to be considered and is interested in attempting to bridge the cultural and language differences between the two parties. This step could greatly enhance the likelihood that the patient will initiate and remain in treatment.

CASE STUDY

The following case example illustrates some of the ways in which the MMPI–2 can be useful in treatment planning. It also underscores the importance of considering cultural factors when making diagnoses and devising treatment plans.

Background Information

Ms. X was a 40-year-old, divorced, Latina woman who had been referred for psychotherapy. She had a lengthy documented history of depression-related difficulties and outpatient psychological and psychiatric treatment, including episodic psychotherapy and brief medication trials.

She had previously reported a large number of physical health problems and concerns, such as chronic fatigue, bodily weakness, joint pain, and difficulty in swallowing. Neurological exams and other tests had been performed to rule out various medical problems and diseases, including myasthenia gravis. At the time of the initial psychotherapy evaluation, she carried a diagnosis of somatization. She previously had been prescribed an antidepressant but had quickly discontinued it, stating that it had caused "visions of horrors." She requested psychotherapy for assistance in coping with her depressive symptoms and with life stresses.

Clinical Impressions After the Initial Psychotherapy Session

During the initial psychotherapy evaluation session, Ms. X reported a history of having "visions" of future events (often involving harm to others) and spoke of having special talents. Her affect was sometimes not congruent to topic, such as when she laughed while describing past events that she had identified as upsetting. Her presentation and reported symptoms were odd and unusual, but it was unclear whether she met criteria for a psychotic disorder.

Differential Diagnosis Issues

It was important to be mindful of the potential impact of cultural factors on the patient's presentation and report of symptoms. The presence of one particular culture-specific syndrome, *ataques de nervios*, was considered. It is a syndrome affecting individuals from Latin American countries and can involve bizarre behavior, hallucinatory experiences, and somatic symptoms all occurring within the context of stressful circumstances (Oquendo, Horwath, & Martinez, 1992; Spitzer, Gibbon, Skodol, Williams, & First, 1994). Certain elements of this syndrome overlapped with the symptoms reported by the patient. Nonetheless, the patient's reported difficulties were not sudden, dramatic, or transient, all of which are associated with *ataques de nervios*. This diagnosis therefore could be ruled out on the basis of these clear qualitative differences.

Because of the lingering lack of clarity surrounding her diagnosis, as well as the fact that her difficulties did not lend themselves to any specific psychological treatment modality, she was asked to undergo psychological testing for the purposes of diagnostic clarification and treatment planning. It was recommended that she complete the MMPI–2, in light of its potential to shed light on her diagnosis as well as to provide information pertinent to treatment planning. Because of her fluency in English, she was administered the English-language form of the instrument.

Results From the MMPI–2
Welsh Code: 1*3"86'27–5490 F'–L/K

Ms. X's MMPI–2 profile was valid and evidenced openness on her part to discussing her difficulties via her responses to the inventory items. The profile was strongly suggestive of the presence of physical malfunctioning and somatic complaints, including the experience of pain. Moreover, the profile indicated that Ms. X's physical problems could worsen during times of severe stress and that she might lack insight into the impact of psychological factors on her physical problems. Correlates of her code type included sensitivity and poignancy, such that she might feel things more intensely than others would. The profile was suggestive of odd and unusual thinking and strange sensory experiences. However, it did not reveal the presence of frankly psychotic symptoms. The profile also showed that Ms. X might be prone to mistrust others and to form shallow interpersonal relationships with the people around her.

Clinical Impressions and Treatment Planning

When the results of the MMPI–2 were combined with the other assessment data, including interview information and qualitative data gathered during other psychotherapy sessions, Ms. X's difficulties appeared to match several *DSM–IV* (American Psychiatric Association, 1994) somatoform disorder diagnoses, including undifferentiated somatoform disorder and pain disorder associated with psychological factors. There was evidence of schizotypal and histrionic personality features as well, although she did not meet full criteria for either personality disorder. Her MMPI–2 profile indicated the presence of beliefs that run counter to those associated with positive treatment outcomes, not the least of which being faith that treatment will bring about positive change. Her overall profile also indicated a lack of psychological insight and likely reluctance to accept psychological explanations of her problems and symptoms. These issues would have clear implications for her involvement in psychotherapy.

The evaluation findings were subsequently shared with Ms. X, including the information regarding her personality disorder traits. She was fundamentally accepting of the feedback and agreed that many of the issues highlighted by the MMPI–2 results were problematic for her. However, she interpreted the personality features as not contributing significantly to any of her personal or interpersonal problems.

A number of treatment planning hypotheses were generated and then tested out during the subsequent course of treatment. One of the most significant was the notion that additional effort might be required to engage Ms. X in psychotherapy, both early on and throughout the later stages of treatment. Her MMPI–2 profile indicated that Ms. X might engage slowly and shallowly in interpersonal relationships, including the one with her therapist. Care clearly should be taken in building and maintaining any therapy relationship. However, when therapists have objective evidence that this issue may be of particular concern with certain patients, they can be attuned to early, subtle indications of problems and can thereby intervene quickly and decisively. Moreover, they can address the issue openly with their patients. For example, when the assessment feedback was provided to Ms. X, the topic of relationship formation was broached with her and it led to a discussion about its potential impact on psychotherapy. She and her therapist agreed to provide one another with ongoing feedback regarding how their relationship was unfolding and what each party could do to enhance it.

There was also the idea that Ms. X would likely resist examining the psychological underpinnings of her physical symptoms and problems and that her unusual thinking might further complicate efforts to alter her beliefs about factors affecting her somatic complaints. When providing her with feedback about the MMPI–2 results, this idea was presented to her, and the door was left open for her and her therapist to discuss how their respective interpretations of her somatic complaints might differ throughout the course of treatment. In the early stages of therapy, in the face of Ms. X's "defensiveness" about the nature of her complaints, the therapist placed less emphasis on connections between her stressors and her physical problems, focusing more extensively on Ms. X's subjective experience. However, as treatment progressed and numerous examples were elicited regarding the interplay of Ms. X's physical complaints and increases in her stress level, there was a firmer basis for the patient to connect the two phenomena. The care that was taken in building the therapy relationship and in being planful about when and how to make such interpretations laid the foundation for this shift to occur.

As the MMPI–2 results and other data had suggested, Ms. X's course of psychological treatment did prove challenging. Potential problems in the therapy relationship were manifested in the patient's frequent cancellation of sessions, often because of "illness." Midway through the course of treatment, she also requested to meet less frequently with the therapist. Because these types of potential difficulties had been anticipated, their impact on the therapy could be managed through acknowledging their likelihood and devising in advance strategies to address them. Ms. X ultimately did remain in therapy for long enough to report a more consistently euthymic mood and greater ability to cope with stress. However, she did terminate psychotherapy abruptly and without first discussing with the therapist her desire to do so.

EXHIBIT 7.1
Highlight: Using the MMPI–2 for Treatment Planning

- The individual validity scales provide important information regarding how well patients have cooperated with the assessment process and how amenable they might be to subsequent treatment. For example, elevations on *L* or *K* can indicate problems with direct communication and with disclosing personal information, which could interfere with psychotherapy progress.
- In interpreting scores on the validity scales, it is important to consider not only the individual scale scores but also the configuration of scores. For example, patients may produce score configurations indicating defensiveness and a desire to fake-good (an *L* or *K* score above 60 with an *F* score below 60) on the one hand or an exaggeration of problems and an attempt to fake-bad (elevations on *F* and low scores on *L* and *K*) on the other hand. In the first instance, patients may not recognize their problems and may not be motivated to discuss them in therapy. In the latter instance, patients may have a hard time focusing on specific problem areas during their treatment sessions.
- The clinical scales can also provide important information regarding treatment openness and readiness, particularly when they are interpreted in conjunction with the validity scales. Lack of motivation for behavioral change is associated with elevations on scales *Hs, Hy,* and Pd. Noncompliance and premature treatment termination may occur within the context of elevations on *Hs, Pa,* and *Ma.* Moderate elevations on *D* and *Pt* can be associated with a positive response to therapy and a favorable treatment outcome.
- Elevations on the content scale TRT can reflect a degree of unwillingness or inability to change that is likely to interfere with therapy progress. High scorers on the content scale WRK tend to struggle with initiating projects and to become easily frustrated or overwhelmed; both of those qualities could have a negative impact on patients' therapeutic progress as well.
- The results of the MMPI–2 can assist the therapist in choosing the best treatment modality for the individual. People with high scores on Si and *Pa* may not be good candidates for group therapy and may profit more from individual therapy. Those individuals with high scores on *K, Hs, D,* and *Hy* may not be good candidates for insight-oriented therapy because of a lack of psychological mindedness.
- It can also be helpful to administer the MMPI–2 several times over a course of therapy, in order to measure symptom change and gauge the degree of improvement in functioning. Repeated administrations of the MMPI–2 allow treatment providers to monitor patients' progress objectively and continually reevaluate the appropriateness of treatment plans. Adaptive administration procedures, a current topic of MMPI–2 research, may facilitate this process.

NEW DIRECTIONS

The literature involving the MMPI–2 continues to evolve. New research is continuously being done that could cast light on variables pertinent to the treatment planning process. The two areas of investigation outlined in the following section could be especially consequential with regard to treatment planning issues (see Exhibit 7.1).

Adaptive Testing

When the MMPI–2 is administered to individuals under standard conditions, they are expected to complete all 567 of the instrument's items, regardless of the specific problems or issues being assessed. Under most circumstances, however, a sizable portion of the test items will seem irrelevant to the individual in question. Standard administration procedures therefore could lead to wasted time, as patients are compelled to read and answer items that do not pertain to them.

One solution to this problem is adaptive testing. Adaptive tests are tailored to the individual such that sets of test items are presented differentially to examinees, in accordance with response patterns. The goals of adaptive testing generally include "administering only those items needed to achieve the fastest answer to the assessment question" and "administering no additional items after the assessment question has been answered" (Ben-Porath, Slutske, & Butcher, 1989, p. 18).

Historically, adaptive testing methods have been applied to such areas as ability assessment. However, they have also been researched in the context of the MMPI and the MMPI–2. Butcher, Keller, and Bacon (1985) introduced the "countdown method" as a means of classifying groups in accordance with whether or not they exceed a given cutoff criterion. Using as an example the MMPI–2's Scale 2 (Depression), once it becomes clear that an examinee is not endorsing enough items in the keyed direction to lead to a T score of 65, the computer program ceases to administer the Scale 2 items to that individual. Indeed, once an examinee has actually met the T = 65 threshold, the program also ceases to administer Scale 2 items.

Adaptive administration procedures have been demonstrated to result in reliable and valid personality-related data when compared to their traditional administration counterparts, with the added advantage of considerable savings in terms of both the number of items administered and the amount of time spent on the testing process (e.g., Roper, Ben-Porath, & Butcher, 1995). The reduced administration time associated with adaptive testing methods could facilitate their use for treatment planning endeavors, particularly for an inventory as lengthy as the MMPI–2. Adaptive testing would enable the treating clinician to obtain valuable data regarding patients' progress without burdening patients with completing the full instrument. Patients are more likely to be amenable to repeated administrations of an adaptive format of the MMPI–2 than to repeated administrations of the full instrument, especially over a lengthy course of psychotherapy. Thus, the adaptive test data could be beneficial in strategizing the course of psychotherapy and could make the process of selecting interventions more purposeful and more strongly rooted in objective evidence.

The Restructured Clinical (RC) Scales

Another area of MMPI–2 research pertinent to the treatment planning issue involves the new RC Scales (Tellegen et al., 2003). The RC Scales were created to make the clinical concepts that underlie them more distinct and separate from one another than is true for their standard clinical scale counterparts. This was achieved through a process involving the following steps: (a) extracting an affective dimension (termed Demoralization) underlying all of the traditional clinical scales; (b) statistically determining the distinctive core features of each of the clinical scales, after the Demoralization variance had been removed; (c) assembling a corresponding set of "seed scales"; and (d) correlating each seed scale with each of the 567 MMPI–2 items in order to create eight RC Scales. There is one RC Scale for each of the clinical scales, with the exceptions of Scale 5 (Masculinity–Femininity, which was excluded because it was originally intended to detect homosexuality, which is no longer considered a disorder) and Scale 0 (Social Introversion, which is not an index of basic psychopathology and which also was not developed using the empirical keying methods used with the other clinical scales). The RC Scales consist of RCd (Demoralization); RC1 (Somatic Complaints); RC2 (Low Positive Emotions); RC3 (Cynicism); RC4 (Antisocial Behavior); RC6 (Ideas of Persecution); RC7 (Dysfunctional Negative Emotions); RC8 (Aberrant Experiences); and RC9 (Hypomanic Activation).

Tellegen et al. (2003) provide data indicating that the RC Scales are at least as reliable as their nonrestructured counterparts and that they are (in general) considerably less saturated with the unifying demoralization component. Data also show that the RC Scales are not correlated as strongly with each other as the clinical scales are. Thus, early indications demonstrate promise for the use of the RC Scales in clinical settings, particularly because of their relative ease of interpretation and their apparent ability to "separate the signal from the noise" in complex patient profiles. Because the RC Scales are unidimensional, any patterns observed among them will be separate from the shared and nonspecific variance that plagues the clinical scales. These qualities could significantly enhance the usefulness of MMPI–2 results for treatment planning purposes, as the RC Scales could provide clinicians with more easily interpreted information about the content of their patients' communications via responses to the test items. However, Nichols (in press) has classified the RC Scales as occupying an "intermediate position" between the traditional clinical scales and the MMPI–2 content scales and as being structurally more similar to the latter than to the former. As a result, he contends that their interpretation is actually somewhat less straightforward than may seem to be the case. That issue aside, note that the RC Scales are newly published.

As a result, further study into their application, especially to treatment planning, is clearly indicated.

CONCLUSION

This chapter has outlined some of the important ways in which the MMPI–2 can serve as an asset to psychotherapy practitioners as they plan their courses of treatment. The existing body of literature supports the instrument's utility for aiding with treatment planning decisions. However, there is clearly room for more extensive research to be conducted. Of particular benefit would be large-scale, randomized, controlled studies in which treatment outcomes could be objectively compared for patients whose courses of therapy were guided by MMPI–2 test results and for those whose courses of therapy were not influenced by such test findings. If the MMPI–2 were consistently demonstrated to benefit patients and clinicians in significant and measurable ways with respect to treatment planning, it would open the door for more emphasis to be placed on treatment planning and for further investigation of the means by which to facilitate it. The established usefulness of the MMPI–2 could only be enhanced in the face of empirical studies that expand and extend clinicians' abilities to gauge patients' openness to, readiness for, and likely ability to benefit measurably from psychological intervention.

8

THERAPEUTIC ASSESSMENT WITH THE MMPI–2

STEPHEN E. FINN AND JAN H. KAMPHUIS

Therapeutic Assessment is a paradigm in which psychological testing is used as the centerpiece of a brief psychotherapeutic intervention. We find it helpful to differentiate between Therapeutic Assessment (TA, with capital letters) and therapeutic assessment (with lowercase letters). The former is a semistructured form of collaborative assessment developed by Stephen Finn and his colleagues at the Center for Therapeutic Assessment in Austin, Texas; and the latter is a term now generally used by various authors for humanistically based assessment methods that aim to positively impact clients. Although TA typically relies upon a variety of tests and methods to address clients' problems in living, it has been practiced and studied extensively using just the MMPI–2 as a focus for in-depth exploration. In this chapter, after a general discussion of TA, we focus on TA with the MMPI–2.

For those who are interested, Finn (2000, 2002a) and Finn and Tonsager (2002) provide many details about the development of TA. Basically, while Finn was in graduate training, he was exposed to Butcher's (1990c) and others' guidelines for giving psychological test feedback to clients. Finn began to notice that some clients seemed to markedly improve after receiving detailed information about their test scores (Finn, 2002a), and he began to experiment with ways to strengthen this phenomenon. Heavily influenced by Sullivanian interpersonal principles, Finn first got the idea of having clients pose questions at the beginning of an assessment that he would address later in a test feedback session (Finn, 2000). Then, Finn and his colleagues began to incorporate into TA techniques of *collaborative psychological assessment* developed by Fischer (1994, 2000), Handler (1995), and others. In collaborative psychological assessment, psychologists try to demystify psychological tests for clients and to involve clients in cointerpreting their test results and specifying how they apply to daily life. Collaborative techniques were adopted into TA because they increased the therapeutic efficacy of psychological assessments for clients (Finn & Tonsager, 2002). In recent years, TA has continued to evolve, adopting a more intersubjective, systemic, and phenomenologic perspective (Finn, 1999, 2002b, 2003, 2005).

HOW IS THERAPEUTIC ASSESSMENT DIFFERENT FROM TRADITIONAL ASSESSMENT?

Finn and Tonsager (1997) contrasted TA with traditional, "information-gathering" psychological assessment on a number of variables, while emphasizing that the two models may be practiced simultaneously. Traditionally, the goals of psychological assessment have been accurate classification and description of clients in order to aid in decision making (e.g., educational placement, treatment planning, employee selection). Therapeutic Assessment retains these aims, while also striving for therapeutic change. Hopefully, at the end of a therapeutic assessment, clients have a new, more accurate, and compassionate understanding of themselves and their problems, so that they feel better about themselves and make better life decisions.

The two models differ also in the procedures they employ. In traditional assessment, psychologists work unilaterally or with referring professionals to identify the kinds of information sought through an assessment, determine which tests should be utilized, observe the client during test administration, interpret test scores, and translate the assessment results into concrete recommendations. In TA, clients are viewed as essential collaborators whose input is invited during each step of the assessment process. For example, clients are asked to list personal questions they wish to have addressed by the MMPI–2 and to notice feelings and associations that take place as they respond to the MMPI–2 items. In subsequent meetings, they are shown their MMPI–2 profiles and are asked to comment on the accuracy of typical, nomothetically based interpretive statements. Assessors and clients then collaborate in extrapolating such information into recommendations and "answers" to the clients' initial questions, and clients may even review and comment upon any written report derived from the assessment.

The role of the assessor is seen differently in the two assessment models. Traditionally, assessors have been taught that they should be "objective observers" and have been cautioned against being too warm or familiar with clients and about mixing therapy and assessment. In TA, assessors are seen as participant–observers in the assessment process; as such, their reactions, associations, and hunches about clients are important clues that help make sense of more structured data. Also, assessors are encouraged to be supportive and personable with clients, since it is believed that a good assessor–client relationship is essential if clients are to risk "trying on" new conceptualizations of themselves and their life situations. Finn (2005) has even argued that collaborative psychological assessment has the potential to heal and influence assessors, as well as clients.

Finally, TA differs from traditional assessment in its overall view of tests and of the assessment process and in what is considered to constitute an "assessment failure." Traditionally, psychologists have viewed psychological assessment as an objective measurement event—akin to getting an EEG or an X-ray—and psychological tests have been seen as scientifically based tools that permit nomothetic comparisons and predictions of clients' behavior outside the assessment setting. An assessment was considered to have failed if inaccurate information was gathered (e.g., because an assessor deviated from standardized administration procedures) or if that information was not interpreted correctly and turned into well-founded recommendations.

In TA, assessors recognize the importance of standardized administration of empirically validated tests. However, psychological assessment is seen as an interpersonal, intersubjective encounter in which the client–assessor relationship inevitably influences the test scores and observations derived from the assessment. Tests are seen as "empathy magnifiers" and as occasions for productive dialogue with clients, which facilitate the assessor's "getting in the client's shoes" and thereby conveying a "new story" to that client and other significant people in his or her life. Even if an assessment collected useful and accurate information about a client, it would be a failure by TA standards if the client felt abused or diminished by the process or outcome of the assessment.

HOW IS THERAPEUTIC ASSESSMENT DIFFERENT FROM OTHER TYPES OF COLLABORATIVE ASSESSMENT?

Therapeutic Assessment shares much in its practice and philosophy with "individualized" psychological assessment as practiced by Fischer

(1994) and with collaborative assessment practices described by Handler (1995), Purves (2002), and others. In fact, Finn, Fischer, Handler, and Purves acknowledge their mutual influence on one another's work, regularly cite one another's papers, and present together at conferences. Therapeutic Assessment differs from these other approaches in following a semistructured series of steps whenever possible. (These steps are described subsequently in regard to using TA with the MMPI–2.) This orderly set of procedures was developed to aid assessors in balancing and simultaneously maximizing therapeutic goals with those of information gathering. Also, the semistructured format of TA helps organize the complex and sometimes overwhelming process of psychological assessment. The orderly sequence of steps facilitates both teaching and learning TA (Finn, 1998) and should make it easier to replicate TA procedures in future research studies.

STEPS IN THERAPEUTIC ASSESSMENT WITH THE MMPI–2

Finn and Martin (1997) and Finn (1996b) provided detailed descriptions of TA with the MMPI–2, along with transcripts of actual sessions. In this section, we summarize the steps in TA with the MMPI–2 (see Figure 8.1) and illustrate each step with an actual case.

Step 1: Initial Session

In the initial session, the client and assessor meet to discuss the goals and context of the MMPI–2 assessment. If the client has been referred for testing by another professional, the assessor reveals (with that person's permission) the questions the referring professional hopes will be addressed by the assessment. Subsequently (or immediately, if the client is self-referred), the assessor and client work together to delineate questions the client has concerning him- or herself or concerning the client's life circumstances, about which the MMPI–2 may be able to provide insights. The assessor collects background information relevant to each of the client's questions, and the assessor and client contract about the practical aspects of the assessment (such as cost, the number and timing of subsequent sessions, and who will receive information about the client's MMPI–2 results). Finally, the assessor addresses any remaining concerns of the client, introduces the MMPI–2, and arranges for the client to complete the test.

By centering the assessment around clients' personal concerns and agendas, TA builds in a motivation for clients to respond to the MMPI–2 in an open and honest fashion. Clients' questions are also very important at the end of the assessment, for they provide "open doors" through which the assessor may reveal difficult-to-hear and sometimes unexpected test find-

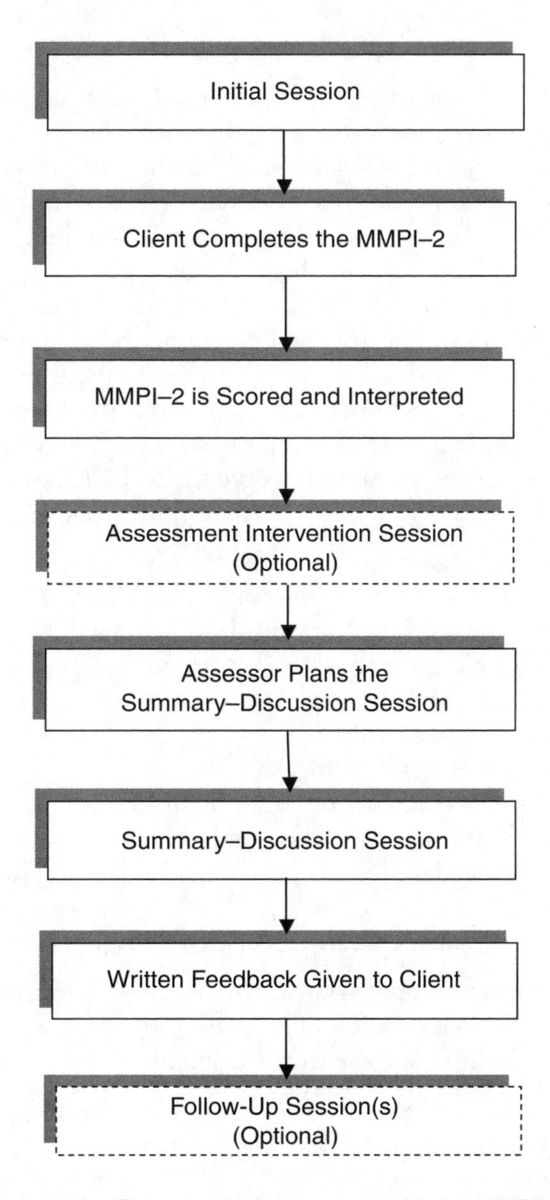

Figure 8.1. Flowchart of a Therapeutic Assessment with the MMPI–2.

ings. As long as an MMPI–2 finding can reasonably be tied to one of the client's assessment questions, the assessor has implicit permission to share the information. Finally, it is believed that helping clients generate questions about their problems engages their curiosity and observing ego; this alone can decrease distress and set the stage for other therapeutic changes to occur.

Case Example

Kamphuis and Nabarro (1999) presented the therapeutic assessment of a traumatized 45-year-old woman, Judith, who had a 20-year history of depression and other psychiatric difficulties. Severe diabetes complicated her psychiatric problems and had resulted in a significant visual impairment, neuropathy, and cardiac disturbances. Over the years, Judith had tried multiple antidepressant medications and various types of intensive psychotherapy. At the time of the assessment, she had just dropped out of a day-treatment program that involved a combination of group therapy and weekly individual therapy. After being told about the procedures of TA, Judith arrived at her first session with Kamphuis (who conducted the assessment) with over 50 handwritten questions she wished to address! As is wise in such instances, Kamphuis worked with Judith to reduce the number of questions to a manageable set, including the following:

What is wrong with me?
Am I depressed or is it more my personality disorder?
When it gets emotional, I am "no longer home." How can I get more control over this, so that I can better stay in touch with my feelings?
What happens when I "block"?
Why is treatment not working?
Am I doing something wrong or is it a misfit?
Is the treatment worse than the problem?
Am I good candidate for group therapy or is individual therapy indicated?
What about physically oriented versus verbal therapies?

The psychiatric resident who was seeing Judith in individual therapy also posed several questions, including the following, which were shared with Judith during the process of the assessment:

Should the therapy focus on the present or be directed at her past?
In other words, should we take the here and now or the past as the focus of our sessions?

As this case illustrates, there is another function served by the client's questions for the MMPI–2: they are an assessment tool in themselves and often foreshadow and assist in making sense of the MMPI–2 profile. This is one reason why Finn (1996b) recommended that assessors record clients' exact wording of their questions. Looking at Judith's questions, we can see that she was struggling to understand the reasons for her life struggles, she was worried that she was to blame for not feeling better after all her treatment, and she lacked a coherent understanding of how her treatment plan would address her condition. In her third question, she appeared to ask about emotional flooding and dissociation and seemed to be searching for an understanding of this phenomenon. In fact, the way she worded the question (i.e., "When *it* gets emotional . . ." rather than "When *I* get emotional . . .") seemed to demonstrate the very dissociative phenomenon she asked about.

Step 2: The Client Completes the MMPI–2

In TA, assessors pay close attention to how the MMPI–2 is introduced to clients and administered. Generally, it is important to begin by explaining that the test is widely used in many different settings and yields information about a range of problems and personality traits. Then the assessor should explain how the MMPI–2 is relevant to the client's questions for the assessment. For example, a client who has asked, "How depressed am I?" may be told that the MMPI–2 has been used in research to measure severity of depression. A client who has asked about recurring problems in intimate relationships may be told that the MMPI–2 yields a great deal of information about personality traits and a person's approach to other people. Again, by referencing the client's personal goals for the assessment and by explaining how the MMPI–2 is relevant, the assessor elicits the client's cooperation and best effort in completing the inventory. Such an action also communicates respect for the client, since the client is "let in" to the assessor's thinking rather than being asked to go along unquestioningly with an undisclosed plan.

Next the assessor shows the client the MMPI–2 booklet and response sheet, reviews the standard instructions, and answers any questions about completing the test. An effort is made to make the administration setting as comfortable for the client as possible. For example, clients are told that they can take short breaks if need be, are offered something to drink, and are encouraged to let the assessor know if they have any questions. Again, such small courtesies communicate the assessor's concern and respect for the client and help create an emotional "holding environment" that is conducive to therapeutic change.

Case Example

With Judith, the standard administration of the MMPI–2 had to be relaxed. She had a visual impairment that prevented her from reading the item booklet or using the (magnified) computerized version of the MMPI–2, and a Dutch-language recording of the items was unavailable. Kamphuis consulted with Judith about other alternatives, and it was agreed that an independent testing assistant would read her the items and subsequently enter her responses. Such an administration procedure is typically frowned upon for fear of distorting a client's test responses. However, Kamphuis believed this was unlikely in Judith's case, given that she had a hand in choosing this option and the two of them had discussed the possibility of her responses being influenced by the presence of the testing assistant.

Step 3: The MMPI–2 Is Scored and Interpreted

In TA, there is great respect for the nomothetically based hypotheses that may be derived from standardized tests; thus, the next step is to score and interpret the MMPI–2 profile as if it is the sole source of information about the client. That is, assessors are asked to first interpret MMPI–2 profiles as if they are blind to the clients' assessment questions and to seek a coherent integration of all the various test scores available for consideration. Finn (1996b) presented one possible outline for integrating such information. Butcher and Williams (1992), Graham (2000), Greene (2000), and Nichols (2001) detail other organizational strategies. After appraising the MMPI–2 independent of a client's questions, assessors then review the profile again, holding the client's questions in mind. At this stage, assessors begin to sketch out tentative answers to a client's questions and to anticipate which of these answers will be most challenging for the client to hear and understand.

Case Example

Judith's basic MMPI–2 profile is presented in Figure 8.2. Exhibit 8.1 shows the main hypotheses derived from the profile, organized as suggested by Finn (1996b). Basically, the profile is the "gull-wing" profile that is typical of women with histories of trauma or dissociation or borderline personality disorder. (Other diagnostic possibilities are indicated in Exhibit 8.1.) It is clear from her responses that Judith feels overwhelmed and highly distressed by serious problems in multiple areas. As we examine the MMPI–2,

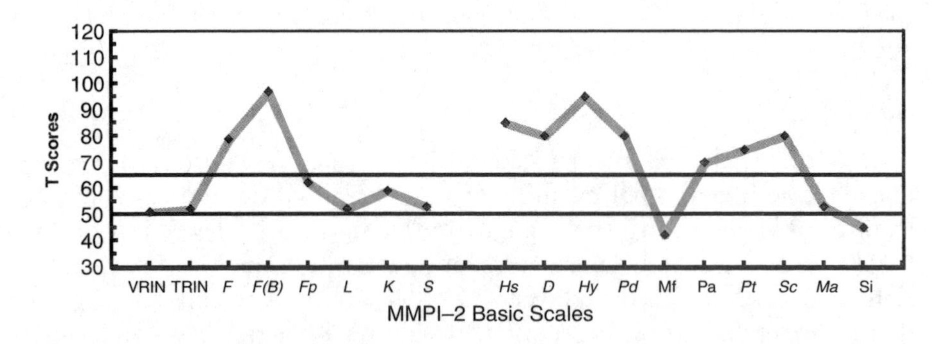

Figure 8.2. Judith's basic MMPI–2 profile. This profile is plotted using the Dutch norms, which are highly similar to the U.S. norms (Derksen, De Mey, Sloore, & Hellenbosch, 1993).

EXHIBIT 8.1
Major Hypotheses Derived From Judith's MMPI–2 Profile

Approach to the Test
She appears to have read and responded carefully to the test items.
She answered openly, and was neither overly self-critical or denying problems.

Amount of Distress and Disturbance
She reported severe emotional distress and severe physical distress.
The profile suggests a severe level of psychological disturbance.

Major Symptoms–Presenting Features
Multiple symptoms and problems, including prominent somatic symptoms, severe depression, anxious worrying, difficulties with emotional control, and lethargy. Some of the somatic symptoms may be unusual, and there is a strong possibility of a thought disorder or of periods of psychosis. Many individuals with this profile have histories of trauma and manifest dissociative symptoms. Many have histories of self-mutilation and multiple suicide attempts. They are easily overwhelmed by their own emotions, especially anger, and may decompensate when emotionally stressed.

Underlying Personality and Relationship Patterns
Similar individuals have extreme low self-esteem (more than the average psychiatric patient) and experience painful self-doubt. They are highly sensitive to criticism and rejection and may perceive rejection where none is present. They tend to be dependent and passive, and they often fail to protect themselves adequately in interpersonal relationships. Many seem wedded to a victim role and feel they have gotten a "raw deal" out of life.

Diagnostic Possibilities
1. Major depression
2. PTSD, dissociative disorder, borderline personality disorder
Rule out: schizoaffective disorder, psychotic depression, and somatization disorder

Treatment Recommendations
Individuals with this profile are known to decompensate in therapies that emphasize emotional uncovering or remembering past traumas; they do best in supportive therapy combined with approaches that teach emotion management skills, such as Dialectical Behavior Therapy.

---

we can begin to empathize with Judith and understand why she would feel confused and discouraged about her treatment. We can also begin to understand why her treatment staff would find it difficult to know how to best help Judith.

Step 4: Assessment Intervention Session

One of the later developments in TA with the MMPI–2 is the use of a separate assessment intervention session—prior to the summary–discussion session—for assessors to introduce and explore hypotheses with clients that they have derived from the MMPI–2 profile. Assessment intervention sessions were modeled after Fischer's (1994) collaborative techniques for "assessment of process" and were first described in writing as part of TA by

Finn and Martin (1997). Hence, Finn (1996b) makes no mention of assessment intervention sessions, but Finn (2003) gives a detailed account of one, including a partial transcript. Assessment intervention sessions are not necessary or advisable for all clients; therefore, we have listed them in Exhibit 8.1 as an optional step.

Basically, in an assessment intervention session, an assessor uses nonstandardized tests or other techniques—such as psychodrama, role-playing, or art projects—to create vivid experiences for clients that may help them understand their main questions for the assessment. Alternatively, standardized tests may be administered following individualized, nonstandardized instructions, as is illustrated in this chapter. Armed with a set of hypotheses derived from the MMPI–2 about the client's conflicts, defenses, and core issues, the assessor attempts to elicit in the assessment session actual instances of the client's problems in living. If such efforts are successful, the client and assessor may then observe, analyze, and discuss those problems as they occur in the assessment setting and then try to generalize any insights to the client's outside life.

As an example, imagine a client whose main assessment question is "Why do I work so slowly compared to others and how can I go faster?" and whose MMPI–2 profile suggests that he has strong obsessive tendencies (e.g., Scale 7 = 90T and OBS = 75T). The assessor may ask the client to complete a paper and pencil task such as the Bender Gestalt test in an assessment intervention session. If the client showed signs of anxiety, perfectionism, and self-criticality during the Bender Gestalt administration, as would be predicted from his MMPI–2 scores, the assessor could then lead the client in observing and discussing these factors and their relationship to the pace of his work. The assessor could even test out possible therapeutic interventions for anxiety (e.g., deep relaxation, negative thought blocking) to see if any successfully enabled the client to work faster on the Bender. If an intervention helped, the client and assessor could then strategize about applying this strategy outside the assessment room in the actual life situations where the client was bothered by his slowness.

In general, assessment intervention sessions are centered on those psychological issues that could be difficult for the client to grasp from an explanation of the MMPI–2 alone. In our clinical work, many clients describe these sessions as having impacted them greatly.

Case Example

Kamphuis chose to explore one particular set of Judith's questions in an assessment intervention session:

> When it gets emotional, I am "no longer home." How can I get more control over this, so that I can better stay in touch with my feelings?
>
> What happens when I "block"?

From Judith's MMPI–2, Kamphuis hypothesized that she was experiencing episodes of emotional flooding, which then led to dissociative lapses and the sense of "no longer being home." He sought a task that could bring such an experience into the room in a controlled way, so that he and Judith could observe and work with her "blocking" and "leaving home." Kamphuis predicted that TAT cards might arouse Judith's emotions, and he chose several cards that typically pull for themes of rejection, loneliness, and abandonment (which the MMPI–2 suggested might be core issues for her). He gave the standard instructions, emphasizing somewhat that Judith should tell emotionally vivid stories, and presented her with Card 13B (a picture of a dejected-looking young boy sitting alone in the doorway of a cabin). The following is from Kamphuis' notes written after the session:

> Judith almost immediately became quite anxious, more so than I had expected. She softly commented that she was not able to do this, and she moved restlessly in her seat in a way I had not seen before. She seemed to try really hard to access her imagination and feelings, but indeed "blocked" and her anxiety gave way to a very flat, absent person, which actually made me quite uncomfortable. It was apparent that the task was too difficult for her, given her degree of emotional overwhelm, and I decided to abort this part of the intervention.

Kamphuis then used a number of techniques commonly employed with individuals who are dissociating to help them get "grounded." He asked Judith to squeeze her fists as hard as she could and to slowly let go of the tension. This was repeated three times. He also asked Judith to stomp her feet forcefully on the floor. Gradually, Judith became more "present" and she and Kamphuis were able to talk about what had happened. Again, from Kamphuis' notes,

> It was hard for her to express what had happened to her when she had tried to respond to the TAT card. She did recognize that it was similar to some of the times she would "sit on the couch, like a Zombie, for hours" after having felt despondent and overwhelmed by emotions. . . . I asked her what else she did [at these times] . . . [S]he indicated that she felt this way often and tended to numb herself with anti-anxiety medication, or hurt herself by scratching her skin, or think about suicide.

Kamphuis then attempted to give Judith a framework for what she had just experienced. Drawing upon his experience with Dialectical Behavior Therapy (Linehan, 1993), Kamphuis drew a diagram for her and introduced the metaphor of an "overflowing bucket," with her being the bucket and the abundance of painful feelings being what was spilling over. He told her,

> When people experience more painful emotions than they can possibly handle, their bucket overflows and they search for an escape, for some means of ending this unbearable state. People choose all kinds of solutions, depending on what they've learned and what works for them. Some choose to use alcohol or drugs, some people hurt themselves,

some engage in risky behaviors, and so on. It sounds like you may choose to numb yourself with medication to get some relief, or to inflict physical pain on yourself to distract yourself from the emotional pain. Or, you flee inward and leave the situation psychologically, so to speak; as you put it, you "block" or are not "home anymore." Does this sound right to you?

When Judith agreed, she and Kamphuis went on to discuss more examples of her dissociating, and they talked about the costs of this method of coping. He then let Judith know that she was not the only one to have these types of difficulties and that many people can learn other, less harmful ways of handling such emotional crises. He shared several ideas of tools other people had found useful, and he asked Judith if she would like to learn how to use such techniques. They ended the session by reviewing their work up to that point and scheduling the time of the summary–discussion session. Judith herself suggested bringing a tape recorder to "be able to listen to it again and share it" with her partner. She asked Kamphuis to be candid and open with her in sharing the assessment results and said that this was the quality she most appreciated in her current psychiatrist.

As is evident from this example, when they are successful, assessment intervention sessions provide a powerful way for assessors to test out ideas they have derived from the MMPI–2 about the client's problems in living. Frequently, such sessions lead to a deeper level of empathy for the client. For example, Kamphuis did not seem to quite grasp Judith's level of fragility and overwhelm from her MMPI–2 but did comprehend it when he saw how she reacted to a single TAT card. Also, assessment intervention sessions provide the opportunity for clients to have someone witness and deconstruct problems that have confused them for years. One senses that Judith felt deeply understood by Kamphuis' naming and calmly explaining her dissociation during the session and that his knowing how to help her get "home again" gave her hope. Her request to bring a tape recorder to the next session seemed positive and possibly indicated that she hoped the assessment would help her partner and others to understand her better too.

Step 5: The Assessor Plans the Summary–Discussion Session

Following the assessment intervention session, the assessor should take time to carefully plan the summary–discussion session with the client. Finn (1996b) gives detailed instructions about this step, but let us review a few major points. First, clients appear to find assessment feedback most useful when it is presented according to how closely it matches their existing ideas about themselves (Schroeder, Hahn, Finn, & Swann, 1993). Early in a summary–discussion session, assessors should relate information that is very close to clients' existing self-conceptions. After this, assessors can proceed to information that is slightly new and different and, finally, to ideas that are likely to conflict with clients' current understandings of their situations. If one begins with this more difficult material, typically clients will react defensively or with anxiety or will get overwhelmed early in the session. If one never broaches difficult topics, the client may decide the test or tester are incompetent or that the information they revealed on the MMPI–2 is too shameful to discuss.

As discussed in Butcher (1990c), the MMPI–2 Content Scales and Harris–Lingoes scales are extremely useful in judging how clients see their own situations, because the items on these scales have a high degree of face validity. Generally, if clients show an elevation on such content-based scales, they will not find it surprising or threatening when the assessor interprets those scores. Conversely, a client with a score on Scale 2 of 80T may be viewed by others as quite depressed; but, if that client scored 60T on DEP and 59T on D1 (Subjective Depression), the assessor would be ill-advised to begin the summary–discussion session by telling the client that the MMPI–2 suggested a severe clinical depression. The client would likely experience such information as confusing and shocking (unless it had been addressed somehow in the assessment information session), which could make it difficult for the client to take in more information after that point.

A second guideline is that assessors should adapt not only the *content* of the session to the individual client but also the *process and tone* of the session. As Finn (1996b) has noted, this basically requires that assessors use the MMPI–2 as an empathic window into the client's experience and then ask themselves, "If I were this person, what would be the best way to tell me about my MMPI–2?" For example, clients with high *F* scores and multiple elevations on the clinical problem scales are generally overwhelmed, and assessors should plan for shorter summary–discussion sessions, structured around a few major points. Clients with 2–7/7–2 code types tend to be internalizing and quite self-critical, and assessors may want to check at the end of a summary–discussion session if such clients have heard any test interpretations as personal indictments. When giving feedback to clients with 4–9/9–4 code types and other scores indicating psychopathic characteristics, assessors should take care not to be too "sympathetic" in their interpretations. Such individuals lose respect for assessors they see as "bleeding hearts" or "easy touches," so a blunt, matter-of-fact presentation style is probably the best. Finn (1996b) gives many other guidelines for tailoring summary–discussion sessions to individual clients according to their MMPI–2 profiles.

Finally, most clients (except for the psychopathic individuals we have mentioned) seem to appreciate some recognition from the assessor that assessment is a vulnerable experience for clients and that they showed some trust by even agreeing to take the MMPI–2. Such comments fit naturally into discussions of the validity scales in open, unguarded profiles. Or an assessor may choose to begin or end the summary–discussion session by expressing such appreciations.

Case Example

As befitting Judith's MMPI–2 and the emotionally overwhelmed state it represented, Kamphuis planned to keep Judith's summary–discussion session quite brief, while trying to address her major questions. He composed a brief preliminary summary—framed in self statements—of what he thought Judith had communicated to him and her psychiatrist through the MMPI–2. He ordered these statements by how closely they seemed to match Judith's view of her situation:

I feel overwhelmed and don't know where to begin.
I feel depressed, despondent, and hopeless and experience many physical problems.
I feel worthless.
My bucket is spilling over with intensely painful feelings, and I am scared of what might happen and of losing control.
I feel lonely and like I am getting a raw deal out of life.

Kamphuis then sketched out answers to Judith's assessment questions and to her referring psychiatrist's question, since he would be present at the session. These tentative answers are presented in Exhibit 8.2. He planned to end the session by emphasizing Judith's strengths, judging that these would be most contrary to her existing self-concept. Finally, Kamphuis reminded himself to go slowly and to look for signs that Judith was dissociating during the session, knowing that it would be better to break things off and resume later than go on when Judith was overwhelmed and unable to process information.

Step 6: Summary–Discussion Session

If there has been an assessment intervention session, the assessor typically begins the summary–discussion session by inquiring about the client's reactions to that session and discussing those. Then the assessor reviews the plan for the session with the client—typically, to discuss and answer the client's questions posed at the beginning of the assessment—and invites the client to interrupt, agree, disagree, ask questions, and share any reactions during the session. With many clients, it is useful to show the MMPI–2 profile next, and orient the client to it. (Finn, 1996b, gives a sample script.) Finally, the assessor begins to review the major findings of the profile and how they relate to the client's assessment questions.

Research confirms our clinical experience by showing that the best method for reviewing test findings with clients is an interactive one (Hanson, Claiborn, & Kerr, 1997) rather than a didactic one. (For this reason,

EXHIBIT 8.2
Prepared Tentative Answers to Judith's Assessment Questions

1. *(From the referring therapist) Should the therapy focus on the present or be directed at Judith's past? In other words, should we take the here and now or the past as the focus of our sessions?*
Therapy should focus on the present, as Judith is currently in crisis. To focus on the past would be something like worrying about the foundation of the house while it is on fire. First, therapy should help make life livable again by building some sense of emotional mastery. In the future, as things have stabilized, it may be useful to examine the origins of Judith's emotional pain and to evaluate what parts of it might be processed.

2. *(From Judith) What is wrong with me? Am I depressed or it is more my personality disorder?*
The MMPI–2 is not a diagnostic instrument per se, but it does give information relevant to determining diagnoses. Even when using antidepressants, you score very high on MMPI–2 scales that measure depression. Most likely, therefore, you are experiencing severe depressive symptoms. The MMPI–2 suggests that your depression may express itself in problems with concentration (e.g., not being able to think clearly, feeling unfocused), loss of pleasure and interest in activities and things around you, a deeply sad despondent feeling, lack of energy, and thoughts about death. However, there are more painful feelings than can be accounted for by depression alone. Your scores on the MMPI–2 are consistent with those found among people with borderline personality disorder and/or who have a history of trauma.

3. *When it gets emotional, I am "no longer home." How can I get more control over this, so that I can better stay in touch with my feelings? What happens when I "block"?*
As we learned during our last session, when things happen that bring up intense or conflicting emotions for you, your "bucket flows over" and then you "block" and/or dissociate as a way of protecting yourself from emotional flooding. Although this is a disturbing and scary experience, the ability to do this probably protected you in the past in situations where you were trapped and overwhelmed and had very few other options. Now, however, you do have different choices available. You can start to recognize warning signals that your emotional bucket is close to overflowing and learn ways to help. You can also learn techniques for "grounding" yourself if you do dissociate. If these tools work, you will be left with the feelings you were working to escape and it's important to know what to do then. There are specific therapies designed to help you successfully manage intense feelings, for example, by learning to soothe yourself, distract yourself, or talk to others to get help "holding" the overwhelming feelings.

4. *Why is treatment not working? Am I doing something wrong or is it a misfit? Is the treatment worse than the problem?*
The standard treatment program is probably too intensive, given how much emotional pain you are experiencing, and may have become a stressor in its own right. It did not help matters that the communication between you and your therapist did not work out well. I do not think you did anything wrong that led to the treatment not working. I think framing the question as you did is an example of looking for faults in yourself. I hope you can catch yourself when that happens and stop it. When people experience too much emotional pain, it is impossible to do effective work in therapy or to process emotional issues. Try not to expect too many things at the same time from yourself—doing so adds to your sense of falling short and to feelings of despondency.

continued

EXHIBIT 8.2
(Continued)

5. *Am I a good candidate for group therapy or is individual therapy indicated? What about physically oriented versus verbal therapies?*
You indicated to me that you had significant experiences in physically oriented therapies. I think such therapies might help you anchor yourself in your body and learn to recognize emotions as they occur. They may also help you to develop some sense of control over your emotions. Right now, I think the specifics of the therapy are less essential than that it provide you with a sense of security and stability that helps you develop new coping skills. Therapy should probably follow a hierarchy or sequence from (a) getting you out of crisis to having a livable life; (b) once life is livable, working on processing feelings; and (c) finally working on more growth-oriented issues.

we now call these types of sessions *summary–discussion sessions*, rather than *feedback sessions*, for the latter term implies a unilateral flow of information from assessor to client.) We suggest that assessors share one piece of information, all the while carefully watching clients' demeanor to judge their reactions. If a client agrees with the finding, the assessor asks for an example of how it is borne out in the client's life and then listens carefully to the example to make sure the client is not simply blindly agreeing to the assessor's interpretation. If a client disagrees, one may ask the client to help modify the finding so it fits with the client's experience. If a client totally rejects a hypothesis derived from the MMPI–2, an assessor has several options. Sometimes, it is useful to restate the finding using different language; at other times, one asks the client if any part of what one has said seems correct. At other times, it is better to simply back off and agree that the test could be wrong. As Finn (1996b) has emphasized, one should *never* argue with a client about the validity of an MMPI–2 finding.

As discussed earlier, the assessor tries to present information in order of how well it matches clients' existing self-concepts, all the while looking for signs of overwhelm or defensiveness from the client. If the client is overwhelmed, it is best to stop and come back later to finish reviewing the remainder of the client's questions. If one is able to cover all the pertinent assessment questions, one moves toward ending the session by inviting other questions and reactions from the client. The assessor typically ends the session by thanking the client again for participating, by mentioning that a written summary will follow, and by inviting the client to attend a follow-up session in 4–6 weeks. Finn (1996b) also suggests that assessors share some way with clients that they felt moved or learned something through working with the client.

Case Example

Kamphuis began his session with Judith by reviewing the plan for the session and proposing a division of roles. He would serve as the "test expert," telling what the MMPI–2 had to say about Judith and her assessment questions. She was the "self expert," whose job it was to see if the results seemed to fit her experience. The psychiatrist, finally, was welcome to give or ask for clarifications or to contribute otherwise. Kamphuis then showed Judith the graph of the basic MMPI–2 profile (magnified so that she was able to see it) and went over the major findings of the MMPI–2 (worded in terms of the self-statements presented earlier). Judith generally agreed with these statements and gave examples of how they applied. Kamphuis noted these additions carefully on his outline for the session. He then reviewed her assessment questions and his tentative answers (see Exhibit 8.2), stopping to ask for Judith's feedback after each one.

Judith stated that she wasn't surprised by the findings, and Kamphuis' impression was that she indeed seemed to take them in stride. The referring psychiatrist chimed in to say that he and Judith had discussed the possibility of her having had traumatic experiences, but that, at present, neither of them were clear on the details of what these might have been. When Kamphuis talked about Judith's being too hard on herself and her believing that she was the sole reason for her treatment impasse, the psychiatrist quickly jumped in to emphasize that point. Judith said that she had not wanted to be a "nag" about her dissatisfactions with treatment; thus, she looked for faults in herself. She agreed, however, that since she had left the treatment program, her day was much less structured and intense, unbearable feelings were pressing, more so than before. She agreed with Kamphuis' formulation that she needed help managing her feelings and that this was the top priority for her work in therapy. She also agreed that her aftercare needed to be focused first on crisis management and that she needed continuity and support most.

When asked for reactions and feedback, Judith said she was most happy that her intense distress had been documented convincingly and clearly. She had not always felt that her emotional pain had been taken seriously and even had questioned herself about whether her urgent desire for help had legitimacy. The psychiatrist said that the assessment was helpful in confirming his impression and in providing a starting point to collaboratively plan Judith's aftercare. Kamphuis closed by talking personally about his experience of Judith's strengths. He had found her to be an intelligent, articulate, and ultimately determined woman, who, once ready, was able to draw lines and stand up for herself. He and Judith joked about how hard it was for her to take compliments, and they said goodbye.

Step 7: Written Feedback Given to Client

In TA, the assessor sends a letter to the client shortly after the summary–discussion session, reviewing the major points from the session and incorporating the client's modifications and examples (noted during

EXHIBIT 8.3

Highlight: Essentials of Therapeutic Assessment With the MMPI–2

- Therapeutic Assessment is a paradigm in which psychological testing is used as the centerpiece of a brief psychotherapeutic intervention.
- Therapeutic Assessment has been used extensively with the MMPI–2 as the main psychological assessment instrument.
- Essential to Therapeutic Assessment is the collaboration between assessor and client throughout the assessment process, most notable in
    - (a) The collaborative formulation of assessment questions, which determine the limits of the observational field for the subsequent assessment;
    - (b) The active participation of the client as the "expert on self" who helps observe and comment on his or her own test performance;
    - (c) The participant–observer stance of the clinician, who shares developing hunches throughout the assessment;
    - (d) The interactive summary–discussion section at the end of the assessment procedure;
    - (e) The written feedback given to the client in the form of a letter that describes the MMPI–2 results in everyday language.
- There is now replicated evidence that Therapeutic Assessment with the MMPI–2 can result in meaningful therapeutic change. Proposed working mechanisms include (a) self-verification, (b) self-enhancement, and (c) self-efficacy–discovery.
- Therapeutic Assessment is likely most beneficial when clients are voluntary participants, are actively seeking for new understandings of persistent problems in living, and are able to meaningfully collaborate in the assessment.
- Therapeutic Assessment offers the least incremental benefits when the desired final product is a diagnostic labeling or a relative standing on predetermined trait levels or when the assessment is involuntary.

the summary–discussion session). In this way, the client sees his or her own impact on the assessment findings. With the client's permission, a copy of this letter is also sent to the referring professional.

Case Example

We have not included Judith's letter in the chapter, as it greatly resembles the text in Exhibit 8.2. Finn (1996b), Finn and Martin (1997), and Finn (2003) provide examples of letters sent to clients at the end of a MMPI–2 assessment.

Step 8: Follow-Up Session(s)

At the summary–discussion session, clients are invited to return at some later date (typically in 4 to 6 weeks) to talk about their later reactions to the assessment and any new questions they have. In our clinical experience, such meetings serve as "booster sessions" in enhancing the beneficial aspects of TA (see Exhibit 8.3).

Case Example

Because of Kamphuis' transition to a different work place, he and Judith did not meet for a follow-up session. However, Judith's psychiatrist did write him several months after the assessment to provide follow-up information. Here are a few excerpts from that document:

> The first and immediately visible result of the assessment was that [Judith] was relieved that she had been acknowledged in her problems. Moreover, the assessment suggested specific guidelines for continued treatment and made it more understandable why the earlier group therapy had been difficult for her. Like many borderline patients, she had learned to see herself as "difficult and impossible" whereas the assessment made her feel understood and taken seriously.
>
> As her treating psychiatrist, I benefited most from the specificity with which this TA addressed the treatment questions. . . . In addition, the TA provided us with a shared frame of reference that reflected major input from the patient herself. . . . After a prolonged and troubled aftercare period (which included a hospital admission), Judith was included in a multicenter structured treatment program for borderline patients, which she felt optimistic about.

WHAT IS THE EMPIRICAL SUPPORT FOR THERAPEUTIC ASSESSMENT?

To date, four controlled studies have investigated the effects of Therapeutic Assessment while using the MMPI–2 as the principal assessment instrument (Finn & Tonsager, 1992; Lance & Krishnamurthy, 2003; Newman & Greenway, 1997; Peters, 2000). Finn and Tonsager (1992) were the first to put their TA model to the empirical test. Sixty-one students who were scheduled for treatment at the University of Texas Counseling and Mental Health Center were randomly assigned to either supportive nondirective counseling (n = 29) or a TA protocol limited to an initial interview and MMPI–2 test administration and test feedback (n = 32). The two treatments were matched for duration, each spanning three clinical sessions, and the groups showed equivalence at baseline in terms of symptomatic distress and self-esteem. Immediately following the interventions, only students who had received therapeutic feedback reported increased self-esteem. The difference between the two groups was substantial as was evident from the Cohen's effect size d of .38 (medium effect size). No immediate effects were observed for symptomatic distress. At follow-up, however, the TA group reported substantially lower symptomatic distress than the control group (Cohen's d = .36) and the improvement in self-esteem was maintained (d = .46). No positive changes were observed for the control group.

As a modified replication, Newman and Greenway (1997) conducted a similar study in Australia, improving on the Finn and Tonsager (1992) design by having the control group take the MMPI–2 as well. This addition ruled out that the observed effects in the Finn and Tonsager study were due merely to the administration of the MMPI–2 per se (rather than to the overall TA protocol, including the MMPI–2 feedback). By and large, the authors replicated the results observed by Finn and Tonsager, albeit with somewhat smaller effect sizes. At follow-up, Cohen's d was .14 and .22 for self-esteem and symptomatic distress effects, respectively. Together, these two studies document that a three-to-four-session semistructured assessment protocol *by itself* can produce marked therapeutic changes, something that had never before been demonstrated in a controlled design. It is worth noting that neither of these studies employed the full set of TA procedures described here, that is, incorporating assessment intervention sessions, written feedback, and follow-up sessions.

One unpublished dissertation has also centered on evaluating the effects of TA-based procedures. Peters (2000) conducted a controlled study on the efficacy of TA among women with eating disorders. She compared TA to information-gathering assessment in a repeated measures design to examine differences in outcome on both general and domain-specific psychopathology. No relative benefits were observed for TA in terms of symptomatology or self-esteem, and neither group evidenced major therapeutic changes. However, on a measure of treatment readiness, women in the therapeutic feedback condition were more likely to seek treatment after the 6-week follow-up measurement. The modest treatment success in this study poses the question as to when (i.e., under what circumstances) TA is more likely to be effective (relative to information-gathering assessment). This question is addressed in the next section, covering therapeutic mechanisms.

Recently, Lance and Krishnamurthy (2003) presented a paper comparing the effectiveness of (a) oral, (b) written, and (c) combined oral and written MMPI–2 test feedback on a multidimensional measure of client satisfaction with assessment (the Assessment Questionnaire—2; Finn, Schroeder, & Tonsager, 1995). The combined feedback approach was superior on overall client satisfaction, and—not surprisingly—was superior to written feedback (only) in terms of the relational experience and superior to oral feedback in terms of new self-insights. Contrary to prediction, oral feedback was less effective than written feedback in terms of sustained new learning and did no better than written feedback in terms of overall satisfaction. This finding underscores the importance of written documents in providing feedback; clients seem to indicate difficulty maintaining the feedback when it is presented orally only. Unfortunately, no measures of psychopathology and self-esteem were included in this study.

Finally, several case studies have been published in which the MMPI–2 was used in a therapeutic assessment (Finn, 1996b; Finn, 2003; Finn & Martin, 1997; Michel, 2002). These reports may be particularly useful in orienting the practitioner to the type of clinical skills that are involved in doing TA. Detailed descriptions of TA, including numerous verbatim statements, were included in the *Manual for Using the MMPI–2 as a Therapeutic Intervention* (Finn, 1996b) as well as in the Finn and Martin (1997) chapter. Both texts provide the reader with a real sense of how a TA proceeds as well as with some hands-on pointers of the technical and practical aspects of TA. Another source is the recently published elaborate TA case study in the context of an impasse in the treatment of a man with ADD (Finn, 2003). Through the collaborative process of the assessment, the client gradually concluded that he did not have ADD, and he and the therapist reached a joint understanding of their next steps in treatment. This case illustrates how collaborative psychological assessment (a) can help clients revise their "stories about themselves and the world" and (b) provides an effective, nonthreatening way for a consultant to intervene in a client–therapist system that has reached an impasse. Michel's (2002) two brief case studies showed how TA with the MMPI–2 can be useful with inpatients hospitalized with eating disorders. In her setting, such assessments were useful in confronting clients' denial about deeper psychological issues, assisting hospital staff in treatment planning, and engaging clients and their families in treatment.

WHAT ARE THE MECHANISMS UNDERLYING THERAPEUTIC ASSESSMENT?

As reviewed earlier, there is now replicated evidence that TA can result in meaningful therapeutic change. What mechanisms might account for the observed positive changes? As with other psychotherapies, little research exists on this question. However, it may be useful to review current theories. Finn and Tonsager (1997) speculated, drawing on their extensive clinical experience, that therapeutic change may result from addressing three fundamental human motives, that is, the need for (a) self-verification, (b) self-enhancement, and (c) self-efficacy–self-discovery experiences. *Self-verification* is obtained when the TA brings about a sense of coherence, of confirmation and validation of one's views of self, others, and the world at large. In the context of TA, a client may experience this self-state when the test feedback underscores how the client's behavior makes sense in light of her or his phenomenal world, for example, the shared understanding of self-destructive behaviors as escape efforts for intolerable feelings. In the case we presented, self-verification seemed evident in Judith's feeling that her problems were taken seriously and were understood by Kamphuis. *Self-enhancement* is experienced to the extent that the TA communicates to the client that he or she is valued, worthwhile, and cared for. Therapeutic Assessment's procedural emphasis on collaboration and the client's key role in providing data and expertise helps foster these experiences. In the case example, Judith's referring psychiatrist mentioned that after the assessment she no longer saw herself as a "difficult patient" but as one who needed a specific kind of treatment. *Self-efficacy* experiences can be derived from the new insights and personal conceptualizations of previously less well-understood problem areas. For example, when current perfectionist attitudes are for the first time tied to early solutions to gain some measure of approval or avoid punishment, an "aha" type experience may be triggered that is quite empowering to the client. In Judith's case, she learned through her assessment about dissociation. Following the assessment, she better understood the cause of such frightening experiences and also learned some techniques to help "ground" herself when she started to dissociate.

As noted however, TA, as other therapies, has not always resulted in far-reaching favorable changes (see, e.g., Peters, 2000). An as yet untested but interesting hypothesis regarding the differential outcomes may be found in Prochaska's transtheoretical model of stages of (psychotherapeutic) change (see, e.g., McConnaughy, DiClemente, Prochaska, & Velicer, 1993; Prochaska et al., 1994). According to this model, clients can be in one of several stages of psychotherapeutic change: precontemplation, contemplation, preparation, action, or maintenance. Particularly relevant to TA may be the distinction between being in the precontemplation stage and being in the contemplation stage. In the precontemplation stage, clients believe it is the environment or other people who need to do the changing. In the contemplation stage, clients are aware of personal problems and are interested in whether these problems can be resolved and whether psychotherapy might be helpful. It seems that in order for TA to result in symptomatic change, clients need some degree of openness and investment in the results of the assessment, a state that is fostered when personal ideas about problem areas are "in flux," no longer perceived as adequate, and in need of revision. A prima facie, voluntary or self-referred assessment seems more likely to satisfy these requirements.

Peters' (2000) (partially negative) findings may be explained along these lines. Her participants were women in an introductory psychology course who took part in the research for course credit; they had been identified as having eating disorders from a survey given to all students in the class. Obviously, these women were not ostensibly seeking help for their eating problems; and, across conditions, fewer than 15% of the women were classified as treatment seeking. In a sense, Peters' assessments might be viewed as semi-involuntary assessments. (The complicated nature of involuntary assessments is discussed later.) No differences were noted between the two conditions on treatment seeking status at pre- nor at postintervention assessment. Interestingly, however, after the 6-week follow-up period, significantly more participants were motivated to seek treatment following TA as compared to those who completed the regular assessment protocol. While not differentially effective in providing symptomatic relief, TA apparently motivated a higher proportion of women with eating disorders to start contemplating treatment. This suggests that TA may help people move along the dimension of stages of change, wherever they start. If a client is in the precontemplation stage, TA may help the client progress to contemplation. For a client already in the contemplation stage, TA may help the client prepare for or actually take action toward change.

One final observation may speak to the mechanisms governing TA. Across the three controlled studies, a delayed effect of TA was noticeable. In both the Finn and Tonsager (1992) and the Newman and Greenway (1997) studies, symptomatic improvement did not emerge until the follow-up assessment, lagging behind the immediate positive effects in self-esteem and hope. Peters (2000) observed that active treatment-seeking behavior did not emerge until after the follow-up period. It appears that perhaps the TA feedback needs some time to "sink in" for it to have its full impact. This finding is also consistent with the superior client satisfaction associated with the inclusion of a written report in the TA protocol (Lance & Krishnamurthy, 2003). Clients seem to indicate that they need time and repeated opportunity to solidify the new insights about themselves. Again, note that none of these studies used the full TA model, including assessment intervention sessions.

WHEN IS THERAPEUTIC ASSESSMENT MORE AND LESS APPLICABLE?

Little research exists on the question of when TA is most effective; however, a few factors have become obvious through our clinical experience.

Forensic or Other Involuntary Assessment

In forensic or other involuntary assessment situations, clients generally do not present with great curiosity about personal motives or problem areas. In a sense, such clients are typically in Prochaska's precontemplation stage (Prochaska et al., 1994). In addition, there are typically powerful interests at stake (e.g., parole, child custody, social security) that are of much greater import and urgency to the client than developing personal insight. Such factors may even work *against* clients developing new ways of viewing themselves and the world. Accordingly, all stages of TA may be compromised. First, collaboratively developing assessment questions is overshadowed by the a priori agenda of the referring party. Frequently, clients will even feel that revealing personal concerns would put them at a disadvantage by exposing issues the referring party could use against them. Second, when taking the test, clients may (sometimes, correctly) believe that too much candor about personal shortcomings and problem areas may decrease the chances the assessment will turn out as they wish. Guarded, less informative test protocols may be the result. Finally, when test feedback is provided, it is likely that the client is most invested in hearing findings that are conducive to his or her cause than anything else.

Notwithstanding, the clinician can try to enlist the client by orienting him or her to the nature of the assessment and what its findings will and will not be used for. Explaining that the test may pick up on an overly positive self-presentation may be part of this orientation. In addition, one might say something like,

> The fact is that we will have to look into these (referral agency) questions, as best we can. If you decide to proceed with the testing, you might as well try to get something out of it for yourself. So, are there any questions about yourself you might be curious about; things you are interested in understanding better about yourself?

Sometimes clients will then come up with issues that are relevant to their personal situation. Another technique is to elicit questions by joining with clients about how they feel misunderstood or mistreated by the referring agency. For example, a mother being assessed for termination of parental rights might be helped to ask,

> Why do people think I'm a bad mother, even though I'm not?

Similarly, an adolescent referred by his parents against his will may ask:

> How can I convince my parents that I'm doing OK and they don't need to worry about me?

Such questions are also useful because they allow the assessor to bring in information about the "persecuting" party's point of view, for example, in the first instance,

> The court seems to believe that you've endangered your children by exposing them to your drug use and drug dealing. What would you say about this concern?

As a side note, we believe it is better *not* to proceed with TA, if at all possible, if the client remains opposed to the entire idea of assessment.

Last, when giving feedback in involuntary assessments, we have found it useful to matter-of-factly report our conclusions and findings and the data we used to derive them, while openly acknowledging that clients may have wished for a different outcome. One may then use Fischer's (1994) technique of inviting the client to write a "minority report" expressing his or her opinion of the conclusions. As Purves (2002) has demonstrated, it *is* possible to conduct TA with involuntarily referred clients in very stressful conditions (i.e., mothers being assessed for termination of parental rights) and for most clients to leave the assessment feeling respected and well-treated. As mentioned earlier, it is even possible that such assessments help some clients to move from a precontemplation stage regarding change to a contemplation or even an action stage.

Classification or Selection

When the main goals of the assessment are classification or selection (e.g., administering an IQ test to see if a child reaches the cutoff for inclusion in a gifted–talented program at school), TA has relatively little incremental value over more traditional forms of information-gathering assessment. In other words: When the desired final product is a diagnostic labeling or a relative standing on predetermined trait levels, straightforward administration of assessment instruments is likely just as productive as TA. On the other hand, a collaborative stance always communicates respect to clients and fosters their investment in the assessment enterprise. Also, it is possible that psychological testing will yield somewhat more accurate data when clients are more invested. Still, when no change is sought, and when the assessment is primarily aimed at obtaining a "snapshot" of current functioning or relative standing, without future therapeutic contact, the added costs of TA may not be exceeded by these benefits.

When Clients Are in Crisis

Sometimes clients are referred for assessment when in a high degree of emotional distress. In these instances, it is a judgment call whether TA (or for that matter, any psychological testing) is the best approach. Many clients who are in immediate crisis need containment, practical advice, and reassurance before they can find any curiosity about themselves or meaningfully engage in a process that fosters self-observation. For example, it would be a major empathic break on the part of a psychologist to ask a highly suicidal client to "reflect on puzzles you have in your life that you would like to explore through an assessment." Similarly, someone who has recently become homeless needs immediate food and housing assistance rather than help "revising existing stories about self and the world"! In such instances, it is best for clients to receive other clinical services first and then proceed with TA when they are calmer and more equipped to tolerate the emotions that are often stirred by this intervention. On the other hand, our experience shows that some clients in long-standing states of crisis and overwhelm benefit greatly from TA and experience it as someone "finally getting to the bottom of things." For example, Finn routinely assesses couples that have spent years feeling dissatisfied with their relationships—sometimes after a great deal of couples therapy—and who present asking, "Is there any hope we can be happy together, and what would it take?" Therapeutic Assessment has proved quite useful in a number of such cases.

Best-Case Scenario

Although a great deal of research is needed to identify the ideal context for TA to produce positive change, we judge it useful at this point for us to put forth our hunches, based on existing studies and years of clinical experience. Therapeutic Assessment seems most likely to yield positive change in the following situations:

1. When clients are voluntary participants in the assessment who believe that the process will be helpful to them in meeting valued goals;
2. When clients have tried other methods of reaching those goals or addressing life problems (e.g., reading self-help books, psychotherapy, following the advice of friends or ministers) and are dissatisfied with the results;
3. When clients are open to the idea that their current ways of viewing themselves and the world are inadequate to explain their life experiences and are searching for new ways of thinking;
4. When clients have not been traumatized previously by experiences with psychological assessment;
5. When clients are cognitively and psychologically able to take part in a process that invites self-observation, curiosity, and introspection (e.g., the client is not acutely suicidal, has food and shelter, and is not in great physical pain);
6. When clients have people who can support them emotionally as they progress through an assessment (e.g., friends, a referring therapist);
7. When major people in clients' lives (e.g., significant others, therapists) are open to new ways of thinking about them and when those individuals are involved in some way in the

assessment (e.g., attending summary–discussion sessions or posing questions to be answered).

CONCLUSION

Therapeutic Assessment is a relatively new brief psychotherapy that uses psychological tests to help clients explore and reach new understandings about their problems in living. The MMPI–2 has been shown in several controlled studies to be an effective centerpiece for Therapeutic Assessment, and detailed instructions and case examples now exist to help clinicians learn the procedures of TA with the MMPI–2. Further research is needed on the mechanisms underlying TA and on the types of clients for whom it is most suited. At this point, TA shows the most promise with clients who voluntarily participate in an assessment in hopes of understanding themselves better and improving their lives.

III

APPLICATIONS OF THE MMPI–2 ACROSS DIVERSE POPULATIONS

9

USE OF THE MMPI–2 IN INPATIENT MENTAL HEALTH SETTINGS

DAVID S. NICHOLS AND BRENTON CROWHURST

It is somewhat surprising that the MMPI/MMPI–2, a product of the inpatient setting, has not received as much attention in terms of its role and use within the context of its origins as would be expected. This chapter seeks to partially redress this gap in the literature of the test by highlighting features of inpatient settings and those who populate them in relation to the tasks the psychologist in such settings is called upon to undertake. Of course not all inpatient settings are alike. Psychiatric services within private or university hospitals differ in important ways from those within Veterans' Administration (VA) facilities, and both differ from publicly funded state hospitals. Average lengths of stay; the proportion of involuntary patients; admission and discharge policies and arrangements; community

The authors extend their thanks to Roger L. Greene, who generously performed numerous statistical analyses for us, thereby saving us time and the embarrassment of numerous errors of fact and interpretation. We and our readers are much in his debt. We also thank Carol Snyder, Librarian at the Oregon State Hospital, for her spirited assistance in securing some references; and we thank David M. Freed for his prompt and wholehearted assistance in the early stages of preparation for this chapter.

support resources and interfaces; the level of education, training, credentials, and experience of the typical professional staff; and their positions within the organizational structure, supervisory arrangements, and routes of accountability give only a rough idea of the kinds and variety of such differences. Despite such differences, the circumstance of residing in an institution charged with providing care, support, and treatment within a medical framework for patients deemed—whether by themselves or others—sufficiently distressed, unstable, incompetent, or dangerous as to be unable to reside, at least temporarily, outside the institution creates its own pattern of similarities as well. It is these similarities that we have assumed if not embraced in this chapter, as we discuss the use of the MMPI–2 in the assessment of psychiatric inpatients. The reader should be aware that the authors' experience in developing this chapter is drawn from state or regional hospitals serving general psychiatric patients. These are our primary points of reference in what follows.

THE TYPICAL INPATIENT SITUATION

Competent assessment with instruments addressing personality and psychopathology requires an appreciation of the range of circumstances that may influence test findings. One of the more important of these circumstances is the setting in which assessment occurs. Although few settings are entirely unique, each comes with its own unique pattern of features that stand to affect the position both examinee and clinician take in the conduct of psychological assessment. For example, the prior probabilities (base rates) of major mental disorders and their symptoms may differ radically from one setting to another. Uncomplicated psychopathy is relatively rare in psychiatric hospitals but common in prisons, whereas for florid schizophrenia the situation is reversed.

The chief difference between patients in most psychiatric hospitals and those in other venues in which mental health services are delivered is that the former receive such services while under compromised status with respect to their civil rights and freedom of choice and movement. Although there are many institutional and individual exceptions (e.g., patients within VA facilities), most psychiatric inpatients are under involuntarily commitment. The laws governing civil commitment vary from state to state. In most, the statutes specify that an allegedly mentally ill person may be involuntarily committed to a state psychiatric facility or to the administrative division responsible for the oversight of such facilities when he or she is judged to fall under these statutes on the basis of one or more of three basic criteria: (a) dangerousness to self; (b) dangerousness to others; or (c) being so gravely disabled as to be unable to provide for basic needs, as for food, clothing, shelter, safety, or emergent medical care.

Involuntary civil commitment is typically initiated by the patient's arrest by police or similar law enforcement authority or when a notification of mental illness alleging that an individual meets criteria for commitment is filed with a probate court of appropriate jurisdiction. The allegedly mentally ill person is notified of the filing and advised of his or her right to be present at a hearing, to be represented by counsel, to have counsel appointed by the court if he or she is indigent, and to cross-examine witnesses. The court then schedules a hearing during which the allegedly mentally ill person is usually examined by two court-selected licensed mental health professionals, typically psychiatrists, and testimony is gathered from interested parties familiar with the patient. (The person may be mandated to appear or taken into custody to ensure his or her appearance at hearing.) Interested parties may include the arresting officer(s); members of the person's family or significant others; friends, neighbors, landlords; or mental health workers having responsibility for and recent contact with the person in the community. If the court determines from the testimony presented that the person meets legal criteria for commitment on the basis of clear and convincing evidence (or some similar guideline), it may issue an order of involuntary commitment, the terms of which may specify a particular duration under which the order will remain in force (e.g., 180 days).

Most jurisdictions provide for some form of emergency detention in which a person may be taken into custody by a police officer, transported, and held in the hospital for several days (typically less than 2 weeks) pending a commitment hearing, if the officer reasonably believes the person to be in need of emergency care and treatment. In some jurisdictions, one or more physicians or psychologists may sign an emergency certificate allowing the apprehension or custody of a person if there is a reasonable belief that the person will meet criteria for involuntary commitment.

Although most of the patient's civil rights remain unabridged under commitment status, and hospitals are typically required to inform civilly committed patients of their rights to petition, appeal, rehearing, the limits of informed consent and confidentiality, access to others via phone and mail, and so forth, many patients lack the degree of insight and perspective necessary to view their circumstances under commitment in other than stark adversarial terms. They may view the notification of mental illness as vengeful; the examining mental health professionals at hearing as intrusive and degrading; the presiding judge as a mere vested instrument of state authority who runs a "kangaroo court"; their own counsel as lazy, uninvested, or in league with the judge or others; and the others present as "false witnesses," whose true aims are betrayal, humiliation, or control. Regardless of the specific attributions and perceptions involved, the involuntarily committed patient is the loser in his or her contest with legal authority, whose rights of self-determination have been diminished to the point that he or she now finds him- or herself at the mercy of the hospital treatment personnel to whom he or she has been assigned for treatment. All this, of course, sets a less than optimal stage for collaboration in an assessment that the psychologist hopes will offer accurate, sensitive results that can contribute meaningfully and constructively to patient understanding, diagnosis, and treatment.

The attitudes that come in the immediate wake of court commitment are often fairly rapidly supplanted as new arrivals adjust to ward routines, become acquainted with peers, and meet the members of their treatment team. Patients are often pleasantly surprised to find themselves in an environment that is predictable and generally supportive, a welcome moratorium and contrast to the daily struggle for existence they may have faced outside the hospital. For others, this adjustment takes longer but is in a similar direction. For a minority, however, the hospital, with its fairly rigid schedules for arising, meals, medications, recreation, and bedtime, and its many rules and procedures, is a confusing and potentially treacherous environment, one in which the behavior of peers or staff are seen as arbitrary, nonsensical, or frightening.

MEDICAL RECORDS

Another important feature of hospital populations is the availability of medical records. The medical record for the index admission, the current "chart," typically includes an admission note with information on the circumstances of admission, the presenting problem—often in the patient's own words, some pertinent history, a mental status examination, and a provisional diagnosis and treatment plan; a developmental and social history; various additional assessments by nursing and activities therapies staff; progress notes; and a log of patient behavior and treatment services by floor staff. In a great many cases, the medical record contains documents from previous psychiatric hospitalizations.

When the medical record includes documents from prior admissions, the assessment clinician stands to gain a fuller appreciation of the patient's developmental, family, achievement, employment, marital, and social history, as well as valuable insights into the course of illness and patterns in the circumstances of previous breakdowns and recoveries. Such documents may also contain information about relatives of the patient who may have been afflicted by mental disorder, their histories of hospitalization, diagnoses, and so on, providing grist for hypotheses about the possible genetic background for the patient's mental disorder. Medical records constitute a rich repository of observations over time by multiple observers with different backgrounds, training, and points of view.

However, as valuable as medical records can be in contributing to a reliable and valid psychodiagnostic assessment, they are always flawed and misleading in one way or another. Observations and descriptions of the patient are diffusely organized in the record, ordinarily requiring a detailed review in order to achieve a level of organization that is conducive to summary. Another problem concerns the language in which observations are expressed. Most staff record their observations in straightforward, descriptive terms. Others, especially among licensed professional personnel, may summarize their observations in interpretive, inferential language, without adequately describing the observations from which their inferences and interpretations arise. The assessment clinician does well to bear these differences in recording style in mind in reviews of the medical record.

Records are rarely complete: some documents may be missing information that they normally contain; some may be missing entirely. The diagnoses listed at times reflect idiosyncratic preferences or habits of the psychiatrist or psychologist who rendered them as much as they do the patient's symptomatology. In some cases, prior diagnoses reflect the conceptions of an earlier era.

The reliability and accuracy of information presented in the social history are limited by the number and reliability of informants. Ideally, the patient will have several relatives or others (e.g., employers) who are accessible and cooperative for interview by the social worker. However, access to such informants is often at least somewhat dependent on the patient, without whose cooperation informants cannot be located. We have seen occasional cases in which the patient's account of history, including such particulars as grades in school, college graduation, marriage and children, occupation and employment, prior hospitalization, was seen as credible and persuasive, only later to be found wildly discrepant from information obtained from a subsequently identified informant in possession of supporting documentation. Finally, erroneous information may find its way into the medical record from observations, overheard conversations, or patient or peer reports that are subsequently recorded by staff.

THE BEARING OF INVOLUNTARY STATUS ON ASSESSMENT

Because of the unique set of circumstances that form the backdrop for psychodiagnostic assessment in inpatient facilities, the persons assessed often possess attitudes and dispositions that differ from clients assessed in outpatient and fee-for-service venues. Some of these circumstances, their potential effects on inpatient assessment with the MMPI–2, and the means by which these effects can be ameliorated are discussed in the following paragraphs.

The most obvious circumstance to potentially affect inpatient psychodiagnostic assessment concerns the patient's legal status and its consequences. Involuntary civil commitment limits freedom of movement and places the patient under the significant control of policies, rules, schedules, and personnel within the institution. In some circumstances, the patient's normally preserved right to communicate with others outside the hospital via mail, telephone, visitors, and passes may be restricted or even suspended.

Perhaps most significantly, the personnel assigned to provide and oversee the patient's treatment within the hospital, including the members of the treatment team, are determined by patterns of hospital census and staff ward assignments, rather than chosen by the patient him- or herself. The situation is thus one in which the patient's contract with his or her treaters is indirect and diffuse rather than immediate and explicit and one that, except in extreme cases, is not subject to cancellation or revocation by the patient.

In this context, then, it is common for patients to feel (realistically) disenfranchised, relatively powerless to enforce their will and preferences on those treating them, apart from certain limited requirements for informed consent; anxious or fearful; uncertain if not suspicious of the extent to which their treaters will respect and be guided by patients' own appraisal of their best interests; and alienation both as a consequence of being involuntarily placed in the company of strangers, both peers and staff, and of being separated from their families, friends, and customary associates. It is therefore to be expected that such feelings may emerge as situational effects in inpatient MMPI–2 protocols. Consider items referencing feeling misunderstood (22), fitful and disturbed sleep (39), believing one is condemned (234), currently feeling much pressure or stress (496), and many other items that may reflect situational influences (e.g., 9, 31, 98, 259, 305, 321, 333, 334, 360, etc.). Along with countless others, any and all of these items may be construed and endorsed by patients with reference not to characteristic and habitual patterns of belief, attitude, and behavior but to the novel and often distressing set of conditions with which they feel surrounded in hospital.

Similarly, items referencing the law and its enforcement (66, 126, 266; ASP [Antisocial Practices]), family and friends (83, 195, 205, 256, 288, 292, 378, 383, 455, 478, 543; see Pd1 [Familial Discord], FAM1 [Family Discord], and FAM2 [Familial Alienation]), and doctors and experts (346, 499) may draw their endorsements from the patient's recent situational experience of apprehension and commitment proceedings, including adverse testimony offered at hearing and antipathy toward assigned treatment personnel, rather than from more stable attitudes and values.

Just as the clinician is well advised to be aware of the patient's general health status and medical history as a context for the interpretation of scales with somatic content (*Hs* [Hypochondriasis], *D*3 [Physical Malfunctioning],

*Hy*4 [Somatic Complaints], *Sc*6 [Bizarre Sensory Experiences], HEA [Health Concerns], HEA1 [Gastrointestinal Symptoms], HEA2 [Neurological Symptoms], HEA3 [General Health Concerns]), so should the current chart be consulted and the patient interviewed to gain specific information about the sequence of events leading up to hospitalization, including details of how the patient was informed that he or she was considered to be mentally ill; how and where the patient was apprehended, detained, and transported to the hospital and by whom; who was present at the patient's commitment hearing; to what each witness testified and the patient's reaction to that testimony; and the patient's perception of the mental health examination and examiners, the performance of the patient's counsel, the conduct and impartiality of the judge, and the overall fairness of the proceedings.

Patients, of course, vary considerably in their tolerance and stamina for inquiry at this level of detail, and there is little to be gained by pressing this agenda on patients who manifest a reluctance to engage it. For those who can tolerate it, however, this reconnaissance can considerably enhance patient–clinician rapport by conveying the clinician's willingness to consider the circumstances of commitment and hospitalization afresh, to manifest an interest in the patient's own account of events, to credit realistic aspects of this account and the questions these may raise when possible, and to seek to place aspects of the patient's account into a larger, less adversarial, alternative context when they cannot be so credited.

These aspects of the clinician's interview should be considered an integral part of preparing the patient for the assessment, leading up to test administration. Several additional considerations must be placed among these preliminaries. The first is the assessment of the patient's overall adjustment to the hospital setting. In general, psychiatric inpatients approached for assessment within the first week or 10 days following admission are less cooperative and are less likely to become engaged with testing than those approached later. Also, for those cooperative with the assessment within this early time frame, the results of testing tend to be less valid and stable than test data obtained later in the admission. The reasons for this are not hard to find. As has already been seen, even when experienced as an enhancement of the patient's overall level of support, hospitalization nevertheless comes with heavy adjustment demands, including orientation to the location of one's room and facilities; becoming familiar with one's roommates, other patient peers, the staff, their names, positions, duties, shifts, and availability; learning the ward schedule and pattern of routines; and demands for other assessments such as nursing and nutritional assessments, physical examinations, X-rays, and so forth. Patients generally experience their first 10 days in hospital as quite "busy." Such concentrated adjustment demands often coincide with—if not stimulate—increased levels of stress.

A second important issue bearing on the patient's adjustment to the hospital setting and, therefore, readiness to cooperate with psychological assessment is medication. Virtually all patients arrive at hospital taking one or more prescribed psychoactive drugs or are started on a medication regimen on or shortly after admission as a part of their initial treatment plan. In most cases, patients suffer one or more side effects of such medication, ranging from the annoying to the debilitating. A complete list of side effects and the specific medications (or classes of medications) that are associated with them is beyond the scope of this chapter, but some of the more common side effects of antipsychotic, antidepressant, and antimanic agents that may interfere with psychological test performance include: anergia and slowing (akinesia), amotivation ("feeling like a zombie"), dizziness or blurred vision, headache, impaired memory and concentration, and so forth. More often than not, such side effects are transient and disappear quickly or may be independently treated, but the timetables by which they may be brought under control vary and some may remain for the duration of treatment. In some cases, side effects are similar to the symptoms under treatment. For example, symptoms of depression such as fatigue and constipation may be difficult to distinguish from the side effects of some antidepressants. To complicate matters further, psychoactive drugs may interact with other medications, psychoactive or otherwise, in ways that confound or exacerbate both desired and side effects and adversely affect patient comfort and ability to cooperate. Such common interactions may occur with antidepressants, antipsychotics, anticonvulsants, thyroid hormone, analgesics, soporifics, antihypertensives, coagulants, diuretics, salycilates (e.g., aspirin), and antihistamines. Under these conditions, the decision to initiate psychological assessment is best postponed until after signs of a satisfactory preliminary adjustment to the ward environment are at hand and the patient's tolerance for and stability on his or her current medication regimen have been established.

THE ENLISTMENT OF COOPERATION

We have already discussed the advantages of interviewing the patient in some detail about the circumstances of admission, both as a means of gaining valuable contextual information for the assessment and as a means of building rapport with the assessment clinician. In many if not most cases, the patient's previous experience with psychologists, as with mental health workers in general, has been less than salutary. Therefore, a clinician who approaches the patient in hospital to seek the latter's participation in assessment typically does so without the benefit of a positive halo effect from earlier encounters.

Wherever possible, assessment should be structured along the lines described in Finn's protocol for therapeutic assessment (1996b; see chap. 8, this volume), including describing the purposes of the assessment (why it is being requested); working with the patient to formulate questions of relevance to the patient him- or herself ("Why am I in the hospital?"), with whom the results of the assessment will be shared; and formulating a plan for the feedback of assessment findings to the patient. Although the usual guidelines for informed consent and confidentiality, including the legal and ethical sanctions that may attach to unauthorized use or release of records, must be observed, the patient should also be made specifically aware that the psychologist's report of the assessment will become a permanent part of the patient's medical record and, thus, will be available to future treatment personnel should rehospitalization be necessary.

ADMINISTRATION

The principles governing the administration of the MMPI–2 in inpatient settings are generally consistent with those covering this process elsewhere, outlined by Friedman, Lewak, Nichols, and Webb (2001); Greene (2000); Nichols (2001); and others. Briefly, those principles honoring standardized instructions; the need for test security; and ensuring reading comprehension, adequate visual acuity and motor control, supervision, and freedom from distractions must be observed. However, the successful administration of the MMPI–2 in psychiatric hospitals requires that the special circumstances of this population be taken into account. Primary among these are the typical, though usually minor, impairments in attention, concentration, memory, vision, susceptibility to distraction and fatigue, restlessness, and motivation secondary to the various mental disorders and to their pharmacological treatment. The availability of alternative formats for administration such as audiotape or computer makes it possible for some patients to complete the MMPI–2 who would otherwise be unable to do so.

Patients vary considerably in their ability to engage and persist with the tasks of assessment. Their motivation to complete the MMPI–2 is rarely strong; hence, adequate preparation, as we have described, is important. Also, even though a minority, some patients will be unable to complete the task in a single sitting, and a few may require multiple sittings spaced over days or even weeks. We have seen valid and useful MMPI–2 protocols that required as much as a month for the patient to complete.

The physical setting for testing should provide comfortable seating and a desk or table at a comfortable height. Unusually short or tall patients may require cushions or alternate seating or tables to ensure comfort. It is best to have the patient face an unadorned wall or other neutral surface—not windows—to minimize distraction. Lighting should likewise be comfortable and illuminate the test materials without glare, to which some patients are especially sensitive.

To a much greater extent than in other settings, the availability of an alert, sensitive, and skilled psychometrist can dramatically enhance the success of testing services for inpatients. At its best, this role requires significant "people skills" in the form of kindness, patience, tact, firmness, availability, and negotiation, in addition to its formal proctoring and scoring functions. Depending on the arrangements within particular facilities, the psychometrist may need to escort the patient to and from the ward, communicate with line staff, log the progress of testing in the medical record, respond to questions or to signs of restlessness or fatigue, escort the patient to toilet breaks, sharpen pencils, assist the patient in consulting a dictionary, hang up clothing, offer minor incentives such as decaffeinated beverages, and in myriad other ways provide supervision and support throughout the testing process. An overview of inpatient assessment with the MMPI–2 is provided in Exhibit 9.1.

THE ASSESSMENT OF VALIDITY AND RESPONSE STYLE

It is beyond the scope of this chapter to review the various validity scales and measures of response style; these are covered in detail in standard sources (Friedman et al., 2001; Greene, 2000; Nichols, 2001). However, in varying degrees, these scales possess features with which the inpatient clinician should be familiar.

As a general caution, all of the scales within this category resist "cut-and-dried" interpretation. All need to be evaluated within the context set by the other scales in this group. Greene (2000) emphasizes the distinction between the consistency and the accuracy of item endorsement, a distinction that is observed here. Briefly, consistency and its measures—VRIN (Variable Response Inconsistency) and TRIN (True Response Inconsistency)—enable an estimate of the extent to which the MMPI–2 items have been read, understood, and responded to in terms of their content. These measures then address the most basic question of protocol validity, "Has the test been taken?" Assuming that their scores, in the context of other scales, are within acceptable ranges, these scales are not suited to judgments about the likely "fit" between the MMPI–2 results as a whole and the symptoms and personality of the patient who produced them. The latter judgments are best made with reference to scales reflecting various aspects of the patient's test-taking attitude (response style), especially as these scales relate to the overreporting versus the underreporting of symptoms and complaints. The scores on the latter scales best support inferences about the *accuracy* of the patient's MMPI–2 protocol in describing him or her.

Although Greene's (2000) distinction is certainly a valid one and an aid in the process of MMPI–2 interpretation, situations arise in practice that

EXHIBIT 9.1
Highlight: Points to Consider in Assessing Inpatients With the MMPI–2

- The nature of the inpatient setting, circumstances, and practical issues in the conduct of assessments need to be considered because the base rates of major mental disorders and their symptoms may differ radically from one setting to another.
- Most psychiatric inpatients are under involuntary commitment. They may view the procedures leading to commitment as illegitimate, as arbitrary and unfair or demeaning. It is common for patients to feel (realistically) disenfranchised and relatively powerless to enforce their will and preferences.
- Response attitudes are important to assess. Persons assessed often possess attitudes and dispositions that differ from clients being evaluated in outpatient and fee-for-service venues.
- An important feature of hospital assessments is the availability of medical records that include, ideally, an admission note, circumstances of admission, pertinent history, a mental status examination, a provisional diagnosis, a developmental and social history, and information about or from previous hospitalizations.
- Important situational factors can influence the assessment. Patients generally experience their first 10 days in hospital as quite "busy." Such concentrated adjustment demands often coincide with, if not stimulate, increased levels of stress. The decision to initiate psychological assessment is best postponed until after signs of a satisfactory preliminary adjustment to the ward environment are at hand.
- Another important issue bearing on the patient's adjustment to the hospital setting and therefore readiness to cooperate with psychological assessment is medication.
- The principles governing assessment in inpatient settings are generally consistent with those covering this process elsewhere. However, the successful administration of the MMPI–2 in psychiatric hospitals requires that the special circumstances of this population be taken into account.
- Assessment should be structured along the lines described in Finn's protocol for Therapeutic Assessment (see chap. 8, this volume), including a description of the purposes of the assessment (why it is being requested) and working with the patient to formulate questions of relevance to the patient.
- Extreme overreporting and underreporting in inpatient settings are relatively infrequent. A large majority of patients appear to report their symptoms and complaints accurately, even when no special efforts are made by the clinician to ensure such accuracy.
- The *F* scale may be elevated in psychiatric populations, more often than not in the range of T80 to T100 or more for code types 28/82, 68/86, 78/87. Such profiles can usually be interpreted to clinical advantage, as long as alertness to the possibility of exaggeration is maintained.
- Underreporting of symptoms does occur in some inpatients. Some investigators have called attention to an association between elevated *L* scores and paranoid phenomena; and, in inpatient settings, the five subscales of the *S* scale can provide information about the attitudes underlying elevations on both *K* and *S* scores.
- The MMPI–2 can be thought of as two inventories, one in which the item responses are encoded in ways that describe complex syndromal rubrics (diagnostically) and another that is more congenial to the patient's experience and outlook, that is, the content.
- The clinician's understanding of the clinical scales and their patterns may be augmented and clarified by scores on content-based scales. In fact, the validities of content scales are comparable to or better than those of the clinical scales. And, content and similar scales (e.g., Harris–Lingoes, PSYC–5, RC) may be even more useful with psychiatric inpatients than the clinical scales because they are viewed as a direct communication between the patient and clinician.

continued

EXHIBIT 9.1
(Continued)

- A number of special scales and indexes have been found to be valuable in clarifying patient symptoms and behaviors—for example, the Paranoid Defensiveness (Pdf) scale, the Schizophrenia Proneness (SzP) scale, and the Paranoia Factors (see Appendix 9.1).
- The types of mental disorders routinely encountered in psychiatric hospitals are notable more for their severity than for their variety. Several diagnostic types are encountered—for example, thought disorders: psychosis, schizophrenia, and delusional disorders; mood disorders: depression and mania; substance abuse disorder, typically with symptoms of psychosis; personality disorders; and severe anxiety disorders, including severe post-traumatic stress disorder.
- The first factor, general distress, is conveniently assessed by a large number of scales. While *A* is the best marker, it runs out of items at ~T80. Other useful markers include scales 7 (raw), *Mt,* Pk, Ps, NEGE, RCDem, and RC7, as well as the content scales ANX, OBS, DEP, LSE, WRK, and TRT.
- The second factor, undercontrol versus overcontrol, is importantly assessed by markers for its two dimensions, emotional and behavioral control. The two primary markers for these aspects are *R* and DISC. Other scales bearing on an assessment of control include scales 9, MAC–R, O–H, INTR, ANG, *D*2, AGGR, Pd2, ASP, ASP2, AAS, and *Re.*
- Suicidality is a routine component of psychodiagnostic assessment and is important given the high base rates for suicidal ideation, threats, and attempts, as well as the success with which suicides are occasionally completed in inpatient settings.
- While assaultiveness and violent behavior are low base rate phenomena even in psychiatric hospitals, a number of indicators of potential assault risk on the MMPI–2 can help to identify the kinds of circumstances under which risk may be elevated.
- Positive and negative indications of psychoticism, as well as delusional symptomatic trends, are assessed by reference to a variety of scales including Scale 8 and its Harris–Lingoes subscales, BIZ, BIZ1, BIZ2, PSYC, RC8, Scale 6, *Pa*1, and RC6.
- While Scale 2 and DEP are both sensitive to depression, Scale 2 is somewhat more reflective of depressive syndromes, whereas DEP better reflects the severity of dysphoric–depressed mood. Other aspects of depressive experience are assessed by reference to INTR, RC2, Scale 9, and Guilt.
- There are no highly specific indicators directly reflecting manic elation, euphoria, and grandiosity. However, the difference between scales 9 and 2 (9 – 2 > 20T) provides a rough index of these qualities. Among other related indicators are *Ma*3, *Ma*4, Si1, FRS, DEP2, LSE, SOD2, INTR, and RC2.
- Disorders of sleep are all but ubiquitous in inpatient settings, with psychiatric disorders serving as both a cause and an effect of sleep disturbance and in relation to both onset and relapse. Six items comprising the Lachar–Wrobel critical item set for sleep disturbance enable a specific description of the patient's complaints regarding sleep.
- Patients who have been prepared for assessment according to the principles of Therapeutic Assessment (Finn, 1996b) are usually eager to learn about their test results and their implications. Patients will have been assisted by the clinician to formulate questions for which the MMPI–2 can provide insight, and addressing these questions early helps capitalize on the therapeutic value that feedback sessions can provide.

can blur it somewhat. In one recent example, a female patient with Wechsler Adult Intelligence Scale—Third Edition (WAIS–III) signs of word-finding difficulty and poor working memory, as well as subjectively reported problems of mental confusion, produced a profile coded 3*2"7186'4+–0/95:, with VRIN = T86, a value that, according to the *Manual* (Butcher, Graham, et al., 2001), would render the profile invalid. Other scale scores included TRIN = T73*F*, *F* = T55, *F(B)* = T58, *Fp* = 41, *L* = 47, *K* = 54, and *S* = 52. True% was 37; and *?* (Cannot Say) was 19. Given these scores and the code, the profile is an extremely poor fit for random, all True, and all False response patterns. In this case, the psychologist, mindful of the limitations of the VRIN scale (see following), elected to interpret based upon the pattern of other scores and because the profile was highly consistent with the patient's stimulus value and self-presentation.

Note that extreme overreporting and underreporting in inpatient settings are relatively infrequent. Whether due to the distress of mental disorder or the distress that attends the disruptions of hospitalization, a large majority of patients appear to report their symptoms and complaints accurately, even when no special efforts are made by the clinician to ensure such accuracy.

Following are brief comments on each of the consistency and response style scales that may help to inform their interpretation in inpatient settings.

VRIN

The mean raw VRIN score for randomly generated MMPI–2 data is 16.75 (below T100), because of the relatively high proportion of asymmetrically scored item pairs (31; 46%). Unfortunately, this score is within a range readily achieved by a significant minority of psychiatric patients who have sought to read the items carefully and respond appropriately. Also, VRIN is most sensitive in the middle range of the True percent (True%–False%) balance. As T%–F% values move toward the extremes, VRIN loses sensitivity (but TRIN gains sensitivity).

Inpatients average slightly higher VRIN scores than normals and show slightly larger standard deviations, and these trends are even stronger among psychotic patients. Scores of T75 and below are generally unremarkable. Low VRIN scores, especially when *F* is high, raise the question of overreporting (Stukenberg, Brady, & Klinetob, 2000).

TRIN

See VRIN. TRIN is maximally sensitive to inconsistency at the extremes of the T%–F% balance.

F (Infrequency)

F is routinely elevated in psychiatric populations, more often than not in the range of T80 to T100 or more for code types 28/82, 68/86, 78/87 (see Greene, 2000). *F* contains a diversity of item content, including paranoid ideation, schizoid underinvolvement, impulsive and antisocial traits, physical symptoms, family enmity, and psychotic processes. The weight of the scale is in the direction of psychotic phenomena. It is considerably less sensitive to random responding than VRIN and TRIN.

In the MMPI environment, *F* was widely considered to elevate too readily, at least among inpatients. In the MMPI–2 environment, it elevates even more rapidly, especially among women. Scores above a raw score of 24 encroach on a range easily reached by random responding, and it may be parsimonious as a matter of practice to avoid interpretation in such cases. But raw scores in a range of 20 to 24 occur with sufficient frequency in valid profiles (as determined by VRIN and TRIN), and rates of true malingering are sufficiently low in (nonforensic) psychiatric hospitals that such profiles can usually be interpreted to clinical advantage, as long as alertness to the possibility of exaggeration is maintained.

***F(B)* (Back Infrequency)**

Like *F*, *F(B)* easily elevates into the T80 to T100 range for 28/82, 68/86, 78/87, and related code types (see Greene, 2000). Unlike *F*, its items are much more reflective of mood than thought disturbance, with content including panic–fear, depression–low self-esteem, suicide–self-harm, alcohol abuse, and family estrangement. Only three items are psychotic in content (3/40 = 7.5%) versus roughly five times as many such items on *F* (~25%). As a concrete illustration: *F(B)* shares three items with BIZ (Bizarre Mentations) but six with DEP (Depression; 15%), while *F* shares 10 items with BIZ (16.7%) but only three with DEP (5%). The two scales correlate at only ~.60 in the restandardization sample but considerably higher in psychiatric samples (~.85), presumably reflecting the greater coincidence of disturbed cognition and mood among persons hospitalized for the treatment of relatively severe mental disorders. Needless to say, the different content emphases of the two scales confounds the intent of *F* and *F(B)* to detect infrequent responding in their two respective halves of the item pool, with *F* being differentially sensitive to infrequent content reflecting thought disturbance and *F(B)* being differentially sensitive to infrequent content reflecting mood disturbance. The confounding of the placement—density of *F* and *F(B)* in different parts of the answer sheet with the content of these scales renders their straightforward interpretation problematic and, potentially, highly misleading. Following the guidelines in the MMPI–2 *Manual* (Butcher, Graham, et al., 2001) poses a significant risk for underinterpreting content scale scores, especially for patients with nonpsychotic mood disturbances, as the latter routinely show large *F(B)–F* differences.

Fp (Infrequency–Psychopathology)

Easily the most sensitive of the *F*-type scales to symptom exaggeration, *Fp* is impaired in both its scaling and its functioning by the inclusion of four *L* items (items more consistent with the denial than the admission of psychopathology!), and four items reflecting severe family enmity (*r* with FAM = .47). The endorsement of *either* subset of these items will elevate *Fp* to a level of T70 or greater. A patient wishing to both affirm moral virtue and admit family enmity, while endorsing no other *Fp* items, will achieve a score of ~T100. Thus, for *Fp* scores of T100 or less, it is always advisable to determine the extent to which these two groups of items have contributed to the elevation and to interpret (or not) accordingly. This task may be eased by referring to the *L* score; for example, when raw *L* = 0, obviously none of the *L* items have contributed to the *Fp* score.

L (Lie)

Among inpatient populations, claiming the kinds of improbable virtues that generate moderately high to very high elevations on *L* is less common than in some other settings. The pattern of *L* greater than *F*, *K*, and all of the clinical scales is associated, though not uniquely, with some defensive paranoid patients, more often than not schizophrenic. In such cases, it is often helpful to examine the endorsed content of *Pa*1 and/or RC6 for ego–syntonic delusional ideation and for other indicators that may betray occult thought disturbance such as BIZ1 > BIZ2 and *Sc*3 > *D*4. PSYC (Psychoticism) > NEGE (Negative Emotionality–Neuroticism) and, especially, Goldberg Index scores greater than 80 tend to produce few false positives for psychosis. Elevations on Scale 5 occur with some frequency among both men and women with this pattern and should be noted when they occur. Rather large FRS (Fears) > CYN (Cynicism) differences are also sometimes seen with this pattern, possibly consistent with the displacement of fears of other people onto phobic objects and situations.

Coyle and Heap (1965) and Fjordbak (1985), among others, have called attention to an association between elevated *L* scores and paranoid phenomena and, in inpatient settings, profiles similar to the one given in Table 9.1 tend to be produced disproportionately by patients who, sooner or later, manifest prominent paranoid features. See the later discussion of the Paranoid Defensiveness scale.

TABLE 9.1
Profile Example

F	*L*	*K*	1	2	3	4	5	6	7	8	9	0
47	71	60	53	51	54	52	49	51	49	50	49	46

K (Correction)

In psychiatric populations, *K* scores tend to fall in a range of T40 to T50 about twice as often as in all other ranges combined, and scores below T40 are not rare. Such scores are, of course, to be expected given the lower socioeconomic and educational level of inpatients, at least in state psychiatric hospitals. Scores above T60 are uncommon, however, and may warrant more detailed investigation in relation to other scales (see Nichols, 2001). Such elevations are usually the result of an underreporting set ($L > K$, $K > Es$ [Ego Strength]). In evaluating scores on the *K*-corrected clinical scales, especially scales 7 and 8, it is important to be mindful of the relative proportions of *K* and clinical scale items in terms of the contribution of each to the total scale score. The patient who attains a raw score of 44 on Scale 8, half of which traces to a raw score of 22 on *K*, is likely to present very differently in terms of overall adjustment and manifest symptomatology from one with the identical Scale 8 raw score but who has endorsed only half as many *K* items.

S (Superlative Self-Presentation)

Given its high correlation with *K* in psychiatric populations (r = ~.88), *S* offers little nonredundant information over *K* (although a recent report by Archer, Handel, & Couvadelli, 2004, is encouraging). However, the five subscales of *S* can provide information about the attitudes underlying both *K* and *S* scores.

Accurate and straightforward interpretation of the MMPI–2 is occasionally compromised by biased response styles in inpatient settings. When the particular response bias is taken into account, however, the test may still yield valuable data. The following example describes a patient whose MMPI–2 was subject to a pronounced bias. While easily identified by the validity scales, the resulting clinical profile was very uncharacteristic of the patient's final diagnosis. Despite posing some challenges for interpretation, careful analysis of the clinical scales produced information that was most helpful in the description and diagnosis of the patient's difficulties.

Case Example 1

Sandra M., 42, was brought to the hospital Emergency by a mobile community mental health outreach team late in November and admitted to Inpatient Psychiatry. The outreach team had gone out to visit Sandra in response to an anonymous call expressing concern about her living in her car. Admission documentation noted Sandra's report that she had been staying in her car for 3 or 4 days with her dog, after being evicted by her roommate. Though initially reluctant to come to the hospital, she was persuaded by the outreach workers to submit to a review of her medications. Sandra had a previous psychiatric history involving several hospitalizations, the most recent in January of the previous year. Her discharge summary noted that she had been admitted in an agitated and manic state, with psychotic symptoms including flight of ideas, auditory hallucinations, and grandiose delusions that she had caused a recent snowfall. She was preoccupied with some ongoing litigation against a former employer for harassment, and there was a suggestion that persecutory ideation was involved in her perception of this. Sandra was described as angry, insightless regarding her difficulties, and noncompliant with treatment. She was diagnosed with bipolar I disorder, anorexia nervosa, and alcohol abuse; and diagnoses from prior hospitalizations were also noted to include cyclothymia and posttraumatic stress disorder (PTSD).

Sandra was most cooperative with the assessment. During the interview, she was pleasant and engaging, inordinately upbeat, effusive, and loquacious. She described concerns about a number of past experiences of abuse and persecution. One of these involved being abducted, as part of a "hazing ritual," by men impersonating police and firefighters, whom she suspected of sexually abusing her while unconscious. She was also concerned about being followed and spied upon by people working for the former employer mentioned previously. Regarding her previous admission, she complained of being "beaten and tortured" while in the hospital. Most recently, Sandra reported being harassed by her roommate. She described this harassment as involving his using homemade electrical devices that worked in conjunction with the metal frame of her bed to deliver electric shocks by remote control to her breasts, conducted through the underwires in her brassiere. In reference to this, she had nicknamed him her "home electrocutor."

Results of the MMPI–2 were coded *56+–9/24:80 137# L+–/K:*. Determining test validity, first, Sandra attended carefully and responded consistently to test items (raw VRIN = 4), with no indications of a "yea-saying," or "nay-saying" bias (T% = 43; TRIN = 10T) or of indiscriminate responding such as may result from reading difficulties, confusion, or carelessness. *L* (T66) was moderately high, suggesting a need to create a favorable impression by putting on a good front through unrealistically denying minor, common human faults and failings out of concern about being negatively evaluated by others. Similarly scoring individuals tend to be morally rigid, naïve, and lacking in insight to the point of being unaware of how they are perceived by others. Under these circumstances, some attenuation of the clinical profile is expected.

Regarding underreporting, *F–K* (–6) does not confirm bias. Neither does *K–Es* (–6) suggest that subjectively perceived adjustment is higher than a more objective estimate. *F* (T75), on the other hand, is only moderately elevated. While this does reflect Sandra's acknowledgment of psychopathology, when psychotic patients fall within this range (T59 to T80), it suggests a degree of intactness that is clearly lacking. When the clinical scales are viewed in the context of the validity scale data and clinical presentation, it appears that the profile has been subject to selective minimization, although there remain elevations that appear clearly relevant, given what is already known of the case.

Scale 6 elevations in the moderate range, as seen here (T67), suggest paranoid symptoms including guardedness, suspiciousness, fearful concern about the malevolent motives of others, and litigiousness, among other attributes. At this level of elevation, a significant minority of inpatients exhibit impaired judgment and disordered thinking, usually involving delusions of reference and persecution. Confirming evidence that her thinking was delusional is found in her elevations on *Pa*1 (T81), PSYC (T78), RC6 (T79), BIZ (T76), and BIZ1 (T120). Further support of delusional ideation came from her elevations on paranoia factors representing her ego–syntonic endorsement of Paranoid Resentment (T74) and Delusions of Control (T120). Support for the view that the severity of Sandra's disturbance falls in the psychotic range is evident from the elevation of PSYC (T78) over NEGE (T45) and BIZ1 (T120) over BIZ2 (T41).

Diagnostically, the MMPI–2 data, to this point, substantiate a psychotic disturbance involving delusional, paranoid thinking. A number of aspects of the data converge to suggest a possible delusional disorder, persecutory type, including the elevations on Scale 6, PSYC, *L* and CYN (T67), as well as the 5–6/6–5 code type, all of which are quite typical. This diagnostic picture, however, is complicated by other features of the profile.

There is an elevation on the MacAndrew Alcoholism—Revised (MAC–R; T75), which is usually interpreted as relating to the presence, history, or potential for alcohol abuse. The Addiction Acknowledgment Scale (AAS; T39; raw = 0) suggests that, if alcohol abuse is an issue, she is either not exhibiting or not acknowledging current abuse or problem consequences attending abuse. Alternatively, the combination of scores on MAC–R and AAS may suggest that MAC–R is a false positive for alcohol abuse. MAC–R is a controversial scale that is more prone to be false positive with certain profiles—those dominated by Scale 9 among them. Further support may be inferred from APS (Addiction Potential Scale), a subtle scale for substance abuse, that (at T30) does not suggest abuse here. If not indicative of alcohol abuse, the interpretation of MAC–R may better be limited to suggesting an energetic, assertive, extroverted, uninhibited, rebellious individual who may be impulsive, aggressive, and resentful of authority. This description accords with the clinical picture and begins to better capture the interpersonal and affective flavor of the case that the scales related to paranoia and thought disturbance failed to touch on.

Further to Sandra's affect, the low Scale 7 (T30) is an unusual finding, suggesting an unstable individual probably manifesting obvious signs of disturbance, particularly of mania (*Ma* [Hypomania]–*Pt* [Psychasthenia] = T29). Viewed in conjunction with the relative elevation of Scale 9 (T59) over Scale 2 (T46), as well as the low scores on Scale 0 (T37) and LSE (Low Self-Esteem; T35), there is mounting support, despite RC9 being a miss (T49), for affective experiences characterized by buoyancy, if not elation, inflated self-regard, turbulent instability, and proneness to agitation. Taking these additional profile features into consideration, rather than a delusional disorder, diagnoses better fitting the data include bipolar I disorder, manic type with psychotic (paranoid) features, or possibly schizoaffective disorder, bipolar type.

It was a matter of concern that Sandra was so undistressed, which aroused a paternalistic desire to protect her from herself. The plethora of scores related to paranoid thinking and emotional instability suggests an individual who is likely to respond with inappropriate reactivity to misperceived or imagined threats. The low scores on Scale 7 and A (Welsh Anxiety; T42), however, suggest the lack of a normal, healthy degree of worry. Together, the data portray a woman who is activated by and inappropriately responsive to misperceptions of risk, yet lacks sufficient anxiety to be appropriately responsive to real risks, such as the consequences that may be occasioned by her own poor judgment. Her lack of awareness of the danger of sleeping in her car in freezing temperatures serves as a good illustration.

That Sandra's apparent lack of regard aroused said paternalistic reaction is, in itself, interesting—perhaps a reflection of implicitly held gender stereotypes. From a perspective of traditional gender roles, it is not "acting like a lady" to react to an intolerable situation (imagined or real) by walking out, "going it alone," and braving the elements. This behavior would seem less unusual for a stereotypically masculine male. Scales related to gender identity reflect her denial of stereotypically feminine identity roles (Mf6 = T43; Scale 5 = T67) and endorsement of stereotypically masculine (Mf1 = 23; GM [Gender Masculine] = T67) attributes of self-confidence, independence, forthrightness, with less tendency to be inhibited by fears, worries, or self-consciousness. Sandra's behavior reflected bad judgment, regardless of gender. That said, however, because she is a woman and her choices were not "ladylike," there was a tendency to overpathologize as symptomatic of some behavior that was substantially influenced by character–identity.

CONFIGURATIONS OF OVERREPORTING AND UNDERREPORTING SCALES

Discussion of the various configurations the so-called validity scales may assume are not undertaken here. An especially useful compendium of *L*, *F*, and *K* patterns is available in Friedman et al. (2001), and detailed information about these and related scales is also available in Greene (2000) and Nichols (2001), among others.

The most common configuration of *L*, *F*, and *K* in inpatient settings is *F* > *L* > *K*, typically with *F* 15 or more T scores greater than *L* and *K*. Indeed, so frequent is this pattern in such settings that marked variations from it, for example, either *L* or *K* > *F*, generally warrant special attention before interpretation proceeds. In particular, depending on other case data, profiles in which *L* or *K* exceed *F* raise the question of ego–syntonic delusional ideation. That is, some patients with this pattern endorse items of obviously delusional content despite a firm set to underreport psychopathology because the pathological nature of such content is transparent to them. Delusions of persecution or control are most common in this context, but the relevant item endorsements are often numerically insufficient to move scales dense with such content (e.g., *Pa*1, RC6) into a position of prominence in the profile. For this reason, it is advisable in such cases to review individual item responses. A set of small factor analytically derived scales, the Paranoia Factors, featuring content for Resentment, Ideas of Reference, Delusions of Control, and Persecutory Ideas/Delusions, is presented in Appendix 9.1, along with their restandardization norms, for this purpose (Nichols & Greene, 2004a).

APPROACHES TO INTERPRETATION: EMPIRICAL–ACTUARIAL VERSUS SELF-REPORT

Meehl's arguments favoring actuarial prediction (1954) and his call for "a good cookbook" (1956) solidified the code-type approach to MMPI interpretation that had already been set in place by Gough (1946) and Hathaway and Meehl (1951a, 1951b), and gave rise to the seminal codebooks by Gilberstadt and Duker (1965) and Marks and Seeman (1963). This emphasis on actuarial bootstrapping sent the importance of MMPI item content, strongly de-emphasized since Meehl's spirited defense of the method of contrasted groups (1945), into virtual eclipse. This situation remained largely in force for nearly 30 years, until the Harris–Lingoes subscales (1955, 1968) and Wiggins (1969) content scales became widely disseminated. The first major attempt to bring the actuarial and content approaches into a coherent theoretical relationship to one another came with Leary's (1956, 1957) interpersonal diagnostic scheme, in which he proposed several levels of measurement. The data from the MMPI clinical scales he categorized as Level I. He conceived data at this level as objective and public, as the overt pressure or impact that the person's interpersonal behavior exerts on others (e.g., the examining psychiatrist), whether in the form of habitual attitudes and preoccupations, traits of character, symptoms, or complaints, that is, the person's social "stimulus value." By contrast, Leary's Level II comprised data reflecting the person's conscious description of self, his or her self-perceptions in terms of traits, behavior, symptoms, and relations with others, that is, the person's phenomenological field. Wiggins' (1969) development of a set of face-valid scales representing the test's major content dimensions clearly advanced the goal of acquiring Level II data through the MMPI.

At this point, any interpretive strategy that does not seek to integrate findings from both actuarially based (the standard clinical scales, other actuarially derived scales such as *Es*, MAC–R, O–H [Overcontrolled Hostility], etc.) and content-based scales (Harris–Lingoes subscales, the MMPI–2 content and component scales, the PSY–5 [Personality Psychopathology Five] scales, factor scales, critical items lists, etc.) is seen to risk significant interpretive error and therefore to fall below a reasonable standard of practice. The strategy of combining and coordinating these two approaches encourages the scales of each kind to be considered within the context set by the scales of the other type. In a limited sense, the MMPI–2 can be thought of as two inventories, one in which the item responses are encoded in ways that are congenial to the complex syndromal rubrics on which the psychopathologically informed clinician relies to perform psychodiagnostic functions, and another that is more congenial to the patient's experience and outlook and allows the latter to be conveyed to the clinician more directly without being "filtered through the strategy of contrasted groups" (Wiggins, 1969, p. 130).

As multivariate models of their respective clinical syndromes, most of the MMPI–2 clinical scales (2, 3, 4, 6, 8, and 9) may be seen to function in ways that are analogous to sets of diagnostic criteria such as those published in the *Diagnostic and Statistical Manual of Mental Disorders* (*DSM*; American Psychiatric Association [APA], 1952), wherein observable differences between patients who may meet the criteria for a given diagnostic category are not required to do so in the same way. We do not here seek, by the way, to stretch the MMPI–*DSM* analogy inappropriately nor to overly stress it but merely to offer a context within which the character of these scales may be better appreciated. In both cases, differences in symptoms, traits, history, and so on, are recognized and codified into a polythetic system of classification that can be seen to strive for a reasonable balance between the goals of adequate intragroup homogeneity to support diagnostic reliability, and adequate coverage such that patients deemed appropriate for classification within a given category can be so classified, despite their differences. Like the *DSM* criteria lists, the MMPI–2 clinical scales contain diverse elements of content indexing aspects of mood, cognition, and behavior that combine with each other in ways intended to model, more or less uniquely, the syndromes that they characterize, even as they allow for such aspects to manifest themselves in different strengths and forms within syndromes, and for similar aspects to be recognized across syndromes. In the case of the MMPI–2, of course, this latter feature is manifested in the fact of shared variances and overlapping items between scales.

A few brief examples may illustrate how the clinician's understanding of the clinical scales and their patterns may be augmented and clarified by scores on content-based scales. Because the Harris–Lingoes scales are, by definition, highly redundant with their parent clinical scales, we focus on the MMPI–2 content scales in these examples, acknowledging that the Harris–Lingoes and PSY–5 scales could be used to illustrate similar points. Indeed, the MMPI–2 clinician will be accustomed to using all three sets of content-based scales in this fashion routinely.

For some code types, such as those coded 273 and combinations, both anxiety and depression are strong correlates; but without reference to ANX (Anxiety) and DEP, it can be difficult to determine which of these may predominate in the individual case.

Scale 7, which has no subscales, carries implications of both anxiety and obsessiveness. It shares six and five items with ANX and OBS (Obsessional Thinking), respectively. Thus, reference to the relative elevations on the latter scales may assist the clinician in understanding the trend of responses to the Scale 7 items. Similarly, Scale 8 contains very few items of psychotic content but does share eight items with BIZ (six on BIZ2). Two of its subscales (*Sc*2 and *Sc*4) are depressively toned.

Finally, some of the clinical scales may raise questions of fears/phobias (scales 1, 7, 8) and anger (scales 4, 6, 8), which may be resolved to some extent with reference to FRS and ANG (Anger).

Accumulated experience dating back at least 30 years (Payne & Wiggins, 1972) has shown that the validities of content scales, considered as a group, are comparable to those of the clinical scales and occasionally may be better. Although valuable in most settings in which the MMPI–2 is used, content and similar scales (e.g., Harris–Lingoes, PSYC–5, the new RC Scales) may be even more useful with psychiatric inpatients, who often have at least some difficulty in the coherent verbal articulation of their symptoms and complaints and who tend, as a group, to be fairly candid in their approach to the MMPI–2. For these reasons, the analysis of content scale scores should always figure in the task of MMPI–2 interpretation in these settings.

CLINICAL SCALES AND CODE TYPES

The basic literature (e.g., textbooks, guides, manuals) of the MMPI–2 is replete with descriptions of the standard clinical scales and their empirical correlates, and these are not reviewed here. Nevertheless, because there are some regularities in the implications for elevations on these scales in inpatient populations, we comment briefly on these if only to make the reader more sensitive to instances in which the scales in this setting do not behave as expected.

Scale 1

In inpatient facilities, *Hs*, like HEA and RC1, appears to function simply as a broad measure of somatization. Elevations are more commonly associated with unusual somatic beliefs, including somatic delusions, than in most other settings.

Scale 2

Scale 2 appears to function largely as it does elsewhere. In code types dominated by Scale 2 (2, 23, 27, 278, etc.), when Scale 9 or, less frequently, Scale 6 elevates moderately, the depression may present with atypically high tension, instability, or motor involvement in the form of agitation.

Scale 3

In inpatient settings, *Hy* (Hysteria) is routinely driven by its depressive and somatic components, *Hy*3 and *Hy*4, respectively; it is unusual for *Hy*1, *Hy*2, and/or *Hy*5 to participate strongly in Scale 3 elevations. When the latter subscales do so participate in profiles dominated by elevations on scales 4, 6, 8, and/or 9 (e.g., 463, 483, 493, etc.), some of the features of the primary code (e.g., hostility, alienation, impulsiveness, respectively) may be attenuated, softened, socialized, or suppressed.

Scale 4

Scale 4 appears to function largely as it does elsewhere. However, Pd1, Pd4, and Pd5 most commonly contribute to elevations; Pd3 does so rarely. Pd2 tends to have fewer malignant–psychopathic connotations than in other settings, often reflecting the kinds of rule breaking that result from deficits in socialization and social incompetence rather than more ingrained or consolidated antisocial dispositions. The same is true of ASP2 (Antisocial Behavior). The items on both reference minor and predominantly juvenile infractions rather than mature antisocial conduct.

Scale 5

Extreme scores are even more unusual for both men and women in inpatient than they are in other settings, presumably because of the lower than average level of educational attainment for most psychiatric inpatients, at least in state hospitals. Scores are usually driven more by the mild neuroticism than by the gender-related interest items. Responses to the latter kinds of items, only about half of the total scale, often are mixed and overinclusive, suggesting identity diffusion or a pessimistic–anhedonic denial of interest in gender-related pastimes and occupations.

Scale 6

Scores of T60 and above should not be overlooked. In inpatient settings, scores on *Pa* (Paranoia) are much more likely to be driven by *Pa*1, especially, and *Pa*2 than by *Pa*3. Although *Pa*3 has implications closely related to the paranoia construct in terms of moral rigidity, self-righteousness, and covertly punitive attitudes, its function in terms of Scale 6 as a whole appears to be one of preventing false negatives for paranoid trends for such code types as 34/43, 36/63, 37/73 or, more generally, when *L* or *K* exceeds *F*. However, the keying of *Pa*3 items (implying trust, confidence, and a lack of cynicism regarding others) may lead to an underestimate of the strength of paranoid trends on the basis of total *Pa* scores among (most) psychiatric patients. Profiles in which *F* exceeds both *L* and *K* are typically associated with suppressed scores on *Pa*3, reducing the total score on Scale 6. Thus, profiles coded 28/82, 48/84, 58/85, 78/87, and 89/98 are almost always more "paranoid" in one way or another than the level of Scale 6 would suggest.

Scale 7

Scale 7 appears to function largely as it does elsewhere.

Scale 8

Scale 8 tends to elevate prolifically in inpatient settings because of family alienation (*Sc*1), severe general alienation (*Sc*1), depressively related pessimism or indifference (*Sc*2), cognitive disruption (*Sc*3), depressively related amotivation (*Sc*4), impulse–emotional undercontrol as seen in both schizophrenia and mania (*Sc*5), and neurologically oriented somatization, also with implications of undercontrol (*Sc*6). Scale 8 is substantially more sensitive to schizophrenia when this disorder is manifested primarily through negative symptoms, in part because it contains so little manifest psychotic content (no more than 15% of items). Elevations suggest schizophrenia most strongly when driven by *Sc*1 and *Sc*3, depression most strongly when driven by *Sc*2 and *Sc*4, and mania most strongly when driven by *Sc*5 and *Sc*6. However, no pattern of subscale scores is known to be inconsistent with any of the latter three disorders. Scale 8 is also routinely elevated in personality disorders unstable enough to require hospitalization, for example, some borderline personality disorders, and in severe substance abuse–toxic conditions such as amphetamine or phenclydine psychosis. McFall, Moore, Kivlahan, and Capestany (1988) found higher scores on *Sc6* and lower scores on *Sc4* among male veteran inpatients with psychotic symptoms and diagnoses as compared to an age-matched sample of outpatients without such characteristics. These findings suggest a crude index for psychoticism in evaluating Scale 8 elevations: *Sc6* – *Sc4*, with positive values suggesting a psychotic basis for such elevations and negative values suggesting depression, anxiety, substance abuse, or personality disorder.

In contrast to Scale 8, RC8 is highly saturated with nonparanoid psychotic content, and thus may be usefully contrasted with Scale 8 to detect a psychotic basis for elevations on the latter scale. In general, when RC8 – Scale 8 is positive, the implications for an active psychotic disorder, usually schizophrenia or disorganized mania, are substantially stronger than when this difference is negative.

Scale 9

Scale 9 appears to function largely as it does elsewhere, but elevations often do not seem well correlated with the severity of symptomatology. That is, some patients can appear severely inflated, hyperactive, and intrusive at relatively low scores (~T70), while others can appear distinctly subdued relative to the former group despite having much higher scores (T90). Distinctly low scores (e.g., at or below T40) in inpatient settings are likely to connote depression, especially unipolar depression, and psychomotor retardation rather than a mere lack of energy, even in the absence of major elevations on Scale 2, DEP, RC2, and so on. There is some clinical lore, inadequately confirmed to this point, that relatively sudden increases in depressed Scale 9 scores in the course of treatment may foreshadow a heightened risk of suicide, suggesting a need for the cautious review of pass requests when this sign is found.

Scale 0

Appearing to function largely as it does elsewhere, Scale 0 tends to be more highly (negatively) correlated with Scale 9 among inpatients than in the restandardization sample. Mood state may often distort the usual trait implications of Scale 0 scores, with Scale 9 pushing scores in a more extroverted direction and Scale 2 pushing them into a range indicating introversion. As a consequence, Scale 0 scores in the context of elevated or depressed mood may vary considerably from those obtained when the patient is tested in a euthymic state.

Scale 0 is contaminated with neuroticism variance, primarily contained in Si3, and is overly sensitive to situational or state effects, social withdrawal, for example. SOD (Social Discomfort) is considerably less contaminated with this variance and may therefore provide a more accurate and stable measure of introversion–extroversion than Scale 0.

The code-type approach to MMPI/MMPI–2 interpretation developed quite rapidly following initial publication of the MMPI. Gough (1946), Guthrie (1949), and Hathaway and Meehl (1951b, from a review of the cases presented in their 1951a) were quick to appreciate that important clinical correlates, some novel, could be gleaned from the two highest clinical scales. As noted earlier, this approach received a substantial boost in 1956 with Meehl's call for "a good cookbook," a call answered in the detailed codebooks of Gilberstadt and Duker (1965) and Marks and Seeman (1963). The data from both books were gathered within inpatient psychiatric facilities. Both are now quite dated, particularly with respect to their diagnostic correlates. The diagnostic guidelines of the time were based on the brief impressionistic criteria of *DSM–I* (APA, 1952), and diagnoses were often determined by psychiatric residents in training. Nevertheless, both books remain highly useful for orienting the MMPI–2 clinician to some of the more common code patterns and a variety of historical ratings and Q-statement correlates. Unfortunately, no similar compendium of code types for inpatients has yet appeared for the MMPI–2. The reader should be aware of the recent extensive report of outpatient MMPI–2 correlates by Graham, Ben-Porath, and McNulty (1999) and discussed by Greene in chapter 10 of this volume.

ANALYSIS OF CONTENT

The items of scales based on relatively homogeneous item content may reside in very different areas within the item pool as represented on the standard answer sheet. For example, the items of the MMPI–2 content scales are heavily concentrated among the last 197 items of the inventory, including half or more of the items appearing on FRS, OBS, ANG, TPA (Type A Personality), LSE, and TRT (Negative Treatment). Only HEA, BIZ, CYN, ASP, and SOD have as many as two-thirds of their items appearing before item 371. The PSY–5 scale items are in an intermediate position, with 34% of their items appearing after item 371. The items of the RC scales, including RCDem, are mostly drawn from the same area as for the standard clinical scales and *L*, *F*, and *K*, with only about 20% of items appearing after item 371. The location of items can be important because the effects of fatigue may render the patient less attentive to their content or lead to the patient's adopting a strategy of overendorsing or underendorsing pathological content in order to complete the test more quickly. Unfortunately, scores on VRIN, TRIN, *F*, and *F(B)* are not entirely reliable for detecting such trends when they occur.

The high face validity of the content (and similar) scales renders them considerably more vulnerable to the effects of extreme response styles, whether underreporting or overreporting, than are the clinical scales. For example, in clinical samples, *K* (and *S*, negative values for *F–K*, etc.) shows a negative relationship with all of the content scales (r = –.50 or higher, and for OBS, ANG, CYN, and TPA, at –.75 or higher). Just as content scale scores are readily suppressed by *K*, so are they prone to inflation by elevations on *F* (and *F – K*, etc.), especially DEP, BIZ, LSE, WRK (Negative Work Attitude), and TRT (r = .70 or higher).

A related problem when it comes to interpreting content scale scores, whether suppressed, inflated, or neither, is their extensive covariation. For example, ANX, OBS, DEP, LSE, WRK, are TRT all intercorrelated at .75 or higher in psychiatric samples because of unusually high levels of nonspecific variance. Correlations with A, the usual marker for such nonspecific (or First Factor) variance, exceed .50 for all of the content scales and, for ANX, OBS, DEP, LSE, WRK, and TRT, exceed .85 in such samples.

The extent of their covariance makes it difficult for the clinician to use these scales to help address questions regarding symptoms that may be commingled in various strengths, such as those reflected in ANX, OBS, DEP, and LSE. It is unusual to find dramatic differences in elevation among these scales. When such differences do occur, however, it can still be difficult to interpret them with confidence. Do such differences indicate clinically significant differences in the strength of, say, anxiety versus depression? Or do they merely reflect normal variation around a baseline determined by the strength of the First Factor? It may be helpful to apply the following rules of thumb in the interpretation of these six scales: First, requiring the scale to exceed A by a certain amount, say 10 T scores, increases the likelihood that the observed elevation, on ANX, for example, reflects that portion of the scale's variance that is uniquely related to anxiety rather than the nonspecific, generalized, discomfort that is common to OBS, DEP, and so on, as well as to ANX. Second, for scales that exceed the level set by the A "index," it is advisable to require relatively large differences in elevation before attempting the differential characterization of symptoms. For example, take a profile in which A = T63, ANX = T75, and DEP = T73. Although the scores on ANX and DEP exceed that on A by an amount that symptoms of anxiety and depression, as opposed to some less differentiated state of discomfort or malaise, are present, little can be said with confidence about their relative strength. However, if, on the other hand, A = T63, ANX = T73, and DEP = T83, the clinician would seem justified in speaking much more confidently about depression as a defining symptomatic feature.

Regarding the MMPI–2 content scales in inpatient settings, ANX, OBS, DEP, HEA, ANG, CYN, LSE, SOD, FAM, and WRK appear to function largely as they do elsewhere. Nevertheless, a few features relevant to their use in inpatient settings may be briefly noted: OBS scores are often suppressed by scales 3 and 4. DEP scores are often suppressed by Scale 3 in combination with Scale 9. Regarding HEA, note the association between HEA2 and *Sc*6. ANG scores are often suppressed by Scale 3; it is somewhat unusual for ANG1 and ANG2 to differ by more than 10 T scores. ANG1 reflects pressures toward impulsive expression at least as much as by anger per se; ANG2 is associated with higher levels of distress than ANG1. CYN scores are often suppressed by Scale 3 when in combination with Scale 4 or Scale 6; it is somewhat unusual for CYN1 and CYN2 to differ by more than 10 T scores. LSE scores are often suppressed by Scale 3 when in combination with scales 4, 9, or 6; LSE1 typically exceeds LSE2 and tends to follow scores on DEP and SOD1. SOD tends to be prominent in the 27, 28, 278, and related code types. SOD1 usually exceeds SOD2 in psychiatric populations and tends to follow scores on LSE1. SOD is less contaminated with neuroticism than Scale 0 and is therefore a somewhat purer measure of introversion–extroversion. FAM tends to be elevated in profiles in which combinations of scales 4, 8, and 2 are prominent; FAM2 usually exceeds FAM1 in psychiatric populations. WRK scores are often suppressed by Scale 3 in combination with Scale 4 or Scale 9 and are pushed up by elevations on scales 2, 6, 7, and 8 and their combinations.

FRS (Fears)

Elevations on FRS2 are relatively uncommon in inpatient settings. FRS1 is commonly elevated and more so in conditions manifesting psychosis than in nonpsychotic states. Most of these items reference vague, nebulous, intangible (empty, dark) situations that allow for the projection of psychotically inspired fears as onto a blank slate. FRS and its component scales are often not elevated by specific fears and phobias; where these are suspected, the items comprising these scales may reveal patterns that are concealed by scale scores. Unusually low scores relative to the other content scales are often associated with fearlessness and recklessness among inpatients.

BIZ (Bizarre Mentation)

Scales 6 and 8 push up BIZ scores in inpatient settings, as elsewhere, and tend to push up BIZ1 relative to BIZ2. BIZ2 is associated with higher levels of distress than BIZ1.

ASP (Antisocial Personality)

Scores on ASP2 often exceed scores on ASP1 by 5 T or more among inpatients, possibly because of histories of minor delinquency, due in most cases to social immaturity rather than to antisocial–psychopathic features. See Scale 4, already discussed. Scores on ASP1 are often differentially suppressed by Scale 3 in combination with Scale 4, relative to scores on ASP2.

TPA (Type A Personality)

Essentially a measure of hostility in inpatient settings, TPA appears to function otherwise largely as it does elsewhere. Scores are often suppressed by Scale 3 in combination with scales 4, 9, or 6. TPA1 is associated with higher levels of distress than TPA2.

TRT (Negative Treatment Indicators)

Not useful among psychiatric inpatients, TRT tends to follow scores on DEP and WRK. TRT1 exceeds TRT2 in the vast majority of cases, not infrequently by as much as 20 T or more. It is rather unusual for TRT2 scores to exceed T60. TRT1 tends to follow DEP and LSE1.

Special Scales

Paranoid Defensiveness (Pdf)

In his description of the development of Scale 6, Hathaway (2000), noted that its "cross-validation was always disappointing, and the published scale was considered weak, although it was the best that could be developed. One factor that seemed to justify at least temporary use of the scale was that there were few false positives" (pp. 54–55). The weakness to which Hathaway refers, then, regards the problem of false negatives. This was the problem addressed in a doctoral dissertation by Holroyd (1964; see also Tellegen, 1964). The Pdf scale was devised with unusual care to discriminate defensive paranoid patients from nonparanoid patients. Holroyd's paranoid patients all produced profiles with Scale 6 less than T65, *F* less than T70, seven of scales 1 to 9 less than T70, and *?* (Cannot Say) less than 20.

Now nearly 40 years old, Pdf has not been widely adopted. Nevertheless, on occasion we have found it highly useful in identifying paranoid patients who produced unelevated profiles and were able to avoid identification on interview. Scores greater than T60 should raise the question of paranoid defensiveness in profiles in which Scale 6 does not exceed T62, no more than two clinical scales exceed T65, and *F* and *K* are less than

T65. As Pdf scores reach T65, paranoid defensiveness may be strongly suspected. Note that these guidelines are intended for psychiatric inpatient settings only. Their application in settings with higher base rates for elevated *L* and *K* scores, within normal limit (WNL) profiles, and lower base rates for severe paranoid disorders, such as employment screening, will result in a very high false positive rate. The Pdf scoring key, with norms for the Minnesota Restandardization Sample, is presented in the appendix to this chapter.

Superlative Self-Presentation (S) Subscales

This set of five subscales for *S* (Butcher & Han, 1995)—Belief in Human Goodness (14 items), Serenity (13), Contentment With Life (8), Patience and Denial of Irritability and Anger (8), and Denial of Moral Flaws (5)—affords a convenient way of assessing the kinds of content that have been endorsed on *S* and, to some extent, *K*.

Schizophrenia Proneness (SzP)

This new scale developed by Bolinskey and colleagues (Bolinskey et al., 2001; Bolinskey, Gottesman, & Nichols, 2003) has shown promise for identifying high-risk subjects who later manifested schizophrenia-related psychoses. Further research is needed to establish the scale's performance in psychiatric inpatient settings, including its ability to identify patients manifesting current signs and symptoms of schizophrenia or cluster A personality disorders (presumably high scores) or, alternatively, patients who have reduced or low liability for developing schizophrenia spectrum disorders (low scores); it is hoped that such research will be forthcoming.

Guilt

The Guilt scale is a set of seven face-valid items. Like all such scales, it is subject to overreporting and underreporting. The scale enables the relatively uncluttered measurement of guilty feelings and sentiments and has proven helpful in the assessment and discrimination of depressive and anxiety disorders. Guilt overlaps Pd5, DEP3, and NEGE by three items each. The Guilt scoring key, with norms for the Minnesota Restandardization Sample, is presented in the appendix to this chapter.

Paranoia Factors

Nichols (2001) noted that one of the Scale 6 subscales, *Pa*1, contains a number of subthemes in its item content. To test this hunch, a set of 24 items, including all of those on *Pa*1, were subjected to factor analysis with Varimax rotation in a sample of 52,543 psychiatric patients. A four-factor solution was retained, with the factors identified as Resentment (six items), Ideas of Reference (six), Delusions of Control (eight), and Persecutory Ideas–Delusions (eight), with minimal overlap. Scoring keys for these four paranoia factors, with norms for the Minnesota Restandardization Sample, are presented in the appendix to this chapter.

MAJOR MENTAL DISORDERS IN INPATIENT POPULATIONS

Given the criteria for involuntary civil commitment, the types of mental disorders routinely encountered in psychiatric hospitals are notable more for their severity than for their variety. Nevertheless, considerable variety exists within each of the diagnostic categories most common to such settings, enough to require discussion in this chapter to be limited to those most likely to be seen by the psychologist specializing in the assessment of personality and general psychopathology. Not addressed, therefore, are myriad disorders that, although they may present with predominantly psychiatric symptomatology, are more appropriately considered within the domain of neurology. These include psychiatric manifestations of Huntington's disease, Alzheimer's disease, multiple sclerosis, traumatic brain injuries, psychiatric excrescences of epilepsy, Parkinson's disease, Tourette's syndrome, and similar conditions. We do not, of course, maintain that personality assessment has no role in the understanding and management of such conditions, only that this role lies outside the concerns of the present chapter. In this section, we describe the most common and representative mental disorders found in inpatient settings in relation to their typical MMPI–2 test patterns and try to highlight the strengths as well as the weaknesses of the MMPI–2 as a potential contributor to diagnostic decision making. Considered are conditions manifested by disordered thinking, disturbed mood, disrupted interpersonal relations, and substance abuse.

Thought Disorders: Psychosis, Schizophrenia, and Delusional Disorder

Psychosis

One of the oldest and still serviceable indicators for psychosis is the Goldberg (1965) index: (*L* + *Pa* + *Sc*) – (*Hy* – *Pt*). This index, using *K*-corrected T scores, best separated psychotics from "neurotics" in Goldberg's research at a cutting score of 45. Given the base rates for psychosis, it is not surprising that scores in inpatient settings tend to run 5 to 10 points higher than this value and are considerably more sensitive for schizophrenia than for other psychotic disorders or manifestations. In general, scores of 70 to 80 should be considered high, and scores of 90 and above, very high. The classic "miss" for this rule is the 38/83 profile and its variants. This index and the other Goldberg rules are discussed in much greater detail in Friedman et al. (2001). A similar but simpler index, *L* + PSYC – NEGE, would presumably perform about as well as Goldberg's index, with scores greater than 55 suggesting a psychotic direction to the profile, but this remains untested.

Schizophrenia

By far the most common mental disorder to require hospitalization at some point in the patient's life is schizophrenia. Patients with this diagnosis typically have extensive psychiatric histories and longer and more frequent hospital stays. Their symptomatic manifestations are legion. Previous efforts to give order to these manifestations by subcategorizing patients into, for example, paranoid, disorganized, catatonic, and undifferentiated subtypes have met with only limited success, with patients frequently crossing subtype boundaries over the course of illness. A simpler and in some ways more robust system of categorization for these patients follows the distinction between positive (hallucinations, delusions, thought disorder–disorganized speech [as manifested by, e.g., derailment, blocking], and bizarrely aberrant behavior) and negative symptoms (affective flattening or blunting, poverty of speech or content of speech, illogicality [alogia], apathy, avolition–amotivation, and social withdrawal). An earlier but still useful review of the MMPI and schizophrenia has been provided by Walters (1988).

The MMPI–2 assessment of schizophrenia is made difficult by the unusually wide range of patterns the profiles of such patients can take. None can rule out this disorder, and none can be considered pathognomonic for it. Indeed, it cannot even be said that there are profiles typical of schizophrenia, so varied are its forms. Nevertheless, there are a number of scales and patterns that are associated with schizophrenia to a degree that is clinically useful.

The first of these is the schizophrenia scale itself, Scale 8. This scale has never performed especially well in identifying schizophrenia. It is known to elevate readily in nonschizophrenic conditions, including severe depressions, disorganized mania, severe personality disorders, and others, and to fail to elevate in well-documented cases of schizophrenia. Nevertheless, its composition and relation to other scales can offer valuable cues to the likely presence and character of this disorder. Items of clearly psychotic content are uncommon on Scale 8, amounting *at most* to perhaps 15% of the total length. Thus, it is relatively less sensitive to the positive symptomatic aspects of schizophrenia than scales with much greater proportions of psychotic content such as BIZ, PSYC, and RC8. On the other hand, Scale 8 is relatively rich in items reflecting negative symptoms, including social withdrawal and alienation (*Sc*1), affective flattening and apathy (*Sc*2), and avolition–amotivation (*Sc*4). The extremity of social withdrawal–alienation is best indexed by the difference between *Sc*1 and Pd4, with the pattern *Sc*1 > Pd4 characteristic of schizophrenia. The items of *Sc*2 and *Sc*4 are depressively toned and, therefore, share variances with Scale 2 and its various subscales, especially *D*1, and *Hy*3, *Pa*2, and with DEP and DEP1. (A more extensive and detailed description of the Harris–Lingoes subscales can be found in Nichols, 2001.)

*Sc*3 is a good measure of cognitive disruption–disorganization, with *Sc*3 > *D*4 being characteristic of thought disorder in schizophrenia, but this pattern also occurs in disorganized mania (although *Sc*2 and *Sc*4 are typically *not* elevated in the latter cases).

*Sc*5 is sensitive to the disintegration of impulse and control in schizophrenia, in which alien or dissociated impulses and urges may gain unfettered control of behavior.

*Sc*6 consists primarily of motor and sensory items, which provide half of the content of HEA2. The content is more neurologic than psychiatric in character. Speculatively, these items may be considered to reflect Meehl's (1962, 1972) "schizotaxia," the central neural deficit he postulated as the inherited substrate of schizophrenia.

As noted earlier, three other scales—BIZ, PSYC, and RC8—are sensitive to the manifest psychotic symptomatology, the positive symptoms, of schizophrenia. All show extensive item overlap. BIZ and PSYC share well over half of their items; two-thirds of the RC8 items overlap with BIZ, and one-half overlap with *Sc*6. Whereas about half of the items on BIZ and PSYC reference paranoid ideation, such items do not appear on RC8 (but do appear on RC6 and *Pa*1). The implications of reality distortion are somewhat stronger for BIZ, especially BIZ1, than for PSYC; however, PSYC has somewhat stronger implications than BIZ with regard to extreme suspiciousness, even though BIZ1 is also often highly elevated in such cases. The relative strength of reality distortion versus suspiciousness may be gauged from the relative elevations of BIZ and RC8, and PSYC, RC6, and CYN2, respectively.

Although elevated scores on BIZ and PSYC are consistent with schizophrenia, they routinely occur in other psychotic conditions, including toxic or substance-induced states and mania, especially when these are florid. Elevations on RC8 may be more specific to schizophrenia, especially when characterized by positive symptoms, but this scale appears to be potentially quite vulnerable to false negatives for negative symptom schizophrenia.

For schizophrenia in general, and paranoid schizophrenia in particular, the difference between BIZ1 and BIZ2 may be an especially strong sign. When both are elevated (to, say, T65), BIZ1 rarely exceeds BIZ2, though cases of paranoid mania will occasionally show this pattern (BIZ1 > BIZ2). The same appears to be true of the pattern RC6–RC8/RC8–RC6 when both are elevated and highest among the RC scales. However, it seems unlikely that this pattern possesses any clear advantages or implications over a distinctive elevation on BIZ alone.

Delusional Disorder

The diagnosis of delusional disorder is always somewhat hazardous because it occurs at a fairly low base rate, even in inpatient facilities. In a general sense, this disorder is defined by the presence of delusional ideation in the absence of features of disorganization and negative symptoms characteristic of schizophrenia and some of the manic syndromes. A minority of cases are subsequently diagnosed with schizophrenia and a smaller fraction with mood disorder. Hallucinations are permitted but rare and usually of olfactory (patient believes he or she emanates a foul or offensive odor) or tactile rather than auditory or visual type. Traditionally, this disorder has been subdivided into erotomanic (de Clerambault's syndrome), grandiose, jealous (Othello syndrome), persecutory, and somatic (e.g., infestation) types. The MMPI–2 is not suitable for identifying erotomanic and jealous types because of limited relevant item content but is sensitive to persecutory delusions. Delusional disorders of grandiose type often resolve to mania.

Because of its low frequency of occurrence, our experience with a wide range of cases of delusional disorder is extremely limited and confined primarily to cases of persecutory type. In principle, the MMPI–2 findings in such cases would be expected to show relatively (but not extremely) high scores on Scale 6 and relatively low scores on measures and indexes of disorganization and negative symptoms. Hence, in general, one would expect relatively high Scale 6 > Scale 8 differences, Pd4 > *Sc*1, *D*4 > *Sc*3, *Sc*2 and *Sc*4 relatively low among the Scale 8 subscales as well as low in absolute terms (e.g., < T55), raw *K* > raw Scale 8, and relatively (but not necessarily extremely) low scores on BIZ, PSYC, and RC8. In particular, diagnoses of delusional disorder would seem all but untenable unless RC6 > RC8. There are no distinct profiles defining this group, but unelevated and moderately elevated Spike 6 profiles, often with *L* > *K* > *F*, have been seen repeatedly in the persecutory type and a few other forms of this disorder. Other profiles are sometimes seen, however (64, 56/65, etc.); but, as in the case of Spike 6 profiles, these are rarely elevated. The differential diagnosis with paranoid personality disorder (PPD) can be quite difficult. The latter cases characteristically generate more elevated profiles for which a few to many of the guidelines already given may not hold. However, the discrimination of these two conditions is more reliably made on base rate, phenomenological features, and history than on profile features.

Mood Disorders: Depression and Mania

Depression

Because of the legal if not institutional criteria for admission, cases of depression seen in inpatient facilities tend to be severe. Most such patients have been committed as dangerous to self on the basis of suicidality or for related problems such as refusing to eat or refusing urgent medical care. The most common depressive syndromes to be distinguished are the unipolar and bipolar subtypes of major depression and secondary depression. Regardless of syndrome, the great majority of cases are symptomatic for depressed mood (usually manifest), psychomotor retardation, and negative beliefs and attitudes (e.g., irrational guilt, ideas of helplessness, hopelessness, and/or worthlessness). A minority of cases show symptoms of psychosis. Among these, delusions of nihilistic coloring such as delusional—or, at least, irrational—guilt (e.g., being responsible for all of the world's evil) and hypochondriasis (e.g., believing one is rotting from the inside; is dead) are most characteristic but also occur in schizophrenia, however rarely. Conversely, hallucinations and delusions, including persecutory delusions, more typical of schizophrenia, also occur in the major depressions, however rarely.

Among the more common mental disorders in psychiatric populations, patients with schizophrenia and substance abuse disorders may be particularly vulnerable to secondary depression, that is, a major depressive episode emerging in the context of an antecedent psychiatric condition.

In contrast to the situation vis-a-vis the MMPI–2 and schizophrenia, patients with depressive disorders tend to generate profiles of much more predictable patterning—and almost invariably with Scale 2 prominent in the profile code. An earlier but still useful review of the MMPI and mood disorders has been provided by Nichols (1988).

The item composition of Scale 2 reflects a wide range of the typical symptoms found in depressive syndromes. *D1* and *D5* (completely contained in *D1*) index the dysphoric mood, anxiety, and general maladjustment and subjective distress of the syndromes. *D2* contains themes of anhedonia or lack of positive emotionality, inhibition, and introversion–social avoidance. *D3* references the vegetative features of depressive syndromes such as loss of appetite, weight change, constipation, and a decline in general health. *D4* is in many ways the "mental" counterpart of *D3*, referencing a sense of decline in cognitive energy and acuity, manifested by problems with attention, memory, concentration, and judgment; in particular, an impaired capacity for spontaneous mental work is noted such that cognitive tasks are experienced as effortful, depleting, and subject to failure.

Several other scales are available to assist in the fleshing out of descriptions of depressive patients/conditions. First among these is DEP, which has repeatedly demonstrated incremental validity for diagnoses of depression and related correlates (Barthlow, Graham, Ben-Porath, & McNulty, 1999; Ben-Porath, Butcher, & Graham, 1991; Ben-Porath, McCully, & Almagor, 1993). DEP1 emphasizes apathy, anhedonia, and lethargy, similar to *D*1, *D*4, and *D*5. DEP2 reflects depressed mood, similar to *D*1 and *D*5. DEP3 reflects guilt and negative self-attitudes (helplessness, hopelessness, uselessness, worthlessness) and is more similar to Pd5 than to the Scale 2 subscales. DEP4 is essentially an incomplete (see items 150, 524, 530) critical items list for suicidal ideation. RC2 and INTR emphasize anhedonia–low positive emotionality, especially in social situations. Both are sensitive to depressive anhedonia, but their discriminative sensitivity for depression versus schizoid and schizophrenic anhedonia is relatively weak. LSE, especially LSE1, emphasizes self-denigration and feelings of worthlessness–uselessness. OBS, which contains no item overlap with either Scale 2 or DEP, reflects primarily indecision. Moderately high scores (~55 to 70) are common in the depressions, but extreme elevations are infrequent and very low scores sometimes occur (impulsive decision making).

The co-occurrence of anxiety and depressive symptoms is common if not modal in severe anxiety and depressive disorders, and decision rules for effectively discriminating these with the MMPI–2 have not been forthcoming. However, some evidence has been found to suggest that guilt feelings predating the current episode may be a strongly discriminating symptom favoring major depressive as distinct from anxiety states (Breslau & Davis, 1985). The MMPI–2 scales most saturated with content suggesting guilt are DEP3 and Pd5. A convenient and somewhat purified content measure of manifest guilt feeling, Guilt, has been devised by one of the authors (DSN) to assist anxiety versus depressive disorder discriminations and is offered here for provisional clinical use but is in need of empirical validation.

In an important but as yet unreplicated study, Bagby, Basso, Nicholson, Bacchiochi, and Miller (2004) found a number of scales that contributed to some common diagnostic discriminations within depressive disorders. As compared with schizophrenics, unipolar depressives scored higher on scales 2, 3, and 4, ANX, DEP, and INTR (Introversion–Low Positive Emotionality) and lower on BIZ and PSYC, whereas bipolar depressives scored higher on scales 2, ANX, and DEP and lower on FRS. As compared with unipolar depressives, bipolar depressives scored higher on scales 9 and DISC (Disconstraint) and lower on INTR.

The latter pattern of differences accords well with clinical experience suggesting a degree of preservation of second factor undercontrol (for which both DISC and, to a slightly less extent, Scale 9, are excellent markers) in cases of bipolar depression; however, it is difficult on present evidence to satisfactorily account for this finding. One complicating factor is the inherent instability of the manic–depressive cycle, such that between manic apogee and depressive perigee, numerous intermediate states occur (Lumry, Gottesman, & Tuason, 1982; for a detailed case example, see Nichols, 1988). Such intermediate states may be reflected in a very large and potentially highly misleading number of profile patterns, from profiles that are within normal limits, suggesting relative euthymia, to patterns more common to personality disorder (e.g., 48/84, 49/94) and less severe anxiety and dysthymic states (e.g., 23/32, 24/42, 27/72, 20/02, 47/74). To put the matter in its simplest and most practical terms, the diagnostic probity of the MMPI–2 in bipolar depression (and mania as well) is unusually dependent on the phase in the patient's mood cycle within which the MMPI–2 is completed. With respect to the Bagby et al. (2004) findings, then, it remains unclear whether the observed differences between their unipolar and bipolar depressives on scales 9, DISC, and INTR are intrinsic to these two kinds of depressed states in their relatively "pure" forms or represent an artifact of the variability of MMPI–2 findings within their bipolar depressed sample resulting from transitional moments, presumably those just approaching, or just departing from, phases of maximal depression at the time their MMPI–2 data were gathered. Nevertheless, a potentially useful index for alerting the clinician to a bipolar "tilt" in cases of depression is DISC – INTR, with positive scores suggesting such a tilt.

Although less dramatic than in bipolar depression, considerable variability is found in the profiles of unipolar depressives. In part, as in the case of bipolar depression, this variability is a function of course as depressed mood waxes and wanes in severity. However, phenomenological manifestations and nosological uncertainties may also play a role in observed variabilities in unipolar depression. With respect to the former, for example, the co-occurrence of somatization and depression appears more common, though by no means modal in these conditions. With respect to the latter, some controversy remains over whether viable subtypes within the broad category of unipolar depression may be distinguished. For example, to take only one distinction that has received considerable attention in the psychiatric literature, Winokur and associates (e.g., Van Valkenburg, Lowry, Winokur, & Cadoret, 1977; Winokur, 1979a, 1979b; Winokur, Behar, Van Valkenburg, & Lowry, 1978; Winokur & Coryell, 1992) have proposed a division of unipolar depression based on the family history of unipolars, between pure depressive disease (PDD)—cases with a family history of depression alone—and depressive spectrum disease (DSD)—cases with a family history of alcoholism and drug abuse, somatization, anxiety, antisocial personality, a personal history of divorce or separation, more nonserious suicide attempts, clearer precipitating events such as rejection, and general social and emotional instability. Subsequent attempts to validate this and similar divisions have resulted in uneven findings, and space limitations preclude a review of such efforts here, but our experience tends to accord with Winokur's distinction at least in the sense that while patients conforming roughly to his PDD description tend to produce profiles of more classically depressive configurations (i.e., 27/72, 28/82, 20/02, 278 and combinations), the profiles of patients similar to his DSD description are much more varied and likely to include scales 1 or 4 in the two- or three-point code (e.g., 12/21, 214, and combinations; 24/42, 243, and combinations; 247 and combinations).

The MMPI–2 is sensitive to numerous aspects of, as well as variations in, depressive experiences. The following example illustrates a case of depressive spectrum disease. When the test data are viewed against the background of the patient's family history, an interpretation strategy emphasizing a content approach reveals the test's sensitivity to some pertinent sequelae of her early experience and personality dynamics that contribute to understanding her symptomatic vulnerability.

Case Example 2. Linda D. came to the hospital Emergency complaining of distress associated with an ongoing depression that had acutely worsened in the days prior to admission due to a marital breakdown. Emergency's report noted increasing marital tensions over an unspecified period of time that precipitously culminated in her husband leaving the marriage and moving out of the home, taking their son with him, one day before admission. Linda was 33 years old, employed, and had been married 5 years to her second husband. The couple's son, one-year-old Jason, is her third child. She shared custody of two other children from her previous marriage.

She was referred for a psychological assessment to augment the understanding of her depression with an exploration of pertinent personality factors related to her current functioning. Linda was cooperative with the assessment. During the interview, she expressed appropriate concern about her difficulties and a motivation to now begin to address issues she felt had contributed to repeated difficulties with depression dating back to childhood.

Linda was the youngest of four, adopted at age 2 by parents with three daughters of their own. Her birth mother reportedly suffered from schizophrenia, and her father died years after the adoption from carbon monoxide poisoning in a suspected suicide. She described a strict family with a mother who meted out punishments frequently and liberally, even for infractions she thought fairly minor, such as whispering in church. She recalls a tense family environment in which she always strove for the approval and affection she felt were lacking. In part, she did this by trying to be "more like my sisters." Unsuccessful in this bid, she felt singled out for more than an equal share of discipline, concluding "I guess I was a bad kid." File documentation makes little mention of the father, except to deny that he was abusive. During the interview, however, she tearfully acknowledged a history of physical abuse by her father. While she did not elaborate on this abuse, she conveyed that it was extensive. She did acknowledge recognizing a pattern of repeated difficulties in her intimate relationships, which she suspected might be attributed to this abuse.

Linda left home by running away at 16 to marry a man she believed was a virgin who lived a "straight life." It turned out he had previously lived with other women and was heavily involved with illicit drugs. She remained married to this verbally abusive man for 5 years, having two children with him by age 18. During the marriage, she experienced two episodes of depression and made two suicide attempts by overdose before soliciting treatment consisting of a couple of courses on antidepressants, which were only partially effective. In the intervening 6 years between marriages, Linda experimented with prescription drugs and often drank five beers per day to "sedate" herself, though she denied ever having a drug or alcohol "problem."

Linda's current episode of depression dated back approximately 1 year to her mother's death from cancer. While she had long been estranged from her mother after leaving home, she had achieved some reconciliation in the last few years of her life. At the time of her mother's death, Linda was already experiencing some emotional difficulties following the birth of her son approximately 6 months earlier. She was not receiving treatment for depression prior to admission though acknowledged using a combination of alcohol and Tylenol with codeine in recent months to "fog out" feelings of disappointment and hopelessness about her marriage. Information on the chart elaborated that Tylenol appeared to be her second choice, after Percocet, for which she did not have a steady supply. Linda described the marital breakdown as related to her depressive mood and bad temper, admitting that she became angry on a daily basis, prompting her to say things she later regretted. She denied that her marriage was abusive but acknowledged often hitting her husband in anger and his pushing her back in response.

On the MMPI–2, Linda responded with average consistency throughout the inventory (VRIN = T45; [*F* – *F(B)*] + VRIN = 9, raw), with no apparent "yea-saying" nor "nay-saying" bias (True % = 51; TRIN = T50). This suggests she attended to items with sufficient care, understood their content, and responded intentionally. She reported considerable distress, primarily associated with disturbing mentation (*F* = T85), although significant affective upheaval (*F(B)* = T77) was also reported. There were no apparent efforts to exaggerate either psychotic (*Fp* = T49) or nonpsychotic (*Ds* = T79) disturbance, nor did she appear to minimize distress (*F–K* = 0, raw), deny minor faults, or present herself as overly virtuous (*L* = T38). By contrast with her ability to accurately report her distress, her perception of an adequate capacity to cope with this turmoil (*K* = T48) overestimated what a more objective measure of adjustment indicated (*Es* = T31; *K* – *Es* = 17).

Five of 10 clinical scales are elevated above T65 in a profile coded 42* 7"8'6+ *013–95/:# F" ' +–/K:L#*. This profile suggests a marked disturbance involving depression (Scale 2 = T90) and anxiety (Scale 7 = T81; ANX = T81) with obsessive uncertainty and indecision (OBS = T71). A psychotic disturbance appears unlikely (Scale 7 > Scale 8; NEGE > PSYC; Goldberg index = 37; BIZ = T47; BIZ1 = 0, raw). Depressive experiences include symptoms of dysphoric mood (DEP = T85; DEP2 = T73; *D1* = T85; *D5* = T83; *Pa2* = T78), anhedonia (INTR = T70; *Sc2* = T86; *Sc4* = T85; DEP1 = T85), depressive ideation (DEP1 = T85) including prominent suicidal ideation (DEP4 = T77), cognitive debility (*D4* = T88; *Sc3* = T74), proneness to guilt (Guilt = T77; DEP3 = T89; Pd5 = T77), low self-esteem and self-criticism (LSE = T76; LSE1 = T66), and vegetative symptoms of weakness, tiredness, fatigue, sleep disturbance (*Hy3* = T79), as well as loss of appetite and weight (*D3* = T70).

Significant anxiety was evident (ANX = T81), and about equally prominent with depression (DEP – ANX = 4). Linda was vulnerable to being easily flustered and overreactive when faced with stress (*Es* = T31), becoming overly upset when frustrated or disappointed (ANX = T81), prone to feeling panic, and fearful of mental collapse. Lacking in self-confidence and persistence (GM = T32; LSE = T76), she was inhibited by ruminative thinking populated with intrusive worries, preoccupation with details, and self-consciousness, which undermined her ability to make and execute decisions. As a result, she felt broadly impaired in her ability to initiate and sustain the effort needed to successfully and efficiently perform tasks expected of her (WRK = T71).

Patients with 427 profiles tend to be at risk for substance abuse, and given her history as well as her acknowledging at least a "medicinal" pattern of alcohol and codeine use, it was obviously important to examine other indicators. While her self-medicating use is perhaps acknowledged in her dissent to item 429, MAC–R (T48), AAS (T61), and APS (T60) were all negative, if marginal, thus failing to strongly implicate the presence, history, or likelihood of substance abuse.

Although she had an average degree of emotional control (*R* = T46), she was less able to contain expressions of rebellious attitudes or inhibit angry impulses (ANG = T72; DISC = T63; Scale 4 – Scale 3 = 34). This anger was experienced as diffuse, rather than circumscribed, alienation (Scale 8 = T76; *Sc1* = T65), and externalized through ego–alien conflicts and problems in the social environment (Scale 4 = T97) manifesting in expressions such as an inordinate readiness to complain and to become impatient, annoyed, or argumentative (ANG2 = T70). Rather than being driven by sadistic hostility (AGGR = T38), however, her low frustration tolerance and quickness to discharge anger were dysphoric in tone, related to negative emotionality, and prone to be accompanied by guilt, remorse, and self-criticism when expressed (ANX = T81; DEP = T85; ANG2 > ANG1; NEGE >AGGR). There was also a passive–aggressive tendency (LSE2 = T69) that was related to the conjunction of her strong need for self-determination (*Ma*4 = T62) with the undermining impacts of her lack of confidence (LSE = T76) and her difficulty in making decisions (OBS = T71) or mobilizing resources (DEP = T85) to take effective actions that would make a difference in her personal or professional roles (TRT = T72; WRK = T71).

Linda harbored continuing resentment about disharmony in her family of origin and a lingering sense of deprivation and hurt (Pd1 = T80). Despite the toxicity of her family environment, she was left feeling ambivalent and unable to completely sever her emotional ties (FAM1 = T67; FAM2 = T68). The legacy of her early family life likely carried over into continued difficulties in her adult family life (FAM = T75), recapitulating the enduring feelings of estrangement from others and lack of a sense of belonging (Pd4 = T70). Her feelings of alienation appeared more sorrowful and poignant than cold and consolidated (Pd4 > *Sc*1). At the time of testing, Linda was given to pessimistic loss of hope (*Sc*2 = T86) and inclined to listless social withdrawal and introversion (INTR = T70). Viewing herself as undeserving, flawed, inadequate, and guilty, she was quite disinclined toward social engagement (LSE = T76; Pd5 = T77; *Sc*2 = T86). Self-doubting and fearful of abandonment, she was also submissively needy and passively dependent (Si = T77; WRK = T71; LSE = T76; GM = T32; NEGE = T72).

Diagnostically, Linda may be best conceptualized symptomatically as exhibiting a unipolar depressive spectrum disease, as well as a substance abuse disorder involving sedatives and analgesics. These symptomatic expressions are seen as occurring in the context of a personality that, typologically, is a mix of depressive, dependent, and passive–aggressive features organized, developmentally, at a borderline level. It is surmised that one cornerstone of Linda's depressive tendencies is a genetic predisposition inherited from her biological father. This episode was precipitated by rejection and abandonment occurring fairly soon after the loss of a mother for whom she had strongly ambivalent feelings. Her vulnerability to this trigger raises the second hypothesized cornerstone of introjective dynamics that include internalization of parental criticism as well as turning unacceptable anger at her parents toward herself. Resulting feelings of inadequacy associated with the former heighten the needs for approval, affection, and support, which foster her inordinate dependency. Shame-reducing needs for atonement associated with the latter lay behind her ingratiating, passive tendencies. This solution to obtaining affection and approval, however, is purchased at a cost of perpetuating the feeling of getting a raw deal. Thus, a vacillating and self-perpetuating pattern is fostered, involving guilty conciliation leading to building resentment leading to open expressions of anger that lead back to guilty conciliation.

Mania

The core symptoms of mania include elated or irritable mood; inflated self-esteem, often to a delusional degree or to the point of grandiosity; increased energy and overactivity; decreased need for sleep; overtalkativeness–pressured speech; behavioral and emotional disinhibition; flight of ideas or the subjective experience of racing thoughts; and decreased attention.

Just as elevations on Scale 2 tend to be the hallmark feature in the profiles of depressives, those of hypomanic and manic patients tend to show Scale 9 as one of the high points. In the case of classic, euphoric mania, Spike 9 profiles are common, with the code 9'+486-13/720: being typical. The extent of euphoria is well indexed by Scale 9 – INTR, social hunger and talkativeness by Scale 9 – SOD, potential recklessness and poor judgment by Scale 9 – ANX, and inflated self-regard–grandiosity by Scale 9 – LSE. In each case, T score differences of greater than 25 are remarkable and, when greater than 45, likely to be dominant in the clinical picture. To this point, no effective MMPI–2 markers have been identified to reference manic irritability (although ANG2 and TPA1, or especially their combination, ANG2 + TPA1, might be considered candidates) or flight of ideas.

Unfortunately, manic cases that conform closely to the symptomatic description given and the typical Spike 9 profile that is generally consistent with such cases constitute only a minority of manic patients as they are encountered in inpatient settings. Even so, patients who are tested near manic apogee are surprisingly consistent for having Scale 9 prominent in the code, along with scales 4, 6, or 8. Conversely, scales 7 and, especially, 2 and 0 tend to be coded low.

Within these general characteristics, some variability occurs. The chief cause of such variability in inpatient populations is psychoticism. Scales 6 (and RC6) and, especially, BIZ, PSYC, and RC8, and, to a lesser extent, Scale 8 reflect psychotic processes in this context, just as they do in schizophrenia. Scale 6 (69/96 profiles and 469 combinations) gives mania a distinct paranoid coloring that, left untreated, may give rise to delusionally inspired retaliatory behavior. In such cases, the absence of a concurrent elevation on Scale 8 (or RC8) may be something of a liability inasmuch as its implications of cognitive disruption and disorganization are unavailable to derail planning and obscure motivation, however delusional. Scales 8 and, to a lesser extent, 4 (89/98, 489 and combinations) give mania a reckless, impulsive, and hostile character. As in the case of schizophrenia, the extent of disruption–disorganization and alienation can be ascertained more precisely with reference to the indexes *Sc*3 – *D*4 and *Sc*1 – Pd4, respectively. Psychoticism in mania reaches its extreme in the 689/869 code type, with pervasive suspiciousness, hypervigilance, multiple and poorly organized delusions, hallucinations, bizarreness, and often violent preoccupations. It is important that the clinician not rely excessively on the empirical correlates of the 68/86 two-point code type, as the 689/869 is a poor fit for many of these. In most cases, the psychoticism is secondary to mania and resolves with the usual antimanic drugs; however, many patients represent such a risk for violence that antipsychotics are needed to gain adequate control and ameliorate their risk to staff, their peers, or others.

Within inpatient settings, psychotic excrescences in mania are the rule rather than the exception and include virtually the full range of psychotic phenomena, including auditory hallucinations; thought disorder, including the so-called first rank symptoms (Schneider, 1959); and grandiose and/or persecutory delusions, among others. Indeed, so salient and preeminent are such phenomena in mania that they commonly overshadow the more distinctive symptoms of the manic syndrome, obscuring the differential diagnosis. Although qualitative differences are occasionally found that can help to arbitrate the differential diagnosis between mania and schizophrenia—notably a degree of bizarreness in speech ("Every time I try to light up a cigarette, a huge wave of communism just seems to go all over everything.") that is exceedingly rare in mania—such expressions are sufficiently infrequent even in schizophrenia as to afford them a differential diagnostic role only occasionally. Considered alone, the extent and extremity of most psychotic manifestations are of little or no value in resolving this differential diagnosis. That is, in gross terms, the typical inpatient manic may be *at least* as psychotic as the typical schizophrenic. Given this state of affairs, it is generally preferable to emphasize symptoms of mood rather than thought disturbance in distinguishing these two conditions, and the MMPI–2 is routinely helpful in this task.

The scales most useful in this regard are Scale 9 itself, scales implicating dyscontrol (DISC, *R* [low], MAC–R, etc.) and extroversion (low scores on INTR, Si, and SOD), and scales suggesting the absence of dysphoric mood and fear (low scores on Scale 2, DEP, RC2, FRS, etc.). RC9 does not appear promising for this purpose because of its excessively oppositional, hostile, and vengeful item content. These features may make RC9 a better fit for certain personality disorders such as aggressively hostile psychopaths or antisocial personalities than for mania, at least in its most commonly encountered forms.

Severe Anxiety Disorders

Anxiety disorders are rather uncommon in inpatient settings unless unusually severe and debilitating or when associated with comorbid symptoms of depression or, occasionally, psychosis. For example, fears and phobias related to social and interpersonal events and situations have a high base rate in psychiatric settings, and their assessment should take into account scores on scales related to introversion and low positive emotionality–anhedonia (Scale 0, SOD, INTR, and RC2). More specific fears and phobias (dark, open spaces, dirt, snakes, fire, etc.) are assessed most readily with reference to the explicit phobic content of FRS, although scale scores are more often than not less informative than individual item responses. In both cases, these kinds of symptoms tend to be ameliorated if not resolved when the primary disorder comes under better control. Similarly, generalized anxiety disorder and obsessive–compulsive disorder are rare in inpatient settings, although their symptoms are not. Indeed, anxiety, tension, worry, apprehensiveness, and obsessionality are, to a greater or lesser degree, ubiquitous among psychiatric inpatients; and compulsive features (though not formal compulsive rituals) are not uncommon. However, as with fears and phobias, these symptoms are usually secondary to another Axis I disorder—for example, recurrent intrusive thoughts and abhorrent images in certain depressions and in some forms of schizophrenia—and are frequently notable in 278 and 78/87 code types. When compulsive behaviors (e.g., hoarding) are present, including such mental compulsions as counting or repeating certain words or phrases (or insisting that their interlocutors repeat them at given intervals; example, "Cool"), these are likely to have either delusional underpinnings or be the product of command hallucinations. On the other hand, histories of obsessive–compulsive disorder among patients with major depression and dysthymia, while uncommon, are not especially rare. The presence of such a history can provide useful guidance in interpreting some MMPI–2 scores such as OBS, ANX, and DEP and the relations among them.

Despite significant and telling recent criticism (Bowman, 1997; Leys, 2000; McNally, 2003; Young, 1995), inpatient diagnoses of posttraumatic stress disorder (PTSD) have continued to occur more frequently in the past 15 years than previously. In most of the cases we have seen, hospitalization was precipitated by depression, suicidal crises, or substance abuse or intoxication; PTSD was rarely the primary diagnosis. Research has shown a good correspondence between Pk (Post-Traumatic Stress Disorder–Keane) scale scores and PTSD symptoms, but this scale has not been found to correspond as well to a history of trauma (e.g., Watson, Juba, Anderson, & Manifold, 1990). Given the unusually high correlation between Pk and the first factor among psychiatric patients (r A × Pk = .93) and even higher correlations with scales 7, 8, and DEP (.95, .94, and .93, respectively), its differential diagnostic value in inpatient settings such as state hospitals is essentially nil. It is possible—though it seems to us unlikely—that its incremental value for identifying cases of PTSD may be enhanced by requiring Pk scores to exceed scores on A by some fixed amount, say 10 to 15 T scores, but this remains to be demonstrated. PTSD and Pk are treated more extensively in chapter 6.

Severe Personality Disorders

Unlike anxiety disorders, personality disorders (PDs) of various kinds are not infrequent in inpatient settings; but, like anxiety disorders, they are usually seen with comorbid symptoms of depression or psychosis, often substance-related. Because the MMPI was developed in a psychiatric hospital to assist in the assessment of major psychiatric syndromes, their manifest symptomatology in particular, the application of the test to the assessment of PDs is relatively recent and, to this point, not well supported by research. An earlier and still useful review of the MMPI and personality disorders has been provided by Morey and Smith (1988).

There are at least two major obstacles to this application in practice. The first is fundamental and concerns the limitations set by the MMPI/MMPI–2 item pool itself. That is, there appear to be areas of item content of relevance to PDs that are simply unavailable within the item pool as it now stands. For one example, items showing a strong statistical association with the first factor of Hare's Psychopathy Checklist—Revised (PCL–R; Hare, 1991) are far too few in number to measure this factor reliably (Nichols & Greene, 2004b). Other examples include items referencing real or imagined abandonment or self-mutilating behavior in borderline personality disorder and items implicating a sense of entitlement, arrogance, and envy, whether experienced subjectively or feeling oneself the object of others' envy as in narcissistic personality disorder. Notwithstanding these limitations, at least three sets of scales have been developed for the assessment of the PDs with the MMPI/MMPI–2 (Ben-Porath & Somwaru, 1993; Levitt & Gotts, 1995; Morey, Waugh, & Blashfield, 1985; Somwaru & Pen-Porath, 1995b). To date, the Morey et al. (1985) *DSM–III* (APA, 1980) personality disorder scales have figured in most of the published research (Guthrie, 1994; Hills, 1995).

The second major obstacle to using the MMPI/MMPI–2 for the assessment of PDs, especially among hospitalized psychiatric patients, is that the more symptomatic determinants of scores, whether on clinical or content-based scales, tend to obscure scores and patterns that may relate more directly to the stable features of personality that characterize personality disorders: Axis II signal tends to be drowned out by Axis I noise. For example, symptomatic depression can overwhelm (or mimic) features of dependent and avoidant PDs; depression, feelings of hopelessness and worthlessness, dependency, and low self-regard are common to both depression (especially unipolar depression) and borderline personality disorder. Similarly, manifestations of psychoticism such as those routinely found in schizophrenia and the mood disorders, especially mania, often mimic or obscure similar features in schizotypal personality disorder. Likewise, the paranoid symptoms found in a variety of inpatients may be seen, usually in attenuated form, in borderline, paranoid, and schizotypal PDs. The successful assessment of personality disorders using the various scales and indexes of the MMPI–2, including specially developed personality disorder scales, may require settings with much lower base rates for general distress and symptomatic behavior than are typical in inpatient settings. There is some confirmation for this suggestion in two reports, one with a mixed sample of in- and outpatients (Hills, 1995), the other an outpatient sample (Guthrie, 1994), in which both found the Morey et al. (1985) PD scales to be more specific than sensitive.

A third difficulty concerns the various comorbidities among the personality disorders themselves, such that multiple diagnoses on Axis II are common, if not the rule, especially among borderline, histrionic, antisocial, and schizotypal PDs. To complicate matters further, concurrent diagnoses involving substance abuse are at least as common among inpatients with personality disorders as among patients carrying major mood or thought disorder diagnoses on Axis I. Given these circumstances, the contribution that the MMPI–2 can make to the assessment of personality disorders in inpatient settings is a modest one.

The majority of Axis II inpatients with personality disorders are found in cluster B and tend to be younger (patients with narcissistic PD are an exception, tending to be of middle age). The borderline PD diagnosis is most common. Cluster A diagnoses are not uncommon but are rarely the focus of treatment in hospital. Cluster C diagnoses are unusual, are almost always associated with a major depressive episode, and are almost never the focus of hospital treatment.

Despite these limitations, it is possible to at least outline certain traits that occur with some frequency in the personality disorders and features of the MMPI–2 with which such traits are associated. One general index that has been proposed for discriminating psychiatric from personality disorders was developed by Goldberg (1972): 2Pd – *Hy* – *Sc*. Goldberg found that a cutting score of 11 best separated a large collection of Axis I and Axis II group profiles. Given that the base rate for Axis I disorders in inpatient settings is so much higher than that for Axis II disorders, it is not surprising that this index performs rather poorly in such settings. Although we have found this index to be usefully orienting in terms of the possibility of personality disorder, especially for cluster B PDs, it generates numerous false positives for PDs among the 46/64, 48/84, 482/428, 274/742/472 code types, and many for the 69/96 and 94 codes as well. As Scale 4 reaches about T80, profiles tend to be classified under this rule as personality disordered regardless of profile configuration or actual diagnosis. Therefore, it must be used with caution.

In general, we have found it more advantageous to approach the assessment of personality disorders from the standpoint of individual traits.

One of these is extroversion, a trait common to the histrionic, antisocial, and narcissistic PDs. Scales 0 and SOD are, of course, saturated with this dimension, although SOD may be preferable because of its greater independence from neuroticism (see Si3). Histrionic personalities tend to score lower than average on these scales and to show a pattern among the Scale 3 subscales in which *Hy*1, *Hy*2, and *Hy*5 exceed scores on *Hy*3 and *Hy*4. CYN tends to be below average. In hospital, however, these patterns are easily disrupted by current distress, such that scales 2, 4, 7, and 8 are elevated in one combination or another. In such cases, *Hy*3 is usually the high point among the Scale 3 subscales. The narcissistic PDs also tend to manifest an extroverted pattern but also tend to show scales 2 and 7 low in the profile code, to elevate Scale 9 (e.g., 39/93 and 59/95 codes, among others), and to produce low scores on LSE (and high difference values on *Ma* – LSE). Antisocial PDs are also extroversive and commonly, but by no means invariably, produce profiles coded 4'9. They tend to elevate DISC, ANG, CYN, ASP, FAM, MAC–R, RC4, and AAS, show very low (i.e., < T40) scores on *Do* and *Re*, low *R*, and usually have DISC as the high point and INTR as the low point (DISC – INTR) among the PSY–5 scales. Because such patients tend also to be extroversive, most of these test signs are also found in manic–hypomanic conditions as well as when the latter are active, making it advisable to retest as these symptoms come under control.

Borderline PDs tend to manifest a highly variable and unstable pattern of symptoms and behaviors. Thus, their MMPI–2 profiles tend to be similarly variable and unstable. At least two or more of scales 2, 4, 6, 7, and 8 are among the clinical scales most commonly elevated, with the 48/84 code type being the most distinctive, though not definitive. Although none of the following test patterns are unique to borderline PD, as a group they are relatively common in this disorder. The conjunction of negative emotionality and emotional and behavioral dyscontrol is one of the hallmarks of borderline PD, and these are reflected in relatively high scores on A, ANX, DEP, NEGE (NEGE generally higher than both ANX and DEP), and DISC and relatively low scores on *R*, respectively. ANX and DEP characteristically exceed OBS (impulsive decision making) and the difference between scales A and *R* (A – *R*) tends to be large. ANG tends to be high, with ANG1 exceeding ANG2 (ANG1 – ANG2). Likewise, FAM is usually high, with FAM1 exceeding FAM2 (FAM1 – FAM2), suggesting a fear of severing relations with family even though these are felt to be conflicted and unsupportive. LSE may or may not be especially elevated, but LSE1 usually exceeds LSE2 (LSE1 – LSE2) because these patients tend to be intolerant of the vulnerability of submission. In a similar vein, feelings of alienation tend to be moderate and poignant rather than severe, and this is reflected in Pd4 exceeding *Sc*1 (Pd4 – *Sc*1). Finally, cognitive processes tend to be more inefficient than disorganized, as reflected in *D*4 exceeding

*Sc*3 (*D*4 – *Sc*3), and tend to be more peculiar, unusual, and referential than frankly psychotic and delusional, as reflected in BIZ2 exceeding BIZ1 (BIZ2 – BIZ1). The reader will understand that these signs are all highly fallible and subject to change with shifts in clinical state. To take only one example, the signs we have mentioned relating to disorganized thinking and psychoticism may reverse for patients suffering micropsychotic states to which they are known to be vulnerable.

The cluster A personality disorders seen in inpatient settings, primarily paranoid and schizotypal PDs, represent continuities with the schizophrenias, especially paranoid schizophrenia, or, occasionally, with delusional disorder. As such they can be extremely difficult to identify and to discriminate from controlled, remitted, or residual schizophrenia. Occasionally, paranoid PDs are seen in the context of inpatient substance abuse services. These patients are often more or less readily identified on the basis of history, observation, and interview. Their interpersonal behavior often manifests such features as self-reference and egocentricity, fears of self-disclosure, and features suggesting concurrent fear and hostility such as suspiciousness, resentment, and a slowness or inability to forgive minor slights and oversights, a readiness to project and transfer blame, hypersensitivity and quickness to take offense, and countersubmissiveness and irritable oppositionality. Thus, their conflicts with others tend to be relatively open and visible. The features of the MMPI–2 tend to follow this pattern, with elevations on Scale 6 that may be driven by any and all of its subscales, on Pd4, *Ma*4, Si3, CYN (both CYN1 and CYN2), TRT2, *Ho*, and low scores on LSE2. When *Hy*2 and *Pa*3 are both elevated, *Pa*3 tends to be the higher; when both are depressed, *Pa*3 tends to be the lower. Scores on PSYC and BIZ likewise vary widely, but PSYC tends to exceed BIZ (PSYC > BIZ). Elevations on any and all of the paranoia factors are not unusual (but scores on Delusions of Control should not exceed scores on any of the other three factors).

Schizotypal PD has either been rare in our experience or has been obscured by Axis I disorder, usually schizophrenia in one manifestation or another. In those few cases we have seen, the only regularities we have noticed are PSYC greater than DISC (PSYC > DISC) and BIZ2 greater than BIZ1 (BIZ2 > BIZ1).

As noted earlier, the cluster C personality disorders are almost never seen in hospital unless in the context of an Axis I disorder, usually depression. Hypothetically, avoidant PD would favor conjoint elevations on the anxiety (scales 7, perhaps 8, *A*, ANX, WRK, etc.) and introversion scales (scales 0, SOD, INTR, etc.), among others; dependent PD: elevations on *Hy*2, *Pa*3 (and *Hy*2 = or > *Pa*3), OBS and LSE2, and low scores on *Ma*4, CYN, and TPA2; obsessive–compulsive PD: elevations on Scale 7, possibly with most of the raw score coming from the *K* correction, and OBS greater than ANX greater than DEP. Again, these are mere speculations and lie outside our clinical experience.

SUBSTANCE ABUSE

Although estimates vary considerably, rates of substance involvement among patients admitted to psychiatric hospitals are generally acknowledged to be very high; about one third to one half or more (e.g., Batki, 1990; Regier et al., 1990). Given these base rates and the tendency of most patients to report accurately, scores on AAS provide the most reliable indication of substance abuse or the absence thereof. Because of its positive covariation with Scale 9 and DISC and its negative covariation with *R*, MAC–R scores can be highly misleading in inpatient settings. The 247 codes are classic false negatives for MAC–R, but false negatives are also commonly seen in other profiles with elevations on scales 2, 3, and/or 0, especially when Scale 9 is low. In contrast, the Scale 9 codes (9, 69/96, 89/98, 689, etc.) are vulnerable to false positive MAC–R scores. Indeed, for inpatient profiles in general, elevations on MAC–R are somewhat more likely to indicate manic or antisocial trends than problems with substance abuse (which is not to say that these are mutually exclusive). More often than not, in those cases for which MAC–R reaches a range suggesting substance abuse, and such abuse is indicated in the patient's history, AAS is concurrently elevated. In other words, the incremental validity of MAC–R over AAS in inpatient settings is limited to nonexistent. The incremental validity of APS over AAS appears likewise to be limited or nil, and profiles in which APS is both elevated and exceeds AAS by 5 T or more are relatively uncommon in any case. Although we have seen too few cases to have drawn conclusions, this pattern, when present, would seem to warrant further investigation to rule out substance abuse. Another sign that appears to be associated with substance abuse is ANG1 + ASP2, with values exceeding 120 often associated with such problems even in the absence (uncommon) of elevations on AAS, APS, or MAC–R.

In terms of common profile types, we have noticed few reliable associations with substance abuse as such or with the types of substance(s) abused. In common with others, we have found elevations on Scale 4 associated with substance abuse and with the variety of substances abused (Greene & Garvin, 1988). However, in inpatient settings, polysubstance abuse appears to be more the rule than the exception, regardless of profile pattern. Such use may be especially profligate in the 482 and 468 codes and their combinations, respectively. We have also noticed some association between Scale 7 and patterns of compulsive use, and between Scale 8 and the use of inhalants/solvents such as paint or gasoline, but could not find documentation of these associations in the literature. A more general treatment of substance abuse is found in chapter 14 of this volume.

SPECIAL PROBLEMS AND ISSUES IN INPATIENT MMPI–2 ASSESSMENT: A BRIEF DIGEST

Distress

The patient's general or overall level of subjective distress, the first factor, is conveniently assessed by a large number of scales: *A*, Scale 7 (raw, especially to the extent that the raw score exceeds the *K* correction), *Mt*, Pk and Ps (Schlenger PTSD), NEGE, and RCDem. The content scales ANX, OBS, LSE, WRK, and TRT, although intended to assess more specific types of distress, are all saturated with this factor. *A*, RCDem, and RC7 are highly sensitive to this broad dimension. Of these, *A* is probably the best marker at moderate to high elevations but begins to run out of items at ~T80 (lack of "top").

Control

The second major factor of the MMPI–2 is a bipolar, undercontrol versus overcontrol dimension. Its two primary markers are *R*, which is biased toward the emotional aspect of this dimension, and DISC, which is biased toward its behavioral aspect. The best general index of this dimension is DISC – *R*, with very high values indicating severe undercontrol and very low values indicating severe overcontrol. Both are about equally related to Scale 9, MAC–R, O–H, and ANG. Scales more closely related to the *R*, or emotional overcontrol, aspect include *D2*, O–H, and INTR, positively, and MAC–R and AGGR, negatively. Scales more closely related to the DISC, or behavioral undercontrol, aspect include Pd2, ASP, especially ASP2, MAC–R, and AAS, positively, and *Re*, negatively.

Suicide

Given the high base rates for suicidal ideation, threats, and attempts—occasionally successful—in inpatient settings, suicidality is a routine component of psychodiagnostic assessment. Virtually none of the code types commonly found in inpatient settings fail to show instances in which some, many, or all of the items with the most obvious suicide content are endorsed, including code types often produced by underreporting. Code types seen in inpatient settings with very high frequency (e.g., 278, 28, 284, 68, and 78) tend to endorse four or five of such items on the average. Glassmire, Stolberg, Greene, and Bongar (2001) found that among a sample of outpatients, responses to six MMPI–2 items—150, 303, 506, 520, 524, and 530—were of incremental value over responses to questions about suicidality on intake interviews. The most convenient index for assessing suicide on the MMPI–2 is DEP4, but this scale contains only five items, two of which do not appear on the Glassmire et al. (2001) list. It is therefore recommended that inpatient MMPI–2 protocols be routinely evaluated for each of the Glassmire et al. and DEP4 items.

Assaultiveness

Assaultiveness and violent behavior are low base rate phenomena even in psychiatric hospitals and have significant determinants other than the kinds of personality and psychopathological variables assessed by the MMPI–2. Such determinants include environmental factors (e.g., ward density [crowding], staff training, and staffing ratios) and certain personality variables of staff (e.g., anxiety proneness, other-directedness, and authoritarianism) that may lead them to adopt coercive, intimidating, provocative, confused, or otherwise aversive and counterproductive postures in interaction with patients. Other individual factors such as histories of assault, other violence, substance abuse, below average intellectual ability, and serum medication levels have also been related to assaultiveness in hospital (e.g., Davis, 1991). Indicators of potential assault risk on the MMPI–2 fall into several categories, including variables related to impaired controls (DISC, low *R*); irritable (ANG2, TPA1) or angry mood, particularly when hotheaded or explosive (ANG, ANG1); aggression and hostility (AGGR, TPA2); hyperactivity and boisterousness (Scale 9); and psychoticism, especially in the form of persecutory delusions (*Pa*1, RC6, the Persecutory Ideas–Delusions paranoia factor) or the mood features noted earlier as a reaction to hallucinations, command hallucinations in particular (BIZ, BIZ1, PSYC, RC8). These indicators are rarely in close alignment, but all can help to identify the kinds of circumstances under which the risk of assault may be elevated. Depression and the absence of hostility and suspiciousness tend to be contrary indicators of assault risk. A rough but convenient broad index is (4 + 6 + 8 + 9) – (1 + 2 + 3 + 7), with positive values indicating heightened risk for assaultive behavior.

The index AGGR – TPA2 appears likely to be of some value in distinguishing whether hostile expressions or actions are rooted in general negative emotionality (negative values) or more predatory or sadistic motivational patterns (positive values) in which such behaviors provide gratifications over and above emotional discharge, including gratifications related to the deliberate infliction of harm or other suffering.

Psychoticism

Positive symptom trends toward psychotic disorganization are most reliably assessed by RC8 and Scale 8, especially *Sc*3, *Sc*5, and *Sc*6, BIZ, BIZ1, and, less strongly, BIZ2 and PSYC. Delusional psychoticism is most reliably assessed by Scale 6, especially *Pa*1, PSYC, RC6, and the three paranoia factors, Ideas of Reference, Delusions of Control, and Persecutory Ideas–Delusions. Psychoticism manifested through negative symptoms is related to Scale 8, especially *Sc*2, *Sc*3, and *Sc*4, INTR, and RC2.

Depression

Scale 2 and DEP are both sensitive to depression, with Scale 2 somewhat more reflective of depressive syndromes because of its inclusion of content related to vegetative symptoms (*D*3) and inhibition (*D*2), and DEP somewhat more reflective of the severity of depressed *mood.* INTR and RC2 are both sensitive to depressive withdrawal and anhedonia. Scale 9 (low) is sensitive to inhibition, passivity, and anergia. The availability of these scales, the component scales for DEP; and Scale 2, the Guilt scale; and *Sc*2, *Sc*3, and *Sc*4 permits a fairly precise and comprehensive description of depressed states.

Elation–Grandiosity

There are no highly specific indicators that directly reflect the elation, euphoria, and grandiosity that are often seen in relatively pure manic states. However, the difference between scales 9 and 2 (9–2 > 20T) provides a rough index of these qualities. Related indicators include high scores on *Ma*3 and *Ma*4, and low scores on Si1, FRS, DEP2, LSE, SOD2, INTR, and RC2. General distress indicators (A, Scale 7, etc.) should be average or below. To the extent that the latter are above average, these qualities are likely to be, at least to some degree, forced or simulated, perhaps in an effort to keep impending dysphoria at bay.

Sleep Disturbance

Disorders of sleep are all but ubiquitous in inpatient settings and are especially prevalent in patients with mood disorders, schizophrenia, and substance use disorders. Patients with major depression, for example, present with disturbed sleep virtually always, usually difficulty in falling asleep, early morning awakening with an inability to return to sleep, and frequent or prolonged awakening in between. Other symptoms, including nightmares, "restless legs," hypersomnia, and excessive daytime sleepiness, are also seen. Psychiatric disorders can be both a cause and a result of sleep disturbance and can be in relation to both onset and relapse (Bootzin, Manber, Loewy, Kuo, & Franzen, 2001; Morin & Edinger, 1999). Moreover, persistent sleep disturbance has been implicated as a risk factor for suicide (Fawcett et al., 1990; Wingard & Berkman, 1983). The only direct means of assessing sleep disturbance on the MMPI–2 are the six items comprising the Lachar–Wrobel critical item set for sleep disturbance, and reference to these items individually enables a specific description of the patient's complaints regarding sleep. Somewhat surprisingly, these items overlap more with ANX than with DEP (3 versus 0), and ANX correlates more highly with these items than does DEP (.78 versus .69).

PROVIDING TEST FEEDBACK

Patients

Patients who have been prepared for the assessment along the lines discussed earlier are usually eager to learn about their test results, the implications of these results for their treatment and length of stay in hospital, and for the purpose of better understanding their problems in living and how these problems may have led to their commitment and hospitalization. If such preparations have followed the principles of Therapeutic Assessment (Finn, 1996b; chap. 8, this volume), the patient will have been assisted by the clinician to formulate questions for which the MMPI–2 can provide insight.

Because patients vary so widely in terms of their ability to attend and absorb information, feedback should be carefully calibrated to the patient's mental status. Some patients will find a single feedback session insufficient to absorb all of the information that the assessment has made available and may require multiple sessions. Similarly, patients vary considerably in their language skills, and it is wise for the clinician to be aware of the level of vocabulary that will provide the patient the greatest access to the feedback provided, as well as sentence length, and the rate and duration of speech used in conveying this information. For patients in whom disturbed thinking figures in their pattern of symptoms or who are interpersonally sensitive on another basis, the possibility for misunderstandings can be especially high. It is therefore helpful to check for these frequently throughout the session in order to ensure that the patient is "receiving" what the clinician is "sending." Finally, an understanding of the significance of insight, or the lack of insight, is essential to providing appropriate feedback.

In acute schizophrenia, for example, the International Pilot Study of Schizophrenia (World Health Organization, 1973), found that lack of insight occurred more frequently than any other symptom; and subsequent research has documented the high frequency of lack of insight in psychotic disorders generally, including psychotic mood disorders (Amador et al., 1994). Furthermore, in schizophrenia, at least, lack of insight may trace more readily to neuropsychological factors, including frontal lobe dysfunction, than to defensiveness (e.g., Kasapis, Amador, Yale, Strauss, & Gorman, 1996). In the light of such findings, it behooves the clinician to appreciate the likely origins of the lack of insight when present and to be aware of the hazards as well as the benefits of the kinds of insight that may flow from test feedback. For example, there is some evidence that among schizophrenics, insight may be associated with increased risk of suicidal behavior (Amador et al., 1996). Patients often find pressures to admit to having a "mental illness" more demoralizing, stigmatizing, or otherwise threatening to their self-esteem than candid and respectful discussions about more concrete problems in living such as difficulties in retaining employment or important relationships; engaging in behaviors that confuse, frighten, or antagonize others; losing track of their concerns; or finding themselves unable to persist toward goals they value. The kinds and scope of questions posed by the patient, both prior to the assessment and during the feedback session, provide the clinician with valuable cues for assessing the range of insights to which the patient is accessible. Insights that support greater participation and collaboration in treatment and follow-up tend to be associated with better treatment outcomes, regardless of whether assent to the "fact" of illness is achieved.

Treatment Teams

As the responsible agent for the patient's care and treatment in hospital, the treatment team is entitled to the proceeds of psychological assessment. However, the psychologist's goals in the assessment process are often more broad than those of the treatment team. The psychologist often wishes for the assessment to illuminate and deepen his or her understanding of the patient as a person in terms that encompass the patient's developmental, educational, social, and vocational history within the context of the traditional rubrics of perception; learning; motivation; and of personality formation, structure, and change that form the relatively unique basis of the psychologist's education and training. In addition, the psychologist typically considers the assessment to fall within the context of a developing psychotherapeutic relationship with the patient, even when the assessment is prompted by referral questions that may be quite narrow. By contrast, the goals for the assessment inspired by the treatment team are typically more focused on specific issues of diagnosis; patient management such as the delineation of various risks, as for suicide or assault; and issues related to privileges, visitors, passes, discharge planning, adherence to prescribed medication regimens, and so on. Because of these differences in the ways the purposes of assessment are understood by the psychologist on the one hand and the rest of the treatment team on the other, providing assessment feedback to the patient's treatment team inevitably involves elements of negotiation and finesse. The psychologist endeavors to be responsive to the treatment team's need for specific information on which to base its decisions, while at the same time approaching the team's questions and concerns in a way that enriches its members' understanding of the patient as an individual, thereby enabling it to reach decisions that contain a greater measure of care, understanding, and wisdom than would be possible without the psychologist's unique contribution.

When provided an appropriate introduction and background by the psychologist, the MMPI–2 can become a convenient shared point of reference for the psychologist and treatment team. Its basic structure and metrics are easily explained and readily conveyed. Its scales, or at least the names thereof, reflect categories that are mostly familiar to psychiatric staff and may be seen to operate in a manner that is roughly analogous to familiar medical equipment such as thermometers. It is also advantageous that the MMPI was developed within a psychiatric setting, that it has a huge research base, and that it is described in recent official psychiatric literature on assessment (e.g., Goldman et al., 2000).

Given the need for the treatment team to focus on more or less immediate patient care concerns, familiarizing the team with the MMPI–2 is a long-term project, one to be accomplished over a period of months. Having profiles and scores available to be viewed by members during treatment team meetings as the patients who produced them are discussed stimulates curiosity and learning. In our experience, treatment teams appreciate having a preview of material that will appear subsequently in the psychologist's written report. They show an interest in patients' MMPI–2 findings and in how the psychologist elaborates and integrates these findings with other parts of the patient database and, most importantly, with team members' ongoing experience of the patient in their day-to-day contacts. These contacts routinely prompt impressions and questions that the psychologist can help set into perspective, and this often leads eventually to questions from team members that specifically address the patient's test results: "What does the MMPI–2 say?"

CODA

It is customary, if at times a bit precious, to speak of the art and science of clinical psychology. In the heyday of logical positivism, Reichenbach (1957) codified this distinction in his well-known contrast between the "context of discovery" and the "context of justification." As Danziger (1990) has pointed out, however, this distinction is not an easy sell today. Kuhn (1970), Feyerabend (1993), and others have made the case that matters of logic and method are as much a part of hypothesis formation (the context of discovery) as inspiration, and that hunch and passion are regulars on the scene in hypothesis testing (context of justification). However, having a distinction blurred may not be sufficient warrant for ignoring it. This chapter is more properly located in the context of discovery than that of justification. Most of its guidelines, qualifications, exceptions, rules of thumb, and so forth are untested outside (our) clinical experience. Like most clinical experience, ours has been informed by due diligence and a desire to be of assistance, by a strong and seasoned interest in test-behavior relationships and a drive to notice and record them, and a desire to see if these relationships persist in subsequent exposure to clinical cases. Like most clinical experience, ours has been acquired in the context of an aspiration to think well, and carefully, about the people we assess, their circumstances, their test data, and about how well our recorded and implicit predictions work out. Like most clinicians, we accept that clinical problems are set and solved in the context of application; that the clinical case information we have about each patient will virtually always be either too little or too much; that our powers of deduction and induction, no matter how rigorously applied, will not save us from error; and that our daily bread will emerge from the oven of the apagoge of Aristotle, the abduction of Pierce, the essential logic of diagnosis: Starting from a rule or set of rules (schizophrenics hear voices; drunks get into trouble on pass), go to a fact (Abel hears voices; Cain gets into trouble on pass), then decide if the fact is such that it should be considered a case under the rule (Abel has schizophrenia; Cain is a drunk). Like all clinicians, we are deceived. People tell us lies; gild the lily; shine us on; put the best (or worst) face on things; misremember events; set us up; pull our legs; pass on misinformation, innocently or willfully; and augment, edit, redact, amend, guess, change the names, and protect the innocent. And, like all clinicians, we deceive ourselves: we are dazzled by or blinded by the penetrating insights of others; we forget about, or are ignorant of, base rates. We remember and record our hits better than we do our misses, find ourselves in the grip of illusory correlates, apprehend resemblances better than we do differences, are seduced by red herrings, and all too often wash down our daily bread of diagnosis with the sweet nectar of confirmatory bias. Moreover, the context of discovery that inpatient psychological assessment provides, its richness as a source of new hypotheses, is less than favorable when it comes to ruling out their competitors.

However much we may ourselves be deceived, we have no wish to deceive our readers. Yet it is inevitable that many of the hypotheses offered here will not fare well in the context of justification. Alas, we do not know which are which. For this we make no apology. We have found the MMPI–2 a trusty ally in our work with psychiatric inpatients. Its complexity and the kinds of crosscurrents so often evident in its myriad scores and indexes have been as challenging as the complexities and crosscurrents within the people we have been called upon to assess. Both have kept us interested! But we can all be fooled. We appeal to others to find ways of sorting the hypotheses offered here into their most appropriate categories, whether wisdom or folly.

APPENDIX 9.1

Pdf—Paranoid Defensiveness (48 Items)

True: 1 6 10 33 63 81 152 157 211 220 223 239 254 261 265 345 372 388 405 416 424
False: 35 38 89 93 116 127 185 196 218 267 285 289 290 304 339 342 344 362 368 398 411 420 430 434 442 444 464
Restandardization Norms: Men: M = 26.82; SD = 5.93
Women: M = 23.95; SD = 6.14.

Guilt (7 Items)

True: 52 82 94 373 390 411 518
False: None
Restandardization Norms: Men: M = 1.75; SD = 1.58
Women: M = 1.71; SD = 1.61.

Paranoia Factors
Resentment (6 Items)

True: 17 22 42 145 234 484
False: None
Restandardization Norms: Men: M = 0.34; SD = 0.75
Women: M = 0.32; SD = 0.71.

Ideas of Reference (6 Items)

True: 251 259 305 333 424 549
False: None
Restandardization Norms: Men: M = 1.01; SD = 1.27
Women: M = 1.08; SD = 1.28.

Delusions of Control (8 Items)

True: 24 144 162 216 228 336 355 361
False: None
Restandardization Norms: Men: M = 0.19; SD = 0.53
Women: M = 0.11; SD = 0.40.

Persecutory Ideas/Delusions (8 Items)

True: 42 99 138 144 216 259 333
False: 314
Restandardization Norms: Men: M = 0.51; SD = 0.94
Women: M = 0.41; SD = 0.84.

10

USE OF THE MMPI–2 IN OUTPATIENT MENTAL HEALTH SETTINGS

ROGER L. GREENE

Before looking at the empirical literature that has examined the impact of the MMPI–2 on treatment planning in outpatient mental health settings, there are several assumptions that need to be made explicit. First, if assessment tools or techniques of some type are not used in planning treatment interventions and evaluating their effectiveness, clinicians will be left to their clinical judgment in making such decisions. The literature on the multitude of problems with clinical judgment have been well documented (cf. Garb, 1998) and do not need to be repeated here other than to say that the actual issue is how to make our assessment tools or techniques better. Second, in a managed-care environment in which limited time and resources are allocated for treatment, it is even more important to optimize the intervention through an accurate assessment of the presenting problem. Rather than spending a number of sessions to allow the client's symptoms to arise spontaneously within the therapeutic alliance, the clinician needs to be making active interventions as quickly and precisely as possible. Third, our assessment tools or techniques can be no better than the criterion being predicted. If "treatment" consists of the clinician trying to enhance the self-esteem of the client or get in touch with feelings, such nebulous goals hardly can be predicted; and it is equally difficult to know if or when the intervention has been successful. Clinicians who are making the interventions need to make them as specific as possible, and then it becomes a very manageable task to find out what variables will predict them. Clear criteria that are measurable at some level have to be the beginning point in this process. Gold-standard criteria are rarely available in any area of intervention initially; but, by bootstrapping the assessment and treatment process, both can work to improve the other. In short, once a problem behavior or symptom can be identified reliably, then it becomes possible to consider what intervention might be appropriate. Monitoring the success of the intervention will highlight areas in which more precise assessment is needed or other variables need to be considered. Introducing these variables then directs the intervention and this feedback process can be continued. Finally, it also behooves us as specialists in assessment to realize that if it were 1940 and we were discussing state of the art in assessment, we would be talking about the MMPI, the Rorschach, and the TAT (Thematic Apperception Test). The fact that in 2005 we still are using these same techniques is mind-boggling. There are few fields in which the advances have been so limited. There is a clear need for significant innovation and creativity within the field of assessment.

Several books have examined the relationship between the MMPI/MMPI–2 and treatment planning. The interested reader should consult Dahlstrom, Welsh, and Dahlstrom (1975), who devoted an entire chapter to the MMPI and treatment evaluation that covers the literature through 1973. Butcher (1990b) has provided a more recent summary of the MMPI–2 in psychological treatment. Rather than review all of the specific statements that could be made about the MMPI–2 in outpatient treatment, only summary statements about major issues are made because of the space constraints for this chapter. The interested reader can refer to the various MMPI–2 sources (Butcher & Williams, 1992; Friedman, Lewak, Nichols, & Webb, 2001; Graham, 2000; Greene, 2000; Greene & Clopton, 2004) for more specific statements about treatment planning with a given scale or set of scales and for the research that supports them. The reader also should review chapter 7 of this volume by Perry, Miller, and Klump for another perspective on this general topic.

THERAPEUTIC ASSESSMENT

The first issue in the administration of the MMPI–2 or any other psychological test is ensuring that the client is invested in the process. A few extra minutes spent answering any questions the client may have about why the MMPI–2 is being administered and how the results will be used in determining the course of treatment will pay excellent dividends. Fischer (1994) has described the process of individualizing psychological assessment in which the client and the clinician collaborate to obtain the desired information. Finn (1996b) has written a splendid text on making the assessment process with the MMPI–2 therapeutic for the client; that text should be mandatory reading for all clinicians. (Chap. 8 of this volume by Finn and Kamphuis provides more depth on this important topic and Lewak, Marks, and Nelson, 1990, have devoted an entire book to this topic.) The major thesis of Finn's text is that the clinician should determine what the client wants to learn from the assessment process and then make sure that the client gets that feedback. Finn also provides specific examples of how clients can be given feedback about troublesome behaviors and symptoms that will be very insightful for the clinician who is just learning this process. If clinicians will follow the procedures suggested by Fischer and Finn, they should find that test-taking attitudes and validity issues become virtually a nonexistent process, because it does not make sense for a client to try to invalidate the MMPI–2 if he or she genuinely wants to learn something from its administration and is an active participant or collaborator in the process.

The importance of ensuring that clients have sufficient intellectual ability and reading skills to complete the MMPI–2 appropriately cannot be overemphasized. One of the primary causes of invalid MMPI–2s is the test taker's inability to read and comprehend the items, which require approximately a sixth- to eighth-grade reading level (Butcher, Dahlstrom, Graham, Tellegen, & Kaemmer, 1989; Butcher, Graham, et al., 2001). Standard, cassette-tape administrations of the MMPI–2 should be used any time that there is reason to suspect that the client's intellectual or reading ability may be inadequate for standard administration in a paper-and-pencil format. If clients are too toxic or neuropsychologically or psychiatrically impaired to complete the MMPI–2 consistently, further assessment or any educational or psychotherapy interventions will need to be delayed until they can function appropriately; clients may not be stable enough initially to be treated on an outpatient basis.

RISK FACTORS FOR OUTPATIENT VERSUS INPATIENT INTERVENTIONS

A number of risk factors must be evaluated when clinicians are deciding whether a client can be treated in an outpatient setting or whether some period of inpatient treatment is necessary: (a) dangerousness to self and others, (b) severe substance abuse or dependence, (c) florid psychotic symptoms, (d) lack of family or community support systems, (e) comorbid severe Axis II disorders, and (f) comorbid severe medical diseases. Most of these factors, particularly the last three, have to be evaluated by the clinician during the initial interview or mental-status examination, but the MMPI–2 can provide additional information even in these circumstances if the client is stable enough to complete the MMPI–2. A number of specific MMPI–2 items relate directly to dangerousness to self (150, 303, 505, 506, 520, 524, 530, and 546) and others (150, 540, 542, 548), severe substance abuse or dependence (264, 387, 429, 489, 511, 527, 544), and florid psychotic symptoms (138, 144, 162, 216, 228, 259, 314, 333, 424), which the clinician can review in assessing these risk factors. (The deviant response for all of these items is "true" except for items 314 and 429.) It is particularly important to make sure that the client's endorsement of these items is consistent with the information presented during the clinical interview. Any discrepancies between these two sources of information, such as reporting dangerousness to self or significant substance abuse or dependence during the clinical interview and not on the MMPI–2 or vice versa, must be investigated and documented carefully.

The items relating to dangerous to self (150, 303, 505, 506, 520, 524, 530, and 546) or others (150, 540, 542, 548) must be examined every time the MMPI–2 is administered, because these areas are an integral part of any treatment plan and not listed in their entirety anywhere on the Pearson National Computer Systems Extended Score Report. Clinicians should check the client's answer sheet to determine the responses to these specific items and decide whether they are worthy of being pursued via an interview. Omitting any of these items also warrants careful review of the client's rationale for not answering them with the assumption that they would have been endorsed in the deviant direction if the client had answered them. In addition, clinicians need to document that they have reviewed the client's responses to these items because they are integral to addressing the client's treatment and any potential litigation that may arise around standards of care.

TEST-TAKING ATTITUDES

If a client is unwilling to comply with completing the MMPI–2 in a consistent and accurate manner, there is little reason to expect that the client will be more compliant with other tasks in treatment. Consequently, clinicians should address such issues directly with the client rather than assuming that the reasons for giving the MMPI–2 are no longer important. If the clinician believes that the information to be provided by the MMPI–2 warrants administration of the test, the client's noncompliance should not be overlooked or dismissed lightly. (There are some aspects of the medical model that clinicians might keep in mind, since physicians rarely omit collecting a blood sample or an urine specimen simply because clients do not want to provide them.)

The MMPI–2 provides a quantitative measure of how clients view their symptomatology. The extensive literature on assessing the validity of this self-description provides valuable information for any intervention. (Chap. 3 of this volume by Bagby, Marshall, Bury, Bacchiochi, and Miller also provides more in-depth coverage of this general issue.) Probably the best documented outcome in this area is that clients who "fake-bad" or exaggerate their symptomatology—which classically has been described as a "plea for help"—are extremely prone to drop out of treatment prematurely across a variety of settings: alcohol and drug treatment, pain management, and so on. (This literature has been summarized in Greene & Clopton, 2004). Alternatively, they may have some reason for exaggerating the severity of their psychopathology that may interfere with their ability to participate in any form of treatment in a meaningful manner.

Clients who minimize the severity of their psychopathology have little internal motivation for treatment because they are not experiencing emotional distress. These clients' psychopathology and deviant behaviors are very chronic and ego–syntonic (not distressing to them), which is reflected by the *lack* of elevation of the MMPI–2 profile; consequently, their behaviors are very difficult to change in short-term treatment, if they can be changed at all. Also, if the person taking the MMPI–2 is not the identified client, he or she is not bothered by the presence of psychopathology in significant others, which does not bode well for any intervention or treatment.

In addition to clients exaggerating or minimizing their report of psychopathology on the MMPI–2, the concordance between the MMPI–2 scores and the client's behavior during the clinical interview and the clinical history must be considered. For example, the clinical presentation may be a clear manifestation of some disorder, say depression, yet when the client takes the MMPI–2, Scale 2 (*D*, Depression) and the content scale of Depression (DEP) are *not* elevated. In such a circumstance, the clinician is being alerted to the need to determine whether the clinical presentation has been misunderstood and, if that is not the case, to find out what the concept of depression means to this client. It is not unusual for clients to say that they are "depressed" when they actually are describing their irritation and frustration with their significant others and/or environmental conditions rather than an internalized mood disorder. Alternatively, clients may present in the clinical interview without any overt manifestations of depression, yet elevate scales 2 and DEP. In this instance, clients are more willing to report their depressive symptoms on the MMPI–2 than directly to the clinician. In this latter instance, the clinician may not realize the severity of the client's symptoms, because the client for whatever reason is unable or unwilling to report them directly. If the clinician fails to utilize some form of assessment with these patients, the clinician is very likely not to implement the appropriate treatment. In all of these instances, appropriate and effective treatment requires determining the concordance between the assessment results provided by the MMPI–2 and the clinical interview and history.

CONTENT-BASED INTERPRETATION

Clients who are willing and able to provide an accurate self-description on the MMPI–2 have good insight into their behavior and can share it openly with the clinician, which augurs well for any therapeutic intervention. Content-based interpretations of the MMPI–2 should reflect accurately the patients' current psychological status in these circumstances.[1]

There are several caveats to keep in mind when using the MMPI–2 content scales (Butcher, Graham, Williams, & Ben-Porath, 1990) in treatment planning. First, the clinician must administer all 567 items so that all of the items on these scales can be scored. Clinicians are well advised to use these scales routinely because they provide valuable information about clients with little additional time required for administration. Second, it is mandatory that clients be able and willing to provide an accurate self-description because the content scales are very susceptible to exaggerating or minimizing the severity of psychopathology due to the face-valid or obvious nature of the items. Third, elevation of the content scales reflects that clients are aware of and willing to report the behaviors that are being assessed by the specific scale. When clients have insight into their behavior and are willing to report accurately, these content scales provide a quick overview of how clients are viewing and responding to their current circumstances. Fourth, the absence of elevation of the content scales can reflect either that the behaviors are not characteristic of the client *or* the client is unaware of or unwilling to acknowledge these behaviors. When the content scales are *not* elevated, clinicians should determine which of these two alternative interpretations is more appropriate. However, clinicians are cautioned about making specific interpretations of *low* scores on the content scales, since no research has validated their correlates. Finally, the relative elevation of the content scales can be used as an index of the importance of that specific content area to the client for planning treatment because of the use of uniform T scores that make the percentiles equivalent across these scales.

[1]In the ensuing sections it will be assumed that the client has endorsed the items accurately, that is, that the client has neither exaggerated nor minimized the description of his or her psychopathology.

The axiom in these circumstances is that treatment cannot be initiated in an area that the client has not recognized as a problem. The MMPI–2 content scales are particularly valuable in this area because they provide an explicit statement of what problem areas are important to the client regardless of how important they may be to the clinician.

When a content scale is elevated at a T score of 65 or higher, the clinician should review the content component scales (Ben-Porath & Sherwood, 1993) to determine the salient components that are producing the elevation. The content component scales are particularly useful in those cases in which an elevation can reflect two very disparate areas of content within the scale that have very different implications for treatment. The best example of this circumstance is that an elevation to a T score of 65 or higher on ANG (Anger) could reflect either ANG1 (Explosive Behavior) or ANG2 (Irritability). The former component scale reflects angry behaviors whereas the latter reflects an irritable mood. A similar situation occurs on ASP (Antisocial Practices) that is composed of ASP1 (Antisocial Attitudes) and ASP2 (Antisocial Behavior). Finally, it is imperative that clinicians know that clients can have raw scores of zero (T = 45) on DEP4 (Suicidal Ideation) and the client still can endorse items with suicidal content (e.g., 150, 505, 524), because all of these items are not found within DEP4.

Clinicians frequently are confronted with MMPI–2s in which the interpretive information for a given scale is or may seem to be contradictory to the information provided by another scale. Several procedures can be followed to resolve such inconsistencies. Probably the best method for resolving such discrepancies involves exploring the issue with the client directly. If the client is not available for some reason and the client has endorsed the items accurately, the MMPI–2 content scales and the specific items that are endorsed should provide a quick means of resolving any discrepancies that may exist with the empirically derived clinical scales that may have a number of different correlates. Clinicians should realize that most, if not all, MMPI–2s will have some minor discrepancies among a few scales so they should not expect perfect concordance. In short, there will be some interpretive challenge in nearly every MMPI–2.

THERAPEUTIC ALLIANCE

The MMPI–2 can provide valuable information for the clinician in how to structure interactions with a specific client. The first step in creating a positive therapeutic alliance is through the use of therapeutic assessment that has already been described. Once that process has been initiated, a number of MMPI–2 scales provide helpful information for the clinician.

Clients who elevate scales 6 (*Pa*, Paranoia) and Cynicism (CYN) tend to be rigid, hypersensitive, and suspicious so that interpersonal contact with them is difficult. Clinicians must maintain their interpersonal distance with these clients and proceed slowly until they can gain their trust and confidence. Confrontational interventions are particularly contraindicated in these clients. Conversely, clients with low scores (T < 50) on scales 6 and Cynicism and elevated scores on Scale 3 (*Hy*, Hysteria) and particularly its subscales of Denial of Social Anxiety (Hy_1), Need for Affection (Hy_2), Inhibition of Aggression (Hy_5), and Poignancy (Pa_2) tend to be overly trusting and find it difficult to consider that others may not have their best interests at heart. These clients tend to be used and abused by others and easily can be abused by the clinician. Group interventions are particularly effective with them so that others can model appropriate social interactions and so that they can learn how to judge the intentions of others.

Clinicians need to be very attentive in monitoring their interactions with clients who elevate Poignancy (Pa_2). These clients are easily bruised and abused in their interactions and unlikely to tell others about their hypersensitivity. It is easy to drive these clients out of treatment by not being aware of these qualities.

Finally, clients who elevate Inability to Disclose (TRT2) are explicitly telling the clinician that treatment is going to be difficult with them. Clinicians need to proceed very slowly with these clients, and the goals need to be modest until some semblance of a therapeutic alliance is established. Cognitive–behavior treatments focused on the behaviors or symptoms that led these clients to treatment are most likely to be successful because of the here-and-now focus.

UNELEVATED SCALES

Frequently the most valuable information in an MMPI–2 profile is the scales that are *not* elevated. The conventional emphasis on the specific clinical, content, and supplementary scales that are elevated can lead clinicians to ignore low-point scales or scales within the normal range. For example, clients who have T scores at or below 50 on scales 2 (*D*) and 7 (*Pt*, Psychasthenia) are not reporting or experiencing any distress over whatever behaviors or symptoms brought them to treatment. Similarly, clients who have low scores on scales 1 (*Hs*, Hypochondriasis), 2, and 3 have few psychological defenses preventing their behaviors or symptoms from being expressed overtly. Clients who have low scores on Scale 9 (*Hy*) have little or no energy to invest in the treatment process. The implications of these low scores for treatment planning should be apparent.

SPECIFIC CLINICAL ISSUES

It is rather typical to organize discussion of the MMPI–2 by categories of scales such as the clinical scales, content scales, and supplementary scales. This organizational structure tends to ignore the common information provided by scales throughout the MMPI–2 that are relevant to a specific clinical issue. This structure also tends to be very general and frequently does not provide the specific information needed for evidence-based interventions within a managed-care environment. Consequently, the organization in the following section is on some of the specific clinical issues that the clinician must evaluate in planning the treatment intervention and how the MMPI–2 can address these issues. Because of space limitations, only the following clinical issues are discussed briefly: (a) somatization, (b) substance abuse or dependence, (c) nature and quality of interpersonal relations, (d) psychotic symptomatology, (e) anger management, (f) mood disturbances, and (g) psychotropic medications. Determination of the relative importance of each of these clinical issues is one of the first tasks that the clinician must accomplish in deciding what type of interventions—and in what order—is needed for this specific patient. Exhibit 10.1 summarizes the major points that clinicians need to consider in planning treatment with the MMPI–2. Following discussion of these clinical issues, a clinical case illustrates their use in planning treatment.

The clinician should look for consistency among the scales that are elevated in deciding the importance of particular clinical issues in treatment planning. Using somatization as an example, if Scale 1 is elevated and it is to be interpreted as reflecting the presence of somatization, other clinical scales—3 or 7—or content scales—Health Concerns

EXHIBIT 10.1
Highlight: Steps for Planning Treatment With the MMPI–2

- Evaluate risk factors for outpatient versus inpatient interventions.
- Therapeutic administration.
- Review dangerousness-to-self-and-other items.
- Review demographic variables.
- Assess test-taking attitudes.
- Determine and interpret code type.
- Evaluate clinical issues:
  - Somatization
  - Substance abuse or dependence
  - Nature and quality of interpersonal relations
  - Psychotic symptomatology
  - Anger management
  - Mood disturbances
  - Need for psychotropic medications
- Integrate MMPI–2 data with clinical interview and history.
- Provide feedback to client and implement treatment.

(HEA)—suggestive of somatization should be elevated. In this same vein, the type of somatic symptoms will be very different if Neurological Symptoms (HEA2) and Bizarre Sensory Experiences (Sc_6) are elevated than if Gastrointestinal Symptoms (HEA1) or General Health Concerns (HEA3), Physical Malfunctioning (D_3) and Lassitude–Malaise (Hy_3) are elevated. If such concordance is not found among somatization scales, some other interpretation of Scale 1 that is consistent with the other elevations or lack thereof must be considered. The more concordance that is found among scales that have the same correlates and/or scale content, the more treatment planning should emphasize this particular clinical issue.

Somatization

The assessment of somatization is one of the real strengths of the MMPI–2 that covers the range from broad, nonspecific symptoms—HEA3, D_3, and Hy_3—to very specific symptoms of medical and neurological disorders—HEA2, Sc_6, and HEA1. Careful review of the client's history is warranted when these latter scales (HEA2, Sc_6, and HEA1) are elevated to determine whether the symptoms reflect past medical conditions that are being well managed or new or undiagnosed conditions. When the client is reporting new or undiagnosed medical conditions, referral for a medical or neurological evaluation is necessary.

Clients who are actually physically ill will endorse their legitimate physical symptoms, but they will not endorse the entire gamut of somatization symptoms represented by these scales. Scale 2 is more likely to be elevated by actual physical illness. If a client with actual physical illness obtains a T score of 75 or higher on Scale 1, there are likely to be somatization features in addition to the physical condition; and the client is probably trying to manipulate or control significant others in the environment with his or her somatization symptoms. Although the client may vehemently argue that the symptoms reflect legitimate physical concerns, the clinician should not ignore the elevation on these somatization scales. The somatization features in these individuals usually are readily apparent despite their protests to the contrary.

Cripe, Maxwell, and Hill (1995) have developed a set of neurological-symptom scales for the MMPI–2 that could be used as a means whereby clients provide the clinician with an indication of the specific categories in which they are experiencing symptoms. The clinician then can explore whether these specific symptoms are the result of the neurological impairment, their reaction to living with the impairment, prior or comorbid psychiatric problems, or more likely some combination of all of these factors.

Somatization also is a crude index of psychological mindedness or sophistication, and typically persons who elevate these scales are uninterested in exploring any psychological reasons for their bodily symptoms. Consequently, significant somatization reflected by elevations on scales 1 and 3 is a negative predictor for outcome in traditional forms of psychotherapy. In these instances, a behaviorally based intervention specific to somatization is warranted (cf. Gatchel & Wesiberg, 2000; Keller & Butcher, 1991; Vendrig, 2000).

Substance Abuse or Dependence

There are three MMPI–2 scales—the Addiction Acknowledgment Scale (AAS; Weed, Butcher, McKenna, & Ben-Porath, 1992), the Addiction Potential Scale (APS; Weed et al., 1992), and the MacAndrew Alcoholism Scale—Revised (MAC–R; MacAndrew, 1965)—and a number of specific items (264, 387, 429, 487, 489, 511, 527, 544) that can be used to assess whether substance abuse or dependence is a treatment issue for the patient. (The deviant response for all of these items is "true" except for item 429.) Since a number of these items are written in the past tense, it is important to determine through the clinical interview and review of the client's history whether the use or abuse of substances is ongoing or reflects earlier behavior patterns. Two items (489 and 511) explicitly ask about current alcohol and drug use and should be explored with clients whenever they are endorsed as being "true." The AAS is a very homogeneous set of 13 items directly assessing substance use and abuse. The APS is a composite of a heterogeneous group of items reflecting the varied consequences of substance abuse that have less of a flavor of resentment and antisocial qualities than might be expected on such a scale. A number of caveats must be kept in mind when using the MAC–R to assess substance abuse or dependence: (a) men score about two raw-score points higher than women across most samples, so different cutting scores will be necessary by gender; (b) clinicians need to be very cautious in using the MAC–R in non-White ethnic groups; (c) hit rates and classification accuracy decrease substantially when clinicians are trying to discriminate between substance abusing and non–substance abusing psychiatric patients, which is a frequent differential diagnosis; (d) hit rates and classification accuracy may be unacceptably low in medical samples; and, probably most important, (e) the MAC–R scale is a general measure of personality that is best described as reflecting impulsive, risk-taking, sensation-seeking behaviors rather than substance abuse per se. Weed, Butcher, and Ben-Porath (1995) have provided a thorough review of all MMPI–2 measures of substance abuse.

Allen (1991) and Greene (1994) have suggested that clients who have high versus low scores on the MAC–R may need different types of treatment. These suggestions are consistent with MacAndrew's (1981) formulation of the differences between high and low scorers on the

MAC–R. High scorers on the MAC–R are more likely to be risk takers who are extraverted and impulsive, and they may have better treatment outcomes in a group-oriented and confrontational program. On the other hand, low scorers are more likely to be risk avoiders who are introverted, withdrawn, and depressed, and they may have better treatment outcomes in a less confrontational and more supportive program. In substance abuse settings, clinicians should be aware that clients who display psychopathic tendencies or who are characterized by denial and minimization of the severity of their psychopathology may be more prone to drop out of treatment, and clinicians should confront these issues directly.

Interpersonal Relations

The client's social orientation, either introverted or extroverted, is assessed very well by scales 0 (Si) and Social Discomfort (SOD); and extreme scores in either direction need to be addressed in the treatment plan. Clients who elevate these two scales seek to stay away from other people, whether individuals or groups, because they feel uneasy and awkward in such situations and because they are happier being alone. They are seen as socially introverted, shy, and withdrawn. Assertiveness training or group therapy is frequently indicated in this instance. These clients may require support from the clinician in the initiation of group therapy because of their discomfort in such situations.

Clients with low scores on scales 0 and SOD are socially outgoing, energetic, and socially facile; thus, they make a good initial impression on others, particularly if Scale 4 (Pd, Personality Disorder) is elevated. Longer exposure to these clients soon reveals, however, their irresponsibility, unreliability, moodiness, and resentment. The clinician should be aware of the favorable initial impression typical of these clients and not be overly influenced by it. Clients with extremely low scores (T scores below 35) on Scale 0 are described as being flighty, superficial in their relationships with others, and lacking any real intimacy. These characteristics are especially likely if the client simultaneously elevates scales 3 and 4. These clients evidence basic deficits in the process of attachment that must be considered in developing the therapeutic alliance and planning any treatment intervention.

Four different scales examine familial relations: Family Problems (FAM; Butcher et al., 1990), Family Problems (Wiggins, 1966), Marital Distress Scale (MDS; Hjemboe, Butcher, & Almagor, 1992), and Familial Discord (Pd_1). A topic that needs to be pursued on the MMPI–2 is the specific nature of the many items relating to family problems and familial discord and whether they pertain to the current familial circumstances or the family of origin.

Scale 5 (Mf, Masculinity–Femininity) also moderates how clients will express the psychopathology that is being tapped by a specific clinical issue. Men who elevate Scale 5 above a T score of 65 will be passive and introverted; and these characteristics decrease the probability of their acting out and increase the probability of their obsessing, ruminating, and fantasizing. Conversely, men who have T scores below 40 on Scale 5 will be active, outgoing, and extraverted; and these characteristics increase the probability of their acting out and decrease the probability of their obsessing, ruminating, and fantasizing. (These same statements will hold for women if their T score on Scale 5 is the opposite of what has been indicated for men.) For example, the treatment plan for a male client with a T score above 65 on Scale 5 should be more cognitively oriented, while a client with a T score below 40 will do better with a more active, behaviorally oriented treatment.

Psychotic Symptomatology

Patients who elevate Bizarre Mentations (BIZ) and, particularly, Psychotic Symptomatology (BIZ1) are reporting a variety of overtly psychotic symptoms that should be readily apparent on even casual interactions with the client; and they are very likely to be the reason that the client is being seen for treatment. Frequently, the issue with these clients is whether they are stable enough to be treated in an outpatient setting. When patients are stabilized on psychotropic medications, the clinician can start to treat the other specific clinical issues.

Clients with less overt psychotic symptomatology are more difficult to identify with the MMPI–2, and the clinician is left with hints on a number of scales and from the clinical history of the probability of a psychotic process. Referral for further evaluation with the Rorschach is warranted in these cases to determine more accurately whether a psychotic process is involved.

Anger Management

A number of MMPI–2 scales—Anger (ANG), Explosive Behavior (ANG1), Irritability (ANG2), Aggression (AGGR), Hostility (*Ho*), and two sets of critical items (Koss–Butcher Threatened Assault and Lachar–Wrobel Problematic Anger)—provide the clinician with important information on how clients manage anger. As clients elevate AGGR and ANG1, they are very likely to have poorly controlled anger and they are prone to angry tirades and destructive outbursts that have the potential to hurt others and damage property. If constrained by external circumstances, they also express their anger in more controlled ways through frequent nagging and teasing and by being stubborn. They frequently report being a helpless spectator to their angry outbursts and may disapprove of their own destructiveness yet feel unable to control their anger. Clients who elevate ANG2 and *Ho* and do not elevate AGGR and ANG1 are more likely to be irritable and grouchy and display anger as a negative mood rather than angry behaviors. In the former instance, anger management is indicated as part of the treatment plan; whereas, in the latter instance, assertiveness training frequently is helpful so that clients can clearly articulate their needs to others.

Mood Disturbances

The initial consideration in the evaluation of the client for a depressive mood disorder is whether the client has general negative affect, which is common to most forms of psychopathology or, specifically, depressive mood. Numerous MMPI–2 scales reflect general negative affect—for example, Welsh Anxiety (*A*), Scale 7, Negative Emotionality/Neuroticism (NEGE), College Maladjustment (*Mt*), Posttraumatic Stress Disorder–Keane (Pk)—and elevations on these scales should not be taken as specific indicators of depressive mood. Also, the primary source of variation in a majority of the MMPI–2 content scales is general negative affect and it should be considered first in the interpretation before the specific content of the individual scale. Consequently, elevated scores on Scale 2 and Depression (DEP) cannot be assumed to reflect depression without consideration of the influence of general negative affect. However, elevations on Low Positive Emotionality/Introversion (INTR), Low Positive Emotionality (RC2lpe; Tellegen et al., 2003), Lack of Drive (DEP1), and Low Motivation (TRT1) reflect significant anhedonia, which is an important marker for depressive mood as well as schizophrenia and psychopathy. In most instances, a review of the clinical history quickly discriminates among these three alternative causes of anhedonia. Elevations on these four scales also reflect a clinical process that has taken some time to develop rather than being an acute reaction to some stressor. In these instances, the clinician and the client will need to realize that it will take some time to see improvement in and alleviate the depressive mood.

Manic mood disorders should be considered any time that Scale 9 (*Ma*) is elevated above a T score of 65 with a careful review of the client's clinical history for mood swings. The probability of a manic mood disorder increases when the client has low scores on scales 2 and 7, as well as the other scales measuring general negative affect—for example, A, Scale 7, NEGE, *Mt*, Pk—and low scores on scales 0 and SOD.

Referrals for Psychotropic Medications

There are numerous instances in which the MMPI–2 profile is suggestive of the need for a referral for psychotropic medications. In making these referrals, the clinician must be aware of whether the client can accurately describe his or her symptoms to the psychiatrist. For example, a patient who has a depressive mood disorder but for whatever reason is unwilling or unable to recognize this depression is unlikely to be assessed accurately by the psychiatrist without appropriate referral information.

Extremely elevated profiles (four or more clinical scales greater than T80) are indicative of significant emotional distress that requires a very active intervention and may even require a brief period of hospitalization to stabilize the patient. If hospitalization is not necessary, some form of antianxiety medication is very likely to be needed to provide relief from the debilitating level of symptoms that are being experienced.

Any time that a mood or psychotic disorder has been identified on the MMPI–2, the clinician should consider referral for a psychiatric evaluation to determine whether initiation of or change in psychotropic medication is needed. Clinicians need to be cautioned again that referrals for medication for depressive mood disorders should be made when the MMPI–2 is reflective specifically of a depressive mood disorder and not general negative affect. Medication in this latter instance probably is not indicated.

Clinical Case Example

The client is a 45-year-old, separated, White male who came to the outpatient clinic to explore his continuing inability to maintain an interpersonal relationship. The woman whom he was currently dating had insisted that he get psychotherapy as a condition for their continuing relationship.

The client had been raised in an alcoholic family, and he started using alcohol and drugs in junior high. He managed to finish high school, although he was using alcohol and drugs on a nearly daily basis. He entered the service after graduation but was discharged within a few months because of his substance abuse. He spent the next 10 years going through a number of relationships and jobs as his abuse of alcohol increased. In his early thirties, he entered alcohol treatment for the first time and he has been sober since then (nearly 14 years). At this same time, he found stable employment and maintained the same job for nearly 10 years.

He was laid off approximately 2 years ago when the economy worsened. He exhausted his unemployment benefits as he waited for his previous employer to rehire him. He started becoming depressed as a result of his inability to find employment and the termination of a relationship that had lasted nearly 2 years. He started sleeping for long periods of time each day,

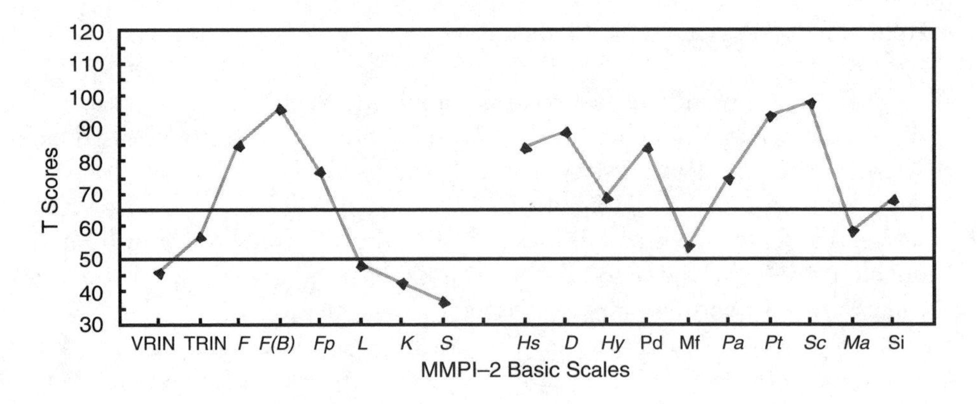

Figure 10.1. MMPI–2 basic validity and clinical scales.

and he gained a significant amount of weight. He also started to frequent adult theaters and to engage in promiscuous sex with both men and women. He was visibly upset about his promiscuity, and the woman with whom he currently was in a relationship was appropriately concerned about the risk of HIV or AIDS. Throughout these stressors, he maintained his sobriety and his active involvement in Alcoholics Anonymous.

The client had rather constant suicidal ideation with a plan that he could implement at any time. His suicidal ideation was monitored on a constant basis, and he was encouraged to enter inpatient treatment for stabilization of his symptoms at any time that he or the therapist felt it was necessary. He refused inpatient treatment and agreed to a no-suicide contract.

The MMPI–2 was administered after the second session to help the clinician in planning the treatment intervention. He endorsed four (303, 505, 506, 520) of the dangerousness-to-self items and none of the dangerousness-to-others items. His endorsement of these dangerousness-to-self items was expected given his clinical history. There are no demographic variables that will impact the interpretation of his MMPI–2. He endorsed the items consistently and accurately and produced a very complex but well-defined 7–8/8–7 code type in which seven clinical scales are elevated above a T score of 65 (Figure 10.1). The initial consideration with a 7–8/8–7 code type is whether there is any indication of a thought disorder. Review of the PSY–5, content (Figure 10.2), content component (Figure 10.3), and Harris–Lingoes (Figure 10.4) scales provides somewhat mixed data on this issue. He slightly elevated the Psychoticism (PSYC = 58) and Bizarre Mentation (BIZ = 57) scales but did not elevate Psychotic Symptomatology (BIZ1 = 44). The lack of elevation of Psychotic Symptomatology and review of his clinical history allowed the possibility of a thought disorder to be excluded from further consideration. The alternative interpretation of a

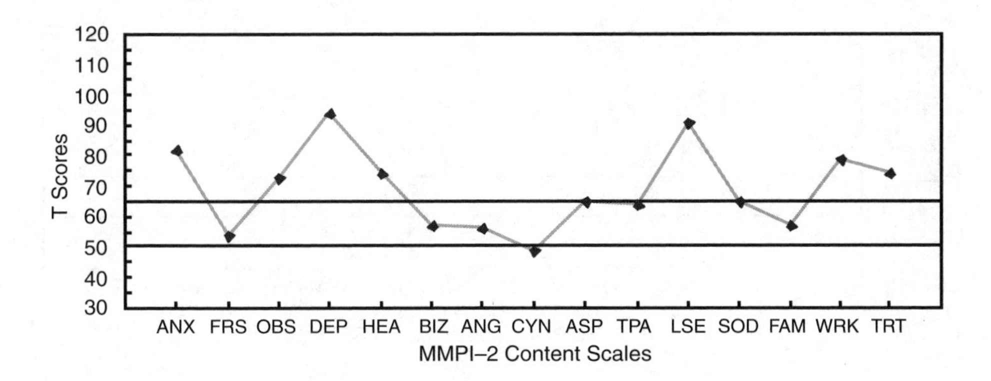

Figure 10.2. MMPI–2 content scales.

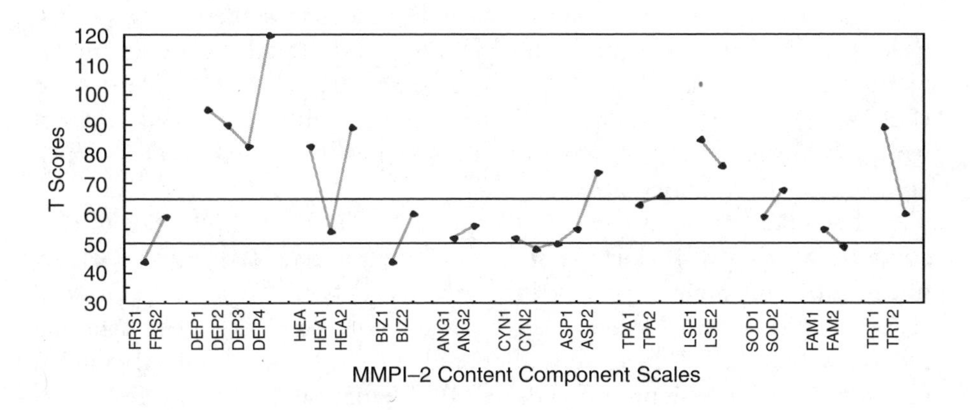

Figure 10.3. MMPI–2 content component scales.

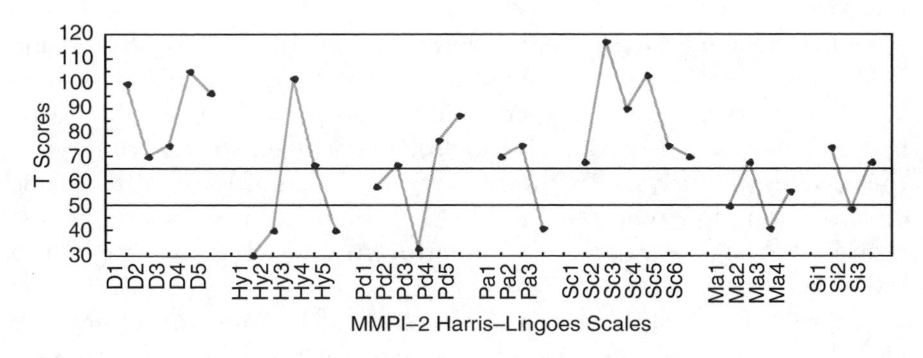

Figure 10.4. MMPI–2 Harris and Lingoes subscales.

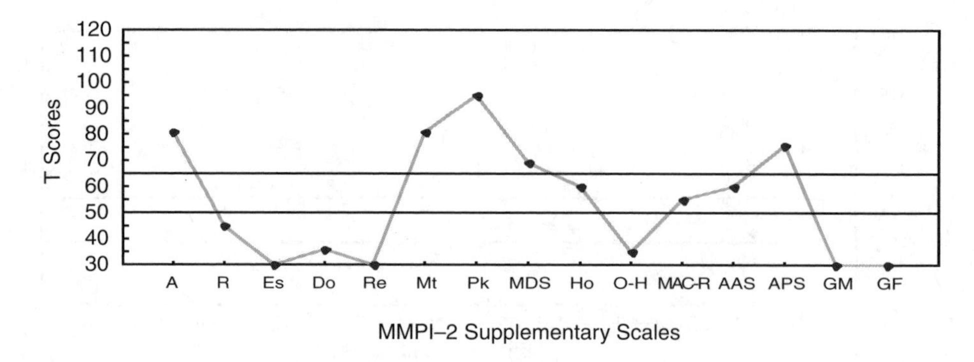

Figure 10.5. MMPI–2 supplementary scales.

7–8/8–7 code type is of a rather severe and intractable depressive mood disorder that is seen throughout the MMPI–2 and already has been documented in his history. The client elevated scales 2 (*D* = 89), Depression (DEP = 94), Introversion or Low Positive Emotionality (INTR = 78), all of which are documenting the severity of his depressive disorder and the presence of significant anhedonia.

The client is significantly introverted: Scale 0 (Si = 68); Social Discomfort (SOD = 65). Somewhat surprisingly, he reported only relatively mild family problems: Family Problems (FAM = 57); Family Discord (FAM1 = 55); Familial Alienation (FAM2 = 49)(see Figure 10.4); Familial Discord (Pd_1 = 58). He is very alienated from others: Social Alienation (Sc_1 = 68); Social Alienation (Pd_4 = 78); Alienation–Self and Others (Si_3 = 68); and for himself: Low Self-Esteem (LSE = 91); Self-Doubt (LSE1 = 85); Submissiveness (LSE2 = 76); Self-Alienation (Pd_5 = 87); Emotional Alienation (Sc_2 = 117). GM (Gender Masculine) and GF (Gender Feminine) were not interpreted.

The client elevated the Addiction Acknowledgment (AAS = 60) and Addiction Potential (APS = 76) scales (Figure 10.5), but he did not elevate the MacAndrew Alcoholism scale (MAC–R = 53). Even though he had over 14 years of sobriety, it should be remembered that a number of these items are written in the past tense (264, 487) and still can be endorsed. The low score on the MAC–R might seem surprising at first thought, but he is very depressed and introverted, which is characterized by low scores.

Based on the MMPI–2 and the clinical history, the client was placed in a cognitive–behavioral treatment for his depression. He currently was taking antidepressant medication that was monitored regularly with his prescribing physician. He also was seen concurrently in group psychotherapy to focus on his alienation from himself and others.

Given his successful history in Alcoholics Anonymous, he was encouraged to attend a self-help group that focused on promiscuous sexual behavior.

The client was followed nearly 1 year in outpatient psychotherapy. His depressive mood gradually improved as a result of the individual and group psychotherapy. He continued to maintain his relationship with his woman friend. Although he was finding it difficult to maintain any length of "sobriety" with his promiscuous sexual behavior, he had a sponsor and continued to attend meetings regularly.

SUMMARY

The MMPI–2 provides an efficient and cost-effective overview of the specific clinical issues that the clinician must evaluate in planning treatment in an outpatient mental health setting. The MMPI–2 also provides a quantitative index of test-taking attitudes that is not available in the clinical interview or with semistructured clinical interviews. Both of these features make the MMPI–2 an excellent choice for the therapeutic assessment of clients in a managed-care setting in which the focus is on evidence-based treatments.

11

USE OF THE MMPI–2 IN MEDICAL SETTINGS

PAUL A. ARBISI AND RICHARD J. SEIME

As initially conceived by Starke Hathaway, the MMPI was intended to be used both in psychiatric settings and in medical settings to improve clinical predication (Hathaway & McKinley, 1940). Items that were ultimately included on the MMPI were derived not only from psychiatric examinations and textbooks but also from "directions for case taking in neurology and medicine" (Hathaway & McKinley, 1940). Consequently, items were intentionally included on the MMPI to tap aspects of a medical patient's clinical presentation and personality. This deliberate inclusion of item content associated with the clinical presentation of medical patients makes the MMPI/MMPI–2 a potent tool in the arsenal of the psychological consultant in medical settings. The MMPI/MMPI–2 has enjoyed wide acceptance among health psychologists (Piotrowski & Lubin, 1990) and physicians for use in the evaluations of medical patients (Swenson, Rome, Pearson, & Brannick, 1965).

Indeed, over 60 years' worth of accumulated data on the MMPI and MMPI–2 in medical settings include literally tens of thousands of individual profiles (Arbisi & Butcher, 2004c; Butcher, Arbisi, Atlis, & McNulty, 2003; Henrichs, 1981). Research using the MMPI to identify clinically relevant features of medical patients has attempted to characterize medical patients in terms of their response to medical conditions and tendency to accurately report physical pain and discomfort (Lees-Haley, English, & Glenn, 1991). Further, scales such as the Low Back scale were developed in order to aid the physician in differentiating between patients complaining of low back pain who had an organic source for that pain and those whose pain complaints were primarily functional in nature (Hanvik, 1951). More recently, the MMPI–2 has been used, in part, to characterize the psychosocial functioning of individuals coping with chronic illness such as human immunodeficiency virus (HIV) infection (Inman Hanlon, Esther, Robertson, Hall, & Robertson, 2002) and systemic lupus erythematosis (Omdal, Waterloo, Koldingsnes, Husby, & Mellgren, 2003).

With the long history and sometimes controversial application of MMPI/MMPI–2-based assessment in medical settings in mind, this chapter attempts to present a practical aid in interpreting the MMPI–2 within medical settings. A selective empirically based review of the literature as it relates to the interpretation of the MMPI and MMPI–2 in medical settings is presented. Specifically, the use of the MMPI–2 in the assessment of psychopathology and substance abuse as manifest in the medicine clinic is discussed. Furthermore, the use of the MMPI–2 in the assessment of chronic fatigue, chronic pain, and screening for organ transplant and surgical intervention is presented. Finally, the use of the MMPI–2 in the identification of personality traits that place individuals at greater risk for coronary heart disease (CHD) and engagement in adverse health-related behavior is also discussed.

THE MMPI–2 AND THE FUNCTIONAL VERSUS ORGANIC DICHOTOMY

Before delving into practical matters related to the use and interpretation of the MMPI–2 in medical settings, it is important to directly address the parameters of the MMPI–2 with regard to the functional versus organic issue. The MMPI clinical Scale 1 (Hypochondriasis) was developed by contrasting 50 cases of "pure" hypochondriasis with the normative group (McKinley & Hathaway, 1980a). In a similar fashion, MMPI Scale 3 (Hysteria) was derived by contrasting psychiatric inpatients who had received the diagnosis of psychoneurosis or hysteria or who had been noted to have characteristic hysterical components to their personality with the normative group (McKinley & Hathaway, 1980b). Further efforts to apply empirical keying in an attempt to differentiate individuals with functional conditions from those with more organic problems were evidenced in the development of the Low Back scale (Hanvik, 1951). Unfortunately, these attempts to identify individuals with functional somatic complaints based on MMPI responses were not entirely successful since individuals who displayed moderate elevations on these scales frequently had well-established objective medical conditions that produced pain and discomfort or reflected actual increases in the severity of medical conditions (Inman Hanlon et al., 2002). Consequently, there have been recommendations to avoid using the MMPI/MMPI–2 in medical conditions to address issues related to pain or somatization (Fishbain, Cutler, Rosomoff, & Rosomoff, 1999; Love & Peck, 1987).

In light of the volume of literature addressing the comorbidity of chronic medical conditions and psychological disturbance (cf. Gatchel, 2004), we feel that the recommendation to avoid using the MMPI–2 to address issues related to pain or somatization is unwarranted. There is convincing empirical evidence for utility of the MMPI–2 in assessing medical patients' suitability for medical procedures and assessing the presence of psychiatric conditions that will influence medical treatment. The MMPI–2 provides a comprehensive view of the presence or absence of emotional distress such as depression and anxiety, as well as personality traits or features that may promote or hinder adaptation to a chronic medical illness (Arbisi & Butcher, 2004c). Furthermore, despite the fact that moderate scale elevation on the MMPI–2 somatic scales (e.g., 1, 3, and Health Concerns) can reflect genuine somatic problems, extreme elevations are associated with somatization and preoccupation with somatic concerns (Barefoot, Beckham, Peterson, Haney, & Williams, 1992; Shekele, Vernon, & Ostfeld, 1991; Wetzel, Guze, Cloninger, Martin, & Clayton, 1994).

USE OF THE MMPI–2 AS A BROADBAND ASSESSMENT IN MEDICAL SETTINGS

The diagnostic questions that confront the clinician working in medical settings are frequently the same as those that are posed in mental health settings. For example, medical patients frequently present to primary care providers with co-occurring mental disorders, including substance abuse, depression, anxiety, and even psychosis (Jackson, Houston, Hanling, Terhaar, & Yun, 2001; Olfson et al., 2002). Often, substance abuse or dependence is first identified through contact with a primary care provider in a medical setting (Roeloffs, Fink, Unutzer, Tang, & Wells, 2001). Moreover, some physical conditions are more frequently associated with depression and suicidal ideation in primary care settings than are other medical conditions (Goodwin, Kroenke, Hoven, & Spitzer, 2003). In particular, congestive heart failure may have a higher associated rate of depression that may contribute to a higher rate of adverse outcomes (Jiang et al.,

2001). Finally, comorbid depression leads to increased health care costs independent of a chronic medical condition (Katon, Lin, Russo, & Unutzer, 2003). Consequently, it is important in both outpatient and inpatient primary care medical settings to provide accurate assessment of mental health issues in order to facilitate the identification and treatment of mental illness. Hence, the use of a broadband measure of psychopathology such as the MMPI–2 can provide information regarding a range of psychiatric conditions that frequently present in medical settings. There are, however, unique aspects associated with assessment within a medical setting in which the MMPI–2 can provide a significant contribution.

According to Sweet, Tovian, and Suchy (2003), the goal of the psychologist performing assessments in medical settings is to contribute to a broader understanding of the patient. This understanding can include the patient's relative psychological assets and weaknesses; evidence of psychopathology that contribute to, are in response to, or are independent of the physical disease process; the patient's emotional response to the illness and medical treatment; and, finally, the identification of preferred coping strategies mustered in response to the medical condition and treatments (Sweet et al., 2003). In addition, the psychologist performing an evaluation in a medical setting can address questions related to the presence of malingering or factious disorder and the interaction between personality, psychological disorders, and medical conditions. As a broadband objective measure of psychopathology and personality, the MMPI–2 can contribute to the goals of assessment in medical settings and help objectively differentiate between what is an expectable reaction to medical illness and a more psychologically complicated response.

USE OF THE MMPI–2 TO IDENTIFY FACTORS ASSOCIATED WITH MALADAPTIVE COPING

In meeting the goals of assessment in medical settings, a consensus has emerged regarding the patient's response to his or her medical condition and the development of pain and disability. Indeed, most contemporary pain experts view the psychological response to medical illness and subjective experience of pain as multidimensional processes (Gatchel, Polatin, & Mayer, 1995). Specifically, a diathesis stress model has been proposed to help understand the unique and multifactorial response that any given individual can manifest to physical illness. The diathesis stress model specifies that preexisting unexpressed individual characteristics such as personality traits or coping patterns become activated by the experience of medical illness and associated pain (Banks & Kerns, 1996; Dersh, Polatin, & Gatchel, 2002). Indeed, MMPI profiles of acutely medically ill patients and those with chronic conditions including nonmalignant pain show distinctive responses to the experience of medical illness and pain (Love & Peck, 1987). Consequently, use of the MMPI–2 in medical settings can help objectively identify personality factors that serve to augment or diminish both emotional and behavioral coping strategies in response to medical illness. Moreover, the MMPI–2 can also assess emotional and psychological resilience by identifying the degree of distress and demoralization that is present both before and after a medical intervention (Tellegen et al., 2003). Finally, the MMPI–2 can help the assessor to objectively describe the individual amenability to treatment and the probability that treatment compliance will be compromised either by personality styles or ongoing substance abuse or dependence issues.

In the remainder of the chapter, we first address general interpretive strategies for the MMPI–2 in medical settings followed by specific discussion of the use of the MMPI–2 in the treatment of chronic pain, organ transplant, bariatric surgery, and health-related behavior.

GENERAL INTERPRETIVE STRATEGIES IN A MEDICAL SETTING

Validity Scale Interpretation

A major advantage in the use of the MMPI–2 over other broadband measures of psychopathology is the presence of effective validity scales that allow the accurate identification of response distortion. There are two basic classes of threats to profile validity detected by the MMPI–2 validity scales: content nonresponsivity and content-response faking (Nichols & Greene, 1997). In the former, the individual fails to respond to the content of items by either failing to respond to the items or responding to the items in a fixed or random manner. The Cannot Say (?) scale identifies a failure to respond to items, and the Variable Response Inconsistency (VRIN) scale and the True Response Inconsistency (TRIN) scale identify random and fixed responding, respectively. In medical settings, clouding of consciousness and compromised attention due to the direct effect of medical illness or of therapeutic agents can lead to an inability to complete the MMPI–2. Of course, protocols in which the patient was unable to attend consistently to the content of the MMPI–2 items should not be interpreted and the MMPI–2 should not be readministered until the patient's mental status has cleared.

Faking-Good

Content-response faking can be a serious problem in medical settings, particularly when the evaluation occurs within the context of a screening process for receipt of scarce medical resources such as a donor organ or access to specialized treatment programs. The more likely and adaptive response under those conditions is a fake-good approach to the MMPI–2 in which the patient presents him- or herself as virtuous and effective and minimizes any psychopathology or distress that may be present. It is critical for the evaluator to have some estimate of the degree to which the patient minimizes psychiatric symptoms and maximizes emotional resilience since the presence of untreated psychiatric conditions can lead to adverse outcomes and increased health care costs. The MMPI–2 contains several scales that provide accurate information regarding minimization and defensiveness (Baer & Miller, 2002). In general, the Lie (*L*) scale and the Correction (*K*) scale both produce large effect sizes when differentiating individuals who are faking-good on the MMPI–2 from those who are responding honestly (Baer & Miller, 2002). Case Example 1 illustrates minimization and defensiveness.

Case Example 1

"*I am fatigued and I ache*." A 54-year-old woman was referred by her primary care provider with a referral question of whether or not depression was playing a role in her fatigue and should be treated or whether her complaints should be addressed further by referral to physical medicine and rehabilitation specialists. The profile shows a defensive response set (see Figure 11.1), with elevations of *L* and *K* on the *S* scale representing what is commonly referred to as a *fake-good profile*. She claimed many virtues and did not report any emotional distress. The basic clinical scales are not elevated; in fact, the overall profile shows no depression per se, but Scale 9

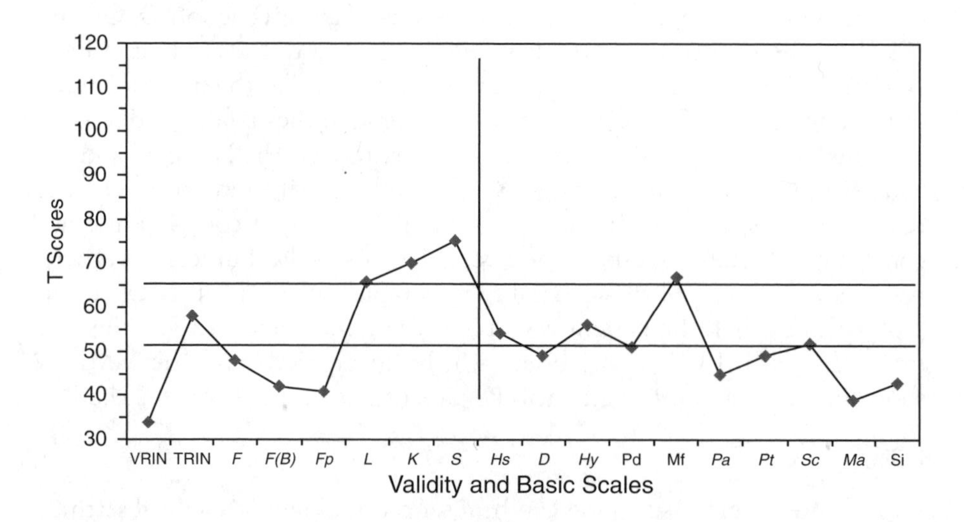

Figure 11.1. Validity and basic scales for 54-year-old woman employed in clerical position.

elevation is consistent with the low energy and fatigue. The clinical scales do not show an excessive preoccupation with somatic symptoms or a configuration of scores that would indicate reinforcement for sick-role behavior. Her willingness to endorse fatigue, muscle pains, and aches was apparent in interviewing her, but she firmly denied emotional problems or problems coping. The elevation on *L* indicates an individual who is not psychologically minded and who is likely to be rigid in her way of approaching problem solving. The clinical scales are not elevated, yet the validity scales provide important information about her coping style, minimization, denial, and "good impression." The MMPI–2 referral question was answered—she is neither currently experiencing depression nor likely to focus on the impact of physical distress on her emotions. The testing supported the primary care provider's notion that a referral to physical medicine and rehabilitation specialists might prove helpful. The MMPI–2 was reviewed with the patient, and our interpretation and recommendations were conveyed to the primary care provider.

Discussion

In some medical settings, the occurrence of defensive MMPI–2 profiles is relatively common. For example, over 20% of patients with end stage pulmonary disease who are evaluated for a lung transplant produced *L* scale scores greater than a T score of 65 (Crews et al., 2003; Ruchinskas et al., 2000; Singer, Ruchinskas, Riley, Broschek, & Barth, 2001). However, only 6.7% produced *L* scale scores equal to or greater than 75 (Ruchinskas et al., 2000). When interpreting the validity of the MMPI–2 within the context of an evaluation for an organ transplant or access to limited medical interventions, the clinician should consider the base rate of elevation on defensiveness scales in that population. The MMPI–2 validity scales are used to provide a dimensional gauge for how much confidence the clinician has in making clinical inferences from the clinical scales. Consequently, in medical settings, as the *L* scale score approaches a T score of 75, inferences regarding the presence or absence of psychopathology become less and less accurate.

Exaggerating and Faking-Bad

In contrast to the denial of psychopathology, feigning of psychopathology is far less likely to occur within medical settings outside of evaluations undertaken for disability purposes. The use of the MMPI–2 in disability evaluations is discussed in chapter 16 of this text. Briefly, feigning of psychopathology or somatic symptoms is more likely to occur in medical settings when there are secondary gain considerations related either to personal injury or to disability compensation (Butcher & Miller, 1998).

Understandably, individuals who have been injured and develop a consequential psychological or psychiatric condition may wish to obtain redress for the incurred pain and suffering, as well as wages lost as a result of the injury. However, litigation and secondary gain can influence symptom presentation and subsequent response to interventions in medical settings and the clinician should be alert for the impact of such response set distortion on clinical presentation (Rohling, Binder, & Langhinrichsen-Rohling, 1995). The MMPI–2 infrequency validity scales (*F*, *F(B)* [Back Infrequency], and *Fp* [Infrequency–Psychopathology]) are quite effective in detecting feigning of psychopathology (Rogers, Sewell, Martin, & Vitacco, 2003; Rogers, Sewell, & Salekin, 1994). In particular, an elevation on the *Fp* scale between a T score of 70 and a T score of 90 suggests exaggeration of existing symptoms whereas an *Fp* scale score greater than a T score of 99 is associated with malingering of psychopathology (Butcher et al., 2001; Rogers et al., 2003).

Unfortunately, the *F* scales are less effective in identifying malingering of physical illness than in identifying the malingering of psychiatric illness. In an attempt to address this problem, a scale was developed for use in personal injury and disability settings to identify malingering of somatic symptoms (Lees-Haley et al., 1991). Despite claims to the contrary, the Fake-Bad scale produces an unacceptably high rate of false positives in both psychiatric settings and in general medical settings (Butcher et al., 2003). Unfortunately, a separate specialized MMPI–2 validity scale that effectively identifies malingering of somatic complaints does not exit. As an alternative, the clinician can look to the relative elevation of MMPI–2 clinical scales associated with somatic preoccupation and report of physical symptoms to determine the likelihood of symptom magnification (Larrabee, 1998).

Elevations on MMPI–2 Scales 1 and 3 in Medical Settings

MMPI–2 scales 1 and 3 are associated with the report of a wide range and unusual combination of somatic complaints and physical symptoms (Graham, 2000). However, what level of elevation on these scales can be expected given genuine medical illness? Individuals who are experiencing medical problems and have sought treatment for those problems are, on average, approximately one standard deviation above the mean on Scale 1 compared with the normative group (Henrichs, 1981). As elevations on scales 1 and 3 increase above this level, the probability that the individual patient is preoccupied with his or her medical condition and reporting unusual combinations of physical symptoms increases (Graham, 2000; Greene, 2000). Increased elevations on scales 1 and 3 suggest a growing influence of functional or nonorganic factors in the maintenance of pain and somatic symptoms. In a compelling finding from a sample of 1,462 patients who underwent a diagnostic coronary angiography, the 13/31 profile was inversely and strongly related to severity of coronary artery disease (Barefoot et al., 1992). In a 10-year study of 2,003 employed middle-aged men, the 13/31 profile was associated with uncomplicated angina pectoris and not associated with the incidence of myocardial infarction and coronary death (Shekele et al., 1991). Consequently, the MMPI–2 scales 1 and 3 are associated with somatic preoccupation that is generally independent of organic pathology as evidenced by objective assessment of disease state.

Despite the aforementioned evidence, a moderate elevation on scales 1 and 3 is to be expected within the context of uncomplicated physical illness. Scales 1 and 3 are elevated approximately one standard deviation above the mean in large groups of medical patients (Henrichs, 1981). Consequently, in medical settings, if scales 1 and 3 are elevated above a T score of 75 in the absence of depression or demoralization, hypotheses regarding functional and emotional components influencing the production and maintenance of somatic complaints can be offered. Case Example 2 illustrates such a situation.

Case Example 2

"*It feels scratchy in my throat.*" A gastroenterologist referred a 62-year-old woman with irritable bowel syndrome and dysphagia. She was having difficulty swallowing and was angry that she was not getting well. She reported feeling "weird," with muscle spasms at the back of her head, feelings of numbness at times in her face, gastric distress with belching, and difficulties swallowing. She denied depressive symptoms, but she was preoccupied with physical problems. An examination of the validity scales (Figure 11.2) shows the high elevation on *L* indicative of a person who sees herself as without faults. The elevations on scales 1 and 3 indicate a high probability that psychological factors are influencing her presentation. She is likely to have very little investment in psychological or behavioral

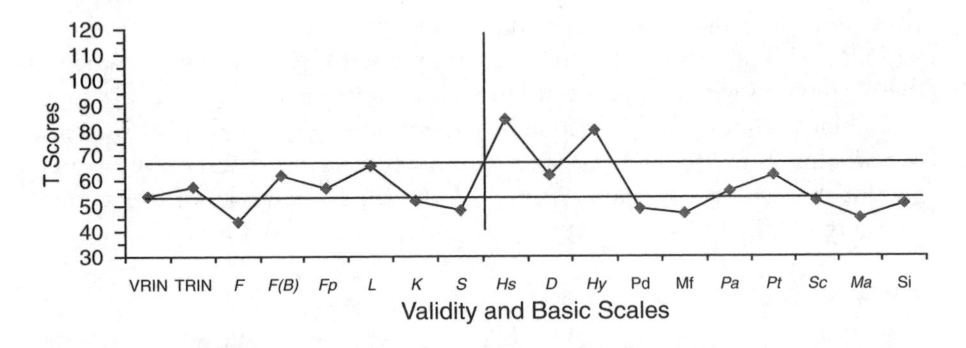

Figure 11.2. Validity and basic scales for 62-year-old woman with irritable bowel syndrome and dysphagia.

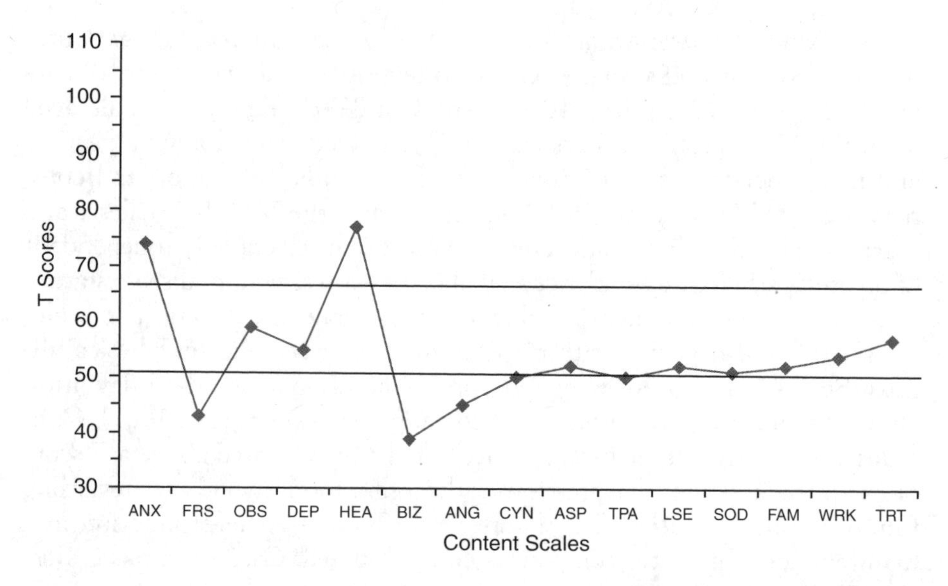

Figure 11.3. Content scales for 62-year-old woman with irritable bowel syndrome and dysphagia.

explanations for her physical distress. The profile suggests a person who will continue to seek a medical remedy for her problems, yet the MMPI–2 profile coupled with elevations of the Anxiety content scale and the Health Concerns content scale (Figure 11.3) point toward psychological factors playing a prominent role in maintenance of the symptoms.

MMPI–2 Indicators of Comorbid Psychiatric Illness in Medical Settings

As mentioned earlier, depression, anxiety, psychosis, and substance abuse frequently present in primary care medical settings. Elevations produced on MMPI–2 scales associated with depression (Scale 2, content scale DEP) and anxiety (Scale 7, content scale ANX), as well as scales associated with thought disorder (Scale 8)—particularly the content scale Bizarre Mentation (BIZ), should be noted (Ben-Porath, Butcher, & Graham, 1991). This should be followed by careful questioning of the patient regarding the presence of these symptoms with an eye toward providing early and effective treatment for a psychiatric condition. Occasionally, patients who are acutely distressed and overwhelmed by life circumstances or an acute psychiatric condition may present through primary care settings. Under these circumstances, elevations on multiple MMPI–2 scales can occur. (See Case Example 3.)

Case Example 3

"I need to get straightened out." A 42-year-old married woman with five children was evaluated at the request of her primary care physician and

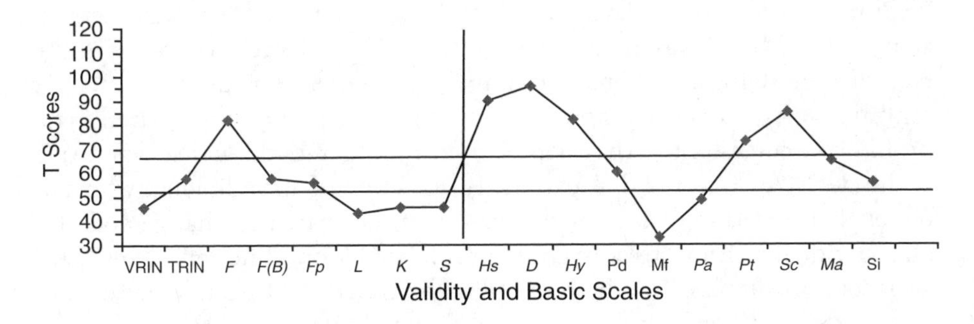

Figure 11.4. Validity and basic scales for 42-year-old woman wanting to be "straightened out."

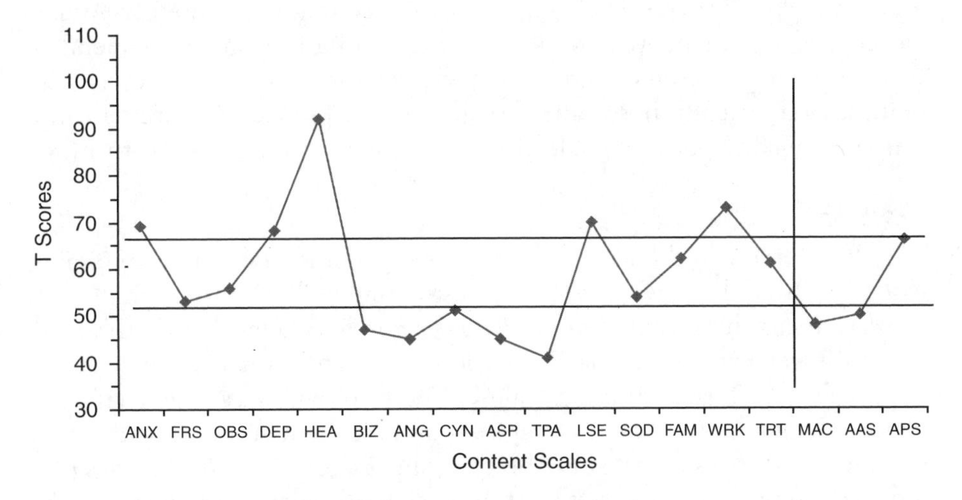

Figure 11.5. Content scales for 42-year-old woman wanting to be "straightened out."

endocrinologist. The endocrinologist's workup had revealed multiple medical issues including history of iatrogenic hyperthyroidism (on thyroid replacement), hyperprolactinemia (amenorrhea off and on since high school), asthma, a history of mood disorder and weight loss, and a history of taking a neuroleptic for distress for 14 years (some fine motor symptoms present suggesting tardive dyskinesia). A major concern for the patient was feeling tired and having trouble sleeping.

The MMPI–2 revealed multiple scale elevations suggesting a somatic focus; significant depression; and possible confusion, disorganization, or psychotic thoughts depicted by the very high elevation on Scale 8 (see Figure 11.4). Her profile certainly indicated significant distress. The content scales (Figure 11.5), especially the low score on Bizarre Mentation, were helpful in ruling out psychotic ideation. The content scales Depression and

Health Concerns were elevated, but she had not been treated for depression. The MMPI–2 was discussed with the patient. Her somatic focus in the face of underlying emotional turmoil; her interpersonal distress; and her chronic worry, insecurity, and sense of alienation were emphasized. The profile was consistent with a person who ruminated and was self-punitive and indecisive. The 1–2/2–1 pattern is reflective of an individual who tolerates high levels of discomfort before being motivated to change and also an individual resistant to a psychological formulation of her problems. This concept was discussed with the patient by describing a tendency on her part to feel bad much of the time and yet not being confident of what she could do to reduce her distress. Her long history of complex medical problems coupled with her MMPI–2 indicating depression, anxiety, rumination, and sense of feeling overwhelmed were evidence that more intensive observation and treatment were warranted. Hospitalization was recommended. In spite of her discomfort and acknowledgment that she would *consider* being psychiatrically hospitalized, she rejected psychiatric intervention. She continued to pursue a medical solution, albeit it at another institution.

Discussion

In addition to the MMPI–2 content scales and Harris-Lingoes scales, examination of the newly developed Restructured Clinical (RC) Scales can serve to focus the interpretation of the profile and help identify the most clinically relevant aspect of the patient's presentation (Tellegen et al., 2003). The RC Demoralization scale (RCdem) provides a single measure of general demoralization and unhappiness and can be used to assess the general level of distress reported by the patient. The remaining RC Scales provide a content-coherent assessment of psychopathology independent of the influence of general distress and demoralization.

Substance Abuse and Dependence

Of particular importance in a medical setting is the presence of substance abuse or dependence. A history of substance abuse or ongoing substance dependence can influence recovery from medical procedures or influence whether a physician prescribes analgesic pain medication. Pain is often undertreated because physicians are appropriately reluctant to prescribe analgesics with a high potential for abuse to individuals who have chemical dependency histories for fear of precipitating a relapse (Rosenblum et al., 2003; Schnoll & Weaver, 2003). On the other hand, unrecognized active chemical dependency can confound treatment in medical settings and limit recovery from medical conditions. The MMPI–2 scales related to substance abuse—MacAndrew Alcoholism—Revised (MAC–R) and the Addiction Acknowledgment Scale (AAS)—provide information related to acknowledged use of substances that can be critical in identifying medical patients who are currently chemically dependent and who are abusing nonprescribed intoxicants (Rouse, Butcher, & Miller, 1999; Stein, Graham, Ben-Porath, & McNulty, 1999; Weed, Butcher, McKenna, & Ben-Porath, 1992). Furthermore, specific MMPI–2 profiles are more likely to be associated with the potential to abuse drugs or alcohol than others (profiles accompanied by significant elevations on Scale 4 or RC4; Butcher & Williams, 2000; Tellegen et al., 2003). Therefore, the use of pain medication in individuals who produce MMPI–2 profiles marked by elevations on scales associated with thrill seeking and impulsivity should be carefully monitored and these individuals provided with support and education to prevent misuse of needed analgesic medications. Figure 11.6 provides a general approach to the interpretation of the MMPI–2 in medical settings.

SPECIFIC APPLICATIONS OF THE MMPI–2 IN HEALTH CARE SETTINGS

Chronic Pain

An emerging consensus regarding the relationship between psychopathology and pain is the acceptance of a diathesis stress model that specifies preexisting unexpressed individual characteristics that become activated by the experience of medical illness and the associated stress of chronic pain (Banks & Kerns, 1996; Dersh et al., 2002). This multidimensional process specifies that a broadband rather than a narrow-focused assessment be adopted when addressing the issue of nonmalignant chronic pain in medical settings. Two fundamental issues are linked to the use of the MMPI–2 in the assessment of the patient with ongoing pain issues. The first relates to the purpose of the assessment: selection for a pain treatment program. The second involves the issue of functional or emotional overlay to pain complaints. In the former case, the MMPI–2 provides important evidence regarding the appropriateness of chronic pain treatment programs and relative benefit from participation in those programs (Alexy & Webb, 1999; Burns, 2000; Vendrig, 1999). In the latter, the question of whether the basis for the report of pain is "organic" or "functional" is often posed when compensation issues are in play (see chap. 16, this volume). As discussed in the introduction of this chapter, the dichotomy posed in this question is a false one and the question should more appropriately be restated as "To what extent do emotional or psychological factors influence the patients' ability to cope with their subjective pain experience?"

Prospective studies of psychological factors in the recovery from physical illness or injury viewed within the context of the diathesis stress model

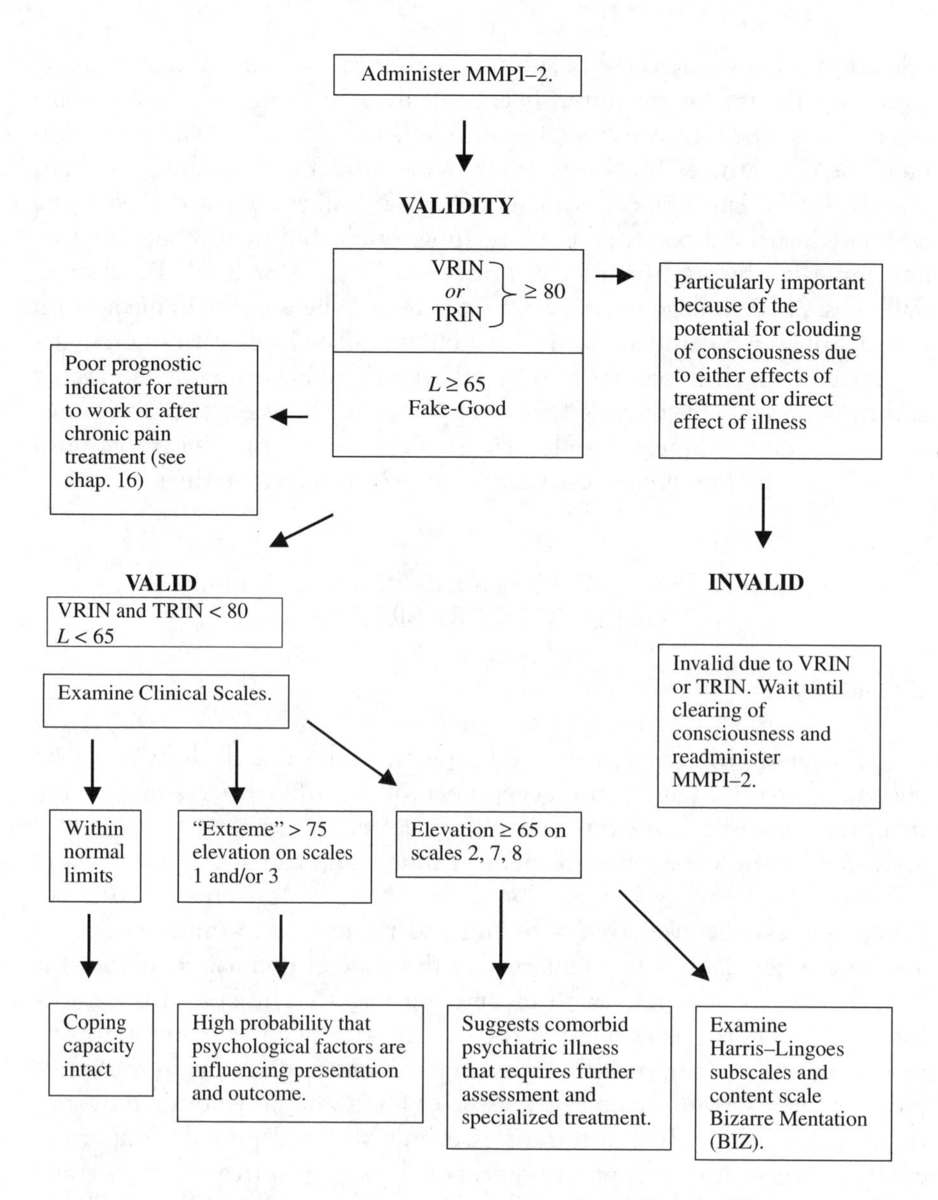

Figure 11.6. Interpretation of MMPI–2 in medical settings—Special considerations.

suggest that MMPI/MMPI–2-assessed psychological dimensions provide useful information for the clinician in medical settings (Fordyce, Bigos, Batti'e, & Fisher, 1992; Imboden, Canter, & Cluff, 1961). In other words, given the multidimensional nature of the emotional response to medical illness and subjective experience of pain, combined with the growing evidence that personality factors influence this response, the MMPI–2 can provide clinicians working in medical settings with important information regarding a patient's adaptive emotional response to his or her medical condition and identify individual characteristics that may impede or promote recovery and adaptation to medical illness and disability.

In support of the role of MMPI-assessed personality dimensions, longitudinal studies have demonstrated that elevation on MMPI–2 Scale 3 is associated with poorer outcomes in treatment of chronic low back pain. In one study, a specific subset of the items on Scale 3 related to the report of lassitude and malaise (*Hy*3) was related to failure to return to work after participating in a chronic pain program in the Netherlands (Vendrig, 1999). In a large group of individuals treated for acute low back injury (within 6 weeks of the initial injury), elevation on Scale 3 predicted continued disability and the failure to return to work a year after initiation of treatment (Gatchel, Polatin, & Mayer, 1995). The elevation on Scale 3 was felt to indicate that the injured patient had developed a passive acceptance of disability (Gatchel, Polatin, & Kinney, 1995). Based on the results of this study, it was concluded that psychosocial variables associated with elevations on Scale 3 played a significant if not preeminent role in the development of disability due to low back injury.

In a prospective study of newly hired Boeing workers, the MMPI Scale 3 was predictive of workers who subsequently went on to develop low back pain and go out on disability (Bigos et al., 1991). Unfortunately, other studies have not confirmed this finding—at least with respect to older individuals. In a 20-year prospective study of Danish men and women, elevations on MMPI scales 1 and 3 at the age of 50 were not associated with the development of low back pain at the age of 70 (Hansen, Biering-Sorensen, & Schroll, 1995). However, elevations on MMPI scales 1, 2, and 3 were present in individuals who had a history of low back pain at the time of initial assessment. This observation suggests that low back pain can precede the elevations on these scales. However, the number of MMPI scales elevated into the clinical range combined with elevations on scales 1 and 3 was found to be associated with poorer functional levels and subsequent disability 6 to 12 years later in patients who suffered from disabling low back pain (Akerlind, HornQuist, & Bjurulf, 1992).

Overall, the weight of the evidence suggests that personality factors associated with the MMPI Scale 3 such as somatic preoccupation and a naïve denial of emotional or interpersonal difficulties lend a vulnerability to the individual toward the development of a chronic pain condition and becoming disabled. (See Case Example 4.)

Case Example 4

"I can't sleep, I want to get off pain medications." A 54-year-old college professor sought comprehensive evaluation and treatment for multiple medical problems. His history included two back surgeries in the prior

5 years, history of myocardial infarction, hypertension, and diabetes. He had been troubled with sleep problems dating back to childhood, which were made worse by back pain. He had been treated for addiction to benzodiazepines. His medical workup included a sleep study that suggested normal sleep with misperception of sleep time and quality. He also had sexual dysfunction and problems with rectal pain involving a rectal fissure.

The MMPI–2 shows highest elevation on Scale 3 with a 3–2 code type. The profile is consistent with his presentation of being fatigued and exhausted, emotionally overcontrolled, and keeping emotions "bottled up." The profile also strongly indicates somatic preoccupation and naïve denial of emotional and interpersonal difficulties. The Harris–Lingoes subscales *D3* (Physical Malfunctioning) and *Hy3* (Lassitude–Malaise) were elevated (see Figure 11.7), yet the patient denied any problem with addiction on the AAS in spite of his history. Based on this MMPI–2 and clinical evaluation, he was referred for cognitive–behavioral intervention for sleep and anxiety and a multidisciplinary program of physical rehabilitation.

Discussion

In general, the population of patients who report chronic nonmalignant pain can be grouped into distinctive clusters based on their MMPI profiles. Using clustering procedures, the MMPI–2 profiles of patients with chronic low back pain form four groups: (a) a depressed pathological group (multiple MMPI–2 clinical scale elevations); (b) a neurotic triad with elevations on the 1, 2, and 3 scales; (c) a conversion V group with elevations on scales 1 and 3; and (d) a within normal limits (WNL) group where no

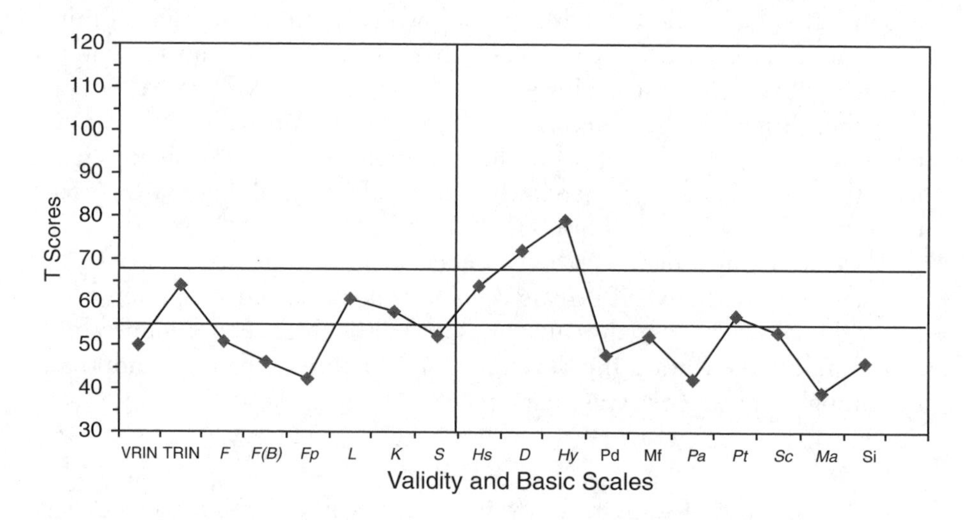

Figure 11.7. Validity and basic scales for 54-year-old man employed as college professor.

MMPI–2 clinical scales are elevated above a T score of 65 (Keller & Butcher, 1991; Slesinger, Archer, & Duane, 2002). These findings have been replicated cross-nationally with the same MMPI profile clusters found in a large group of Australian chronic pain patients (Strassberg, Tilley, Bristone, & Oei, 1992). There is also strong evidence to support differential outcomes across these groups after treatment in chronic pain programs. In general, the WNL group shows the best outcomes and the "pathological" group—marked by multiple MMPI scale elevations—the poorest (McCreary, 1985; Naliboff, McCreary, McArthur, Cohen, & Gottlieb, 1988). At follow-up, after completion of an inpatient chronic pain program, individuals with multiple scale elevations reported higher levels of pain and higher degrees of functional disability (Naliboff et al., 1988). Elevations on MMPI scales associated with depression and general distress predicted levels of self-reported disability independent of pain intensity ratings in chronic pain patients (Millard & Jones, 1991).

With respect to outcome after surgical intervention, the WNL and the neurotic triad group reported better outcomes, including decreased pain, increased physical activity, and a return to work (Riley, Robinson, Geisser, Wittmer, & Smith, 1995). However, the relationship between MMPI profile elevations and outcome may be complicated by the timing of the surgery. The impact of psychological factors on the outcome of spinal surgery may be more important in the prediction of outcome in less well defined injuries or in surgeries that have been delayed. Severe emotional distress is not necessarily a poor prognostic factor if the disk herniation is well defined and surgical intervention occurs shortly after injury or diagnosis (Carragee, 2001). Consequently, the degree of emotional distress as reflected by the overall MMPI–2 profile is a poor prognostic indicator for successful completion of chronic pain programs and the presence of such a profile points to the need for more intensive psychological or psychiatric intervention.

Beyond the obvious impact of psychopathology or emotional distress on the medical patient's response to intervention, what does the MMPI–2 assess that is relevant for the clinician regarding the pain experience? Although the MMPI–2 is associated with outcomes, it does not appear to be directly predictive of improvement in physical parameters after injury as much as improvement in the emotional response to the physical injury. That being said, emotional factors clearly impact recovery from injury (Carragee, 2001). Reported stress at the time of a work-related injury predicted poorer outcome and lower self-reported recovery even after controlling for the extent of the injury (Oleske, Andersson, Lavender, & Hahn, 2000). Consequently, behavioral and emotional factors are important in predicting recovery. In a study conducted in the Netherlands of chronic pain patients, the MMPI–2 scores on admission were found to be unrelated to physical measures of outcome but did reflect the emotional response to the treatment program (Vendrig, Derksen, & De Mey, 2000; Vendrig, 1999). The MMPI–2 was unrelated to categorical variables associated with objective physical function or return to work, but positive emotionality and extraversion were predictive of the emotional aspects of treatment outcome such as satisfaction with the treatment program and emotional improvement but unrelated to perceived pain intensity (Vendrig et al., 2000).

Chronic Headache

The MMPI–2 has been used to evaluate psychological factors that contribute to headache sufferers seeking medical attention and the degree of disability experienced as a result of the headaches (Zeigler & Paolo, 1995, 1996). In a comparison of 51 patients seeking medical assistance for headache with 53 controls not seeking medical assistance, and after controlling for headache intensity, elevations on scales 1, 2, 3, 7, and 0 were the only distinguishing feature of those seeking help (Ziegler & Paolo, 1995). In a follow-up study, again controlling for headache severity, a discriminant function analysis showed self-reported disability from headache and elevations on Scale 3 distinguished help seekers from those not seeking help (Ziegler & Paolo, 1996). The importance of examining Scale 3 elevations on the MMPI–2 again is underscored.

Temporomandibular Disorders (TMD)

The MMPI–2 has shown promise in differentiating those who cope effectively or are more dysfunctional in coping with another prevalent and chronic medical condition, temporomandibular disorder (TMD), a painful condition affecting the jaw, face, and neck. Temporomandibular disorder involves the combination of physiological and psychological factors in symptom presentation and symptom exacerbation (Bernstein & Gatchel, 2000). Epker and Gatchel (2000) studied 322 patients with TMD and categorized patients based on the Multidimensional Pain Inventory (Kerns, Turk, & Rudy, 1985) as either adaptive copers or dysfunctional-distressed. The dysfunctional-distressed group had significant elevations (elevations equal to or greater than 65) on scales 1 and 3 and had a "conversion V" pattern on scales 1, 2, and 3. In a follow-up study of predictor variables in TMD treatment outcome, Bernstein and Gatchel (2000) carefully assessed patients with research criteria to determine presence of TMD and, based upon the research demonstrating Scale 3 elevations in chronic pain populations, used Scale 3 of the MMPI–2 as a sensitive measure of psychosocial functioning. Pain intensity was measured on a scale that calculated current, worst, and average pain on a 0 (least) to 100 (most) scale. Patients were classified into one of four categories: (a) Scale 3 elevation and TMD, (b) Scale 3 elevation alone, (c) TMD alone, and (d) no Scale 3 elevation or TMD diagnosis. The category of patients with presence of both Scale 3 elevation and TMD diagnosis had the highest pain intensity. Additionally, the presence of both Scale 3 elevation and TMD had a negative impact on treatment outcome.

Chronic Fatigue and Chemical Sensitivity Syndromes

Syndromes that involve fatigue as a symptom are often encountered in medical referrals and have been the subject of research with the MMPI and MMPI–2. For example, 57 patients diagnosed with systemic lupus erythematosus (SLE) were studied. Systemic lupus erythematosus is a disease with chronic inflammation, multiorgan involvement, and immunological abnormalities for which fatigue is a major issue in morbidity (Omdal et al., 2003). Fatigue was assessed with a self-report fatigue scale, and a stepwise regression analysis showed that MMPI–2 scales 2 and 3 were the most powerful variables for explaining fatigue scores. The MMPI–2 scores of the patient cohort showed general elevations on scales 1, 2, and 3.

In a study of chronic fatigue syndrome (CFS) patients using the MMPI, Schmaling and Jones (1996) contrasted 53 CFS patients with 43 healthy controls. Scales 1, 2, 3, and 8 were elevated into the clinical range in the CFS group, although 13% of the profiles were within normal limits. The authors concluded that the MMPI could be helpful in guiding treatment in that those patients who denied emotional distress (scales 1 and 3) or who displayed cognitive complaints (Scale 8) were more likely to resist psychological treatment and would benefit more from cognitive-behavioral training and multidisciplinary treatment. In contrast, those showing distress (as indicated by elevations on scales 2 and 8) would be more receptive to psychological intervention. Another study used the MMPI–2 to examine group difference in patients with either chemical sensitivities or chronic fatigue (Fiedler, Kipen, DeLuca, Kelly-McNeil, & Natelson, 1996). Included in the study were 18 CFS patients, 23 patients with multiple chemical sensitivities (MCS), 13 patients with chemical sensitivities (CS), and 18 normal controls. For 44% of MCS, 42% of CS, and 53% of CFS patients, the 1–3/3–1 code types (scores less than or equal to 65) were most frequently observed, suggesting psychological distress expressed as somatic symptoms. Of note, the mean *L* scale score was higher in the MCS and CS subjects. The authors suggested that defensiveness may be associated with higher levels of physiological reactivity, which, in turn, may produce more somatic symptoms.

Organ Transplant

The MMPI and MMPI–2 have long been used to evaluate candidates' emotional and psychological suitability for organ transplant. The presence of significant emotional distress, emotional instability, certain personality traits, and ongoing substance dependence or abuse can influence quality of life, need for adjunctive treatments, and medical compliance in patients awaiting organ transplants (Singer et al., 2001). Noncompliance is a major cause of late post-transplant mortality and morbidity and leads to more frequent postoperative hospitalizations (Stilley, Miller, Gayowski, & Marino, 1998). Thus, evaluation of distinctive personality traits and overall emotional distress in patients awaiting organ transplants to facilitate specialized or more intensive psychological intervention will improve success rates and quality of life for patients undergoing transplant.

Emotional distress and depression can be significant problems for a subset of patients awaiting transplants. Ninety patients with end-stage obstructive lung disease who were referred for a psychological evaluation to determine suitability for lung transplant produced a mean MMPI–2 profile with elevations on scales 1 and 3 (Crews et al., 2003; Ruchinskas et al., 2000; Singer et al., 2001). Interestingly, 23% produced an elevation on the *L* scale greater than or equal to 65 and 6.7% produced an *L* scale score greater than or equal to 75. Forty percent of the group reported significant depression as reflected by an elevation on the MMPI–2 2 scale greater than or equal to 65 (Ruchinskas et al., 2000). In a combined sample including the previous sample, 243 patients with end-stage pulmonary disease who received an MMPI–2 as part of a pre-transplant evaluation produced a mean elevation above T65 on scales 1 and 3. Again, 22% produced elevations on the *L* scale greater than 65 and 37% produced elevations on Scale 2 greater than a T score of 65 (Singer et al., 2001). These studies illustrate the fact that, although mean profiles of profoundly medically ill patients awaiting lung transplants reflect an understandable degree of somatic focus and concern with physical health, a significant subset are reporting seriously depressed mood and a sense of demoralization, which should become the focus of intervention to improve quality of life and effective coping. Of note, a significant percentage of candidates awaiting a lung transplant produced defensive MMPI–2 profiles suggesting a tendency to put their best foot forward in an adaptive attempt to obtain a life-extending medical procedure. Nonetheless, nearly 7% produced profiles that reflected such a high degree of defensiveness as to preclude any MMPI–2-based inferences regarding the presence or absence of psychopathology.

In a controlled study of veterans awaiting liver transplants, 51 patients who had taken an MMPI–2 as part of a pre-transplant evaluation were compared with 26 veterans who had other medical conditions and had been referred for a psychological evaluation. The subjects awaiting liver transplants were less distressed and reported less psychopathology in general than the controls who were referred for psychological evaluations. Nonetheless, the transplant candidates produced elevations on the MMPI–2 scales that form the neurotic triad (scales 1, 2 , and 3; Stilley et al., 1998). Finally, men and women awaiting cardiac transplants appeared significantly more distressed on the MMPI–2 than did the patients detailed who were awaiting lung or liver transplants. A large group of men produced mean MMPI–2 scale elevations above 65 on scales 1, 3, 7, and 8. Based on the mean scale scores, the well-defined code type for the group of men awaiting cardiac transplant was a 37/73 (Trunzo, Petrucci, Carter, & Donofrio, 1999). Women awaiting cardiac transplant produced elevations above a T score of 65 on scales 1, 7, and 8 in which the average score on Scale 1 was significantly elevated above the scores on scales 7 and 8 (Trunzo et al., 1999). These findings again point to the presence of clinically significant distress and demoralization in patients awaiting cardiac transplant that could very likely have an impact on recovery and compliance with post-transplant medical care.

Bariatric Surgery

With the growing prevalence of morbid obesity in our society, an increasingly common procedure for the treatment of this chronic condition has become gastric bypass surgery. Although an effective method for management of morbid obesity, not all patients who undergo the procedure maintain the expected weight loss (Benotti & Forse, 1995). Moreover, a large percentage of those who undergo the procedure continue to experience serious complications 13 to 15 years after surgery (Mitchell et al., 2001). As is the case with organ transplant surgery, the MMPI/MMPI–2 is commonly used to screen for suitability to undergo bariatric surgery and attempts have been made to identify presurgical MMPI profiles that are associated with compliance and outcome (Barrash, Rodriguez, Scott, Mason, & Sines, 1987; Lauer, Wampler, & Lantz, 1996).

The attempts to identify positive surgical outcome based on MMPI–2 profiles have not uniformly met with success. However, the MMPI–2 continues to be a useful tool in identifying surgical candidates who are at risk for poor outcomes due to the presence of psychopathology or personality traits that would compromise compliance. Candidates for gastric bypass surgery on average display a high degree of psychopathology as reflected by the MMPI–2 (Glinski, Wetzler, & Goodman, 2001). The mean MMPI–2 profile of 1,027 individuals evaluated for surgical intervention to treat morbid obesity was marked by elevations on scales 1, 3, and 2 (Maddi, Khoshaba, Persico, Bleecker, & VanArsdall, 1997). Of those individuals awaiting surgery, 13.2% produced *L* and *K* scale scores above 65. Forty-five percent of the sample produced elevations on Scale 1, 40.6% on Scale 3, and 32.5% on Scale 2. Additionally, 23% produced elevations on Scale 4, 21.5% produced elevations on Scale 7, and 19.4% produced elevations on Scale 8 (Maddi et al., 1997). These findings indicate that a large percentage of morbidly obese patients presenting for evaluation prior to a surgical intervention are experiencing a significant level of distress marked by anxiety and depression. This distress may in part be a function of the difficulty experienced coping with a chronic illness, because, following surgical intervention, the level of psychopathology as assessed by the MMPI–2 significantly declines indicating an improvement in emotional status (Maddi et al., 2001). Thus, the MMPI–2 demonstrates a sensitivity to change in emotional status and distress after weight reduction surgery for treatment of morbid obesity.

In sum, the use of the MMPI–2 as part of a multimodal screening process for candidates awaiting treatment for organ transplants or bariatric surgery is primarily as a tool to identify the presence or absence of psychopathology and personality traits that would impact compliance with treatment protocols and recommendations. Specifically, it is important to examine the MMPI–2 profile for elevations on scales such as 2 and DEP that are significantly above those of the reference population (e.g., individuals who are awaiting bariatric surgery) for evidence of psychopathology. Further, defensive MMPI–2 profiles based on *L* or *K* elevations above 65 are not particularly unusual; however, elevations above a T score of 75 on those scales are meaningful and preclude inferences regarding the presence or absence of psychopathology in those candidates.

HEALTH-RELATED BEHAVIORS

Over the past 20 years, there has been a renewed interest in the identification of MMPI–2-defined personality variables in the prediction of medical illness. In no small part, this interest was spurred by early studies that demonstrated a link between Hostility and Type A behavior and risk for coronary artery disease (CAD; Barefoot, Dahlstrom, & Williams, 1983; Williams et al., 1980). With the creation of several large prospective data sets, questions relating to the causal link between personality traits and the development of medical disease are being examined (Barefoot, Peterson, et al., 1989; Kawachi et al., 1998; Kubzansky, Sparrow, Vokonas, & Kawachi, 2001; Siegler et al., 1990). Similarly, the MMPI has been used in a large-scale study to determine if optimism–pessimism as measured by the MMPI was associated with increased risk for mortality over a 30-year period. A pessimistic explanatory style was associated with a 19% increase in risk of development of medical disease (Maruta, Colligan, Malinchoc, & Offord, 2000).

Coronary Artery Disease

Coronary artery disease (CAD) has received the most attention, and a number of personality factors and traits measured by the MMPI/MMPI–2 have been implicated in the development of CAD. These MMPI/MMPI–2-derived personality factors include hostility, anger, Type A personality, depression, dominance, and optimism–pessimism and have all been shown to be related to longer-term survival and the risk for the development of CAD (Barefoot, Dodge, Peterson, Dahlstrom, & Williams, 1989; Barefoot, Peterson, et al., 1989; Kawachi et al., 1996, 1998; Kubzansky et al., 2001; Sesso, Kawachi, Vokonas, & Sparrow, 1998; Siegman et al., 2000).

The Hostility (*Ho*) scale was initially developed to predict the relationship between classroom teachers and students (Cook & Medley, 1954). Individuals who received high scores on the Cook–Medley Hostility scale experience higher levels of anger in interpersonal situations; are more likely to be overtly hostile and appear unfriendly; and are suspicious, cynical, and untrusting (Graham, 2000). The scale appears to tap aspects of anger, cynicism, hostility, and neuroticism (Blumenthal, Barefoot, Burg, & Williams, 1987; Han, Weed, Calhoun, & Butcher, 1995). Hostility as measured by the MMPI–2 Cook–Medley Hostility scale was prospectively associated with increased risk for coronary artery disease and overall mortality in groups of attorneys, physicians, older adults, and younger adults (Barefoot et al., 1983; Barefoot, Dodge, et al., 1989).

Recently, attempts have been made to specify the causal mechanisms by which hostility leads to cardiovascular mortality. One approach is to identify whether individuals who are more prone to hostile expression have greater exposure to cardiovascular risk factors that thereby lead to increased mortality. In support of the exposure to independent risk factor hypothesis, high Hostility scores of individuals while in college or an increase in Hostility scores from college to midlife were found to predict the presence of health-related risk factors such as social isolation, obesity, and a high-fat diet, as well as smoking and consumption of caffeine (Siegler et al., 2003; Siegler, Peterson, Barefoot, & Williams, 1992). The relationship between CAD and hostility is complex in that Hostility scores were positively related to lower education, higher total caloric intake, body mass index, the ratio of hip size to waist size, and higher serum triglycerides (Niaura et al., 2000).

Hostility appears to have a direct effect on hypertension, an independent risk factor for CAD. Young adults who scored higher on *Ho* and a measure of time urgency were more likely to develop hypertension 15 years later than those who scored lower on these measures (Yan et al., 2003). Under acutely stressful conditions, sustained elevation in blood pressure appears to be related to *Ho* elevation. Individuals who were categorized as high hostile or low hostile on the basis of their scores on the *Ho* scale were exposed to an interpersonally challenging task in which they were asked to solve an anagram while being interpersonally harassed. Participants who scored higher on *Ho* were more likely to produce sustained increases in blood pressure, heart rate, and cortisol response under the harassment condition than did the low *Ho* participants (Suarez, Kuhn, Schanberg, Williams, & Zimmermann, 1998). In a separate study, subjects who were high on *Ho* produced sustained increases in blood pressure after exposure to a film clip depicting racial discrimination when compared with subjects who scored low on *Ho* (Fang & Myers, 2001).

As demonstrated, the relationship between hostility and the risk of developing cardiovascular disease is likely dynamic and involves an interaction between the personality trait of hostility and affective emotional states. Interleukin-6 plays a central role in the development of atherosclerotic cardiovascular disease (ASCVD) through the stimulation of processes contributing to plaque buildup and has been shown to be a predictor of the onset and development of ASCVD in healthy individuals (Suarez, 2003). An interaction was observed between depression and hostility and plasma levels of interleukin-6 in healthy nonsmoking men. Men who were high on the Cook–Medley Hostility scale and who scored above a 10 on the Beck Depression Inventory had higher plasma interleukin-6 levels than men with lower scores (Suarez, 2003).

Hostility-related psychological factors tapped by the MMPI–2 scales Type A Personality (TPA) and Anger (ANG) are also related to the risk for CAD (Barefoot, Peterson, et al., 1989; Siegel et al., 1989, 1990; Williams et al., 1988). The MMPI–2 TPA content scale contains sets of items related to time urgency, anger, and competitiveness (Butcher, Graham, Williams, & Ben-Porath, 1990). Individuals high on TPA are described by their spouses as acting bossy, being critical and irritable, and becoming upset by unexpected events (Butcher et al., 1990). The TPA scale contains two components: impatience and competitiveness (Ben-Porath & Sherwood, 1993). In comparison, the ANG content scale is more associated with direct expression of anger and loss of control associated with significant interpersonal maladjustment (Butcher et al., 1990). Both MMPI–2 content scales ANG and TPA have been implicated in increasing the risk of developing CAD. The TPA scale as assessed by the MMPI–2 was found to be associated with increased risk of coronary heart disease independent of anger, cynicism, and hostility (Kawachi et al., 1998). The MMPI–2 TPA scale, time urgency, competitiveness, and hostility taken together increased the risk for coronary heart disease (Kawachi et al.,

1998). Others have argued that Type A personality in and of itself does not directly increase the risk of arteriosclerosis and coronary heart disease but increases exposure to behaviors that serve as independent triggers for that process (Gallagher, Sweetnam, Yarnell, Elwood, & Stansfeld, 2003). However, a more recent study found that two components of Type A behavior—time urgency and hostility—assessed in young adulthood were directly associated with a dose response increase in long-term risk of the development of hypertension 15 years later (Yan et al., 2003). This relationship was independent of other risk factors including age, gender, race, alcohol consumption, and level of physical activity. The mixed findings related to risk for hypertension and TPA behavior was felt to be related to the failure in other studies to clearly isolate and identify the components of Type A behavior—time urgency and hostility—that were most important in directly lending an increased risk for CAD (Yan et al., 2003).

The MMPI–2 ANG content scale is defined by the expression of overt anger and hostility. Individuals who are high on ANG become angry easily, yell, and appear grouchy and irritable. They are described as moody and become annoyed easily (Butcher et al., 1990). In a longitudinal study of 1,881 community-dwelling male veterans, elevations on the ANG content scale were associated with a two- to threefold increase in the risk of coronary heart disease and angina pectoris on average 7 years after the administration of the MMPI–2 (Kawachi et al., 1996). This relationship remained significant even after adjusting for risk factors such as cigarette smoking.

Smoking Cessation

One of the most important risk-related behaviors is smoking, which has been linked to increased mortality and morbidity due to a variety of health conditions including CAD and lung cancer. MMPI-assessed personality variables have been shown to be associated with the initiation of smoking and with cessation of smoking. Smoking behavior was examined in a group of male medical students who were followed up after 25 years. Medical students who never smoked had lower scores on the MMPI *L* and Pd scales than smokers. Furthermore, physicians who had successfully quit smoking had lower scores on MMPI scales 9 and 4 than those who continued to smoke. This suggests that smoking initiation is associated with greater sensation seeking and rebelliousness and cessation is associated with decreased impulsivity and rebelliousness (Barefoot, Smith, Dahlstrom, & Williams, 1989). In a more representative prospective study of college students, similar scales were associated with initiation of smoking for both men and women—high scales 9, 4, and *Ho* and low Social Introversion (0). In addition, successful smoking cessation was best predicted by low scores on *Ho* for both genders (Lipkus, Barefoot, Williams, & Siegler, 1994).

As has been abundantly demonstrated in the preceding section, MMPI–2-measured personality variables are clearly tied to the initiation and maintenance of maladaptive health habits such as smoking and the risk of developing CAD. Consequently, information related to an individual's premorbid personality risk factors can be used in developing early preventive interventions to modify behavior and learn more effective coping strategies to decrease the chance of developing coronary heart disease. Moreover, use of the MMPI–2 to assess these personality variables prior to initiation of educational programs to promote positive health habits can identify those individuals who will require specialized interventions to achieve the goal.

CONCLUSION

Our intent in this chapter was to demonstrate that the MMPI–2 is a valid and effective assessment tool for use in health care settings. A further goal was to provide the clinician practicing in medical settings with suggestions for the interpretation of the MMPI–2 in reaching decisions regarding the patient's ability to effectively cope with a medical illness or procedure and to benefit from various interventions. The cases in this chapter represent typical clinical presentations of medical patients and illustrate how the MMPI–2 was helpful in discerning the contribution of emotional distress to symptom presentation or, in contrast, the denial of any emotional distress and the impact of such denial on the patient's presentation. It is important that feedback be provided directly to patients about the MMPI–2 in order to foster good care and compliance. The instrument provides an opportunity for clinicians to validate the distress experienced by a patient and serves as a vehicle to discuss with the patient the behavioral, psychological, and attitudinal factors that influence coping and resilience (Finn, 1996b). The MMPI–2 can help patients to adopt a new model for understanding and dealing with their situation or reinforce that treatment be sought for emotional distress and maladaptive coping. In addition, feedback regarding the MMPI–2 shared with the referring health care provider can frequently result in a shift in the perception of the patient so that a more collaborative relationship can be fostered between the patient and his or her providers. It should not be surprising given the rich history and empirical tradition of the MMPI–2 in medical settings that the results from an MMPI–2-based assessment can have a powerful impact on both the patient and health care provider perspectives and attitudes toward one another.

Exhibit 11.1 contains a summary of the major points from the chapter that are related to the interpretation of the MMPI–2 in medical settings.

EXHIBIT 11.1
Highlight: Main Issues for the Interpretation of the MMPI–2 in Medical Settings

- Rather than indicating whether the patient's complaints are functional in nature, the MMPI–2 provides important information regarding the influence of emotional or psychological issues on the presentation of physical complaints. In other words, the MMPI–2 provides the practitioner with an objective means of identifying emotional and psychological factors that may influence medical illness.
- Personality traits or disorders can hamper compliance with medical treatment and recovery from illness. On the same token, normative emotional response to medical illness or invasive treatment can be misinterpreted as suggestive of personality disturbance. Therefore, the objective assessment of personality traits and coping styles is critical when concerns arise over these issues in medical settings. Under certain circumstances, such as gaining access to scarce medical resources or treatments, it is understandable for a medical patient to provide a positive self-presentation and appear more emotionally resilient than perhaps he or she actually is. It is useful to quantify the degree of defensiveness and minimization present by examining the *L, K,* and *S* scales to determine how similar or dissimilar the particular patient is in his or her approach to the evaluation when compared with others awaiting similar treatments or interventions.
- The average elevation on scales 1 and 3 in medical settings is a T score of 60. As scales 1 and 3 increase to above 65, the probability that emotional factors are influencing the report of physical pain and somatic complaints increases. Elevations on MMPI–2 scales associated with depression, anxiety, or thought disorder within the context of a medical condition suggest the presence of psychiatric illness and point to the need for intervention.
- Patients participating in chronic pain treatment programs produce four broad groups of MMPI–2 profiles: (a) a within normal limits group; (b) a group with elevations on scales 1 and 3; (c) a group with elevations on scales 1, 2, and 3; and (d) a pathological group with multiple clinical scale elevations.
- The MMPI–2 is an objective tool used to screen candidates awaiting treatment for organ transplants or bariatric surgery for the presence or absence of psychopathology and personality traits that could impact compliance with treatment protocols and serve to hamper recovery from surgery.
- Hostility as assessed by the MMPI–2 *Ho* scale has repeatedly been shown to be associated with increased risk for the development of coronary artery disease (CAD). This increased risk appears mediated through a direct effect on hypertension by maintaining the physiological response to anger-evoking life events. Moreover, higher hostility as assessed by the MMPI–2 *Ho* scale is indirectly associated with risk for CAD by increasing exposure to health-related risk factors such as social isolation, obesity, a high-fat diet, smoking, and consumption of caffeine.

12

USE OF THE MMPI–2 IN NEUROPSYCHOLOGICAL EVALUATIONS

CARLTON S. GASS

A neuropsychological evaluation would be incomplete without an assessment of personality and emotional status. This portion of the evaluation is particularly challenging because of the complexity of human behavior and the limited amount of exposure the clinician has to the examinee. The assessment process involves the integration of data derived from various sources, including the clinical interview, behavioral observation, collateral reports, and psychological tests (Gass, 2002b). These diverse sources provide "snapshots" of information taken from different angles and perspectives. The MMPI (MMPI–2; Butcher, Dahlstrom, et al., 1989) has been one of these widely used sources for more than 60 years. No assessment tool, technique, or interpretive approach is infallible. The MMPI–2 has many critics within the field of neuropsychology, many of whom rely exclusively on interview and observational data, sometimes incorporating a shorter measure of emotional status. Nevertheless, the MMPI–2 is the most popular and extensively researched psychological test in the world, and the amount of empirical literature on the MMPI–2 in neuropsychological settings far surpasses that based on any other personality measure. From the standpoint of clinical practice, surveys indicate that it is, by far, the most often used personality measure in neuropsychological settings (Lees-Haley, Smith, Williams, & Dunn, 1996; McCaffrey & Lynch, 1996).

Historically, neuropsychology has devoted more attention to brain-based cognitive and sensorimotor functions than to matters of personality and emotional status. In clinical settings, many neuropsychologists underestimate the importance of personality assessment and fail to pursue it through formal measurement. However, there are many reasons why the measurement of psychological status is important in a neuropsychological evaluation. First, psychological problems, such as depression and anxiety, commonly result from brain dysfunction, regardless of the type of brain disease. Myriad causes exist, including lost behavioral competencies and diminished access to rewarding experiences. Cerebral damage can cause receptive and expressive communication disorders, changes in the viscera and autonomic nervous system, changes in emotional experience and mood, and changes in emotional memory (Heilman, Bowers, & Valenstein, 1993). The frequency of such problems is great enough to warrant routine and careful assessment. The second reason for formal measurement is to ensure the detection of underlying psychological conditions that masquerade as neurological dysfunction. Somatoform disorders, for example, often include pseudoneurological symptoms such as numbness, paralysis, imbalance, incoordination, diplopia, visual impairment, weakness, dysphagia, seizures, amnesia, or other forms of dissociation. Related to this is the need to address the problem of malingering, which can be manifested in the feigning of emotional, cognitive, or somatic symptoms (Berry & Butcher, 1998; Larrabee, 1998, 2000). Third, the cognitive difficulties and subjective complaints that commonly trigger a neuropsychological referral are often symptomatic of an unrecognized emotional disorder and not structural brain damage (Gass & Apple, 1997; Gass & Russell, 1986). For example, a significant amount of unique variance in performance on popular measures of attention and memory can be accounted for by MMPI–2 indexes of anxiety and depression (Gass, 1996b). Performance efficiency on some neuropsychological tests can be systematically lowered by emotional factors that, unless measured, cannot be accounted for (Gass, Ansley, & Boyette, 1994), thereby increasing the likelihood of misdiagnosis.

Accurate assessment of emotional status is essential in neuropsychology because proper intervention is contingent on problem identification. In some cases, individuals use self-report instruments such as the MMPI–2 as a vehicle to convey serious problems that they will not otherwise disclose. Bill was a 42-year-old inpatient who was 2 weeks post-left-frontal stroke, with residual telegraphic speech. He had a prior left-frontal CVA (cardiovascular accident) 2 years before, which left him with a mild right hemiparesis. Bill lived with his wife and was working as a mechanic. He was evaluated by the neurology service and referred for neuropsychological evaluation. In the interview, the patient stated that he was mildly depressed over having had a second stroke. However, when queried, he minimized the significance of this "disappointment." On the MMPI–2, his results suggested a very different picture (see Figures 12.1 and 12.2).

Bill produced high scores on scales 1, 2, 3, 7, and 8 and endorsed items that refer to suicidal behavior. An immediate follow-up feedback session and interview were conducted, in which he admitted having a clear and specific plan to shoot himself with his revolver out of a sense of hopelessness and frustration about his seemingly intractable medical condition. At this point, staff members were able to intervene to prevent a negative outcome. There are many other less dramatic examples of this general principle: People often use self-report instruments to convey problems that they may not bring up or admit to in an initial interview.

The reverse phenomenon sometimes occurs, too. Some people adopt an exaggerated or defensive posture in answering MMPI–2 items, and the

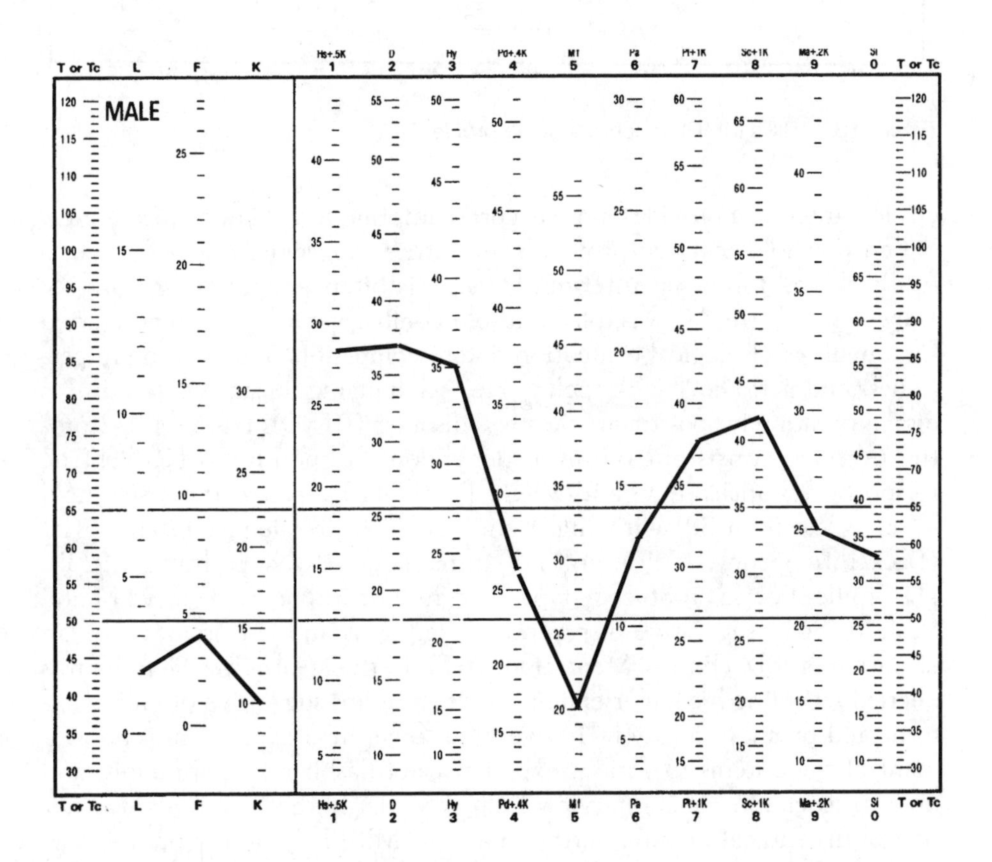

Figure 12.1. Bill's MMPI–2 basic clinical profile.

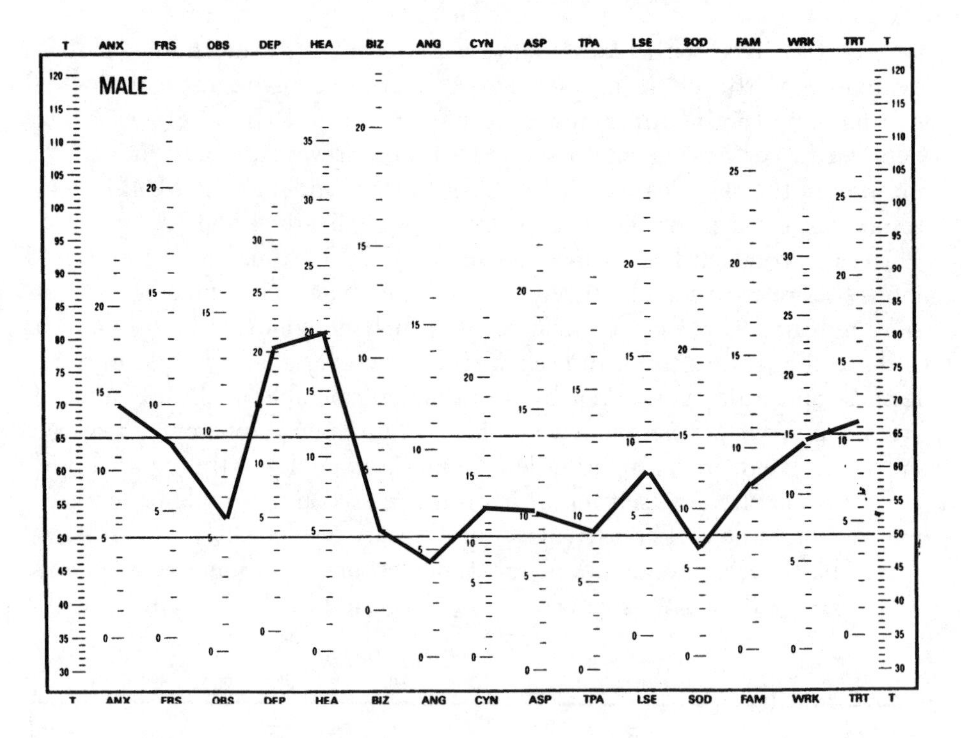

Figure 12.2. Bill's MMPI–2 content scale profile.

clinical interview provides more accurate information about the examinee. When psychological test protocols are either exaggerated or defensive, a feedback and follow-up interview session is often enlightening (Gass & Brown, 1992). Mr. W. was a 57-year-old combat veteran who was referred for a neuropsychological evaluation due to complaints of increasing forgetfulness and periodic "blank spells." He was applying for an increase in his disability rating for posttraumatic stress disorder (PTSD). His MMPI–2 profile revealed consistent (content-dependent) responding (TRIN [True Response Inconsistency] and VRIN [Variable Response Inconsistency] T score less than 80) with high scores on *F* (Infrequency; 110T), *F(B)* (Back Infrequency; 108T), and *Fp* (Infrequency–Psychopathology; 92T). His profile showed an 86 code type, with high scores on Scale 8 (94T) and Scale 6 (86T) suggestive of psychotic symptoms and corroborated by an elevation on BIZ (Bizarre Mentation; 76T). In the feedback session, he was queried regarding his endorsement of critical items suggestive of hallucinations and paranoid ideation. In every instance, he attributed his endorsement of these items to various experiences of flashbacks, nightmares, and drug intoxication. This interview helped to clarify that psychosis was not part of his clinical picture. Furthermore, his MMPI–2 validity profile, particularly the high score on *Fp*, strongly suggested symptom exaggeration, especially in light of the compensation context of this examination.

In my experiences with practitioners, I have often encountered five errors involving MMPI–2 interpretation. The common errors include (a) inflexibility in the format of test administration, (b) ignoring valid protocol information due to validity scale misinterpretation, (c) overestimating the significance of high scores on the MMPI–2 clinical scales for neuropsychological test performance, (d) confusion over the interpretation of high scores on somatic-related scales (1, 2 , 3, and 8), and (e) failure to fully utilize the MMPI–2 content scales (Butcher, Graham, Williams, & Ben-Porath, 1990). These issues are addressed in this chapter.

INCREASING THE PROBABILITY OF OBTAINING VALID MMPI–2 PROTOCOLS

Medical patients are occasionally defensive in answering questions that pertain to emotional status. A strategy to help prevent this is to provide the examinee with a rationale for the use of the MMPI–2. One example is, "This inventory is a routine part of our test battery, and it provides important information about feelings and attitudes." Due to its length, short forms of the MMPI–2 have been proposed. Under certain circumstances, an accurate short form may offer advantages that outweigh the loss of comprehensiveness (Dahlstrom & Archer, 2000). Initial data on the proposed 180-item format were promising, but further analyses revealed that this form was very unreliable as a basis for predicting clinical code types, identifying the high-point scale, or predicting scores within 5 to 10 T score points on most of the clinical scales (Gass & Luis, 2001b; Gass & Gonzalez, 2003). Current data suggest that a standard interpretation of the 180-item short form is likely to be inaccurate. However, in the event that a patient can complete only 180 items, the clinician can obtain a limited amount of information about general problem areas using the conservative guidelines outlined by Gass and Gonzalez (2003). Of course, the optimal approach to MMPI–2 use involves a full administration of all 567 items, which provides a detailed and relatively comprehensive picture based on the basic, content, and supplementary scales. If this cannot be accomplished, the clinician can administer the first 370 items, which are sufficient for complete scoring of the basic clinical profile and Harris–Lingoes subscales (Harris & Lingoes, 1968).

Some patients find it easy to complete the MMPI–2, some are incapable, and a third group of individuals can complete it but only with special assistance. The most widely used administrative format requires a level of reading ability that many neuropsychological referrals do not have. Although most examinees exceed the required sixth-grade reading level, 13% of those over age 65 have some form of visual impairment, and almost

8% have severe impairment (blindness in both eyes or inability to read newsprint even with glasses). Presbyopia, cataracts, age-related macular degeneration, glaucoma, and diabetic retinopathy are common problems in the ever-increasing older population. Brain-related problems with acquired alexia, visuoperceptual impairment, headache, and poor visual attention affect people of all ages. A viable alternative to the standard MMPI–2 administration is the audiocassette format sold by National Computer Systems, and this is available in both English and Spanish. The standard MMPI–2 answer sheet contains small print, but the clinician can compose a more readable large print answer sheet on which the examinee circles "True" or "False" for each item.

During MMPI–2 administration, it is important to unobtrusively observe the examinee to ensure that the test procedures are being followed. This is especially critical in the case of individuals who have more severe cognitive impairment and who are more likely to lose the instructional set. Despite instructions to the contrary, examinees sometimes skip items or fail to match the statement number with the item number on the answer sheet. Monitoring can help prevent this. Most examinees who successfully complete the first several items are able to complete the remainder of the test, though an additional session may be required due to fatigue or other discomfort. In some instances, however, the examinee shows increasing difficulties as the testing continues, requiring the clinician's intervention.

The MMPI–2 is best administered in a controlled environment free of distraction, including input from spouses, family members, friends, or fellow patients. On several occasions, I discovered that the patient's spouse was answering the questions for the patient. When confronted, the spouse explained, "I wanted to make sure you got the right answers. He's not going to tell you the truth." On one occasion I administered the MMPI–2 to six inpatients in one room. After I left the room, they decided to use a democratic approach, voting on how to answer each item. In several instances, examinees left the hospital with the MMPI–2 booklet in hand. The MMPI–2 should not be given outside of a controlled testing environment because one can never be sure who really took the test or what influences may have intervened (Pope, Butcher, & Seelen, 1993).

INTERPRETATION OF THE VALIDITY SCALES

Protocol validity is not invariably a black and white issue. Rather than simply classifying a protocol as valid or invalid, it is often necessary to ask, "What valid information can be extracted from this profile?" The validity scales primarily reveal response consistency and test-taking attitude. The original validity scales also provide a basis for inferences about extratest behaviors and, in particular, amenability to psychological treatment (Butcher, 1990b). The following discussion focuses on common problems involving Cannot Say (*?*), and scales *L* (Lie), *F*, and *K* (Correction).

Cannot Say (?)

This score is the number of items that were either unanswered or answered with both "True" and "False." The most common explanation for unanswered items is a reluctance to disclose information (defensiveness). However, confused individuals sometimes score high (10 or more) on this measure. This is typically because they do not understand the meaning of the item. The impact of Cannot Say depends on the number of omitted items and where these items are located on the test. If 10 or more items are omitted within the first 370 items, one should expect a lowering of scores on some of the basic scales. The higher the Cannot Say score, the lower (and more distorted) the resulting profile. However, item omissions do not always necessitate discarding a protocol. For example, all of the basic profile information is contained in the first 370 items, so any item omissions after Item 370 tend to lower content and supplementary scale scores but do not affect scores on the basic profile, including the Harris–Lingoes subscales. In addition, regardless of the Cannot Say score, elevated scores on any clinical scales suggest problem areas that require attention. The clinician should attempt to have the examinee answer all or nearly all of the omitted items on the MMPI–2.

L (Lie) Scale

This 15-item scale measures naïve defensiveness and an attempt to appear extremely virtuous, well-controlled, and free from commonplace human frailties. The impact of naïve defensiveness (T greater than 60) is usually to lower scores on some of the clinical scales. However, high scores on clinical scales sometimes occur even in defensive protocols, and these scores indicate problem areas that should be addressed. Scores above 60T on *L* suggest a rigid and ineffective style of coping with problems, denial, limited self-awareness, and limited insight into the manner in which one's behavior affects others. In brain-damaged samples, scores on *L* have been linked with the extent of cognitive impairment (Dikmen & Reitan, 1974, 1977; Gass & Ansley, 1994). In a mixed neurological sample, scores on the *L* scale were mildly predictive of the degree of neuropsychological impairment on the Average Impairment Rating scale, $r(144) = -.27$, $p < .005$ (Gass, 1997). Individuals who have brain damage and score high on the *L* scale underestimate their acquired cognitive deficits, make poor decisions, and take on tasks that are beyond their capability.

F (Infrequency) Scale

This scale was designed to detect deviant ways of responding, but it is best recognized for measuring degree of openness in reporting problems. These problems may be real, embellished, or completely faked. Scores on Scale *F* are sensitive to a variety of situations, including severe psychopathology, symptom feigning or exaggeration, random responding, and atypical item interpretation (Arbisi & Ben-Porath, 1995). Many clinicians erroneously discard protocols that have high *F* or *F(B)* scale scores (T greater than 80) on the grounds of suspected faking-bad. In many clinical settings, such scores commonly reflect severe psychopathology, and the protocols are quite valid. Of course, other reasons such as exaggeration, malingering, and content-independent responding should be ruled out. A high *F* or *F(B)* score does not, in itself, invalidate a protocol, since extreme scores occur in the presence of severe psychopathology (Graham, Watts, & Timbrook, 1991). Indiscriminate responding must be ruled out (VRIN and TRIN must both be less than 80T). Severe psychopathology is more likely if a high score on *F* is accompanied by a low *Fp* (T less than 80). In the presence of a high score on *F* (T greater than 80), a high *Fp* score suggests possible symptom exaggeration or faking. In the absence of a high *F* scale score, a high *Fp* score may be a less reliable indicator of symptom fabrication (Gass & Luis, 2001a). In personal injury settings involving claims of brain injury, some individuals feign emotional pathology resulting in very high *F*-scale scores (Berry, Wetter, Baer, Youngjohn, et al., 1995), whereas others restrict their faking to cognitive and somatic symptoms of brain damage (Greiffenstein, Gola, & Baker, 1995; Larrabee, 1998). Although the latter obtain higher scores on scales 1 and 3, they do not typically produce high scores on the *F*, *F(B)*, or *Fp* scales.

K Scale

This scale measures sophisticated defensiveness and a desire to portray oneself as psychologically well-adjusted and emotionally healthy. Contrary to the interpretive practice of many clinicians, scores on *K* (and other scales) are largely independent of the examinee's educational background. Data from the MMPI–2 normative study demonstrate that level of education has virtually no influence on MMPI–2 scores. High scores on *K* (T greater than 60) are associated with a denial of behavioral and emotional problems and lower scores across the clinical profile. Physical problems, however, may be reported, yielding higher scores on 1 and 3. The high *K* scorer denies a need for psychological intervention and is reluctant to discuss feelings. Protocols with elevated *K*-scale scores are sometimes deemed invalid and subsequently ignored, even when high scores exist on one or more of the clinical scales. In these cases, the elevated scores on the clinical scales suggest problem areas that should not be overlooked. For example, the 13 and 49 code types are sometimes found in defensive protocols, and the associated behavioral correlates of these code types are typically applicable in these cases. The presence of the high *K* score does not invariably mean that the entire clinical profile should be ignored. It does indicate, however, that other psychological problems may exist that were unreported and that low or normal-range scores across the clinical scales cannot be accepted as valid indicators of psychological status.

MMPI–2 SCORES AND NEUROLOGICAL TEST PERFORMANCE

The diagnostic efficacy of neuropsychological tests depends, in part, on their specificity in detecting underlying brain dysfunction. To the extent that emotional factors interfere with neurobehavioral performance, inferences regarding brain-based abilities are more uncertain. The influence of emotional status is sometimes obvious and observable. Examples include an examinee who angrily throws the test stimulus on the floor and storms out of the office or voices preoccupations and begins to cry. In these situations, the examinee is not fully engaged in the testing process and the obtained results have doubtful validity. In the majority of cases, the influence of emotionality, if present, is subtle and unobservable and the examinee appears to be fully engaged in the examination. A key interpretive concern is whether poor or mediocre performance on neuropsychological tests can be attributed to emotional factors.

Clinicians commonly interpret deficient cognitive test performance in the light of an examinee's psychiatric diagnosis or presumed emotional status. Robert is a 57-year-old retired attorney who presented with complaints of word-finding difficulty and problems recalling the names of familiar people. These difficulties had emerged insidiously about 1 year prior, shortly after he went through a bitter divorce. He acknowledged that his marital breakup was rather difficult for him to handle emotionally, though he nevertheless maintained his normal active lifestyle, including working out at the gym and playing tennis several times a week. His medical history is unremarkable for any major illnesses or surgeries. He denied any history of substance abuse, head trauma, vascular disease, anoxia, or toxic exposure. He denied any recent family history of dementia. The neuropsychological test findings revealed overall borderline impairment of Robert's mental abilities, with mild impairment in the areas of retentive memory, visuoconstruction, and confrontation naming. Sensorimotor functions were intact bilaterally, with no asymmetry. On the Wechsler Adult Intelligence Scale—Third Edition (WAIS–III), he achieved a Full Scale IQ of 112, a Verbal Scale IQ of 120, and a Performance IQ of 104. His MMPI–2 profile

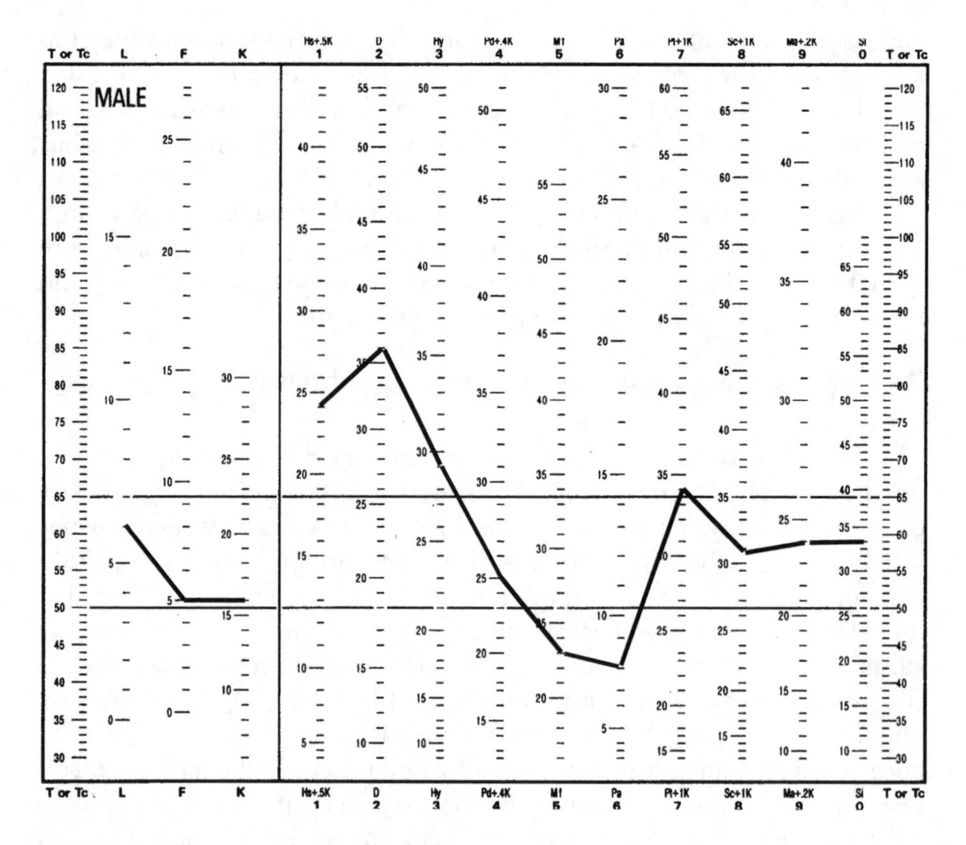

Figure 12.3. Robert's MMPI–2 basic clinical profile.

is shown in Figures 12.3 and 12.4. None of his supplementary scale scores exceeded 65T.

Does Robert have underlying brain dysfunction? The MMPI–2 revealed that, despite his attempt to appear highly proper and virtuous, he is very depressed and reports many physical symptoms and concerns about his health. What is the likelihood that Robert's observed deficits are secondary to his depression? Many clinicians who view such cases place heavy diagnostic weight on high MMPI–2 scores, not only to identify psychological problems (which is appropriate) but also to infer an absence of underlying brain pathology. Not surprisingly, MMPI–2 scores that suggest high levels of depression, anxiety, or other problems of a psychological nature are often the basis for inferring an emotional impact on neuropsychological test performance. This common practice is based in logic and an appreciation of the fact that cognitive inefficiency can arise from emotional difficulties. Unfortunately, this interpretive approach has very little empirical foundation.

Research involving the widely used Halstead–Reitan Neuropsychology Battery (HRNB; Reitan & Wolfson, 1993), which includes concurrent

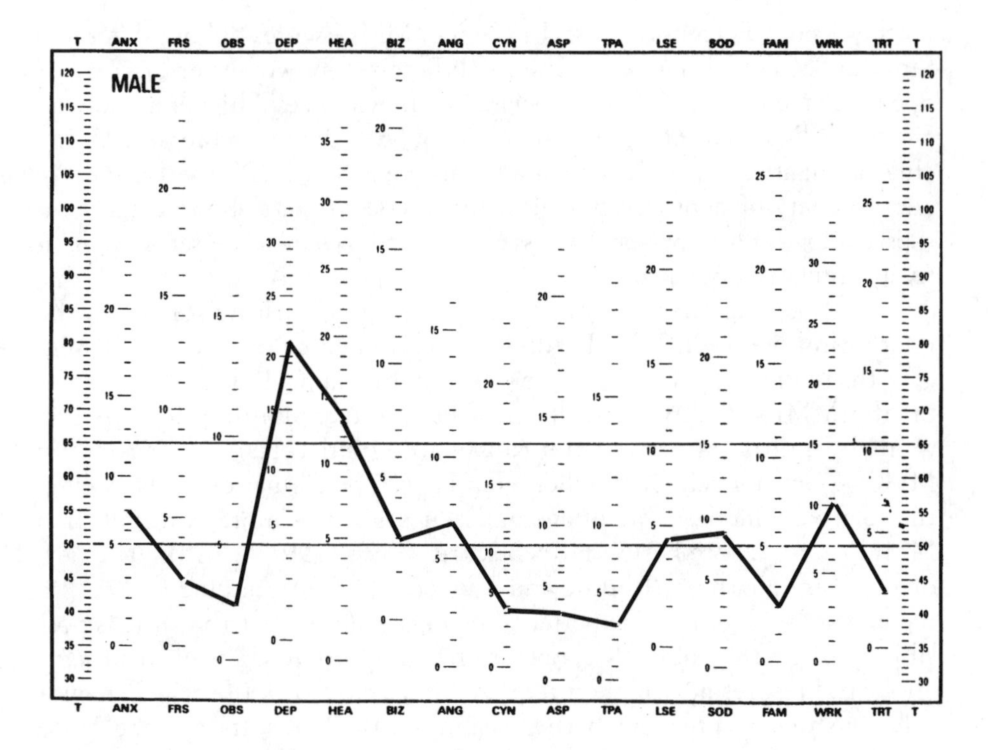

Figure 12.4. Robert's content scale profile.

administration of the MMPI, has examined correlations between performance on HRNB tests and MMPI scores on the basic clinical scales. Heaton and Crowley (1981) examined this issue in 561 patients who were referred to their laboratory for neuropsychological evaluation. Correlations between the Average Impairment Rating on the HRNB and the MMPI basic scales ranged from –.09 (*K*) to .33 (Scale 1), none accounting for as much as 11% of the variance in neuropsychological test performance. Calsyn, Louks, and Johnson (1982) examined correlations between the MMPI and HRNB in a sample of normal individuals and found no statistically significant relationships. In stroke patients, only modest relationships were found between MMPI variables and neuropsychological test performance (Gass & Ansley, 1994).

Gass (1991a) investigated the potential impact of MMPI variables on performance across each of the individual tests that comprise the HRNB. This sample was 105 neuropsychological referrals who were judged to be neurologically intact by staff neurologists using interview data and any diagnostic procedures deemed necessary. The composite MMPI profiles of high and low scorers on each of the HRNB tests were contrasted, and they were found to be the same except in the analysis of high versus low scorers on the Speech Perception Test. In general, MMPI scores did not differ as a function of performance on the HRNB tests. However, errors on the Speech Perception Test were associated with evidence of higher anxiety on Scale 7. Zillmer and Perry (1996) factor analyzed the test scores of 225 psychiatric inpatients who had been administered the MMPI, the Rorschach, and a variety of neuropsychological tests. Their results showed that neuropsychological and personality assessment indexes measure separate, relatively unrelated domains.

Although further investigation is warranted, existing studies on the relationship between MMPI scores and performance on the HRNB suggest that clinicians should be conservative in appealing to high scores on the MMPI–2 clinical scales as a basis for explaining poor performance on this battery of neuropsychological tests. Scores on the MMPI–2 are not reliable predictors of HRNB performance. In fact, even the relatively modest role of age and education was more powerful than MMPI scores in predicting HRNB scores (Gass, 1991a). In their review of this general topic, Reitan and Wolfson (1997) concluded, "As we have often said, clinical experience makes it quite clear that if it is possible to elicit the subject's cooperation and effort to do well, neuropsychological test results can be interpreted in a framework of brain–behavior relationships, even though the patient's MMPI results may be quite deviant" (p. 16).

Neuropsychologists frequently employ performance measures that are not part of the HRNB, and the manner in which emotional factors may influence scores on these tests warrants systematic investigation. The Logical Memory and Visual Reproduction subtests of the Wechsler Memory Scale are prime examples of popular tests that often play an important role in differential diagnosis. In order to be of diagnostic value, a memory test must be differentially sensitive to the effects of emotional factors and cerebral pathology. The relative influence of neurological versus emotional status on attention and memory test performance was examined by Gass (1996b) using a sample of neuropsychological referrals. These were 80 neurologically intact psychiatric patients and 48 patients with a recent history of traumatic brain injury. The findings of this study can be summarized as follows. The unique variance accounted for by several MMPI–2 measures of confused or unusual thinking, anxiety, and fearfulness was 22% (Visual Reproduction), 16% (attention span), 13% (Logical Memory), and 5% (list learning, selective reminding format). Unlike previous findings pertaining to the HRNB, this study found evidence that psychological factors may exert a distinct and important impact on attention span and visuographic memory, and a significant though slightly more modest effect on verbal–narrative memory. The importance of MMPI–2 variables in predicting performance on tests of attention and verbal learning was recently corroborated by Ross, Putnam, Gass, Bailey, and Adams (2003) using a sample of 381 psychiatric and head-injured neuropsychological referrals.

The content scale FRS (Fears) seems to have the strongest and most consistent association with neuropsychological test performance, especially in relation to nonverbal, visuospatial tasks. This scale measures the extent of highly specific fears, such as the sight of blood, high places, snakes, mice, and water, as well as a general disposition toward fearfulness. In the study already described (Gass, 1996b), FRS scores were predictive of performance on the Visual Reproduction subtest of the Wechsler Memory Scale—Revised ($r = -.40$). In another study, FRS scores were predictive of performance on several measures of executive functioning. Using a sample of 70 neuropsychological referrals, all of whom were judged to be neurologically intact, Gass, Ansley, and Boyette (1994) found that higher scores on FRS predicted poorer performance on the Design Fluency Test ($r = -.48$), Wechsler Intelligence Scale for Children—Revised (WISC–R) Mazes ($r = -.40$), and the Controlled Oral Word Association Test ($r = -.36$, $ps < .01$). One possible explanation of these findings is that FRS measures a tendency toward situation-specific anxiety and that this anxiety is elicited in the testing situation. Support for this hypothesis was found in a study of neuropsychological examinees who completed the Test Anxiety Profile (TAP; Oetting & Deffenbacher, 1980) in addition to a comprehensive neuropsychological test battery (Gass, 2002a). Test Anxiety Profile scores were associated with global performance on the WAIS–R (Full Scale IQ, $r = -.35$) and HRNB (Average Impairment Rating, $r = -.30$, $ps < .001$).

INTERPRETATION OF THE SOMATIC-RELATED MMPI–2 CLINICAL SCALES

Evaluating the Effects of Neurological Symptom Reporting

Scales 1, 2, 3, and 8 contain physical and cognitive symptom items that are a source of confusion and controversy when the MMPI–2 is used with people in medical and medicolegal settings. In neuropsychological settings, group studies show that these scales typically show the highest elevations (Wooten, 1983). The interpretation of scales 2, 3, and 8 can be facilitated by examining the scores on the Harris–Lingoes subscales. In brain-impaired samples, high scores on Scale 2 are most commonly associated with complaints of physical malfunctioning (*D*3) and mental dullness (*D*4). High scores on Scale 3 are most often linked with prominent elevations on lassitude–malaise (*Hy*3) and somatic complaints (*Hy*4). On Scale 8, high scores are usually due, in part, to reports of cognitive difficulties (*Sc*3) and bizarre sensory experiences (*Sc*6). These types of somatic and cognitive complaints are common in brain-injured individuals who report their symptoms of central nervous system (CNS) disease. Unfortunately, the extent to which scores on these subscales are reflective of psychological disturbance, as opposed to CNS symptom reporting, is unknown. A high subscale score can be achieved through the positive endorsement of different items, only some of which are sensitive to CNS pathology. Thus, high scores on these subscales could reflect psychopathology, neurological symptom reporting, or both.

In developing the MMPI, McKinley expressed an interest in measuring neurologic as well as psychiatric symptoms. Hathaway and McKinley (1940) identified several item clusters of MMPI items reflecting "general neurologic" (19 items), "cranial nerve" (11 items), and "motility and coordination" (6 items). Using the empirical keying method of scale construction with carefully defined psychodiagnostic groups, these CNS items were assigned along with other MMPI items to the various clinical (psychopathology) scales. Sound psychometric principles are seriously challenged when these scales are applied to patients who, having bona fide CNS symptoms, differ in a relevant and systematic way from the psychiatric patients used in the criterion groups to construct the scales. In brain-injured samples, neurologically sensitive items constitute a distinctive source of variance in MMPI responses (Gass, 1991b, 1992). At one extreme, some authors recommend ignoring the presence of these neurologically sensitive items or their potential profile effects when evaluating brain-impaired individuals. Some authors opt for a crystal ball approach, recommending a reliance upon vaguely defined "clinical judgment," but they fail to provide specific guidelines. At another extreme, some authors argue that the MMPI–2 as applied to brain-injured patients is essentially uninterpretable because of the confounding influence of neurological symptom reporting and the resulting inflation of scores across the clinical scales. They go so far as to suggest using rationally (not empirically) selected MMPI–2 items as a neurological symptom checklist.

A sensible approach to MMPI–2 use with brain-impaired patients requires a systematic examination of the potential impact of neurologically sensitive item endorsement on MMPI–2 profiles. This can be accomplished by inspecting the examinee's responses to these items, singling out the items that were answered in the keyed direction, and calculating the effects of their endorsement on the clinical profile. The original MMPI–2 profile, scored in the standard way, can then be compared with the "corrected" profile (Arbisi & Ben-Porath, 1999; Gass, 1991b, 1992). To the extent that the two profiles are similar, the clinician can have greater certainty regarding the profile's accuracy as a reflection of emotional status and personality characteristics. To the extent that the two profiles differ, the clinician has to proceed more cautiously, knowing that there is a higher likelihood of artifactual score elevation. In either case, unless this interpretive method is followed, the clinician is left with the highest degree of uncertainty regarding the potential influence of neurological symptom reporting.

A fundamental question is, when assessing the brain-impaired patient, which items on the MMPI–2 are most likely representative of neurological symptoms? Different approaches have been used to identify these items, and these approaches yield diverse but overlapping results. Not all methods of item identification hold equal validity. For research purposes, the simplest approach has relied on expert opinion in item selection. However, this approach is inherently unreliable because experts disagree among themselves and may be biased by extraneous influences. An expert's opinion about any given item may change overnight. This is an empirical issue that requires an empirical solution. Although imperfect, a statistical approach is more objective than subjective judgments and it makes much better sense. An optimal statistical solution to this problem was proposed by Kendall, Edinger, and Eberly (1978), who refined a previously devised MMPI correction for use with spinal cord injury patients. These authors outlined a rigorous empirical methodology for identifying MMPI items most sensitive to symptoms of spinal cord injury. This general strategy of item identification was adopted by Gass for closed-head injury patients (1991b) and with stroke victims (1992). Using a sample of 75 traumatic brain-injury patients, none of whom were compensation seeking, 14 items were identified after they passed four successive empirical hurdles: discriminative power, frequency of positive endorsement, homogeneity, and face validity. First, responses to each item sharply distinguished the 75 patients from the MMPI–2 normative sample (*ps* < .001). Second, every item was endorsed by at least 25% of the head-injured patients. Third, the items comprised a unitary factor. Fourth, the content of the items showed face validity as representing physical and cognitive symptoms related to brain damage.

The 14 items that emerged are 31, 101, 106, 147, 149, 165, 170, 172, 175, 179, 180, 247, 295, and 325. The scored direction appears in Table 12.1, which can be used to tabulate the influence of these items on the overall clinical profile. First, items that are answered in the keyed direction can be circled across their respective row. Second, in a columnwise manner, the number of circled items are added to obtain the raw score impact on each of the relevant clinical scales. These scores are then subtracted from the full scores on the clinical scales to provide an adjusted score for comparison. The neurologically sensitive items refer to distractibility, forgetfulness, headache, difficulties with speech, reading problems, tremor, imbalance, numbness, and motoric weakness. This set of items, as applied to bona fide traumatic brain-injury patients, has received empirical support in several studies. The unitary nature of these items in a

TABLE 12.1.
MMPI–2 Correction Table for Traumatic Brain Injury

Item	*F*	1	2	3	4	7	8	9	0
31 True	—	—	31T	31T	31T	31T	31T	—	31T
101 True	—	101T	—	101T	—	—	—	—	—
106 False	—	—	—	—	—	—	106F	106F	106F
147 True	—	—	147T	—	—	147T	147T	—	—
149 True	—	149T	—	—	—	—	—	—	—
165 False	—	—	165F	—	—	165F	165F	—	—
170 True	—	—	170T	—	—	170T	170T	—	—
172 True	—	—	—	172T	—	—	—	—	—
175 True	—	175T	175T	175T	—	175T	—	—	—
179 False	—	179F	—	179F	—	—	179F	—	—
180 True	180T	—	—	—	—	—	180T	—	—
247 True	—	247T	—	—	—	—	247T	—	—
295 False	—	—	—	—	—	—	295F	—	—
325 True	—	—	—	—	—	325T	325T	—	—
Sum	___ *F*	___ 1	___ 2	___ 3	___ 4	___ 7	___ 8	___ 9	___ 0

head injury sample was supported by Barrett, Putnam, Axelrod, and Rapport (1998), who reported a Cronbach's alpha coefficient of .80. The specificity of the 14 items to traumatic brain injury (TBI) was investigated by Edwards, Holmquist, Wanless, Wicks, and Davis (1998) using a sample of predominantly non-compensation-seeking TBI patients. These authors sought to determine whether the positive endorsement of these 14 items by head-injury patients might reflect preexisting psychological problems. After completing the MMPI–2, if an item was answered in the scored direction, each patient (*N* = 20) and a significant other (*N* = 20) were asked (independently) if the problem had been present before the head injury or if was a result of the head injury. The authors went through each of the positively endorsed correction items and inquired about the origin of the symptom that was being reported. In nearly every instance, injury victims and their relatives independently reported that the correction items were endorsed by the patient specifically because of problems resulting from the injury. Consider an example—Item 179: "I have had no difficulty in keeping my balance in walking." Thirteen of the patients answered "false" and, in the interview, all 13 of them attributed the imbalance to the head injury. Sixteen family members were interviewed independently and asked about the patient's answer to this item. All 16 family members attributed the symptom to the head injury. Across the 14 items, the patients were 10 times more likely to attribute the endorsed problem to the head injury than to their preinjury status. Similarly, their significant others independently attributed the item endorsements to the head injury about 13 times more often than to preinjury status. Overall, 109 of 119 endorsements of the 14 items were attributed to the head injury, supporting the specificity of the correction when applied to TBI patients. To date, no other study that has attempted to address the specificity of the correction has examined individual cases in this careful and detailed manner.

The 14-item correction was examined in a sample of 67 inpatients who were consecutive admissions to a general hospital immediately following a TBI (Gass, Luis, Rayls, & Mittenberg, 1999). Exclusionary criteria included recent substance abuse and a history of either neurological or psychiatric disorder. Upon admission, these patients were administered the Glascow Coma Scale (GCS) and had CT scans. An incidental finding in this study was the fact that the endorsement frequency on the 14 MMPI–2 correction items was positively related to injury severity on the GCS ($r = .26$) and findings on the CT scan ($r = .26$, $ps < .05$). These findings provide empirical support for the 14-item correction. Nevertheless, they are unexpected and surprising given the well-established weak relationship between the number of symptom complaints and degree of brain injury, whether estimated on the basis of GCS scores, radiological findings, duration of loss of consciousness or post-traumatic amnesia (Bornstein, Miller, & van Schoor, 1988). It is surprising to find a correlation between the amount of symptom reporting and estimates of injury severity, particularly when these estimates are typically crude and temporally separated from the time of symptom (MMPI–2) reporting by highly variable time periods, ranging from several weeks to many years. To complicate matters, mild-head-trauma patients with questionable injuries commonly report more symptom complaints than bona fide brain-injury patients (Berry, Wetter, Baer, Youngjohn, et al., 1995; Youngjohn, Burrows, & Erdal, 1995; Youngjohn, Davis, & Wolf, 1997). Furthermore, retrospective reports of injury severity made by mild-head-injury litigants with large financial incentives and symptoms persisting up to 7 years post-incident (e.g., Brulot, Strauss, & Spellacy, 1997) have doubtful validity and are completely misleading and irrelevant for assessing the validity of an MMPI–2 correction.

Rayls, Mittenberg, Burns, and Theroux (2000) investigated the question of whether the 14 correction items are reflective of neurological versus emotional symptoms in the same sample of acute head injury cases described previously (Gass et al., 1999). They reported several major findings. First, the acutely injured patients endorsed correction items in a manner that was statistically independent of their measured level of distress surrounding their accident. Second, on retesting after several months, they endorsed the correction items much less frequently, commensurate with their recovery. Based on their data, these authors concluded that as applied to acute and mild head injury, the correction initially reflects an impact of neurological symptom reporting. However, in *mild*-head-injury patients, after several months have passed, a continuing endorsement of these items probably reflects problems with psychological adjustment. This conclusion is consistent with the recommendation that the correction *not* be used with uncomplicated mild-head-injury cases in whom persistent complaints exist well beyond the normal recovery period. The correction is applicable when brain damage exists, as in acute mild brain trauma, but not after the individual recovers and cerebral compromise has dissipated.

As a general rule, clinicians are advised to first establish that there is sufficient evidence of brain dysfunction before evaluating the profile effects of the 14-item correction. The 14 items cannot possibly be reflective of neurological symptoms unless there is underlying neurological impairment. By implication, the correction is inappropriate for application with subjects who are involved in litigation or seeking compensation for symptoms that persist months or years following uncomplicated mild head injury. In most of these cases, there is ample reason to doubt the presence of brain dysfunction. Instead, the ongoing symptomatic complaints are usually related to psychological factors, motivational pressures, incentives to acquire compensation, and other important aspects of their medicolegal context (Reitan & Wolfson, 1997; Youngjohn, Davis, & Wolf, 1997). Interestingly, researchers who have recommended against using the correction based their conclusions largely on studies using primarily litigating mild-head-injury or personal injury clients for whom the correction is inappropriate (Brulot et al., 1997; Dunn & Lees-Haley, 1995). In a clinical setting, once brain dysfunction is established—whether through clinical history, neurological examination, or other neurodiagnostic methods—the correction factor can be used to gauge the potential impact of neurological symptom reporting on the MMPI–2 profile. Finally, the correction items are somewhat sensitive to various types of psychopathology, particularly somatoform disorders, and should be interpreted cautiously in individuals who have premorbid or comorbid emotional disturbances or substance abuse. In these cases, a minor or nil corrective impact increases the clinician's confidence in the validity of elevated scores on scales 1, 2, 3, and 8.

In contrast to closed head injury, the determination of structural brain damage is often more clearly made in cases of cerebrovascular disease, or stroke. Stroke is one of the most common neurological conditions that presents with a variety of physical and cognitive sequelae. Scores on the somatic-related scales of the MMPI–2 are commonly elevated in stroke patients to an extent suggestive of somatoform disorder, often contrary to any other evidence. The major source of variance distinguishing the MMPI–2 responses of stroke patients from normals is a cluster of items that refer not to emotional problems but to difficulties such as paresthesia, numbness, speech changes, reading difficulties, tremor, poor health, ataxia, weakness, and poor concentration. Using the same previously described statistical procedures, Gass (1992) identified 21 stroke-sensitive items that are most prominently represented on scales 1 (12 items) and 3 (13 items). The association of these items with stroke was corroborated in a follow-up study of 50 CVA patients (Gass, 1996a). The influence of the endorsement of these items on the profiles of individual stroke patients can be examined systematically for the purpose of gauging the potential impact of neurological symptom endorsement on profile elevations (Gass, 2000). To the extent that the original profile and the "corrected" profile are similar, the clinician has greater confidence that traditional code types and scale correlates apply. Conversely, if the two profiles are substantially different, then there is a greater likelihood that the traditional interpretive literature, based on psychiatric patients, will be inaccurate. In this case, very cautious interpretation is warranted.

Case Illustration

Betsy is a 49-year-old high school teacher who awakened one morning with marked weakness and a tingling sensation in her right arm and leg. Her speech was dysarthric but otherwise normal. She had a headache and dizziness that subsided after several hours. She denied having any other symptoms. Her past medical history was unremarkable. A brain scan revealed evidence of infarction in the left cerebral hemisphere, specifically in the posterior limb of the internal capsule extending into the corona radiata, dorsolateral thalamus, and body of the caudate nucleus. She was referred for a neuropsychological evaluation 2 months later while undergoing rehabilitative therapies.

Betsy's neuropsychological examination revealed mild to moderate impairments in right-hand motor speed (finger tapping), grip strength, and tactile performance. Her ability to retain verbal–narrative information showed mild compromise. Her speech was still mildly dysarthric. Intelligence testing revealed deficits in working memory and verbal conceptual reasoning. Her executive, visuospatial, and other language functions were intact. Betsy produced the MMPI–2 profile shown in Figure 12.5. Betsy's validity scale configuration suggests that she approached the MMPI–2 items in a frank, open manner, producing a valid clinical profile. She endorsed a number of problems and concerns.

Her MMPI–2 clinical profile (elevations on scales 1, 2, 3, 4, and 8) suggests excessive bodily concerns, numerous vague somatic symptoms, and undefined complaints such as gastric upset, fatigue, pain, and physical weakness. Such individuals are typically selfish, egocentric, and narcissistic. They are emotionally overcontrolled, negativistic, defeatist, unhappy, and demanding of attention. The presence of five elevated scores on the clinical scales might raise concern regarding the potential impact of psychological factors on her neuropsychological test performance. However, there is

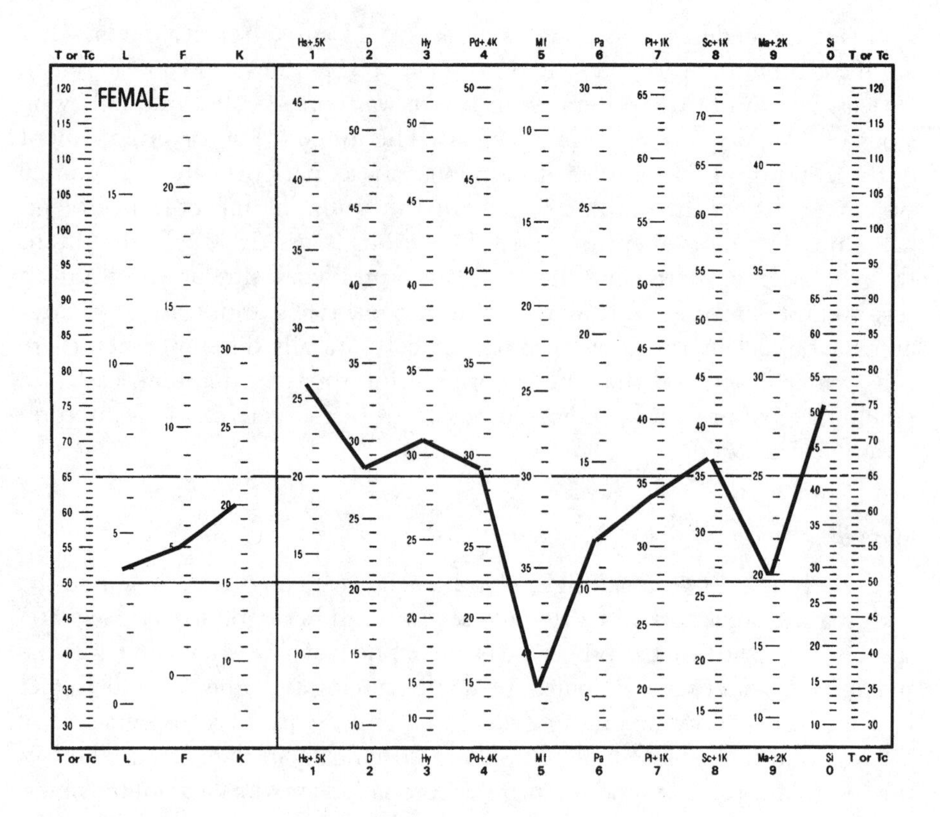

Figure 12.5. Betsy's MMPI–2 basic clinical profile.

little empirical basis for making this inference, and Betsy was fully cooperative throughout the examination.

Betsy endorsed in the scored direction 14 of the 21 MMPI–2 items that have been associated with stroke (Gass, 1992, 1996a). The items include references to work incapacity (10), poor concentration (31), paresthesia (53), dysarthric speech (106), poor health (141, 148), reading difficulties (147), fatigue (152), dizzy spells (164), memory lapse (168, 229), pain (224), numbness (247), and visual difficulties (249). These could conceivably reflect physical symptoms of stroke; and, as such, they might have limited psychodiagnostic significance.

The solid line on the basic clinical profile graph in Figure 12.6 represents Betsy's profile after accounting for her endorsement of the 14 stroke-related items. The contrast reveals an impact of 19T on scales 1 and 3, 11T on Scale 2, and 10T on Scale 8. With the exception of Scale 0, the adjusted profile is within normal limits. In this case, the discrepancy between the original and adjusted profiles is great enough to raise uncer-

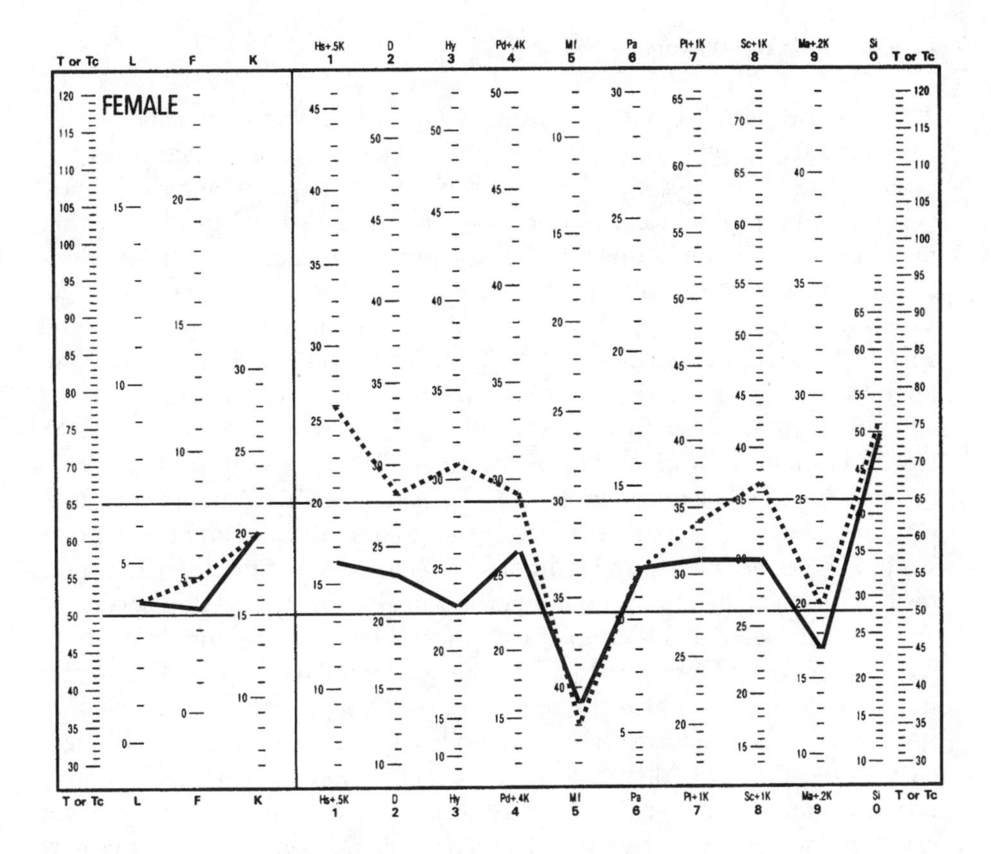

Figure 12.6. Betsy's MMPI–2 basic clinical profile with correction (solid line).

tainty regarding the validity of inferences derived from Betsy's original clinical profile. The clinician has less confidence in these inferences and must rely more heavily on other sources of information. Had Betsy endorsed fewer correction items, the discrepancy would have been less. In this scenario, the clinician could more confidently rely on a standard profile interpretation. The content scale results, which are generally less affected by neurological symptom reporting, were valid (*F(B)* = 54T, VRIN = 46T, and TRIN = 58T). Betsy's scores on the MMPI–2 content scales were all within the normal range except for her score of 70T on Health Concerns (HEA). The HEA scale is much more sensitive to CNS damage than are the other content scales. An inspection of the component scales (Ben-Porath & Sherwood, 1993) is helpful in refining the interpretation of content scale results. In this case, the elevated score on HEA was strongly affected by Betsy's disclosure of neurological symptoms (HEA2 = 93T) and, to some extent, general health concerns (HEA3 = 72T).

Use of the Harris–Lingoes Subscales

Patients with brain disorders of any type are likely to report neurological symptoms on psychological inventories. The extent to which this compromises standard interpretation is a problem that requires empirical investigation. The problem exists not just with the MMPI–2 but with other measures as well, including the Personality Assessment Inventory, Beck Depression Inventory, and the Symptom Checklist 90–R (Prenger, 2000; Woessner & Caplan, 1995, 1996). In addition to traumatic brain injury and stroke, the need for cautious MMPI–2 interpretation has been addressed in relation to multiple sclerosis (Nelson, Elder, Tehrani, & Groot, 2003) and epilepsy (Ansley, Gass, Brown, & Levin, 1995; Bornstein & Kozora, 1990; Derry, Harnadek, McLachlan, & Sontrop, 1997). In the absence of a diagnostic-specific set of neurologically sensitive MMPI–2 items, the clinician should carefully consider the Harris–Lingoes subscales and the content scales. These measures provide limited assistance in estimating the degree to which neurological symptom reporting might affect scores on several of the clinical scales. For example, one can be more confident that a high score on Scale 2 (T greater than 75) reflects the usual behavioral correlates in a neurological patient if the scores are relatively higher on subscales *D*2 (psychomotor retardation), or *D*5 (brooding). This is because *D*1 (subjective depression), *D*3 (physical malfunctioning) and *D*4 (mental dullness) contain some neurologically sensitive items that do not necessarily reflect psychopathology. Higher scores (T greater than 75) on Scale 2 are usually indicative of depressive symptoms, regardless of the subscale results. This is also true regarding high scores on the content scale DEP (depression), which has relatively few neurologically related physical and cognitive symptom items. Conversely, depressive symptoms are less likely to exist if DEP is less than 60T.

High scores on Scale 3 can be interpreted in the standard way with greater confidence if relatively higher scores exist on the Harris–Lingoes subscales that are free of neurologically sensitive item content. These subscales are *Hy*1 (denial of social anxiety), *Hy*2 (need for affection), and *Hy*5 (inhibition of aggression). The clinician must be more cautious with interpretation if the brain-impaired individual elevates *Hy*3 (Lassitude–Malaise) or *Hy*4 (somatic complaints), because some of the items on these subscales can reflect neurological impairment rather than psychiatric symptoms. Symptoms of a somatoform disorder are more likely to be present in the brain-damaged individual if the score on Scale 3 is quite high (T greater than 75) and prominent in the profile configuration.

Many factors can contribute to a high score on Scale 8, and brain-impaired subjects often endorse items that reflect blank spells (229), distractibility (31), speech changes (106), poor concentration (325), reading difficulty (147), memory problems (165), problems walking (179), anosmia (299), tinnitus (255), numbness (247), and paralysis or weakness (177, 295). Greater confidence can be placed in the standard interpretation of Scale 8 if relatively high scores are present on Harris–Lingoes subscales that have the fewest neurologically sensitive items. These include *Sc*1 (social alienation), *Sc*2 (emotional alienation), *Sc*4 (lack of ego mastery, conative), and *Sc*5 (lack of ego mastery, defective inhibition). Cautious interpretation is recommended if Scale 8 is marginally elevated (60T to 70T) and high scores are present on *Sc*3 (lack of ego mastery, cognitive) or *Sc*6 (bizarre sensory experiences), because these subscales have some items that can reflect symptoms of CNS impairment. In contrast to Scale 8, the content scale BIZ is a more specific measure of psychotic symptoms. Psychotic symptoms are much less likely to be present if BIZ is less than 65T. In a valid protocol that is free of symptom exaggeration, a high BIZ score (T greater than 70) suggests the presence of psychotic symptoms in a brain-injured or neurologically intact patient.

Malingering Brain Injury

Ample evidence indicates the existence of diverse approaches to feigning brain-injury symptoms on self-report measures such as the MMPI–2. Individuals who fake or exaggerate symptoms of brain injury can choose an approach that calls attention to emotional difficulties, physical problems, cognitive difficulties, or any combination therein. Any given clinical or forensic setting may attract malingerers who tend to favor one particular approach; and, not surprisingly, the research literature shows mixed findings that are partly a function of divergent sampling characteristics. The MMPI–2 *F* scales (*F*, F(B), and *Fp*) are all sensitive to the feigning of psychological symptoms and emotional pathology in brain injury (Berry, Baer, Rinaldo, & Wetter, 2002; Berry, Wetter, Baer, Youngjohn, et al., 1995; Dearth et al., in press; Heaton, Smith, Lehman, & Vogt, 1978). However, many malingerers feign physical and cognitive symptoms of brain injury while attempting to hold in check any appearance of severe psychological disturbance. In these cases, scores on scales 1, 2, and 3 are frequently extreme (T greater than 80), whereas scores on the *F* scales are not particularly elevated.

The Fake-Bad Scale (FBS; Lees-Haley, English, & Glenn, 1991), which was designed to detect malingerers involved in personal injury claims, is comprised of 43 items that include somatic symptoms, unusual beliefs, and deviant attitudes. The scale shares 14 items with Scale 3 and 13 items with Scale 1. The FBS is sensitive to the problem of somatic malingering, which is common in personal injury and other medicolegal settings (Greiffenstein et al., 1995; Larrabee, in press; Ross, Millis,

Krukowski, Putnam, & Adams, in press). Unfortunately, the FBS appears to be sensitive to a variety of other conditions across a variety of clinical settings (Butcher, Arbisi, Atlis, & McNulty, 2003). In particular, scores on the FBS do not distinguish malingerers from individuals with somatoform disorders. Yet, these disorders are commonplace in the personal injury arena and may account for a majority of cases with persisting post-concussion symptoms (Youngjohn, Burrows, & Erdal, 1995). In view of this lack of specificity, the term *fake-bad* is a misnomer with unfortunate connotations. The scale might be more accurately labeled *somatic exaggeration*.

USE OF THE MMPI–2 CONTENT SCALES

The content scales were designed using rationally constructed items with transparent meaning. In this regard, these scales are quite different from the basic clinical scales, which were designed by applying the empirical keying approach to items, some of which have subtle content. Practically speaking, the content scales provide a much more direct means by which the examinee intentionally conveys problem areas and their magnitude to the clinician. This information is very useful in providing patients with feedback regarding their MMPI–2 results. In addition, whereas the validity scales assess openness in symptom reporting, the content scales reflect in more specific detail how the client wants to appear. For example, the well-defended client may emphasize psychological health in the areas of anger management and social comfort level by scoring very low (T less than 40) on scales ANG (Anger) and SOD (Social Discomfort), respectively. The malingering individual may attempt to accentuate an appearance of psychosis as evidenced by a prominent elevation on BIZ. The content scale profile reveals elements of impression management that are undetectable using the validity scales alone.

Some clinicians who use the MMPI–2 base their interpretive inferences almost exclusively on the basic clinical scales without paying sufficient attention to content scale information. Yet, in many cases, the content scale profile sheds interpretive light on the meaning of high scores on the more heterogeneous basic clinical scales (Butcher, 2002c). For example, the Depression (DEP) scale may provide clearer and more direct information regarding general distress, worry, and unhappiness than Scale 2 because scores on Scale 2 are more likely to be elevated by self-reported physical problems and cognitive difficulties. One component of the DEP scale, Suicidal Ideation (DEP4), provides critical information regarding the probability of self-destructive ideation or intentions. Depressive symptoms often include low self-esteem (LSE); and, though inferences regarding self-esteem can be based on the basic clinical profile, this dimension is more directly assessed by the content scale LSE. High scores on Scale 7 may be attributable to generalized anxiety, obsessional thinking, fears and phobias, or any combination of these. Scores on the content scales Anxiety (ANX), Obsessional Thinking (OBS), and Fears (FRS) can provide assistance in interpreting the meaning of an elevated score on scale 7.

The HEA scale yields high scores (T greater than 65) in about 50% of brain-injured patients (Gass, 1999). Analysis of the component scales in these cases usually reveals a prominent elevation on HEA2, indicating the major contribution of neurologically related item endorsement to the HEA score. High scores on Scale 8 are not necessarily indicative of psychotic symptoms. Many variables influence the score on Scale 8, including neurological symptom reporting (Bornstein & Kozora, 1990). Unlike Scale 8, scores on the BIZ scale are largely unaffected by the endorsement of common neurological symptoms. In addition, because of its homogeneous item composition, BIZ is generally more effective than Scale 8 in identifying psychotic symptoms (Ben-Porath, Butcher, & Graham, 1991). Social anxiety and discomfort are often suggested by high scores on scales 8 and 0, but these important personality characteristics are more directly assessed by the SOD scale. Inferences can sometimes be derived from the basic clinical scales regarding an individual's level of anger. However, a person's degree of control over anger is directly addressed by the ANG scale.

CONCLUSION

The evaluation of personality characteristics and emotional status is a critically important yet often neglected component in neuropsychological assessment. It is essential in neuropsychological diagnosis, patient care, and treatment planning. Although most neurobehavioral assessment tests and techniques focus on specific cognitive and sensorimotor functions, psychological factors play the major role in determining a person's adaptation to the surrounding environment and, more generally, to quality of life. This chapter reviewed various issues and common difficulties involving the use of the MMPI–2 in neuropsychological settings. It is appropriate to do so, given the fact that this instrument has established itself over many decades as a useful tool in this assessment process, having the advantages of broadband measurement (comprehensiveness), inclusion of validity scales that assess test-taking attitude, and an extensive research base related to neuropsychological practice. Some of the controversy over the use of the MMPI–2 with brain-injured patients is perhaps unnecessary as long as the test is used properly as part of a multimodal evaluative approach that includes behavioral observation, interview data, and collateral reports. Within this assessment context, clinicians can expand their use of the MMPI–2 in terms of administrative feasibility, interpretive comprehensiveness, and descriptive accuracy. (See Exhibit 12.1.)

EXHIBIT 12.1
Highlight: Use of the MMPI–2 in Neuropsychological Assessment

- A neuropsychological evaluation is incomplete without an assessment of personality and emotional status.
- The use of a comprehensive self-report instrument such as the MMPI–2 holds many advantages. For example, some patients use the MMPI–2 to disclose significant problems that they will not bring up or acknowledge in a clinical interview.
- Profile invalidity can result from the ill-advised use of proposed short forms of the MMPI–2, inadequate preparation of the examinee, inadequate supervision over the testing session, or exclusive reliance on the standard written administration of the MMPI–2 with examinees who have limited reading ability. Reading difficulties can be circumvented through the use of the audiotape format.
- Profile validity is not invariably an all-or-none issue. In many cases, the question is not, Is the profile valid or invalid? The proper question is, What valid information can be extracted from this profile? For example, individuals sometimes "fake-good" on the MMPI–2 but still reveal selected problem areas that require attention.
- Scores on the MMPI–2 are not reliable predictors of performance on neuropsychological tests. In the absence of corroborative observational evidence, clinicians should be reluctant to use elevated MMPI–2 scores as an explanatory basis for poor performance on neuropsychological tests.
- Scales 1, 2, 3, and 8 contain items that are sensitive not only to psychopathology but also to symptoms of central nervous system impairment. A sensible approach to MMPI–2 use with brain-impaired patients requires a systematic examination of the potential impact of neurologically sensitive item endorsement on MMPI–2 profiles.
- Neurologically sensitive items were identified using a rigorous four-step statistical procedure for traumatic brain injury (Gass, 1991b) and stroke (Gass, 1992). By exposing the potential impact of neurologically sensitive item endorsement, the application of the correction factor assists the clinician in addressing the uncertainty inherent in interpreting elevated profiles produced by brain-impaired individuals.
- Correction use applies to individuals with bona fide brain impairment. It is inappropriate in cases in which symptoms persist months or years following uncomplicated mild head trauma. In view of the fact that correction items are somewhat sensitive to psychological disturbance, cautious interpretation is required in brain-injury cases involving comorbid or premorbid psychopathology or substance abuse.
- In evaluating the MMPI–2 profiles of brain-impaired individuals, the Harris–Lingoes subscales provide some assistance in estimating the extent to which neurological symptom reporting might affect scores on scales 2, 3, and 8.
- The malingering of brain-injury symptoms on the MMPI–2 can selectively showcase (a) severe psychological disturbance, (b) physical problems, (c) cognitive deficits, or any combination therein. Scale *F* is sensitive to the first type, and scales 1, 3, and HEA are sensitive to the second type.
- High scores on the Fake-Bad Scale (FBS; Lees-Haley, English, & Glenn, 1991) occur in cases involving the malingering of physical symptoms, but they also occur in a variety of other clinical conditions. The FBS does not appear to distinguish malingerers from individuals with somatoform disorders, which are commonplace in the personal injury arena.
- The MMPI–2 content scales provide information that helps the clinician refine and supplement clinical scale interpretation.

13

USE OF THE MMPI–2 IN CORRECTIONAL SETTINGS

EDWIN I. MEGARGEE

This chapter discusses the use of the MMPI–2 (Butcher, Dahlstrom, Graham, Tellegen, & Kaemmer, 1989) in corrections, that is, with convicted felons tested in criminal justice settings. It does not deal with forensic issues such as evaluating competency to stand trial or determining legal sanity at the time of offense. The primary focus is on areas in which the use of the MMPI–2 in corrections differs from its application in mental health and nonclinical settings.

A BRIEF HISTORY OF THE MMPI IN CORRECTIONS

The original MMPI (Hathaway & McKinley, 1943) has been used in criminal justice and correctional settings for over 60 years. In the early 1940s, before the original MMPI was even completed, Doris Capwell

(1945) used the scales that were then available to assess the personality characteristics of delinquent girls; and, shortly after its publication, Fry (1949) applied it to male and female state prisoners. The original MMPI and its successors, MMPI–2 and MMPI–A, have been used with adult criminals and delinquents ever since.

In the early 1950s, Hathaway and Monachesi (1963) investigated the ability of the original MMPI to forecast subsequent delinquency. In studies involving thousands of Minnesota youths, Hathaway and Monachesi identified "excitatory" and "inhibitory" scales that were reliably associated with increased and decreased risks of delinquency. Meanwhile, other investigators derived dozens of new scales for the original MMPI, many of which assessed factors relevant to correctional classification such as prison adjustment and recidivism.

In the 1960s, a number of studies evaluated the usefulness of the standard and specialized MMPI scales in prisons, training schools, and other criminal justice facilities; and multivariate studies sought the best combination of MMPI scales to predict criteria such as responsiveness to prison educational programs and parole success (Megargee & Carbonell, 1995).

In the early 1970s, Megargee empirically derived an MMPI–based classification system for criminal offenders using the statistical method of hierarchical profile analysis (Megargee, 1977; Megargee & Bohn, 1979). Hailed as defining the "state of the art" in correctional classification (Gearing, 1981, pp. 106–107), Megargee's classification system has been the subject of over 100 studies that have demonstrated its reliability, validity, and utility in criminal justice classification. After the MMPI–2 was published, the original MMPI–based classification system was revised so it could be used with the MMPI–2s of male and female offenders in probation, parole, corrections, and forensic mental health settings (Megargee, 1994, 1997; Megargee, Carbonell, Bohn, & Sliger, 2001). Recently, a special correctional report was published that includes interpretive statements and critical items specifically designed for correctional settings along with the 10 Megargee profile types and the MMPI–2 data that have proved most useful in criminal justice settings (Megargee, 2000).

THE NATURE OF ASSESSMENT IN CORRECTIONAL SETTINGS

Obviously, many differences exist between correctional and other settings. Four of the most salient are (a) the volume of cases, (b) the degree of legal accountability required, (c) the nature of the offender population, and (d) the consequent need to maintain security.

Volume of Cases

In the United States, corrections is a growth industry and has been for decades. Since 1970, the number of adult men and women confined in state and federal prisons has increased 684% and the rate of incarceration per 100,000 has increased 476% (American Correctional Association, 2004). Each year in the United States more than 12 million individuals are admitted to jails; and, on any given day, 6.6 million adults are under some form of correctional supervision and over 2 million of them are behind bars (Harrison & Beck, 2003; Harrison & Karberg, 2003). Needless to say, staffing and budgets have not kept pace with this exponential growth in the correctional population.

Offenders who are detained or incarcerated in jails and prisons must be screened for mental illness, developmental disabilities, self-destructive tendencies, and their potential for dangerous or violent behavior, after which case managers must determine which facilities and programs are best suited to their particular needs. Later, in jurisdictions in which parole is an option, it must be determined if, when, and under what conditions those imprisoned should be released (American Association for Correctional Psychology, Standards Committee, 2000; Anno, 1991; National Commission on Correctional Health Care, 2003a, 2003b).

Many offenders are emotionally disturbed or mentally ill. The Bureau of Justice Statistics (BJS) recently reported that 283,800 (16%) of the state and federal adult prisoners could be considered mentally ill, and another 15% to 20% require mental health services or interventions at some time during their incarceration (Anno, 1991). In addition to those with emotional disturbances, many have histories of and require treatment for alcohol or substance abuse (Anno, 1991; Beck & Maruschak, 2001; Ditton, 1999; Mumola, 1999). Along with factors such as age, gender, education, and criminal offense, each prisoner's psychological condition and personality characteristics should play an important role in these management decisions and treatment plans. Thus, assessment is of paramount importance, and the sheer numbers involved dictate that only the most cost-effective techniques can be used.

Legal Accountability

Few psychologists receive closer scrutiny than those working in criminal justice and correctional settings. Because prisoners are completely dependent on the institution for their health care, the correctional health care delivery system is subject to external and even judicial review. Strict standards for the assessment and treatment of prisoners have been established by the courts and by organizations such as the American Association for Correctional Psychology (AACP) and the National Commission for Correctional Health Care (NCCHC). These standards require that prisoners have access to mental health services; and they stress the need for assessment by capable and appropriately credentialed mental health personnel using instruments that are reliable, valid, and suitable for correctional settings (AACP, 2000; NCCHC, 2003a, 2003b).

Because incarcerated criminal offenders are involved in the judicial system, correctional psychologists may be called on to testify in court regarding their evaluations. They must be prepared to explain their findings to a judge or jury and be able to defend their choice of tests as well as their administration and interpretation of these instruments when cross-examined (Pope, Butcher, & Seelen, 2000).

Given the MMPI–2's position as our preeminent objective personality assessment device (Butcher & Rouse, 1996), it is not difficult for correctional psychologists to justify its use with criminal offenders; indeed, it would be more difficult to defend omitting it from a test battery. However, most MMPI and MMPI–2 interpretive research has been carried out in clinical and mental health settings, which differ in many ways from correctional facilities. Correctional psychologists must be able to demonstrate that their procedures and interpretations are supported by empirical research with criminal populations tested in criminal justice and correctional settings.

The Nature of the Clientele

Probably the most significant difference between corrections and other settings is the antisocial nature of the clientele. In most settings, we can assume that an MMPI–2 assessment is a cooperative enterprise in which the client and the clinician share the basic goal of developing an accurate appraisal of the respondent in order to help with his or her treatment. Not so in the criminal justice system. Many criminal offenders are deviant and disruptive. They may view the MMPI–2 assessment as an adversarial situation in which the psychologist is "the man," another authority to be outwitted. Therefore, correctional psychologists have to adapt their MMPI–2 administrations and interpretations to the realities of the prison setting.

Need for Security

The need to maintain security affects correctional practice in many ways. One is the need to provide for the physical security of the mental health staff. With regard to the MMPI–2, this means making sure that tests are administered in suitable settings by well-trained proctors who can maintain control of the testing situation. The security of test data, reports, and assessment files must also be maintained. In prisons, inmates should not be used to administer, score, or file test data; and reports should not be left where they may be seen (or stolen) by inmate clerks or cleaning crews.

Assessment Questions in Correctional Settings

Although correctional psychologists must be prepared to deal with the full range of referral questions that they would encounter in a free-world mental health facility, most assessment in corrections focuses on three issues: (a) mental health screening, (b) risk assessment, and (c) needs assessment.

Mental Health Screening

The AACP (2000) and the NCCHC (2003a, 2003b) standards for mental health services in jails and prisons stipulate that each new admission to a jail or prison must receive a mental health screening immediately upon entering and before being placed in a cell or holding area with other inmates. This should entail a direct examination of the new inmates as well as a review of whatever paperwork accompanied them to the new facility. This initial mental health screening is often done in conjunction with a brief health screening by health care workers or specialty trained correctional staff (Anno, 1991). Any indication that an offender is in need of mental health care requires a referral for a more thorough examination by a mental health professional.

One of the things the MMPI–2 does best is identify mentally ill or emotionally disturbed people. Unfortunately, in jail settings where large numbers of people are admitted at all times of the day and night, the volume of new admissions and the limited resources available generally preclude the routine use of the MMPI–2 in the initial screening. However, the MMPI–2 can certainly aid in the more thorough mental health assessment of those new admissions who are identified as possibly having mental health problems.

Convicted offenders sentenced to prison generally go first to a reception center for a comprehensive evaluation. In these settings, where the volume of cases is smaller and the time available is greater, the MMPI–2 is often administered to all new admissions.

Risk Assessment

Risk appraisal is an essential component of correctional assessment. It involves evaluating the danger offenders pose to the community, to the correctional staff, to their fellow inmates, and to themselves. Policy dictates that new arrivals be assigned to the least-restrictive facility that matches their needs for security and control. In the federal system and in most states, security levels typically range from maximum security penitentiaries through medium security correctional institutions down to minimum security open camps. Within institutions, the more predatory offenders should be identified and separated from those most likely to be preyed upon (Levinson, 1988).

The assessment of the potential for violent behavior is a difficult and complex task, one for which personality tests such as the MMPI–2 are not very well suited (Heilbrun & Heilbrun, 1995; Megargee, 2002). A major problem is that interpersonal violence is largely influenced by situational factors that tests cannot appraise. Moreover, the low base rates for violence, even in correctional settings, magnify the effects of false positive errors (Kamphuis & Finn, 2002). Nevertheless, Bohn (1978, 1979) was able to reduce the rate of serious assaults in a medium security federal correctional institution by 46% by using Megargee's MMPI–2–based offender classification system (Megargee et al., 2001) to separate the more predatory offenders from those most likely to be victimized. While the MMPI–2 can thus make a contribution to risk assessment, it is best employed in conjunction with case and criminal history data, as well as with narrowband instruments more specifically focused on dangerous behavior such as Hare's (1991) Psychopathy Checklist—Revised (PCL–R) or Bonta and Motiuk's (1985) Level of Supervision Inventory (LSI). In forensic mental health settings, Harris, Rice, and Quinsey's (1993) Violence Risk Appraisal Guide (VRAG) and Webster, Douglas, Eaves, and Hart's (1997) Historical, Clinical, and Risk Management (HCR–20) instrument have proved useful in Canada and the United Kingdom (MacPherson & Jones, 2004). (For a more detailed discussion of risk assessment in corrections, see Megargee, 2003, pp. 370–375.)

Needs Assessment

The next step is to determine each prisoner's management and treatment needs. The goal of treatment is to maximize the likelihood that former convicts will become responsible and productive citizens and family members once they return to their communities. If the correctional system is to rehabilitate inmates, each offender's educational, vocational, emotional, and mental health needs must be appraised and individual management and treatment programs formulated.

Needs assessment includes psychological appraisals to identify those most in need of and likely to benefit from mental health interventions, as well as cognitive and motivational assessments to determine their need for and ability to profit from educational programming or vocational training. The MMPI–2 is especially useful in these appraisals. Based on their MMPI–2 profiles, Megargee et al.'s (2001) empirically derived classification system divides offenders into 10 types that have been found to differ significantly in their adjustment to prison and in their response to correctional programs; and the MMPI–2 Criminal Justice and Correctional Report (Megargee, 2000) provides scales assessing their need for and response to various types of programming.

THE MMPI–2 IN CORRECTIONS

This section discusses the actual use of the MMPI–2 in corrections. It concentrates on four areas in which the correctional usage of the MMPI–2 differs from its application in other settings: (a) administration, (b) validity screening, (c) code-type interpretation, and (d) using the Megargee classification system and the Criminal Justice and Correctional Report. The section concludes with a case example.

Administration of the MMPI–2 in Correctional Settings

Volume of cases, legal accountability, the nature of the clientele, and the need to maintain security all combine to make the administration of the MMPI–2 in correctional settings different from most free-world assessments. Because of the large numbers of inmates who must be tested in many settings, group testing is often necessary. It is best to test inmates in small groups of no more than 15 or 20 respondents and to have at least two people present to administer the test. If one proctor must leave the room for some reason, such as escorting a respondent to the rest room, the other(s) can supervise the group. The proctors should be well trained, highly motivated, and able to project a friendly air of confident authority while at the same time maintaining control of the testing session.

Respondents should be screened prior to the testing session, perhaps as part of the cognitive assessment, for their ability to read English at least at the sixth-grade level. Special arrangements may have to be made for those who have difficulty reading; whose primary language is not English; and who have visual, auditory, or other disabilities. (See chap. 18 by Garrido and Velasquez on interpreting Hispanic MMPI–2s and chap. 19 by Butcher et al. on using the MMPI–2 with other cultural and national groups.)

An appropriate setting that is secure and free from distractions should be provided. Whether computerized or paper-and-pencil administration is used, the work spaces should be arranged to afford each respondent with some measure of privacy. In addition to adequate supplies of the materials to be used in testing, the testing room should have an internal phone line so that no-shows can be located, and there should be an inmate-accessible rest room in the vicinity.

Examiners should adhere to the ethical standards of the AACP (2000) by informing respondents at the outset of the purpose of the testing and of any limits on confidentiality and by securing appropriate informed consent. Accountability requires that the administration closely adhere to the standard MMPI–2 test administration procedures, especially if the psychologist in charge may some day have to testify about the MMPI–2 findings, because deviations from standard practice may have to be justified and their effects assessed. It is especially important for the proctor to establish the identity of the respondents; some inmates are not above sending a "ringer" to take the examination for them. Needless to say, inmates should never be given an MMPI–2 to complete back in their living units.

The MMPI–2 should be administered in its entirety. Although a number of so-called "short forms" have been devised, after reviewing numerous studies, Butcher and Williams (2000, p. 24) concluded, ". . . none were found to provide sufficient information and were not recommended for clinical use."[1]

To ensure reliability, answer sheets should be scored by computer using an established program rather than by hand, especially if the Megargee classification system is to be used. With computerized scoring, it is important to preserve the "chain of evidence" from the respondent to the scanner to the final output so that in court you can testify with certainty that the profile in question came from the answer sheet that the litigant filled out. This can be done by having the proctor initial or otherwise identify each answer sheet as soon as it is completed. All test data must be kept in secure files. Inmate labor should never be used to score MMPI–2s, nor should inmates have any role in processing or filing test data or results. (See Megargee, in press, for a detailed discussion of how to administer the MMPI–2 in criminal justice and correctional settings.)

Screening for Validity

In corrections, as in other settings, once MMPI–2s are scored they must be inspected to determine whether they were completed correctly. General procedures for establishing profile validity are discussed in chapter 3 by Bagby et al. In this chapter, we focus on the issues peculiar to validity screening in correctional settings.

---

[1]In exceptional circumstances, it is possible to administer the first 370 items of the MMPI–2 or MMPI–A, which include all the items needed to score validity scales *L* (Lie), *F* (Infrequency), and *K* (Correction) and the 10 standard clinical scales, and to classify the profile into its Megargee type. However, this procedure results in the loss of all the other validity scales as well as the supplementary and content scales. Moreover, since it is a departure from standard practice, it is incumbent on the clinician to disclose and justify this alteration. If time is an issue, it is far better to schedule two or more administrations so that the MMPI–2 can be completed in its entirety.

In corrections, as in other settings, the primary threats to profile validity are (a) incomplete profiles, (b) nonresponsive answering, and (c) distorted or dissimulated responding.

Incomplete Profiles

Incomplete profiles are those on which more than 30 items are not answered or are unscorable because both the True and False options were filled in. The Cannot Say (?) raw score is the total of all the unanswered and unscorable items. Normative research with correctional samples indicates that male and female federal and state prisoners are no more likely to omit items or mark them both True and False than their free-world counterparts (Megargee, in press). Therefore, the same exclusion criteria can be used with correctional as with other samples. Profiles on which the raw score on ? is equal to or greater than 30 should be considered invalid and uninterpretable. Those on which ? is equal to 10 through 29 should be interpreted cautiously. In addition, no scale on which less than 90% of the items have been answered should be interpreted. If answer sheets are inspected as they are turned in, those with ? scale scores equal to or greater than 10 can be identified and salvaged by having the respondent fill in the missing items.

Nonresponsive Answering

Nonresponsive answering occurs when the respondent answers randomly or in some fixed pattern such as all True, all False, or an alternating True and False pattern. On the original MMPI, the primary defense against nonresponsive answering was the *F* or Infrequency scale, consisting of those original MMPI items answered in the keyed direction by less than 10% of the original derivation samples. On MMPI–2, several new scales have been added to detect nonresponsive answering: Back *F* [*F(B)*], Variable Response Inconsistency (VRIN), and True Response Inconsistency (TRIN).

The MMPI–2 Infrequency Scales in Correctional Settings. Criminal offenders are not known for their high tolerance for frustration. On the original MMPI, all the *F*-scale items appeared among the first 300 items, which were printed on the front side of the answer sheet. When offenders discovered upon turning over the answer sheet that they had another 266 items to answer, many would begin to answer hastily to get through the test, some without even reading the items. Scale *F*, with all its items on the front, was unable to detect these impatient individuals.

On the MMPI–2, Scale *F* has been supplemented by Scale *F(B)* consisting of infrequently answered items on the latter half of the test. This improvement makes it possible to identify those respondents who get bored and begin to answer nonresponsively halfway through the test.

A more serious problem is the fact that criminal offenders who are answering conscientiously can nevertheless obtain elevated scores on scales *F* and *F(B)* by virtue of their atypical lifestyles. An inspection of the item content of the *F* scale shows that offenders who (a) feel that people are out to get them, (b) feel that they have been victimized by others, (c) do not express warm feelings of love and admiration for their parents, or (d) admit to having stolen things or having been in trouble at school or with the law will obtain elevated scores.

Recent item analyses of the *F* and *F(B)* scales among incarcerated male and female state and federal prisoners showed that more than half of the items did not meet the basic requirements for inclusion on an Infrequency scale because they were answered in the keyed direction by more than 10% of the offenders (Megargee, 2004). The content of these items strongly suggests that incarcerated felons answer these items in the deviant direction not because of carelessness or reading difficulties but, instead, because of their lifestyles and present circumstances.

Psychologists working in inpatient mental health units encountered a similar problem with the responses of psychiatric patients who were truthfully reporting bizarre and atypical symptoms. They dealt with it by constructing a new Infrequency–Psychopathology (*Fp*) scale comprised of items rarely answered by psychiatric patients (Arbisi & Ben-Porath, 1995). Unfortunately, our research indicates that male and, to a lesser extent, female prisoners also obtain elevated *Fp* scale scores, so using *Fp* in correctional settings does not solve the problem. Therefore, we have constructed a new 51-item Infrequency–Criminal (*Fc*) scale. The items are listed in Appendix 13.1. The initial validation research on this experimental scale indicates that it effectively identifies prisoners' random and malingered profiles (Mathews, Gassen, & Pietz, 2004; Megargee, 2004).

The MMPI–2 Inconsistency Scales in Correctional Populations. Whether they are exhibiting extreme psychopathology on the one hand or defensiveness on the other, offenders who read and understand the MMPI–2 items should respond reliably. The VRIN and TRIN scales were devised to identify inconsistent responding. Although there is as yet little research on the validity of these scales in corrections, our normative research on VRIN indicates that criminal offenders obtain mean scores in the normal range (Megargee, in press; Megargee, Mercer, & Carbonell, 1999). Therefore, it is probably safe to use the VRIN cutting scores recommended for other settings in correctional settings. Research with TRIN indicates that prisoners have somewhat elevated mean scores (T = 58 for men and T = 57 for women), so we should probably be more cautious when interpreting TRIN.

Recommended Cutting Scores for Detecting Incomplete and Nonresponsive Answering. Correctional psychologists should rely more on the MMPI–2 VRIN and TRIN scales than they do on *F*, *F(B)*, or *Fp* to detect nonresponsive answering. Based on our normative research with criminal offenders' MMPI–2s, as well as the published guidelines for samples of nonoffenders (Butcher, Graham, Ben-Porath, Tellegen, Dahlstrom, & Kaemmer, 2001), the MMPI–2 profiles of criminal offenders should be considered invalid and uninterpretable if any of the following signs are found:

1. Cs ≥ 30 (raw)
2. VRIN ≥ 80T
3. TRIN ≥ 80T
4. T% or F% ≥ 90%

Profiles with any of the following signs should be interpreted cautiously:

1. Cs = 10 through 29 (raw). No scales with Response % < 90% should be interpreted.
2. VRIN = 65T through 79T inclusive
3. TRIN = 65T through 79T inclusive

MMPI–2s characterized by nonresponsive answering should be readministered after the reason for the problem has been determined and corrected.

Distorted or Dissimulated Responding

Most clients who are tested in criminal justice settings probably hope to convey a particular impression or secure some desired outcome through their MMPI–2 responses. Given the high stakes involved in correctional and forensic assessments, the possibility of positive or negative dissimulation (such as "faking-good" or "faking-bad") should always be considered (Berry, Baer, Rinaldo, & Wetter, 2002). Indeed, Gallagher, Ben-Porath, and Briggs (1997) reported that 13% of the inmates tested on intake into a maximum security reception center later admitted that they had intentionally distorted their self-presentation on the MMPI–2 in some fashion. Convicted offenders hoping to be placed on probation or released on parole usually want to make a favorable impression, while prisoners hoping for single cell placement, psychological treatment, or a transfer from a correctional to a mental health setting may feel it is better for them to appear disturbed. The issue for correctional psychologists is not whether the respondent sought to put a positive or negative spin on his MMPI–2 responses. Instead, the primary concern should be whether the profile has been altered or distorted to the point where interpreting or classifying it would give an inaccurate or misleading picture of the respondent.

Both over- and underreporting of symptoms are threats to the validity of the MMPI–2. The rationally developed MMPI–2 content scales, for which the purpose and meaning are more obvious than the empirically derived clinical scales, are probably most susceptible to distortion. A number of studies have investigated deception on the original MMPI and on the MMPI–2, but investigations using criminal or correctional samples are rare. (See Bagby et al., chap. 3, this volume).

Overreporting of Symptoms and Malingering. The MMPI–2 infrequency scales *F*, *F(B)*, and *Fp* and the *F–K* index are the primary indicators of malingering on the MMPI–2. Unfortunately, as we have seen, the infrequency scales are often elevated in correctional samples. Moreover, other factors such as random responding and severe psychopathology can also elevate the infrequency scales. Berry et al. (2002, p. 275) caution, "With rare exceptions, a patient should never be labeled a malingerer on the basis of a single finding. Rather, increasing confidence may be gained as multiple lines of evidence from various sources and diverse methods converge on the conclusion that self-reported symptoms are being exaggerated, fabricated, or misattributed." They further warn, ". . . *the presence of malingering does not rule out the possibility of psychopathology*" [italics in original].

Underreporting of Symptoms. Underreporting occurs when respondents intentionally or unintentionally paint a more favorable picture of their adjustment and situation than seems warranted on the basis of a thorough objective evaluation.

The MMPI–2 has three regularly scored scales designed to detect protocols answered in an overly favorable manner: *L* (Lie), *K* (Correction), and *S* (Superlative Self-Presentation), as well as the *F–K* index. Like the overreporting scales, the scales designed to detect positive dissimulation have more than their share of possible confounds. The most pervasive is the possible influence of a nay-saying response bias, since all of these scales have a majority of their items keyed False.

Recommended Cutting Scores for Detecting Biased Responding. While recognizing that the context of the assessment and base rates should be considered in diagnosing over- or underreporting and that more research needs to be done on distorted responding among criminal offenders, the MMPI–2 profiles of criminal offenders that have been screened for content nonresponsive (CNR) responding should *probably* be considered invalid and uninterpretable if any of the following signs are found:

1. $F \geq 115T$
2. $Fp \geq 100T$
3. $L \geq 80T$
4. $F - K \geq +16$ (raw)

Profiles with any of the following signs should be interpreted cautiously:

1. $F = 90T$ through $114T$
2. $Fp = 90T$ through $99T$

3. L = 65T through 79T
4. $K \geq 70T$
5. $S \geq 70T$
6. $F - K$ = +11 through +15

Defensive or fake-good profiles on which all the clinical scales are within normal limits should be viewed skeptically. This skepticism should extend not only to the scale elevations but also to the code-type and the Megargee type classification. On the other hand, any noteworthy elevations on the clinical or content scales take on added significance. If, for example, offenders who are attempting to portray themselves in a favorable light nevertheless obtain T scores greater than 70 on scales 4 and 8, it is reasonable to suppose that these scales might have been even higher if the offenders had responded more candidly; it is troubling if an offender who is trying to make a good impression obtains clinically elevated scores on content scales such as ASP (Antisocial Practices) or ANG (Anger).

Code-Type Interpretation

Many clinicians rely heavily on code types when interpreting the standard scales of the MMPI–2.[2] Most authorities exclude scales 5 and 0 and limit coding to the eight "basic" scales: 1, 2, 3, 4, 6, 7, 8, and 9. However, James Panton, who did much of the original MMPI research in adult correctional settings, included all 10 "standard" scales. Because of the importance of scales 5 and 0 among criminal offenders, I also include them.[3]

Dozens of researchers have explored the correlates of various original MMPI and MMPI–2 codes in inpatient psychiatric settings and outpatient mental health clinics. The results of these empirical investigations have been collated in comprehensive guides to MMPI and MMPI–2 interpretation, and they form the basis for many computerized interpretive programs.

Three drawbacks to relying on code-type interpretation in correctional settings are (a) the lack of reliability in the operational definitions of code types, (b) the fact that many criminal offenders' profiles cannot be coded when strict classification criteria are used, and (c) the fact that there are insufficient data on the correlates of code types among criminal offenders.

Unreliability of the Operational Definitions of Code Types

Authorities differ on the degree of elevation and definition required for a code to be meaningful. Some, such as Butcher and Williams (2000),

[2] "1-point" codes refer to the most elevated scale in the profile, while "2-point" codes refer to the two highest-ranked scales. Some schemes even go on to interpret 3- and 4-point codes.
[3] Scale 5 is second only to Scale 4 as the most frequent high-point code among female prisoners (Megargee et al., 1999).

restrict code typing to clinically elevated scales equal to or greater than 65T. Others, such as Graham (2000), maintain that it is more important that code types be well defined with the coded scales being at least five points higher than the other scales in the profile. McGrath and Ingersoll (1999) recently reviewed the 10 most extensive empirical investigations of MMPI high-point code systems. They reported finding ". . . striking diversity across studies in the rules used for the definition of high-point codes. Researchers varied almost every aspect of the coding strategy, including whether the order of code scales was considered, how profiles that met criteria for more than one code group were handled, and whether minimum elevation was required. Except for basing rules on which scales are most elevated, not one element of the code definition strategy has been constant across all these studies" (p. 162). Given the need for accountability in criminal justice assessments, this lack of agreement on the operational definition of code types is troubling.

Inability to Code Many Offenders' MMPI–2s

Unfortunately, when strict criteria for code-type classification are utilized, many criminal offenders' MMPI–2 profiles cannot be coded. Everyone agrees that the higher the elevation and the greater the definition, the more a code type will resemble those used in the empirical studies that ascertained the attributes associated with the various high-point and two-point codes and the more likely it is that the person who produced the profile will share the characteristics of the criterion groups. However, the stricter the classification criteria, the fewer the number of profiles that can be coded.

Among male offenders, only 65% of the MMPI–2 high-point codes and 42% of the 2-point codes are clinically elevated, only 49% of the high-point and 28% of the 2-point codes are well defined, and only 39% of the high-point and 16% of the 2-point codes are both clinically elevated and well defined. Among female offenders, 80% of the MMPI–2 high-point and 55% of the 2-point codes are clinically elevated, only 51% of the high-point and 32% of the 2-point codes are well defined, and only 46% of the high-point and 24% of the 2-point codes are both clinically elevated and well defined (Megargee et al., 1999). Moreover, some of the restricted and well-defined profiles belong to rare code types for which correlates have not been investigated. Clearly, there are drawbacks to interpretive schemes that apply to only a fraction of the profiles encountered in a setting.

Insufficient Research on the Correlates of Criminal Offenders' Code Types

Another troubling aspect of relying on code types to interpret the MMPI–2 profiles of criminal offenders is the fact that all the major studies of the correlates of MMPI–2 codes have been conducted in free-world settings such as inpatient psychiatric units and outpatient community mental health clinics. Until more extensive code-type research has been conducted in correctional settings, I feel more comfortable using criminal offenders' code types as a source of clinical hypotheses about the client than I do in relying on them as the foundation for my interpretation.

The Megargee MMPI–2–Based Offender Classification System

Fortunately, correctional psychologists do not have to rely on code-type interpretation. Instead, we have an alternative interpretive system empirically derived on offenders tested in criminal justice and correctional settings that is more reliable and comprehensive than code-type analyses. This is the Megargee MMPI–2–based offender classification system that was first developed for the original MMPI in the 1970s (Megargee, 1977; Megargee et al., 1979) and later extended to MMPI–2 (Megargee, 1994; 1997; Megargee et al., 2001).

Description of the Megargee System

Derived from cluster analyses of criminal offenders' original MMPIs, the Megargee system is comprised of 10 types labeled with neutral, alphabetic names: *Able*, *Baker*, *Charlie*, *Delta*, *Easy*, *Foxtrot*, *George*, *How*, *Item*, and *Jupiter*. These neutral names were originally adopted so that our understanding of the characteristics of each type would be based solely on the accumulated empirical data without the added connotations associated with more descriptive labels. The neutral labels also contribute to security because they are not pejorative and convey no information to inmates who may discover their designation, unlike terms such as *mentally disturbed* or *psychopathic*.

The classification of individual MMPI–2 profiles into Megargee types is based on a complex set of rules that considers all aspects of a profile—not just the two highest scales but the entire configuration including overall elevation, slope, and low scale patterns. Thus, the system substitutes overall profile types for high-point code types. Its strength lies in the following factors: (a) the 10 profile types were empirically derived through cluster analyses of criminal offenders' profiles, (b) approximately 95% of the valid MMPI–2 offender profiles can be classified, and (c) the characteristics of these types have been empirically determined over the course of more than 30 years of research with thousands of criminal offenders. The system thus satisfies the need for accountability emphasized at the outset of this chapter.

Construction of the MMPI–2–Based System.[4] The data used in the initial derivation and validation of the MMPI–2–based typology were obtained at the Federal Correctional Institution (FCI) at Tallahassee,

[4]Readers wishing a comprehensive description of this research should consult Megargee et al. (2001).

Florida, which was then a medium security prison for youthful male offenders ages 18 to 27.

Hierarchical profile analysis, a clustering technique that considers all aspects of an MMPI profile, was applied to three different samples, each consisting of 100 offenders' original MMPI profiles. The same basic clusters were found in each of the three samples. Subsequent replications of these hierarchical analyses by independent investigators using the MMPIs of male and female federal, state, and local prisoners have yielded the same basic groups (Megargee et al., 2001).

Classifying MMPI–2 Profiles Into Megargee Types. After determining that clinicians familiar with the results of the cluster analyses could reliably assign individual offenders' MMPI profiles to the clusters, the next step was to formulate operational definitions of each group so that other clinicians or computers could reliably assign individual MMPI profiles to the types. A complex set of classificatory rules was devised and computerized.[5]

Although it is possible to classify profiles by hand, most users prefer to utilize computerized classifications, especially if there are many profiles to be classified. The Megargee type classification can be obtained in the computerized MMPI–2 Criminal Justice and Correctional Report (Megargee, 2000) along with the "level" of classification: high, medium, low, or minimal. The higher the level, the more likely the respondent's characteristics will resemble the modal attributes of the group.

Determining Characteristics of the Types. Our next task was to determine empirically the characteristics of each of the 10 groups. We initially used data gathered on 1,213 male youthful offenders who had completed the MMPI on intake to the FCI. After being classified according to the typology, they were compared on a broad array of measures derived from presentence investigation reports; individual structured interviews; prison and medical records; and a number of personality, ability, and aptitude tests (Megargee et al., 2001). Additional insights into their characteristics were obtained by comparing the adjectives the members of each group used in describing themselves, as well as the descriptive adjectives applied by staff psychologists who had interviewed the offenders.

Subsequent research contrasted measures of the groups' behavior, adjustment, and achievements over the course of their confinement as assessed by ratings, reports, and observations of their institutional adjustment, disciplinary infractions, educational progress, and work performance. In post-release follow-up studies, their subsequent criminal activity was also assessed (Megargee et al., 1979). Overall, 140 of the 164 comparisons

[5]The rules for classifying the original MMPIs and the MMPI–2s of male and female offenders can be found in appendixes B, C, D, E, and F of Megargee et al. (2001).

proved to be statistically significant. These studies were recently replicated using MMPI–2 (Megargee et al., 2001).

The patterns of statistically significant differences on all of these measures were used to formulate modal descriptions of each type and to suggest strategies for their optimal management and treatment, focusing on the best setting, the most suitable change agent, and the most appropriate treatment techniques. These descriptions and prescriptions proved to be useful guides for management and treatment. For example, as noted earlier, Bohn (1978, 1979) achieved a 46% reduction in serious assaults by using the system to separate the most predatory offenders from those whose MMPI classifications suggested they were most likely to be victimized.

Once the system was published (Megargee, 1977), numerous other researchers began investigating the characteristics of the types. The system was also extended to women, among whom nine clusters were identified; and the characteristics of the female types were investigated and compared with those of their male counterparts. We recently collated the findings of all these independent studies and integrated them with our own studies characterizing the types over the years (Megargee et al., 2001).

Generality of the Megargee System. Independent investigators have reported the successful application of the MMPI–2–based system among both male and female adult offenders in probation, parole, and correctional settings.[6] Within corrections, this system has been utilized in federal, state, military, and local facilities with security levels ranging from minimum to maximum. It has also been used in halfway houses, community restitution centers, forensic mental health units, and local jails. The specialized populations to which the system has been applied include death row inmates, people who have threatened the president of the United States, and mentally disordered sex offenders (Megargee et al., 2001). Typically 90% to 95% of the valid MMPI–2 profiles can be classified, and the proportions of profiles falling into the 10 types are remarkably stable across correctional facilities.

Modal Descriptions of the 10 Megargee MMPI–2 Types

The 10 offender profile types are briefly described in the following sections. Although anyone's profile can be classified into one or more of these types, these statements were derived exclusively on adult criminal offenders and should only be applied to this population. More detailed descriptions and summaries of the data on which these characterizations are based can be found in Megargee et al. (2001). The mean profiles of male and female offenders in each of the Megargee types can be seen in Figure 13.1.

[6]The system cannot be used with juvenile offenders tested with the MMPI–A.

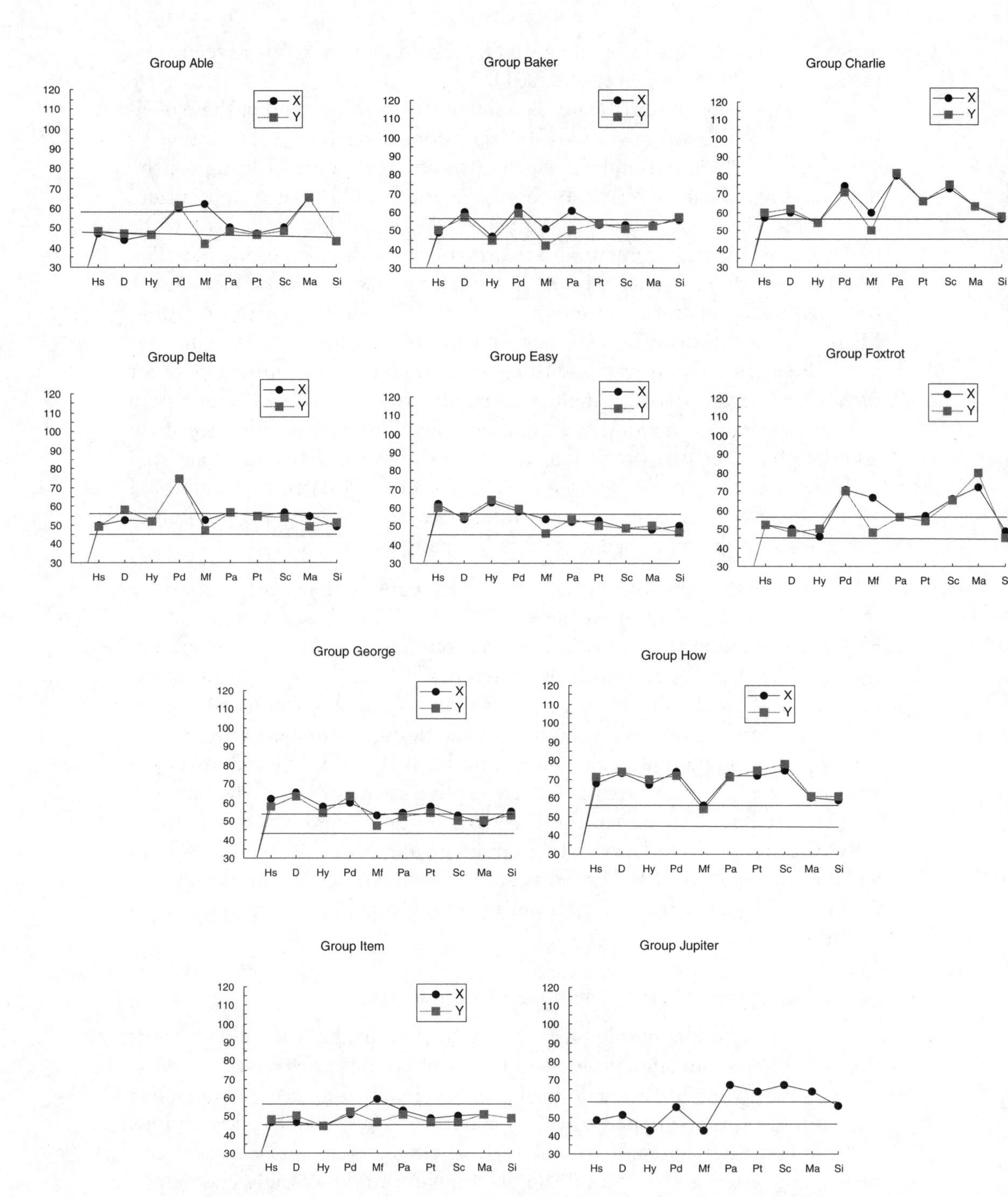

Figure 13.1. Mean profiles of male and female prisoners classified into the 10 MMPI–2 types.

Type Able. Group Able is characterized by a low profile with moderate peaks on scales 4 and 9 and low scores on Scale 0 and, among men, Scale 5. Offenders in Group Able typically come from families that are more stable and less deviant than most of the other offender groups. Better educated and relatively well adjusted, they are socially skilled and ascendant. However, they lack internal inhibitions and controls. Easily bored, with low frustration tolerance, they engage in reckless and impulsive behavior with little thought for the consequences. They chafe under strict rules, doing better in more lenient settings. Ables require strict change agents who can resist their manipulations. They have a high rate of recidivism.

Type Baker. Group Baker has a low MMPI–2 profile with modest elevations on scales 2, 4, and 0 (see Figure 13.1). Although their family backgrounds are somewhat less favorable than most of the types, Bakers are average[7] with regard to education, employment history, and prior criminal records. Offenders in Group Baker tend to be anxious, shy, and socially inhibited. They often have drinking problems and may benefit from substance abuse interventions such as 12-step programs. Socially awkward and somewhat passive–aggressive, they may be victimized or exploited by other inmates and need supportive help adjusting to incarceration. Bakers have a relatively high rate of recidivism.

Type Charlie. Group Charlie has a sharply elevated MMPI–2 profile with peaks on scales 4, 6, and 8 (see Figure 13.1). Charlies come from very adverse family backgrounds with high rates of social deviance. They typically had many problems in school, poor employment histories, and extensive criminal records, with the highest rates of violence of any Megargee type. Often emotionally disturbed, they have lifelong patterns of maladjustment and social deviance. Hostile, suspicious, and misanthropic, they do not get along well with others. They do poorly in prison, where they have more aggressive incident reports than any of the other groups. They use sick call frequently and require extensive clinical services. Distrustful and sensitive to any perceived unfairness, Charlies need clear contingencies and scrupulous adherence by staff to stated rules and policies. Charlies require mental health evaluations for possible thought disorders and may need to be placed in protective segregation or transferred to a forensic mental health facility.

Type Delta. Group Delta has an elevated "spike 4" MMPI–2 profile (see Figure 13.1). Deltas typically come from disorganized, deviant, socially marginal family backgrounds. Frequently charming and often relatively

[7]Terms such as *above average*, *average*, and *below average* refer to comparisons with the other MMPI–2 offender types comprised of incarcerated felons. See Megargee et al. (2001) for the actual data and analyses on which these comparisons are based.

bright, they may make a good first impression; but over time their manipulativeness, impulsivity, irresponsibility, and exploitation of others causes their interpersonal relations to deteriorate. Deltas often did well in school but poorly in the workplace. They typically have extensive juvenile and adult criminal records. They are low in socialization and high in egocentricity, having deviant value systems. They do poorly in prison, receiving many disciplinary infractions and poor evaluations, especially from work supervisors. They use sick call extensively and may prey on weaker inmates. They require firm limits from strong change agents who must convince them of the inappropriateness of their behavior. Their recidivism rates are average or better.

Type Easy. Group Easy has a low MMPI–2 profile with modest elevations on scales 3 and 4 (see Figure 13.1). Group Easy is superior to most of the other Megargee types. They are the best adjusted and least deviant of the groups, coming from the most stable and cohesive family backgrounds. As a group, Easies have the most favorable school and vocational backgrounds, although, considering their advantages, they may be underachievers. In general, they have the most benign criminal histories, although some settings report having some Easies who have committed crimes of extreme violence. In general, Easies have the most favorable interpersonal relations and the least aggressiveness of all the types. They have few difficulties in prison and little need for high security or extensive programming. Their recidivism rate is the lowest of all the types.

Type Foxtrot. Group Foxtrot's elevated MMPI–2 profile slopes up sharply to the right with 4, 8, and 9 being the highest scales (see Figure 13.1). Foxtrots' developmental families were chaotic and disorganized, cold, rejecting, unstable, deviant, and deprived. Although they have average educational attainment, Foxtrots experienced many adjustment problems in school and they have poorer vocational histories, more marital instability, and more drug abuse than most of the groups. Their criminal histories are more extensive, and they have high rates of violent crimes and drug offenses. Foxtrots are cold, tough, aggressive, and egocentric. They sometimes attract weaker followers whom they lead in a deviant direction. In prison, they receive many disciplinary infractions for their antisocial attitudes and aggressive behavior. Foxtrots require structured settings and active programs with clear contingencies. They are difficult to change and have high recidivism rates.

Type George. Group George has a moderately elevated MMPI–2 profile with moderate peaks on scales 2 and 4 (see Figure 13.1). Georges typically come from working- or lower-class families that are average with respect to stability and social deviance. Georges have average school and employment records, but their criminal histories are more extensive than most, with a relatively high rate of alcohol-related offenses. Although they are somewhat anxious, they get along well with others and mind their own business. More dependable than most, they do well in correctional education programs. Because they do not cause many problems, it is easy for staff to overlook Georges, so they often emerge unchanged and have high rates of recidivism. They may benefit from more programming, especially if they have alcohol-related problems.

Type How. Group How has a highly elevated MMPI–2 profile with several scales in the clinical range but no particular pattern of high scales (see Figure 13.1). Hows come from highly deprived families with extensive social pathology. Their IQs are lower than most of the groups, and they have difficulties in school and in employment settings, but their criminal histories are not as extensive as those of some of the other groups. Hows are characterized more by emotional maladjustment and disturbance than they are by antisocial or aggressive tendencies. They have the highest rate of prior mental hospitalizations of all the types. They have difficult interpersonal relations and adjust poorly in prison, utilizing many clinical services including sick call. They require mental health evaluations and programming and may need protective segregation or transfer to a mental health facility.

Type Item. The most frequent of the 10 Megargee types, Group Item's MMPI–2 profile is within normal limits and has no particular pattern of elevations (see Figure 13.1). Items come from superior homes relative to the other types. Their families are more stable and cohesive and have less social deviance. Average in intelligence, Items do well in school and have few job-related difficulties and relatively benign criminal histories. They tend to be older than most offenders at the time of their first arrest and have minimal juvenile histories. Items get along well with others and, as a group, do not have major health or adjustment problems. They adjust well in prison, have few disciplinary problems, and receive good evaluations from correctional staff and work supervisors. They have a low rate of recidivism. Based on their tested personality patterns, Items do not need a very secure setting or extensive programming; although, for some, the nature of their offenses may dictate otherwise.

Type Jupiter. Group Jupiter, which is found only among male offenders, has an MMPI–2 profile that slopes sharply up to the right with elevations on scales 7, 8, and 9 (see Figure 13.1). Jupiters come from unfavorable family backgrounds and have relatively poor educational achievement. However, they do better than one would expect on the job and have average criminal histories. Somewhat anxious and maladjusted, Jupiters nevertheless get along well with others. Less aggressive than most, they are rather passive, avoid hostile encounters, and do not cause trouble. In prison, their work supervisors view them more favorably than do the correctional officers. Jupiters need individualized programming to deal with their many deficits, but they do better than one would expect given their background and have average rates of recidivism.

The MMPI–2 Criminal Justice and Correctional Report

The computerized MMPI–2 Criminal Justice and Correctional Report was developed to simplify the practitioner's interpretive task. It provides the Megargee type classification along with profiles and scores on the MMPI–2 validity, standard, and content scales, as well as selected supplementary scales especially relevant to the assessment of criminal offenders. The *User's Guide* (Megargee, 2000) provides guidelines for interpreting all the various MMPI–2 scales and indexes in criminal justice and correctional settings along with descriptions of the 10 types.

The most innovative aspect of the report is a set of interpretive statements that are directly relevant to correctional risk and needs assessment. Offenders are evaluated on nine behavioral dimensions and nine possible problem areas based on their Megargee classification and their T scores on relevant clinical, content, and supplementary scales. The report also indicates whether offenders endorsed any critical items relevant to self-destructive or suicidal ideation and behavior. All the cutting scores and interpretive statements are based on cutting scores and correlates determined through empirical research with criminal offenders, most of whom were tested in correctional settings.

Assessment of Behavioral Dimensions

This section of the Criminal Justice and Correctional Report (Megargee, 2000) evaluates each respondent on nine behavioral dimensions that are germane to assessment in criminal justice settings. These dimensions were chosen because (a) they are relevant to risk and needs assessment and (b) because MMPI–2 can reliably and validly differentiate criminal offenders on these dimensions. They include the following:

- D-1: Apparent need for mental health assessment or programming
- D-2: Indications of socially deviant behavior or attitudes
- D-3: Extraversion; need for social participation
- D-4: Leadership ability or dominance
- D-5: Likelihood of hostile or antagonistic peer relations
- D-6: Indications of conflicts with or resentment of authorities
- D-7: Likelihood of mature, responsible behavior; positive response to supervision

D-8: Likelihood of positive or favorable response to academic programming

D-9: Likelihood of positive or favorable response to vocational programming

On each of these nine scales, an offender is evaluated as being Above Average (High), Average (Moderate), or Below Average (Low) *relative to other criminal offenders*. Thus, while most offenders would probably be rated as High in social deviance (D-2) relative to the general population, when they are compared with other criminal offenders, some individuals' MMPI–2s indicate that they are only Medium or Low on this dimension.

The proportions of offenders rated as High, Medium, or Low on the various behavior dimensions vary across settings. For example, among prisoners confined in maximum security institutions, there should be more rated High on the social deviance dimension than there are among a sample of probationers. Similarly, more clients in a forensic mental health facility should be evaluated as needing mental health assessment or programming than would be the case in the general population of a medium security correctional institution.

Identification of Possible Problem Areas

In this section of the report, criminal offenders are screened for Possible Problem Areas indicated by the MMPI–2. In contrast to the behavioral dimensions on which every respondent is evaluated on every scale, in this section only those problem areas suggested by an individual's MMPI–2 are flagged.

These statements are designed to discriminate criminal offenders from one another rather than from the general public. Therefore, there are no "Barnum-type" messages that would apply to all felons, such as "Probably gets into legal difficulties." Problem areas that cannot be validly assessed by the MMPI–2, such as the likelihood of interpersonal violence or escaping from custody, are also not included on this list. The nine possible messages that may appear include the following:

P-1: Possible difficulties with alcohol or substance abuse

P-2: Possibility of thought disorder

P-3: Possibility of depressive affect or mood disorder

P-4: May use sick call extensively

P-5: Possibility of overcontrolled hostility

P-6: May manipulate or exploit others

P-7: Possibility of problems with anger control

P-8: Possibility of awkward or difficult interpersonal relationships; may be passive and submissive

P-9: Possibility of family conflict or alienation from family

The use of the words *possible* or *possibility* in these messages underscores the fact that these statements constitute hypotheses for clinicians to check out in an interview or by referring to the case history, staff observations, or other tests. The cutting scores that have been established make it likely that there will be more false positives than false negatives. The actual true and false positive rates will, of course, differ from one setting to the next as a function of the base rates for various difficulties.

Critical Items Suggesting a Potentially Self-Destructive Frame of Mind

The report includes 22 critical items, the manifest content of which could suggest a self-injurious or self-destructive frame of mind. Any items endorsed in the deviant direction are printed out on the report. Clinicians should follow up on these items in interviews with respondents to determine what they meant by these answers. This is especially true if clients have endorsed several such items and if their scores on MMPI–2 scales 2 and DEP suggest depression.

Interpreting Criminal Offenders' MMPI–2s: A Case Example

We conclude by presenting a case illustrating how the MMPI–2 may be used as part of the initial mental health screening of a newly admitted prisoner, Frankie, who is a 32-year-old divorced White male. In actual practice, the inferences derived from his MMPI–2 should be regarded as hypotheses to be tested by and integrated with other sources of information when they become available, including Frankie's present legal situation; his criminal record; his case history; and the results of interviews and other tests of intellectual, cognitive, and personality functioning (Megargee, 2003). The advantage of the MMPI–2 is that it can provide reasonably accurate estimates early in the classification process which can help guide the rest of the mental health assessment.

We proceed with the following sequence of steps:

1. Determine the validity of the MMPI–2 profile.
2. Classify the profile into the best Megargee type, determine the level of fit, and use this as the initial basis for our interpretation.
3. Interpret the 10 basic clinical scales, noting Frankie's pattern of high and low scores and, if possible, his 1- or 2-point code type. Whereas the interpretation of Frankie's Megargee type is based exclusively on its correlates with various criteria among criminal offenders, the interpretation of his scores on the clinical and other MMPI–2 scales is primarily derived from research conducted in free-world settings that may or

may not generalize to corrections. They thus complement the Megargee type interpretation. Detailed discussions of the interpretation of criminal offenders' scores on the MMPI–2 clinical, content, and supplementary scales can be found in Megargee (2000, in press).

4. Examine the 15 content scales, noting the pattern of high and low scores and use them to further refine the interpretation.
5. Examine the pattern of scores on the selected supplementary scales and use them to further refine the interpretation.
6. Consider the nine Behavioral Dimension scales, any Possible Problem Areas, and critical items relating to self-destructive behavior.

Figure 13.2 displays the first page of Frankie's MMPI–2 Criminal Justice and Correctional Report, containing his scores on the nine regularly scored validity scales and the 10 standard clinical scales, along with other indexes including the code type and the Megargee type classification and level.

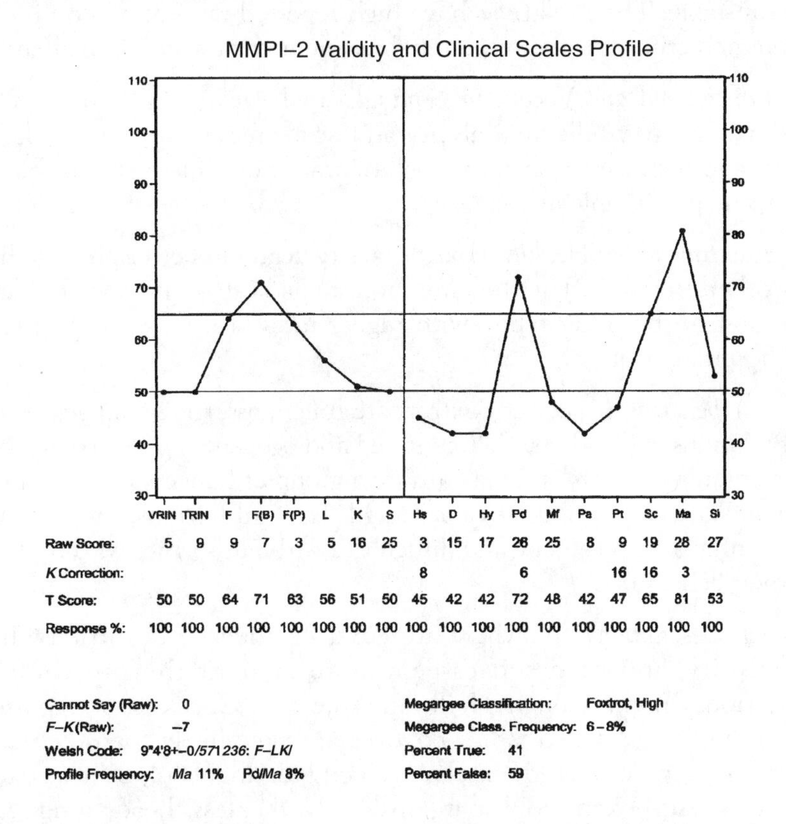

	VRIN	TRIN	F	F(B)	F(P)	L	K	S	Hs	D	Hy	Pd	Mf	Pa	Pt	Sc	Ma	Si
Raw Score:	5	9	9	7	3	5	16	25	3	15	17	26	25	8	9	19	28	27
K Correction:									8			6			16	16	3	
T Score:	50	50	64	71	63	56	51	50	45	42	42	72	48	42	47	65	81	53
Response %:	100	100	100	100	100	100	100	100	100	100	100	100	100	100	100	100	100	100

Cannot Say (Raw): 0
F–K (Raw): –7
Welsh Code: 9"4'8+–0/*571 236*: *F–LK/*
Profile Frequency: *Ma* 11% Pd/*Ma* 8%

Megargee Classification: Foxtrot, High
Megargee Class. Frequency: 6–8%
Percent True: 41
Percent False: 59

Figure 13.2. Frankie's validity and clinical scales profile from the MMPI–2 Criminal Justice and Correctional Report. Copyright 2000 by the University of Minnesota.

Ascertaining Validity

The first step is to ascertain the validity of Frankie's profile. Because Frankie answered all the MMPI–2 items (Cs = 0) and his scores on the other clinical scales are within acceptable limits, we can conclude that his overall profile is valid. However, the moderate elevation on Scale *F(B)* suggests that Frankie may have become careless toward the end of the test.

Interpreting the Megargee Type

Step 2 is to ascertain Frankie's Megargee type classification. The report shows Frankie's profile to belong to Type Foxtrot at the High level. A detailed description of Type Foxtrot can be found in Megargee et al. (2001, pp. 277–292), and a more concise summary is located in the Correctional Report *User's Guide* (Megargee, 2000, pp. 64–66). In these sources, Foxtrots are described as follows.

Background. As was noted earlier, Foxtrots come from family backgrounds marked by discord, deviance, and rejection. Foxtrots' marriages are often unstable. Their relatives have high reported rates of mental hospitalizations and criminal offenses, often for violent crimes and drug offenses.

Educational and Vocational Aptitudes and Abilities. Foxtrots are typically average in intellectual ability and academic achievement, but they often have histories with many behavioral and adjustment problems in school and poor employment.

Adjustment and Health. Foxtrots are typically in better physical health than other offenders, but they are more maladjusted and socially deviant than most of the other types, with higher rates of drug abuse and psychiatric hospitalizations.

Interpersonal Relations. Foxtrots are tough, assertive, and aggressive in their relations with others. Self-centered and egocentric, they try to control and manipulate others and may attract a group of hangers-on who do their bidding. With their criminal values and lack of inhibitions, they frequently have conflicts with the law and difficulties with authorities who try to control their behavior.

Self-Descriptions. Nowhere are Foxtrots' tough egocentricity, hypermasculinity, and high self-esteem more evident than in their self-descriptions on the Gough–Heilbrun Adjective Checklist as reported in Megargee et al. (2001, p. 282). Foxtrots are *more* likely than offenders in other groups to describe themselves as being daring, cool, cautious, tough, suspicious, outspoken, cold, outgoing, jolly, reckless, headstrong, clever, interested in many things, courageous, and hard-hearted. They are *less* likely than the men in other groups to describe themselves as trusting, affectionate, soft-hearted, worrying, warm, understanding, efficient, responsible, helpful, gentle, sentimental, sympathetic, logical, obliging, and sensitive.[8]

Psychologists' Description. While Foxtrots described themselves in terms that they no doubt felt were favorable, their psychologists used more negative adjectives, describing them less favorably than any of the other types. They rated Foxtrots as being *more* hasty, irresponsible, dissatisfied, impulsive, unstable, hard-hearted, self-centered, headstrong, disorderly, apathetic, aggressive, moody, irritable, pleasure-seeking, and stubborn. They were *less* likely to depict Foxtrots as easygoing, capable, friendly, mannerly, calm, good-natured, clear thinking, cooperative, peaceable, adaptable, unassuming, tactful, sociable, dependable, and honest.

Personality Patterns. Personality assessments show Foxtrots to be impulsive, self-centered, irresponsible, attention-seeking, aggressive, and hedonistic, with deficient socialization and few inhibitions. They embrace a strong macho persona and deny any softness, sensitivity, or anxiety. They are high in assertiveness, self-confidence, and self-esteem. With their verbal skills, they can be persuasive and effective.

Correctional Adjustment. In prison, Foxtrots have more rules infractions than most of the other groups and spend more time in disciplinary segregation, often for offenses involving aggression or violence. Bohn (1979) regarded them as one of his "predatory" groups and separated them from the more vulnerable inmates. Although their social skills enabled some to relate adequately with correctional officers, work supervisors gave them uniformly bad evaluations; and they did not do especially well in educational programming.

Implications. Foxtrots are manipulative, self-centered, and aggressive. They are out for what they can get and are apt to bully or exploit weaker inmates. They require structure, strict limits, and strong supervision. Their prognosis for change is poor and they have high rates of recidivism.

Interpreting Frankie's Clinical Scales and Code Type

Frankie's highest MMPI–2 clinical scores were on scales 9 (T = 81), 4 (T = 72), and 8 (T = 65), giving him a 9"4' two-point code. Consistent with the implications of being in Group Foxtrot, individuals with 94 code types have been found to be amoral with deficient ethical values. They have a low tolerance for frustration and like to stir up excitement when

[8]Adjectives are presented according to the magnitude of the differences in endorsement frequency between Foxtrot and the overall mean of the entire sample.

they are bored. Their impulsive risk taking often involves them in a wide range of deviant and delinquent behavior resulting in repeated arrests, family discord, and marital problems, all of which they blame on society's stupid rules or the behavior of others. Although they are smooth and socially skilled, their interpersonal relationships are shallow and exploitative as they seek to manipulate and outsmart those whom they encounter (Megargee, in press). In clinical settings, psychiatric inpatients with 49/94 profiles are typically diagnosed with sociopathic or psychopathic personality disorders. A cardinal feature is their relative lack of anxiety or guilt over their transgressions and their apparent inability to learn from experience despite better-than-average intelligence. When confronted with an obstacle, they try to manipulate or con their way around it, blaming any difficulties on others or on situational circumstances.

Frankie's score of 65 on Scale 8 suggests that he is more antisocial and more alienated from others than the typical 49 code-type individual. Frankie's lowest scores were on scales indicating demoralization and discomfort, indicating that he is not motivated for change or for treatment.

Interpreting Frankie's Content Scales

Frankie's content scales profile, presented in Figure 13.3, is further evidence of Frankie's social deviance, criminal values, and lack of anxiety

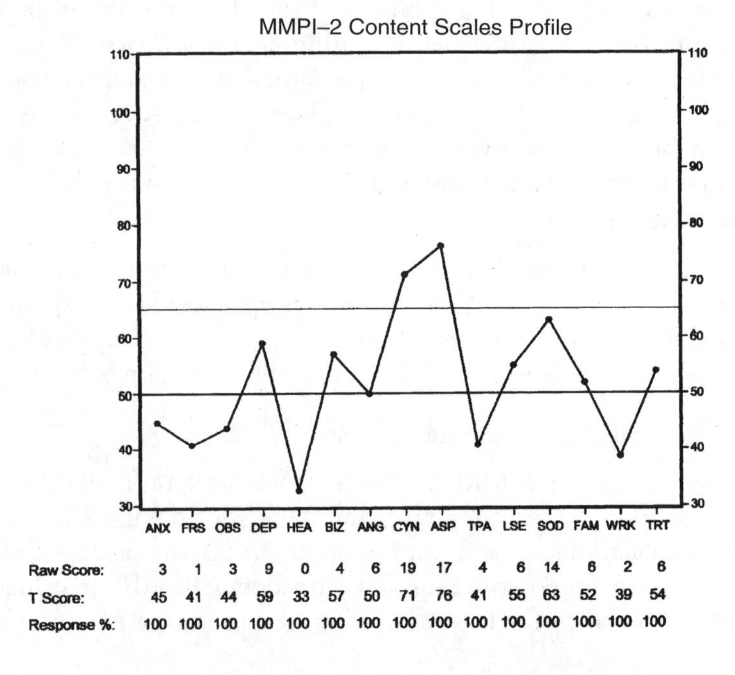

Figure 13.3. Frankie's content scales profile from the MMPI–2 Criminal Justice and Correctional Report. Copyright 2000 by the University of Minnesota.

or depression. His highest scores are on scales ASP (T = 76) and CYN (Cynicism, T = 71). His score on Scale ASP demonstrates that Frankie openly acknowledges his antisocial attitudes and values and frankly admits engaging in illegal behavior. Frankie's score on Scale CYN indicates that he thinks others share his cynicism and that he believes that they, like him, are only out for themselves. This pattern strongly suggests that Frankie's illegal behavior is ego–syntonic and stems from his criminal values rather than from any neuroses or situational pressures.

Frankie had T scores of 45 or less on content scales ANX (Anxiety), FRS (Fears), OBS (Obsessiveness), HEA (Health Concerns), and WRK (Work Interference). These low scores indicate that Frankie is not suffering from the demoralization, depression, physical ailments, and general malaise assessed by these measures; and they suggest that he is not experiencing the sort of discomfort that would motivate him to seek changes through psychotherapy.

Interpreting Frankie's Supplementary Scales

In order to reduce the cost to users, the Criminal Justice and Correctional Report only includes seven supplementary scales that are especially useful in corrections and that do not correlate highly with the clinical and content scales. Five assess special symptom patterns: MAC–R (MacAndrew Alcoholism Scale—Revised), APS (Addiction Potential Scale), AAS (Addiction Acknowledgment Scale), O–H (Overcontrolled Hostility), and MDS (Marital Distress Scale). [Since Frankie is not married, MDS was not scored; however, the fact he is divorced speaks for itself.] Two scales assess positive aspects of interpersonal functioning: *Do* (Dominance) and *Re* (Responsibility).

Frankie's supplementary scale profile is presented in Figure 13.4. Frankie obtained an elevated score only on MAC–R (T = 69). The MAC–R score can reflect criminal and antisocial attitudes and behavior as well as excessive use of alcohol. Given the fact that Frankie's scores on APS (T = 33) and AAS (T = 56) were not elevated, it seems likely that Frankie's MAC–R elevation is associated with his criminality more than with drinking problems. Nevertheless, his use of alcohol or drugs should be investigated.

Interpreting Frankie's Behavioral Dimensions and Possible Problem Areas

Frankie's pattern of scores on the nine Behavioral Dimensions is consistent with our picture of him as an antisocial criminal who is difficult to deal with as opposed to being either an offender who is emotionally disturbed or an average individual who succumbs to temptation or is driven into crime by external situational factors (see Figure 13.5).

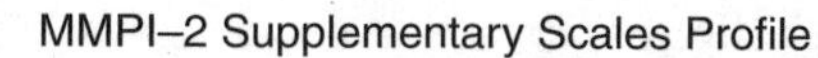

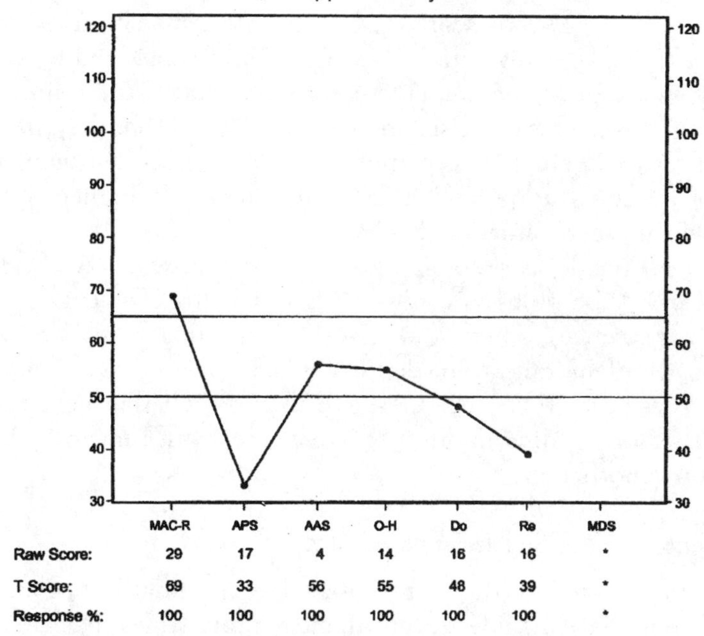

Figure 13.4. Frankie's supplementary scales profile from the MMPI–2 Criminal Justice and Correctional Report. Copyright 2000 by the University of Minnesota.

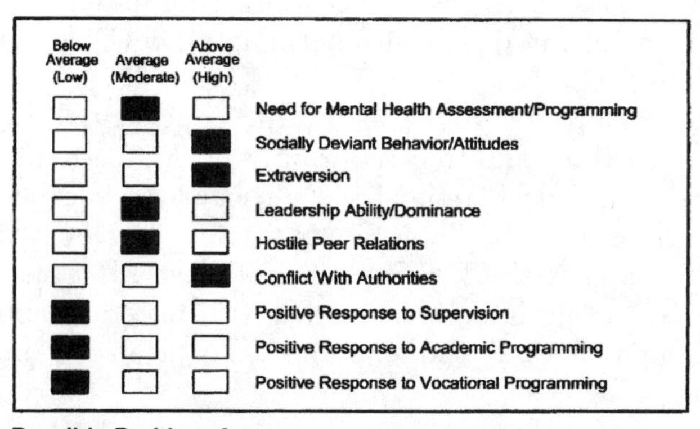

Possible Problem Areas

The following possible problem areas require further assessment:

- Possible difficulties with alcohol or substance abuse
- May manipulate or exploit other inmates
- Possibility of family problems or alienation from family

Figure 13.5. Frankie's behavioral dimension scales and possible problem areas, from the MMPI–2 Criminal Justice and Correctional Report. Copyright 2000 by the University of Minnesota.

Behavioral Dimensions. Based on his group membership and scores on the MMPI–2 clinical, content, and supplementary scales, Frankie was evaluated as being Above Average or High on the scales for (a) "Socially deviant behavior/attitudes," (b) "Extraversion," and (c) "Conflict with authorities." These scales reflect the amoral, criminal values and consequent authority conflicts associated with his membership in Group Foxtrot as well as the outgoing social behavior associated with elevations on Scale 9.

Frankie was evaluated as being Average or Moderate relative to other offenders on the Behavior Dimension scales for (a) "Need for mental health assessment or programming" (again reflecting the fact that he appears socially deviant rather than emotionally disturbed), (b) "Leadership ability and Dominance," and (c) "Hostile Peer Relations." As noted earlier, Frankie's extraversion and leadership may enable him to attract a group of followers, which his antisocial and criminal values suggest he will lead in the wrong direction.

Frankie was assessed as Below Average or Low on the scales for (a) "Positive response to supervision," (b) "Positive response to academic programming," and (c) "Positive response to vocational programming," further indicating that he will probably be difficult to work with and that he is not presently amenable to or likely to benefit from educational or vocational programming or therapeutic interventions. If, as in many institutions, the demand for programs and services exceeds their availability, the MMPI–2 data suggest that Frankie should be given lower priority for such programming, should he request it, than others who are more likely to benefit from it. It is, of course, possible that his attitudes may change over time, so Frankie should periodically be reassessed to note any changes that may occur as a result of incarceration.

Possible Problem Areas. The MMPI–2 evaluations flagged three possible problem areas:

1. "Possible difficulties with alcohol or substance abuse." This warning reflects Frankie's elevated score on MAC–R. It is tempered somewhat by his scores on AAS and APS. However, Foxtrots have a high rate of substance abuse so prudence dictates further evaluation of this area, beginning with Frankie's case history.
2. "May manipulate or exploit others." Staff members will have to be on the guard to avoid being "conned" by Frankie, and they must also be alert to any attempts on his part to take advantage of weaker inmates.

3. "Possibility of family conflict or alienation from family." Frankie probably comes from a discordant family and may blame them for some of his difficulties. Staff should monitor Frankie's behavior during and after any family visits, because such contacts may anger or antagonize him rather than being a source of encouragement or support.

Critical Items. Frankie endorsed seven critical items, numbers 85, 303, 407, 506, 520, 526, and 546, the manifest content of which suggests self-destructive thought or behaviors. These items are printed out on his Criminal Justice and Correctional Report and should be followed up in interviews. However, the item numbers and Frankie's elevated score on *F(B)* (T = 71), as well as his low scores on scales 2 (Depression, T = 42) and DEP (Depression, T = 59) suggest that Frankie may have become impatient and started answering nonresponsively toward the end.

CONCLUDING REMARKS

Correctional facilities are total institutions that are responsible for all aspects of their residents' well-being, including their health and safety. The AACP (2000) and the NCCHC (2003a, 2003b) standards call for mental health screening as soon as possible after admission, sometimes even before medical, mental health, and criminal record data are available. Using group testing and on-site computerized scoring and interpretation, the MMPI–2 can provide a comprehensive array of clinical data and flag potential problems early in the assessment process.

After the initial mental health screening, risk and needs assessments must be carried out to determine whether offenders pose a danger to themselves or others and to assess their need for and ability to profit from a wide array of correctional settings and programs. The MMPI–2 can provide data relevant to risk assessment and needs assessment that will help inform management decisions and programming planning.

To be legally accountable, correctional assessments must be reliable and valid. Given its stature as our most widely used and thoroughly researched objective personality test (Butcher & Rouse, 1996), practitioners will have no difficulty justifying their use of the MMPI–2 in correctional assessment. However, accountability also requires that the interpretive principles and techniques used in correctional assessment be validated on criminal offenders tested in criminal justice settings. Correctional psychologists should base their analyses and interpretations of offenders' MMPI–2s primarily on research conducted in correctional settings and only secondarily on inferences extrapolated from free-world findings. Exhibit 13.1 summarizes some of the important points to consider when interpreting MMPI–2s in correctional settings.

Needless to say, no assessment should be based exclusively on one instrument administered at a single point in time. MMPI–2 interpretations should be checked against and integrated with other sources of information including clinical interviews, physical and mental health records and reports, case and criminal history data, and the results of other tests, as well as the observations of experienced correctional personnel, an all too often neglected resource. Do not neglect your clinical sensitivity. In assessing the dangerousness of a convicted felon, you are wise to pay attention to the sensation of your hair rising on the back of your neck as well as to your perception of scales 4, 6, and 8 rising from the offender's MMPI–2 profile.

EXHIBIT 13.1
Highlight: Important Considerations in Using the MMPI–2 in Correctional Settings

- Offenders who are detained or incarcerated in jails and prisons must be screened for mental illness, developmental disabilities, self-destructive tendencies, and their potential for dangerous or violent behavior, after which correctional authorities must determine the facilities and programs best suited to their particular needs.
- Each new admission to a jail or prison should receive a mental health screening immediately upon entering and before being placed in a cell or holding area with other inmates.
- Accountability demands that correctional psychologists must be able to demonstrate that their procedures and interpretations are supported by empirical research with criminal populations tested in criminal justice and correctional settings.
- Risk appraisal involves evaluating the danger offenders pose to the community, to the correctional staff, to their fellow inmates, and to themselves. Policy dictates that new arrivals be assigned to the least restrictive setting that matches their needs for security and control. In risk assessment, the MMPI–2 is best employed in conjunction with case and criminal history data, as well as with narrowband instruments specifically focused on dangerous behavior.
- Needs assessment includes psychological, cognitive, and motivational appraisals to identify those most in need of and likely to benefit from mental health interventions, educational programming, and vocational training. The MMPI–2 is especially useful in these appraisals.
- Administration of the MMPI–2 in a correctional setting should abide by the ethical guidelines established by the American Association of Correctional Psychologists (AACP, 2000) and adhere to the standardized procedures set forth in the MMPI–2 *Manual.*
- By virtue of their lifestyles and circumstances, prisoners answering truthfully may nevertheless obtain elevated scores on the MMPI–2 infrequency scales, *F, F(B),* and *Fp.*
- Cutting scores based on correctional samples should be used in assessing the validity of prisoners' MMPI–2s.
- Three drawbacks to relying on code-type interpretation in correctional settings are (a) the lack of reliability in the operational definitions of code types, (b) the fact that many criminal offenders' profiles cannot be coded when strict classification criteria

are used, and (c) the fact that there are insufficient data on the correlates of code types among criminal offenders.

- Megargee's empirically derived classification system divides offenders into 10 types based on their MMPI–2 profiles. Approximately 95% of offenders' valid MMPI–2s can be classified into these groups, which have been found to differ significantly in their backgrounds, histories, educational and vocational achievements, and emotional adjustment, as well as in their adjustment to prison and their response to correctional programs. Based on these findings, descriptions of the groups and recommendations for management and treatment have been formulated that have been found useful in a wide range of correctional settings.
- The Criminal Justice and Correctional Report utilizes the Megargee classification and scores on the MMPI–2 clinical, content, and supplementary scales to make interpretive statements relevant to mental health screening and needs and risk assessment.

APPENDIX 13.1

List of Items for the MMPI–2 Infrequency Criminal (Fc) Scale

True: 11, 18, 24, 72, 92, 96, 114, 144, 150, 162, 198, 216, 228, 252, 270, 282, 291, 294, 303, 312, 319, 322, 323, 324, 329, 332, 336, 355, 361, 387, 468, 478, 506, 520, 530, 555.

False: 2, 78, 90, 102, 108, 109, 126, 192, 210, 260, 276, 318, 343, 404, 561.

14

ASSESSING ALCOHOL- AND DRUG-ABUSING CLIENTS WITH THE MMPI–2

KEVIN R. YOUNG AND NATHAN C. WEED

Substance abuse and dependence have long been areas of intense research interest and concern, as they are among the most common problems seen by practicing mental health care workers. The latest estimates of prevalence from the Substance Abuse and Mental Health Services Administration (SAMHSA, 2002) indicated that almost half of the population had consumed some form of alcoholic beverage in the prior month, with nearly one fifth of the general population reporting they had consumed five or more alcoholic beverages in a single sitting within the prior month. Furthermore, 12.6% of the population reported having used an illicit drug within the last year, with cocaine (1.9%) and cannabis (9.3%) being the most frequently used. Given these prevalence rates, it is not surprising that substance-related disorders are highly comorbid with other *Diagnostic and Statistical Manual of Mental Disorders, Fourth Edition, Text Revision* (*DSM–IV–TR*; American Psychiatric Association [APA], 2000) diagnoses, with 15.7% of all adults with any diagnosed mental disorder also meeting criteria for a substance abuse disorder (SAMHSA, 2002).

Researchers have long sought to identify patterns among substance-abusing and substance-dependent clients in terms of gender, substance of abuse, length of use or abuse, intensity of use or abuse, and familial history of abuse, with the goal of identifying relatively homogeneous groups within substance-abusing populations. These groups, if they were found to exist, could then be studied to help select and formulate focused treatment strategies. A number of psychosocial factors have been hypothesized to differentiate among substance-abusing clients, including: levels of depression, anger, and anxiety; the presence and severity of antisocial tendencies; and the presence of any comorbid psychopathology.

Thus, the purpose of clinical assessment of substance-abusing clients can be seen as twofold: first, to identify and evaluate the pattern of substance use and abuse; and second, to assess the associated personality and psychopathology factors known to be related to substance use and treatment outcome. When the assessment task is viewed in this way, it is easy to see how the MMPI–2 offers many advantages over other substance abuse measures. The MMPI–2 does, of course, contain a number of scales that are designed explicitly to assist in the screening and evaluation of substance abuse problems, such as the MacAndrew Alcoholism Scale—Revised (MAC–R), the Addiction Potential Scale (APS), and the Addiction Acknowledgment Scale (AAS). However, many other assessment instruments, such as the Michigan Alcoholism Screening Test (MAST; Selzer, 1971) and the Substance Use Disorders Diagnostic Schedule (SUDDS; Harrison & Hoffmann, 1989), have similar aims, have extensive research support, and are often much quicker to administer. What these instruments typically do not offer is the capacity to assess (a) test-taking attitudes that may affect client responding, and (b) the personality and psychopathological factors known to complicate and maintain substance abuse and to bear upon treatment planning and outcome. A major advantage of using the MMPI–2 with substance-abusing populations is its ability to evaluate these behavioral and personological dimensions along with patterns of substance use and test-taking attitudes.

The purpose of this chapter is to provide clinicians with a practical guide for interpreting the MMPI–2 with substance-abusing clients. In many ways, of course, strategies for interpretation of the MMPI–2 should not differ markedly across clinical populations. However, there are some interpretive issues that for a substance abuse population need to be underscored. We begin by reviewing such issues surrounding MMPI–2 administration and test-taking styles. We then describe in detail the widely used MMPI–2 substance abuse scales (MAC–R, AAS, and APS) and review some illustrative research literature on these scales. Next, we highlight MMPI–2 assessment of a number of clinical issues associated with substance abuse treatment planning. We conclude with a general interpretive strategy for the MMPI–2 in substance abuse settings and provide two case examples of how the MMPI–2 may be used in assessment of clients with substance abuse problems.

TEST ADMINISTRATION ISSUES ASSOCIATED WITH SUBSTANCE-ABUSING CLIENTS

Along with the many traditional concerns involving administration of the MMPI–2 that apply to nearly all settings (e.g., reading level, supervision of administration, etc.), there are some specialized test administration concerns above and beyond those typically encountered that arise in assessment of clients that may be abusing drugs or alcohol. For instance, the MMPI–2 validity scales, particularly the family of *F* (Infrequency) scales and the inconsistency scales (VRIN [Variable Response Inconsistency] and TRIN [True Response Inconsistency]), can be especially useful in substance abuse settings when a test user is concerned about possible intoxication or mental impairment at the time of test administration. Although care should be taken to optimize test-taking conditions before the MMPI–2 is administered, occasionally the test user will not have direct knowledge about a client's sobriety at the time of testing. Intoxication at the time of test administration, of course, may result in confusion or impaired cognitive functioning and may thus invalidate the results of the assessment (Sobell & Sobell, 1990).

Often, in settings in which substance abuse is at issue, clients' difficulties may be connected to legal issues. Therefore, before test administration, the confidentiality of clients' responses to the MMPI–2 and the limitations of this confidentiality need to be discussed with examinees. More generally, of course, the test user should always seek to increase the probability that the client fully cooperates with the assessment process by informing the client before administering the MMPI–2 of why the test is being administered and how the results will be used (Finn, 1996b). It is reasonable to assume that the likelihood of an interpretable and informative MMPI–2 protocol is maximized when the client feels like a collaborator in the assessment process and when the client can trust that the results of the assessment will be used to address relevant goals and concerns.

RESPONSE-STYLE ISSUES ASSOCIATED WITH SUBSTANCE-ABUSING CLIENTS

Another area of concern with substance-abusing clients that can be particularly salient is the question of whether they will honestly and accurately report their difficulties in a self-report questionnaire. Although this concern can be alleviated to some degree by securing client cooperation as suggested in the preceding section, some may question whether a self-report questionnaire is appropriate in a substance-abusing population given the frequent legal complications and the potential for unconscious or conscious response distortion. The test user should be aware that research on the MMPI–2 has supported its use across a wide variety of clinical contexts, including those in which there is substantial tendency to distort self-report. In an illustrative study, Babor, Steinberg, and Anton (2000) used the data collected in Project MATCH to compare self-report measures of substance-abusing behavior and biological indicators of substance abuse. Results from this study indicated that, along with the known advantages that self-report questionnaires have over collateral reports from knowledgeable others and biological tests (chief among ease of acquisition), they also found that self-report questionnaires were moderately associated with both collateral reports and biological tests. Furthermore, self-reports showed higher correlations with each of the other two data-collection methods as intensity of alcohol abuse rose. The authors do acknowledge potential bias in self-report in the form of the press for social conformity and simple forgetting, though these are phenomena that may be evaluated with the MMPI–2 validity scales.

Careful evaluation of response style, usually centering on interpretation of the MMPI–2 validity scales, is important for determining whether the examinee has produced an interpretable protocol. Other chapters in this book (especially chap. 3) have detailed common strategies for assessment of response style. There is, however, an interesting research literature on response style as evaluated in a substance abuse clinical setting. For example, Isenhart and Silversmith (1997) found that the validity scales of the MMPI–2 could differentiate among groups of alcohol-abusing subjects in two samples of inpatient substance abusers at a Veterans Administration medical center. Cluster analysis of MMPI–2 results identified three "types" of subjects, distinguished by: an exaggerated response style (very high *F*, low *K* [Correction]), a straightforward response style (elevated *F*, low *K*), and a defensive response style (average *F*, slightly above average *K*). Subsequent analysis also demonstrated that the "defensive" subgroup had significantly lower scores on the *DSM–III–R* (APA, 1987) substance abuse severity scales. These response styles differed slightly from similar groupings identified previously by Butcher (1990b), in that a highly virtuous, perfectionistic, and defensive group (high *L* [Lie] and *K*, low *F*) was not identified in the sample. The authors speculate that one possible reason for this was that the subjects were assessed pretreatment, and elevated scores on the *K* scale typically are seen in the posttreatment stage of successful therapy.

One of the more influential recent theories in clinical psychology has been the Stages of Change model, proposed by Prochaska and DiClemente (1982, 1986). This theory posits that clients progress through a sequence of stages when initiating and completing behavioral change. Miller and Tonigan (1997) developed an instrument—the Stages of Change Readiness and Treatment Eagerness scale (SOCRATES)—designed to assess the motivation of a given client for change. This instrument was then factor-analyzed using 1,726 subjects from the baseline sample of Project MATCH. Results suggested three factors, labeled Taking Steps, Recognition, and Ambivalence, which roughly correspond to the three cluster types identified by Isenhart and Silversmith (1997). Although Miller and Tonigan did not provide information regarding the global functioning of subjects producing elevated scores on each factor, the content of the Taking Steps factor suggests a level of awareness and behavioral control consistent with higher scores on the *K* and *L* validity scales of the MMPI–2. Although this interpretation may be intriguing, given its current lack of empirical support, clinicians should not use the MMPI–2 validity scales alone as an indicator of a client's motivation for change. However, the interpretation does suggest that elevated scores on the family of *F* scales and lower scores on the defensiveness triad (*K*, *L*, and *S* [Superlative Self-Presentation]) may raise concerns about treatment adherence and outcome.

THE MMPI–2 SUBSTANCE ABUSE SCALES

Although numerous MMPI–2 scales possess clinical correlates of relevance in the assessment of substance abuse, only three widely used scales are designed specifically to evaluate substance abuse problems: the MacAndrew Alcoholism Scale—Revised (MacAndrew, 1965), the Addiction Potential Scale (Weed, Butcher, McKenna, & Ben-Porath, 1992), and the Addiction Acknowledgment Scale (Weed et al., 1992). In this section, we describe the development of these scales, highlight illustrative validity research, and identify interpretation strategies.

The MacAndrew Alcoholism Scale—Revised (MAC–R)

Development of the MAC–R

Of the three most commonly used substance abuse scales on the MMPI–2, the MAC–R (Butcher et al., 2001; MacAndrew, 1965) has been in existence the longest. In fact, it has been one of the most heavily researched scales on the MMPI (Gantner, Graham, & Archer, 1992; Greene, 1994; MacAndrew, 1981). MacAndrew originally developed his scale for use with the MMPI. In a sample of 400 male outpatients, he compared MMPI item responses between those seeking treatment for alcoholism and those receiving psychiatric treatment for other problems, and identified the items that best distinguished between these groups. Before he finalized his scale, which came to be known as the MacAndrew Alcoholism Scale (MAC), however, he discarded items that had direct reference to substance abuse, reasoning that a scale without such items may be less susceptible to attempts to conceal substance abuse problems. During the revision of the MMPI, four of the original 49 MAC items were deleted because of objectionable content. Because many test users had come to rely on interpretations of raw MAC scores, four comparable items were selected from the MMPI–2 item pool to replace the lost items. The revised scale became known as the MacAndrew Alcoholism Scale—Revised (MAC–R).

Like nearly all scales developed via this empirical contrast group methodology, the internal consistency of the MAC–R is poor, owing to the fact that its items cover a wide range of content. One factor analysis of the MAC–R item intercorrelations (Weed, Butcher, & Ben-Porath, 1995) suggests that the MAC–R contains item dimensions including: cognitive impairment, school maladjustment, harmful habits, interpersonal competence, risk taking, and masculine interests. Of all the scales on the MMPI–2, the MAC–R scale correlates most highly with the other MMPI–2 substance abuse scales, the AAS and the APS, and with scales that measure problems with impulse control: Pd, *Ma,* and ASP. Not surprisingly, research on external correlates of MAC–R seems to indicate that its scores are most strongly correlated with (a) problems related to substance abuse and (b) various manifestations of behavioral dyscontrol, including risk taking, exhibitionistic behavior, social extroversion, and aggression.

Note that despite its prodigious research base, controversy has existed about the use of the MAC as a measure of alcoholism proper (Gottesman & Prescott, 1989; Schwartz & Graham, 1979). It is generally accepted (Greene, 1994; Levenson et al., 1990; MacAndrew, 1981; Schwartz & Graham, 1979) that the MAC–R is not measuring alcoholism *per se* or even personality traits that are exclusive to alcoholics. Further, as Graham (2000) points out, there is little evidence to suggest that MAC–R scores can predict the development of substance abuse problems in persons not currently abusing substances. However, among all the many scales commonly scored on the MMPI–2, the MAC–R repeatedly appears as one of the strongest correlates of clinically significant substance abuse problems.

Illustrative Research With the MAC–R

Levenson et al. (1990) investigated the correlates of the MAC in a normal population. The authors sampled 1,117 males in the Normative Aging Study and compared those participants who reported having a problematic pattern of drinking ($N = 102$) to those who did not report having a history of drinking problems ($N = 976$) with 23 men excluded as lifetime abstainers. The results of the study supported the notion that the MAC is measuring personality characteristics broader than substance abuse. Individuals who had a history of arrest and had drinking problems possessed the highest average scores on the MAC. However, individuals who had been arrested but did not report a history of problem drinking and those who had not been arrested but did report a history of problem drinking produced mean scores on the MAC that were virtually indistinguishable. All three of these groups had significantly higher scores on the MAC than individuals who reported neither a history of arrests nor drinking problems. These results seem to support the hypothesis that the MAC (and its revision, MAC–R) is in fact measuring personality traits that correlate highly but not exclusively with substance abuse, such as a tendency toward risk-taking behaviors. Again, high scores on the MAC–R should be interpreted not as necessarily indicating the presence of alcohol abuse problems but, rather, as suggestive of personality characteristics associated with substance abuse.

The Addiction Potential Scale (APS) and the Addiction Acknowledgment Scale (AAS)

Development of the APS

The APS (Weed et al., 1992) was designed to be a collection of MMPI–2 items that maximally and uniquely characterize individuals with substance abuse problems. Like the MAC–R, it was hoped that this scale would reflect personality dimensions and life situations associated with substance abuse and would be of use both to researchers investigating and practitioners assessing such problems. The APS was derived empirically, using methods similar to those employed in the construction of the MAC.

The development of the APS began simply as an attempt to modify the MAC–R empirically, taking advantage of the new MMPI–2 item pool. By substituting the weakest of the existing MAC–R items with the strongest of the new items, it was hoped that the MAC–R could be improved upon while preserving continuity with the older scale. Three large samples collected as part of the MMPI Restandardization Project were used in the development of the APS: (a) the MMPI–2 normative sample, (b) a sample of psychiatric inpatients, and (c) a sample from an inpatient substance abuse treatment program. The development of APS started with an examination of every MMPI–2 item for its potential to replace old items. To be considered as a useful item candidate, it had to meet one of two conditions: (a) that it be endorsed *more* frequently by members of the substance abuse sample than in both the normative sample and the psychiatric sample; or (b) that it be endorsed *less* frequently by members of the substance abuse sample than in both the normative and the psychiatric sample. A minority of 180 of the 567 MMPI–2 items met either of these conditions. For the remainder of the items, the endorsement frequencies in the substance abuse sample fell in between the endorsement frequencies of the psychiatric and normative samples. Surprisingly, this latter condition was also characteristic of the majority (29 of 49) of the MAC–R items. At this point, the goal of continuity with MAC–R was abandoned in favor of using the best possible set of items to be found in the item pool, regardless of the items' inclusion in the earlier scale. The candidate pool of items for the new scale became the 180 items that met these criteria.

Next, the consistency and magnitude of these items' ability to discriminate between groups were considered. Four group comparisons were devised: (a) male substance abuse versus male normative, (b) female substance abuse versus female normative, (c) male substance abuse versus male psychiatric, and (d) female substance abuse versus female psychiatric. To be considered further as a candidate for inclusion in the empirical APS, an item was required to discriminate groups beyond a minimum effect size in each of these four comparisons, and beyond a predetermined "substantial" effect size for at least three of the four group comparisons. The MMPI MAC items that discriminated between groups at or beyond this level in just two of the four comparisons were also considered candidates, because they presumably met similar standards in the development of the MAC. Forty-six items met these criteria. Finally, as with the MAC, items with obvious reference to alcohol or other drug abuse were discarded, as were items that possessed negative correlations with the total scale score. Seven items were dropped at this step. The remaining 39 items were preserved and named the Addiction Potential Scale.

Like MAC–R, the item content of the APS is heterogeneous. Weed et al. (1995) found the following content dimensions in a factor analysis of item intercorrelations: Harmful Habits, Positive Treatment Attitudes, Forthcoming, Hypomania, Risk Taking, and Passivity. Scores on the APS are not as strongly related to dimensions reflecting behavioral dyscontrol as are scores on the MAC–R. Its strongest correlates with other commonly scored MMPI–2 scales include the other substance abuse scales (AAS and MAC–R) and scales reflecting self-criticism and distress (*L*, *Pt* [Psychasthemia], ANX [Anxiety]).

Development of the AAS

To complement the APS, which by design contains no items with content obviously related to substance abuse, Weed et al. (1992) developed a second scale consisting entirely of items whose content directly suggests problems with substance abuse. Whereas the construction of APS began with an empirical search through the MMPI–2 item pool, the construction of the AAS began with a rational search through the MMPI–2 item pool for items with content directly indicating substance abuse problems. Fourteen such items were located. Three items not contributing to internal consistency were dropped and were replaced by two items that improved scale internal consistency and that were judged to be consistent in content with the items already identified. The AAS comprises these final 13 items. None of these items is on APS, but the two scales are moderately intercorrelated.

Interpretation of the APS and the AAS

A review of the research on the APS and the AAS to date (some of which is reviewed in Weed et al., 1995) suggests the following about the scales' psychometric properties:

1. Though internal consistency of the APS is low (true of most empirical scales), the AAS is internally consistent and relatively unidimensional; and both scales have acceptable test–retest reliability.
2. Three different lines of evidence—correlations with other MMPI–2 scales, clinical group discrimination studies, and correlations with external criteria—support the convergent and discriminant validity of the APS and the AAS as measures of substance abuse.
3. The AAS, though only 13 items long, appears so far to be substantially more effective than either the APS or the MAC–R at detecting substance abuse problems in a variety of settings and with a variety of populations (e.g., see Greene, Weed, Butcher, Arredondo, & Davis, 1992).
4. Some of the content dimensions underlying the APS items may be more related to characteristics of the sample from which the APS was developed (such as treatment readiness) than to substance abuse in general.

For clinical use, the contrasting construction methodologies of the APS and the AAS suggest different interpretive approaches. As a multidimensional empirical scale, the APS is best interpreted probabilistically, with high scores suggesting a high probability of psychological problems similar to those of the substance abuse sample with which the APS was derived. Given the scale's construction, we would expect that an individual with significant psychological difficulties in addition to problems with substance abuse would obtain a lower score on the APS than an individual would whose problems are focused around substance abuse. The AAS, of course, can also be interpreted probabilistically. However, given its construction and unidimensionality, a high score on the AAS can be interpreted simply as open admission to a number of problems related to substance abuse. Research to date suggests that a high score on the AAS is the best single indicator on the MMPI–2 of substance abuse problems. Test users may also employ the AAS as a list of critical items, noting what specific problems related to substance abuse are endorsed by the examinee.

The AAS and the APS have only been in existence since 1992, and abundant evidence already exists supporting their utility, along with the MAC–R, in the clinical assessment of substance abuse. Interpretation of these scales and other MMPI–2 indicators is already standard practice in the assessment of substance abuse and is reflected in computerized interpretive systems (e.g., Butcher, 1991). Interpretation of MMPI–2 protocols produced within a substance abuse setting often begins with an analysis of the substance abuse scales themselves. Higher scores on these scales not only have been associated with the *probability* and *severity* of substance abuse disorder but also may indicate personality characteristics relevant to the treatment-planning process.

Illustrative Comparative Research Studies on the MMPI–2 Substance Abuse Scales

Rouse, Butcher, and Miller (1999) investigated the relative diagnostic abilities of the AAS, the APS, and the MAC–R in an outpatient clinical sample of 460 clients, 68 of whom had a substance abuse diagnosis. Results from the study indicated that a combination of the AAS and the MAC–R produced the greatest level of diagnostic accuracy and that the AAS alone performed better than either the MAC–R or the APS alone.

Stein, Graham, Ben-Porath, and McNulty (1999) also examined the ability of the three substance abuse subscales to detect substance abusers, using an outpatient sample from a community mental health center (N = 833). In contrast to prior studies, the authors investigated the incremental validity of the AAS and the APS above and beyond the MAC–R in predicting substance abuse status. Consistent with prior results, the AAS showed greater incremental validity than did the APS. Additionally, the AAS outperformed both the MAC–R and the APS in terms of the amount of meaningful variance contributed to the prediction of substance-abusing status and in terms of the diagnostic hit rate of substance-abusing status.

ASSESSMENT OF ISSUES RELEVANT TO SUBSTANCE ABUSE TREATMENT

When assessing a client with substance abuse concerns, MMPI–2 protocol interpretation should not focus on the substance abuse scales alone. In fact, when substance abuse is the identified reason for referral, it is commonly the case that a client's pattern and severity of substance use are the facets of clinical presentation that are already understood best. Therefore, case conceptualization and treatment planning for clients in substance abuse settings are often informed best by careful analysis not of the MMPI–2 substance abuse scales but of the MMPI–2 scales that address the personal, social, and psychopathological variables that complicate or maintain substance use behaviors and that interfere with attempts to recover.

Such variables can be roughly categorized into *emotional variables* such as depression and anger, *cognitive variables* such as motivation to change and level of functioning, *social variables* such as social support and interpersonal style, and *comorbid psychopathology*. These categories are not mutually exclusive but are instructive and can be useful when interpreting an MMPI–2 profile.

Emotional Variables

Level of depression has been demonstrated (Gottheil, Thornton, & Weinstein, 2002) to be associated with substance abuse treatment outcome. Patients with higher levels of depression have been shown to have better outcomes than those with lower levels of depression when treated using highly structured treatment protocols such as most cognitive–behavioral treatments. The MMPI–2 provides the clinician with several scales providing information on relative level of depression. Clinical Scale 2 (*D*), the DEP (Depression) content scale, and the LSE (Low Self-Esteem) content scale can provide the most direct information regarding the relative level of depressive symptoms. Additionally, the new Restructured Clinical scales (Tellegen et al., 2003) may be of use in assessing both general demoralization (RCd) and low positive emotionality (RC2).

Another example of an emotional variable that has been shown to be related to treatment outcome among substance-abusing clients is anger (Fuller & Allen, 2000; Kadden, Longabaugh, & Wirtz, 2003; Mattson, Babor, Cooney, & Conners, 1998). Anger and poor impulse control have also been implicated in multiple typology studies conducted with alcohol-abusing patients. Clinical Scale 4 (Pd; Psychopathic Deviate) and the Anger (ANG), Antisocial Practices (ASP), and Type A Personality (TPA) content scales each may be interpreted as being indicative of anger or impulse control difficulties that may cause individuals to be vulnerable to substance abuse, or serve to maintain problems with substance abuse. Clinical Scale 4 is often prominent in the profile of a substance-abusing client. Studies (e.g., Finn, Sharkansky, Brandt, & Turcotte, 2000) have shown that Pd is among the most frequently elevated scales seen among individuals with substance abuse difficulties, along with clinical scales 2 (*D*) and 9 (*Ma*; Hypomania).

Cognitive Variables

The category of cognitive variables includes considerations of both capacity and style. As an example of the former, Ciraulo, Piechniczek-Buczek, and Iscan (2003) describe the cognitive impairment that sometimes occurs as a result of excessive substance abuse and that can interfere with the formation of effective strategies for coping during treatment of substance abuse. Although intellectual and neuropsychological assessments are the most appropriate means for identifying such cognitive impairment, note that a number of MMPI–2 scales (e.g., the *F* scales, the inconsistency scales, and the *Sc* scale) are sensitive to cognitive confusion. Elevations on validity scales in MMPI–2 protocols produced by individuals with severe and chronic patterns of substance abuse may reflect confusion and impaired cognitive efficacy that does not remit during periods of sobriety.

Many MMPI–2 scales are sensitive to cognitive styles and attitudes that are relevant to treatment planning. For example, elevations on scales *L* or *Pa* (Paranoia) may indicate cognitive inflexibility; elevations on scales *Pa, Sc* (Schizophrenia), BIZ (Bizzare Mentation), or the PSY–5 (Personality Psychopathology Five; Harkness, McNulty, & Ben-Porath, 1995) may reflect autistic thinking patterns; elevations on scales *D*, DEP, LSE, or RC2 may reflect not only depressed mood or general demoralization but also cognitive symptoms of depression that may contribute to negative expectations about treatment; elevations on the Negative Treatment Indicators content scale may reflect attitudes about treatment that are counterproductive in a therapeutic context.

Social Variables

A third cluster of variables relevant to substance abuse treatment planning involves interpersonal style and resources. As most forms of treatment involve some sort of interpersonal involvement, it is often important in treatment to be able to anticipate what stylistic variables may present obstacles or serve as strengths in the formation of therapeutic relationships. Scales 0 and SOD provide information about general social orientation and may indicate to what extent a client is likely to feel comfortable in a social therapeutic context. Elevations on scales Pd, CYN (Cynicism), and *Pa* may indicate that cynicism or mistrust or both are likely to color therapeutic interactions. Scores on scales 4, FAM (Family Problems), and MDS (Marital Distress Scale) may reflect the amount of social support the client can rely upon during treatment.

Comorbid Psychopathology

Finally, it is important to consider the relevance of any comorbid psychopathology that may complicate the clinical presentation of substance abuse (Ciraulo et al., 2003) or that may warrant particular attention in treatment planning. The ability of the MMPI–2 to identify symptoms and behavioral tendencies that are part of psychopathological syndromes is, of course, one of its great strengths.

A GENERAL MMPI–2 INTERPRETIVE STRATEGY WITH ALCOHOL- AND DRUG-ABUSING CLIENTS

Although the MMPI–2 can provide a broad, general description of the personality and psychopathological characteristics of the examinee, it is most useful when the interpretive question is narrowed. That is, rather than asking of the MMPI–2, What is my client like?, more useful questions may be, To what extent does my client acknowledge abuse of alcohol?, Does my client appear to be motivated to engage in psychotherapy?, or even, In what manner might my client's interpersonal style serve as an obstacle to success in group therapy? Because such focused questions depend upon the circumstances of the assessment and the particular situation of the client, no single approach to MMPI–2 interpretation serves all purposes equally well. However, in the preceding sections, we have described a number of the interpretive focal points that are common in the assessment of alcohol- and drug-abusing clients with the MMPI–2 (some of these are highlighted in Exhibit 14.1). We next summarize these elements in the form of a general strategy.

First, the test user must work to optimize conditions of MMPI–2 administration, ensuring that it is not compromised by acute intoxication or misunderstandings about the purpose of testing. Second, the test user should perform a careful examination of the MMPI–2 validity scales to come to an understanding of how the examinee approached the test (motivations, confusions, compliance, openness, acknowledgment of problems), first determining whether the protocol is interpretable and then determining what qualifications may need to be placed on the inferences drawn from the test results. Third, the test user should examine scores on the MMPI–2 substance abuse scales: the AAS, the APS, and the MAC–R. Elevations on the AAS can be interpreted as direct report by the client of problems associated with substance use; elevations on the APS and the MAC–R indicate endorsement of attitudes, behaviors, or symptoms that have been associated with substance-abusing populations. Finally, the MMPI–2 profile should be interpreted in light of the emotional, cognitive, and social variables that may cause or maintain substance abuse problems or that have implications for treatment planning, considering also whether there are complicating comorbid conditions that may affect the focus of treatment. The following two case examples (fictionalized accounts based on actual clinical cases) illustrate how elements of this general interpretive strategy may be integrated.

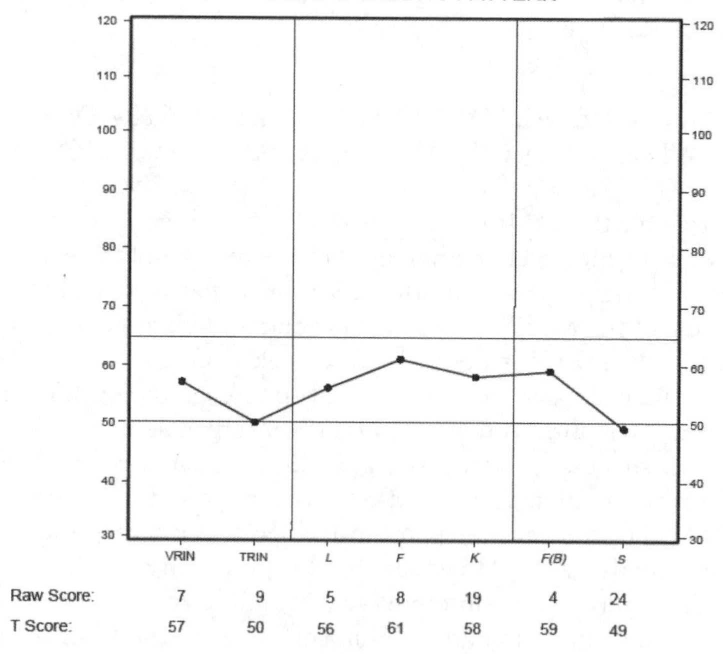

Figure 14.1. Case Example 1 validity scales profile. MMPI–2 Validity Pattern. From *MMPI–2 Minnesota Report: Adult Clinical System—Revised Interpretive Report.* Copyright © 1989, 1993 by the Regents of the University of Minnesota. All rights reserved. Used by permission of the University of Minnesota Press.

Case Example 1: Felix

The MMPI–2 profiles presented in Figures 14.1 and 14.2 were produced by Felix, a 43-year-old loan officer who presented for court-ordered treatment after a DUI conviction. Felix reported that his conviction for driving under the influence represented a lapse of judgment on his part and that his drinking habits are not the primary concerns in his life. In fact, Felix claimed that his drinking habits are one of the few methods he has of coping with what he terms "my otherwise miserable life." Felix lives alone, is not involved in a relationship at this time, and has not been involved in a relationship for the past 10 years—a matter that causes him great concern. One of his primary goals in life was to start a family, but he reported having been unable to find anyone who was willing to marry him, despite two marriage proposals while he was in his mid-twenties. Felix stated that when he used to go drinking with his college roommates he frequently met women but he never seemed to measure up to their expectations and they eventually broke off the relationships. As Felix got older, his friends began to get married and he found himself gradually accompanied by fewer and fewer people to the bar, until he was eventually going alone.

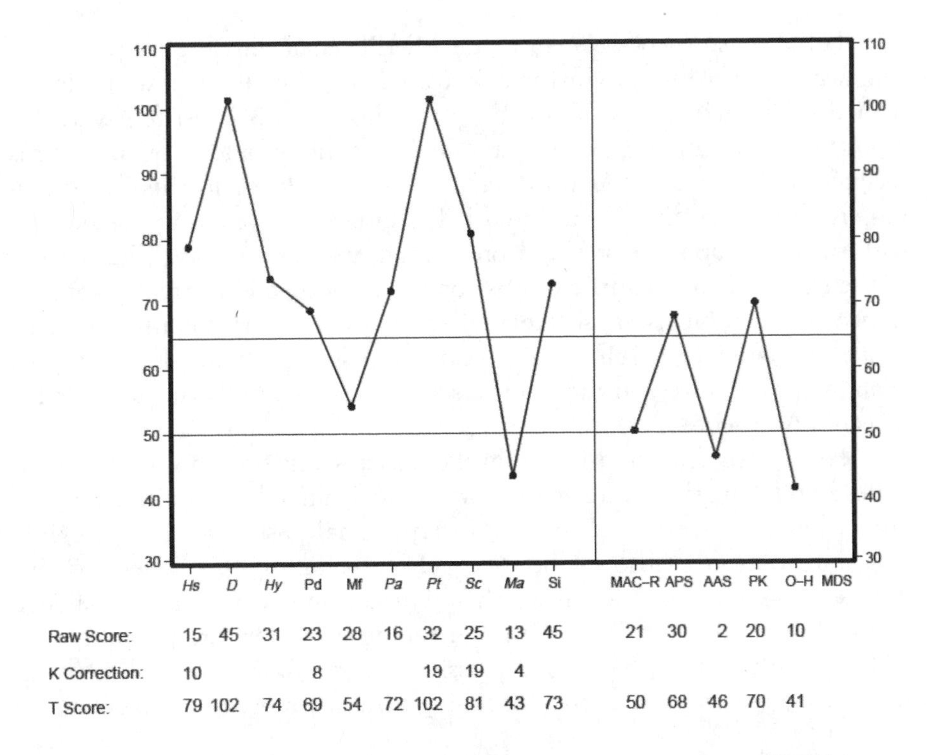

Figure 14.2. Case Example 1 clinical and substance abuse scales profile. From MMPI–2 Basic and Supplementary Scales Profile. *MMPI–2 Minnesota Report: Adult Clinical System—Revised Interpretive Report.* Copyright © 1989, 1993 by the Regents of the University of Minnesota. All rights reserved. Used by permission of the University of Minnesota Press.

Felix reported that he currently goes to the bar "every chance I get" (usually five or six nights a week), where he sits alone, usually speaking to nobody, including the wait staff, who he believes are repelled by him. A typical night at the bar involves nursing six or seven drinks from 6:00 p.m. until closing, sometimes while reading the newspaper want ads and fantasizing about how his life might have turned out differently. He reported that he is rarely drunk when he leaves the bar and so feels little need to call a cab; he drives himself home most nights and goes directly to bed.

Although Felix does not regard drinking as the major problem in his life, he voices no resistance to the court-ordered treatment. He is open with the examiner about his unhappiness with life, and this openness is also reflected on his MMPI–2 validity scales, on which he produced no significant elevations. Scores on VRIN and TRIN suggest consistent responding, with neither an acquiescent or nay-saying response style. Scores on *L*, *K*, and *S* scales suggest no attempt to minimize his troubles, and his *F* scale score indicates no unusual response pattern.

Felix's pattern of scores on the MMPI–2 substance abuse scales is somewhat surprising, given his acknowledgment in interview of almost daily drinking. His low score on the AAS, however, is consistent with his report that his drinking behavior results in few life problems outside of his recent conviction. Although his MAC–R score is low, most likely reflecting an absence of the disinhibited risk-taking style sometimes associated with substance abuse, his APS score is high, indicating that he responded to the MMPI–2 in a manner that is common among clients treated for substance abuse problems, most likely reflecting the APS item content dimensions associated with self-criticism and admission of personal flaws. An examination of scores on the clinical scales helps clarify the meaning of his elevated APS score.

Felix is reporting an intense level of distress. His extreme elevations on scales 2 and 7 suggest severe anxiety and worry, vulnerability, guilt, depressed affect, low self-esteem, self-blame, interpersonal passivity, and inflexible thought processes. Although he may feel motivated to seek relief from his distress, his feelings of low self-worth and defeatism may present a challenge in treatment. Concerns with Felix's drinking behaviors are probably best addressed in the context of his depressive symptoms, as it is likely that his substance use serves as a method of coping with his emotional distress.

Case Example 2: Linda

Linda is a 22-year-old Caucasian female referred by her college for an assessment following an arrest for public drunkenness after she delivered a heated, profanity-laced tirade when the campus police attempted to escort her home after an evening event. She had been evicted from the dormitories during her sophomore year for fighting with a roommate after a night of drinking alcohol. Linda acknowledges both episodes but claims they were "blown out of proportion." She reports that her greatest difficulty at present is in figuring out "what the hell I want to do with my life." Although Linda is one week from graduation with a degree in criminal justice, she has not yet made any attempt to find employment. Linda found her internship work in the legal system "stupid and dull" and disliked the tedious, detail-oriented paperwork for which she was responsible. Although Linda's principal plans following graduation are to "hang out with friends," she admits to some anxiety about her prospects. Linda also reports that she feels quite resentful of both her parents and her professors at school, who she feels are trying to force her to "be something I'm not."

Linda does not believe she has problems with substance abuse. She reports drinking three or four beers per night about 10 nights per month and reports that she "rarely" gets drunk when she drinks. She smokes approximately one marijuana cigarette per month at parties and denies

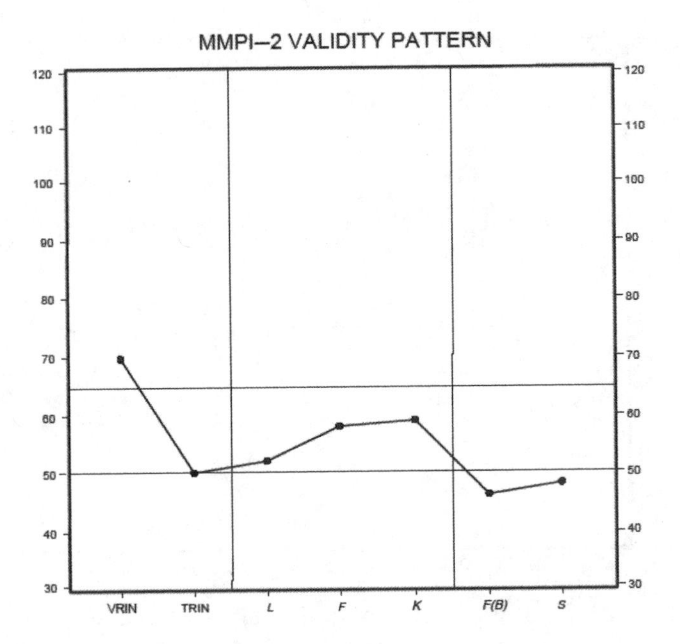

Figure 14.3. Case Example 2 validity scales profile. From MMPI–2 Validity Pattern. *MMPI–2 Minnesota Report: Adult Clinical System—Revised Interpretive Report.*

other drug use. Although she initially reported believing that the evaluation was "stupid" and "just something to get through," she quickly warmed up to the prospect of "finding out what makes me tick." Principally, she hoped to learn whether "there is a job in this world for someone like me." Although she was informed that a comprehensive vocational assessment was beyond the scope of the current evaluation, she remained interested in the results of the evaluation and seemed genuinely invested.

The validity scales for the protocol produced by Linda suggest an open and honest response style, consistent with observations about her apparent investment in the evaluation (see Figure 14.3). Her score on VRIN indicates that she was inconsistent in some of her responding, but there is little reason to believe that this was the result of confusion or intoxication at the time of testing. Furthermore, scores on the other validity indexes indicate that whatever inconsistency was apparent in her responding did not result in an unusual or distorted response pattern. Linda's score on the *K* scale is consistent with her self-report that her current problems are minor and manageable.

Linda's scores on the MMPI–2 substance abuse scales indicate that Linda does not view herself as having significant difficulties with substance abuse (see Figure 14.4). However, the elevated score on the APS suggests that Linda possesses many of the personality characteristics typical of

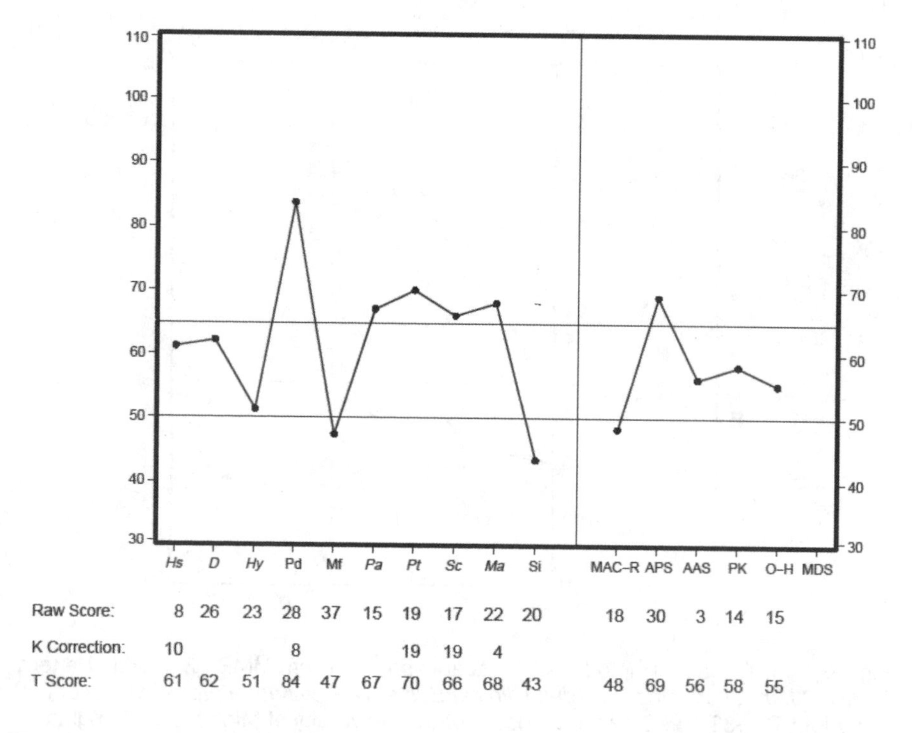

Figure 14.4. Case Example 2 clinical and substance abuse scales profile. From MMPI–2 Basic and Supplementary Scales Profile. *MMPI–2 Minnesota Report: Adult Clinical System—Revised Interpretive Report.* Copyright © 1989, 1993 by the Regents of the University of Minnesota. All rights reserved. Used by permission of the University of Minnesota Press.

substance-abusing clients. Her scores on the MMPI–2 clinical scales suggest what these characteristics are. Her most prominent elevation is on clinical Scale 4, which suggests a tendency toward excitement seeking, acting out, anger, and difficulties with impulse control. These behavioral tendencies likely play a role in her pattern of substance use and in her unconstrained misbehavior while under the influence of alcohol. This scale elevation also may help explain her dissatisfaction with the aspects of her internship work that require careful attention to detail.

During test feedback, although she was impatient with a general description of the MMPI–2 profile, she seemed to enjoy herself, pointing immediately to the visually dramatic Scale 4 elevation, grinning and blurting out, "Wow! What does *that* mean?" She readily acknowledged a tendency to act on an angry impulse, elaborating that "it only gets worse when I drink." When discussion turned to her career options, she seemed pleased when the examiner pointed out how she may prefer a job that involved more hands-on activities and less paperwork. The remainder of the session focused on the generation of possible career paths. She accepted a referral to the career counseling office.

SUMMARY

Although many assessment tools are available for evaluating problems associated with substance abuse, the MMPI–2 offers some important advantages for practitioners who work with clients in substance-abusing populations. The MMPI–2 validity scales can be used to provide information about both mental status and test-taking attitudes, either of which may affect the quality of information obtained during assessment. The MMPI–2 substance abuse scales measure not only direct reporting of substance abuse problems but also behavioral patterns and lifestyle characteristics often associated with substance abuse. The other clinical, content, and supplementary scales on the MMPI–2 provide a rich context for understanding the emotional, cognitive, social, and psychopathological factors that cause or maintain substance abuse problems and that have implications for treatment planning. All together, these sets of MMPI–2 scales comprise a potent instrument for assessing alcohol- and drug-abusing clients.

EXHIBIT 14.1
Highlight: Important Considerations in Using the MMPI–2 With Substance-Abusing Clients

- *Prevalence of substance abuse:* Substance abuse is both highly prevalent and comorbid with other psychological conditions. Therefore, assessment of substance abuse and associated characteristics is often necessary even when they are not the presenting problems.
- *Test administration:* The possibility of intoxication during test administration should be considered. Efforts should be made to secure cooperation of the examinee before test administration by explaining the importance and relevance of the MMPI–2.
- *Response style:* Variability in client insight regarding substance abuse problems, and complications associated with legal involvement make careful examination of validity scales an important part of MMPI–2 interpretation in substance-abusing populations.
- *MMPI–2 substance abuse scales:* There are three principal MMPI–2 scales used to assess substance abuse. The Addiction Potential Scale (APS) and the MacAndrew Alcoholism Scale—Revised (MAC–R) are empirically developed scales that measure personality patterns and behaviors statistically associated with substance abuse. The Addiction Acknowledgment Scale (AAS) is a rationally derived scale that measures direct report of problems with substance use.
- *Treatment planning with the MMPI–2:* Although the MMPI–2 substance abuse scales are useful for identifying substance abuse problems, case conceptualization and substance abuse treatment planning with the MMPI–2 often focus on clinical, content, and supplementary scales that assess emotional, cognitive, and social variables that may cause or maintain substance abuse and that may affect treatment outcome.

15

PERSONNEL SCREENING WITH THE MMPI–2

JAMES N. BUTCHER, DENIZ S. ONES, AND MICHAEL CULLEN

The history of objective personality assessment in the United States began with a personnel selection application. During World War I, Woodworth (1920) developed the Personal Data Sheet, a paper–pencil questionnaire addressing emotional adjustment issues, in an effort to screen out mentally unsuited draftees from the army. After the war ended, personality questionnaires became a widely explored approach to personality assessment. The use of psychological tests in making personnel-related decisions is an appropriate professional activity for psychologists to undertake and a valuable contribution to the employment process. Several psychological adjustment factors have been considered important for personnel practitioners to address in assessing clients for responsible positions of public trust. Examples of these psychological adjustment factors include emotional stability; judgment and public responsibility; ability to deal with situations that induce extreme stress; capability of dealing effectively on an interpersonal level for jobs that require teamwork (e.g., airline flight crews); and the presence of severe personality disorders or other psychological disorders that may result in rule violations, careless and impulsive behavior patterns, and so forth.

In a number of occupations, such as those of police and fire personnel or nuclear power plant employees, employers are obliged to conduct extensive personnel evaluations and background checks in order to assure the public that the persons hired are emotionally stable and responsible. For example, in almost half of all states in the United States, the screening of police applicants using a clinical instrument such as the MMPI is mandated by law (Association of Directors of Law Enforcement Standards and Training, 2000). In the case of police applicants, the purpose of this psychological screening is to identify and screen out those applicants who may be at risk for engaging in a broad range of undesirable behaviors. These unwanted behaviors comprise an amalgam of antisocial characteristics that may or may not reflect or be a product of a serious clinical condition requiring treatment or intervention. They include behaviors such as drug and alcohol abuse, evidence tampering, perjury, excessive use of force, fire arms misuse, embezzlement, theft from property rooms, accepting bribes in exchange for restricted information about upcoming police raids, agreeing not to apprehend known offenders, or not testifying against offenders. Recent investigations of police corruption in Los Angeles and New York suggest that the incidence of these destructive police behaviors may be on the rise (Glover & Lait, 2000; Mollen, Baer, Evans, Lankler, & Tyler, 1994).

Although most personnel evaluations involving the use of personality-based measures are in employment screening (usually after the person has been deemed qualified for the job and made a preliminary offer), other situations require the assessment of existing employees. Some of these assessments include: fitness-for-duty evaluations for employees who have experienced work-related problems with a psychological element; evaluations to aid employees to obtain counseling for a mental health problem such as substance abuse (e.g., in an employee assistance program); evaluations to determine if an employee is suitable and emotionally stable for a higher-level position such as for advancement to captain in a police department; an assessment of an employee's mental state in a work compensation claim; or assessments of reliability in applicants for security clearances for sensitive jobs. See Exhibit 15.1 for a summary of factors central to selecting psychological procedures for personnel screening.

RESEARCH ESTABLISHING THE MMPI'S USE IN PERSONNEL SETTINGS

A review of the research supporting MMPI use was published by Rouse and Butcher (1995). This review of the use of the test in personnel and educational applications found over 570 articles and books on the

EXHIBIT 15.1
Highlight: Important Factors in Choosing Psychological Tests for Personnel Screening

- Tests that are used as a general emotional screening instrument in personnel selection should meet the highest professional standards in terms of accepted professional criteria of utility, validity, and reliability.
- The tests need to be *objective* in structure to ensure that decisions are based on defensible criteria rather than on procedures that are interpreted by "clinical impressions."
- The tests used in employment should be administered, scored, and interpreted according to the highest test administration standards. It is important that decisions concerning emotional stability be made by experienced professionals with both a clinical psychological and a personnel screening background in using tests with "normals."
- The tests used in establishing emotional stability need to be *fair* to all applicants. This means that they have been demonstrated to work equally well for women and minorities. Research on the test should substantiate any claims of fairness to women and minority applicants.
- An instrument that is being used as a standard in personnel selection should have alternate forms in other languages that may be spoken by applicants; for example, in areas where many applicants come from Spanish-speaking backgrounds, the test could be administered in the appropriate language.
- Any test serving as a standard for personnel decisions should be demonstrated to have a substantial *research base for interpretation* with normal range populations such as police applicants. The test should have clear and widely established interpretive strategies for use with applicants.
- The tests need to have a demonstrated *validity in predicting* personality and mental health problems that are considered detrimental to the job, for example, impulsive and irresponsible behavior, difficulties in social and interpersonal relationships, and antisocial attitudes and behavior.
- The test scales used in the evaluation need to have demonstrated test reliability. That is, tests need to have an available research literature demonstrating that the measures are psychometrically reliable.
- To ensure that applicants are not dismissed unfairly or inappropriately from the applicant pool on the basis of psychological tests, a review process or an appeals panel should be implemented to give a "final review" for applicants that are being rejected.

Source: Butcher (1999b).

topic across a wide variety of settings (police, fire personnel, airline pilots, military, nuclear power plant employees, air traffic controllers, and medically related occupations). Space limitations in this chapter do not permit the full documentation of the MMPI and MMPI–2's use in personnel applications; however, the reader is referred to several articles that provide evaluations of the empirical research in a number of personnel settings (e.g., Butcher, 1979, 2002a; Beutler, Storm, Kirkish, Scogin, & Gaines, 1985; Derksen, Gerits, & Verbruggen, 2003; Fulkerson, 1957; Hiatt & Hargrave, 1988a; Schofield, 1953).

THE MMPI AND COUNTERPRODUCTIVE POLICE OFFICER BEHAVIOR

One of the most extensive personnel applications today, police applicant screening (which has been widely researched) is addressed in some detail to provide examples of the ways that the MMPI–2 has been used in the assessment of applicants. Recent surveys estimate that at least 36% of police agencies surveyed use the MMPI for selection purposes (Drees, Ones, Cullen, Spilberg, & Viswesvaran, 2003). Given the extensive use of the MMPI in police selection and the potential damage that can ensue when officers engage in counterproductive behaviors, an important concern is how well the MMPI fulfills its intended purpose of identifying problem officers. Several studies have examined how well scales from the MMPI predict various indexes of police officer counterproductivity. Using *violence* as a criterion, Hargrave, Hiatt, and Gaffney (1986) found that a discriminant function based on the Psychopathic Deviate (Pd), *F* (Infrequency), and Hypomania (*Ma*) scales and a scale measuring sensitivity to Social Introversion (Si) successfully classified 75% of officers into a group whose members had admitted to being involved in two or more non-job-related fights prior to applying to be a police officer and a group whose members did not make any such admissions. Using absences as the criterion, Shusman, Inwald, and Landa (1984) found that the MMPI MacAndrew Alcoholism Scale (MAC) successfully differentiated a group of officers who had been absent from work on three or more occasions during a 10-month probationary period from a group of officers who were absent on fewer than three occasions. Unfortunately, for some criteria, studies have yielded inconclusive results. For instance, while some researchers have found that the MMPI Hypomania scale is a useful predictor of car accidents (e.g., Marsh, 1962; Azen, Snibbe, & Montgomery, 1973), other researchers have found that completely different scales or no scales at all predict this criterion (Beutler et al., 1985).

Studies investigating the links between MMPI scale scores and disciplinary days are numerous. Costello, Schneider, and Schoenfeld (1996) found that combined scores on the MMPI *F*, Psychopathic Deviate, and Hypomania scales correlated .223 with the number of disciplinary suspension days for officers who had been on the force for at least 3 years. These results suggest that traits such as impulsivity and rebelliousness may be modestly good predictors of a general counterproductivity criterion. This suggestion is buttressed by research by Bartol (1991), who found that a discriminant function based on the *L* (Lie), Psychopathic Deviate, and Hypomania scales correctly classified 74% of officers to a group whose members had remained on the force since their time of hire and a group whose members were either dismissed for cause or who voluntarily resigned due to a failure to meet departmental expectations of job performance. Further support for the importance of the trait of impulsivity in predicting counterproductive acts comes from research by Hiatt and Hargrave (1988b), who found that the Hypomania scale significantly differentiated between a group of officers who had received at least one significant disciplinary action during job tenure and a group of officers who had received no such actions. The effect size for the Hypomania scale in this study was .46, indicating that offending officers achieved higher scores on this scale.

In apparent contrast to these findings, Scogin, Schumacher, Gardner, and Chaplin (1995) found that one year following graduation from the police officer academy none of the MMPI scales were predictive of the dichotomized criteria of whether one or more or zero verbal, written, or vehicular reprimands had been received or of whether one or more citizens' complaints had been received. Note, however, that the data in this latter study, unlike that in the earlier studies, were collected after only one year of police work. Thus, it is possible that given more time officers might have displayed more counterproductive behaviors and thereby changed the results.

Recently, Cullen and Ones (2003) investigated the predictive validity of MMPI clinical scales in relation to a number of counterproductive and corrupt police behaviors, including drug and alcohol abuse, evidence tampering, perjury, excessive use of force, fire arms misuse, embezzlement, theft from property rooms, accepting bribes in exchange for restricted information about upcoming police raids, and agreeing not to apprehend known offenders or not to testify against offenders. Results indicated that scores on the Psychopathic Deviate scale were positively related to police corruption and that scores on the Hypochondriasis (*Hs*), Psychopathic Deviate, Schizophrenia (*Sc*), and Social Introversion scales were positively related to police counterproductivity.

Although studies investigating the relationship between MMPI scales and counterproductive police behavior do not yield identical findings, they do suggest some meaningful trends. In particular, replicated results for the Hypomania scale and the Psychopathic Deviate scale in relation to a number of diverse criteria, including violence (Hargrave et al., 1986), disciplinary days, and termination (Bartol, 1991; Costello et al., 1996; Hiatt & Hargrave, 1986), suggest the utility of traits such as impulsivity, rebelliousness, and hostility as predictors of a general counterproductivity criterion. In another context, a recent study of psychopathic and narcissistic personality styles in psychiatrists provides additional support for the MMPI Psychopathic Deviate scale in assessing personality problems. Garfinkel, Bagby, Waring, and Dorian (1997) conducted a follow-up evaluation of 70 first-year psychiatric residents who had taken a battery of psychological tests including the MMPI between 13 and 17 years earlier during their residency training. At the follow-up, two psychiatrists had had their licenses revoked because of repeated sexual boundary violations with their patients.

Both psychiatrists who lost their licenses were found to have significant character pathology (high Pd scores) on the MMPI.

Recently, Cullen, Ones, Viswesvaran, Drees, and Langkamp (2003) conducted a meta-analysis of the original MMPI for predicting job-relevant police behavior. The predictors included all of the MMPI clinical scales, as well as the *L*, *F*, and *K* (Correction) scales; and the criteria were overall job performance, disciplinary actions, and the decision about whether to select or reject police applicants. In conducting this meta-analysis, the authors utilized all published and unpublished studies up until 2003. They made corrections for unreliability for the criteria of overall job performance as well as corrections for range restriction in the MMPI scales. As expected, results indicated that the Pd scale predicted who would be hired, with an estimated population effect size of .34. In addition, there was some evidence that the Lie, Psychopathic Deviate, Psychasthenia (*Pt*), Hypomania, and Masculinity–Femininity (Mf) scales were valid predictors of overall job performance, with estimated validities of .17, .20, .17, .18, .18, and .17, respectively. However, due to the small number of studies included in this meta-analysis, it was not possible to reach any definitive conclusions by inspecting the credibility intervals.

ASSESSMENT OF DEFENSIVENESS

In personnel selection, the possibility that job applicants may present themselves in a socially desirable manner raises three key issues. One concern is that if response distortion takes place on personality-based selection measures because people are trying to present themselves in a desirable manner, the criterion-related validities of personality–performance relationships are in fact lower than they appear (Hough & Schneider, 1996). If social desirability does influence criterion-related validities, there are several ways it could do so. First, social desirability could moderate those validities. In this case, different criterion-related validities would be observed for groups of individuals who do not fake on personality measures and for those who do fake on those tests. In the personality domain, this question has been addressed on a number of occasions. Generally, results indicate that social desirability does not appreciably moderate criterion-related validities (Barrick & Mount, 1996; Hough, 1998; Hough, Eaton, Dunnette, Kamp, & McCloy, 1990). In the integrity-testing domain, Ones, Viswesvaran, and Schmidt (1993) found in their meta-analysis that, in respect to studies using predictive strategies and applicant samples, the predictive validity of integrity tests was .41 in relation to job performance and that there was no room for moderators to influence that relationship.Social desirability could also act as a mediator or suppressor variable. If social desirability were a mediator of the integrity–performance relationship, then partialing social desirability would lead to a dramatic decrease in the validities of personality tests. In contrast, if it were a suppressor variable, partialing social desirability would lead to an increase in the criterion-related validities of personality tests. These effects can be investigated by partialing social desirability from integrity–performance relationships and observing whether validities change. When these social desirability corrections have been made, results have generally yielded no change in criterion-related validities (Hough, 1998; Ones & Viswesvaran, 1998). Thus, it would appear that social desirability is neither a strong mediator nor a suppressor variable.If social desirability does not act as a moderator, mediator, or suppressor of integrity, the last remaining question is whether social desirability changes the rank ordering of applicants (this is particularly pertinent for measures that are used to rank applicants). Social desirability could change the rank order of applicants but not significantly affect overall criterion-related validities if it only changed the rank order of individuals at the higher end of the distribution of scores. If social desirability does affect such rank order changes, then it still has the potential to result in unfairness in the hiring process. Since some selection systems employ a top-down selection strategy, social desirability could lead to the hiring of many individuals who have lower scores on their integrity tests than they appear to have.

Some studies have demonstrated that social desirability can indeed change the rank order of applicants (e.g., Zickar, Rosse, Levin, & Hulin, 1997). Assuming that social desirability can affect the rank ordering of applicants, the important question is, what should be done about it? One option is to make social desirability corrections. The assumption in making these corrections is that we will be able to recover an individual's true score on the integrity instrument. If we can recover an individual's true score on the integrity test with these corrections, we will be able to make selection decisions based on this score alone. Such a result would increase the fairness of a selection system that uses integrity tests.

Unfortunately, some research suggests that such corrections do not help researchers to recover an individual's "true" score on personality tests. Using a within-subjects design, Ellingson, Sackett, and Hough (1999) examined the proportion of correct selection decisions made (a) when social desirability corrections were made and (b) when they were not made to personality instruments completed by participants instructed to fake-good on those inventories. Correct decisions were construed as selection decisions that would have been made on the basis of the same personality instruments completed when those same participants were asked to complete them honestly. Results indicated that at a variety of selection ratios, social desirability corrections unsystematically resulted in more correct decisions on some occasions and more incorrect decisions on an equal number of occasions.

In summary, although many of the original fears of the effect of social desirability on personality scale validities have been proven to be unfounded, there remains the important concern that social desirability may change the rank ordering of applicants, leading to nonoptimal selection decisions in many cases. It remains the task of researchers to devise a solution to this pressing problem. Keep in mind that with respect to MMPI–2 applications ranking of applicants is not a factor because the test is not usually used in this way.

Approaches to Understanding Defensive Responding With the MMPI–2

The detection of invalidating response conditions is important in all personality assessment situations that rely extensively on the individual's self-report. This is particularly important in personnel selection situations in which applicants for desirable jobs attempt to present themselves in an overly favorable light. Test defensiveness is the most common type of problem responding that employment practitioners encounter in that the applicant will minimize problems to such an extreme degree or present such a favorable picture of his or her adjustment as to invalidate the test. Test defensiveness and virtue claiming are common test-taking strategies in employment assessment and interview situations in personnel settings. Most job applicants attempt to put their best foot forward when they apply for a job. Pick up any "guide" written to aid job seekers and you will note that advice handed out to job applicants is geared toward making a good impression on prospective employers.

Two major MMPI–2–based approaches for appraising defensiveness and increasing honesty on the MMPI–2 are (a) validity scales designed to measure test-taking attitudes, such as the MMPI–2 *L* scale developed by Hathaway and McKinley (1940), the *K* scale developed by Meehl and Hathaway (1946), and the Superlative Self-Presentation scale (*S*) developed by Butcher and Han (1995); and (b) retesting under altered instructions—a procedure designed to lower defensiveness. Both of these strategies are described in detail in the following paragraphs.

Detecting Defensive Responding—The Superlative Self-Presentation Scale

The use of the *L* scale and the *K* scale to detect defensive responding is widely known because these scales have been used in MMPI interpretation since the 1940s. More recently, an additional measure was developed in a personnel setting in an effort to improve the detection of defensive responding and to study possible sources of defensive responding. In a study aimed at developing a measure for detecting excessively defensive and invalidating self-reports on the MMPI–2 among airline pilot applicants, Butcher and Han (1995) developed the Superlative Self-Presentation or

S scale. This scale addressed defensive responding in situations in which "test defensiveness" could be an important motivating condition.

In the construction of the S scale, Butcher and Han (1995) used as developmental samples 274 male airline applicants and the MMPI–2 normative sample (N = 1,138 men and 1,462 women). The normative research study included a sample of 822 normal couples that had taken the MMPI–2 and had rated each other on 110 personality variables that were used to identify potential correlates for the scale. The items for the S scale were empirically selected by examining item response differences between the airline pilot applicants—who tend to describe themselves in superlative terms in order to impress examiners—and normative men from the MMPI–2 restandardization sample. Next, the scale was refined by using internal consistency methods to ensure high scale homogeneity. The S scale was validated initially using the rating data available from the MMPI–2 standardization project noted earlier. The scale was shown to have a number of behavioral correlates reflecting the presentation of oneself as a well-controlled, virtuous, and problem-free person.

Finally, to evaluate whether the scale can address different motivations to deny problems, a set of S subscales was developed. The items were found to cluster into five distinct subgroups based on an item factor analysis of the 50-item scale (S). This analysis yielded five factors that were named *Beliefs in Human Goodness*, *Serenity*, *Contentment With Life*, *Patience–Denial of Irritability and Anger*, and *Denial of Moral Flaws*. Five subscales based on the components of the S scale emerged in the analysis:

1. *Beliefs in Human Goodness:* The items in this subscale deal with likely unrealistic values or goals and the assertion of vague, unrealistically positive attitudes about people in general.
2. *Serenity:* This subscale includes items that assert being calm and relaxed even in a stressful environment, having a characteristically low experience of tension or stress, and never worrying about anything.
3. *Contentment With Life:* These items emphasize an extremely positive view of one's life situation and an absence of self-doubt.
4. *Patience–Denial of Irritability and Anger:* These items address the person's claim that he or she never gets mad or becomes impatient with other people.
5. *Denial of Moral Flaws:* The items on this scale claim high moral values and the absence of habits such as using marijuana or using alcohol excessively.

In interpreting the S scale, the practitioner is encouraged to examine the relative elevations on the S subscales when the S scale is elevated. The relative elevation on particular subscales may provide the practitioner with clues as to ways the applicant might have expressed defensiveness.

Subsequent research on the *S* scale has shown it to be one of the strongest indicators of defensive responding (Archer, Handel, & Couvadelli, 2004; Bagby, Nicholson, et al., 1999; Bagby et al., 1997; Crespo & Gomez, 2003; Lim & Butcher, 1996). Moreover, one study reported that there were differences between people being evaluated in different settings on the *S* subscales: For example, airline pilots tended to show elevations on all of the *S* subscales and parents involved in child custody disputes tended to be elevated on *S4* (Patience–Denial of Irritability and Anger) and *S5* (Denial of Moral Flaws; Butcher, 1998a).

Retesting of Applicants to Reduce Defensive Responding Under Altered Instructions

Job applicants, as well as many people taking the MMPI–2 in forensic settings, approach the test items defensively—invalidating the results—in an effort to present a very favorable picture of themselves. Research has shown that giving applicants an opportunity to retake the test after informing them that they have invalidated their initial testing as a result of defensiveness can result in more usable test results (Fink & Butcher, 1972; Butcher, Morfitt, Rouse, & Holden, 1997). Butcher et al. (1997) found that about two-thirds of job applicants produced valid results when the test was readministered with the information that they had invalidated the initial test as a result of test defensiveness and were being allowed to retake the test. They were informed that the test contained means of detecting defensiveness; thus, they were encouraged to be honest in their responding during the retest. About 15% of the retest cases produce clinically significant results in the readministration; this suggests that some people do indeed mask psychological problems in their initial testing. The retest procedure has been employed effectively in a number of personnel contexts, and other studies have replicated the original Butcher et al. (1997) study (Cigrang & Staal, 2001; Gucker & McNulty, 2004).

Case Example. The results of a retest administration to lower defensiveness are shown in Figures 15.1 and 15.2. The applicant for an airline pilot position invalidated his initial testing as a result of defensive responding (see Figure 15.1). He was retested after being informed that his initial test was invalidated due to test defensiveness. He was provided the recommended retest instructions (see Butcher et al., 1997) and encouraged to respond to the items in a nondefensive manner. The resulting MMPI–2 profile was both valid and interpretable, and the second profile shows possible psychological problems that need to be given consideration.

One may wonder why the altered instructions could not simply be used in the initial assessment because many applicants are, in fact, defensive on the testing; and, as noted earlier, the test defensiveness clearly

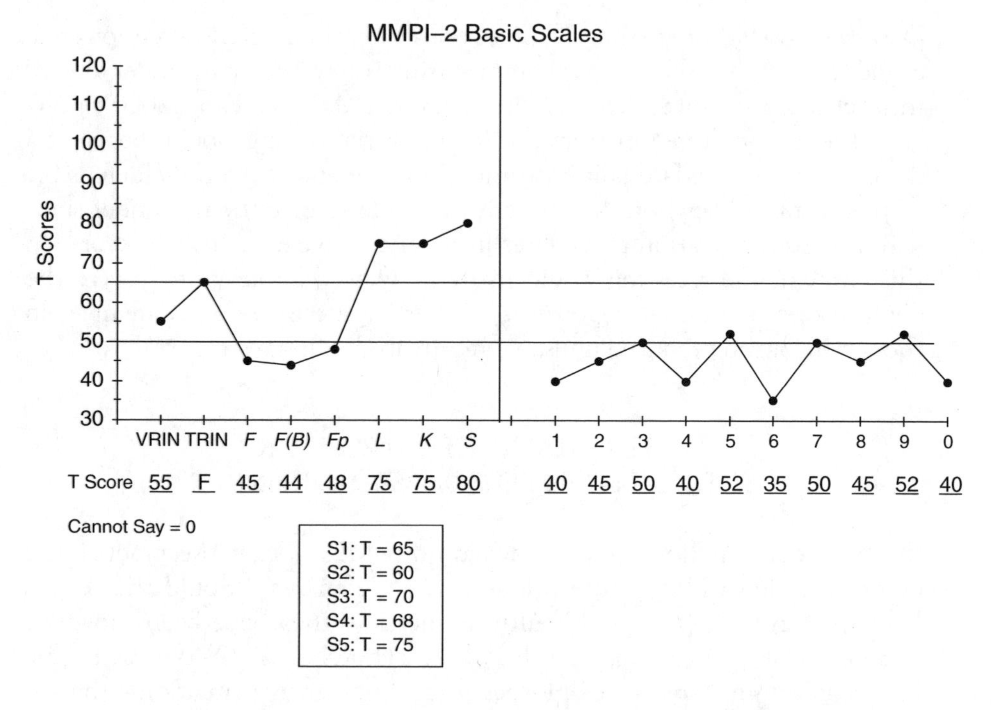

Figure 15.1. Initial MMPI–2 validity and clinical profile of a defensive airline pilot applicant.

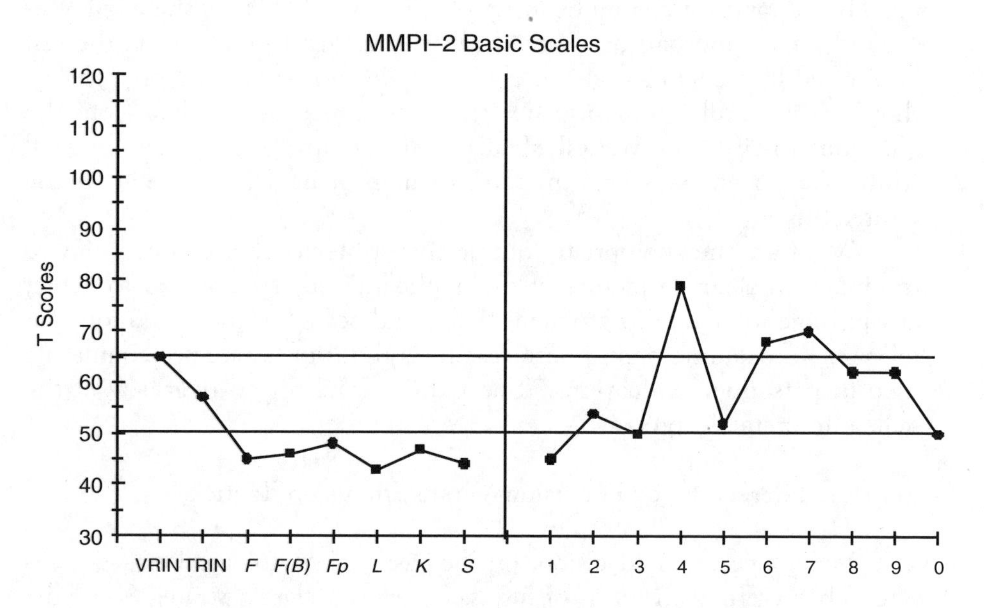

Figure 15.2. MMPI–2 validity and clinical retest profile of a defensive airline pilot applicant following instructions to reduce defensiveness.

masks psychopathology that becomes apparent when defenses are lowered. Some research has shown that administering the test initially under altered instructions does lower defensiveness (Butcher, Atlis, & Fang, 2000); however, the use of altered instructions in the initial testing would represent a deviation from standard administration practice and may not be defensible in the event of litigation. It is usually desirable to give the test under standard test administration procedures in order to have a defensible record. In this context, the retesting would likely be viewed as an effort to give the applicant an additional opportunity to participate in the assessment even though he or she produced unusable results in the first testing.

INTERPRETIVE STRATEGY FOR THE MMPI–2 IN PERSONNEL SCREENING

Once an applicant has produced an MMPI–2 that the practitioner determines is valid and interpretable (nondefensive), would the results likely be sensitive to mental health problems as they have been shown to be in clinical settings? Research has shown (Butcher, 1979) that when the MMPI is administered to employees in a nondefensive situation—that is, when they were not being screened for employment but were already employed, they tended to respond in a straightforward manner acknowledging a broad range of mental health problems. About 23% of the employees showed some symptoms or mental health adjustment problems on the test as assessed by elevations on the clinical scales—a percentage of problems that is comparable to mental health surveys such as the data from the National Institute of Mental Health Catchment Area epidemiological study (Regier et al., 1984) on rates of mental health problems in the United States.

What are the appropriate interpretive strategies that can be followed to obtain an accurate picture of the applicant's adjustment and to detect any possible work-related problems that could occur? In the discussion that follows, we examine appropriate test interpretation strategies commonly used in personnel evaluations. (See Exhibit 15.2 for an overview of the scale interpretation process.)

Personnel Screening by Exclusion Versus Inclusion Tactics

Making personnel decisions on the basis of psychological test scores is often characterized in terms of *inclusion* versus *exclusion* strategies. Under inclusion strategies, an applicant would be considered eligible for the desired position if his or her test scores on a particular variable were in a range that suggested positive qualities needed for the job, such as having high scores on an IQ test that would qualify the person for a position that

EXHIBIT 15.2
Highlight: Interpretation of the MMPI–2 in Personnel Settings

- Personality assessment is often mandated in personnel evaluations for which public responsibility and emotional stability are key to the occupation.
- To be recommended for use in personnel evaluations, a test should possess a substantial and relevant research base.
- The defensiveness that is common among applicants needs to be addressed.
- The applicant's performance on Scale *S,* particularly the relative performance on *S* subscales, can provide an appraisal of the applicant's defensiveness.
- Retesting under instructions to be less defensive can significantly improve the applicant's cooperativeness in providing personality information.
- The use of non-*K*-corrected profiles in interpretation should be avoided at this time because most of the validity studies on MMPI–2 in personnel screening have used *K*-corrected scores.
- Psychological tests are often used in personnel screening situations to detect negative characteristics that would exclude the applicant from the successful applicant pool. For example, a significant elevation on the Pd scale would suggest likely behavior problems; thus, the applicant would be rejected from the position because of these negative characteristics.
- Research has supported several MMPI–2 scales in assessment of counterproductive behavior among police applicants, particularly the Pd, the *Ma,* and the MAC–R scales.
- Tests can also be used in screening to identify candidates that possess positive attributes thought to be important to the job. For example, a high score on the Ego Strength scale and an average Si score on the MMPI–2 suggest that the individual is likely to manage stress well and work well with others.
- Evaluate any negative personality factors that may suggest rule violations or acting-out behavior (e.g., high elevations on ASP [Antisocial Practices], Pd, or DISC [Disconstraint]) or that may suggest a disruptive lifestyle resulting from substance use problems (e.g., high elevations on MAC–R, APS [Addiction Potential Scale], or AAS [Addiction Acknowledgment Scale]).
- High scores on Pd, ASP, or the Authority Problems Harris–Lingoes subscale can suggest authority conflicts.
- Assess the capability of working with others using measures such as the Si scale (particularly high scores suggest social avoidance) and measures of aggressive interpersonal style such as the DISC, Pd, Type A, and ANG (Anger) scales.
- Evaluate possible stress management problems including symptoms of negative affect, depression, hypersensitivity, and social ineffectiveness and particularly high scores on *D* (Depression), *Pt,* NEGE (Negative Emotionality–Neuroticism), and Si.

requires a particular level of intelligence. This approach to interpretation of the MMPI–2 in personnel settings examines potentially positive characteristics based on certain scale elevations or, in some cases, lack of elevation. For example, to determine whether a person would be assertive in interpersonal situations one might look for high scores on *Do* (Dominance) and low scores on Si. For a summary of possible personality characteristics that can be addressed by MMPI–2 scales, see Table 15.1.

Using exclusion rules, an applicant would be eliminated from the acceptable applicant pool if test scores were elevated in a range that is typically associated with negative characteristics such as personality problems, emotional instability, or addiction. For example, a score of 80 on the

TABLE 15.1
Overview of MMPI-Based Personality Characteristics Central to Personnel Setting Applications

		MMPI–2 factors	Relevant sources
Nondefensive approach to dealing with conflicts/ relationships	• Nondefensive; not rigid, or evasive in dealing with others • Effective in dealing with conflict • Tends not to be self-defensive under pressure	• Score on the *S* scale below a T of 69 • *L* and *K* score below 64 • *Hy* (Hysteria) and *Pa* (Paranoia) scale in the normal range, equal to or less than a T of 64	Bieliauskas (1980); Binder, Mayman, & Doehrman (1974); Burish & Houston (1976); Butcher & Han (1995); Ganellen (1994); Newberry (1967)
Stress tolerance/ emotional control	• Does not panic under stress • Makes appropriate decisions under pressure • Does not react to stress with negative behaviors such as alcohol abuse, physical symptoms, and so on	• Within interpretive limits on validity scales • Not overly defensive or inconsistent in response pattern • Absence of profile elevations on clinical and content scales • Substance abuse indicators in low range • Interpersonal indicators such as MDS (Marital Distress Scale) and Si within an acceptable range	Bartol (1991); Ben-Porath (1990b); Biondi et al. (1986); Butcher (2002a); Carr & Graham (1996); Cimbura (2000); Cook & Wherry (1950); Cook et al. (1996); Heilbrun (1984); Hjemboe & Butcher (1991); Kasl (1970); Merbaum (1977); Oetting (1966); Sommer & Lasry (1984); Taylor (1958); Thomas-Riddle (2000); Torki (2000)
Acceptance of feedback, supervision	• Does not externalize blame • Does not become defensive when criticized • Accepts authority	• Pd, *Ma,* and ASP within normal limits • *Pa* scale within the normal range, neither too high or extremely low • *K, S,* and *L* within the normal range • Low score on Authority Problems subscale and DISC	Butcher et al. (1990); Finn (1996a); Harris & Lingoes (1968); Harkness, Royer, & Gill (1996)

TABLE 15.1
(Continued)

		MMPI–2 factors	Relevant sources
Good impulse control	• Thinks situations through before acting • Avoids making rash decisions	• Pd and *Ma* within the normal range (below 65T) • APS below 65T • Disconstraint scale within the normal range	Graham (2000); Harkness, McNulty, Ben-Porath, & Graham (1999); Weed, Butcher, & Ben-Porath (1995)
Positive attitude/ absence of negative attitudes	• Demonstrates positive social skills • Does not hold an overly cynical view of others • Shows trust • Takes difficult circumstances in stride	• Low score on *Pa* (below 65T) • Low score on CYN (Cynicism), *Ho* (Hostility) • Shows no problems with anxiety or depressed mood • NEGE not elevated	Aston & Lavery (1993); Banreti-Fuchs (1975); Chansky & Bregman (1957); Cole (1956); David (1968); Ekman, Friesen, & Lutzker (1962); Gilbride & Hebert (1981); Gough (1949); Gough, McClosky, & Meehl (1952); Han, Weed, Calhoun, & Butcher (1995); Harkness, McNulty, Ben-Porath, & Graham (1999); Jensen (1957); Kennedy, Nielson, Lindner, Turner, & Moon (1960); Schofield (1953)
Integrity	• Trustworthy • Does not bend rules to suit own interests • Shows no problems with authority • Accepts responsibility for own actions	• No elevation on ASP • No elevation on Pd, especially the Authority Problems scale • *Pa* not elevated at 65T or above • Substance abuse scales within the normal range (no greater than 60T) • *Re* (Responsibility) score greater than 60T	Butcher et al. (1990); Gough et al. (1952); Harris & Lingoes (1968); Weed et al. (1995)

(*continued*)

TABLE 15.1
(Continued)

		MMPI–2 factors	Relevant sources
Dependability/ reliability	• Not a procrastinator • Careful at tasks • Free of personality problems, such as impulsivity, that could create difficulties on the job	• Normal range validity pattern • Scales 4, 7, ASP, and WRK (Negative Work Attitudes) in the normal range (below 65T) • Substance abuse indicators below 60T • Scale 9 below 70T • Elevations on *Es* (Ego Strength), *Re*	Derksen et al. (2003); Graham (2000); Weed et al. (1995); Zuckerman & Link (1968)
Shows initiative/ achievement motivation/ leadership	• Can work without supervision • Energetic • Absence of disabling psychopathology	• Absence of severe psychopathology • For example, has low scores on clinical dimensions such as depression, anxiety • Si score below 60T • Ma score a high point, but not extremely elevated	Armilla (1967); Butcher & Williams (2000); Carson et al. (1966); Cardwell (1982); Dubno (1961); Hargrave et al. (1986); Harrell & Harrell (1973); Hartshorne (1956); Kelly (1974); Sobchik (1989); Williamson et al. (1952)
Conforms to rules and regulations	• Follows rules and regulations • Respects authority • Followed recommended testing procedures	• Cannot Say less than 2 • DISC score at or below 64T • Pd and ASP at or below 64T • No Authority Problems subscale elevations • *Ma* within normal range	Butcher et al. (1990); Harkness, McNulty, Ben-Porath, & Graham (1999)
Anger control	• Restrained • Shows no interpersonal relationship problems • Low tendencies toward reactive aggression	• ANG score within the normal range • Pd below 65T • AGGR (Aggressiveness) within the normal range • *Pa* and *Sc* within the normal range • *Ho* less than 55T	Biaggio & Godwin (1987); Blumenthal, Barefoot, Burg, & Williams (1987); Butcher et al. (1990); Carr & Graham (1996); Clark (1994); Ernst, Francis, & Enwonwu

TABLE 15.1
(Continued)

		MMPI–2 factors	Relevant sources
			(1990); Greene, Coles, & Johnson (1994); Han et al. (1995); Harkness, McNulty, Ben-Porath, & Graham (1999); Kinder, Curtis, & Kalichman (1986); Leiker & Hailey (1988); O'Laughlin (1994); Schill & Wang (1990); Strassberg (1997); Williams (1980b)
Adaptability/ flexibility	• Shows the capacity to change behavior to meet new demands • Accepting of new job demands • Can work on more than one task at a time	• *Pt,* ANX (Anxiety), OBS (Obsessiveness) below 65 T • *Ma* score above 50 • Low *D* score • Si score below 60	Armilla (1967); Campos (1989); Fulkerson (1956, 1957); Hargrave et al. (1986); Hiatt & Hargrave (1988a, 1988b)
Vigilance/ attention to detail	• Can maintain a steady pace • Does not become impatient or irritable under routine or repetitive tasks	• *Ma* score below 65T • Low AGGR scores • Pd below 65T • Low OBS and *Pt* (i.e., not excessively focused upon detail)	Adair (1964); Butcher et al. (1990); Harkness, McNulty, Ben-Porath, & Graham (1999); Hilakivi, Alihanka, Airikkala, & Laitinen (1992); Hoffmann (1970); Strauss, Brandt, & McSorley (1986); Wink & Donahue (1997)
Interpersonal sensitivity	• Aware of the feelings of others • Capable of dealing with interpersonal issues in an effective manner • Refrains from rude or offensive comments	• Si score below 65T • *Pa* score below 65T • *Pt* and *D* below 65T • For males, Mf score above 50T; for females, Mf score below 65T	Graham, (2000); Guetrer (1994); Libet & Lewinsohn (1973); Nair (1974); Williams (1980b)

(*continued*)

TABLE 15.1
(Continued)

		MMPI–2 factors	Relevant sources
Interpersonal interest/social concern	• Shows interest in being with others • Concern for others	• For males, Mf above 60T; for females, Mf below 60T • Si scores below 55T • *Pa* below 60T • Pd and *Ma* below 65T	Blackburn (1971); Brophy (1996); Gough et al. (1952); Williams (1980b); Zuckerman (1972)
Teamwork/ capability of working with others	• Developing and maintaining good working relationships • Acceptance of authority and supervision • Positive approach to problems	• Low score on *Ho* • Low score on Authority Problems • Below 60T on Cynicism • Si score below 60T • No interfering clinical elevations (e.g., *D,* Pd, *Pt*) • No cognitive aberrations as found in *Pa* and *Sc* • Accepts responsibility—low Pd, *Pa* • High *Re* and *Es*	Butcher et al. (1990); Cook & Medley (1954); Gough et al. (1952); Graham (2000); Harris & Lingoes (1968)

Ma scale would suggest likely impulsivity and lack of judgment. This latter strategy is often used with a pathologically oriented instrument such as the MMPI–2 with its extensive focus on work-negative behaviors. We next examine a case of a police department applicant with a history of acting out problems.

Case Example: Police Department Applicant

Applicant: W. J.
Age: 25
Education: 16 years

W. J. was an applicant for a position as a police officer for a police force in a suburb of a large Midwestern metropolitan community. As part of the application process, he was interviewed and administered the MMPI–2 (see Figures 15.3 and 15.4) and a check of his motor vehicle record and financial records were obtained.

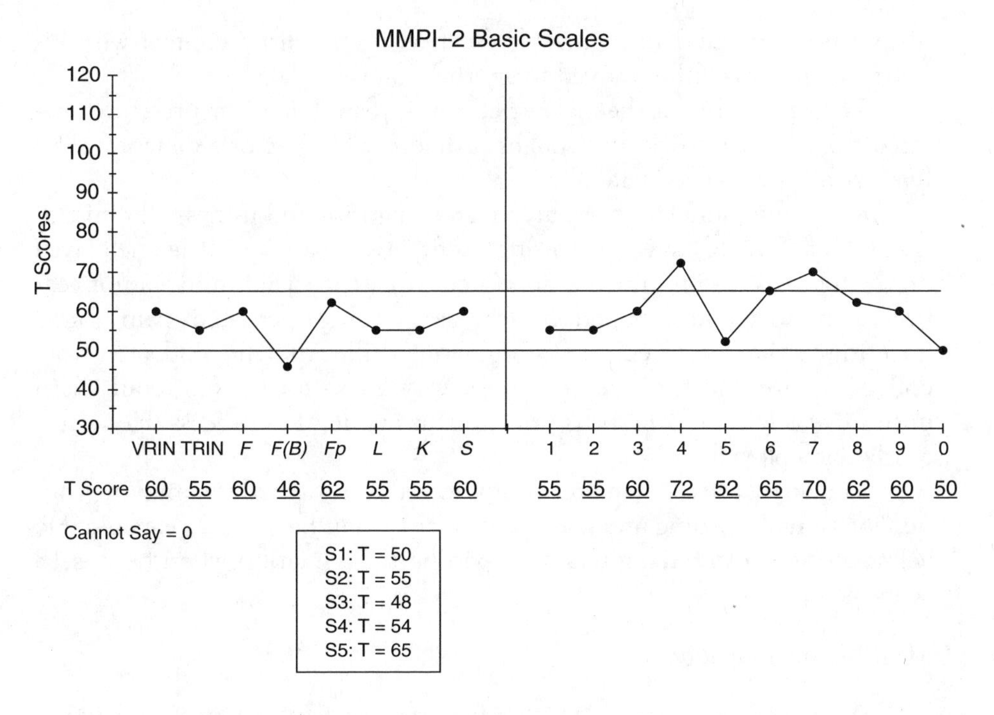

Figure 15.3. MMPI–2 validity and clinical profile of a police applicant.

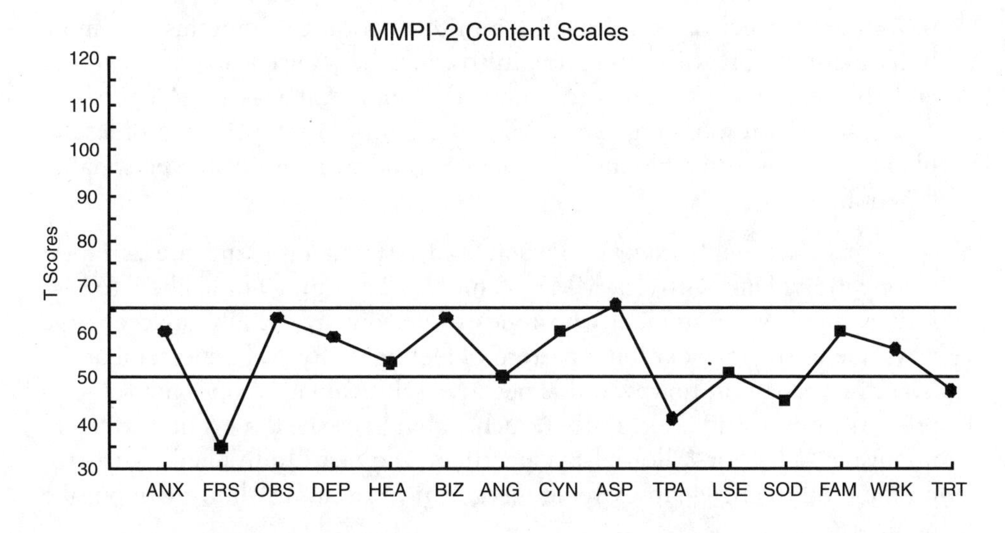

Figure 15.4. MMPI–2 content scale profile of a police applicant.

Mr. J. was the youngest of three children. His parents were divorced when he was 9 years of age following several years of family turmoil. He was raised by his mother, a middle-school teacher. His two older siblings had already graduated from high school and were out of the home at the time of his parents' divorce. During his adolescence, he had little contact with his father because his father moved to another state.

The applicant has been married for 4 years but is, at present, separated from his wife who has sought a divorce. He has one daughter who lives with his estranged wife.

Mr. J. completed a liberal arts degree majoring in business administration with a C (2.40) average. During his first two years of college, he played on the football team; however, he was cut from the squad in his junior year because he was unable to perform well as a result of persistent pain from a knee injury that occurred during a practice drill. After he graduated from college, he worked for 2 years as a security guard for a large retail chain until he was laid off 3 months prior to this application process. He is currently unemployed.

The applicant's driving record indicated that he had two moving traffic violations (speeding and careless driving) when he was 20 years old. He acknowledged also having had an "open bottle" violation when he was 18 years old.

MMPI–2 Interpretation

Validity Considerations. The applicant's initial MMPI–2 was invalid as a result of test defensiveness. He was given the opportunity to retake the test under instructions encouraging him to respond to the items in a more frank manner. On the second administration, he showed no defensiveness and the resulting profiles were valid; the applicant was more open and cooperative in responding to the MMPI–2 items. His MMPI–2 profiles are likely to be interpretable and represent a good estimate of his personality functioning.

Personality and Behavior. Personal adjustment problems are common among individuals with this MMPI–2 profile. The applicant is likely to be a rather impulsive individual who tends to act out in socially unacceptable ways. He or she may exhibit a pattern of feeling guilty and remorseful about his or her behavior; however, this negative self-evaluation does not serve to prevent future acting out. Rather, such individuals show a cyclic pattern of impulsive behavior followed by superficial remorse. Individuals with this profile tend to engage in extreme self-gratification in an almost compulsive manner.

Some individuals with this profile develop physical symptoms and feelings of anxiety following their periods of acting out. This tension and anxiety appear to be temporary and do not seem to deter future excesses. Individuals with this profile tend to be rather dependent and quite insecure. They manipulate other people to secure their own ends. They may express superficial guilt about having taken advantage of other people.

Some individuals with this profile appear quite helpless and unable to manage their problems following periods of acting out. In these situations, they may seek reassurance and support from people around them.

This MMPI–2 pattern indicates periods of acting out followed by feelings of superficial guilt and shame about this behavior. It appears to be a repetitive, enduring pattern. Many persons with this profile show a pattern of antisocial and antiauthority attitudes.

Possible Employment Problems. Law enforcement applicants with this extreme MMPI–2 profile should be carefully evaluated in employment assessment. Personality or adjustment problems are likely to occur. Authority problems and lack of social judgment may be factors in poor job performance.

Individuals with this MMPI–2 profile tend to encounter problems because of their impulsive behavior. Personal, work-related, and family problems are common. These individuals also tend to be quite manipulative and are usually able to get people to give them a second or third chance to do better. Their pattern of acting out, however, is likely to continue.

Given the MMPI–2 elevations and the history of problem behavior, the applicant was not recommended for employment.

SPECIAL CONSIDERATIONS IN MMPI–2 INTERPRETATION IN PERSONNEL SETTINGS

Nongendered T Scores for MMPI–2

Many personality measures, such as the MMPI–2, have been developed using gender-specific norms—that is, men are compared with men and women with women. This standard interpretive procedure results, at least in part, because the original work of Hathaway and McKinley (1940) noted that there were some gender differences found in some of the comparison samples they used in developing the original MMPI, although these were minor. Throughout the MMPI's history, gender-specific norms have been used in interpretation.

However, in some personnel selection situations, the use of gender-specific norms has been questioned. Comparing men with men and women with women can give the appearance of exclusiveness in the selection process and can be considered possibly unfair to women because a different standard is being used for men and women. Furthermore, the Civil Rights Act of 1991 has made the use of gender-specific norms illegal within group norms. In order to address this issue, gender-neutral norms (rather than gender-specific norms) were developed in a study with the MMPI–2

(Tellegen, Butcher, & Hoegland, 1993). On most scales, the differences between the T scores were minimal—and a given raw score produced similar T scores for both distributions. More recently, Ben-Porath and Forbey (2003) used the MMPI–2 normative sample to provide nongendered scores for most MMPI–2 scales. Note that T scores generated from one set tend to be highly comparable to those generated from the other norms.

Cautions in Using Unproven MMPI–2 Measures in Personnel Screening

Some measures that have been developed for the MMPI–2 have not been found to be effective in personnel screening. This could be because of the general mind-set among applicants to present defensively or perhaps because the scales have been insufficiently researched with this population to allow confident interpretation.

Use of Non–K-Corrected Profiles in Personnel Screening

As described in chapter 2, the *K* weights were developed by Meehl and Hathaway (1946) in an effort to improve the discrimination of cases in a psychiatric setting by correcting some clinical scales to detect psychopathology in patients who were overly defensive during the administration. At the time, five MMPI scales (*Hy*, Pd, *Pt*, *Sc*, and *Ma*) were found to work more effectively by adding a portion of the *K* scale to the raw score. Although most authorities conclude that the *K* scale has been shown to be effective at detecting defensive responses and problem denial (Butcher & Williams, 2000; Graham, 2000; Greene, 2000), the *K* weights have not been proven uniformly valuable in correcting for defensiveness (Archer, Fontaine, & McCrae, 1998; Sines, Baucom, & Gruba, 1979). Empirical efforts to improve the correction factor by modifying the weights have not proven effective. Weed (1993) attempted, albeit unsuccessfully, to increase the discriminative power of the correction for defensive profiles by using different weights. However, he found no other combination of weights to be effective at increasing the discrimination.

Most MMPI studies since 1946 have been conducted using *K*-corrected T scores. Butcher and Tellegen (1978) and Butcher, Graham, and Ben-Porath (1995) encouraged researchers to include non-*K*-corrected scores in MMPI validity research so that ultimately non-*K*-corrected scores could be confidently included in interpretive approaches to the test. However, validity research has not yet produced a sufficient validity database to support the interpretation of non-*K*-corrected scores for most applications, including personnel decisions.

What are the differences between *K*-corrected and non-*K*-corrected profiles? When comparing *K*- and non-*K*-corrected profiles on clients, we find in most instances that there is not much difference between the two methods. In these cases, the profile shapes and elevations between the two profiles are often comparable. Research too has demonstrated that there are usually no differences between *K*-corrected and non-*K*-corrected scores when external criteria (such as therapist's ratings) are used to verify their accuracy (Barthlow, Graham, Ben-Porath, Tellegen, & McNulty, 2002), although this conclusion has not always been obtained (Detrick, Chibnall, & Rosso, 2001). In some instances, non-*K*-corrected profiles can appear dramatically different from the *K*-corrected profile and can result in a different code type. The practitioner needs to be aware that, in some cases when the *K* is elevated and *K* correction is applied, some of the clinical scale elevations (e.g., on *K*-corrected scales such as *Sc* or *Pt*) can be accounted for by the elevation on *K* alone. That is, the person may have actually endorsed few (or none) of the other items contained on the scale. In such cases, the practitioner is then provided with an interpretive dilemma—which of the two profiles should be used in the interpretation.

The current state of the research suggests that even though the *K* scale does not operate as a correction for defensiveness as Meehl and Hathaway (1946) had hoped, the practice of correcting for *K* in interpreting profiles still continues in MMPI–2 use because much of the empirical research supporting test interpretation of the clinical scales involves *K*-corrected scores. In personnel screening, the non-*K*-corrected profile has not been sufficiently researched to serve as a confident basis for interpretation. The interpreter has a much more extensive research base for interpreting the *K*-corrected profile than for the non-*K*-corrected profile.

At this point, we know that *K*-corrected scores operate successfully as a sign that the person has approached the assessment task in an overly favorable manner. Therefore, a T score on *K* that exceeds the 70T level is not likely to be useful in providing self-reported personality information to enter into the decision process. Defensive profiles in this range should not be interpreted (or included into research studies) because interpretive errors can occur in profiles that have had a lot of *K* added to them.

The O–H Scale

The O–H (Overcontrolled Hostility) scale (Megargee, Cook, & Mendelsohn, 1967) was developed for use in forensic assessments as a measure of overcontrolled aggression, which is the tendency of some people to be so overcontrolled in dealing with conflict that they are actually unable to deal with severe emotional conflict when it occurs. These people lose control and act out in aggressive ways, such as killing someone in a sudden rage. This scale was developed empirically using as the developmental sample men who had acted out in extreme and uncontrolled ways.

Although this scale addresses the control dimension well (people who have high scores on O–H tend to be emotionally repressed or overcontrolled), it does not assess the "acting-out" component sufficiently to complete the picture for predicting aggression. In other words, a high O–H score measures overcontrol but does not assess aggression. The base rate of high scores on O–H in applicants for employment is high because they tend to present themselves in a highly socialized manner producing high scores on the O–H scale on average. For example, the average score of airline pilot applicants (Butcher, 1994b) on the O–H scale is 62T. Most applicants produce an elevated score on O–H indicating a picture of overcontrol or, rather, socialization; but a high score does not address hostility, either overt or suppressed.

The Restructured Clinical Scales

The Restructured Clinical (RC) Scales (Tellegen et al., 2003) were developed in an effort to improve the traditional clinical scales by reducing item overlap, lowering scale intercorrelation, eliminating subtle items, and improving convergent and discriminant validity. The RC Scales were recommended as supplemental measures and not intended to replace the original clinical scales (see also the discussion in chap. 1). The scales were developed through several steps:

1. Development of the "Demoralization scale." The authors removed items from the eight clinical scales that tended to be influenced by a set of general maladjustment items. Initial construction aimed to capture "demoralization," a factor that was viewed as common to most clinical scales, resulting in concept overlap.
2. Constructed "seed" scales for the eight clinical scales by removing the demoralization component. Other items were removed for other reasons, for example, the "correction" items that the original authors included on Scale 2.
3. Derived the RC Scales by including other related MMPI–2 items. This was accomplished by correlating the "seed" scales with the entire MMPI–2 item pool to obtain other items that measure the basic constructs.
4. Conducted both internal and external validity analyses to further understand the operation of the scales.

The authors provided analyses of the RC Scales' internal validity and predictive validity with mental health patients from the Portage Path Outpatient Sample (Graham, Ben-Porath, & McNulty, 1999) and two inpatient samples from an unpublished study by Arbisi and Ben-Porath (as cited in Tellegen et al., 2003) showing that the RC Scales have an equal or greater degree of association to external behavioral correlates as the traditional clinical scales. Although the initial publication of the RC Scales did not present information on the relationships of the RC Scales and other widely used MMPI–2 measures such as the MMPI–2 content scales, recent data (Forbey, Ben-Porath, & Tellegen, 2004) suggests a high degree of relationship between some RC Scales and the MMPI–2 content scales. The scale construction strategies used in the development of the RC Scales ensured that the scales were unidimensional in scope and homogeneous in content, similar to the MMPI–2 content scales. At this point, the extent to which the RC Scales operate like the MMPI–2 content scales is not known. If the RC Scales turn out to function in a manner similar to that of the MMPI–2 content scales, then they may have more limited applicability in settings like personnel screening in which the obvious item content is somewhat transparent and clearly avoided by persons wishing to make a good impression.

As noted by the RC Scale authors (Tellegen et al., 2003), the RC Scales are not viewed as replacements for the MMPI–2 clinical scales; rather, they are only a means of refining interpretation. However, some scales are so different from the original scale as to require a new nomological network for interpretation. For example, the reconstruction of Scale *Hy* as a cynicism scale may have substantially altered the scale's utility as a "refinement" measure of Scale 3; there is actually a high negative correlation (–.42) between the RC3 scale and its parent scale, *Hy*, indicating that they are really different scales. Nichols (in press) refers to this change in the measurement focus of the scales as "construct drift." The data and analysis Nichols provides suggest that the RC3 scale is not measuring the constructs addressed by the *Hy* scale, a scale that is often the primary elevation for personnel applicants. In personnel settings, an elevation on the *Hy* scale reflects a personality style that is comprised of the reliance upon denial and repressive defenses to deal with conflict situations. Extreme scores on Scale 3 are interpreted as reflecting a personality style in which the person is superficial and possesses ineffective means of resolving interpersonal conflict situations other than by using, for example, somatic symptoms. The reshaping of this scale to measure cynicism (a construct that is already measured well by the MMPI–2 content CYN scale) may limit its usability as a refinement measure for the *Hy* scale because the content of the scale has been substantially modified away from the original.

The initial validation studies for the RC Scales included inpatient and outpatient samples but have not been studied systematically in the assessment of applicants in personnel settings. There is some early indication (Butcher, 2003c) that the RC Scales may underrepresent problems in personnel settings, that is, they often do not reach the interpretive level (T = 65) even when the clinical scale is elevated to a T score greater than 65—a situation that often affects content scales as a result of the saturation of obvious psychopathology items. The RC Scales should not be used for making employment decisions until a substantial number of validity studies are available in personnel settings.

SUMMARY

Objective personality assessment has a long history, which began with the development of a personnel selection program for the U.S. military in World War I. Personality assessment has subsequently expanded greatly with the development of many assessment procedures and has been used in many different applied contexts. Personality tests are widely used in government and business to appraise the suitability of applicants for various critical occupations. Moreover, in a number of occupations, such as police, firefighters, and nuclear power plant employees, employers are obliged to conduct extensive personnel evaluations.

The MMPI–2 is widely used in government and industry to assess personality factors for job placement. The test provides clues as to possible unsuitable personality characteristics, for example, counterproductive and corrupt police behaviors, including drug and alcohol abuse, evidence tampering, perjury, excessive use of force, fire arms misuse, embezzlement, and theft from property rooms. Research linking certain MMPI scale scores and disciplinary days are numerous. Studies have provided evidence that the Lie, Psychopathic Deviate, Psychasthenia, Hypomania, and Masculinity–Femininity scales were valid predictors of overall job performance.

Test defensiveness among job applicants is a common type of problem; thus, the detection of invalidating response conditions is important in all personality assessment situations that rely extensively on the individual's self-report. Among personality questionnaires, the MMPI–2 provides the broadest and most extensive scales for detecting defensiveness in job applicants. The traditional MMPI scales *L* and *K* are effective at detecting virture claiming and defensiveness on the test. A newer scale, the *S* scale, was developed in a personnel screening context to assess defensiveness. The *S* scale contains five subscales that can aid the practitioner in examining possible motivations for defensive responding on the test.

An important method for reducing the defensiveness of applicants is to retest defensive applicants who invalidate their initial test. Research has shown that giving applicants an opportunity to retake the MMPI–2 after informing them that they have invalidated their initial testing as a result of defensiveness can result in more usable test results. About two-thirds of job applicants produced valid results when the test was readministered with modified instructions. Moreover, about 15% of the retest cases produce clinically significant results in the readministration, suggesting that this procedure can detect applicants with MMPI–2–based psychopathology upon retesting. Once a valid, interpretable MMPI–2 protocol is obtained, standard test interpretation strategies and inferences can be drawn in personnel evaluations as in other MMPI–2 contexts.

16

USE OF THE MMPI–2 IN PERSONAL INJURY AND DISABILITY EVALUATIONS

PAUL A. ARBISI

Claims for federal disability through the social security system have steadily increased over the last decade with the number of workers receiving disability benefits climbing from 3 million in 1990 to 5.42 million currently. Further, between 1999 and 2003, the initial claims for disability increased from 457,823 to 592,692 (for current figures, see: http://www.ssa.gov/finance). The reason for this increase in disability awards is multifaceted but clearly tied to economic conditions and the broadening of the definition of *disability* to include mental health problems. In fact, back trouble and mental stresses are the two most frequently cited reasons for disability claims both for social security benefits and through private insurers. In the Veterans Benefits Administration, 500,000 veterans receive medical care and disability payments for posttraumatic stress disorder (PTSD) with a large number of veterans continuing to apply for benefits based on claims related to PTSD (National Center for Veterans Analysis and Statistics, 1995). Additionally, clients may present to psychologists for treatment after a personal injury resulting from an accident or a hostile work environment. Thus, the increasing rates of disability claims and the regularity with which individuals suffer personal injuries suggest that psychologists will frequently see patients who present with problems that may serve as the basis for a claim of disability or compensation. Consequently, the practicing psychologist must become familiar with disability issues and be prepared to support assertions made during the course of evaluation and treatment related to causality and the nature of the psychological injury and subsequent disability. Objective measures of psychopathology such as the MMPI–2 can greatly assist the practitioner in making judgments regarding the validity of a claim of disability, support an opinion regarding the level of distress that may lead to compromised adaptive functioning, and serve as a cause of damages.

GENERAL ISSUES RELATED TO DISABILITY OR PERSONAL INJURY EVALUATIONS

Disability and personal injury evaluations differ from psychological evaluations—for which the focus is diagnosis or treatment planning—in several important ways. (Exhibit 16.1 summarizes the contextual aspects of psychological evaluations conducted for disability or personal injury.) First, the mental health professional's client may not be the person that is being evaluated. For example, often an attorney in the context of a dispute over a disability award will refer a claimant to a psychologist for an evaluation. As part of the referral, the claimant may have signed a release specifying that the recipient of the report is to be the attorney and not the claimant. Likewise, if an insurance provider contacts the psychologist to provide an examination, the claimant often waives his or her right to see the report and the examiner is specifically prohibited from sharing an opinion or discussing the findings with the claimant. The insurance company may not make the report available to the claimant or may, in fact, only release the report to the claimant's attorney during the course of discovery.

EXHIBIT 16.1
Highlight: Contextual Aspects of Psychological Evaluations Conducted for Disability or Personal Injury

- The client is the person or agency who contracted with the examiner to conduct the evaluation and is not necessarily the individual being evaluated.
- Frequently, a treatment relationship is not established and, in fact, is often explicitly excluded.
- The evaluation may be perceived as adversarial by the examinee.
- The work product and conclusions generated from the evaluation will be carefully scrutinized and judged.
- Deliberate attempts to distort or alter the clinical presentation may be present.

Although it is relatively clear who the client is when the claimant is referred from an attorney working on behalf of an insurance carrier or the Veterans Benefits Administration for a compensation and pension examination, the client of record is less clear under other circumstances. For example, within the Veterans' Administration (VA) health care system, any evaluation for PTSD may be a disability evaluation since the establishment of an independent diagnosis of PTSD outside of the official disability examination process is thought to lend credibility to the veteran's claim. Thus, veterans are frequently directed by their veterans' service officer, a Veterans Benefits advocate, to present to a VA mental health center and request an evaluation for PTSD. A similar scenario can occur when individuals who are injured in an accident are instructed by their attorney to seek treatment. The evaluation and subsequent treatment may serve as the foundation for a claim of consequential emotional injury.

An *independent psychological examination* (IPE), an examination provided by an unbiased psychologist with no prior relationship with the examinee, often specifically precludes the development of a treatment relationship; that is, the referral source may stipulate that the examiner not provide recommendations, advice, or any treatment to the claimant. Finally, someone most certainly carefully scrutinizes the evaluation. Decisions regarding the award of disability benefits or monetary compensation after a personal injury are based on the treatment records and the evaluation completed by the treatment provider. The records generated as a result of the contact with the litigant are released to the disability carrier or to the court to aid in making a decision regarding compensation or disability award. Often, another medical expert examines those records to determine whether the diagnosis and resulting treatment are appropriate and consistent with published guidelines. Further, if a dispute arises over the disability carrier's decision and the proceedings become adversarial, an independent mental health professional is likely to review those records to determine if the assessment was properly conducted and the conclusions reached regarding diagnosis, treatment, and subsequent disability are reasonable.

Unlike psychological evaluations focused on treatment planning or diagnostic clarification, evaluations within the context of personal injury or disability may be adversarial. For example, the examiner, despite claims of independence, is often perceived by the examinee as an agent of the insurance carrier or of the federal government. Further, when the evaluation occurs within the context of an IPE, the claimant has most likely undergone an earlier evaluation conducted by his or her care provider and has already received a diagnosis. The IPE is scheduled because a dispute has arisen between the care provider/claimant and the disability carrier over the claimant's reported degree of disability and the carrier's perception of the level of claimed disability. Consequently, the claimant may respond to the examination in a hostile and uncooperative fashion, providing information only grudgingly and with great reluctance.

Finally, in evaluations for which disability or compensation could become an issue, the deliberate distortion of self-report is always a possibility. Compensation can serve to influence the report of symptoms and response to treatment in the direction of prolonging treatment and limiting recovery (Rohling, Binder, & Langhinrichsen-Rohling, 1995). Individuals who undergo disability evaluations have claimed that they are impaired by a mental or nervous disorder and are unable to perform the substantial and specific duties of their occupation. As a result, the claimant is requesting benefits that may include treatment for the mental or nervous disorder and monetary compensation that will partially replace lost wages. Additionally, within the Veterans Benefits Administration and the Social Security Administration, receipt of permanent disability may include educational benefits for dependents. Consequently, the possibility always exists that the claimant is attempting to obtain tangible benefits for assuming the sick role and is either exaggerating or fabricating symptoms in order to reach this goal.

Conducting disability evaluations or treating clients involved in personal injury disputes places the clinician in the unfamiliar position of being seen by one of the parties in the dispute as biased and co-opted by the other party or as an advocate who will work to advance the client's agenda. Therefore, the process by which the examiner arrives at an opinion regarding the presence or absence of a disabling condition and associated pain and suffering demands great care. It is imperative that any opinion provided regarding these issues be based upon objective and well-validated measures of psychopathology and distress. The use of such measures allows the examiner to defend against charges of bias and provides a firm foundation for diagnostic decisions and subsequent opinions regarding disability and emotional distress.

In conclusion, psychological evaluations that take place within the context of disability determination or personal injury are qualitatively different than evaluations that occur for the purpose of diagnosis or treatment planning. Consequently, the examiner must adopt a different approach to these evaluations by becoming a critical thinker and relying on objective measures of response bias and psychopathology rather than relying on clinical judgment and the unquestioned acceptance of the evaluee's self-report.

Use of the MMPI–2 in Disability and Personal Injury Evaluations

Given that the evaluation of individuals who have suffered a personal injury or who claim disability are often adversarial, secondary gain is always a consideration, a high level of scrutiny is involved, and the use of an objective and well-standardized psychometric instrument is required. The MMPI–2 represents such an instrument and has been widely used for such purposes (Butcher & Miller, 1998; Pope, Butcher, & Seelen, 1999). The reason for the continued and widespread use of the MMPI/MMPI–2 in disability and personal injury evaluations is that the instrument provides several advantages for the examiner over clinical judgment alone. The use of actuarial or objective data in clinical judgment has been actively promoted for many years with early studies clearly demonstrating the benefit of the use of such data (see Meehl, 1954). More recent meta-analyses have demonstrated the utility of psychological instruments in the assessment of emotional or nervous conditions and have shown that the effect size of this contribution is equivalent to those found for commonly accepted medical diagnostic tools (Grove, Zald, Lebow, Snitz, & Nelson, 2000; Myer et al., 2001). Despite the well-documented advantage of psychological instruments in improving clinical judgment, clinicians are often reluctant to use such data—especially when the data do not correspond with their clinical impression (Arbisi, Murdoch, Fortier, & McNulty, 2004). The failure to integrate objective information—particularly with respect to detection of self-report bias—can lead to erroneous decisions and inappropriate denial of claims or award of compensation.

Issues Addressed in Disability Evaluations

The psychologist who is evaluating an individual who has suffered an injury or is claiming disability is often focused on establishing a diagnosis and defining the impact of that diagnosis on the claimant's ability to carry out activities. The examiner may be asked to opine whether the current level of disability is the direct result of the claimed psychiatric condition. Disputes tend to arise over the existence of a specific psychiatric diagnosis or whether, if present, the psychiatric condition leads to the alleged level of disability claimed. The examiner is required to conduct a diagnostic evaluation based on review of medical records and a face-to-face clinical interview. It is advisable to use standardized assessment procedures including focused structured interviews and self-report instruments such as the MMPI–2 to arrive at diagnoses (Rogers, 2001). Unfortunately, the validity of structured interviews can be compromised by intentional defensiveness and malingering. Consequently, the MMPI–2, with the presence of effective validity scales, is an important if not essential complement to either a structured or unstructured clinical interview in the evaluation of disability and personal injury. (See Exhibit 16.2 for a summary of issues addressed in disability or personal injury evaluations.)

Another frequently posed question to the examiner relates to the adequacy of treatment provided to the claimant. Given that the claimant

EXHIBIT 16.2
Highlight: Issues to Be Addressed During the Disability or Personal Injury Evaluation

- Establish that a psychiatric condition occurred and resulted in impairment (injury) or disability.
- Address the degree to which the psychiatric condition is present currently and the adequacy of current and past treatment provided for the condition.
- Establish the presence or absence of "secondary gain"; that is, estimate the accuracy of the individual's self-report.
- Address causality; that is, did the injury lead directly to the development of the psychiatric/psychological condition and result in impairment?
- Address aggravation; that is, did the injury aggravate a preexisting psychiatric/psychological condition that contributes to a greater degree of impairment or disability?

is presenting him- or herself as injured and in need of financial compensation as a result of the presence of a psychiatric condition, the permanency of disability is often at issue. Further, if the person is totally or partially disabled by the condition, have the treatments and interventions provided to date been necessary and adequate? Regarding the adequacy of treatment, over the past decade the American Psychiatric Association (2002) has published practice guidelines for several conditions that are frequently the source of a disability claim or mental condition resulting from an injury. It is helpful to familiarize oneself with these published guidelines to aid in reaching a determination regarding the adequacy of care and treatment.

The presence of secondary gain is almost always an issue when conducting personal injury or disability evaluations. Often, the examiner is asked to indicate the extent to which secondary gain plays a role in the claimant's presentation. On the face of it, the answer is obvious for all disability or personal injury evaluations because secondary gain issues are clearly involved and play a role in symptom presentation (see Binder & Rohling, 1996; Rohling et al., 1995). A more meaningful question—and one that can be addressed within the context of the evaluation—is, to what extent is secondary gain influencing the presentation of symptoms and report of impairment? The MMPI–2 is uniquely useful in addressing this question. Indeed, the MMPI–2 is probably more useful than other broadband measures of psychopathology because it contains a number of well-established validity scales that accurately assess response distortion (Baer & Miller, 2002; Rogers, Sewell, Martin, & Vitacco, 2003). The validity scales contained in the MMPI–2 provide dimensional information for the examiner regarding the extent to which the self-report of the claimant is distorted. Because secondary gain is always present in disability evaluations, the MMPI–2 can provide a reasonably objective assessment of the influence of secondary gain. That is, examination of the MMPI–2 validity scales can indicate to the examiner whether inferences made about the claimant's degree of disability based on the accuracy of self-report are reasonable or whether the self-report is so distorted that it is impossible to accept the self-report as an accurate representation of the current clinical condition.

Finally, causality is frequently a disputed issue with regard to the development of disability. The dispute generally arises when an event occurs at one time and a disabling psychiatric or psychological condition occurs or worsens sometime later. Within the workers' compensation system, whether the work-related injury caused or substantially contributed to the claimed psychiatric condition is always at issue. Causality is also implied when the claimed disabling condition is PTSD, consequential depression, or substance dependence as a result of a personal injury or work-related injury. Using an objective broadband measure of psychopathology such as the MMPI–2 can provide the examiner with information regarding the current symptom presentation. Further, the claimant's current MMPI–2 profile, if valid, can be compared to groups of individuals with the condition, such as PTSD, to determine how consistent the claimant's presentation is to others with that condition.

To summarize, the use of broadband objective measures of psychopathology can assist the evaluator in addressing questions posed by the referral source because the individual claimant's response can be compared to other well-defined groups of individuals who share the same diagnosis or medical condition or were injured in the same manner. In so doing, the examiner can document how comparable the claimant's self-report and symptom presentation are to those groups.

Because the MMPI was initially developed for use with psychiatric populations, it is a particularly well-suited measure to use when conducting disability and personal injury evaluations. Further, the MMPI and the MMPI–2 have been used for the past 50 years in the evaluation of medical patients; therefore, individual profiles can be compared with those of large groups of psychiatric inpatients (Arbisi, Ben-Porath, & McNulty, 2005a; Gilberstadt & Duker, 1965; Marks & Seeman, 1963), psychiatric outpatients (Graham, Ben-Porath, & McNulty, 1999b), and medical patients (Henrichs, 1981), including chronic pain patients (Keller & Butcher, 1991; Slesinger, Archer, & Duane, 2002). Consequently, when using the MMPI–2 in disability or personal injury examinations, the evaluator has access to a rich breadth of comparative data and is able to objectively determine how similar or dissimilar the claimant's current self-report is relative to a specific reference group. If challenged, the actuarial inferences derived from the MMPI–2 can be supported by reference to these large data sets as well as to the 50 years of accumulated empirical research undergirding the instrument (Pope et al., 1999).

Validity Considerations

"It is probably indefensible to render expert testimony regarding the likelihood of malingering without psychological test data bearing on this question" (Schretlen, 1988). A common request from the referral source to the examiner is to speak to the presence of malingering or "secondary gain." Because the MMPI–2 contains well-supported validity scales that objectively assess both exaggeration and minimization of self-report, the instrument is the obvious choice to assess the issue of response distortion when this question is raised (Baer & Miller, 2002; Lally, 2003; Rogers et al., 2003; Rothke et al., 2000). Indeed, the MMPI–2 provides objective evidence regarding the presence of malingering and supports testimony provided in court regarding the presence of such a response set (Pope et al., 1999).

Several general issues require comment prior to a more detailed discussion of MMPI–2 validity in disability or personal injury evaluations. Often, individuals who are undergoing these evaluations have retained counsel to assist in processing their claim or to serve as an advocate in their lawsuit. When counsel is retained, the possibility of coaching regarding the clinical presentation, as well as how to avoid detection by the MMPI–2 validity scales, must be considered (Wetter & Corrigan, 1995). Indeed, in surveys of attorneys, the majority felt that it was their duty to advise their clients not only that the MMPI–2 contained validity scales but also how to minimize the chance that misrepresentation of their clinical state would be detected by the MMPI–2 (Wetter & Corrigan, 1995). In a review of studies in which college students or graduate students were directed to fake a psychiatric disorder and either were given no coaching or were provided with information regarding the MMPI–2 validity scales, effect sizes were reduced substantially and individuals provided with coaching were better able to elude detection by the MMPI–2 validity scales than were individuals who were not provided with coaching (Bagby, Nicholson, Buis, & Bacchiochi, 2000; Bury & Bagby, 2002; Rogers et al., 2003; Storm & Graham, 2000; Viglione et al., 2001; Wetter, Baer, Berry, Robison, & Sumpter, 1993). Nonetheless, with the exception of the Viglione et al. (2001) study, the standard fake-bad validity scales (*F* [Infrequency], *F(B)* [Back Infrequency], and *Fp* [Infrequency–Psychopathology]) were effective in identifying individuals who were feigning a psychiatric condition. In a recent meta-analysis of the detection of faking with the MMPI–2, the *F* family of scales demonstrated the largest effect sizes in differentiating between clinical samples and groups asked to feign psychopathology (Rogers et al., 2003). Specifically, the *Fp* scale had a comparatively large effect size and a relatively narrow range of cut scores across diagnostic and clinical groups.

To summarize, although evidence exists from surveys of attorneys that a significant proportion feel it is in their clients' best interest to provide specific information about psychological instruments and psychiatric symptoms, providing information regarding symptoms of illness does not improve the ability to avoid detection when malingering. However, when information is provided regarding the MMPI–2 validity scales, it becomes more difficult to detect individuals who are malingering.

Threats to Profile Validity

In general, two possible threats to profile validity are assessed on the MMPI–2: content nonresponsivity and content response faking (Nichols & Greene, 1997). These are broad response dimensions that, if extreme, will completely prevent any inference drawn from the MMPI–2 regarding the presence or absence of symptoms and their association with psychological injury.

Content nonresponsivity refers to the failure of the examinee to respond reliably to the content of MMPI–2 items. The most basic form of content nonresponsivity is to simply fail to respond to the item and move to the next item on the inventory. The claimant's failure to respond to items is recorded on the MMPI–2 by tallying the total number of omitted items. This tally is termed *Cannot Say* (?) and is reported on the MMPI–2 summary sheet. Generally, if the number of omitted items exceeds a total of 30, the profile should be considered uninterpretable (Butcher et al., 2001). On the other hand, Graham (2000) argues that ? totals above 7 should be considered questionable. The scales on which the omitted items fall and the content of the omitted items should be scrutinized to determine whether the claimant is refusing to respond to items associated with a particular content area (Graham, 2000). Failure to respond to an excessive number of items on the MMPI–2 can be the result of confusion or reading problems as well as obfuscation or oppositionality. Because disability evaluations are often viewed by the claimant as adversarial, failure to respond to items may reflect oppositionality. Explaining to the claimant that it is in his or her best interest to cooperate with the evaluation because failure to do so will be documented in the report is often enough to elicit a willingness to respond to the omitted items.

Another form of content nonresponsivity is careless responding. Carelessness is assessed on the MMPI–2 by the Variable Response Inconsistency (VRIN) scale. The VRIN scale is composed of pairs of items with similar content. Item pairs that are scored in a mutually exclusive direction are indicative of careless responding; that is, an elevation above a T score of 80 on the VRIN scale indicates that the claimant is not reading the items carefully and is randomly responding to the items without apprehending the meaning of the items. As with the omission of items, a failure to respond to the items carefully can indicate confusion or compromised reading ability. Another possibility is that the examinee was not cooperative and failed to take the evaluation seriously. If the VRIN scale score falls above a T score of 80, the profile is uninterpretable and no inferences regarding the claimant's clinical condition should be made.

A second type of inconsistent responding occurs when the examinee adopts a fixed response set and responds either True or False without attention to the content of the item. The True Response Inconsistency (TRIN) scale is constructed of sets of MMPI–2 item pairs for which responding either True to both items or False to the pair of items would constitute an incompatible set of responses. If this scale is elevated above a T score of 80, this indicates that the individual either adopted a fixed nay-saying response set or a fixed acquiescent response set, and the profile should not be interpreted. As with the VRIN scale, an elevated TRIN scale can result from confusion or cognitive limitations as well as carelessness or oppositionality. By relying upon test-independent information, these alternatives can be readily evaluated and the most plausible explanation for the elevated TRIN can be determined.

Fake-Bad Response Set

An issue more directly related to disability and personal injury evaluations and the question of secondary gain is that of content response faking. This response set occurs when the claimant deliberately attempts to distort his or her clinical presentation by appearing either less symptomatic (faking-good) or more symptomatic (faking-bad) than actually is the case. The MMPI–2 contains a range of scales that were developed to detect content response faking. Since there is an understandable tendency to emphasize the depth and breadth of medical problems or psychopathology while undergoing a disability or personal injury evaluation in order to convince the examiner of the legitimacy of the claim, it is critical that the examiner has the means to objectively quantify the self-report bias. Compensation- or disability-seeking claimants are understandably more likely to alter their self-presentation in order to forward their personal agenda than are treatment-seeking patients for whom relief from emotional distress or turmoil is the only agenda. Given the differential prevalence of deliberately distorted self-report in compensation-seeking patients, it is a mistake to assume—simply because someone is applying for disability or claims an injury—that he or she is malingering. Similarly, it is a mistake to accept that whatever a claimant reports about the presence or absence of symptoms and impairment should be taken as accurate. Although a certain degree of symptom emphasis may be common in claimants seeking disability benefits, there appears to be an underlying dimension of response faking or malingering that, in the extreme, results in a completely distorted and nonrepresentative clinical presentation (Rogers et al., 2003; Strong, Greene, & Schinka, 2000). Because the MMPI–2 validity scales associated with malingering and faking-good provide dimensional information regarding the response set, the examiner is able to estimate the degree of confidence she or he has in the clinical inferences made from the MMPI–2 given the claimant's response set.

The standard fake-bad scales contained on the MMPI–2 include the *F*, *F(B)*, and *Fp* scales. All three of these scales adopt a rare or unusual symptom strategy for the detection of malingering (Rogers et al., 2003). These scales contain items that are infrequently endorsed by different comparison groups. The *F* scale was developed by identifying items that were endorsed by fewer than 10% of the original Minnesota normative group. The scale was retained on the MMPI–2, although four items were dropped and several items no longer met the less than 10% endorsement rate in the MMPI–2 normative group. The *F(B)* was developed to identify items from the back half of the MMPI–2 that were endorsed by fewer than 10% of the MMPI–2 normative group. Although both of these scales are effective in the detection of malingering of psychopathology, both scales can also be elevated due to genuine distress and severe psychopathology (Arbisi & Ben-Porath, 1995).

The *Fp* scale is also an infrequency scale but differs from *F* and *F(B)* in that the items contained on the scale are infrequently endorsed not only by the MMPI–2 normative group but also by large independent groups of psychiatric inpatients. The *Fp* scale was developed by identifying items that were infrequently endorsed (less than 20%) by both psychiatric inpatients and the normative sample. That is, the 27 items contained on the *Fp* are unusual items infrequently endorsed by even the most severely disordered psychiatric patients confined to inpatient psychiatric facilities as well as by individuals who are not experiencing psychiatric or psychological problems. The *Fp* scale is generally independent of psychiatric diagnosis and less influenced by the presence of severe psychopathology than either the *F* or the *F(B)* scale (Arbisi & Ben-Porath, 1997). The *Fp* has support for the detection of malingering within the context of disability evaluations for both combat-related PTSD and PTSD resulting from industrial accident (Bury & Bagby, 2002; Franklin, Repasky, Thompson, Shelton, & Uddo, 2002).

When both *F* and *F(B)* are elevated, the examiner should consult *Fp* to determine if the scale is elevated. If *Fp* is elevated above a T score of 70, this indicates that the examinee is exaggerating severe emotional disturbance and demoralization. As the T score approaches 100, confidence in the accuracy of self-report diminishes and the examiner's ability to make accurate clinical inferences based on the clinical scales of the MMPI–2 decreases. At a T score of 100, the correct classification rate is 98% when discriminating between psychiatric patients who responded honestly to the MMPI–2 and psychiatric inpatients who were feigning a psychiatric condition (Arbisi & Ben-Porath, 1998). Consequently, scores at or above 100 on the *Fp* scale are associated with malingering of psychopathology and invalidate the profile. In a forensic setting, a T score of 100 on the *Fp* had a positive predictive power of 1.0 in predicting malingering as defined by the Structured Interview for Reported Symptoms (SIRS; Lewis, Simcox, & Berry, 2002; Rogers, Bagby, & Dickens, 1992). Indeed, in a recent meta-analysis of the detection of malingering with the MMPI–2, Rogers et al. (2003) recommended the use of the *Fp* scale over other MMPI–2 fake-bad scales because the false positive rate at T scores of 100 is quite low and the cut score for prediction of malingering remains stable across a variety of clinical settings and psychiatric conditions.

Other less widely used or validated fake-bad scales can be scored on the MMPI–2 (see Gough's Dissimulation revised scale). One such scale that deserves special mention due to the claims made for the utility of the scale in detection of malingering in personal injury claims is the Fake-Bad Scale (FBS; Larrabee, 1998; Tsushima & Tsushima, 2001). The FBS was developed by selecting MMPI–2 items on a rational basis that were thought to discriminate individuals who were feigning physical illness and disability as a result of a personal injury (Lees-Haley, English, & Glenn, 1991). Additionally, the scale was thought to identify individuals who were feigning PTSD as a result of a personal injury from those who responded honestly to the MMPI–2 (Lees-Haley, 1992). Despite claims that the scale has merit for detecting malingering in personal injury and disability evaluations, at recommended cut scores the scale was shown to yield unacceptably high rates of false positives across a wide range of clinical settings (Butcher, Arbisi, Atlis, & McNulty, 2003). The FBS demonstrated what appeared to be gender bias in that far more women than men were identified as malingering based on the published cut score recommendations. Additionally, in a separate study, the FBS was ineffective in discriminating between a group of workers who developed PTSD as a result of a work-related injury and a group of university students who were asked to feign PTSD (Bury & Bagby, 2002). Consequently, results from these studies as well as from the Rogers et al. (2003) meta-analysis indicate that the FBS should not be used as a means of identifying individuals who are faking-bad on the MMPI–2 regardless of the setting.

Case Example of Faking-Bad: Case of Malingered PSTD

Mr. Z is a 34-year-old licensed practical nurse who has been completely disabled for the past 3 years after incurring a work-related injury to his neck and back when assaulted by a geriatric patient. While employed at a nursing facility for demented patients, Mr. Z was providing care for a demented patient who became agitated and aggressive. During the course of attempting to restrain and control the patient, Mr. Z was grabbed by the patient around the neck and choked. Other staff came to his aid and helped restrain the patient. Mr. Z was taken to a local emergency room where he was examined and an MRI of the neck and back was obtained. No structural changes to his neck or back had occurred, and he was released with the diagnosis of neck strain and was taken off work for a couple of days. Subsequently, when Mr. Z attempted to return to work, he complained of an inability to see patients and the fear that he would be assaulted again. His symptoms increased to include nightmares, "flashbacks," and avoidance of all elderly males. Mr. Z was referred to a therapist and psychiatrist who diagnosed PTSD and took him off work. Despite 3 years of aggressive therapy, Mr. Z has been unable to return to work in any capacity, including roles that require no patient contact. An IPE was requested in order to confirm the diagnosis and degree of disability as well as speak to the adequacy of treatment.

Figure 16.1 shows Mr. Z's MMPI–2 profile results. Mr. Z produced an MMPI–2 that was marked by elevations on *F* and *F(B)*. The *Fp* scale score exceeded a T score of 100. With a low VRIN scale score and an *Fp* above 100T, Mr. Z very carefully endorsed items that even the most severely disturbed psychiatric patients do not endorse. This response set suggests that Mr. Z deliberately attempted to feign a psychiatric illness; therefore, inferences based on the MMPI–2 clinical scales regarding Mr. Z's condition are not possible.

Fake-Good Response Set

The opposite of exaggerating or faking-bad is denying or minimizing problems by presenting oneself as without fault and overly virtuous. Within the context of disability evaluations or personal injury claims,

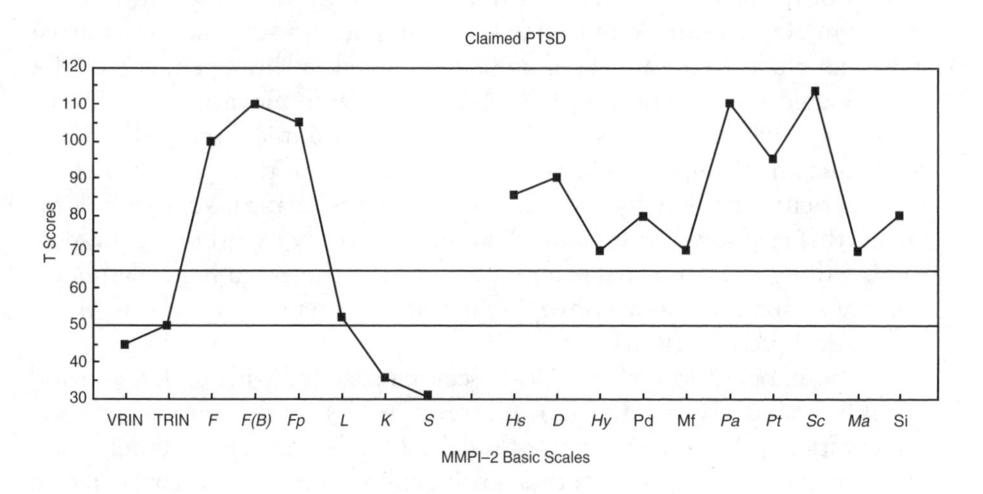

Figure 16.1. Mr. Z's MMPI–2 profile results.

the minimization or denial of difficulties would appear to be counterproductive if the goal is to obtain compensation or benefits. Therefore, it is somewhat surprising to find claimants responding to the MMPI–2 in a defensive fashion during the disability or personal injury evaluation. Despite the counterintuitive nature of a defensive response set within this context, this response set can occur and is more likely to be adopted when the source of disability is noncompensable. For example, substance dependence is not independently a compensable condition under Social Security Administration or Veterans Benefits Administration rules. However, other conditions such as depression or PTSD are compensable. It is reasonable and adaptive for claimants to simultaneously emphasize certain aspects of their condition while de-emphasizing others. For example, in order to increase the chances of obtaining compensation, a veteran seeking service connection for PTSD who is alcohol dependent and meets criteria for antisocial personality disorder would be best served by denying problems associated with substance dependence and denying work difficulties due to authority problems and solely attributing his inability to hold a job and ongoing chronic sleep disturbance to PTSD.

A pattern of defensive responding may also be observed in a worker's compensation evaluation when a claimant is reporting psychiatric symptoms, pain, and distress associated with a work-related injury. Emphasizing somatic concerns and depression and minimizing maladaptive personality traits and substance abuse are more likely to support the claim that the work-related injury was the principal cause and directly contributed to the development of the psychiatric condition and somatic concerns. If, on the other hand, the employee was forthcoming about all aspects of his or her clinical presentation, then he or she would run the risk of having the examiner and—more important—the administrative judge conclude that the symptoms experienced are independent of the work-related injury. Thus, an MMPI–2 profile with elevations on one or more of the defensiveness scales accompanied by clinical scale elevations represents an attempt to selectively report aspects of the claimant's clinical experience while denying other, potentially relevant psychopathology. Given this response pattern, the examiner can only report what the person is willing to acknowledge and indicate that there is a high likelihood that the claimant is not conveying a complete representation of his or her clinical presentation.

The standard MMPI–2 validity scales associated with underreporting or faking-good are the Lie (*L*), Correction (*K*), and Superlative Self-Presentation (*S*) scales. Elevations on the *L* scale indicate a rather unsophisticated denial of psychopathology, including denial of minor character flaws and failings that most people readily acknowledge. An elevation on the *L* scale indicates that the claimant is presenting him- or herself to be highly virtuous and morally upright (Graham, 2000). Rather than assessing the denial of faults and personal failings, the *K* scale assesses the degree to which the individual is denying psychological problems and emotional distress (Graham, 2000). High scores on the *S* scale indicate the denial of psychological problems, beliefs in human goodness, claims of serenity, contentment with life, patience, and denial of moral flaws (Butcher & Han, 2000). The *S* scale was developed by contrasting applicants for pilot positions at a major airline with the MMPI–2 normative group. An elevation on the *S* scale represents an attempt to present oneself as well adjusted, competent, and effective while also denying significant psychological problems. In a recent meta-analysis of fake-good scales on the MMPI–2, the *L* and *K* scales demonstrated the largest effect sizes when discriminating between groups of individuals instructed to respond honestly and those instructed to fake-good (Baer & Miller, 2002). The results for the *S* scale were less consistent, with some studies demonstrating incremental improvement for *S* in prediction of impression management and defensiveness compared to the *L* and *K* scales and with other studies failing to find such improvement (Baer & Miller, 2002; Bagby, Nicholson, Buis, Radovanovic, & Fidler, 1999; Lim & Butcher, 1996).

The failure to fully disclose on the MMPI–2 as indicated by an elevated *L* scale is a poor prognostic indicator for successful treatment of injured workers. Indeed, an elevation on the *L* scale in claimants suffering chronic pain as a result of a work-related injury is associated with a failure to return to work after treatment through a work-hardening program (Alexy & Webb, 1999). Further, individuals participating in a comprehensive chronic pain treatment program who had an *L* scale elevation performed poorly on a wide range of outcome measures compared to participants who had lower scores on *L* (Burns, 2000). Therefore, the unsophisticated denial of minor faults and the claim of excessive virtue as assessed by the MMPI–2 *L* scale appear to bode poorly for a return to work after injury and the development of subsequent chronic nonmalignant pain.

USE OF THE MMPI–2 IN THE EVALUATION OF PERSONAL INJURY OR DISABILITY CLAIMS DUE TO PSYCHIATRIC ILLNESS

The overall approach to the interpretation of the MMPI–2 within the context of the disability evaluation is very similar to the general interpretive approach described by the authors of the leading MMPI–2 interpretive guides (Butcher & Williams, 2000; Graham, 2000; Greene, 2000). However, a slight adaptation to the general interpretive guidelines is used in that a more hierarchical interpretation is adopted, moving from the overall level of distress engendered in the profile to the specific report of symptoms, followed by a description of the means that are mustered to psychologically cope with the stress of the injury.

INFLUENCE OF LITIGATION ON DISABILITY AND IMPACT ON MMPI–2 FINDINGS

What effect does the establishment of a disability claim or entering into litigation after a personal injury have on the MMPI–2 profile? In general, without a prospective evaluation, it is impossible to definitively establish the impact of litigation on self-report as reflected in the MMPI–2 profile. However, several studies provide clues that can be used to assess the impact of litigation on reported psychological stress (Fow, Dorris, Sittig, & Smith-Seemiller, 2002; Gallagher et al., 1995; Levenson, Glenn, & Hirschfeld, 1988). Workers who had been receiving workers' compensation benefits in excess of 6 months and who were rated by compensation counselors as ready to return to work underwent a psychological evaluation as part of a vocational-planning evaluation. The mean MMPI–2 clinical scale score for this group fell below 70 and, therefore, was not generally consistent with significant emotional disturbance (Patrick, 1988). On the other hand, injured workers who were receiving workers' compensation benefits had a poorer response to treatment than did workers who were not receiving compensation. Scores on scales 1, 2, and 3 on the MMPI–2 did not decrease as significantly for participants in the chronic pain treatment program who were receiving workers' compensation when compared with scores of participants with other types of insurance sponsorship (Fow et al., 2002). Individuals who chose to litigate after a personal injury produced higher elevations on MMPI–2 clinical scales 1, 2, and 3 than disabled patients who chose not to litigate (Lanyon & Almer, 2002). In contrast, individuals who reported a late postconcussive syndrome after minor head injuries produced more defensive and less elevated MMPI–2 profiles within the context of an independent neuropsychological evaluation when compared with their own pre-injury profiles (Greiffenstein & Baker, 2001). Consequently, compensation-seeking status and litigation, as well as emotional distress stemming from disability, can serve to influence the relative elevation on MMPI–2 clinical scales by both decreasing and increasing elevations depending upon the circumstance of the evaluation.

The context within which a psychological evaluation takes place can influence the retrospective report of emotional and intellectual function. For example, litigants reported better premorbid cognitive and intellectual performance and better emotional adjustment after a mild injury than were documented in contemporaneous records (Greiffenstein, Baker, & Johnson-Greene, 2002).

Current Adjustment and Degree of Overall Manifest Distress

The first step after the validity of the MMPI–2 protocol is established is to examine the number and relative elevation of the clinical scales to determine the current level of adjustment and degree of subjective distress. This provides the examiner with an overall objective estimate of the degree of maladjustment and distress associated with the injured litigant's condition. The mean score on the eight clinical scales was found to be the best indicator of maladjustment in outpatients based on self-reported symptom severity and clinicians' ratings of severity and level of functioning in psychiatric outpatients (Graham, Barthlow, Stein, Ben-Porath, & McNulty, 2002). Moreover, the newly developed Revised Clinical scale, Demoralization (RCd), can also provide additional information related to the degree of general maladjustment and demoralization. An RCd T score equal to or greater than 75 suggests that the claimant may be experiencing significant emotional discomfort and may report feeling overwhelmed and incapable of coping with the current demands and challenges that face him or her consistent with a disabling psychiatric condition (Tellegen et al., 2003). Consequently, individuals claiming disability as a result of a psychiatric illness would be expected to produce MMPI–2 profiles marked by a significant degree of distress and maladjustment as evidenced by clinical scale elevations and an elevation on RCd. If a within normal limits (WNL) profile is produced or a profile is produced that is marked by elevations on scales associated with somatic preoccupation—but without an elevation on the RCd scale—then there is less likelihood that the reported condition is resulting in psychiatric symptoms of sufficient magnitude to lead to disability.

Once the subjective level of distress and maladjustment is established, examination of the clinical scale elevations and profile configuration establishes the symptom presentation and the consistency of objective self-report with the claimed cause of the disability.

MMPI–2 CLINICAL AND CONTENT SCALE INTERPRETATION IN DISABILITY AND PERSONAL INJURY EVALUATIONS

Given a valid and interpretable MMPI–2 profile, the examiner can have confidence in making inferences derived from the relative elevations of the MMPI–2 clinical, Restructured Clinical (RC), content, and supplementary scales regarding the presence or absence of psychiatric symptoms.

Depression and Anxiety

Both depression and anxiety are psychiatric conditions that frequently occur as a consequence of a personal injury and can serve directly as the source of a disability claim. In the case of a physical injury, comorbid affective disturbance can increase the overall level of disability and impairment through a synergistic relationship with the primary condition. For example, individuals with chronic pain resulting from an automobile accident may develop depression and claim that the combination of depression and chronic pain results in impairment and disability. The MMPI–2 profile should reflect the presence of an affective disorder through elevations on Scale 2 and the Depression (DEP) content scale in the case of depression, and elevations on Scale 7 and the Anxiety (ANX) content scale in the case of anxiety. The MMPI–2 Clinical Depression scale and the DEP content scale are moderately accurate in identifying patients with major depressive disorder (Ben-Porath, McCully, & Almagor, 1993; Gross, Keyes, & Greene, 2000). Moreover, specific MMPI–2 profiles such as 278/872, 27/72, and 87/78 are frequently associated with the diagnoses of depression and anxiety in both outpatient and inpatient psychiatric settings (Arbisi, Ben-Porath, & McNulty, 2003a; Graham, Ben-Porath, & McNulty, 1999).

Thought Disorder

The MMPI–2 content scales can help in interpreting observed elevations on the clinical scales. With multiple clinical scale elevations that include an elevation on Scale 8, examination of the Bizarre Mentation (BIZ) content scale is particularly useful in determining whether a thought disturbance is present. The BIZ scale adds incrementally to the clinical scales in prediction of psychosis and in discriminating between major depression and schizophrenia (Ben-Porath, Butcher, & Graham, 1991). Indeed, the MMPI–2 content scales have demonstrated incremental validity (the prediction of extratest clinical criteria is improved) over the clinical scales in both outpatient and inpatient settings (Archer, Aiduk, Giffin, & Elkins, 1996; Barthlow, Graham, Ben-Porath, & McNulty, 1999; Ben-Porath et al., 1993). Therefore, reference to the content scale and the content component scales can greatly enhance and refine the examiner's ability to characterize the claimant's report of symptoms and associated distress (Ben-Porath & Sherwood, 1993).

Case Example: A 25-Year-Old Woman Injured While at a Sporting Event

Ms. M is a 25-year-old, unmarried high school graduate who was employed full time as a waitress at the time of her injury. She and a group of friends were attending a professional sporting event when the team mascot threw a promotional ball into the crowd. Ms. M had turned to talk with a friend and the ball struck her on the side of the face above the left eye. She was startled and rapidly turned toward her companion who had his elbow extended. Ms. M's face came in contact with her companion's elbow and she suffered an injury to her mouth. Ms. M received immediate attention from on-call emergency personnel. She complained of headache and pain in her front tooth. Her companions took her to the hospital where she was evaluated and released. Later, it was discovered that she had fractured her front tooth. She developed nightmares and intrusive images related to the incident in which she felt as if she was being pursued by a "demonic" team mascot. Further, over the course of several weeks, she began to believe that she was being followed and was in danger from malevolent agents. Ms. M reported sleep disturbance, and she eventually refused to leave her apartment because she felt too uncomfortable in public. A psychiatric evaluation was undertaken, and the diagnosis of PTSD was made. Ms. M was unable to return to work and was subsequently hospitalized on two occasions for psychiatric treatment. A personal injury lawsuit was initiated claiming emotional injury in the form of PTSD resulting from the negligent actions of the team mascot.

Figures 16.2–16.4 show Ms. M's MMPI–2 profiles for the basic scales, the content scales, and the RC Scales, respectively. Ms. M responded to the MMPI–2 in a relatively careful fashion. She endorsed item content associated with serious psychiatric illness in a manner consistent with patients who have genuine, serious, psychiatric illness. The clinical profile

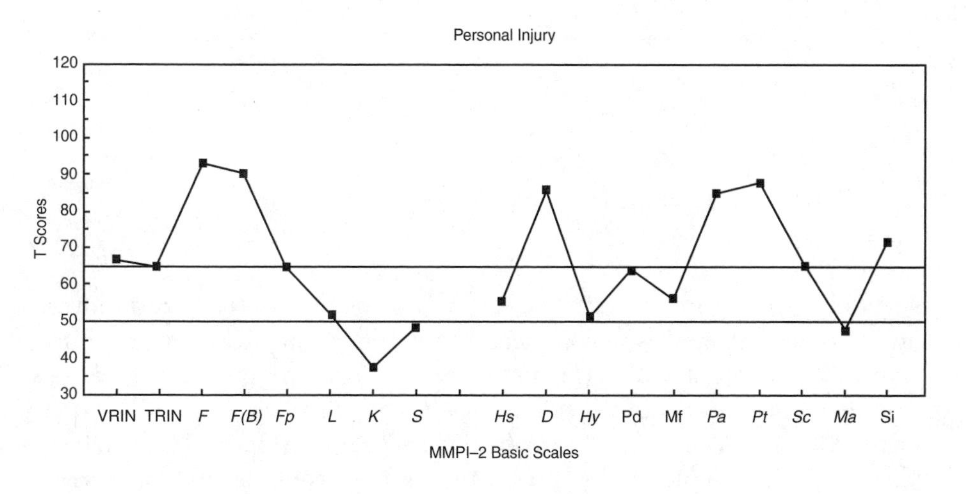

Figure 16.2. Ms. M's MMPI–2 basic scales profile.

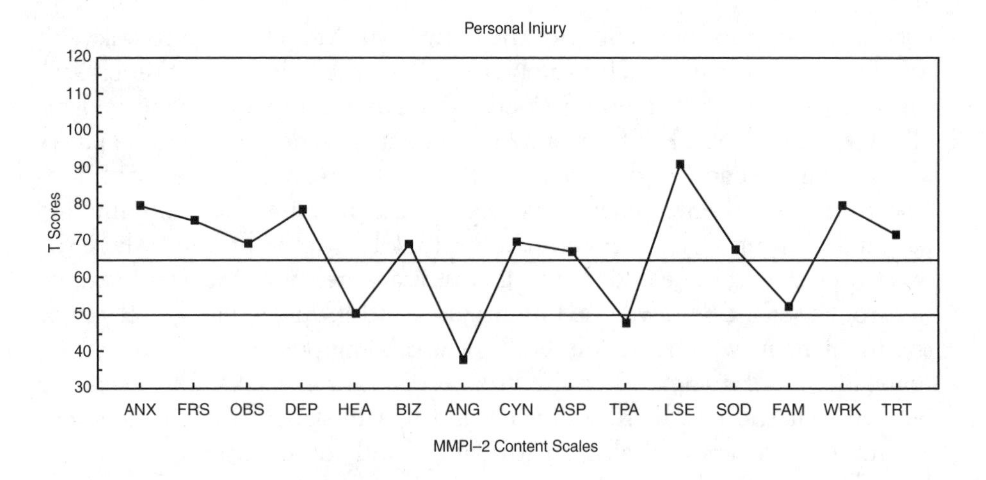

Figure 16.3. Ms. M's MMPI–2 content scales profile.

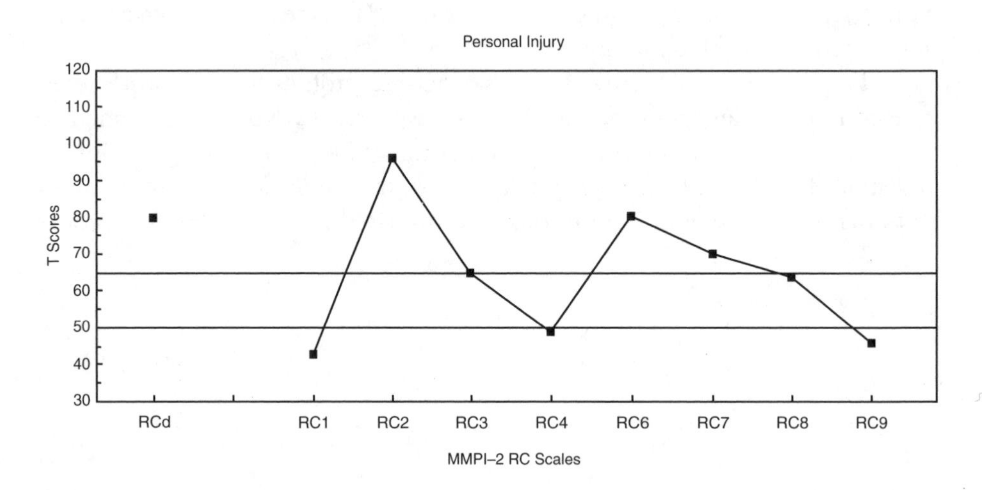

Figure 16.4. Ms. M's RC Scales profile.

suggests profound distress marked by depression, anxiety, rumination, and—somewhat surprisingly—ideas of reference and paranoia. Examination of the content scales (Figure 16.3) confirms the presence of depression, general anxiety, and specific fears, along with bizarre sensory experiences. In this case, examination of the RC Scales (Figure 16.4) helps to clarify the clinical picture by accounting for the overall level of distress and demoralization. As expected, Ms. M is extremely distressed and feels overwhelmed and unable to cope with the challenges in her life. She reports a number of symptoms consistent with the core features of depression, including the inability to experience pleasure from activities, lack of energy, and pessimism. Note that she is also reporting frankly paranoid experiences that likely reach psychotic proportions. Despite an elevation on the RC Scale Dysfunctional Negative Emotions suggesting underlying anxiety, the capacity to ruminate and worry, and increased sensitivity, it is not the most salient feature of the profile. Although Ms. M's MMPI–2 profile indicates that she is clearly psychiatrically ill, the profile is more consistent with thought disorder and depression than with PTSD. Although women who develop PTSD after sexual or domestic abuse can produce elevations on scales 6 and 8, these elevations are not generally associated with psychotic symptoms as is the case in the current profile. Consequently, the event involving the team mascot was unlikely to be the direct cause of her psychiatric condition and may have simply corresponded with the onset of a serious psychiatric condition. A more thorough examination of Ms. M's behavior in the months and weeks leading up to the event would be useful in supporting or refuting the preceding hypothesis.

Restructured Clinical (RC) Scales

The RC Scales seem to provide assistance in clarifying MMPI–2 profiles marked by multiple scale elevations in psychiatric settings. The RC Scales can be used to augment the interpretation of the clinical scales much as the Harris–Lingoes subscales are used to clarify the interpretation of clinical scale elevation. For example, an individual applying for Social Security Disability benefits produces an MMPI–2 profile marked by primary elevations on scales 2, 7, and 8, all falling within a range of 5 T score points, accompanied by secondary elevations on scales 4 and 6 at T scores above 65. The obtained 278/728 code type represents a mixed diagnostic picture associated with tremendous emotional turmoil and the possible occurrence of brief acute psychotic episodes, despondency, and ruminative thoughts of suicide (Graham, 2000). The profile reflects distress and emotional turmoil marked by depressed and anxious mood with accompanying confusion and alienation. Further, the secondary elevations point to anger, poor impulse control, and perhaps persecutory ideation or paranoia. The presence or absence of psychotic thinking would need to be ascertained through examination of the BIZ content scales and the Harris–Lingoes subscales. The elevations on scales 4 and 6 could be due to a great deal of manifest emotional distress but could also reflect antisocial attitudes and paranoia. Through reference to the associated RC Scales—Demoralization, Low Positive Emotions (RC2), Antisocial Behavior (RC4), Ideas of Persecution (RC6), Dysfunctional Negative Emotions

(RC7), and Aberrant Experiences (RC8)—the examiner can determine if the relative scale elevations are related primarily to general distress and demoralization or to the unique facets of the individual clinical scales reflecting thought disturbance, paranoia, or antisocial behavior. In this way, the examiner can decide to emphasize or de-emphasize aspects of the profile to provide a more accurate interpretation of the claimant's current psychological state.

A note of caution regarding the RC Scales is that care must be taken in relying upon the RC Scales in the interpretation of MMPI–2 profiles produced within the context of disability or personal injury evaluations that solely involve a medical condition. In contrast to findings from both inpatient and outpatient psychiatric settings in which the RC Scales show promise in clarifying the MMPI–2 profile interpretation, there are as yet no published data regarding the incremental contribution of these scales in medical settings (Tellegen et al., 2003). Consequently, the contribution of the RC Scales in interpreting MMPI–2 profiles produced in medical settings remains tentative and awaits further research.

In summary, examination of the RC Scales within the context of multiple elevations on the MMPI–2 clinical and content scales can be particularly useful in objectively identifying the presence of discrete psychiatric or psychological symptoms independent of distress and demoralization.

Substance Abuse and Dependence

The abuse of alcohol or other controlled substances often plays a role in the continuation of disability after a work-related injury. Development of dependence on prescribed analgesics can limit return to full-time employment after a disabling injury. Consequently, the capacity of the MMPI–2 to assess whether substance abuse or dependence is a factor in the failure to recover from an injury is a distinct advantage in the use of the MMPI–2 in personal injury or disability evaluations. The MMPI–2 contains three scales designed to identify individuals who were abusing alcohol or drugs from groups of individuals who were not abusing intoxicants. The MacAndrew Alcoholism Scale (MAC) was developed to differentiate male alcoholic patients from nonalcoholic psychiatric patients. The MAC was intended to be a subtle scale so items that directly dealt with excessive drinking were removed (Graham, 2000). The Addiction Potential Scale (APS), developed by Weed, Butcher, McKenna, and Ben-Porath (1992), was modeled after the MAC, utilizing the MMPI–2 item pool to empirically identify personality characteristics and lifestyle patterns specifically associated with alcohol and drug abuse. A third scale, the Addiction

Acknowledgment Scale (AAS), was rationally derived by identifying items with content obviously related to substance abuse problems (Weed et al., 1992). In general, the AAS has demonstrated superiority in detecting substance abuse across a wide range of populations, including outpatient mental health settings and university settings (Clements & Heintz, 2002; Stein, Graham, Ben-Porath, & McNulty, 1999). In particular, the AAS scale emerges as the best single predictor of independently diagnosed substance abuse and consequently shows significant potential as a screen for substance abuse both in outpatient mental health settings and among psychotherapy clients (Clements & Heintz, 2002; Rouse, Butcher, & Miller, 1999). Within the context of personal injury or claim of disability, any elevation on the AAS scale above a T score of 60 warrants comment and triggers further evaluation of substance abuse and dependence; this is because the individual is clearly acknowledging problems with drug or alcohol use and such use will likely impact the claimant's ability to participate in rehabilitative services.

Posttraumatic Stress Disorder

Posttraumatic stress disorder (PTSD), a psychiatric condition that frequently results in the claim of disability, warrants special mention because this condition is cause of action both in personal injury cases and in claims for veteran disability benefits. In fact, PTSD is one of the most frequently claimed medical conditions resulting in disability within the VA system (National Center for Veterans Analysis and Statistics, 1995). The MMPI–2 can serve an important role in the assessment of PTSD within the context of a disability evaluation or personal injury claim due to the extensive empirical support the instrument has for use in the evaluation of PTSD in disability determinations (Bury & Bagby, 2002; Franklin et al., 2002). MMPI–2 profiles of patients with PTSD have been well described for military veterans, former prisoners of war, victims of assault, victims of sexual abuse, and accident survivors (Bury & Bagby, 2002; Elhai, Frueh, Gold, Gold, & Hamner, 2000; Engdahl, Eberly, & Blake, 1996; Lyons & Wheeler-Cox, 1999; Morrell & Rubin, 2001; Sapp, Farrell, Johnson, & Ioannidis, 1997; Scheibe, Bagby, Miller, & Dorian, 2001; Sillanpaa, Agar, & Axelrod, 1999; Sutker & Allain, 1996; Weyermann, Norris, & Hyer, 1996). Further, the MMPI–2 contains a scale (Pk, Keane PTSD) that is associated with PTSD diagnosis in combat veterans (Keane, Mallyo, & Fairbank, 1984; Lyons & Wheeler-Cox, 1999) but is less effective in identifying PTSD resulting from noncombat-related trauma (Morrell & Rubin, 2001; Perrin, Van Hasselt, & Hersen, 1997; Scheibe et al., 2001).

Unfortunately, given the rather diffuse nature of symptoms and frequent occurrence of comorbid psychiatric conditions associated with PTSD, there is no single common code type or set of clinical scales that distinguishes MMPI–2 profiles produced by individuals with PTSD from the MMPI–2 profiles produced by individuals with other psychiatric disorders. However, mean profiles produced by patients diagnosed with PTSD have certain elements in common and are more frequently represented by specific code types. The pattern of scale elevation and common code type appears to vary based on the type of traumatic event that led to the development of PTSD. For combat veterans with PTSD, the most frequently occurring code type is the 278/728 three-point code (Arbisi, Ben-Porath, & McNulty, 2005b; Lyons & Wheeler-Cox, 1999; Wetter et al., 1993; Wyermann et al., 1996). These three scales also appear to differentiate individuals who developed PTSD after a workplace accident from those who do not develop the disorder (Scheibe et al., 2001). There is growing evidence that underlying coping strategies mustered in response to traumatic events can influence the clinical presentation of PTSD (Miller, Grief, & Smith, 2003). In the case of combat-related PTSD, two reliable clusters of MMPI–2 profiles represent externalizing and internalizing coping patterns developed in response to trauma exposure. These clusters reflect relative low pathology, the presence of externalizing behavior marked by other-directed aggression and hostility (elevations on clinical scales 4, 9, and PSY–5 [Personality Psychopathology Five] Aggression) and more internalized expression of distress associated with depression and increased anxiety (elevations on clinical scales 2 and 7, scale 0, and PSY–5 Low Positive Emotionality; Miller et al., 2003).

On the other hand, the 278/728 code type is generally not the modal profile for non-combat-related PTSD although certainly can be produced in individuals with non-combat-related trauma. For example, victims of domestic abuse often elevate Scale 6 as well as scales 8, 1, 2, and 7 on the MMPI–2 (Morrell & Rubin, 2001). Survivors of childhood sexual abuse who present with PTSD in adulthood can produce elevations on MMPI–2 scales 4 and 8 as well as scales 2 and 7 (Elhai et al., 2000). Thus, the cause of the trauma as well as the response to the trauma can influence the presentation of PTSD symptoms as reflected in MMPI–2 scale elevations and profile configuration.

A scale developed specifically to identify PTSD in combat veterans on the original MMPI, the Pk scale, can be of use in identifying individuals with PTSD within the context of disability evaluations. The Pk scale was developed empirically by comparing the item responses of Vietnam combat veterans on inpatient psychiatric units who were diagnosed with combat-related PTSD with Vietnam combat veterans without PTSD and other male psychiatric patients (Keane et al., 1984). Although the recommended cutoff (raw score of 28) on the Pk scale produces a reasonably accurate discrimination of veterans with PTSD from veterans without PTSD, the cutoff yields an unacceptably high rate of false positives (Greenblatt & Davis, 1999; Lyons & Wheeler-Cox, 1999; Munley, Bains, Bloem, & Busby, 1995). Independently, the Pk scale was ineffective in distinguishing veterans with PTSD from veterans with schizophrenia or depression (Greenblatt & Davis, 1999). However, when Pk was combined with the MMPI–2 scales 8, Bizarre Mentation, and Anxiety, it accurately classified 70% of the inpatient veterans (Greenblatt & Davis, 1999).

With regard to non-combat-related PTSD, the use of the Pk scale is more problematic. Despite reports of the utility of the Pk scale in the assessment of PTSD resulting from non-combat-related traumatic events (Knisely, Barker, Ingersoll, & Dawson, 2000; Korestzky & Peck, 1990; Morrell & Rubin, 2001; Perrin et al., 1997), other studies have failed to support the utility of the Pk scale in identifying PTSD resulting from non-combat-related traumatic events (Miller, Goldberg, & Streiner, 1995; Scheibe et al., 2001). A recent well-controlled study examined the use of the MMPI–2 in identifying PTSD due to work-related accidents and found that the Pk scale was ineffective in differentiating accident victims with and without PTSD (Scheibe et al., 2001).

The variability of effective cut scores on the Pk across settings and type of trauma and the inability of the Pk scale to effectively discriminate patients with PTSD from those with other psychiatric conditions are likely due to the fact that a substantial portion of the variance on the Pk scale is accounted for by negative affectivity. In other words, the Pk scale is an index of general maladjustment and undifferentiated emotional distress (Miller et al., 1995). Therefore, the Pk scale—although sensitive to the presence of PTSD—is not specific for PTSD and should not be relied on in isolation to support a diagnosis of PTSD (Graham, 2000).

In sum, it is essential for an MMPI–2 profile that is interpreted as consistent with PTSD to contain evidence, beyond a high level of general distress, for anxiety as reflected by elevations on scales 7, content ANX, and RC7. Without some objective evidence of anxiety presented through the MMPI–2 responses, making the case that PTSD is present is very difficult.

For further clarification, note that the MMPI–2 profiles produced by individuals suffering from PTSD appear to differ based on the traumatic event that precipitated the syndrome. Further, specific MMPI–2 PTSD scales developed for combat-exposed veterans do not perform as well in identifying non-combat-related PTSD.

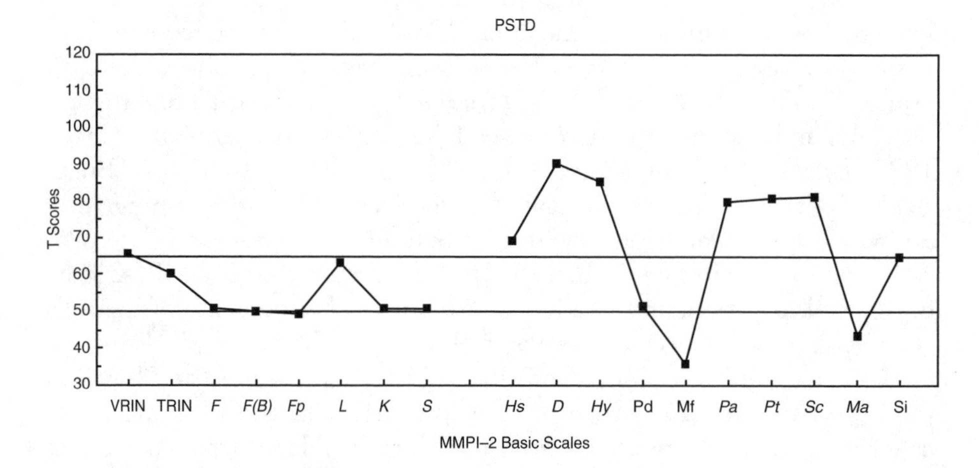

Figure 16.5. Ms. Y's MMPI–2 basic scales profile.

Case Example: PTSD in a Pediatric Nurse

Ms. Y was a 38-year-old registered nurse who was claiming she was unable to function in her capacity as a private pediatric nurse. For the previous 5 years, Ms. Y had been the proprietor of a business that provided in-home nursing care for children. She had two other employees and spent approximately 25% of her time managing the business. The remaining 75% of her time was devoted to direct patient care. Approximately 1 year prior to the evaluation, Ms. Y, accompanied by her husband and two children, were walking in a local park when her youngest child, a 5-year-old son, was struck by a bicycle and thrown to the pavement, striking his head. Ms. Y provided first aid and CPR until paramedics arrived. Unfortunately, her son died a few hours later from his injuries. Since the accident, Ms. Y has had difficulty sleeping and is troubled by nightmares related to the event, and she has intrusive thoughts regarding the accident that she tries to put out of her mind or ignore. Further, she is unable to provide direct nursing care to children because this reminds her of her son's death and her inability to do anything to save his life. She experiences tremendous guilt over her inability to save her son's life and does not trust herself to discharge her duties with other children in her care.

Figures 16.5 and 16.6 show the MMPI–2 profiles generated by Ms. Y. Ms. Y responded carefully to the MMPI–2 in a relatively open manner, although she did present herself in an overly virtuous and socially conforming manner by denying commonly acknowledged per-

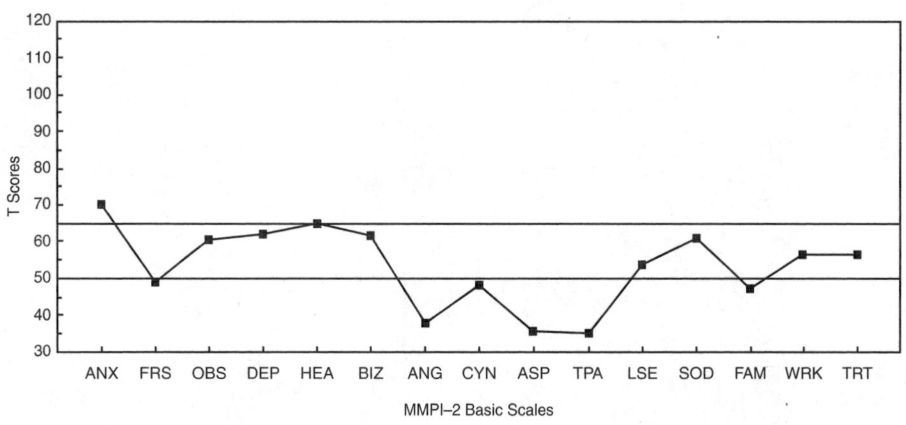

Figure 16.6. Ms. Y's MMPI–2 content scales profile.

sonal flaws and failings. She tends to focus on physical problems and difficulties, often ignoring emotional or psychological factors that are playing a role in her life. She reports a wide range of somatic complaints and simultaneously reports depressed mood, anxiety, and rumination. She feels quite sensitive and sees the world as a dangerous and threatening place where she must remain watchful and vigilant. Thus, her attempts to defend against underlying dysphoria, tension, and anxiety through the use of repression, denial, and somatic preoccupation are only moderately successful. Indeed, the content scale Anxiety is elevated indicating that Ms. Y feels nervous, is worried and apprehensive, has trouble concentrating, and may complain of sleep disturbance. Consequently, the profile is broadly consistent with PTSD. Figure 16.7 presents general interpretive guidelines for the MMPI–2 in disability or personal injury evaluations.

MMPI–2 EVALUATION OF INJURED WORKERS

Workers who become disabled as a result of on-the-job injuries are subject to benefits under state statutes regulating workers' compensation. These statutes vary from state to state, and the type of work-related injury covered under workers' compensation also varies from state to state. For example, in a number of states, workers cannot receive benefits for a primary mental or emotional injury without having experienced a physical injury. A major depressive disorder brought on by a stressful work environment or PTSD

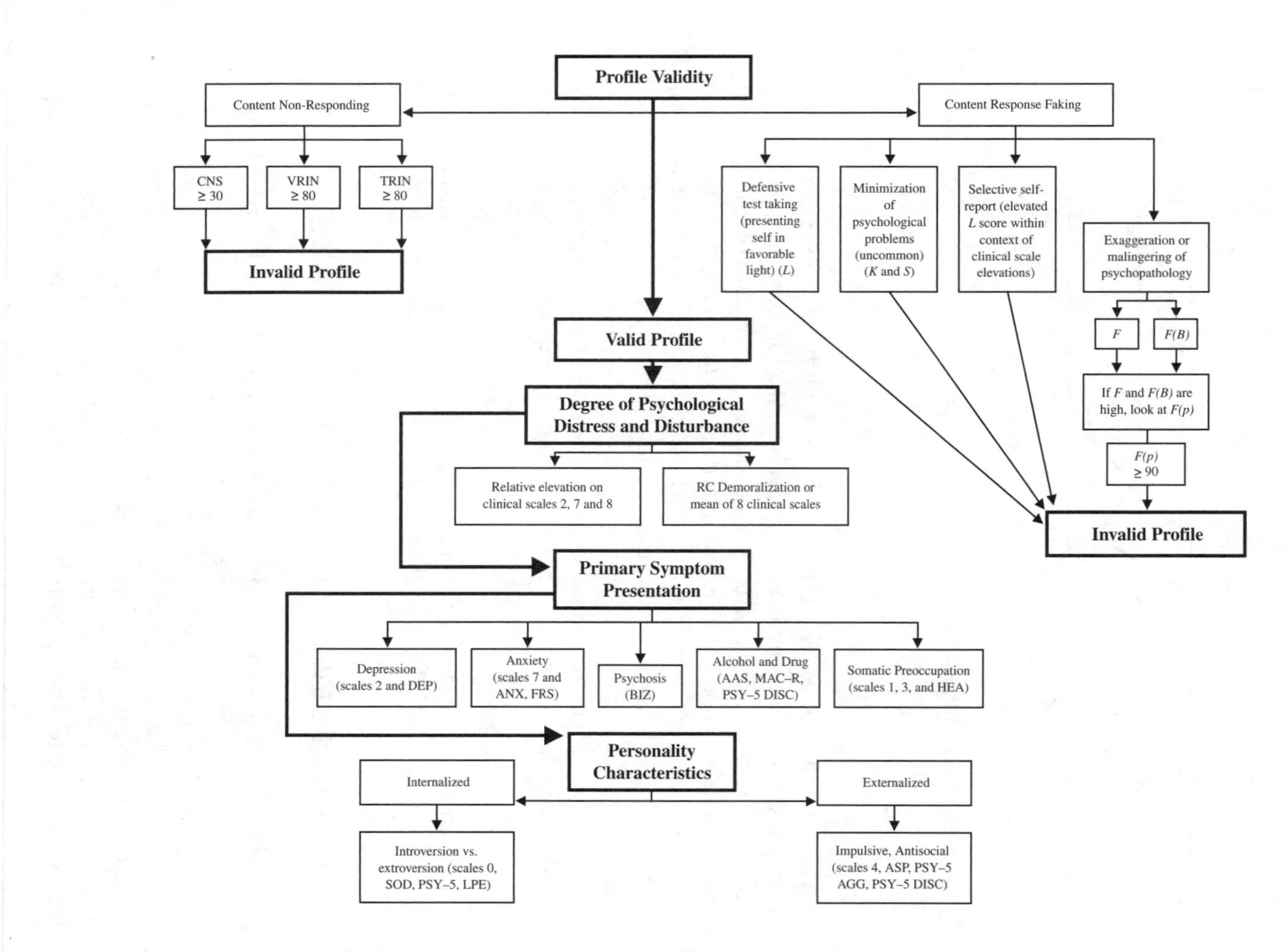

Figure 16.7. Interpretation of the MMPI–2 in disability or personal injury evaluations

resulting from an armed robbery that did not result in physical harm would not be considered a work-related condition in some states. However, if the mental or emotional condition occurred as a result of a physical condition caused by a job-related injury, then treatment and disability resulting from the mental disorder would be covered under workers' compensation statutes. Examples of such secondary mental or emotional conditions that frequently become the subject of workers' compensation claims are (a) a major depressive disorder stemming from a chronic pain condition caused by a work-related back injury and (b) PTSD resulting from an armed robbery at a bank where the clerk was struck in the head and injured. Workers' compensation in all jurisdictions would cover treatment and disability resulting from both the depression and PTSD under those conditions.

In some jurisdictions, case law has recently broadened the scope of injuries covered under workers' compensation to include the aggravation of a preexisting psychiatric or psychological condition by the work-related injury. The aggravated psychological or psychiatric injury can then be used to reach an overall permanency rating with respect to the work-related injury. Consequently, psychological or psychiatric factors can play a significant role in worker compensation awards by being either directly compensable or contributing to the overall disability claimed by the injured worker. To summarize, the workers' compensation evaluator will be asked to address the following issues:

1. *Causality:* Did the work-related injury cause or aggravate a psychological condition?
2. *Degree of disability:* Does the psychological condition result in a partial or complete inability to perform the employee's occupation?
3. *Permanency:* If disabled, is the employee temporarily or permanently disabled by the psychological condition?

Finally, the examiner may be asked to specify the period and duration of time the employee was disabled by the work-related injury and, if permanently disabled, based on statutory ratings, to specify a rating of partial or total disability.

To clarify, workers' compensation statutes in most jurisdictions allow for a psychological injury to be considered work-related if a work injury directly caused or aggravated a previously existing psychiatric condition. Further, even a preexisting stable psychological condition resulting in some impairment can be combined with impairment associated with a work-related physical injury in reaching a total disability and permanency rating.

The use of the MMPI–2 in disability evaluations as a result of workers' compensation claims can aid in establishing the presence or absence of the claimed condition and in determining the relative degree of emotional distress reported by the claimant. However, attributing direct causality solely through examination of an MMPI–2 profile produced by an injured worker is not possible (Butcher & Miller, 1998). Nonetheless, the MMPI–2 can serve as an objective measure of the injured worker's self-report. The report of somatic symptoms, pain, and emotional distress as reflected by the response to the MMPI–2 can be compared with MMPI–2 profiles produced by other industrially injured workers seeking compensation and by medical patients with the same type of injury. The examiner can make probabilistic inferences regarding causality based on the similarity or dissimilarity of the MMPI–2 profile to the various comparison groups. For example, if the profile produced by the injured worker is not typically found among injured workers or if the profile is much more elevated than that typically found in injured workers, then the chance that the injured worker's presentation is due solely to the consequences of a work-related injury is diminished.

On average, industrially injured workers tend to produce MMPI profiles marked by elevations on scales 1 and 3 (Pollack & Grainey, 1984). In comparison to individuals who had private insurance, those who were applying for disability through workers' compensation had more elevated MMPI profiles and thus appeared more disturbed. In a group of 200 individuals seen for psychiatric evaluation related to workers' compensation litigation, 15% produced a within-normal-limits (WNL) MMPI profile. Of those who produced elevated profiles, 38% produced the following two-point codes: 12/21, 13/31, and 23/32 (Hersch & Alexander, 1990; Repko & Cooper, 1983). Consequently, a significant proportion of MMPI profiles produced by injured workers involved in workers' compensation litigation indicates some degree of somatic preoccupation accompanied by depressed mood. An additional 12% of the workers' compensation claimants produced 28/82 and 68/86 code types (Hersch & Alexander, 1990; Repko & Cooper, 1983). These five code types were also the most frequently produced code types in workers referred for a psychological evaluation by company medical personnel for company benefits pending the outcome of claims filed for workers' compensation (Hersch & Alexander, 1990).

The mean MMPI profile of 100 consecutive workers' compensation patients seen within a year of injury for psychological evaluation included elevations on scales 2, 1, and 3 (Repko & Cooper, 1985). Elevations produced by individuals seeking disability are higher on these scales compared to non-disability-seeking medical patients. For example, 766 men and 298 women who applied for Social Security Disability benefits as a result of nonpsychiatric conditions produced MMPI profiles that were significantly higher than those of a group of 14,306 general medical patients seen at a larger tertiary care medical facility (Shaffer, Nusbaum, & Little, 1972). The mean code type for the men who applied for Social Security benefits was 1,

2, 3 and for the women 1 and 3 (Shaffer et al., 1972). In comparison to the general medical patients, elevations on the clinical scales fell in the clinical range in the group of individuals applying for social security disability (Shaffer et al., 1972). Thus, the MMPI profiles of individuals applying for disability benefits appear significantly more pathological than profiles produced by medical patients receiving care in general medical settings.

Injured workers produce fairly stable MMPI–2 profiles over time. The MMPI–2 profiles of injured workers referred for a psychological assessment after suffering a work-related injury remained relatively stable over a 21.3-month interval (Colotla, Bowman, & Shercliffe, 2001). Ninety-four workers were administered an MMPI–2 on two occasions spanning an average of 21.3 months. The workers were claiming a psychological injury secondary to a work-related incident. Thirty-two percent claimed PTSD after an accident or criminal incident and 20% claimed disability due to chronic pain. The remainder claimed disability due to closed head injury or other psychological problems such as depression or anxiety (Colotla et al., 2001). The observed test–retest reliability coefficients for the MMPI–2 scales of the injured workers were only slightly lower than those found for the MMPI–2 normative sample. Further, across the time interval, high point elevations were observed on scales 1 and 3 and content scale HEA with secondary elevations on scales 2, 7, and 8 at the first administration and scales 2, 6, 7, and 8 at the second administration. The mean MMPI–2 profile at the second administration suggests a higher level of depression as reflected in significant increases on scales 2 and 7 (Colotla et al., 2001).

In the preceding study, the observed increase in distress as reflected in the increase in MMPI–2 clinical scales is likely due to the fact that workers who underwent a second evaluation had not recovered from their injury and as a result were being evaluated a second time. Those individuals who experienced an improvement in symptoms would obviously not be seen for follow-up and quite likely reported an improvement in overall level of distress. Consequently, this may have contributed to the observed stability in MMPI–2 profiles over time. Nonetheless, despite an average increase in the level of distress, the self-report of these compensation-seeking injured workers remained remarkably consistent over time, suggesting that MMPI–2-assessed symptoms of injured workers are quite reliable (Colotla et al., 2001).

The length of time an individual remains disabled may contribute to an observed increase over time in general psychological distress as reflected in elevation on the MMPI Depression scale. Industrially injured workers who were disabled for a period of less than 2 years had lower MMPI Scale 2 mean scores than those who had been disabled for a period of greater than 2 years (Levenson et al., 1988). This difference was attributed to the adverse impact of disability and chronic pain, because there were no differences observed between the groups across a range of psychosocial variables.

It was concluded that the MMPI was sensitive to the impact of disability on the psychological function of the injured worker.

Work-Related Low Back Injuries

Unfortunately, the relative level of disability and the subsequent ability to return to work are not entirely related to the pathoanatomic findings and are felt to involve social and psychological factors, including compensation status, stress, and lifestyle factors. For example, even after controlling for the severity of the injury, the level of reported stress at the time of the work-related injury predicted the level of self-reported disability due to low back pain (Oleske, Andersson, Lavender, & Hahn, 2000). Low back pain as a result of work-related injury is one of the most frequently reported reasons for workers' compensation claims in the United States (Bureau of Labor Statistics, 2003). Recovery from low back injury is complicated and involves a variety of factors. For example, even with recent advances in spinal surgery, which involve shorter hospital stays and less invasive procedures, prediction of outcomes is complicated. Among patients who are brought to surgery relatively soon after the injury with well-defined disk herniation, severe emotional distress does not appear to predict poor outcome (Carragee, 2001). However, among individuals with less well-defined herniation or in cases in which there has been a delay in coming to surgery, severe emotional distress at the time of surgery is associated with a poorer outcome and increased disability (Carragee, 2001).

Given the clear involvement of nonanatomic factors in the recovery from injury, it is essential that a broadband measure such as the MMPI–2 be used in the assessment of disability related to work injury to determine the relative contribution of psychological factors in the continuing disability. As referenced earlier, the mean MMPI profile for individuals receiving workers' compensation benefits involves elevations on the 1, 2, and 3 scales. This is the same profile configuration seen with chronic pain populations (Keller & Butcher, 1991; Slesinger et al., 2002).

Within the context of a workers' compensation disability evaluation, the relative elevation of the MMPI–2 scales is the most salient issue. Given the observation that clinical scales 1, 2, and 3 are frequently found to be elevated into the clinical range on MMPI–2 profiles of injured workers, the question for the examiner is, In comparison to other medical patients, how much higher or lower are these scales elevated in the current case? If the scales are significantly higher than the average or if the MMPI–2 profile is not typically observed in injured workers, the examiner can then speak to the factors empirically associated with the particular scale elevation or MMPI–2 profile configuration that impacts recovery from the work-related injury and either promotes or hinders continued disability. For example, an injured worker who produces an elevation on scales 1 and 3 above a T score of 90 is more likely to report a wide range of physical problems and concerns that occur in response to emotional stress than an injured worker who produced an MMPI–2 profile with elevations on the 1 and 3 scale at a T score of 67.

In several studies, using a prospective design, an elevation on the MMPI Scale 3 appears to predict failure to return to work. In a large sample of 421 patients suffering acute lumbar pain, elevation on Scale 3 predicted disability and failure to return to work a year after the injury and initial report of pain (Gatchel, Polatin, & Kinney, 1995). Further, in 87 unemployed workers with low back pain referred to an orthopedic back pain clinic, lower scores on MMPI scales 1 and 3 predicted return to work 6 months later (Milhous et al., 1989). This finding was replicated with a larger group of disability-seeking low back patients receiving care through a university low back clinic for which Scale 3 contributed to independent psychosocial factors in predicting return to work after 6 months of treatment (Gallagher et al., 1989). In contrast, higher scores at time of admission to a chronic pain treatment program on scales 2 and 3 were associated with greater improvement in pain and function at time of discharge (Kleinke & Spangler, 1988). Although Scale 3 was positively associated with higher reports of pain, there was no relationship to improvement in symptoms per se. Compared with individuals who were not being treated for a work-related injury, individuals receiving workers' compensation benefits reported a greater number of symptoms and higher pain ratings both at entry and at discharge (Kleinke & Spangler, 1988). In sum, the MMPI–2 can identify psychological factors in workers suffering low back injuries that hinder recovery and promote continued disability, especially when the neuroanatomical findings are less well defined.

Prediction of Disability Among Industrially Injured Workers

Early in the history of the MMPI, attempts were made to develop scales from the MMPI item pool that would identify individuals whose pain complaints were nonorganic or functional in nature (Hanvik, 1951). These attempts proved to be unsuccessful, primarily because of the complex nature of the pain experience and the unreasonable goal of distinguishing between pain that is the physiological result of injury and pain that is the result of psychological, social, and cultural factors (Keller & Butcher, 1991; Love & Peck, 1987; Vendrig, 2000). More recently, a more nuanced understanding of the pain experience and the recognition of multidimensional contribution to that experience have developed (Chibnall & Tait, 1999; Gatchel, Polatin, & Mayer, 1995; Vendrig, 2000).

In general, workers who have been injured on the job and who have failed to recover produce elevations on the 1, 2, and 3 scales of the MMPI–2 (Gandolfo, 1995; Levenson et al., 1988; Repko & Cooper, 1983). Much of the evidence for this generalization comes from workers suffering from low back injuries and associated chronic pain. Low to moderate elevation on MMPI–2 clinical scales 1 and 3 are common among individuals with low back pain associated with objective findings (Sherman, Camfield, & Arena, 1995). However, high elevations on these scales are suggestive of functional factors involved in the failure to recover from the injury (Love & Peck, 1987; Vendrig, 1999). Because the 1, 2, and 3 scales of the MMPI–2 assess somatic preoccupation, depressed affect, discouragement, and the tendency to respond to emotional stress through the development of somatic complaints and pain, this finding is not surprising because there is compelling evidence to support the contribution of psychosocial and personality factors in the failure to recover from a low back injury (Chibnall & Tait, 1999; Gatchel & Gardea, 1999). Consequently, the MMPI–2 does provide important information related to factors that impair recovery from physical injury.

To clarify, the MMPI–2 can provide information regarding emotional factors that may hinder recovery from work-related injuries. For example, an elevation on Scale 3 is associated with failure to return to work after a low back injury. Moreover, the association between an elevation on Scale 3 and failure to return to work was found prior to the occurrence of the work-related injury.

Prospective studies exploring MMPI–2 variables that are associated with a failure to return to work after a work-related accident and failure to benefit from a chronic pain treatment program identify personality characteristics that are tapped by Scale 3 (Fordyce, Bigos, Batti'e, & Fisher, 1992; Gallagher et al., 1995; Vendrig, 1999). Overall, injured workers who fail to recover from their injury and who become involved in workers' compensation litigation produce higher elevations on MMPI–2 scales associated with somatic preoccupation and depression. Profiles tend to be stable and increase over time in disabled workers. From the perspective of the disability examiner, it is important to examine the relative elevation of the MMPI–2 clinical scales to determine if the profile is typical of injured workers and consistent with the type of injury reported. Moreover, the absolute elevation of scales associated with somatic preoccupation—such as clinical scales 1 and 3 and content scale Health Concerns—is important. If these scales are highly elevated—two standard deviations above the mean of hospitalized medical patients (T = 60 on scales 1 and 3; Henrichs, 1981)—the probability that psychosocial and personality factors are significantly influencing the report of pain and disability increases substantially (see chap. 11, this volume, for more information on chronic pain).

SUMMARY

Since 1984, the rates of non-elderly Americans receiving Social Security Disability or Supplemental Security Income have doubled. Specifically, between 1983 and 1998, disability awards for mental disorder or disease of the musculoskeletal system grew by 60% (Autor & Duggan, 2001). These trends, taken together with an associated increase in workers' compensation claims based on mental disorders and litigation based on emotional damages sustained after a personal injury, suggest that practicing psychologists, even those who do not specialize in disability evaluations, will frequently be faced with the prospect of either evaluating or treating a client who is seeking compensation after an injury. It is important that both the disability specialist and the psychologist in general practice understand the ramifications of such claims and the impact of litigation or compensation seeking on the assessment process and subsequent treatment. A thorough, objective, psychological evaluation is essential when faced with the injured client. This chapter presented evidence in support of the use of the MMPI–2 in the evaluation of injured clients and provided practical recommendations and guidelines for MMPI–2 interpretation under those circumstances. There are several advantages to incorporating the MMPI–2 as an essential component in an evaluation of injured clients related to the objective nature of the instrument. The MMPI–2 contains validity scales that provide an objective and reliable measure of the accuracy of the evaluee's self-report. The individual MMPI–2 profile can be compared with the mean profiles of individuals suffering from similar injuries or psychiatric conditions to objectively quantify the relative level of distress associated with the claimed condition and to determine whether the profile is broadly consistent with profiles produced by others suffering from the claimed condition or injury. The use of the MMPI–2 in disability or personal injury evaluations decreases the subjective component of clinical judgment and provides a standardized measure upon which the examiner can base an opinion. Thus, the psychologist can readily defend his or her opinion regarding the presence or absence of disorder and associated disability.

IV

SPECIAL CONSIDERATIONS IN MMPI–2 INTERPRETATION

17

COMPUTER-BASED ASSESSMENT WITH THE MMPI–2

MERA M. ATLIS, JUNGWON HAHN, AND JAMES N. BUTCHER

Over the past 50 years, computers have become an integral part of psychological assessment. Although initially their role was limited to scoring, in more recent decades computer-based test administration and interpretation have grown substantially in their scope and popularity. A number of authors have discussed the advantages and disadvantages of computer use in psychological practice (Butcher, 1987; Groth-Marnat, 2000; Moreland, 1985b; Matarazzo, 1986; Watkins & McDermott, 1991). Computers can provide an objective, reliable, and cost-efficient way to administer, score, and interpret psychological tests (see Table 17.1). They can avoid or minimize subjectivity in compiling of interpretive material and can provide expert consultation by rapidly incorporating information from a large number of sources. At the same time, computer-based administration may not be equivalent to other assessment formats and may impact test takers' scores in a variety of ways, such as by test takers having a greater willingness to disclose personal information (Butcher, 2003a; Moreland, 1987). Computerized reports based on poorly validated psychological tests may appear more valid than they actually are due to professional appearance and reliability. Even when valid interpretive data are available for a

TABLE 17.1
Advantages and Disadvantages of Computer-Based Psychological Test Administration, Scoring, and Interpretation

Advantages	Disadvantages
Objectivity—No observer effects are present; the test is not subject to interpreter bias.	*Format non-equivalence*—Differential impact of computerized format on test scores (e.g., impact of higher test anxiety or higher openness in responses) may occur.
Reliability—The content of outcome and interpretation is consistent across many administrations.	*Overestimation of validity*—Due to professional look and reliability, reports may appear more valid than they actually are.
Standardization—Administration, scoring, and results are produced consistently for every test taker.	*Barnum effect*—Interpretive statements may be so general that they would apply to virtually anyone.
Economy—Scoring time is significantly reduced, which in turn can lead to monetary savings; making copies of a computer program is cheaper than training another professional.	*"Black box" problem*—Scoring and interpretive rules are not always available to consumers, which can make validation and decisions about the efficacy of each system difficult or impossible.
Consultative role—Interpretation can incorporate expertise of multiple individuals.	*Too many systems*—An overabundance of scoring and interpretation packages is available, with little information about their validity.
Assistance for special populations—Potential advantages exist for test takers with visual and auditory disabilities.	*Ethical concerns*—Ease of administration and scoring can create a higher potential for misuse (e.g., access of nonqualified users to interpretive reports and decreased security of items and individual test scores).
Efficiency in updating—Once the system is created, it may be easier to update and incorporate experience of multiple experts, making extensive training for every human interpreter unnecessary.	*Time-consuming to create*—Quality computer-based interpretive systems can take 2–6 years to develop (not including all the time needed for validation studies).
Innovative presentation—Alternatives are available for visual/virtual, interactive, and/or adaptive administration of traditional test items.	*Potentially aversive user response*—Clients and clinicians may be impacted by negative attitudes, fears, higher test anxiety, and feelings of depersonalization.
Advantage in validation process—It may be easier to validate a computer system than the interpretive schemes of individual psychologists.	
Potentially positive user response—Clients may be more likely to disclose certain sensitive information to a computer.	

particular test, computer-based systems do not guarantee that their approaches to integrating the data are valid. Consequently, choosing among an ever growing number of available systems can be quite a challenge. How can one maximize the advantages and evaluate the potential problems for a computer-based system? What features make the utilization of such systems most beneficial?

In this chapter, we attempt to answer the preceding questions through discussion of the computer-based MMPI–2. First, we describe the history of the computerized MMPI and MMPI–2. Then, the summary of research on equivalence of the computer-based and paper-and-pencil reports is followed by discussion of new developments in the computer-based administration of the MMPI–2. Next, a practical case example is described. We conclude this chapter with a list of suggestions on how to incorporate computer-based MMPI–2 data with other sources of information about the client.

HISTORY OF THE COMPUTER-BASED MMPI AND MMPI–2

Compared to other personality tests, the MMPI has a long, well-established tradition in computerized assessment. Since the early 1960s, at least 14 computerized interpretive systems were made commercially available (Eyde, Kowal, & Fishburne, 1991). The vast majority of such systems have been mostly *nonintegrative*, or consisting of a series of sentences or phrases, each of which was constructed to interpret a particular test or a scale (Vale & Keller, 1987). The first MMPI interpretive system was developed by Mayo Clinic to generate a profile of scale scores and several interpretive statements from a total of 110 possibilities, most of which were based on behavioral correlates for single-scale elevations (Rome et al., 1962; Pearson, Rome, Swenson, Mataya, & Brannick, 1965). The report was scored using special IBM cards that could be marked by the test taker and read into the computer by the scanner. The Fowler Report, developed at the University of Alabama, expanded the Mayo Clinic's strategy by creating a program that generated a three-page narrative report from a library of interpretive statements based on correlates associated with single-scale elevations (Fowler, 1966, 1968). In 1965 the Roche Psychiatric Service Institute made the Fowler system commercially available through the first national mail-in MMPI computer-based interpretation service. During the 17 years of its existence, about 1.5 million reports were scored, which suggests that about one fourth of the eligible psychologists and psychiatrists in the United States used the service (Moreland, 1985a). In the mid-1960s, the Behaviordyne Report was produced by Finney (1966); Finney's program produced an interpretive narrative of 100 statements from a repertory of about 1,000 statements to describe the conscious or unconscious processes and typical patterns of interpersonal relationships. As noted by Sundberg (1985), the report also provided a list of diagnostic impressions selected according to the most likely fit with the *Diagnostic and Statistical Manual of Mental Disorders, Third Edition* (*DSM–III*; American Psychiatric Association, 1980).

The programming logic of nonintegrative computer-based systems is relatively simple; however, configural or score pattern interpretations are rarely included, which makes the nonintegrative interpretive reports more likely to be contradictory, repetitive, and blind to score interaction effects. With the accumulation of code-type data and publication of several MMPI "cookbooks," integration of more than one scale score into a computerized narrative became feasible. Caldwell (1970, 1978) incorporated his expertise and empirical data (Chase, 1974) into constructing interpretive statements based on code-type correlates. His computerized narrative report featured sections on treatment planning, early-childhood correlates of profile types, and alternative diagnoses listed in order of "most likely" to "least likely" fit (Greene, 1980). The Lachar Interpretive system published by the Western Psychological Services (Lachar, 1974b) offered extensive data on how the system was created, including algorithms for generating narrative statements based on empirical information for a large number of code types. *Marks Adult MMPI Report* published by Applied Innovations also provided interpretive statements along with explicit descriptions of how each individual statement was generated (Duthie, 1985). It also provided diagnostic suggestions based on the *DSM–III* diagnoses. Another computerized interpretive system prepared by Leon M. Morris and Jack R. Tomlinson using the Colligan, Osborne, Swenson, and Offord (1983) norms, incorporated the *DSM–III* terminology and included statements regarding the test taker's social, vocational, and academic functioning, as well as statements related to assertiveness and forensic implications of test findings.

Incorporating code-type data into computer-based interpretations does not guarantee that all the relevant behavioral correlates will be appropriately integrated. *Omnibus* systems are specifically designed to interpret an entire profile of scale scores or a battery of scale scores in an integrative fashion (Vale & Keller, 1987). One way to create an omnibus system is to model the decision process of an expert clinician or to create empirically tested decision trees that incorporate actuarial data from research on behavioral correlates. To accomplish this goal, some researchers have explored the development of statistical decision rules to improve classification of the MMPI profiles into clinically useful categories. For example, the Goldberg Index attempted to model reasoning of an expert clinician by developing mathematical prediction models to classify MMPI profiles into either psychotic or neurotic categories. Once the human expert's classification rules were specified and programmed, the computerized program outperformed the original expert (Goldberg, 1970, 1972). Kleinmuntz (1964, 1975) modeled expert reasoning by creating a logical decision tree to sort MMPI profiles into *adjusted, maladjusted,* or *unclassified* categories. The sequential decision rules were based on hours of the clinician's tape-recorded verbalizations as he sorted profiles of 126 college students. Consistent with Goldberg's findings, once the decision rules were programmed, the computer produced a better hit rate than the original decisions made by the expert clinician (Kleinmuntz, 1964, 1975).

Computer-based interpretive reports attempt to incorporate at least some of the empirically tested decision rules as well as the most recent code-type data such as the FASTTEST developed by Miller, Johnson, Klingler, Williams, and Giannetti (1977). Another system, the Minnesota Report (Butcher, 1990a), makes use of available empirical research, including the empirical code-type studies described by Gilberstadt and Duker (1965); Marks, Seeman, and Haller (1975); and Graham, Ben-Porath, and McNulty (1999) to provide correlates for various MMPI–2 scale and code-type elevations. The report uses several interpretive schemes and selects a narrative report sequence depending upon setting. The three settings from which reports can be generated are (a) clinical and alcohol/drug, (b) personnel, and (c) forensic. Once the user selects the setting with which to compare the client's profile, then the interpretive subroutines are selected. In generating a report, the program first checks to determine if the profile is valid and interpretable based on validity scale elevations. Then it searches to determine if the generated profile is a well-known code type. If yes, then the interpretation is based on the code-type configuration. If the profile is not a well-defined, well-known code type, then the program checks whether any scale scores are elevated. If yes, then a linear combination of scale scores is used to come up with predictive and descriptive statements about the test taker. If profile falls within normal limits, the results are interpreted in terms of vocational issues, social relationships, and health problems. The program for each setting for the Minnesota Report contains hundreds of pages of interpretive text in order to provide a report for all clients.

VALIDITY OF NARRATIVE, COMPUTER-BASED INTERPRETATIONS

As noted earlier in this chapter, high reliability is among the primary advantages of computer-based administration, scoring, and interpretation. According to the *American Psychological Association Guidelines for Computer-Based Tests and Interpretations* (American Psychological Association [APA], 1986), "a well-designed statistical treatment of test results and ancillary information will yield more valid assessments than will an individual professional using the same information" (p. 9). This acknowledgment stems from research on statistical and clinical prediction starting with a monograph by Meehl (1954), who argued that the actuarial/statistical predictions were more valid than those based on subjective clinical decisions. Consequent empirical investigations indicated that objective assessment procedures are equal or superior to subjective approaches (Dawes, Faust, & Meehl, 1989; Goldberg, 1965, 1970; Grove & Meehl, 1996;

Kleinmuntz, 1975). In a meta-analysis of 136 studies by Grove, Zald, Lebow, Snitz, and Nelson (2000), the statistical prediction was estimated to have about 10% accuracy advantage over clinical prediction.

Despite the advantages of statistical prediction, it is important to keep in mind that not all computer-based assessment is actuarial. Sines (1966) defined statistical prediction as "the empirical determination of the regularities that may exist between specified psychological test data and equally clearly specified socially, clinically, or theoretically significant non-test characteristics" (p. 135). Computerized assessment based on the work of an expert clinician who developed his or her interpretations based on published research and extensive clinical experience still involves clinical judgment and is not actuarial in nature. Nonetheless, incorporating the expertise of a particular clinician into a computer-based interpretive system should not be viewed as a disadvantage. For the vast majority of tests, including a well-researched instrument such as the MMPI–2, data on base rates and empirically validated statistical prediction rules are not available for every scale and profile configuration. Consequently, the MMPI–2 computer-based interpretation systems typically attempt to incorporate actuarial and expert approaches into their narrative reports.

One of the first studies investigating the quality of computer-based narrative reports was conducted by Fowler and Miller (1969), who asked practicing clinicians to provide the global ratings of their computer-based interpretive system. In response to the question, "How would you sum up the value of this service to you?" 98% of all participants provided favorable responses. Similar "consumer satisfaction" studies have provided an overwhelming support for the computer-based interpretative systems with an estimated median global accuracy rating of 78.5% (Moreland, 1987). Despite being useful in guiding improvements of the computer-based interpretive systems, reviewers tend to agree that these studies often fail to control for the P. T. Barnum effect; that is, the interpretive systems may be characterized as accurate because the interpretive statements are so general that they would apply to virtually anyone (Moreland, 1987).

In an effort to improve the "consumer satisfaction" design, a few studies compared the computer-generated narrative MMPI reports with "criterion" narratives of the MMPI produced by human interpreters (usually clinicians). In such studies, computerized reports are frequently judged to be equal or better than average when compared to interpretations of similar profiles produced by expert clinicians. For example, a study of 262 airline pilot applicants investigated the validity of the computerized MMPI in personnel screening by comparing evaluations of expert clinicians and application of the computer-generated decision rules (Butcher, 1988). For each applicant, the overall level of psychological adjustment was rated by experts as *adequate*, *problems possible*, or *problems likely*. The computer-generated decision rules were also used to classify applicants' adjustment into five categories: *excellent*, *good*, *adequate*, *problems possible*, and *poor*. Although no kappa values were calculated and no external criteria were provided to evaluate the relative accuracy of each rating method, in ratings of the overall adjustment of pilot applicants there was a strong agreement between the expert clinicians and the computer. In 26.7% of all cases, computer rules and clinicians were in agreement on the possibility of problems being present. Over 60% of applicants who were rated as *problems likely* by the expert clinicians were also classified as *poor* by the computer-generated rules (Butcher, 1988).

In a cross-cultural study investigating the validity of computer-generated MMPI–2 narratives, clinicians in Australia, France, Norway, and the United States were asked to administer the translated versions of the MMPI–2 to their patients seen for psychological evaluation or therapy (Butcher, Berah, et al., 1998). The MMPI–2 responses were then scored and interpreted using the Minnesota Report (National Computer Systems, 1982) based on the U.S. normative sample. All clinicians estimated the percentage of accurate computer-generated MMPI–2 descriptions for each of their patients and responded to questions about how to improve the narrative report. They also rated each section of computer-based MMPI–2 narratives as *extensive*, *more than adequate*, *adequate*, *some*, or *insufficient*. Clinicians from all four countries found that Validity Considerations, Symptomatic Patterns, and Interpersonal Relations sections of the Minnesota Report output provided the most useful information about their patients. Few raters classified the narrative reports as inaccurate or inappropriate. Among the 87% of all narrative reports, 60% of computer-generated narrative statements were rated as appropriate (Butcher, Berah, et al., 1998).

One serious methodological limitation of "criterion" studies is that they do not account for the possibility that the validity of clinicians' interpretations might be low enough to allow the computerized reports with poor validity to be judged as accurate (Butcher, Perry, & Atlis, 2000; Moreland, 1987). Moreland (1985b) pointed out that in studies involving global accuracy ratings it is often quite difficult or even impossible to obtain estimates of inter-rater reliability. In addition, clinicians are often asked to provide their judgment about the accuracy of narrative reports without explaining their reasoning or verifying the accuracy of their judgments by questioning the test takers themselves or by seeking other sources of criterion information such as family members' or physicians' reports. In developing or improving a particular computer-based interpretive system, global accuracy ratings may not be as useful as evaluations of individual interpretive statements (Moreland, 1985b).

Eyde et al. (1991) conducted one of the best studies to date incorporating a number of Moreland's methodological suggestions. These researchers used case histories and self-report questionnaires as a criterion against which narrative reports generated by seven MMPI computer interpretation systems were evaluated. Twelve raters evaluated six MMPI–2 protocols carefully selected from a pool of active-duty male patients at the Walter Reed Army Medical Center between 1983 and 1985. A pair of Black and White patients who were matched for 7/2 (Psychasthenia–Depression) code type and a pair of Black and White cases who had all clinical scales in the subclinical range (T scores less than 70) were assigned to all raters. Each rater was also assigned one of the unique 12 pairs of cases matched for race, MMPI spike, or a code type. Clinicians rated the relevance of each sentence in all narratives and estimated the global accuracy of each interpretive report. In their final global ratings, the raters showed strong agreement for each of the common cases and in evaluating the overall accuracy of the narratives of the seven systems. The subclinical normal cases rated by all clinicians had a high percentage (median 50) of unreadable sentences, while the percentage of unreadable sentences for the 7/2 code-type common cases was low (median 14). For the unique code types, the sentence-by-sentence results were consistent with the global ratings of the seven systems. The three systems with the highest rank order were the Minnesota Report (Pearson Assessments, formerly National Computer Systems; NCS, 1982), the Caldwell Report (Caldwell, 1970, 1978), and the Lachar Interpretive System (Lachar, 1974), with the median accuracy rates across the 12 raters 49%, 46%, and 33%, respectively. A potential explanation for differences in findings for the subclinical normal and clinical cases may come from the fact that the clinical cases were inpatients for whom more detailed histories were available. Also, since the length of time between the preparation of the case histories and the administrations of the MMPI varied, changes in acute symptoms over time could not be controlled (Eyde et al., 1991).

Shores and Carstairs (1998) further investigated the validity of the computer-based Minnesota Report (NCS, 1982) in a simulation study designed to determine the report's accuracy in identifying faked MMPI–2 profiles. Three groups of 18 college students were asked (a) to portray themselves in unrealistically good light (fake-good), (b) to portray themselves in unrealistically bad light (fake-bad), or (c) to read the standard instructions from the MMPI–2 test booklet. The results of the study supported the validity of the Minnesota Report in identifying invalid profiles. In the fake-good condition, 94% were classified correctly with only one profile misclassified as "normal." In the fake-bad condition, the Minnesota Report classified 100% of the MMPI–2 profiles correctly. For profiles completed under standard instructions, 78% were classified as "normal" and 22% were classified as faking-good (Shores & Carstairs, 1998).

To summarize, research into computer-generated narrative reports for the MMPI and MMPI–2 generally has found that the interpretive statements contained in them are comparable to clinician-generated statements. In addition, there is evidence to suggest that the computer-based MMPI–2 reports are relatively successful in classifying profiles in clinically meaningful ways—such as being able to successfully identify invalid profiles or screen applicants in personnel settings. However, there are also indications that not all computer-based programs are equally valid and that there is great variability in their ability to provide useful narrative reports (Williams & Weed, 2004).

EQUIVALENCE OF COMPUTER-BASED AND PAPER-AND-PENCIL FORMATS

Most MMPI and MMPI–2 data were and still are collected using the paper-and-pencil version of the instrument. It is only reasonable to inquire whether the computerized format produces enough of a difference in testing conditions to impact the scores and their interpretation. Differences between the two administration formats may exist for several reasons. During a computer-administered test, examinees are presented a limited number of items at a time and may have no way of knowing how many items are on the test. This may prompt more careful attention to each item, which may in turn impact the meaning of test takers' responses and subsequent interpretation of test results (Moreland, 1987). The content of items may also have a differential effect when administered on the computer. For instance, there is considerable evidence to suggest that test takers may be more comfortable disclosing sensitive personal information to a computer (Carr, Ghosh, & Ancil, 1983; Davis, 1999; Duffy & Waterton, 1984; Koson, Kitchen, Kochen, & Stodolsky, 1970; Salgado & Moscoso, 2003; Wallace, 1999). Consequently, when compared to a conventional testing format, greater openness in responding may result in more elevated profiles for the computer-administered MMPI (Bresolin, 1984).

In light of potential differences in administration formats, a number of studies have investigated the equivalence of computer-based and paper-and-pencil MMPI and MMPI–2 (Biskin & Kolotkin, 1977; Jemelka, Wiegand, Walker, & Trupin, 1992; Lambert, Andrews, Rylee, & Skinner, 1987; Lushene, O'Neil, & Dunn, 1974; Pinsoneault, 1996; Schuldberg, 1988; Watson, Juba, Anderson, & Manifold, 1990). Overall, the bulk of evidence indicates that the differences between computer and paper-and-pencil administrations are generally small and, if present, non-equivalence is small enough to be of little practical consequence. Finger and Ones (1999) supported this conclusion in their meta-analysis of 14 studies that were conducted between 1974 and 1996 and used the computerized MMPI or MMPI–2. The T-score mean differences between the two test formats across studies were negligible. Since the cross-form correlations were reliably near 1.00, the authors concluded that there is little impact of computer administration on the MMPI scores (Finger & Ones, 1999).

RECENT DEVELOPMENTS: COMPUTERIZED ADAPTIVE TESTING

Adaptive Testing and Item Response Theory

An important feature of quality psychological assessment is parsimony. Since the information obtained from most psychological tests comes from responses to their items, it is crucial that the assessment questions are answered with the smallest possible number of highly efficient items. In traditional psychological testing, everyone receives the same items, which could be too easy or too difficult for a particular test taker. While easy items may dampen motivation, overly difficult items may lead examinees to omission of responses or random guessing (Watkins & McDermott, 1991). Consequently, traditional testing may present a restricted range of accuracy for nonaverage test takers.

An *adaptive test* is a tailored, individualized test that can provide an optimal amount of information with minimal cost. An adaptive instrument can determine when enough information has been collected to estimate the trait of the examinee accurately. The goal of an adaptive test is to achieve parsimony by providing the optimal number of items, and this goal can be obtained by "adjusting the item coverage to the response characteristics of individual test takers" (Anastasi, 1988, p. 314). During the adaptive test administration, the first administered item is scored immediately to determine the difficulty and discrimination level of the next item. If an examinee answers that item in a predetermined direction, the next item to be administered will be a more "difficult" one or the one designed to assess the hypothesized domain more deeply. If the examinee fails to respond in a predetermined direction, the second administered item will be an "easier" one or one created to sample a slightly different aspect of the same domain. The third item is administered and scored in the same manner and is chosen based on the responses from the previous two items. An adaptive test is discontinued sooner than its traditional counterpart because it ensures that only items appropriate for the examinee's level are presented, making the process of obtaining the information about each examinee most efficient.

To date, most adaptive testing strategies have been based on item response theory (IRT; Weiss, 1985). In IRT, the conditional probability of the response to an item for different levels of an underlying latent trait or ability is estimated. For example, if an individual has a high latent trait, the probability of that person responding to an item in the keyed direction is greater. The relationship between the probability of the item endorsement and the latent trait can be graphically expressed in an S-shaped curve, called an item characteristic curve (ICC). One of the goals of the IRT analysis is to find the most accurate ICC curve for each test taker, delineating the best regression estimate between the probability of the item endorsement and the latent trait (Weiss & Yoes, 1988). Ability to estimate the measurement precision for each test taker provides the IRT with a major advantage over the classical testing theory (Hulin, Drasgow, & Parsons, 1983). In classical testing theory, measurement precision can be assessed by a uniform standard error of measurement. In contrast, measurement precision in IRT can be indexed by a conditional standard error of measurement based on a test information curve rather than assuming a global standard error across all trait levels. As a result, IRT allows gaining maximum precision across individuals with different latent trait levels.

Computerized Adaptive Testing

An adaptive test can be administered by computer. In computerized adaptive testing (CAT; Weiss, 1985), computers administer items, score the responses, select the next items based on the responses to the previous items, and determine if the optimal amount of information has been obtained and thus terminate the test. Most CAT is composed of three components: (a) a procedure for estimating an examinee's ability or trait level, (b) a procedure for selecting items that are most informative for each individual with different trait levels, and (c) a termination criterion to determine the discontinuing point (Waller & Reise, 1989). Starting from an item of predetermined difficulty, the preprogrammed computer decides if an examinee answered in the keyed or nonkeyed direction, then selects the next item that can provide maximal information about the person's latent trait. The computer automatically discontinues this algorithm if the termination criterion is satisfied.

The major advantage of CAT over conventional testing is its supreme efficiency and precision. Computerized adaptive testing participants are provided with only the items that are necessary to measure the assessment questions, and they do not have to take the redundant or inappropriate items. As a result, test length and time can be significantly reduced (Brown & Weiss, 1977; Kiely, Zara, & Weiss, 1983; McBride & Martin, 1983; Moreno, Wetzel, McBride, & Weiss, 1984). Also, the individualized, tailored test items for each individual in CAT can ensure the same degree of precision for all the examinees (Weiss & Vale, 1987). If everybody has to answer all items regardless of his or her status on the trait being measured, in order to maximize the overall precision of the test, test developers must adjust the item difficulty to the average level of all potential test takers.

Hence, examinees with very high or low ability may not be measured as precisely as those with average ability. In contrast, the individualized CAT allows each test taker to receive items that are selected for that particular individual, even when that individual's performance is at the extreme ends of the distribution. Consequently, all examinees are tested with superior measurement precision.

MMPI–2 Applications of Computerized Adaptive Testing

Despite the evidence for high efficiency in CAT applications of the IRT, some authors have argued that the IRT assumption of an underlying unidimensional latent trait is problematic when applied to psychometrically heterogeneous measures (Butcher, Keller, & Bacon, 1985; Weiss & Suhdolnik, 1985). The two underlying assumptions of the IRT are (a) the IRT model used for parameter estimation must adequately fit the data, and (b) all the test items assess a single underlying latent trait (Hulin et al., 1983). Most personality and clinical tests are designed to measure multiple, frequently overlapping domains. The MMPI–2 and its empirically keyed clinical scales are the prime example of this problem. Realizing the difficulty of applying CAT to heterogeneous tests, Ben-Porath, Waller, Slutske, and Butcher (1988) suggested to either (a) restrict the effort to apply CAT to the tests that are unidimensional in nature, or (b) develop an alternate method that can replace IRT to apply CAT in multidimensional personality tests.

Waller and Reise (1989) followed the Ben-Porath et al. (1988) recommendation and demonstrated that application of CAT to the unidimensional tests or to individual scales from a multidimensional measure can be successful. These researchers showed that the IRT–based CAT model can be used effectively for the 34-item Absorption scale from the Multidimensional Personality Questionnaire (Tellegen, 1982), a homogeneous scale designed to assess hypnotic susceptibility (Tellegen & Atkinson, 1974). Waller and Reise (1989) tested two different strategies of the IRT–based CAT. In the *fixed-test-length* (FTL) adaptive testing strategy, the participants were provided with a fixed number of individualized items hypothesized to be appropriate for their trait level. The FTL strategy saved as many as 50% of the test items with little loss of accuracy. When classification is the goal of the assessment, the *clinical-decision* (CD) adaptive testing allows the computer to provide estimated latent trait levels for each item and compare them with the predetermined cutoff score. Waller and Reise (1989) found that the CD strategy identified individuals with an extreme level of Absorption trait using just 25% of the available 34 items.

Despite the support for effective use of IRT–based testing with relatively homogeneous measures, Waller and Reise (1989) also cautioned that "strict attention to the dimensionality of the assessment instrument must be paid to ensure the integrity of the procedure" (p. 1057). Unless the unidimensionality assumption has been met beforehand, the IRT–based CAT strategies may not be applicable to other personality tests. To test the dimensionality of the MMPI, Carter and Wilkinson (1984) have applied a one-parameter IRT model to the MMPI validity and clinical scales. Their analysis showed that the one-parameter IRT model fit poorly to the MMPI items for all the validity and clinical scales except Scale *L* (Lie), indicating that most of the MMPI validity and clinical scales are multidimensional in nature and do not satisfy the unidimensionality assumption of the IRT. The content scales of the MMPI, however, may be good candidates for applying the IRT–based CAT strategies because they were designed to possess high internal consistency (Butcher, Graham, Williams, & Ben-Porath, 1990).

Ben-Porath et al. (1988) tested the applicability of the IRT–based CAT strategies to relatively homogeneous MMPI–2 content scales. The IRT parameter estimates for the MMPI–2 Depression (*D*) and Cynicism content scales were obtained from 1,000 subjects who were part of the MMPI–2 normative sample. For the FTL strategy, the trait estimates from the short form of the Depression scale correlated almost perfectly (r = .99) with trait estimates derived from the full scale scores, producing more than 50% in item administration saving. For the CD strategy, individuals with below-cutoff scores received less than 30% of the full scale, with little loss of accuracy. Consistent with Carter and Wilkinson (1984), the researchers concluded that, while the IRT–based CAT strategies with the MMPI–2 clinical scales could not be used due to their multidimensionality, clinical-decision and fixed-test-length adaptive testing are promising approaches for the content scales (Ben-Porath et al., 1988).

Countdown Method

Since the multidimensional nature of the MMPI–2 clinical scales violates the IRT assumptions, Butcher et al. (1985) proposed the *countdown method* as an alternative nonpsychometric approach to IRT–based adaptive testing. Two strategies in the countdown method have been suggested (Ben-Porath, Slutske, & Butcher, 1989; Butcher et al., 1985). The first strategy, *classification procedure* (CP), is most useful when the assessment question is simply to know whether the responses of the test takers fall below or beyond the cutoff scores. To illustrate, if a psychiatric screening instrument consists of 30 items and a score of 20 is a cutoff value to classify clinically meaningful elevation, then a person who does not endorse the first 11 items (and thus will endorse fewer than 70 items) cannot be classified within the deviant group. Yet, if a participant endorses 20 items, then the person is positively classified into the "deviant" group and no additional items will be administered. In the *full scores on elevated scales* (FSES) strategy, the machine terminates the administration only when scale elevation is "ruled out," in other words, when the responses exceed the cutoff values. Thus, if an individual reaches clinical elevation, all items in that scale are administered to obtain the full score on that scale. Ben-Porath et al. (1989) pointed out that cost minimization in the countdown method can be achieved by administering items in the order of the endorsement rate. For example, the main purpose of the FSES strategy is to rule out scale elevation. Consequently, one can first administer the items that are less likely to be endorsed in the keyed direction (e.g., Depression). If an examinee endorses the items that are less likely to be endorsed by depressed individuals, one can more quickly rule out the possibility of scale elevation for that examinee.

Using the real-data simulation technique, Ben-Porath et al. (1989) explored the potential advantage of applying the countdown method to the MMPI. The applicability of both the CP and the FSES strategies were tested, using two personnel-selection samples (n = 470) and two clinical samples (n = 232) from four different settings in Minnesota and Ohio. To maximize item cost savings, they first administered 150 least frequently endorsed items and then went on to the remaining items. The results were promising—up to 31.3% of the items in the CP strategy and up to 31.1% of the items in the FSES strategy could be saved (Ben-Porath et al., 1989).

Roper, Ben-Porath, and Butcher (1995) expanded Ben-Porath et al.'s (1989) methodology to compare the computerized adaptive MMPI–2 based on the countdown method to the conventional booklet version of the MMPI–2 in a sample of 571 undergraduate college students. Three versions of the MMPI–2 were administered: a booklet version, an adaptive computerized version, and a conventional computerized version. The same format was administered twice: each participant took the booklet and adaptive computerized versions (in counterbalanced order) or took the conventional and adaptive computerized versions (in counterbalanced order). Roper et al. (1995) found few statistically significant differences between the mean scale scores of the computerized adaptive and conventional MMPI–2, suggesting that the two administration methods were equivalent. Mean item savings of the computerized adaptive version were remarkable, producing item savings of 30% to 34%. Furthermore, in addition to the two versions of the MMPI–2, study participants completed the Beck Depression Inventory (BDI; Beck, Ward, Mendelson, Mock, & Erbaugh, 1961), the Anxiety and Anger scales from the State–Trait Personality Inventory (STPI; Spielberger, 1979), and the Symptom Checklist Revised (SCL–90–R; Derogatis, 1983). Correlations between the MMPI–2 scores and the criterion measures were quite comparable for the computerized adaptive and conventional MMPI–2, indicating that the changes in the MMPI–2 administration did not affect its criterion validity.

Handel, Ben-Porath, and Watt (1999) further explored the validity of the countdown method in a study of 140 Veterans Administration hospital patients entering an addictions program. All participants took the MMPI–2 twice after being randomly assigned one of the two conditions: computerized conventional test–retest (n = 72) or computerized conventional–computerized adaptive (n = 68). The researchers compared the correlations between conventional and adaptive MMPI–2 scales with scores on criterion measures including NEO–PI–R (Neuroticism, Extraversion, and Openness–Personality Inventory—Revised) scales (Costa & McCrae, 1992), the BDI (Beck et al., 1961), the Self-Report Personality Questionnaire (SCID–Q; First, Spitzer, Gibbson, & Williams, 1995), the Aggression Questionnaire (AQ; Buss & Perry, 1992), and the fifth edition of the Addiction Severity Index (ASI; McLellan, Kushner, Metzger, & Peters, 1992). Consistent with Roper et al. (1995), the results showed promising comparability of the computerized adaptive MMPI–2 based on the countdown method. The mean scale scores of the computerized adaptive and conventional MMPI–2 were quite comparable. Although some statistically significant differences were found between computerized adaptive and conventional versions on certain clinical and content scales, most of these differences were within the five T-score points and, therefore, were not clinically meaningful. With respect to criterion validity, none of the correlations between the MMPI–2 and the criterion measures were significantly different when the computerized adaptive and conventional booklet versions were compared. Moreover, Handel et al. (1999) found that the loss of information due to the change of administration was minimal. The researchers concluded that this mode of adaptive testing has minimal impact on the test validity, ensuring the feasibility of applying the countdown method to the development of the adaptive MMPI–2.

Limitations of Adaptive MMPI–2 Testing

The main advantage of an adapted test administration of the MMPI–2 is to abbreviate test administration—reducing the amount of time required to arrive at an interpretable set of scores. In most cases, an adapted version provides an extraction of the full MMPI–2, providing only one or two of the most salient clinical scale scores. As a shortened administration, the adaptive version of the MMPI–2 is, in many respects, similar to other "short forms" of the test; thus, many of the criticisms of the short forms of the MMPI–2 can be raised with respect to adaptive administration (Butcher & Hostetler, 1990).

In most MMPI–2 applications, however, time considerations are secondary and a thorough psychological assessment is needed. For example, in a forensic personal injury setting in which the main goal is veridical evaluation of symptoms and problems, one would want to use the most comprehensive and validated form of the test. Similarly, in a personnel selection situation evaluating applicants for a position of public trust, such as airline pilot or police personnel selection, the practitioner would want to use the full form of the test in order to have the established validity research apply. Therefore, when time is not a primary consideration or when a comprehensive reliable assessment is needed, then an abbreviation of the test through an adaptive version becomes disadvantageous and a full version of the instrument must be used.

To summarize, a number of studies suggest that the computerized adaptive version of the MMPI–2 has the potential to produce savings in items and time with minimal loss of test validity for the peak clinical scale scores. Adaptive versions of the MMPI–2 content scales based on both the IRT and the countdown method were found to be valid and generally equivalent to the traditional paper-and-pencil and computer-administered versions. Although the IRT–based CAT for the MMPI–2 clinical scales appears to be problematic due to the item heterogeneity of many MMPI–2 clinical scales, for the clinical scales the computerized adaptive MMPI–2 based on the countdown method can provide a valid alternative to IRT–based approaches (Ben-Porath et al., 1989; Handel et al., 1999; Roper et al., 1995). Despite the benefits of using an adapted version of the test, some clear limitations remain. In particular, compared to a full MMPI–2 administration, adaptive testing allows only a limited view of the client's personality and problems.

OTHER COMPUTER-BASED APPLICATIONS: THE MMPI–2 AND THE INTERNET

The widespread use of Internet technology and resources has created some pressure for test publishers to make available online administration, scoring, and interpretation of psychological tests. In recent decades, substantial growth has occurred in the dissemination of information related to mental health and the provision of mental health services (Buchanan, 2002; Buchanan & Smith, 1999; VandenBos & Williams, 2000). However, validation of Internet-based services—including assurance of equivalence in testing conditions, normative equivalence, and similarity in test-taking attitudes—is lagging behind the technological expansion. The MMPI–2 has seen only limited use on the Internet. One exception is the Flemish–Dutch MMPI–2, which was standardized using an Internet-based data collection (Sloore, Derksen, De May, & Hellenbosch, 1996). The Flemish–Dutch standardization committee collected 1,244 questionnaires through the University of Amsterdam Telepanel, a computer-guided, data-gathering system that loaned a computer and a modem to each of 1,630 households throughout Holland in exchange for their weekly participation in various surveys. Although the standardization sample may not have been fully representative of the Flemish–Dutch population because they were quite familiar with the use of computers, their demographic characteristics closely resembled the general population in Holland. A number of similarities were found between the U.S. normative and Flemish–Dutch MMPI–2 administrations, suggesting that the two versions are generally equivalent (Sloore et al., 1996). One potential application of the University of Amsterdam study is allowing qualified users such as licensed clinicians or registered research study participants to have Internet-based secure access to the MMPI–2 administration, scoring, and interpretation. Limited secure access would allow for even faster test processing and would eliminate the need for additional software installation and upgrades. Despite the encouraging results by Sloore at al. (1996), making the MMPI–2 widely available through the Internet does not appear feasible at this time due to significant non-equivalence issues and ethical concerns regarding test security. Some of the problems with administering clinical tests like the MMPI–2 on the Internet have been described by Butcher, Perry, and Hahn (2004). They suggested four problem areas that require attention if Internet applications of clinical tests are to be developed:

1. *Importance of ensuring that test-taking attitudes are equivalent to the normative sample:* The test administration differences cannot be assumed to produce equivalent test results. Pasveer and Ellard (1998) reported that administering tests on line resulted in problems worth serious consideration, such as multiple submission of records by the same test taker. Some research has suggested that different test-taking situations may produce different test results (Buchanan & Smith, 1999). It would, therefore, be important to ensure that Internet test administration strategies would not produce results different from results obtained through standard administration procedures. Unfortunately, Internet-administered versus booklet-administered tests have not been widely studied; and, as pointed out by Buchanan and Smith (1999), equivalence between the two administration procedures cannot be ensured.

2. *Importance of ensuring that test norms are appropriate for the specific Internet application:* Some research has suggested that tests administered on the Internet produce different results than those administered under standard conditions (Buchanan & Smith, 1999). Many available standardized tests have norms that are based on a sample of individuals who took the test under controlled conditions. The use of test norms developed under standard conditions requires that persons being compared on the norms be tested under similar conditions. Relatively few traditional psychological tests have been developed through the Internet assessment procedures. The one exception was the Dutch-language version of the MMPI–2 noted earlier, which was standardized through an Internet

normative program (Sloore et al., 1996). Since most available instruments have not been developed through an online testing program, Internet administration creates serious non-equivalence concerns. Changing the administration procedures can make the standard test norms inappropriate.

3. *Importance of assurances that the Internet-administered test is valid:* The use of any psychological test for making decisions about people is predicated upon the test having demonstrated reliability and validity. As noted earlier, one cannot be confident that an Internet-administered procedure will measure the same constructs in the same way as standard paper-and-pencil administration. Confident test use requires assurance that the test correlates are comparable to established results. Although some evidence has been reported that Internet-administered tests have construct validity when compared to tests by traditional administration procedures (Buchanan & Smith, 1999), the support for such conclusions is minimal.

4. *Need for ensuring test item security:* Test security must be ensured before the items are made available through the Internet. The lack of security of documents sent through the Internet is notoriously questionable. Numerous examples exist of "hackers" being able to easily obtain access to highly secure bank, government, and business files. Most commercially available psychological tests are copyrighted, and test publishers protect copyright by either refusing permission to use or by allowing only limited use of test items. Some test publishers have tightened their security over test items by refusing to allow psychologists to cite them even in scientific publications with a more restricted audience range. To safeguard against unauthorized use by unqualified individuals, American Psychological Association (APA, 1986) guidelines for psychological test interpretation services identified the MMPI–2 and its computerized reports as B1-level tests available only to fellows, members, and associate members of the APA, as well as licensed psychologists, physicians, and marriage and family therapists. Making the MMPI–2 available on the Internet could result in nonqualified persons obtaining the test, thus violating copyright regulations and the *Code of Ethics* of the American Psychological Association (APA, 1986).

Case Example

Susan, a 30-year-old office manager, completed the MMPI–2 as part of her presurgical psychological evaluation for a gastric bypass operation. She was referred to the bariatric surgery program by her primary care physician as a means of treating her obesity. Susan has had a problem with her weight since childhood. Her current weight is 240 pounds, which is an estimated 120 pounds overweight for her height. Over the years, she has attempted numerous diets but has been unable to reduce her weight without regaining. Within the past year, she developed symptoms of hypertension and an irregular heartbeat, prompting her physician to recommend an intestinal bypass operation. In addition to obesity, Susan has a history of alcohol abuse. She indicated that she used to drink alone to reduce her work-related tension. Within the past 5 years, she has completed two inpatient alcohol abuse programs. She reported being abstinent from alcohol since completion of her most recent substance abuse treatment program 12 months ago. Susan currently smokes two packs of cigarettes a day—a habit she has had since she was 14 years old.

Susan is the youngest of three children. Her older sisters are 12 and 14 years her senior. Their mother died when Susan was 5 years old. She was raised by her father and her stepmother, who married her father 6 months after his wife's death. Her father is now deceased. With the exception of her long-standing weight problem, Susan's medical history is unremarkable. She completed high school—although she was not a strong student academically—with mostly Cs and some Ds. She did not consider going to college and participated in a work-study program instead. Throughout high school, she did not engage in social activities at school and did not date, in large part because she was self-conscious about her weight problem. During high school and subsequent years, she had difficulty making friends and, according to her report, was interested in having more male friends but her relationships with males were superficial. She has been employed by the same real estate agency for 7 years. Initially, she was employed as a secretary but for the past 2 years she has been an office manager—a job that involves greater responsibility and involvement with her coworkers. She reported feeling a lot of pressure on the job and indicated that she finds that her superiors are not supportive of her and tend to be overly demanding. She works long hours and is often called on to manage work details over weekends.

Susan was 30 minutes late for the psychological evaluation, explaining that she had some difficulty getting around the building. She had a noticeable limp, tending to drag her right foot. She was dressed casually and appropriately for the season but appeared somewhat uncomfortable in her large loose-fitting dress as she sat down. She was spontaneous and talkative, at times to the point of being tangential and off track. During the interview, she expressed a great deal of anger toward her older sisters, who she feels are unsympathetic to her health problems. The MMPI–2 was administered after the interview.

Figure 17.1 shows Susan's MMPI–2 validity scale pattern, Figure 17.2 shows Susan's MMPI–2 clinical and supplemental scales, and Figure 17.3 shows her content scales. The computer-based interpretive section generated by the Minnesota Report for the General Medical setting (Butcher, 2003b) is shown in Appendix 17.1.

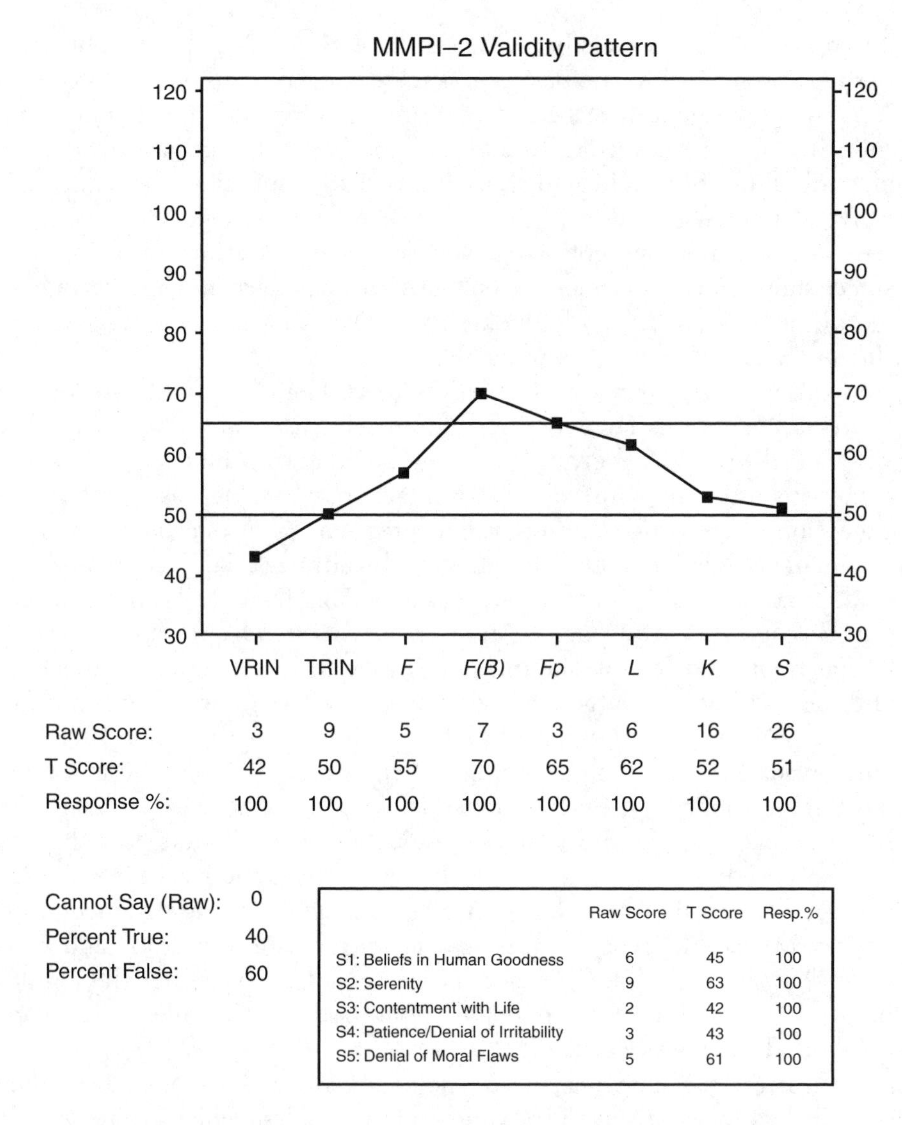

Figure 17.1. MMPI–2 validity profile for a 30-year-old office manager referred for a bariatric surgery evaluation.

THE MMPI–2 COMPUTER-BASED INTERPRETIVE REPORT

A recently created database of the MMPI–related references available between 1940 and 2001 contained close to 14,000 citations (Butcher, 2001). Since this vast amount of information is not conveniently organized for efficient use, it is impossible for a clinician to commit to memory or keep up with all of the relevant empirical information for various profile types. Consequently, the MMPI–2 computer-based

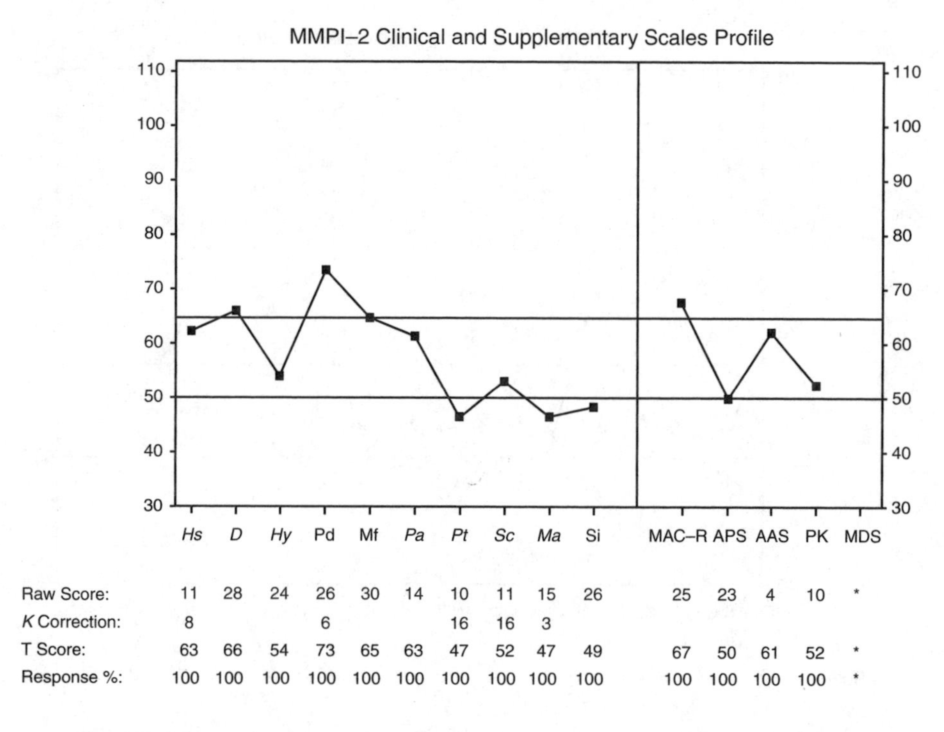

	Hs	D	Hy	Pd	Mf	Pa	Pt	Sc	Ma	Si	MAC–R	APS	AAS	PK	MDS
Raw Score:	11	28	24	26	30	14	10	11	15	26	25	23	4	10	*
K Correction:	8			6			16	16	3						
T Score:	63	66	54	73	65	63	47	52	47	49	67	50	61	52	*
Response %:	100	100	100	100	100	100	100	100	100	100	100	100	100	100	*

Welsh Code: 4'25+16–38/079:L–FK/

Profile Elevation: 58.1

*MDS scores are reported only for clients who indicate that they are married or separated.

Figure 17.2. MMPI–2 clinical and supplemental scales for a 30-year-old office manager referred for a bariatric surgery evaluation.

interpretive report can be seen as an electronic textbook or a resource database that can provide a summary of the most likely personality descriptors or symptoms relevant to a particular case. The computer-based interpretive report conveniently organizes the empirical information into standard clinical categories such as "interpersonal relationships" and "treatment recommendations." Information from the MMPI–2 computer-based report can also be used effectively in treatment planning and in providing test feedback to clients (Butcher, 1997b, 2002b; Finn & Tonsager, 1992).

All features of the MMPI–2 computer-based report are created to help clinicians to get the most realistic and most efficiently constructed picture of their clients' psychological issues as well as the most reliable estimate of test validity. However, even with all the advantages, such reports must be used with caution (Butcher, 2002b). No computerized report is designed to replace clinical judgment, including the ability to integrate all the available data. It is essential that clinicians have a good working knowledge of the MMPI–2 in order to properly evaluate the relative accuracy and relevance of the computer-generated report.

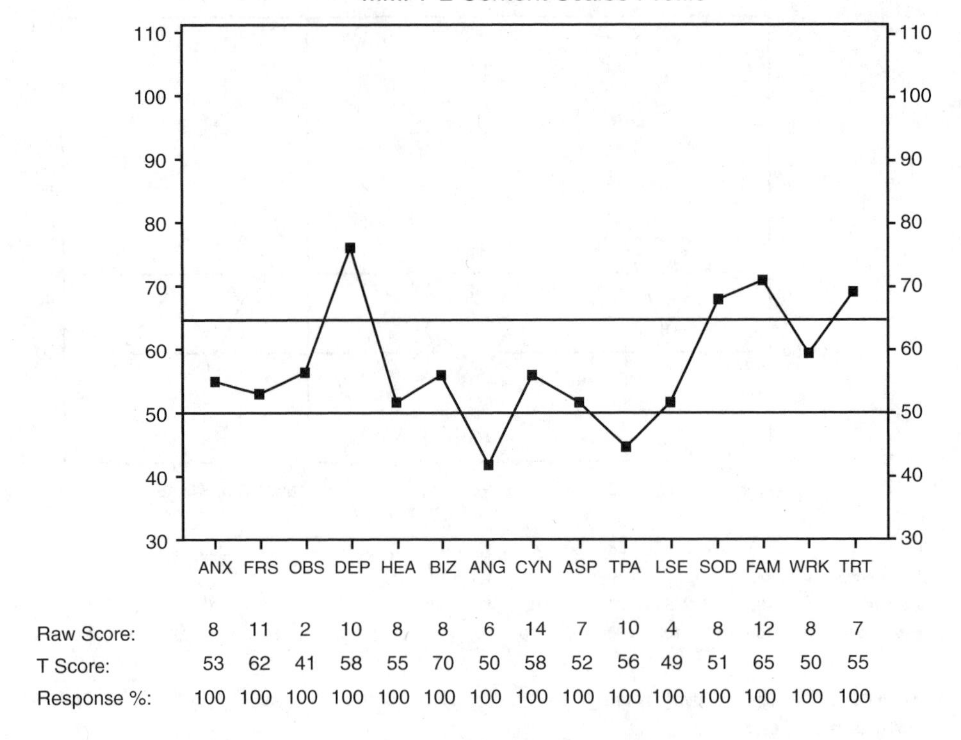

Figure 17.3. MMPI–2 content scales for a 30-year-old office manager referred for a bariatric surgery evaluation.

Practitioners without the proper training in MMPI–2 interpretation will be vulnerable to making "Barnum-like" statements that can make it difficult to discriminate among clients or to draw accurate conclusions, which in turn can lead to inappropriate and potentially harmful treatment.

Using the Interpretive Report

We recommend the following strategy as an effective means of incorporating the information from the computer-based MMPI–2 report into a more comprehensive clinical picture of a particular client:

1. The large number of validity indexes on the MMPI–2 is quite advantageous for computer-based interpretation. To illustrate, True Response Inconsistency (TRIN) and Variable Response Inconsistency (VRIN) scales involve complex scoring and are subject to clerical errors when scored by hand. One study found that, despite their high interscorer reliabilities (0.97 to 1.00), the rate of hand-scoring errors was 7% demonstrating that, whenever possible, these scales should be scored by the com-

puter (Iverson & Barton, 1999). The Minnesota Report (Butcher, 2003b) provides scoring for *L*, *F* (Infrequency), *K* (Correction), Cannot Say (?), VRIN, TRIN, *F*1, *F*2, *Fp* (Infrequency–Psychopathology), and *S* Superlative Self-Presentation. The interpretive report contains a section on profile validity and issues a warning if the profile cannot be scored or appears invalid. In Susan's case, the MMPI–2 validity pattern (Figure 17.1) and the Profile Validity section of the narrative report (Appendix 17.1) show that her test results are in the interpretable range. She has a slight elevation on the Back Infrequency *F(B)* scale, suggesting that she endorsed more difficulties on the second half of the test.

2. The MMPI–2 interpretive database consists primarily of information from the extensive work published on the empirical correlates of the clinical scales. Since many profiles will have elevations on a single clinical scale, clinical scale correlates (summarized in the Symptomatic Patterns section of the narrative) are particularly valuable in the computerized MMPI–2 interpretation system. As shown in Figure 17.2, Susan's clinical scale elevations of T equal to or greater than 65 were on scales 4 (Psychopathic Deviate; Pd), 2 (Depression), and 5 (Masculinity–Femininity). The Minnesota Report (Butcher, 2003b) appropriately identified scales 4 and 2 as central to the Symptomatic Patterns section of the computer-based narrative report (Appendix 17.1).

3. Since the early development stages, MMPI researchers found that more than one clinical scale is elevated for many test takers. Given that interpretation of such profiles must take into account all scale elevations, configural interpretation became preferable over scale-by-scale analysis. As a result, the empirical literature on the correlates of the MMPI and MMPI–2 code types has been extremely important in designing computer-based interpretations. Nonetheless, practitioners must keep in mind that (a) empirical correlates for the entire range of code types have not been sufficiently explored; (b) MMPI–2 profiles contain information beyond code types from scales such as the Social Introversion (Si) and MacAndrew Alcoholism—Revised (MAC–R) scales; (c) code-type information does not apply to all settings—for example, some information about 4/9 profile types may apply more specifically to correctional or forensic settings. These limitations mean that, for profile types that have not been widely studied (for example the 2/9–9/2 code), the MMPI–2 computer-based reports go beyond strict actuarial interpretation by incorporating clinical experience accumulated by the MMPI–2 experts and sometimes described in published case reports.

The focus on configural interpretation implies that it may be helpful to look at elevations of additional scales before reading the interpretive narrative report in order to make sure that this valuable information gets incorporated with other hypotheses about the test taker's functioning. In the context of prospective bariatric surgery, Susan's substance abuse history and cigarette smoking are particularly relevant due to the possibility that her substance use would have a negative impact on her postsurgical adjustment. Thus, her MMPI–2 scores on additional substance abuse scales should be closely considered. The Diagnostic Considerations section of the narrative report states that Susan's elevated MAC–R score is indicative of her substance abuse potential (Appendix 17.1). Note that the computer-based narrative report does not always acknowledge scores that are within normal limits but that are also relevant to profile interpretation. In such cases, the clinician's MMPI–2 background becomes particularly important. To illustrate, Susan's scores on the Addiction Potential Scale (APS) and the Addiction Acknowledgment Scale (AAS) were within normal limits, which is consistent with her self-report of being abstinent for about 1 year since she completed her most recent alcohol abuse treatment program. Since the MAC–R measures addictive potential and does not measure current use or abuse of substances, Susan's APS and AAS scores highlight our certainty in interpretation of the MAC–R elevation.

4. The Profile Frequency section of the Minnesota Report (Butcher, 2003b) contains recently updated base-rate information (Appendix 17.1). Base-rate data can inform us about how "different" and how "extreme" an individual profile is when compared to the population of profiles in a particular clinical setting. For instance, knowing that a particular patient's profile is a relatively common occurrence can provide a clinician with additional confidence in his or her profile interpretation. At the same time, certainty in making predictions from a given profile decreases when the base rate of such a profile type is small (Finn & Kamphuis, 1995). Thus, knowing that a patient's scale score elevation is quite rare should prompt the practitioner to seek additional information about this patient. As can be seen from the Profile Frequency section (Appendix 17.1), Susan's 2/4–4/2 code type and an elevation on the MAC–R are quite rare in the general population but are not uncommon in clinical settings, particularly with respect to substance abuse treatment programs. However, with respect to Scale 4 (Pd) elevation, Susan's profile appears to be relatively rare among medical patients. Therefore, in the follow-up interview with this patient, the examining clinician should be prompted to explore Susan's substance abuse history as well as her potential for impulsive acting-out behavior and poor judgment.

5. The Minnesota Report (Butcher, 2003b) provides interpretive reports for the General Medical, Personnel, Criminal Justice and Correctional (designed to be used with inmates and offenders in the criminal justice system), and Forensic settings. For some settings, information about additional scales or classification systems is also available. For example, the Personnel Report is tailored to six specific occupations (law enforcement, firefighters and paramedics, medical and psychology students, nuclear

power facilities workers, airline pilots, and seminary students) and provides occupation-specific mean profiles based on more than 18,000 cases. Most of the setting-specific information is typically included in the Profile Frequency section. As noted in the last paragraph of that section (Appendix 17.1), Susan's elevation on Scale 4 is relatively rare. However, given that her profile is not well defined, in her case the two-point code-type information may not be relevant.

6. The Profile Stability section of the report (Appendix 17.1) is an important indicator of whether a client's behavior is likely to change in the future. A number of MMPI researchers recommend that profiles be classified as "well-defined" for cases in which the lowest scale used to define the code type is at least five T-score points higher than the next highest scale (e.g., Ben-Porath & Tellegen, 1995; Graham, Timbrook, Ben-Porath, & Butcher, 1991; Graham et al., 1999; Tellegen & Ben-Porath, 1993). Imperfect reliability of the MMPI is one of the main reasons for this recommendation. Differences of less than five T-score points are difficult to interpret because they are within the standard error of measurement for the scales. Consequently, well-defined profiles tend to be more stable over time. As indicated by the narrative report, Susan's profile is not well defined, which suggests that the relative elevation of her clinical scales could shift if she retested with the MMPI–2.

7. The Interpersonal Relations, Diagnostic Considerations, and Treatment Considerations sections of the narrative report are other sources of hypotheses about the client. These sections were constructed using a broad range of sources including behavioral correlates for code types and individual scales such as the Si scale. For example, consistent with information obtained during Susan's interview, her Diagnostic Considerations section points out that she is currently experiencing interpersonal difficulties and acknowledging excessive use of addictive substances.

8. In addition to validity, clinical, and content scale scores, the Minnesota Report (Butcher, 2003b) provides a Supplemental Score output, which includes Harris–Lingoes subscales, Content Component scores, and a list of Koss–Butcher critical items. Supplemental output can provide some additional insight into what factors may be contributing to elevations on the clinical and content scales. For instance, Susan's T score of 65 on FAM (Family Problems) appears to be related to her feelings of alienation from her family as suggested by her T score of 77 on the Familial Alienation (FAM2) subscale.

Additional Recommendations

Once the preceding eight points have been considered, the clinician should write down a list of hypotheses about the client to be followed up in subsequent meetings with the client. Following is an example of a hypotheses summary based on Susan's MMPI–2 computer-based narrative report and the bariatric surgery context.

- Among the key questions with respect to bariatric surgery are, To what extent is the client going to physically and psychologically benefit from the surgery? and, What are some of the factors that may interfere with successful recovery? In particular, bariatric surgery is likely to be associated with a great deal of stress, especially during the first few weeks after the surgery. Significant dietary and lifestyle changes, as well as potential for serious side effects if the strict regimen is not followed, require that Susan's depression, impulsivity, and ability to communicate with others (e.g., seek social support and constructively interact with her health care providers) are thoroughly assessed.
- Susan was open to sharing her difficulties on the MMPI–2. However, as noted in the Treatment Considerations Section, her long-term adjustment problems may be resistant to psychological treatment. This may mean that her level of insight into her difficulties is limited. Her view of her relationships with others appears to support this assertion. In particular, her limited social contacts, alienation from her family, and anger at her coworkers expressed during the interview are suggestive of poor interpersonal skills. According to the MMPI–2 report, she may be interpersonally dependent and manipulative but sees herself being confident in social situations.
- She reports being somewhat depressed and unhappy with herself. This is not surprising in the light of her chronic weight problems and the likely poor self-image. According to the MMPI–2 report, her depressive symptoms are likely to dissipate once situational stressors (e.g., weight problem and interpersonal conflicts) are removed. Nonetheless, further investigation of her past and present depressive symptoms is warranted.
- The MMPI–2 report suggests that she may be impulsive and prone to acting-out behavior. Exploring more specifically her tendency "to act without thinking" would be beneficial, especially in light of her depression (e.g., history of suicide attempts and other self-harm behaviors).
- Given the stress of bariatric surgery, her drinking, impulsivity, and depression patterns are likely to be intertwined. Investigating how she reacts to stress would be important. This concern is particularly relevant because she has reported drinking

alcohol alone to reduce stress. Also, given that she spends long hours at work and finds her superiors unsupportive of her difficulties, how is she going to cope with having to take time off of work for the surgery? How likely is she to get depressed, resume drinking, or act out impulsively?

- As noted by the MMPI–2 report, she has reported some "bizarre ideas," which may be indicative of problems with thinking. Going over the Koss–Butcher critical items (e.g., Mental Confusion and Persecutory Ideas categories) or reviewing her endorsement pattern on the BIZ (Bizarre Mentation) content scale may be helpful in clarifying her thinking patterns.

SUMMARY AND FUTURE DIRECTIONS

The MMPI and MMPI–2 have a long, well-established tradition of computer-based assessment. Use of the MMPI–2 computer-generated scoring and interpretive reports appears to be highly advantageous as there is evidence to support their accuracy and equivalence when compared to scoring and reports generated by clinicians and via traditional paper-and-pencil administration. Of course, using computer-based reports is not without its challenges. In order to make proper use of computer-generated MMPI–2 reports, practitioners must be able to incorporate other sources of extratest data in addition to having training in the MMPI–2 interpretation (see Exhibit 17.1).

In the context of the history and current trends described throughout this chapter, what might be the future of the MMPI–2 computer-based assessment and interpretation? We anticipate that, in the fine tradition of the "empirical manifesto" (Butcher, 2000b; Meehl, 1945), there will be continued investigation regarding whether the computer-generated results predict behaviors similar to data generated by other methods. As more research on the code-type behavioral correlates is generated, the interpretive statements library, interpretive rules for the MMPI–2, and—eventually—MMPI–3 computer-based interpretive systems will become more elaborate.

One of the greatest current impacts on psychological assessment comes from managed-care companies (Groth-Marnat, 2000). In light of the MMPI–2 multiple validity indexes and an ever-growing, setting-specific empirical data base, it is likely that the MMPI–2 computer-based reports will become even more elaborate and specialized to particular settings (e.g., forensic, correctional, personnel selection). Managed-care environments also increase the demands to maintain better integration between assessment and treatment, which in turn increases the need for more empirically validated treatment planning recommendations. Therefore, we expect that the

EXHIBIT 17.1

Highlight: General Considerations for Computer-Based Assessment With the MMPI–2

- Over the past 50 years, computers have become an integral component of psychological interpretation in personality assessment.
- The MMPI has a long, well-established tradition in computerized assessment history beginning in the 1960s.
- More recent MMPI–2 computer-based interpretive systems attempt to integrate empirically tested decision rules and code-type correlates, as well as base-rate and setting-specific information.
- Research into computer-generated narrative reports for the MMPI and MMPI–2 has found that the interpretive statements contained in them are comparable in relevance and accuracy to clinician-generated statements.
- There is evidence to suggest that not all computer-based MMPI and MMPI–2 programs are equally valid and that there is great variability in their ability to provide useful narrative reports.
- Computer-administered MMPI and MMPI–2 tests appear to provide the same information on clients as paper-and-pencil test administrations.
- Computer programs have been developed to adapt test administration of the MMPI–2 (e.g., through item response theory or the countdown method) to abbreviate test administration and to reduce the amount of time required to arrive at an interpretable set of scores. There is evidence to support the validity of adaptive testing; however, because a great deal of information available in the MMPI–2 is sacrificed for the sake of brevity, whenever possible, a full version of the test must be used.
- Internet technology and resources have prompted a desire among some psychologists to obtain tests through online administration, scoring, and interpretation. However, for clinical tests such as the MMPI–2, problems such as the lack of reliability and validity data of Internet applications and such as the need to ensure test item security have deterred online availability. Protected testing sites for administration could be developed in the future to provide a more secure means of Internet applications.
- Computer-based MMPI–2 reports conveniently organize the vast amount of information into summaries of symptoms most likely to be relevant to a particular client.
- A number of studies indicate that automated decision rules often outperform those generated by clinicians. At the same time, a computer-based report is designed not to replace clinical judgment but to assist practitioners in generating valid hypotheses about the test takers.
- In the use of computer-based MMPI–2 reports, it remains essential that practitioners have proper training in MMPI–2 interpretation.

Treatment Recommendations section of the computer-based MMPI–2 reports will expand and become integrated with other sources of information about clients, including setting-specific information. Last, but not least, although the role of clinicians in integration of multiple sources of information about the clients will remain quite important, computer-based assessment and interpretation technology developed for the MMPI and the MMPI–2 will move toward integration of quantitative and qualitative data. Overall, we see the future of computer-based MMPI–2 assessment as hopeful and believe that over time its development will continue to follow the world's rapid expansion of computer technology.

APPENDIX 17.1

The following text is the computer-generated narrative section from the Minnesota Report for a 30-year-old office manager referred for a bariatric surgery evaluation.

Profile Validity

Her response to the traditional MMPI–2 validity scales (*L*, *F*, and *K*) was within the normal range. Her performance on the MMPI–2 clinical scales is likely to be a good indication of her present personality functioning.

Symptomatic Patterns

The MMPI–2 clinical profile configuration that includes Scales *D* and Pd was the prototype used to develop this report. This scale configuration is not well defined. Interpretation of the profile should take into consideration other clinical profile elements, particularly the scales that are close in elevation to the prototype scales. The client's MMPI–2 clinical profile suggests a number of psychological problems. She reported being somewhat depressed, tense, and dissatisfied with herself. However, personality problems including impulsivity, poor judgment, and acting-out behavior may be central in her clinical picture.

She may behave irresponsibly at times and blame others for problems she becomes involved in. There is some indication from her profile code that she may reduce tension with pleasure-oriented behavior, such as overuse of alcohol or medication.

The client has diverse interests that include activities that are not traditionally associated with her gender. Women who score high on Mf are somewhat unusual compared with other women. They endorse item content that is typically seen as representing extreme masculine interests.

In addition, the following description is suggested by the content of the client's item responses. According to her response content, there is a strong possibility that she has seriously contemplated suicide. She views herself as being confident in social situations, and she tends to be exhibitionistic and forceful in expressing her views. She has endorsed a number of unusual, bizarre ideas that suggest some difficulties with her thinking.

Profile Frequency

Profile interpretation can be greatly facilitated by examining the relative frequency of clinical scale patterns in various settings. The client's high-point clinical scale score (Pd) occurs in 9.5% of the MMPI–2 normative sample of women. However, only 4.7% of the sample have Pd scale peak scores at or above a T score of 65, and only 2.9% have well-defined Pd spikes. This elevated MMPI–2 profile configuration (2–4/4–2) is very rare in samples of normals, occurring in less than 1% of the MMPI–2 normative sample of women.

She scored relatively high on MAC–R, suggesting the possibility of a drug- or alcohol-abuse problem. The base rate data on her profile type among residents in alcohol and drug programs should also be evaluated. This MMPI–2 profile configuration contains the most frequent high point, the Pd score, among alcohol- and drug-abusing populations. Over 26% of the women in substance-abuse treatment programs have this pattern (McKenna & Butcher, 1987).

Available contemporary frequency information on mental health patients can also provide useful comparisons for patients being seen in medical settings. In this section, frequencies of high points or two-point codes on a broad range mental health and health care clients are reported regardless of elevation to typify cases from a variety of settings. Then, frequencies are given from a different perspective on scores that are well defined and elevated above a T score of 65.

Taking into account the relative frequency this profile high point in diverse clinical settings can be useful in clinical interpretation. The relative frequency of this high-point profile peak in the NCS Pearson combined sample of clinical patients (Atlis, Butcher, & Hahn, 2002; N = 41,495 women) is informative. 14.84% of women have this high point when a given profile elevation is not established in advance. The Pd spike is the most common peak score in the combined sample of women.

Moreover, looking at scale elevation in a different light by considering cases with elevated and well-defined scores, 6.7% of the women have the Pd spike at or above a T score of 65 and as a well-defined pattern. This elevated MMPI–2 two-point profile configuration (2–4/4–2) is found in 4.34% of the women in the combined NCS Pearson clinical sample (Atlis, Butcher, & Hahn, 2002) when scale elevation is not considered, and 1.3% are well-defined cases at or above 65T.

Medical patients from the NCS Pearson Archival Data Set (N = 2,635 women; Atlis, Butcher, & Hahn, 2002) with a high-point Pd score are found in 6.87% of the sample regardless of elevation and 2.96% of the sample have Pd as a well-defined spike at or above a T score of 65. This elevated MMPI–2 two-point profile configuration (2–4/4–2) is found as high-point pair in 2.62% of the women in the NCS Pearson Medical patient sample (N = 2,635; Atlis, Butcher, & Hahn, 2002), and 0.61% are well-defined cases at or above 65T.

Profile Stability

The relative scale elevation of her highest clinical scale scores suggests some lack of clarity in profile definition. Although her most elevated clinical scales are likely to be present in her profile pattern if she is retested at a later date, there could be some shifting of the most prominent scale elevations in the profile code. The difference between the profile type used to develop the present report and the next highest scale in the profile code was 3 points. So, for example, if the client is tested at a later date, her profile might involve more behavioral elements related to elevations on *Hs* (Hypochondriasis). If so, then on retesting, she might report more physical complaints.

Interpersonal Relations

She is probably somewhat dependent and tends to manipulate relationships for her own ends. She also seems somewhat hedonistic and may act out impulsively at times.

She has an average interest in being with others and is not socially isolated or withdrawn. She meets and talks with other people with relative ease and is not overly anxious at social gatherings.

Diagnostic Considerations

She is likely to be experiencing some interpersonal difficulty at this time. Her depressed mood needs to be taken into consideration. She shows some elements of a personality disorder and acting-out behavior. Her unusual thinking and bizarre ideas need to be taken into consideration in any diagnostic formulation.

She appears to have a number of personality characteristics that have been associated with substance abuse or substance use problems. Her scores on the addiction proneness indicators suggest that there is a possibility of her developing an addictive disorder. Further evaluation for the likelihood of a substance use or abuse disorder is indicated. In her responses to the MMPI–2, she has acknowledged some problems with excessive use or abuse of addictive substances.

Treatment Considerations

Her depressive symptoms might improve in therapy or with a reduction in her situational stress. However, individuals with this profile tend to have some long-term adjustment problems that are repetitive and tend to be resistant to psychological treatment. Her personality style is not easily altered.

Her item content suggests some family conflicts that are causing her considerable concern at this time. She feels unhappy about her life and resents having an unpleasant home life. Psychological intervention could profitably focus, in part, on clarifying her feelings and conflicts about her family.

Her acknowledged problems with alcohol or drug use should be addressed in therapy.

NOTE: This MMPI–2 interpretation can serve as a useful source of hypotheses about clients. This report is based on objectively derived scale indices and scale interpretations that have been developed in diverse groups of patients. The personality descriptions, inferences, and recommendations contained herein need to be verified by other sources of clinical information because individual clients may not fully match the prototype. The information in this report should most appropriately be used by a trained, qualified test interpreter. The information contained in this report should be considered confidential.

18

INTERPRETATION OF LATINO/LATINA MMPI–2 PROFILES: REVIEW AND APPLICATION OF EMPIRICAL FINDINGS AND CULTURAL–LINGUISTIC CONSIDERATIONS

MARIA GARRIDO AND ROBERTO VELASQUEZ

Over the past 30 years, a number of important studies have been conducted that explore the use of psychological assessment techniques with U.S. Latinos/Latinas (Velasquez & Callahan, 1992; Velasquez, Garrido, Castellanos, & Burton, 2004). These studies represent the ongoing work of researchers, scholars, and practitioners who work with Spanish-speaking or bilingual U.S. Latinos/Latinas and who are concerned with the adequacy, appropriateness, and limitations of techniques in the proper assessment, diagnosis, and treatment planning of this population. Historically, much of this work has followed the conclusions of Padilla and Ruiz (1973, 1975), whose review of psychological testing and assessment with Latinos/Latinas identified a tendency to minimize or even neglect the impact of cultural differences on test findings. At the heart of this work has been the key issue of cultural competence in all aspects of the assessment process, that is, choice of assessment technique, appropriate administration, and interpretation. In light of the fact that today, Latinos/Latinas constitute the largest and fastest-growing ethnic and linguistic minority in the United States, the work of those concerned with the culturally competent psychological assessment of Latinos/Latinas has become that much more crucial.

The MMPI/MMPI–2 and MMPI–A have been the most widely used personality assessment instruments with many cultural groups including Latinos/Latinas (Greene, 1991; Velasquez, Ayala, & Mendoza, 1998). The more recent studies on the use of the MMPI–2 with this population encompass a wide range of applications such as inpatient and outpatient assessment and a variety of forensic applications (e.g., Ben-Porath, Graham, Hall, Hirschman, & Zaragoza, 1995). Important work has been conducted as to the culturally competent administration of the instrument (Velasquez et al., 1997; Velasquez, Ayala, et al., 2000; Velasquez, Maness, & Anderson, 2002), with particular attention to issues of language use and preference/proficiency (Velasquez, Chavira, et al., 2000).

However, beyond language and cultural considerations relevant to the assessment process itself lies the *key issue of culturally competent interpretation of Latino/Latina MMPI–2 findings*. Therefore, the purpose of this chapter is to focus on the interpretation of Latino/Latina MMPI–2 findings by incorporating what we have learned from the empirical work produced so far with our observations as practitioners dedicated to the psychological assessment of this group. We offer interpretive guidelines that have assisted us in our MMPI–2 interpretations of Latino/Latina profiles and that we hope can be useful to other practitioners who engage in this work.

This chapter contains three major sections. The *first section* is a review of empirical MMPI/MMPI–2 findings with U.S. Latinos/Latinas. In this review, we highlight the main research and methodological issues that have characterized the study of MMPI/MMPI–2 use with Latinos/Latinas. We also provide an overview of the main cultural and linguistic considerations in the interpretation of the MMPI–2 in light of the diversity and heterogeneity of the U.S. Latino/Latina population. In the *second section*, we offer interpretive guidelines that incorporate research findings, sociocultural considerations, and clinical experience in the interpretation of specific MMPI–2 scales. The *third section* presents case studies drawn from our clinical experience with inpatients, outpatients, forensic clients, and bilingual clients. The cases are discussed by highlighting interpretive issues and guidelines that clinicians should consider in their own work.

REVIEW OF KEY MMPI AND MMPI–2 FINDINGS WITH U.S. LATINOS/LATINAS

Historically, research with the MMPI and MMPI–2 with Latinos/Latinas has been characterized by many of the methodological issues that have affected research of these instruments with other non–White ethnic minority groups in the United States. Greene (1987) has clearly articulated these methodological issues in the application of the MMPI and, most recently, the MMPI–2 (Greene, 2000).These issues have had inevitable implications for the interpretation of the resulting profiles. Likewise, in their extensive review of research on the original MMPI with U.S. minorities, Dahlstrom, Lachar, and Dahlstrom (1986) enumerated several factors that have affected profile interpretation. We review these issues separately for the MMPI and the MMPI–2.

The MMPI

As discussed by Greene (1987) in his review, much of the MMPI research with ethnic minorities has involved what he calls a prototypical approach to comparing differences between groups without attending to the magnitude or implications of such differences for purposes of profile interpretation or to the possible impact of these differences for the empirical correlates of the scales. Greene goes on to delineate a number of methodological issues that, much like the use of the prototypical approach, have had implications for the interpretation of Latino/Latina profiles. Among those issues and their implications are the lack of specificity provided by researchers concerning the basic sociodemographic characteristics of study participants (including ethnic group membership and identification), limited (if any) discussion of profile validity, and a general lack of consideration of potential moderator variables. In his review of Latino/Latina–White comparisons, comprised of MMPI studies conducted between 1970 and 1985, Greene (1987) observed a lack of pattern to the findings except for a trend toward higher *L* (Lie) scale and lower Scale 5 scores among Latinos/Latinas. This finding has been obtained in MMPI–2 research to date (Hall, Bansal, & Lopez, 1999).

A review of MMPI studies involving Latinos/Latinas by Dahlstrom (1986) more specifically illuminates the impact of the methodological issues already enumerated in the interpretation of MMPI profiles. The findings of several studies reviewed by Dahlstrom (e.g., Montgomery & Orozco, 1985; Murphy, 1978; Padilla, Olmedo, & Loya, 1982) reveal a tendency to overpathologize Latinos/Latinas in the interpretation of MMPI profiles when factors such as acculturation and socioeconomic status (SES) are not taken into account and when, as a result of subject matching, the profiles were found to be comparatively similar. In fact, studies where matching for acculturation and SES was employed revealed the largest differences to be on scales *L* and 5. Additionally, Dahlstrom's (1986) review of studies with Latinos/Latinas between 1970 and 1985 reveals a tendency to focus on only basic scales. This, in our opinion, neglects important dimensions of behavior and functioning as well as opportunities to identify whether any existing profile differences are primarily a function of group differences or could be accounted for by other factors. These studies have been valuable in alerting MMPI/MMPI–2 users that observed differences probably should be interpreted not as a result of ethnic group membership exclusively but, rather, as also accounted for by extratest factors that may impact ethnic minorities.

The MMPI–2

The potential effects of extratest factors on the MMPI profiles of ethnic minorities, as discussed by Greene (1987) and by Dahlstrom et al. (1986), have continued to be important in discussions of MMPI–2 profiles. Greene (1987) examined the effects of age, gender, education, and marital status on MMPI–2 profiles and concluded that the effects of age were generally limited and mainly consisted of 5 to 8 T-point increases in scales 1, 3, HEA (Health Concerns), 2, and DEP (Depression) up to age 60. Simultaneously, there were 5 to 10 T-point decreases in scales 4, 6, and 9 with increased age. Virtually no effects of age were found among the content scales. People in the 18 to 19 age group were observed to elevate several scales 5 to 10 T points over those in the 20 to 29 age group. Greene cautions, however, that these results may reflect cohort effects rather than age differences. In fact, in a large-sample study, Butcher et al. (1991) found virtually no effects of age on MMPI–2 profiles.

As for gender, Greene (1987) found that women tended to endorse more items on scales 1, 2, 3, 7, and 0, based on raw score comparisons with men. Men endorsed more items only on Scale 9. Women also endorsed more items on most content scales. Men had higher raw scores on CYN (Cynicism), ASP (Antisocial Practices), and TPA (Type A Personality). Similarly, gender produced differences in the supplementary scales, with women endorsing more items on scales associated with anxiety, posttraumatic stress, and college maladjustment whereas men endorsed more items on all of the scales associated with substance use difficulties. However, the differences were found to be rather small.

Level of education was found to have a larger impact on MMPI–2 results than age or gender. In general, those with 10 or fewer years of education were found to have higher T scores on their profiles than those with 11 or more years of education in both the clinical and normative samples.

As for marital status, Greene (1987) found virtually no effects within the MMPI–2 normative sample or the clinical sample.

Greene's (1987) review of studies involving comparisons by ethnicity in MMPI–2 profiles covers Black–White, Hispanic–White, and Native American–White comparisons. The existing studies on Black–White comparisons with the MMPI–2 reveal very few differences. For instance, Timbrook and Graham (1994) found that among nonclinical subjects, Black men scored higher on Scale 8 than Whites, and Black women scored higher on Scale 5. In psychiatric samples, Blacks had higher scores than Whites on scales 6 and 8 (Arbisi, Ben-Porath, & McNulty, 2002). Furthermore, these authors, as well as McNulty, Graham, Ben-Porath, and Stein (1997), found no Black–White differences in the correlations between MMPI–2 scales and external correlates.

As for Hispanic–White comparisons, the MMPI–2 studies reviewed by Greene (1987) indicate the existence of fewer differences in normal samples than with the MMPI, with few studies that involve clinical samples. The only differences that have appeared reliably have been on scales *L* (Latinos/Latinas tend to score higher than Whites) and 5 (Latinos/Latinas tend to score lower than Whites; Hall et al., 1999). Therefore, firm conclusions as to the existence of differences between Whites and Hispanics may not yet be justified given the need for additional research with clinical and other nonnormative groups. Note, however, that many of the new studies involving Hispanic–White comparisons on the MMPI–2 and involving intra-Hispanic group differences are still in the form of unpublished papers, dissertations, and theses, and thus are not readily available to practitioners and other researchers for analysis. Therefore, even though the work is ongoing, conclusions concerning the existence of Hispanic–White differences should be approached all the more carefully as a result of this relative lack of published work (Velasquez et al., 2004).

Comparatively more differences have been identified between Whites and Native Americans when normative groups were compared on the MMPI–2 (e.g., Greene, Robin, Albaugh, Caldwell, & Goldman, 2003; Robin, Greene, Albaugh, Caldwell, & Goldman, 2003), consistent with findings with the MMPI as described by Greene (2000); but the empirical correlates of the scales apply equally well. Moreover, Greene et al. (2003) explored empirical correlates of MMPI–2 scales among Native Americans and found significant correlations between scale elevations and several symptoms. Therefore, the MMPI–2 differences identified previously appear to correspond to actual symptoms among the Native American participants rather than just test bias.

Greene (1987) further cautions users of the MMPI–2 to be alert to the impact of sociodemographic variables, the impact of participants' ethnic identification, the validity of the profile, and whether there are any empirical correlates of any group differences that are found. No less important is the setting where the evaluation is conducted (i.e., employment, forensic), as respondents may have motivational reasons to underreport or overreport symptoms depending on what is at stake as a result of the evaluation.

The MMPI–2 and U.S. Latinos/Latinas

The methodological issues described by Greene (1987) and Dahlstrom (1986) have implications for Latino/Latina MMPI/MMPI–2 interpretation, especially when researchers do not afford them the appropriate consideration in their research design. For Latinos/Latinas, in particular, specificity as to basic sociodemographic characteristics and as to ethnic group membership and identification is extremely important given the considerable heterogeneity of Latinos/Latinas in their national origins and circumstances of migration (Padilla, 1992).

The MMPI restandardization project was carried out in response to the need to provide current norms, develop a nationally representative normative sample, provide minority representation, and update item content (Greene, 1991). The wording of the items was also modified in order to reduce cultural bias. This resulted in the publication of the MMPI–2 (Butcher, Dahlstrom, Graham, Tellegen, & Kaemmer, 1989). The large normative sample of the MMPI–2 (N = 2,600) included Black, Latino/Latina, Native American, and Asian participants in proportions consistent with 1980 census data along variables such as age, gender, and, to some extent, ethnicity. Nevertheless, Latinos/Latinas are underrepresented in this sample—especially those with less than a high school level of education. Additionally, the Latino/Latina sample (n = 35 men, n = 38 women) was obtained primarily from one geographic area of the United States (Southern California), further limiting the sample's ability to represent the heterogeneity of U.S.Latinos/Latinas. Analyses of MMPI–2 profile differences between White men and women and their Latino/Latina counterparts (employing the normative sample), have revealed some differences by ethnicity, with Latinos/Latinas obtaining higher scores. The differences have been found to be small (Lopez & Weisman, 2004).

Whitworth and McBlaine (1993) were the first to publish an MMPI–2 study with nonclinical Latino/Latina and White participants and in which the clinical and content scales were analyzed. This study revealed that Latinos/Latinas obtained higher *L* scale scores and also revealed differences in Scale 5, consistent with studies with the original MMPI. Other differences by ethnicity and gender were identified yet were considered to be very small.

This finding concerning scales *L* and 5 has been substantiated by Hall et al. (1999). In their review of 31 years of comparative MMPI/MMPI–2 research, the authors conclude that, in the aggregate, MMPI/MMPI–2 differences between White, Black, and Latino are quite small, with robust effect sizes found in differences between Whites and Latinos on scales *L* and 5. Specifically, these authors examined effect sizes from 13 investigations involving Latino and Euro-American males in a variety of clinical and forensic settings. A total of 169 effect sizes were reported. Hall et al. (1999) found the difference on Scale *L* to represent a moderate effect size ($d = .21$), with Latinos obtaining higher scores than their Euro-American counterparts. However, they found the difference in Scale 5 to represent the largest aggregate effect size in their study ($d = -.34$), with Latinos obtaining lower scores on Scale 5 than their Euro-American counterparts. The authors recognize that this finding by itself does not indicate the existence of extratest differences in behavior between White and Latino males. Interestingly, they report that this difference in Scale 5 has been observed in studies involving matched and unmatched samples. In spite of the apparent consistency of these findings, the authors offer important cautions for the interpretation of research findings derived from meta-analytic studies. In particular, such studies are based on the inclusion of investigations that meet specific methodological characteristics, thus potentially excluding many other relevant investigations. Moreover, it is important to remember that because Scale 5 does not measure "psychopathology" per se, but may reflect educational or cultural/familial differences between Latinos and others, Scale 5 differences between Latinos and others may not impact assessment of psychopathology as much as point to some personality style differences.

In sum, and of special relevance for the interpretation of MMPI–2 profiles of Latinos/Latinas, the findings by Hall et al. (1999) indicate that, as a general approach to personality assessment with Latinos/Latinas, the MMPI–2 provides comparable personality assessment information for both Latinos/Latinas and non-Latino/Latina Euro-American respondents. We believe that the general comparability of the findings for these groups enables us to consider the MMPI–2 to be an appropriate measure for the assessment of Latinos/Latinas and also to suggest ways in which its interpretation with Latinos/Latinas can be further refined as required by linguistic, cultural, social, or migration circumstances.

Ongoing research with the MMPI–2 indicates that Latinos/Latinas appear to obtain profiles that are generally similar to those of non-Latino/Latina White test takers (Greene, 2000). This finding applies to research with the English version of the instrument and with normative (nonclinical) groups (see Velasquez et al., 2002). More recently, MMPI–2 research with Latinos/Latinas has focused on exploring the comparability of the English and Spanish versions of the MMPI–2 (Velasquez, Chavira, et al., 2000). Studies with bilingual college students resulted in nearly identical profiles in the English and Spanish versions. The same authors looked at the comparability of different Spanish versions, finding a high degree of similarity in the resulting profiles among college students. Nevertheless, there continues to be a need to explore these issues with clinical groups.

MMPI–2 and Latino/Latina Heterogeneity: Migration, Cultural Identification, and Language Issues

The recognition among researchers and practitioners of the heterogeneity of Latinos/Latinas has prompted further research into the adequacy of the existing Spanish-language translation of the MMPI–2 in use in the United States (Garcia & Azan-Chaviano, 1993). This heterogeneity pertains to an individual's level of identification with his or her Latino/Latina origins, the circumstances of migration, and language use and preferences. Therefore, both researchers and clinicians must be aware of and address this in their methodologies and clinical interventions.

In line with Padilla (1992), this text's chapter 19 authors Butcher, Mosch, Tsai, and Nezami caution clinicians to consider the circumstances under which a client being assessed with the MMPI–2 has migrated to the United States and what that client's level of adaptation/acculturation to a new, complex culture might be. Specifically, it is not unusual for individuals who are evaluated shortly after having arrived in the new culture to reflect comparatively higher levels of distress than those who have been in the new culture for a longer period of time. Research by Velasquez et al. (2002) strongly suggests this. Other authors (e.g., Deinard, Butcher, Thao, Moua Vang, & Hang, 1996) have documented the importance of understanding the impact of adaptation and acculturation processes on the psychological functioning of individuals from other cultures as reflected in their MMPI–2 profiles. Additionally, Comas-Diaz and Grenier (1998) point out that many immigrants (and especially immigrants of color) become ethnic minorities upon relocation to North America and are likely to experience discrimination along with being perceived as inferior by the nonminority community because of their lack of political power. In this context of sociopolitical power differentials, these immigrants are under pressure to adapt to the host culture and to be a person of color in the new culture. According to the authors, these pressures lead to the development of coping strategies to deal with the adaptation challenge described here. In turn, these strategies may be manifested in the results of tests standardized in the host culture and may inaccurately portray these immigrants in a less-than-positive light.

For instance (and as is discussed in more detail in the next section), many Latinos/Latinas obtain elevations in the *L* scale of the MMPI–2. This has often been interpreted by various researchers (e.g., Velasquez et al., 2004) as an effort to appear socially competent and to not "air one's dirty laundry" to others outside the family or to a professional who may not be Latino/Latina. The disclosure of potentially negative personal characteristics or attitudes by Latinos/Latinas is widely seen as bringing shame to the individual and the family and as increasing the risk of being perceived as inferior in a social context that is already challenging for these immigrants. As indicated by Butcher (1996a), higher *L* scale scores have also been observed among some European groups when compared to the U.S. norms, which suggests that cultural differences also impact these groups' scores. Without knowledge of how these migration and sociopolitical factors may impact the evaluation, it is tempting to limit the interpretation of a high *L* scale score among Latinos/Latinas to stating that it reflects a defensive lack of cooperation with the evaluation or moralistic naïveté. Indeed, several researchers advocate contextual assessment (e.g., Dana, 1993) and ethnocultural assessment (Comas-Diaz & Jacobsen, 1987).

Briefly, these are approaches to the clinical assessment (including the careful use of psychological testing) and diagnosis of culturally diverse clients that take into account the assessment of level of acculturation, use of the client's preferred language, use of assessment devices that are culturally syntonic, and providing culture-specific feedback on the results (Dana, 1993). Ethnocultural assessment is a stage-based contextualized approach that takes into consideration the influence of the migration experience on the individual and how this experience might have influenced the development of a cultural identity (Comas-Diaz & Jacobsen, 1987). This approach is especially useful in the assessment of clients who are in the process of cultural transition, adaptation, and acculturation—as many Latino/Latina immigrants are.

Additionally, there is great heterogeneity among Latinos/Latinas in their level of identification with their culture of origin and their level of identification or acceptance of the host culture. Comas-Diaz (2001) describes what she calls a "taxonomy of ethnic terms" along with specific names that Latino/Latina groups employ to identify themselves. This taxonomy is framed in a historical and sociopolitical context that helps inform the relationship between a given Latino/Latina group and the dominant culture and that often reflects the dialectic between oppression and self-determination among these groups. As an example, Comas-Diaz describes for those of Puerto Rican origin at least three designations, each one representing a distinct balance of identification with and acceptance of island-origin identity and values and U.S. mainland identity. An additional level of complexity in ethnocultural identification is exemplified by those who are also of African descent.

Questions of language dominance, fluency, and language preference are extremely important in any kind of assessment and especially when discussing emotional issues (Centeno & Obler, 2001; Perez-Foster, 1998). Perez-Foster (1998) draws from psychoanalytic theory to describe an individual's mother language as the site of basic desires and emotions. As such, it is conceivable that an immigrant who is fully bilingual may spontaneously choose to employ his or her native language in those instances in which a translated term for the emotional experience would not convey the same meaning or intensity. Likewise, Perez-Foster describes language as an organizer of experience. Drawing on early social science, linguistic, and anthropological knowledge, she indicates that a culture's language has been understood to bring into focus those aspects of the physical, interpersonal, and experiential environment that are uniquely important in the life of that culture. Language, then, becomes not only a collection of symbols for communication but also the basis of a template through which people of a culture could organize their environment.

In their discussion of bilingualism as it pertains to Latino/Latina clients, Centeno and Obler (2001) remind us of the complexities of assessing whether a client is bilingual and indicate the existence of three dimensions of bilingualism that clinicians should examine: (a) language modality (e.g., reading, speaking), (b) language level (e.g., vocabulary, sentence comprehension), and (c) language context (e.g., formal versus informal). Clearly, a client may have different levels of proficiency in each dimension for each language. The authors also describe a number of designations that highlight the complexity of bilingualism, though they are not reviewed here in detail. Nevertheless, one designation described by Baetens Beardsmore (1986) is particularly relevant to this discussion. This author describes receptive bilinguals as those individuals who have an adequate understanding of a second language—in spoken or written form—but do not necessarily master conversational or written forms of the second language. Therefore, the assessment of proficiency in both the native and second language becomes critical when a bilingual client is assessed with a measure like the MMPI–2.

Clinicians who work with clients who may be receptive bilinguals are especially compelled to obtain some measure of language proficiency for these clients. Those who employ the MMPI–2 (or virtually any other measure) with Latinos/Latinas who have lived in the United States for a period of time must be aware of the distinction between an individual's proficiency in basic interpersonal communication skills (BICS) and cognitive–academic language proficiency (CALP; Cummins, 1984). As described by Cummins, basic interpersonal communication skills are associated with the ability to use language conversationally in everyday communicative contexts, whereas cognitive–academic language proficiency is a more complex level of language proficiency that is associated with reading, reading comprehension, written expression, and a generally more conceptual use of language, all of which emerge with formal schooling. In the absence of learning disabilities or other adverse conditions, this level of competency tends to develop over a period of several years. Therefore, while it is possible for some Latinos/Latinas to converse in English fairly fluently after living in the United States for a relatively short period of time, it may not be appropriate to use the English version of the MMPI–2 with them if their proficiency in the nonconversational use of English is not sufficient.

MMPI–2 Translation/Adaptation Issues

It is also appropriate to consider translation issues in evaluating the use of the instrument with Latinos/Latinas. The translation and adaptation of an instrument always raise the concern of the equivalence of a measure when used cross-culturally (see Exhibit 18.1). As clearly articulated by Butcher, Mosch, Tsai, and Nezami in chapter 19 of this text, the adaptation of a psychological assessment instrument for application in a different linguistic and cultural context requires that linguistic equivalence is achieved. The authors cite the work of Sechrest, Fay, and Zaida (1972), who described this equivalence as including vocabulary and idiomatic and grammatical–syntactical equivalences. Reaching equivalence requires that the

EXHIBIT 18.1
Highlight: Interpretation of the MMPI–2 With Latinos/Latinas

- Research on the use of the MMPI/MMPI–2 and MMPI–A with Latinos/Latinas over the past 30 years reveals that these are the most widely used personality assessment instruments employed with this group. Much of the research during that period of time has focused on considerations of cultural competence in the use of this instrument, specifically, reasons for its administration to Latino/Latina clients, choice of linguistic version for appropriate administration, and considerations as to the meaning of items for Latinos/Latinas representing different nationalities, among others. More recently, attention is being focused on the culturally competent *interpretation* of MMPI–2 findings with Latinos/Latinas.
- Researchers and clinicians should be alert to the methodological characteristics of research that discusses MMPI–2 findings with Latinos/Latinas, as the conclusions resulting from this research are likely to influence how MMPI–2 profiles are subsequently interpreted. This is especially important in light the fast-paced growth of the Latino community in the United States and its heterogeneity.
- Moderator variables (or extratest factors not related to group membership) must be considered when clinicians wish to interpret MMPI–2 findings from Latino/Latina clients in a culturally competent manner.
- The most recent studies indicate that there are very few robust differences between the MMPI–2 profiles of Latinos/Latinas and non-Latinos/Latinas. These differences are seen mostly on scales *L* and 5. The (clinical) significance of even small differences should be considered by clinicians within a culturally relevant context for their clients.
- When clinicians interpret MMPI–2 profiles of Latino/Latina clients, they may optimize their interpretations by considering alternative, culturally related explanations to observed scores. This will enrich the interpretive statements and make them more relevant to the goal of reaching appropriate treatment plans.
- Considerations of cultural background and of a number of moderator variables will influence the way in which MMPI–2 profiles of Latino/Latina clients are interpreted for their validity characteristics as well as for their clinical and content profile configurations.

translation is accurate (Allen & Walsh, 2000). According to Okazaki and Sue (1995), the linguistic equivalence of a test is important to ethnic minorities of a country, even when they speak the dominant language of the host society. Likewise, variations may occur within the same language use, such as the distinction between White English and Black English (Helms, 1992). The fact that most standardized instruments in use in the United States are written in (standard) White English raises the concern as to whether the items retain the same meaning across groups. This concern is likely to be amplified when an instrument is translated into an altogether different language, as it is critical that the conceptual equivalence of the measure is preserved in both the original and other language versions (Butcher, 2004).

To this end, Brislin (1993) discusses multistage translation–back translation as a method to ensure equivalency. Likewise, and as a result of concerns over the lack of a standard protocol for the translation of the MMPI, Butcher (1996a) has outlined a translation–back translation strategy followed by field testing in order to determine the acceptability of the instrument. Going beyond issues of linguistic equivalence, however, Butcher suggests that the newly translated instrument is compared with the original to determine the adequacy of the American norms and, if indicated, that local norms are developed. Handel and Ben-Porath (2000) indicate that, owing to Butcher's recommendations, current translations of the MMPI–2 have improved considerably and can generally be considered to be linguistically equivalent to the original. Nevertheless, the authors recognize the existence of language variability within same-language cultures. Among Spanish-language speakers, this is especially well illustrated. The authors highlight that Spanish versions such as those in use in Mexico, Chile, and Argentina may not be appropriate for use with other Spanish-speaking subgroups, such as those from Caribbean countries. For instance, Velasquez and Burton (2004) list a number of idioms of distress employed primarily by Chicano–Mexicano men in therapy that may not necessarily be understood by a Spanish-speaking therapist of a different Latino nationality. A similar situation is described by Rogler (1999) as it applies to Puerto Ricans.

Language use and level of acculturation have been thought to influence MMPI–2 results, as suggested by a number of recent studies. For instance, Fantoni-Salvador and Rogers (1997) identified differences between two groups of psychiatric inpatients (Mexican American and Puerto Rican), suggesting the existence of possible differences between these groups in the expression of psychopathology. Likewise, level of acculturation has been thought to affect MMPI–2 scales *L*, *F* (Infrequency), and 5 of Latinos/Latinas (e.g., Canul & Cross, 1994; Chavira, Montemayor, Velasquez, & Villarino, 1995; Hernandez, 1994; Lessenger, 1997; Mendoza-

Newman, 1999). The authors of these studies, however, recognize that the findings on acculturation tend to be mixed and that this is an area of Latino/Latina MMPI–2 research that warrants further study.

Recent studies by Lucio, Ampudia, Duran, Leon, and Butcher (2001) and by Lucio, Palacios, Duran, and Butcher (1999) caution test users not only to employ the linguistic version of the MMPI–2 that is most appropriate to the client but also to consider employing norms developed in the country of origin for Latinos/Latinas that have been in the United States for no more than 5 years. Neglect of these considerations may result in what Rogler (1999) has described as insensitivity in mental health research and application. He warns of the threats to the validity of an instrument as a result of neglecting to understand specific idioms of distress and of applying concepts cross-culturally that are not sufficiently similar in two different cultures.

More recently, MMPI–2 research with Latinos/Latinas has turned toward the adequacy of the existing norms as applied to this group. An example is the work of Lucio, Reyes-Lagunes, and Scott (1994), who developed a Spanish-language version of the MMPI–2 for use in Mexico. This has been followed by the development of specific Mexican norms (Lucio et al., 2001) that would be representative of the urban population from various regions of Mexico. In their comparison of their norms with the U.S. norms, the authors found significant differences accounted for by nationality (effect sizes greater than .40) in several validity and clinical scales for men and women. While, overall, these norms are similar to the U.S. norms, the authors indicate that in the case of the Mexican population it would be preferable to employ the local norms as they appear to account for cultural factors.

Clearly, the task of achieving the adaptation of an instrument to another language goes beyond just translation and into considerations of language equivalence, which may in turn impact the validity of the obtained results. These considerations regarding the quality of an instrument's language adaptation are, in our opinion, central to the appropriateness of the interpretive statements that are derived from it.

Profile validity is another central consideration in the interpretation of Latino/Latina MMPI/MMPI–2 profiles. As is discussed in more detail in the next section, numerous studies with Latinos/Latinas have found a tendency for these profiles to reflect an effort toward positive self-presentation, expressed in *L* scale scores that are often higher than those of non-Latino/Latina White subjects. This tendency toward overly positive self-presentation has been linked to Latino/Latina sociocultural values associated with social desirability, acquiescence, and unwillingness to disclose personal matters especially to non-Latinos (Marin & VanOss-Marin, 1991). Likewise, the impact of moderator variables for Latinos/Latinas must be recognized. Socioeconomic status, level of education, and cognitive ability have been examined as moderators in the interpretation of MMPI/MMPI–2 profiles (Velasquez et al., 2002). For Latinos/Latinas, it would also be important to consider the potential effects of migration and migratory circumstances, experiences of discrimination, acculturation (as well as acculturative stress), and any other relevant background experiences that could impact emotional functioning. These experiences may include extreme poverty, war, trauma, or persecution in the country of origin (Falicov, 1982; Garcia-Preto, 1982; Santiago-Rivera, Arredondo, & Gallardo-Cooper, 2002).

The studies reviewed here provide researchers and clinicians with important guidelines and cautions as to the culturally competent interpretation of the MMPI/MMPI–2. First, we agree with Hall et al.'s (1999) conclusion that equivalence in MMPI–2 profiles is not equal to equivalence in extratest behaviors in "real-world" environments. Therefore, while group differences may be small, they may not necessarily be trivial in their implications and need to be addressed in the interpretation. This warning also reminds us of the ongoing need for research that explores the empirical correlates of MMPI–2 findings, as recommended by Greene (2000). Second, the authors remind us that in spite of finding few ethnic differences in psychopathology (based on epidemiological data), it is possible that the instruments currently available are not sufficiently sensitive to detect differences that may exist. This potential lack of sensitivity evokes the distinction between *etic* and *emic* approaches to cross-cultural research. Briefly, this is the distinction between approaches based on universal assumptions about human experience that transcend races and cultures (etics) and those based on indigenous, culture-specific assumptions of experience (emics; Triandis, 1994). As discussed by Triandis, psychologists who work across cultures strive to understand behavior in terms that are meaningful to a specific culture and also to compare such findings to other cultures from an external perspective. This also underscores the importance of translation, conceptual, and metric equivalence of measures in order to achieve meaningful comparisons between groups. Therefore, researchers should be alert to conceptual characteristics of their measures that may make them pseudoetic and therefore not sufficiently sensitive to meaningful differences. Finally, we support the author's call for additional within-group research.

For clinicians, it is important to consider the various aspects of culture and, especially, issues of ethnocultural identity, language use, and value orientation that may be reflected in MMPI–2 profiles. Given the rapid growth, development, and dynamics of contemporary Latino/Latina U.S. populations, both clinicians and researchers should recognize not only the impact of the cultural values that we have long been familiar with but also the potential challenges to those values as a result of acculturation experiences and stressors (Vega, 1995). This also requires that both clinicians and researchers pay special attention to within-Latino/Latina group characteristics in language use, concepts of emotional health and distress, and relationship with the broader society.

SOME INTERPRETIVE GUIDELINES FOR MMPI–2 SCALES

We next offer a series of interpretive guidelines for the validity, clinical, and content scales of the MMPI–2 in the context of the sociocultural values that most often characterize Latino/Latina respondents. As described here, adherence to socially and culturally sanctioned ways of interacting within the cultural group and with the broader society may have an impact on the interpretation of MMPI–2 profiles of Latinos/Latinas. We encourage clinicians and researchers who interpret Latino/Latina MMPI–2 profiles to consider these guidelines in formulating interpretive statements. In particular, we believe that consideration of these guidelines may help prevent test users from reaching inaccurate conclusions or conclusions that may reflect stereotypical or even overpathologized views of Latino/Latina clients.

In addition to the influence of sociocultural tendencies, the manner in which Latinos/Latinas approach structured inquiries, surveys, and other forms of research may also have implications for the validity and characteristics of MMPI–2 profiles. Marin and VanOss-Marin (1991) have reviewed several studies (e.g., Hui & Triandis, 1989) in which Latinos/Latinas have been found to employ extreme response sets (i.e., "yea-saying" or "nay-saying"). This tendency has been identified especially among Latinos/Latinas with lower levels of acculturation. The authors also point out that the use of acquiescent response sets and socially desirable responses have been identified as characteristics of Latinos'/Latinas' approach to research instruments. These tendencies, described in the study of measures other than the MMPI–2, are likely to have implications for the validity of Latino/Latina profiles. While the MMPI–2 has various scales to detect extreme response sets, social desirability, and other forms of inconsistent responding (e.g., TRIN [True Response Inconsistency], VRIN [Variable Response Inconsistency]), there is still a lack of research concerning the influence of culture on these scales for Latinos/Latinas (Cuellar, 1998).

A review of the sociocultural values relevant to Latinos/Latinas suggests several key considerations that should be included in any interpretive task. As described by Garcia-Preto (1982) and Santiago-Rivera et al. (2002), most Latinos/Latinas hold a diverse array of beliefs in spirituality. Many hold devotions to the saints of the Catholic faith, which is still dominant among Latinos/Latinas. However, some Latino nationalities (especially of Caribbean origin) practice spiritism, santeria, or other variations of African origin religions. The deep influence that spirituality has in the frame of reference of Latinos/Latinas is manifested, for instance, in popular, everyday expressions such as "Si Dios quiere" (if it's God's will). Another example, especially among Latino/Latinas who adhere to a more traditional value orientation, is the belief in the power of saints to influence outcomes, especially in times of adversity such as instances of physical or mental illness. Therefore, endorsement of MMPI/MMPI–2 items related to these beliefs may have an effect on test indicators associated with unusual experiences—or even psychotic symptoms—and may be inaccurately interpreted as an indication of severe psychopathology. In particular, this may have implications for the interpretation of scales 8 and BIZ (Bizarre Mentation).

In addition, many Latinos/Latinas place considerable importance on the quality of interpersonal relationships as opposed to individualism, a quality often referred to as "personalismo." Personalismo has been described as a characteristic of a collectivistic worldview (Levine & Padilla, 1980).This term also encompasses values such as those of dignity and interpersonal respect. At the heart of this value is the high level of regard for inner qualities and self-worth, as opposed to material achievement, and interdependence, as opposed to individualism in interactions with others. This tendency is closely related to the need to present a dignified self and to not reveal personal problems publicly, especially to someone outside the family network. Therefore, adherence to this sociocultural value may have implications for the interpretation of Scale *L*. Indeed, the disclosure of personal problems would bring shame ("verguenza") upon the individual *and* his or her family. By not considering the potential impact of this sociocultural imperative, the interpretation of an elevated *L* score may be limited to stating that it is due to an effort to look good, defensive noncooperation with the evaluation, or naãveté in describing personal behavior.

Related to the concept of personalismo is the expectation that Latinos/Latinas are socially competent and comfortable around their families and social networks. Velasquez et al. (2004) have observed elevations in Scale 0 among Latinos/Latinas who report feelings of alienation from the mainstream culture and even from their cultural groupof origin.Therefore, for Latinos/Latinas, the interpretation of scores on Scale 0 should take into account the existence of difficulties beyond internally experienced social anxiety or discomfort.

Latinos/Latinas also may find it comparatively more acceptable to endorse items related to somatic and health concerns than to endorse items directly related to symptoms of emotional distress. Therefore, this may result in higher scores on scales such as *Hs* (Hypochondriasis) and HEA (Velasquez et al., 2004).

Many Latinos/Latinas uphold a strong alliance and loyalty to their families (both nuclear and extended), a value known as *familismo*. As described by Marin and Triandis (1985) and Falicov (1998), familismo derives from a collectivistic worldview that values the sharing of responsibilities, emotional and financial support when needed, and participation in decision making.Interdependence as opposed to independence tends to be fostered. Direct, personal contact with members of the nuclear and extended family is valued over other forms of communication such as telephone calls (Hurtado, 1995). It may be inferred that Latinos/Latinas who do not have this level of access to their family systems owing to migration or other circumstances may experience emotional or other adjustment difficulties. In fact, a study involving Latino prison inmates in which MMPI–2 characteristics and predictors of institutional adjustment were explored found that content scale FAM (Family Problems) was the strongest single predictor for number of disciplinary infractions among Latino immates (Garrido, Gionta, Diehl, & Boscia, 1998). This suggests that for this group a history of family distress has a strong, negative impact on the ability to adjust to incarceration and possibly other adverse situations. It could also be inferred that a positive relationship with family may serve as a supportive, grounding influence for Latino inmates and that the absence of this support may havesevere negative effects on their adjustment. Content scale FAM was not a significant predictor for either Euro-American or Black inmates.

The clear demarcation of male and female roles within the family has long characterized traditional Latino families. The concepts of *machismo* and *marianismo* are most readily associated with the understanding of gender roles among Latinos/Latinas and are likely to have important implications for the interpretation of Scale 5 on the MMPI–2. Briefly, machismo refers to a Latino man's responsibility, loyalty, and integrity to his family, his community, and his friends rather than to the often-described emphasis on virility and chauvinism that has characterized other definitions of machismo (Morales, 1996). On the other hand, marianismo refers to the expectation that women adopt a nurturing, pious, virtuous, and humble role in the family (Lopez-Baez, 1999). More recently, however, there is debate as to the extent to which Latinos/Latinas adhere to these gender assumptions in contemporary society. With respect to Scale 5 findings on the MMPI–2, recent studies have found that Latinas show more variability on this scale than men, who tend to obtain scores below 50T (Anderson, 1999; Anderson, Fernandez, Callahan, & Velasquez, 2001; Anderson, Velasquez, & Callahan, 2000). In fact, Anderson (1999) has reported T scores between 60 and 65 among college-educated Latinas. This suggests that for these women there is less adherence to traditional gender role expectations, possibly as a function of increased independence from their families and of pursuing professional advancement.

Last, among Latinos/Latinas, the expression of aggression and emotional distress reflects clear cultural rules. Specifically, it is not unusual that many Latinos/Latinas report somatic symptoms under which may be sources of emotional distress such as depression, anxiety, interpersonal, or family conflict.

We have organized our presentation of the scales and their interpretive possibilities from a Latino/Latina perspective in Appendix 18.1. Each section *describes* the meaning of elevated scores (T greater than 65) for the scale and includes a series of *interpretive issues* to be considered for Latino/Latina profiles. The content of this appendix follows interpretive procedures from Butcher et al. (1989), Velasquez et al. (1998), Marin and VanOss-Marin (1991) and our collective clinical observations derived from more than 20 years of use of the MMPI and MMPI–2 with Latinos/Latinas.

CASE EXAMPLES

In this chapter, we present three case examples that illustrate several interpretation issues or challenges that clinicians are likely to encounter when evaluating Latino/Latina and bilingual and bicultural clients with the MMPI–2. The purpose of presenting these cases is to highlight the importance for practicing clinicians of being aware of the ways in which their bilingual and bicultural clients utilize language to describe their emotional distress. This may, in turn, help clinicians make informed decisions concerning which version of the MMPI–2 is the most appropriate one to interpret in a given situation. Other cases are included to illustrate issues of profile validity and of the potential impact of extratest variables (e.g., circumstances of migration) on the MMPI–2 profiles of Latino/Latina parents involved with child protective agencies.

As these cases illustrate, selecting an inappropriate language version of the MMPI–2 or not administering the inventory in a second language when appropriate may result in inaccurate profile interpretations. Oftentimes, resulting profiles may reflect a heightened degree of psychopathology and much more impaired functioning than would be reflected by a profile administered in a language that could facilitate a more accurate expression of emotional functioning. Other aspects of MMPI–2 interpretation that can be affected by the language in which the test is administered include level of self-disclosure, the distinction between pathological functioning and culturally sanctioned value assumptions, and the distinction between severe psychopathology and interpersonal distress. Solutions to address interpretive challenges are also proposed.

Case Example 1: Ana

Ana, a 26-year-old Puerto Rican, monolingual, Spanish-speaking mother, had been referred for a parenting evaluation by the state child protective agency. Allegedly, she had neglected her younger child (age 3) and left him in the care of inappropriate caretakers. Her oldest child, age 6, was with his father at the time of the referral. Ana had lived in the mainland United States for 3 years at the time of the referral.

Ana herself was raised by and lived with—during alternating periods of time—her mother, her grandparents, and other relatives. She and her siblings witnessed severe domestic violence between her mother and her boyfriends. Ana distinctly recalled having very little parental or other adult supervision. Ana also reported having been sexually molested during childhood and physically abused by her own partners. She reported being bothered by symptoms of depression and anxiety with post-traumatic features, has had several suicide attempts, and has experimented with drugs.

Ana's initial behavioral presentation was suspicious, angry, and confrontational—especially toward the child protective caseworker who was handling her case. She was also resistant toward the evaluation, but it was possible to eventually enlist sufficient cooperation from her to complete it. In particular, Ana voiced concerns about language and communication barriers between her and her caseworker as well as concerns about what she described as unreliable interpreter services. She felt that she could be taken advantage of or deceived due to her lack of proficiency in English.

Among other instruments that strongly indicated Ana's high level of stress in her experience as a parent and an interpersonal and emotional life dominated by experiences of conflict, Ana was administered the MMPI–2 in Spanish. Her validity and clinical profiles show considerable levels of distress with a relatively low level of defensiveness (L = 60, F = 120, K (Correction) = 30). The high F score (extremely exaggerated and bordering on invalidity) likely reflects a "call for help." Although the profile should only be interpreted with caution, there are multiple elevations in scales that could reflect some concerns she is having with respect to suspiciousness, anger, impulsivity, and unusual thoughts. In the absence of obvious signs of thought disorder, the elevations on scales 6 (T = 98) and 8 (T = 83) appear to capture Ana's experiences of suspiciousness (especially toward the child protective agency) and alienation from her family, as well as her low levels of trust. Additionally, an elevation in Scale 5 is noted at T = 81. It is possible that this elevation is accounted for by Ana's need to be a survivor at her home of origin in light of the chronic disruption there. Ana also needs to survive in a host society in which her own safety has been threatened by partners, in which she has had to interact with a child protective bureaucracy, and in which she does not feel in control of her situation due to her inability to effectively communicate in English. Traditional interpretations of elevations in Scale 5 for women state that they can be unfriendly, domineering, and aggressive. While these characteristics were portrayed by Ana's presentation, it is important to consider the impact of her adverse family background and present circumstances on her overall functioning.

Case Example 2: Juan

Juan is a 27-year-old male who was asked by his mother to come to therapy. His mother indicated that her son is currently living with a girlfriend who is pregnant by him. She also noted that "Juan is very good-looking, self-centered, poorly motivated, aggressive, macho, and angry." She also suspected that he may be abusing drugs or alcohol, although he denied this to her. She noted that Juan has been very angry since childhood because she and Juan's father were divorced and she married Juan's padrino or godfather (he was also married and left his wife for her). She stated that Juan may benefit from therapy, especially since he was about to become a father.

Juan was administered the MMPI–2 after the intake because he appeared to be very charming yet defensive and guarded. He indicated that he did not need therapy because he was happy in his current situation, which was his girlfriend being pregnant. Yet, he had a bruise on his face, which suggested that he might have gotten into a fight. When asked about the bruise, he stated that he had recently fought his girlfriend's ex-boyfriend because he found him at their apartment and he was being abusive toward her.

A review of Juan's MMPI–2 profile indicated that it was valid and interpretable. His validity scales reflected a rather open approach or demeanor with the *L* and *K* scales at 39T and the *F* scale at 51T. Juan's performance on the clinical scales indicated only two elevations—on the Pd (Psychopathic Deviate) and *Pa* (Paranoia), yielding a "6–4 code type." In addition, his Mf (Masculinity–Feminity) scale was low relative to the Pd and *Pa* scales at 50T. The only two scales elevated on the content scales were the BIZ (70T) and the ANG (Anger; 74T) scales indicating both unusual beliefs and significant anger and hostility. In spite of denying any type of substance use, the three substance-related scales were elevated: MacAndrew Alcoholism Scale—Revised (MAC–R; 73T), Addiction Acknowledgment Scale (AAS; 70T), and Addiction Potential Scale (APS; 73T). On the Personality Psychopathology Five (PSY–5) scales, Juan obtained elevations on the Aggressiveness (AGGR; 74T) and Negative Emotionality–Neuroticism (NEGE; 64T) scales, supporting the presence of both aggression and negativity. A review of the Harris–Lingoes subscales indicates elevations on the Pd1 (Familial Discord), the *Pa*1 (Persecutory Ideas), and the *Ma*4 (Ego Inflation) scales. On the Content Component scales, Juan obtained elevations on the DEP1 (Lack of Drive), the ANG1 (Explosive Behavior), the ANG2 (Irritability), the ASP2 (Antisocial Behavior), and the TRT1 (Low Motivation) scales.

Collectively, the results of the MMPI–2 are consistent with his mother's description of him. The results also point toward an individual who is likely to hold very traditional beliefs and ideas about sex roles, including his girlfriend's, and is likely to be inflexible and resistant to treatment. The results of the MMPI–2 were shared with Juan at the subsequent therapy session. Juan became very defensive and guarded when asked to talk about issues such as substance use. While admitting to using various illegal substances on a regular basis, he minimized the effects on his personality and well-being.

Case Example 3: Antonio

Antonio is a 29-year-old, monolingual, Spanish-speaking, South American native who was referred for a parenting evaluation by a state child protective agency. Together with his wife, he is the father of two children ages 3 years and 8 months. The infant child had been found to have a leg fracture, which doctors described as "consistent with physical abuse." Antonio and his wife vehemently denied that either one of them had ever hurt the child physically and attributed the fracture to their infant son having his leg caught, accidentally, in the safety bars of his new crib. At the time of the referral, the two children were in foster care and the parents were able to visit them regularly.

Antonio described his own upbringing as "very positive, I grew up in a close-knit family where discipline was not physical punishment." Antonio had decided to migrate to the United States with his wife in search of better economic conditions. He soon found that his lack of English proficiency prevented him from pursuing employment in his field of study and, at the time of the evaluation, was working in a rather low-paying position. He consistently highlighted his wife as a good mother. Antonio added that using a crib was a new experience for them because their limited finances did not allow them to purchase one for their older son. Therefore, that child slept with them during infancy, a practice that Antonio described as "normal" among people of limited means in his native country. As such, they were not aware of the need to add a protective bumper to the crib in order to prevent the type of injury their infant sustained.

Among other assessment instruments, Antonio completed the Spanish version of the MMPI–2. Antonio approached the inventory by portraying himself in a highly positive light ($L = 95$, $F = 59$, $K = 70$). This "good impression" profile is relatively common in persons being evaluated in custody cases. Keep in mind that the client is likely to be presenting a highly favorable view of himself in the evaluation. Even this defensive profile also reveals difficulties related to depression ($D = 75$) and related to experiencing emotional distress through somatic symptoms ($Hs = 80$). This is in line with his reports of reduced appetite; and he asserted, "If you don't know how well your children are being taken care of, or how well they are eating, you don't feel like eating either . . . I also have more headaches, just don't feel right." The expression of emotional distress via somatic and health concerns is further confirmed in the MMPI–2 by the elevation in the HEA content scale (T = 75). Interestingly, Antonio's Scale 5 score (T = 65) may appear to be higher than expected for Latino males but may be indicative of his sensitivities and attachment to his children and his real experience of distress upon being separated from them and may also be associated with other aspects of his personal background such as his relatively high level of education.

SUMMARY AND CONCLUSIONS

In this chapter, we have reviewed a number of significant considerations in the interpretation of MMPI–2 findings with Latinos/Latinas. Additionally, we have reviewed research that investigates MMPI–2 findings among Latinos/Latinas, paying special attention to the methodological qualities of these investigations. Our review of those studies has highlighted the importance of employing appropriate methodologies to the conclusions derived from the findings, which will in turn shape the interpretive guidelines applied to the group being studied.

We have also suggested interpretive guidelines for MMPI–2 findings within a framework that considers sociocultural values, language use and proficiency, approach to structured assessments and to situations involving disclosure, culturally prescribed gender roles, and the impact of migration and acculturation processes. Finally, we have presented clinical case examples. In these cases, we illustrate how key aspects of culture and language use have informed our clinical interpretation of Latino/Latina MMPI–2 profiles and have contributed to the formulation of treatment plans. Taken together, our work with Latinos/Latinas who have been assessed with the MMPI–2 suggests the following conclusions:

1. Both clinicians and researchers are encouraged to critically examine the methodological characteristics of MMPI–2 research with Latinos/Latinas. It is especially important to examine the level of specificity in the study concerning sample composition, language use, Latino/Latina nationality, and the migration status and circumstances of the participants in such research.
2. Clinicians must consider numerous moderator variables that may impact MMPI–2 results of their clients. These extratest factors separate from group membership include but may not be limited to socioeconomic status, level of education, migration circumstances, acculturative pressures, and experiences of discrimination in the host society.

3. Likewise, both clinicians and researchers who work with Latinos/Latinas must consider the role of culturally prescribed attitudes and approaches to situations that require or expect disclosure or in which the quality of self-presentation is important. In this respect, it is important to identify tendencies toward extreme response sets and toward highly positive self-presentation and to interpret them considering how the respondent's culture may have influenced these tendencies.
4. In general, research indicates that the MMPI–2 and its Spanish translation and adaptations do not tend to portray Latinos/Latinas unfavorably. The existing research (e.g., Hall et al., 1999) indicates the existence of few robust differences between Latinos/Latinas and non-Latinos/Latinas.
5. Clinicians who work with bilingual Latinos should exercise care in their choice of language version of the MMPI–2. The appropriate choice may require that language proficiency assessment is performed.
6. In spite of the existence of only a few differences, it is still important for clinicians to evaluate the significance of these differences for their clients' adjustment.

APPENDIX 18.1

INTERPRETIVE HYPOTHESES FOR MMPI–2 VALIDITY AND CLINICAL SCALES FOR LATINOS/LATINAS.

L (Lie) Scale

Description

- This scale indicates the approach to the test. High scores are associated with test resistance, lack of insight, unrealistically positive self-presentation, or lack of sophistication in creating a positive personal impression.

Interpretive Issues

- *L* tends to be higher among Latinos than among non-Latino White clients. Is it deliberate deception? Social desirability?
- Consider Latino tendency to positive self-presentation in structured inquiries and by non-Latinos.
- Consider the need to protect self and family from shame, to preserve dignity, and in light of what is at stake (e.g., custody).
- Level of acculturation matters: less acculturation is related to higher *L* than vice versa.

F (Infrequency) Scale

Description

- *F* is associated with unusual, generally serious symptoms; exaggeration of symptoms; possible malingering; and profile invalidity when elevated.
- Elevations can be associated with poor reading comprehension, confusion, test resistance, or lack of cooperation.

Interpretive Issues

- For elevated scores, consider possible reading problems and/or unfamiliarity with test and response format.
- If *Sc* (Schizophrenia) is also elevated, consider the possibility of endorsement of items related to spirituality.
- Consider possible effect of an all-true response set.

K (Correction) Scale

Description

- This scale is associated with willingness to self-disclose.
- Elevated scores are associated with reluctance to self-disclose, reliance on denial, or lack of insight.

Interpretive Issues

- Consider possible reluctance to self-disclose, especially if score on *L* is also elevated.
- As with *L*, consider the need for positive self-presentation, maintaining dignity, and concerns about being found mentally ill.

F(B) (Back Infrequency) Scale

Description

- Items are similar to those of *F*, but are located in the last half of the inventory.
- Elevated scores are interpreted similarly to elevations in *F*.

Interpretive Issues

- Consider reading problems, confusion, length of the instrument, and other issues that also affect interpretation of *F*.

VRIN (Variable Response Inconsistency)

Description

- This scale assesses inconsistent, indiscriminate, random responding to the inventory. High VRIN scores are associated with confusion, poor reading, level, careless approach to the test, or legitimate psychopathology.

Interpretive Issues

- Consider problems with reading level and comprehension, confusion as to format of the test, and other issues that affect the interpretation of *F*.

TRIN (True Response Inconsistency)

DESCRIPTION

- This scale is an additional index of response consistency (or inconsistency) based on the tendency to give mostly True or mostly False responses.
- This scale indicates the existence of response sets—either acquiescent or nay-saying.

INTERPRETIVE ISSUES

- If elevated as mostly True, consider possible tendency to be acquiescent in test responses and structured inquiries.
- Consider the possibility that respondents may have had many of the experiences described in the inventory.

Scale 1: *Hs* (Hypochondriasis)

DESCRIPTION

- This scale is associated with excessive concerns about health.
- Elevations are associated with exaggeration of physical problems, pessimism, bitterness and demandingness, self-centeredness, overreaction to problems, or bizarre somatic delusions.

INTERPRETIVE ISSUES

- Consider culturally congruent ways of channeling emotional distress via somatic problems; physical sensations such as heat rising from upper body to the head when angry, stressed, or disappointed.
- Consider cultural rules concerning anger control/repression that may lead to somatization.

Scale 2: *D* (Depression)

DESCRIPTION

- This scale indicates withdrawal, despondency, slowness of thought and action, suicidality, low energy and concentration, subjective sadness, inadequacy, and being overwhelmed by problems.

INTERPRETIVE ISSUES

- Consider history of depression but also the effects of migration and acculturation pressures such as language competency, different customs, intergenerational issues (parenting challenges), and others.
- Consider the availability of social supports and the status of family relations.

Scale 3: *Hy* (Hysteria)

Description

- This scale indicates denial, dissociation, flirtatiousness, naïveté, low insight, physical symptoms when distressed, being uninhibited, and exhibiting tantrum behavior.

Interpretive Issues

- Consider (see *Hs*) culturally congruent expression of distress via physical symptoms and incidence of "ataque de nervios" when in acute distress.
- Consider culturally congruent behaviors of expressiveness, gregariousness, and personalismo.

Scale 4: Pd (Psychopathic Deviate)

Description

- This scale indicates authority conflicts, antisocial actions, aggressive behavior, poor judgment, irresponsibility, substance abuse, instability, superficial relationships, recurrent work and marital problems, and impulsivity.

Interpretive Issues

- Consider family distress/disruption; authority issues for younger Latinos/Latinas coping with acculturation issues at home and socially; survival-related behaviors for Latinos/Latinas in light of legal status problems; and possible social and self-alienation.

Scale 5: Mf (Masculinity–Feminity)

Description

- Males: Low scores are associated with traditional male interests, aggression, crudeness, self-confidence, and recklessness; opposite for high scores.
- Females: Low scores are associated with dependency, submissiveness, traditional feminine interests, and helplessness; opposite for high scores.

Interpretive Issues

- Males subscribe to traditional role of assuredness and of defending family honor; low scores are a consistent finding with Latino males.
- Females: If high scores, consider effect of acculturation, and educational and professional environments on younger Latinas. Also, consider role of single mothers/family providers.

Scale 6: *Pa* (Paranoia)

Description

- This scale indicates misinterpreted social situations, anger, hostility, externalization of blame, mistaken beliefs, thought disorder, and ideas of reference.

Interpretive Issues

- Consider issues related to legal status, real or perceived discrimination, and feeling like "I have to do more and be better than nonminorities to be regarded positively."
- Consider culturally congruent orientation to value/trust individual relationships more than relationships with official institutions.

Scale 7: *Pt* (Psychasthenia)

Description

- This scale indicates anxiety, depression, fearfulness, rumination, feelings of guilt, superstitious phobias, worrying, being tense, and being moralistic.

Interpretive Issues

- Consider impact of separation from family supports.
- Consider adherence to culturally sanctioned mores, expectations, and roles.
- Consider adherence to spiritual beliefs, folk healing, or even spiritism.

Scale 8: *Sc* (Schizophrenia)

Description

- This scale indicates unusual beliefs, thought disorder, withdrawal, delusions, hallucinations, and social seclusion.
- This scale indicates poor contact with reality, bizarre behavior, and religious concerns.

Interpretive Issues

- Consider possible migration/acculturation experiences affecting relationship with self and broader society (alienation).
- Consider culturally congruent ways of coping considered "unusual" in host culture.
- Consider adherence to devotions, saints, spirituality, and other rituals that assist in coping with distress.

Scale 9: *Ma* (Hypomania)

Description

- Characteristics of this scale are gregariousness, impatience, talkativeness, impulsivity, restlessness, euphoria, being over-extended, poor temper control, hyperactive, expansive, and excess activity.

Interpretive Issues

- Consider culturally valued sociability, gregariousness, and outgoingness.
- Consider the need to improvise in daily life out of necessity.
- Consider multiple responsibilities held for parents, children, extended relatives, and others.

Scale 0: Si (Social Introversion–Extroversion)

Description

- This scale indicates submissiveness, low self-confidence, introversion, shyness, insecurity, aloofness, and withdrawal.

Interpretive Issues

- Consider effects of acculturative pressures and migration on individuals who would otherwise be more outgoing.
- Consider adaptation to workplaces and whether there are feelings of inadequacy due to language barriers or other cultural differences.

19

CROSS-CULTURAL APPLICATIONS OF THE MMPI–2

JAMES N. BUTCHER, SONIA COELHO MOSCH, JEANNE TSAI, AND ELAHE NEZAMI

Traditionally, the study of cultural influences on personality and psychopathology has been relegated to different subareas of anthropology. With the exception of a few renegade scientists and clinicians, psychologists and psychiatrists have begun only recently to think seriously about cultural influences on personality and psychopathology. This is partly because of demographic trends that guarantee increasing exposure to and contact with immigrant and ethnic minority populations (U.S. Bureau of the Census, 1992) and partly because of advances in technology that facilitate international communication. In this chapter, we discuss the importance of examining personality and psychopathology across cultural and ethnic groups and the advantages to using objective personality instruments in such examinations; we review methodological problems that arise when adapting such instruments for international use; and we present technical solutions that address problems to such examinations. Finally, we present the MMPI–2 as a useful tool for assessing personality and psychopathology in different cultural and ethnic groups and discuss instruments for which most of the methodological problems have already been resolved.

WHY STUDY CULTURE, PERSONALITY, AND PSYCHOPATHOLOGY?

Understanding the influence of culture on psychological processes is important for several reasons. Psychology and psychiatry are fields that originated, for the most part, in Western culture. As a result, many of the existing conceptions of "human behavior" not only are derived from the observation of Western samples but also are products of Western epistemology. In order to test the validity of such observations and ensure that they are indeed describing *human* behavior rather than the behavior of specific Western populations, these psychological constructs must be examined with other cultural samples. Moreover, examining the behavior of members of other cultures may make salient particular aspects of Western behavior that have largely gone unnoticed by Western social scientists. For example, the study of anxiety disorders in other cultures has revealed that eating disorders such as anorexia nervosa and bulimia are specifically Western phenomena (Prince, 1983; Swartz, 1985).

From a practical standpoint, it is highly likely that in occupational, social, and clinical settings, we will come into increasing contact with individuals from cultural backgrounds different from our own. For example, in mental health care settings, clinicians are coming into greater contact with ethnic minority groups (Sue & Sue, 1990). Although the rates of mental health service utilization vary across ethnic minority groups in the United States (Sue et al., 1991), the overall percentage of refugee, immigrant, and American-born ethnic minority individuals seeking health care services is on the rise. O'Sullivan, Peterson, Cox, and Kirkeby (1989) and Russell et al. (1996) have found that ethnic matching of therapist and client results in higher ratings of client functioning. These findings suggest that being of a different cultural background than one's clients may limit one's ability to assess optimal client functioning. Although it is unclear whether more optimal assessments of client functioning are indeed more accurate, these findings suggest that knowing when culture does and does not influence personality and psychopathology is important for accurate diagnosis and treatment.

CULTURE AND PERSONALITY

The study of cultural influences on human behavior raises the related issue of individual differences that exist independent of culture. For example, how do we determine whether an individual's emotional expression is a result of his or her cultural heritage or a result of his or her personality? The tension between cultural and personality influences raises other questions: (a) Is personality universal or culture-specific? (b) Do the same personality traits manifest themselves differently across different cultural contexts? (c) How do culture and personality interact to influence behavior? (d) Can we measure personality across cultural groups? These issues become particularly relevant when we consider the wide use of personality instruments in occupational, academic, and health settings. For example, an international corporation that utilizes personality instruments to screen its potential employees may mistakenly use standards that reflect abnormal behavior in one culture and normal behavior in another. As a result, potential employees may be incorrectly deemed ineligible for specific occupations.

Few empirical studies of culture and personality exist. Among those that do, most suggest cross-cultural similarities in the underlying personality structures (Benet & Waller, 1995; Butcher & Pancheri, 1976; Church & Katigbak, 1989; Narayanan, Menon, & Levine, 1995). Although even fewer studies have examined the psychological correlates of different personality dimensions (Greene, 1987), some findings suggest that these correlates are also of similar cultures. For example, Yamaguchi, Kuhlman, and Sugimori (1995) found that members of American, Korean, and Japanese cultures who were more allocentric (oriented toward the group) were also more affiliative, were more sensitive to rejection, and demonstrated a lower need for uniqueness. Clearly, more work needs to be conducted in this area. Previously, one of the greatest challenges to conducting this type of work was the lack of instrumentation to measure personality across different cultural groups. The international adaptations of the MMPI and MMPI–2, the most widely used clinical personality assessment instruments, meet this challenge.

CULTURE AND PSYCHOPATHOLOGY

Is there a common *human* core to psychopathology, or is mental illness culturally constructed? Is "abnormal" behavior culturally defined? Can we treat mental illness cross-culturally, or are specific treatments for mental illness restricted to specific cultures? Anthropologists, epidemiologists, psychologists, and psychiatrists vary in their beliefs regarding the influence of culture on mental illness. Although epidemiological evidence suggests that similar syndromes of depression and schizophrenia can be found across cultures (Good & Kleinman, 1985; World Health Organization, 1973), there is some evidence suggesting that patients' symptom presentation and conceptualizations of illness vary across cultures. For example, in China, depressed patients have been described as emphasizing their somatic symptoms more than their affective symptoms and as seeking medical rather than psychological/psychiatric treatment for their conditions (Kleinman, 1986). Forms of anxiety and other related disorders appear to vary more than depression and schizophrenia across cultures (Butcher, Narikiyo, & Bemis-Vitousek, 1992). Some suggest that many "culturally bound syndromes" or "recurrent, locality-specific patterns of aberrant behavior and troubling experience" (American Psychiatric Association [APA], 1994, p. 844) may be different cultural manifestations of anxiety disorders. For example, "taijin kyofusho," an intense fear that one's body is offensive to others (APA, 1994, p. 845) may be an anxiety disorder found only in Japan, a culture in which not offending others is a dominant cultural value.

Attempts to understand how culture influences psychopathology have faced difficult methodological challenges. Perhaps the largest obstacles involve measuring and identifying psychopathology in different cultural contexts. By their very nature, clinical interviews that are typically used in diagnosis are fraught with biases that may differ across interviewers, across interview sessions, and across cultures. Cultural differences in definitions of "abnormal" behavior make Western clinicians cautious about imposing diagnostic criteria derived from Western culture on other cultures (Butcher, Narikiyo, & Bemis-Vitousek, 1992). Moreover, given the variability in how diagnoses are made even within the same cultural context, mere diagnoses without a description of specific symptomology tell us little about whether the syndromes themselves are the same across cultures.

USING WESTERN INSTRUMENTS IN CROSS-CULTURAL, CROSS-ETHNIC SETTINGS

Objective personality instruments may help reveal cultural differences and similarities in personality and psychopathology. The structured and standardized format of objective personality instruments makes them easy to administer and reduces the variance and bias that can be introduced with the clinical interview. Moreover, data on their reliability and validity can be easily obtained and measured. On the other hand, objective personality instruments are also culture-specific in that the items included on the inventories may have one meaning in Western culture and may have an entirely different meaning in another culture. As a result, personality profiles that are indicative of psychopathology in one culture may imply something quite different in another culture. In addition, it is possible that the standardized format of the instrument is foreign to some cultural groups and, therefore, may also jeopardize the validity of results.

While acknowledging that objective personality instruments are products of the culture in which they were devised, we believe that these Western instruments can be used as a starting point for understanding personality and psychopathology in different cultures. Medicinal treatments that may originate in the United States are often adapted for other cultural groups by adapting administration instructions and, perhaps, even using the drug content based on what is known about the biochemical functioning of other cultural groups. Similarly, Western psychometric instruments may provide the foundation for study, such as the study of personality and psychopathology across cultural groups. Correctly adapting Western instruments for use in international settings, however, is not easy. Cultural informants and translators must be employed to critique, identify, and adapt items that may be culturally invalid. When administrating such instruments, clinicians must pay particular attention to the way in which the instrument is introduced to the patient and must create a testing situation that promotes valid responding by the examinee. Finally, examinees' responses should be carefully interpreted within their cultural context. Exhibit 19.1 summarizes cultural factors that need to be considered when interpreting MMPI–2s with clients from different cultural backgrounds.

In the next section, we review the methodological problems that arise when adapting objective personality instruments for use across cultures. We also present established solutions to such problems. This section provides a guide to adapting Western instruments internationally.

METHODOLOGICAL PROBLEMS AND TECHNICAL RESOLUTIONS IN ADAPTING OBJECTIVE PERSONALITY INSTRUMENTS

The process of adapting objective personality tests for the purposes of examining personality and psychopathology across cultures has illuminated numerous methodological issues and problems. Ensuring *equivalence* between translated versions of an objective personality instrument or ensuring that the two versions of the instrument are indeed asking the same questions and measuring the same concepts is perhaps the greatest challenge. The initial version of the test originating in the "source" culture is translated and adapted for use in the "target" culture. For example, teams of researchers have translated the English-language MMPI–2 used in the United States, the source culture, for use in Russia, the target culture. Under the general rubric of "equivalence" fall many different subtypes that vary in their level of focus. For example, at the literal translation level, *linguistic equivalence* refers to items conveying the same literal meaning in both versions. At the conceptual level, *construct equivalence* refers to similar concepts being conveyed in both versions of the instrument. At a psychometric level, *equivalence* refers to both instruments possessing similar psychometric properties. Each type of equivalence represents a specific set of problems that arise when adapting instruments internationally. The following

EXHIBIT 19.1

Highlight: Cultural Factors to Consider in Interpreting MMPI–2s With Clients From Different Cultural Backgrounds

- In contemporary society, practitioners increasingly come into contact with clients from cultural backgrounds different from their own. In psychological assessment with persons from different cultural backgrounds, the practitioner needs to be acutely aware of possible cultural factors influencing the testing.
- Knowing when culture does and does not influence personality and psychopathology (and the results of testing) is important for accurate diagnosis and treatment.
- Patients' symptom presentation and conceptualizations of illness can vary across cultures. Some disorders such as depression can manifest differently in patients with different cultural backgrounds, for example, as somatization in ethnic Chinese.
- Western-derived instruments, such as the MMPI–2 (if properly translated and adapted), can be used as a starting point for understanding personality and psychopathology of persons with different cultural backgrounds.
- It is important to ensure *equivalence* between translated versions of an objective personality instrument and the original.
- A great deal of research and clinical applications have suggested that the MMPI–2 can readily be adapted to other languages and that the U.S. norms may be used for other cultures to determine the effectiveness of the instrument.
- Culture-specific norms may be more acceptable if the in-country performance on U.S. norms appears deviant by research. The question as to whether one should develop country-specific norms for a translation needs to be evaluated in the early stages of a test adaptation.
- Most researchers who have collected new country-specific norms (e.g., in Holland, France, Italy, Israel, Mexico, Chile) have found that the raw scores tend to fall close to the U.S. norms.
- Numerous studies have suggested that the MMPI–2 is measuring the same constructs across cultures.
- Clinical case evaluations from different cultures have typically found that MMPI–2–based profile interpretations that were developed from a U.S. perspective typically result in meaningful conclusions about clinical patients who are tested in other languages and cultures.
- Cultural factors may not be the only variables operating to cloud assessments in the multicultural context. The process of acculturation needs to be taken into consideration. More recently arrived immigrants are often experiencing the stress of being uprooted from their homes and may show psychopathology that is transitory.
- MMPI–2 scores will typically be more elevated in individuals who have recently migrated than they are for persons of the same background who have had more time to assimilate.
- The adaptation process can be significantly disturbed by stressful environmental events that serve to make a refugee's adjustment to a new environment more troubling and more difficult for the assessment process.

discussion describes the types of equivalence targeted in cross-cultural research with objective personality instruments and presents proposed solutions that have been implemented with international adaptations of the MMPI and MMPI–2. The procedures used by cross-cultural MMPI–2 researchers are based on the recommendations of Brislin (1986); Brislin, Lonner, and Thorndike (1973); Butcher and Pancheri (1976); Butcher and Han (1996); and other authors.

Methodological Problem 1: Linguistic Equivalence

Linguistic equivalence, the most basic level of equivalence between translated versions of a psychological test, refers to items and instructions that communicate the same meanings in both forms of the instrument (Butcher, 1996a). Sechrest, Fay, and Zaida (1972) identify different types of linguistic equivalence, including *vocabulary equivalence, idiomatic equivalence, and grammatical–syntactical equivalence*. These authors suggest that in order to ensure vocabulary equivalence, translators well versed in the everyday language of the prospective test takers—not necessarily "dictionary language" (p. 44), which may be elevated or pedantic—should be used. Idiomatic equivalence is a particularly challenging type of equivalence given the embeddedness of idioms in our speech patterns and the difficulty of finding completely accurate translations (Sechrest et al., 1972). When translating idioms, it is suggested that the level of the target language idiom be comparable to the level of the source language expression in complexity and formality (Sechrest et al., 1972) and that the use of the idiom along with the (parenthetical) literal translation may add clarity (Brislin, 1970; Rosen, 1958; Werner & Campbell, 1970). Grammatical–syntactical equivalence refers to the challenge of finding appropriate verb forms, nouns, and pronouns, as well as matching voice and tense (Butcher, 1996a; Sechrest et al., 1972). Avoiding rare expressions and abstract terms is also suggested as a means of achieving greater linguistic equivalence (Butcher, 1996a). In general, most authors suggest the use of both a literal translation and a nonliteral translation that may more closely match the meaning of the item. Although using both literal and nonliteral translations increases the length and complexity of the instrument, it is preferred to the possibility of distorting the meaning of the items themselves.

Technical Solution: Initial Translation

The process of ensuring linguistic equivalence is accomplished by initial translation from the source to the target language, then the back translation by independent linguists from the target to the source language, as has been conducted in international adaptations of the MMPI and MMPI–2. The initial translation from the source to the target language is performed by a team of bilingual translators, well versed in both languages. Bracken and Barona (1991) recommend the use of translators who are truly bilingual and sufficiently familiar with both languages. Butcher, Lim, and Nezami (1998) recommend the use of independent translators with collaboration and discussion after the initial translation. Also, sufficient experience with both cultures is important, for example, 5 years of living in each country or some such equivalent experience. With international adaptations of the MMPI–2, many initial item translation problems have been made easier since item level improvements were implemented with the

1989 revision. These item level improvements eliminated many idiomatic, rare, and obscure expressions that existed in the original MMPI.

Back Translation

The next phase of the adaptation process to achieve linguistic equivalence that has been recommended by many authors (Bracken & Barona, 1991; Brislin, 1970; Brislin et al., 1973; Butcher & Pancheri, 1976; Rosen, 1958; Sechrest et al., 1972; Werner & Campbell, 1970) is the independent retranslation of translated items back to the source language in order to determine if the translated items retain their meaning. At this point, items that were difficult to translate are discovered and translated again. This translation–back translation repetition should continue until the discrepancies between the source language version and the back-translation version are reduced (Bracken & Barona, 1991). The use of different translation–back translation teams may increase the efficiency of this problem-solving process. Experience with international adaptations of the MMPI–2 has shown that at the first back translation, approximately 10% to 15% of translated items fail this first step and require retranslation (Butcher, 1996a). This translation–back translation process continues until all problematic items are satisfactorily translated; this process is considered a crucial step in any translation endeavor.

Methodological Problem 2: Construct Equivalence

A second methodological problem concerns construct equivalence, or the generalizability across cultures of the personality variables or constructs being examined (Butcher, 1996a). This type of equivalence has been described as "conceptual equivalence" or "construct equivalence" to denote that the concepts implied by the translated and original items are similar in nature (Sechrest et al., 1972). Personality variables may differ in form and quantity across cultures, and constructs may not have the same psychological meaning across cultures (Butcher, 1996a). For example, the construct of "gregariousness," as it refers to someone in the American culture who is sociable and likes companionship, is not readily applicable to the Melanesian people of Dobu Island, who show noticeably fewer social, affiliative behaviors (Butcher & Pancheri, 1976).

Technical Resolution: Bilingual Test–Retest Studies

Attempts to achieve generalizability of constructs from a sample from one culture to another sample from a different culture are addressed by bilingual test–retest studies. These studies require a group of bilinguals to take the English form and the translated version of the test within 1- to 2-week intervals (Butcher, Nezami, & Exner, 1998). The two forms of the test cannot simply be administered to two separate monolingual groups in order to assess translation equivalence unless it can be assumed that both groups possess equal distributions of the traits in question (Hulin, 1987). With the bilingual test–retest design, the variance resulting from individual differences is removed, as it would be with any other test–retest design of short intertest intervals. Thus, the variance due to language and all interactions involving language suggest nonequivalency in the translation (Hulin, 1987). The bilinguals' data are analyzed in a manner that is similar to the analysis in a test–retest study design to determine if the two tests can be considered to be alternate forms (Butcher, Derksen, Sloore, & Sirigatti, 2003). Bilingual individuals may not be representative of the two monolingual populations that are involved because of different cognitive and semantic structures (Hulin, 1987); therefore, it is important to conduct further research on the monolingual populations—such as the research discussed in subsequent sections on (a) developing a culturally appropriate normative base and (b) validation studies.

Methodological Problem 3: Psychometric Equivalence

The next methodological problem in cross-cultural research involves achievement of psychometric equivalence, which refers to an instrument possessing similar psychometric properties in different cultures (Butcher & Han, 1996). This type of equivalence may be demonstrated through examination of the internal structure of the instruments via factor analysis and through studying item endorsement patterns among similar groups (e.g., college students from the two cultures), as is discussed later in this chapter. Theoretically, similar groups should have similar patterns of responding cross-culturally. Related to psychometric equivalence is *scalar equivalence* or the idea that two instruments express scores on the same scale or to the same level of intensity (Butcher & Han, 1996). For example, if the MMPI–2 Social Introversion (Si) scale in the source language has a T score of 80 and the same level of social introversion (a T score of 80) is achieved on the target language translation, then scalar equivalence has been demonstrated. Scalar equivalence is demonstrated by administering the test to similar groups in both cultures in order to determine if similar scores on the same scales are achieved; for example, "normals" from two cultures have similar scores as do "clinical cases" from two cultures.

Technical Resolutions: Equivalency Studies and Development of Appropriate Norms

The procedures used to examine levels of psychometric equivalence cross-culturally involve equivalency studies based on factor analytic techniques and item response theory. An additional step in ensuring psychometric equivalence is the development of a culturally appropriate normative base.

Factor analysis is the technique that examines the similarity of latent factors in order to assess whether the test has a similar structure across different cultural groups (Ben-Porath, 1990a; Brislin et al., 1973; Butcher & Pancheri, 1976; Irvine, 1979). Factor comparisons should be made with the use of objective indexes rather than by subjective inspection of factor loadings (Barrett, 1986; Ben-Porath, 1990a; Hui & Triandis, 1985; Nunnally, 1978; Poortinga, 1989). Several possible methods are available for this purpose, including the (a) *congruence coefficient*, (b) *factor score correlations*, and (c) *confirmatory factor analysis*, which we summarize briefly. For a more detailed discussion of these methods, see Butcher and Han (1996). (a) The congruence coefficient (Tucker, 1951) represents an index of agreement between two factor loadings, ranging from +1 (perfect agreement) to 0 (no agreement) to –1 (inverse agreement). This factor convergence score is relatively easy to calculate (compared to factor score correlations and confirmatory factor analysis) but, unfortunately, is not sensitive to differences in the mean level of the loadings and is influenced by the sign of the loadings (Butcher & Han, 1996). (b) Factor score correlations—also termed the "comparability coefficient" by Everett and Entrekin (1980)—were first described by Nunnally (1978). This index is a measure of factor similarity, as opposed to similarity in factor loadings, and consists of correlations between two sets of factor scores. Since factor score correlations will be uncorrelated across factors extracted from the same solution (unlike factor loadings), it is likely that these scores will allow for a discernible convergent–discriminant pattern (Butcher & Han, 1996; Watson, Clark, & Tellegen, 1984). (c) Confirmatory factor analysis (Joreskog, 1971; Gorsuch, 1983) requires the acquisition of information about the number of factors, the relationships between factors, and the size of the factor loadings for the test when administered repeatedly to the source culture. The next step is to extract the same solution in the target culture's data and then test the model for its goodness of fit; chi square analyses will allow the rejection of the hypothesis that the model fits the data. This method will indicate if the model fits the data but, unfortunately, will not allow a factor-by-factor comparison to determine which factors replicate and which do not (Walkey & Green, 1990). Because the various factor analytic methods possess unique advantages and disadvantages, most authors recommend using multiple methods for comparing factor structures across the target and source culture's data (Butcher & Han, 1996).

Item response theory (IRT) is an innovative approach that is beginning to be explored in the investigation of psychometric equivalence between test translations (Butcher & Han, 1996; Hulin, 1987). The trait being assessed, in theta units, and the responses to the item measuring that trait are specified by an S-shaped function, referred to as an *item characteristic curve* (ICC). These ICCs are used to summarize conditional probabilities of specified responses conditioned on the trait assessed by the item. By examining the ICCs for two different language versions of an item, it is possible to determine the equivalence of the item meanings in relation to theta. For example, it is possible by examination of the ICC of an item tapping "social introversion" to determine (a) how well an item measures that trait in terms of its ability to discriminate between different levels of introversion, (b) how difficult or extreme the item is and the level of introversion required to respond affirmatively, and (c) the probability of a keyed response for individuals who are low on introversion. The disadvantage to using item response theory as it is applied to the MMPI–2 is that item response theory assumes unidimensional scales, which makes it not applicable to the multidimensional clinical scales of the MMPI–2. (However, it is more applicable to the homogeneous content scales.)

Development of a Culturally Appropriate Normative Base

When translating the MMPI–2 to other languages, U.S. norms may be used for these other cultures if the two sets of data from their respective "normal" populations are within the standard error of measurement (e.g., Ellertsen, Havik, & Skavellen, 1996). However, culture-specific norms may be more acceptable if U.S. norms cannot be applied because the cultures are too different in their responses to the test items (Avila-Espada, 1996; Gillet et al., 1996; Lucio-G. & Reyes-Lagunes, 1996; Rissetti, Himmel, & Gonzalez-Moreno, 1996; Sloore, Derksen, De Mey, & Hellenbosch, 1996). A representative group of nonclinical subjects in the target country should serve as the normative group, as well as native subjects from known clinical groups.

Methodological Problem 4: Psychological Equivalence

Although items may be translated correctly in a linguistic sense from the source to the target language, convey the same construct, and even possess similar psychometric properties, the items may not possess *psychological equivalence*. Psychological equivalence refers to the similarity in meaning or cultural significance of test items (Butcher, 1996a). Sechrest et al. (1972) address this issue in terms of *experiential equivalence* or the conveyance of concepts that are familiar to the real experiences of the target and source cultures. For example, the test item "I would like to be a florist" may not be accurately translated in terms of its psychological meaning to non-Americans because flower shops are not found in many parts of the world (Sechrest et al., 1972). Similarly, the psychological significance of someone having an interest in selling flowers arranged into aesthetically pleasing, creative ways for decorative purposes may reflect adherence to feminine stereotypes in one culture and interest in being a florist in another. Related to the idea of psychological equivalence is the issue of *functional equivalence*, which means that the function of a behavior in one culture is equivalent to the function of a behavior in a different culture even though the behaviors themselves may be different. For example, smiling is indicative of embarrassment in many Asian cultures, whereas in many Western cultures smiling indicates pleasure (Butcher & Han, 1996). Thus, "smiling" in Asian cultures may be more functionally equivalent to averting eye contact and blushing in the American culture.

Technical Resolution: Validation Studies

The psychological equivalence of cross-cultural versions of an objective personality instrument is examined through validation research, as has been done with international versions of the MMPI–2 (Butcher, Derksen, et al., 2003). This procedure involves administration of the translated version to known groups in the target culture and the same known groups in the source culture in order to examine whether similar test patterns are correlated with similar outcomes across cultures. For example, U.S. college students, psychiatric patients, and prison inmates would be compared to their subgroup counterparts in the target country. Theoretically, similar groups should respond similarly to their respective versions of the test. If the two versions of the test similarly predict group membership across cultures, external validity is demonstrated. Groups of college students have frequently been used in validation research; they are usually available to researchers, are familiar with the test-taking format, and tend to produce relatively normal range profiles similar to U.S. college students (Butcher, 1996a).

INTERNATIONAL APPLICATIONS OF THE MMPI AND THE MMPI–2

Early in its long life, the MMPI was adapted for use in many other countries by mental health professionals—for example, in Germany by Sundberg (1954), in Italy by Reda (1948), and in Japan by Abe (1959). Over the next decades, the MMPI came to be very widely adapted (about 150 translations) and widely used in 46 other countries. Several reasons accounted for the broad international use of the MMPI, many of which concern the method issues already described.

- Following World War II, clinical psychology as a profession experienced broad international development bringing with it a need for valid personality assessment instruments.
- The MMPI was found to be a relatively easy instrument to translate and carried with it an interpretive experience base that ensured effective clinical adaptation in a broad range of settings.

- The psychometric properties of the original MMPI were shown to be equivalent over different language translations. Scale reliability and factorial invariance provided assurances of measurement equivalence.
- Once translated and adapted in the host country, the MMPI proved to have external validity in its new surroundings (Butcher & Pancheri, 1976; Butcher & Clark, 1989; Cheung & Song, 1989).

The MMPI and the MMPI–2 have been widely adapted around the world (Arbisi & Butcher, 2004c; Butcher, 2004). Three recent reviews of research and clinical applications provide a perspective on the broad use of the instrument around the world: (a) research in Europe (Butcher, Derksen, et al., 2003), (b) applications in Asia (Butcher, Cheung, & Lim, 2003), and (c) use of the MMPI and MMPI–2 in Cuba (Mendez-Quevedo & Butcher, in press).

Revision of the MMPI

After several decades of use, however, the MMPI item pool came to be viewed as somewhat dated (e.g., "I like tall women"). Moreover, the norms for the test were thought to be outmoded and overly narrow for the range of populations in which the instrument was used (Butcher, 1972). The instrument underwent a major revision during the 1980s, and two revised versions of the instrument were published; the MMPI–2 for adults was published in 1989 (Butcher, Dahlstrom, Graham, Tellegen, & Kaemmer, 1989), and the MMPI–A[1] for adolescents was published in 1992 (Butcher, Williams, et al., 1992).

The major features of the MMPI revision were the following:

- *Item level improvements:* The language of some items was revised because items of the MMPI were awkwardly worded or outmoded in expression or content (e.g., "I like Lincoln better than Washington"). Some objectionable or irrelevant (unused) items were deleted from the instrument.
- *Additional items were included in the revised forms to assess a broader variety of problems:* A number of additional problem areas such as suicide assessment, substance abuse, family relationships, treatment compliance, and work behavior were included to address a broader range of clinical problems than the original instrument included.

[1]The discussion in this chapter focuses only on the MMPI–2 and does not address the MMPI–A, the adolescent form of the instrument. The MMPI–A (published in 1992) has already undergone a number of translations and adaptations for: China, France, Greece, Italy, Israel, Korea, Mexico, Norway, and Russia; there is also a Spanish-language version of the test for the United States.

- *New, nationally representative norms were collected:* MMPI response data on a total of 2,600 (1,138 men and 1,462 women) were collected to serve as norms for MMPI–2. These participants were randomly selected from across the United States. The samples were balanced in terms of ethnicity (African American, Hispanic, American Indian, and Asian American) in order to obtain an unbiased general norm set.
- *Substantial samples of diverse patient and nonpatient groups were collected:* Several separate studies were conducted including samples of inpatient psychiatric patients, chronic pain patients, substance abusers, outpatients, couples in counseling, potential child abusers, and prison inmates. In addition, several other samples of "normals" (airline pilot applicants, military personnel, college students, and older men) were studied. This increased generalizability of the MMPI to different groups.
- *New scales were constructed:* The MMPI–2 revision program included the development of a number of new measures to broaden the range of psychological assessment with the instrument. Several new validity scales were developed: *F(B)* (Back Infrequency), two consistency scores (VRIN [Variable Response Inconsistency] and TRIN [True Response Inconsistency]), and *S* (Superlative Self-Presentation); a new set of MMPI–2 content scales was developed (Butcher, Graham, Williams, & Ben-Porath, 1990) to address important content dimensions in the MMPI–2; and several special problem scales were developed including the Addiction Potential Scale (APS), the Addiction Acknowledgment Scale (AAS), and the Marital Distress Scale (MDS).

International Adaptations of the MMPI–2

Since its publication in 1989, the MMPI–2 has become available in 24 languages and several research projects are under way in other languages including Hindi, Rumanian, Croatian, and Portuguese (see Appendix 19.2 for a listing of translators and translations). An inspection of these completed international efforts provides the reader with a perspective on the broad range of test adaptation efforts with the MMPI–2 that have been implemented across the world (Butcher, 1996a). In this section, the research on the MMPI–2 that has been conducted to date is summarized according to the following topic areas: (a) translation procedures, (b) bilingual equivalence studies, (c) in-country normative efforts, and (d) external validation research efforts. Each topic area addresses the methodological issues and technical resolutions already described. Keep in mind that the amount of progress from one country to another varies depending on the researchers' previous familiarity with the original MMPI as well as resources available. Some of the projects that have been published (Almagor & Nevo, 1996; Gillet et al., 1996; Han, 1996; Pancheri, Sirigatti, & Biondi, 1996; Rissetti et al., 1996; Sloore et al., 1996) are extensive research programs that cover a long period of development and involve extensive data collection. Other projects are not as well developed but include extensive applied data collection programs (Casullo & Samartino, 1996; Pongpanich, 1996) that focus more on clinical application and less upon psychometric research. Still others (Kokkevi, 1996; Nezami & Zamani, 1996; Soliman, 1996) are in the early stages of their adaptation efforts. All demonstrate the (potential or demonstrated) usefulness of the MMPI in different cultural settings.

Translation

The MMPI–2 items were significantly improved during the MMPI restandardization (Butcher et al., 1989) making the job of item translation much easier for MMPI–2 translators than their earlier counterparts. Most of the translations have employed translation–back translation procedures as recommended earlier in this chapter.

Bilingual Test–Retest Studies of the MMPI–2

As recommended by test-translation researchers (Butcher & Pancheri, 1976), the bilingual test–retest study is an important step in test adaptation to demonstrate test equivalency. Most of the bilingual retest projects that have been described in the literature to date (e.g., with Hmong, Icelandic, Hebrew, Italian, French, Spanish, and Vietnamese) have found the MMPI–2 scales to operate similarly when the inventory is administered to bilinguals in both languages. In this equivalency research, the researchers administer both the translated version and the English-language version to a group of bilinguals, usually in a counterbalanced manner. Overall, the research to date has shown that whether the items are answered in English or in the translated language the resulting scale scores are generally equivalent, usually within 1 or 2 T score points of the U.S. norms (Almagor & Nevo, 1996; Deinard, Butcher, Thao, Moua Vang, & Hang, 1996; Pancheri et al., 1996; Rissetti et al., 1996; Sloore et al., 1996).

Normative Research

The question of whether one should develop country-specific norms for a translation needs to be evaluated in the early stages of a test adaptation. If the MMPI–2 translation is equivalent and the culture is generally within the industrialized Western tradition, a separate norm set may not be required and the U.S. norms may serve well in conducting clinical patient evaluations. The new U.S. norms that were developed for the MMPI–2 made the instrument more readily adaptable in other countries. The revised MMPI–2 norms are based on a more diverse population in the United States, which, incidentally, also brought the general norm much closer to other international samples as well. (On the original MMPI, most international samples had highly elevated scores because the original MMPI norms were set too low, even for assessments in the United States. (See Butcher & Pancheri, 1976.) Many MMPI–2 test adapters have reported that the scale scores in the target country were within the standard error of measurement for the scales according to norms based on the U.S. normative population (e.g., in Norway and Iceland).

There are reasons, of course, other than psychometric necessity, that a test adapter in another country may need to develop in-country norms—the most salient of which is "political." That is, it may be important for a researcher to develop separate norms for the test to be accepted by practitioners in the host country. Regardless, most of the researchers who have collected new country-specific norms (e.g., in Holland, France, Italy, Israel, Mexico, and Chile) have found that the raw scores tend to fall close to the U.S. norms.

Validation Studies

In this section, we address research that has been aimed at exploring the predictive and descriptive equivalence of the MMPI–2 scales in applied settings. These studies are grouped as follows: internal validation efforts, external validity studies, and studies addressing the accuracy of computer-based reports cross-culturally. All suggest that the MMPI–2 is measuring the same constructs across cultures.

Internal Validity. As with the early research with the original version of the MMPI (Butcher & Pancheri, 1976), studies reporting on the factor analyses of the MMPI–2 scales in other national research projects have found comparable factor structures to research of the MMPI–2 in the United States. Usually a four-factor solution, regardless of national sample, emerges when the 10 traditional MMPI standard scales are included in the analysis. This research leads one to conclude that a good translation of the MMPI–2 will likely produce an equivalent factor structure in target countries (Ben-Porath, 1990a; Butcher & Han, 1996; Emiru, 2003; Watkins, 1989). The four factors are usually named anxiety, overcontrol, masculinity–feminity, and social introversion.

Convergent Validity. Researchers examining discriminant validity in psychiatric settings in other countries (e.g., researchers in France, Italy, Mexico, Chile, Norway, and Israel) have reported results that are comparable to clinical validity studies in the United States. Patients with similar problems in other countries tend to produce MMPI–2 profiles that are also similar (Almagor & Nevo, 1996; Ellertsen et al., 1996; Gillet et al.,1996; Lucio-G. & Reyes-Lagunes, 1996; Rissetti et al., 1996). In addition, Han (1996), using personality ratings of Korean college students completed by a close personal acquaintance, found that the scale elevation tended to result in behavioral descriptors for the MMPI–2 scales that were similar to those the research in the United States has shown.

Interpretive Accuracy. Clinical case evaluations from different cultures have typically found that MMPI–2–based profile interpretations that were developed from a U.S. perspective generally result in meaningful conclusions about clinical patients who are tested in other languages and cultures (Almagor & Nevo, 1996; Butcher, Berah, et al., 1998; Butcher, Nezami, & Exner, 1998; Soliman, 1996; Pongpanich, 1996;). See also the subsequent case example in which the Farse MMPI–2 (Nezami & Zamani, 1996) was administered to a client living in the United States and scored and interpreted (by computer) using English-language norms.

As noted in the case example that follows, similar interpretive results are obtained when the test is interpreted by computer rather than by a clinician. Computer-based interpretive reports tend to show close interpretive congruence when applied to patients in other cultures. One important feature of a structured personality measure like the MMPI–2 is that the scores can be interpreted by objective and automated procedures—even by an electronic computer. The use of computers to interpret objective psychological tests such as the MMPI–2 has become broadly accepted in clinical psychology in the United States (Butcher, 1995) and in international settings (Fowler & Butcher, 1987; Pancheri & Biondi, 1987). Several studies have evaluated the effectiveness of computer-based interpretive reports at describing behavior and personality in cross-cultural settings (Berah et al., 1993; Butcher, Nezami, & Exner, 1998; Gillet et al., 1996).

Butcher, Berah, et al. (1998) found that computer-derived MMPI–2 reports showed high generalization validity when applied to psychiatric patients in other countries. In this study, patients from several countries (Norway, Australia, France, and the United States) were administered the MMPI–2. Their answer sheets were processed by electronic computer, and a computer-based narrative personality description was generated. This report was then given to the clinician for review. The clinician was asked to rate the accuracy and completeness of the report in describing his or her patient. That is, the clinician was instructed to rate whether the specific elements of the interpretations that were provided appropriately described the patient's symptoms and behaviors. After reviewing the narrative report, the therapist provided an appraisal of the "overall accuracy" of the narrative report in describing the client. Clinicians' ratings of the computer-based reports indicated that 66% of the records were found to be accurate 80% to 100% of the time and 87% of the reports were rated as accurate in

60% of the cases. This high level of judged accuracy of computer-based reports across these diverse international clinical settings indicated that automated personality-based descriptions derived in one country have utility when applied in other countries.

CASE EXAMPLE

Referral Problem

The patient, Mr. T., is a 40-year-old, married, Iranian immigrant to the United States who was in counseling for marital problems. He has lived in the United States for 22 years. This is his first marriage but his wife's second marriage; they are in the process of divorce. Mr. T. is seeking the divorce because he sees his wife as very unsupportive and so preoccupied with her own emotional adjustment problems as to disrupt the marriage. The client has been in outpatient mental health treatment for the last 6 months. At present, he is being evaluated prior to beginning psychoanalytic therapy.

Family and Parental Relationships

Mr. T.'s relationships to his family of origin were extremely difficult for him while he was growing up. His parents had great difficulty getting along with each other; they argued a great deal and were never supportive of their children. His parents were divorced when he was very young. His father, who maintained custody of the children, remarried shortly afterward to a woman who was cruel toward the children. Mr. T.'s stepmother had many psychological adjustment problems and abused the patient both physically and emotionally. The only support he felt when he was growing up was from his paternal grandmother whom he saw occasionally.

Marital Relationship

As a young man, Mr. T. felt abandoned by his mother and neglected by his father, while being abused by his stepmother. He felt he had no choice but to grow up fast and come to the United States where he could develop on his own. He married his present and only wife through arrangements that were made by his family in Iran (arranged marriages are common in traditional Iranian families). However, his hope for an ideal marriage with an educated woman (his wife had been a dentist in Iran before migrating to the United States) was shattered when he came to realize that his wife has chronic psychological problems that interfered with their relationship. His wife has a borderline personality with anger as the primary mode of showing emotions. She gets violent and physically attacks her husband. She has significant issues with controlling anger and aggression and is labile. The extreme psychological adjustment problems she has reminds Mr. T. of his mother and stepmother. His marital discord is so intense that he feels the only solution is to get divorced.

Symptoms and Behavior

Mr. T. has been successful in his business career as a risk management consultant. No work-related problems were noted. He completed an undergraduate degree in business administration and has been working in a managerial position for several years. He reports no problems related to his work—only difficulties in his marital relationship. He has been a heavy smoker in the past, but he has been trying to quit. He still relies on cigarettes and excessive food intake to deal with stress. He has had a weight problem and has continued to struggle with overeating. He reportedly is emotionally isolated and does not have many friends, spending a great deal of time alone. Mr. T. was administered the MMPI–2 in Farsi, and his profiles are shown in Figures 19.1, 19.2, and 19.3. A computer-based MMPI–2 report is provided in Appendix 19.1 to provide an empirical description of the symptoms and behavior as shown by the MMPI–2.

CONFOUNDING EFFECTS OF STRESS AND CULTURE: ASSESSMENT OF PEOPLE IN TRANSITION

The MMPI–2 is often used in the United States to evaluate persons who are from a different country, language, and cultural background (e.g., in a correctional setting for an immigrant who has committed a crime or in a mental health facility for an individual who has been admitted in need of mental health services). In some cases, the MMPI–2 version from the client's native country may be used in the assessment and the profile may be interpreted using norms from the country of origin—for example, the Mexican norms (Lucio, Ampudia, Duran, Leon, & Butcher, 2001).

Additionally, cross-cultural assessments are often conducted in situations in which the individuals being evaluated are in a state of intense turmoil as they transit from one life situation to another as refugees. Being a refugee or immigrant from one culture to another complex society such as the United States requires great life change and a broad adaptation to roles and demands in the new environment. Research has shown that this cross-cultural evaluation may be complicated further by the process of immigration itself, and the stress of transition can have a major impact on an individual's psychological adjustment and the way in which he or she responds

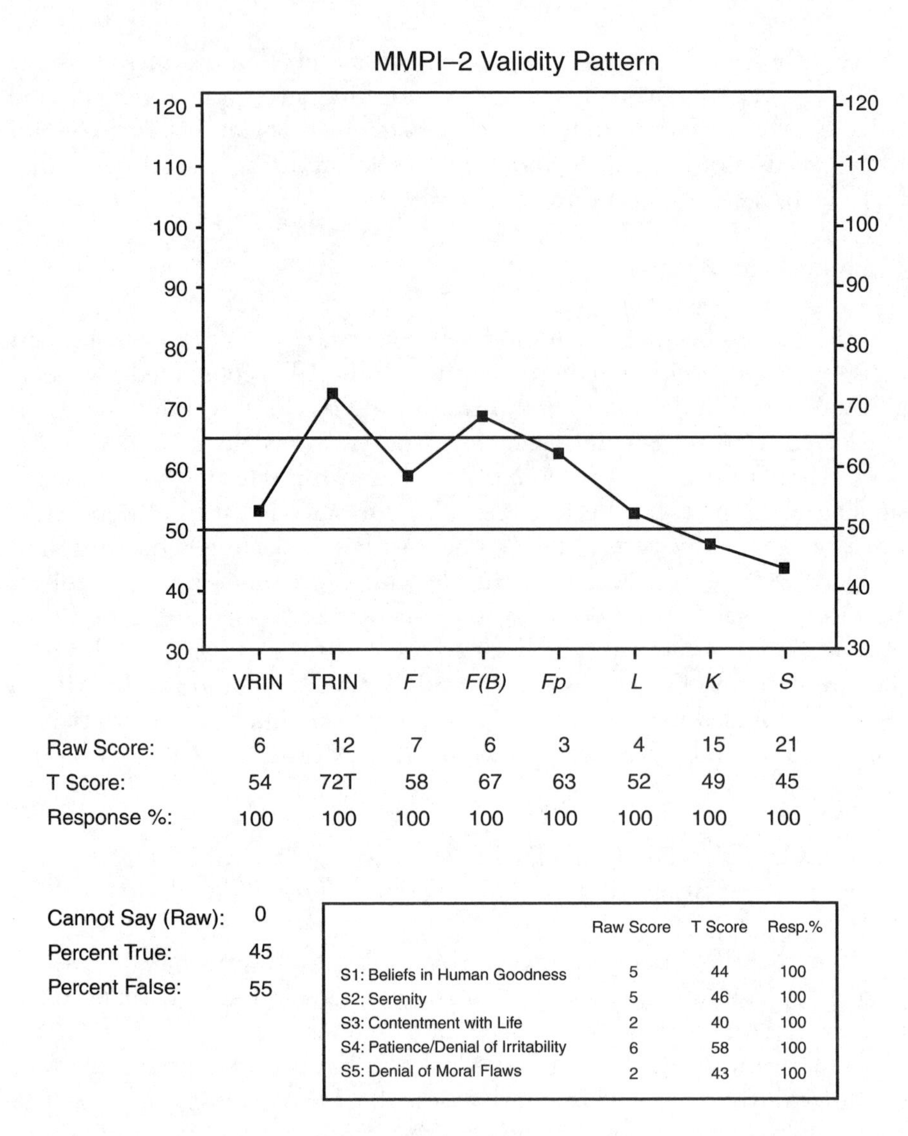

Figure 19.1. MMPI–2 validity scale pattern of Mr. T.

to MMPI–2 items. Several studies using the MMPI–2 have been published that suggest that persons being evaluated shortly after their arrival in the United States show more general psychopathology than those of the same ethnic group who have been in the United States longer (Azan, 1989; Deinard et al., 1996; Sue, Keefe, Enomoto, Durvasula, & Chao, 1996; Tran, 1996; Velasquez, Maness, & Anderson, 2002); these evaluations reflect to an extent the adjustment problems that result when people move to a new and different culture. This situation requires that the psychologist consider a number of factors in the evaluation. Conducting a psychological evalua-

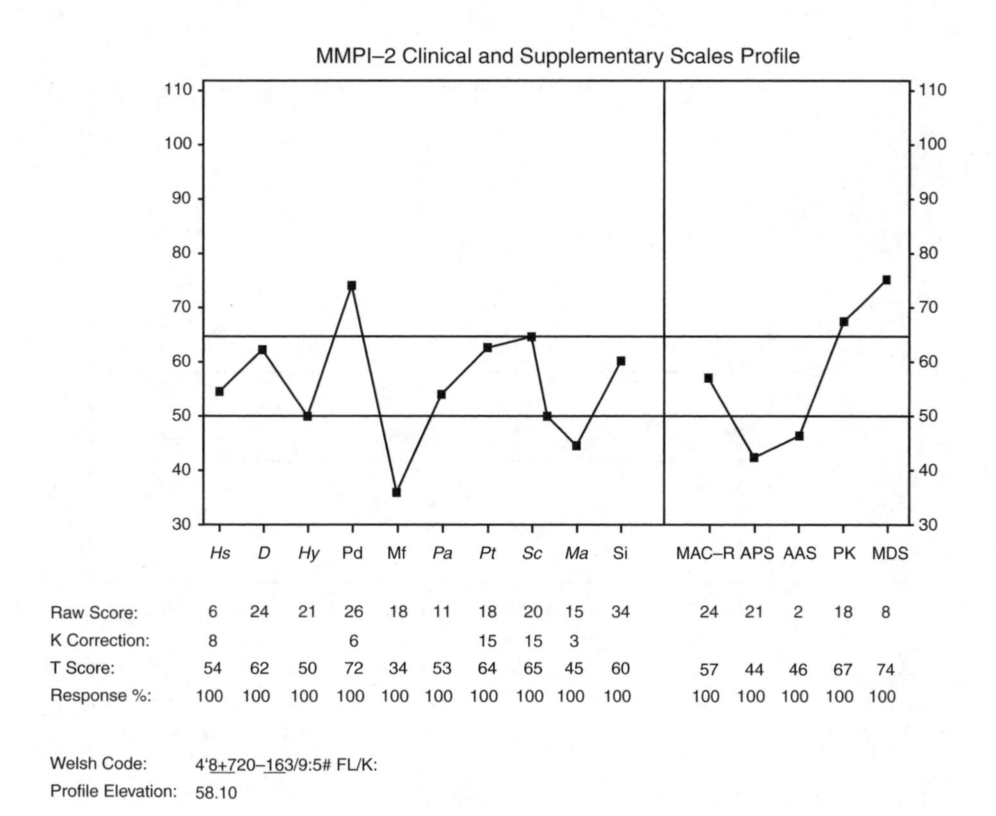

Figure 19.2. MMPI–2 clinical and supplemental scale pattern of Mr. T.

tion on a person who is in the process of acculturating into a new society requires that the psychologist take into consideration the fact that the person may not be sufficiently acculturated to the "American ways" to collaborate fully with the evaluation.

The acculturation process can be severely affected by current events as well. For example, in a 5-year study of refugees from Ethiopia and Somalia, the Refugee Population Study (Halcón et al., 2004; Jaranson et al., 2004; Spring et al., 2003) interviewed 1,134 refugees living in the Twin Cites of Minnesota several times over a 5-year period with respect to their mental health adjustment and their adaptation to the United States. Many of these refugees had, prior to immigration, experienced severe war trauma and many had been tortured in their home countries. Although general cooperativeness was obtained throughout the study (which used indigenous interviewers who were themselves refugees), there were periods in which current environmental circumstances made the data collection extremely difficult. Following the trauma of 9/11, the immediate backlash against foreigners (especially Muslims) produced great consternation within the

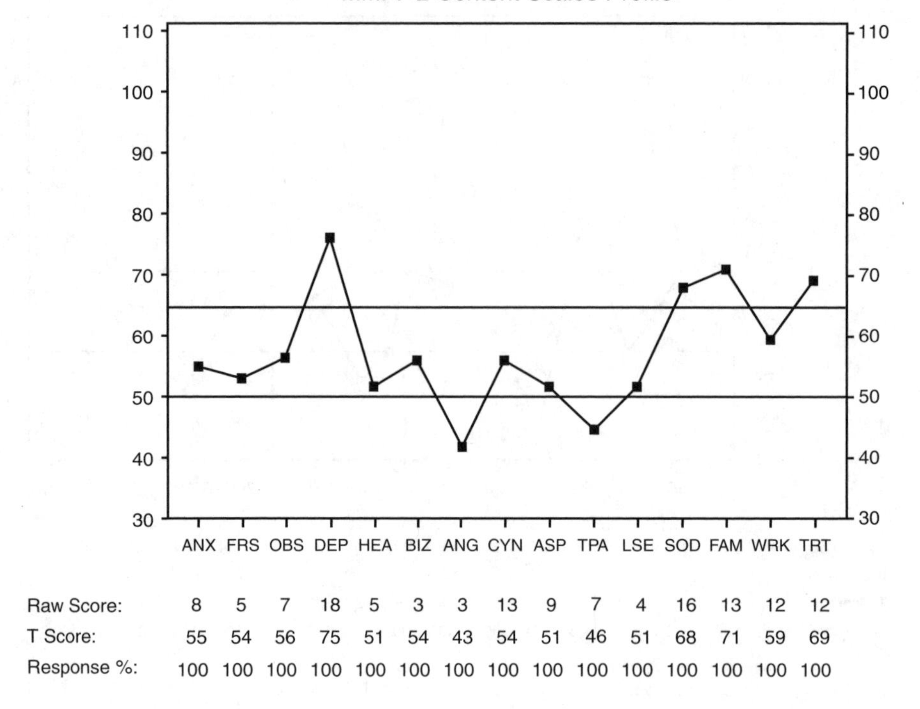

Figure 19.3. MMPI–2 content scale pattern of Mr. T.

research sample causing a number of people to cancel appointments or show great reluctance to talk with interviewers for fear of government retribution or deportation. The pace of project interviews slowed considerably because the participants lacked trust as a result of the felt threat from the FBI, local citizens, and the police and attention from the media in the Twin Cities.

Psychologists conducting psychological evaluations on recently immigrated clients need to take into consideration their life circumstances and the stress they may be undergoing, in addition to attending to cultural differences.

SUMMARY

Examining personality and psychopathology across cultural and ethnic groups is important for our scientific understanding of human behavior and has tremendous applications in a variety of clinical, occupational, and social settings. The use of Western-culture-derived personality instruments can provide the foundation for studying personality and psychopathology across cultures. The most widely used clinical personality inventory in international settings is the MMPI–2, which—like its predecessor, the MMPI—has been widely adapted abroad. The MMPI–2 covers a wide range of clinical problems pertinent to clinical assessment in many cultures and provides practical clinical diagnostic information, even in countries that are culturally different from the United States. This chapter has highlighted the complexities of adapting personality instruments for use cross-culturally, and the technical solutions that have been proposed and used in foreign language adaptations of the MMPI and MMPI–2 have been outlined. The procedures used to achieve *linguistic equivalence*, or semantic equality, are the initial translation by a team of experienced bilinguals and the back translation by an independent group of bilingual translators. The next step of demonstrating *construct equivalence*, that the two instruments tap the same concepts, is addressed through bilingual test–retest studies in which a group of bilingual examinees take the two forms of the instrument within short time intervals. *Psychometric equivalence*, or both versions of the instrument possessing similar psychometric properties, is achieved by equivalency studies using factor analytic methods and item response theory and also through the development of a culturally appropriate normative group. Last, the *psychological equivalence* of the two instruments, or the relevance and similarity in psychological meaning of the items, is investigated with validation research in which the same subgroups are compared with each other; for example, U.S. college students are compared with German college students.

This chapter described the recommended procedures for translating and adapting the MMPI–2 into other languages. A number of international MMPI–2–based research programs were highlighted. It was noted that the MMPI–2 is relatively more easy to adapt than the original version of the instrument because of the item level improvements in content and because of the more relevant contemporary normative population. The MMPI–2 items are viewed as culturally relevant and straightforward to translate into equivalent statements in other languages. In some languages, the content of a few items needs to be altered in order to make them relevant for the target population.

A number of MMPI–2 test adaptation programs have reported the results of bilingual retest studies as a means of demonstrating equivalency across cultures. Although test translators have typically developed separate norms in the target culture, many researchers have found that scale scores in the target country were within the standard error of measurement for the scales in the U.S. normative population. Both internal factor analytic studies and external validity studies of the MMPI–2 scales have demonstrated extensive generalization validity in other countries. Because of its objective interpretation format, assessments based on the MMPI–2 apply well in cross-cultural adaptations. Moreover, computer-derived MMPI–2 interpretations, as with clinically based reports, appear to have a high degree of accuracy when applied to patients from other countries. Computer-based reports derived from interpretive strategies developed for the United States were rated as highly accurate by clinicians when they were applied in several other countries.

Given the high equivalency of the MMPI and MMPI–2 across cultures, we believe it to be a useful task in understanding cultural influences on personality and psychopathology. It is with instruments such as the MMPI and the MMPI–2 that we hope the answers will be revealed to fundamental questions regarding how individuals interact with their cultural contexts, what abnormal human behavior is universally, and what is culture-specific.

APPENDIX 19.1

The following text is the computer-generated MMPI–2 narrative summary of Mr. T.'s personality evaluation. (See the discussion of the Minnesota Report in chap. 17.)

Profile Validity

This is a valid MMPI–2 profile. The client was quite cooperative in describing his symptoms and problems. His frank and open responses to the items can be viewed as a positive indication of his involvement with the evaluation. The MMPI–2 profile is probably a good indication of his present personality functioning and symptoms.

Symptomatic Patterns

The clinical scale prototype used to develop this report incorporates correlates of Pd (Psychopathic Deviate) and *Sc* (Schizophrenia). Because these scales are not well defined in the clinical profile (the highest scales are relatively close in elevation), interpretation of the clinical profile should not ignore the adjacent scales in the profile code. The client's MMPI–2 clinical profile suggests that he is experiencing psychological problems at this time. This profile type reflects long-standing personality traits that are likely to lower his adaptability. He seems to be somewhat unconventional and alienated from others. He may also be somewhat unpredictable and impulsive at times, and he may act out in socially unacceptable ways and have a generally marginal life adjustment. He may be irritable and touchy in interpersonal contexts, appearing aloof and distant to others. Individuals with this pattern tend to act out their problems in an antisocial manner.

This client seems to lack the cultural interests that are characteristic of individuals with his educational level. He has a rather limited range of interests and seems to prefer mechanical things or practical activities to artistic or cultural pursuits. He appears to be more involved with exclusively male-oriented activities than with interpersonal relationships, and he may even reject activities that involve interpersonal contact. He appears to be insensitive and intolerant of others. He is likely to be a narrow-minded and closed person who is uninterested in the expression or discussion of feelings.

In addition, the following description is suggested by the content of the client's item responses. He has endorsed a number of items suggesting that he is experiencing low morale and a depressed mood.

Profile Frequency

Profile interpretation can be greatly facilitated by examining the relative frequency of clinical scale patterns in various settings. The client's high-point clinical scale score (Pd) occurs in 9.1% of the MMPI–2 normative sample of men. However, only 3.3% of the normative men have Pd as the peak score equal to or greater than a T score of 65, and only 1.9% have well-defined Pd spikes. This elevated MMPI–2 profile configuration (4–8/8–4) is very rare in samples of normals, occurring in less than 1% of the MMPI–2 normative sample of men.

The relative frequency of this profile in various outpatient settings is useful information for clinical interpretation. In the National Computer Systems (NCS) male outpatient sample, this is the most frequent high-point clinical scale score (Pd), occurring in 17.8% of the sample. Additionally, 10.9% of the male outpatients have the Pd spike at or above a T score of 65, and 7% have well-defined Pd spikes. This elevated MMPI–2 profile configuration (4–8/8–4) is found in 1.6% of the men in the NCS outpatient sample.

Profile Stability

The relative elevation of his clinical scale scores suggests that his profile is not as well defined as many other profiles. That is, his highest scale or scales are very close to his next scale score elevations. There could be some shifting of the most prominent scale elevations in the profile code if he is retested at a later date. The difference between the profile type used to develop the present report and the next highest scale in the profile code was one point. So, for example, if the client is tested at a later date, his profile may involve more behavioral elements related to elevations on Pt. If so, then on retesting, intensification of anxiety, negative self-image, and unproductive rumination may become more prominent.

Interpersonal Relations

He seems to have some difficulties getting along in society and in interpersonal relationships, and he may be aloof and insecure. He tends to be moody, and his nonconforming behavior may place a strain on relationships at times. He is probably behaving in unpredictable and erratic ways that may produce a great deal of marital strain.

He is somewhat shy, with some social concerns and inhibitions. He is a bit hypersensitive about what others think of him and is occasionally concerned about his relationships with others. He appears to be somewhat inhibited in personal relationships and social situations, and he may have some difficulty expressing his feelings toward others.

His very high score on the Marital Distress Scale suggests that his marital situation is quite problematic at this time. He has reported a number of problems with his marriage that are possibly important to understanding his current psychological symptoms.

The content of this client's MMPI–2 responses suggests the following additional information concerning his interpersonal relations. He views his home situation as unpleasant and lacking in love and understanding. He feels like leaving home to escape a quarrelsome, critical situation and to be free of family domination.

Diagnostic Considerations

He has reported a number of personal problems and maladaptive attitudes that are consistent with a personality disorder diagnosis. His self-reported tendency toward experiencing depressed mood should be taken into consideration in any diagnostic formulation.

Treatment Considerations

Mental health patients with this MMPI–2 pattern tend to be somewhat difficult to approach therapeutically because of their characteristic social alienation. The client's immature, unconventional lifestyle may make it difficult for him to establish a treatment relationship. He may feel that mental health professionals cannot understand his situation. Individuals with this profile also tend to act out impulsively and create problems for other people. Intense environmental stress and multiple problems may make treatment goals such as personal insight seem inconsequential.

Any treatment plans involving psychotropic medication should be carefully considered because some potential for medication abuse is reflected in this profile.

The item content he endorsed indicates attitudes and feelings that suggest a low capacity for change. His potentially high resistance to change may need to be discussed with him early in treatment in order to promote a more treatment-expectant attitude.

Examination of item content reveals a considerable number of problems with his home life. He feels extremely unhappy and alienated from his family. He reports that his home life is unpleasant and that he does not expect it to improve. Any psychological intervention will need to focus on his negative family feelings if progress is to be made.

NOTE: This MMPI–2 interpretation can serve as a useful source of hypotheses about clients. This report is based on objectively derived scale indexes and scale interpretations that have been developed in diverse groups of patients. The personality descriptions, inferences, and recommendations contained herein need to be verified by other sources of clinical information because individual clients may not fully match the prototype. The information in this report should most appropriately be used by a trained, qualified test interpreter. The information contained in this report should be considered confidential.

APPENDIX 19.2

MMPI–2 TRANSLATIONS

Arabic

Abdalla M. Soliman
Department of Psychology
Faculty of Education
United Arab Emirates University
AL-AIN, PO Box 17771
United Arab Emirates
97-13-5063310, (fax) 97-13-656457

Chinese

1. Fanny Cheung
Chinese University of Hong Kong
Department of Psychology
Shatin, N.T. Hong Kong
852-2-6096498
(fax) 852-2-6035019
(E-mail) fmcheung@cuhk.edu.hk

2. Song Wei Zhen
Institute of Psychology
Chinese Academy of Sciences
PO Box 1603, Postcode 100012
Beijing, China

Croatian

Naklada Slap

Czech

Testcentrum, a subsidiary of Hans Huber Verlag, Bratislava

Danish

Dansk, 1997

Dutch/Flemish

1. PEN Test Publishers
PO Box 6537
6503 GA Nijmegen, the Netherlands
31-24-3240884
(fax) 31-481-465867

2. Hedwig Sloore
Free University of Brussels
Department of Psychology
Pleinlaan 2
Brussels, Belgium
32-2-629-2516, (fax) 32-2-6292489
(E-mail) hsloore@vnet3.uub.ac.be

Ethiopian

Tenbit Emiru
Department of Psychology
University of Minnesota
Minneapolis, MN 55455
(E-mail) Emir0001@tc.umn.edu

Farsi

Translation by Elahe Nezami (University of California) and Reza Zamani (University of Tehran)

French

ECPA, 25 rue de la Plaine
75980 Paris, Cedex 20, France
33-1-40-09-62-62
(fax) 33-1-40-09-62-80

French–Canadian

Canadian Customers Contact

Multi-Health Systems
65 Overlea Boulevard, Suite 210
Toronto, Ontario M4H 1PI
416-424-1700

U.S. Customers Contact

Pearson (National Computer Systems)
5601 Green Valley Drive
Bloomington, MN 55437-1099
1-800-627-7271
(fax) 952-681-3259

German

Dr. Jurgen Hogrefe
Verlag Hans Huber
Langgass-Strasse 76
CH-3000
Bern 9
Switzerland
41-31-242533 (fax)·41-31-243380

Greek

Anna Kokkevi
Department of Psychiatry
Athens University Medical School
Eginition Hospital
72-74 Vassilissis Sopphias Avenue
Athens, 11528 Greece
33-1-721-7763
(fax) 30-1-724-3905

Hebrew

Moshe Almagor (972-4-344321)
University of Haifa
Faculty of Social Sciences
Mount Carmel, Haifa 31905, Israel
972-4-240-111, (fax) 972-4-246814
or 240966

Hmong

Customer Service
Pearson (National Computer
Systems)
5601 Green Valley Drive
Bloomington, MN 55437-1099
1-800-627-7271
(fax) 952-681-3259

Icelandic (Old Norse)

University of Iceland in 1995
Solvina Konrads and Erlendur
Haraldsson and Jakob Smari
University of Iceland
Hrisholti 7
210 Garoabae, Iceland

Indonesian

Translator: Lena Halim
PEN, Nijmegen
(E-mail) magdalenah@fp.
atmajaya.ac.id

Italian

1. Roberto Mattei
Organizzazioni Speciali
Via Scipione Ammirato 37-50136
Firenze, Italy
55-660-997, (fax) 55-669-446

2. Saolo Sirigatti
Dip. Psicologia
Universita di Firenze
Via S. Niccolo, 93, Italy
39-55-2491618
(fax) 39-55-2345326

3. Paolo Pancheri
CIC Edizioni Internazionali
5a Cattedra di clinica Psichiatrica
36, Viale Dell' Universita
00185 Roma Italia
39-6-902-49244 x501
(fax) 39-6-3210494

Japanese

Noriko Shiota
Department of Psychology
Villanova University
Villanova, PA 19085
610-519-7772, (fax) 610-519-4269

(Translation by Noriko Shiota and Lee Anna Clark)
Publisher: Nihon Bunka

Current Researcher/Norm Developer

Dr. Takashi Hayama
Mental Health and Welfare
Division
Minato-Chop NAKA-KU
Yokohama 231-0017-JAPAN
(Phone) +81-45-671-3935
(fax) +81-45-681-2533
(E-mail) xn3t-hym@asahi-net.or.jp

Korean

Kyunghee Han
Maumsarang Co. Ltd.
Kyunghee Han and JeeYoung Lim

Latvian

Translation by Zinta Sarma

Norwegian

Bjorn Ellertsen
University of Bergen
Clinical Neuropsychology
Arstadveien 21
Bergen, Norway N-5009
47-55-29170, (fax) 47-55-589873
Publisher: Norwegian Psychological Association

Romanian

Translation by Michael Stevens

Russian

1. Vladimar Martens
Institute of Biophysics
Zilapistnaya 46
Moscow, 182 Russia

2. Victor Koscheyev

Spanish

Argentina

Maria Casullo
University of Buenos Aires
Faculty of Psychology
Tucuman 2162, 8th Floor A
1050 Buenos Aires, Argentina
541-953-1218, (fax) 541-49-4332
(E-mail) casullo@insinv.psi.uba.ar

Chile

Fernando J. Rissetti
Departamento de Salud Estudiantil
Pontificia Universidad
Catolicia de Chile
JV Lastarria 65
Santiago, Chile SA5
(fax) 562-638-0638
(E-mail) frissett@lascar.puc.cl

Mexico

1. Manual Moderno
Av Sonora 206
Col. Hipodromo, 06100
Mexico, DF
52-5-265-1100
(fax) 52-5-265-1162

2. Emilia Lucio G. M. and Isabel Reyes-Lagunes
Corregidora 30-1
Col. Miguel Hidalgo Tialpan
CP 14410
Mexico, DF
525-665-6325, (fax) 525-528-5253

Spain

Alejandro Avila-Espade
Universidad de Salamanca
Department of Psychology

United States

1. Customer Service
Pearson (National Computer Systems)
5601 Green Valley Drive
Bloomington, MN 55437-1099
1-800-627-7271
(fax) 952-681-3259

2. Alex Azan
Florida International University
Student Counseling Services
University Park-GC 211
Miami, FL 33199
305-348-2880, (fax) 305-348-3448

3. Rosa Garcia-Peltoniemi
Center for the Victims of Torture
717 East River Road
Minneapolis, MN 55455
612-626-1400, (fax) 612-626-2465

Thai

La-or Pongpanich
Psychiatric Department
Army General Hospital
Bangkok, Thailand
(fax) 66-02-245-5702
or 66-02-245-5641

Turkish

Dr. Merla Culha
Koc University
Cayir Caddesi No. 5
Istinye, 80860
Istanbul, Turkey
212-229-3006 x502
(fax) 212-229-3602-229-50

Swedish

Psykologiforlaget
Stockholm

Vietnamese

Pauline Tran
1258 Capistrano Lane
Vista, CA 92083
619-630-1680, (fax) 619-630-1680

MMPI–A TRANSLATIONS

Chinese

Fanny Cheung
Chinese University of Hong Kong
Department of Psychology
Shatin, N.T. Hong Kong
852-2-6096498
(fax) 852-2-6035019
(E-mail) fmcheung @cuhk.edu.hk

French

ECPA
25 rue de la Plaine
75980 Paris, Cedex 20, France
33-1-40-09-62-62
(fax) 33-1-40-09-62-80

Greek

Anna Kokkevi
Department of Psychiatry
Athens University Medical School
Eginition Hospital
72-74 Vassilissis Sopphias Avenue
Athens, 11528 Greece
33-1-721-7763
(fax) 30-1-724-3905

Hebrew

Hoshe Almagor (972-4-344321)
University of Haifa
Faculty of Social Sciences
Mount Carmel, Haifa 31905, Israel
972-4-240-111, (fax) 972-4-246814
or 240966

Italian

Roberto Mattei
Organizzazioni Speciali
Via Scipione Ammirato 37-50136
Firenze, Italy
55-660-997, (fax) 55-669-446

Korea

Jeeyoung Lim
802-501 Hanjin APT
Jeongdun-Maul
193 Jeongja-Dong, Boondang-Gu
Sungnam-City, Kynuggi-Do
South Korea
822-729-9191
(fax) 822-729-9082
(E-mail) mmpi2@samsung.co.kr

Norwegian

Bjorn Ellertsen
University of Bergen
Clinical Neuropsychology
Arstadveien 21
Bergen, Norway N-5009
47-55-29170, (fax) 47-55-589873

Russian

Dr. Mera Atlis
601 Van Ness Apartment #109
San Francisco, CA 94102

Spanish

Mexico

1. Manual Moderno
Av Sonora 206
Col. Hipodromo, 06100
Mexico, DF
52-5-265-1100
(fax) 52-5-265-1162

2. Emilia Lucio G. M. and Isabel Reyes-Lagunes
Corregidora 30-1
Col. Miguel Hidalgo Tialpan
CP 14410
Mexico, DF
525-665-6325, (fax) 525-528-5253

United States

Pearson (National Computer Systems)
5601 Green Valley Drive
Bloomington, MN 55437-1099
1-800-627-7271
(fax) 952-681-3259

Thai

La-or Pongpanich
Psychiatric Department
Army General Hospital
Bangkok, Thailand
(fax) 66-02-245-5702
or 66-02-245-5641

REFERENCES

Abe, M. (1959). MMPI O kanshite mita nichibeijin paasonarichi no hikaku [Comparison of personalities between Japanese and Americans through the MMPI]. *Owaki Yoshikazu Kyoju 35-nen kinen shinrigaku ronbunshu*.

Adair, A. V. (1964). *A comparative study of performance on the* Pt *scale of the MMPI and a visual vigilance task*. Unpublished Master's thesis,Virginia State College.

Aerts, I. (2001). *Borderline persoonlijkheidsstoornis: Onderzoek naar MMPI–profielen* [Borderline personality disorder: Investigation of MMPI profiles]. Brussels, Belgium: Vrije Universiteit, Sfdeling Klinische Psychologie.

Akerlind, I., HornQuist, J. O., & Bjurulf, P. (1992). Psychological factors in the long-term prognosis of chronic low back pain patients. *Journal of Clinical Psychology*, *48*(5), 596–605.

Aldwin, C. M., Levenson, M. R., & Spiro, A. (1994). Vulnerability and resilience to combat exposure: Can stress have lifelong effects? *Psychology and Aging*, *9*, 34–44.

Alexy, W. D., & Webb, P. M. (1999). Utility of the MMPI–2 in work-hardening rehabilitation. *Rehabilitation Psychology*, *44*(3), 266–273.

Allen, J. P. (1991). Personality correlates of the MacAndrew alcoholism scale: A review of the literature. *Psychology of Addictive Behaviors*, *5*, 59–65.

Allen, J., & Walsh, J. A. (2000). A construct-based approach to equivalence: Methodologies for cross-cultural/multicultural personality assessment research. In R. H. Dana (Ed.), *Handbook of cross-cultural and multicultural personality assessment*. Mahwah, NJ: Lawrence Erlbaum Associates.

Almagor, M., & Nevo, B. (1996). The MMPI–2: Translation and first steps in its adaptation. In J. N. Butcher (Ed.), *International adaptation of the MMPI–2* (pp. 487–505). Minneapolis: University of Minnesota Press.

Amador, X. F., Flaum, M., Andreasen, N. C., Strauss, D. H., Yale, S. A., Clark, S. C., & Gorman, J. M. (1994). Awareness of illness in schizophrenia and schizoaffective and mood disorders. *Archives of General Psychiatry*, *51*, 826–836.

Amador, X. F., Friedman, J. H., Kasapis, C., Yale, S. A., Flaum, M., & Gorman, J. M. (1996). Suicidal behavior in schizophrenia and its relationship to awareness of illness. *American Journal of Psychiatry*, *153*, 1185–1188.

American Association for Correctional Psychology, Standards Committee. (2000). Standards for psychological services in jails, prisons, correctional facilities, and agencies. *Criminal Justice and Behavior*, *27*, 433–494.

American Correctional Association. (2004). *2004 Directory: Adult and juvenile correctional departments, institutions, agencies and parole authorities*. Lanham, MD: Author.

American Psychiatric Association Steering Committee on Practice Guidelines. (2002). *American Psychiatric Association practice guidelines for the treatment of psychiatric disorders compendium*. Washington, DC: Author.

American Psychiatric Association. (1952). *Diagnostic and statistical manual of mental disorders* (1st ed.). Washington, DC: Author.

American Psychiatric Association. (1980). *Diagnostic and statistical manual of mental disorders* (3rd ed.). Washington, DC: Author.

American Psychiatric Association. (1987). *Diagnostic and statistical manual of mental disorders* (3rd ed., rev.). Washington, DC: Author.

American Psychiatric Association. (1994). *Diagnostic and statistical manual of mental disorders* (4th ed.). Washington, DC: Author.

American Psychiatric Association. (2000). *Diagnostic and statistical manual of mental disorders* (4th ed., text revision). Washington, DC: Author.

American Psychological Association. (1986). *American Psychological Association guidelines for computer-based tests and interpretations*. Washington, DC: Author.

American Psychological Association. (1994). *Publication manual of the American Psychological Association* (4th ed.). Washington, DC: Author.

American Psychological Association. (2001). *Publication manual of the American Psychological Association* (5th ed.). Washington, DC: Author.

American Psychological Association. (2002). *Ethical principles of psychologists and code of conduct*. Washington, DC: Author.

Anastasi, A. (1988). *Psychological testing* (6th ed.). New York: Macmillan.

Anderson, U. (1999). Validation of the MMPI–2 Masculinity–Femininity scale with Latino men and women: Preliminary findings. *The SDSU McNair Journal, 6,* 70–77.

Anderson, U., Fernandez, S., Callahan, W. J., & Velasquez, R. J. (2001, May). *Validation of the MMPI–2 Masculinity–Femininity Scale with Latino men and women*. Paper presented at the Annual Symposium on Recent Developments in the Use of the MMPI–2, Minneapolis, MN.

Anderson, U., Velasquez, R. J., & Callahan, W. J. (2000, August). *Sex roles, cultural differences and Mf scores of Latinos*. Paper presented at the Annual Meeting of the American Psychological Association, Washington, DC.

Angleitner, A., & Wiggins, J. S. (Eds.). (1985). *Personality assessment via questionnaires: Current issues in theory and measurement*. New York: Springer.

Anno, B. J. (1991). *Prison health care: Guidelines for the management of an adequate delivery system*. Chicago: National Commission on Correctional Health Care.

Ansley, J., Gass, C. S., Brown, M. C., & Levin, B. E. (1995). Epileptic and nonepileptic seizure disorder: A comparison of MMPI–2 profile characteristics [Abstract]. *Journal of the International Neuropsychological Society, 1,* 135–136.

Arbisi, P. A., & Ben-Porath, Y. S. (1995). An MMPI–2 infrequent response scale for use with psychopathological populations: The Infrequency–Psychopathology scale, *F(p)*. *Psychological Assessment, 7*(4), 424–431.

Arbisi, P. A., & Ben-Porath, Y. S. (1997). Characteristics of the MMPI–2 *F(p)* scale as a function of diagnosis in an inpatient sample of veterans. *Psychological Assessment,* 9(2), 102–105.

Arbisi, P. A., & Ben-Porath, Y. S. (1998). The ability of Minnesota Multiphasic Personality Inventory—2 validity scales to detect fake-bad responses in psychiatric inpatients. *Psychological Assessment, 10*(3), 221–228.

Arbisi, P. A., & Ben-Porath, Y. S. (1999). The use of the Minnesota Multiphasic Personality Inventory—2 in the psychological assessment of persons with TBI: Correction factors and other clinical caveats and conundrums. *Neurorehabilitation, 13*, 51–59.

Arbisi, P. A., & Ben-Porath, Y. S. (2000). An MMPI–2 infrequent response scale for use with psychopathological populations: The Infrequency–Psychopathology scale, F(p). In J. N. Butcher (Ed.), *Basic sources on the MMPI–2* (pp. 163–176). Minneapolis: University of Minnesota Press.

Arbisi, P. A., Ben-Porath, Y. S., & McNulty, J. (2002). A comparison of MMPI–2 validity in African American and Caucasian psychiatric inpatients. *Psychological Assessment, 14*, 3–15.

Arbisi, P. A., Ben Porath, Y. S., & McNulty, J. (2003a). Empirical correlates of common MMPI–2 two-point codes in male psychiatric inpatients. *Assessment, 10(3)*, 237–247.

Arbisi, P. A., Ben-Porath, Y. S., & McNulty, J. (2003b). Refinement of the F(p) Scale is not necessary: A response to Gass and Luis. *Assessment, 10*, 123–128.

Arbisi, P. A., Ben-Porath, Y. S., & McNulty, J. L. (2005a). *MMPI–2 correlates of psychiatric inpatients*. Unpublished manuscript.

Arbisi, P. A., Ben-Porath, Y. S., & McNulty, J. L. (2005b). *The ability of the MMPI–2 to detect feigned PTSD within the context of compensation seeking.* Unpublished manuscript.

Arbisi, P. A., & Butcher, J. N. (2004a). Failure of the FBS to predict malingering of somatic symptoms: Response to critiques by Greve and Bianchini and Lees-Haley and Fox. *Archives of Clinical Neuropsychology, 19*, 341–345.

Arbisi, P. A., & Butcher, J. N. (2004b). Relationship between personality and health symptoms: The use of the MMPI–2 in medical assessments. *International Journal of Clinical and Health Psychology, 4*(3), 571–595.

Arbisi, P. A., Murdoch, M., Fortier, L., & McNulty, J. (2004). The relationship between MMPI–2 validity and award of service connection for PTSD during the compensation and pension evaluation. *Psychological Services, 1*(1), 56–67.

Archer, R. P., Aiduk, R., Giffin, R., & Elkins, D. E. (1996). Incremental validity of the MMPI–2 content scales in a psychiatric setting. *Assessment, 3*(1), 79–90.

Archer, R. P., Fontaine, J., & McCrae, R. R. (1998). Effects of two MMPI–2 validity scales on basic scale relations to external criteria. *Journal of Personality Assessment, 70*, 87–102.

Archer, R. P., Handel, R. W., & Couvadelli, B. (2004). An evaluation of the incremental validity of the MMPI–2 Superlative (S) scale in an inpatient psychiatric sample. *Assessment, 11*(1), 102–108.

Archer, R. P., Handel, R. W., Greene, R. L., Baer, R. A., & Elkins, D. E. (2001). An evaluation of the usefulness of the MMPI–2 F(p) scale. *Journal of Personality Assessment, 76*, 282–295.

Armilla, J. (1967). Predicting self-assessment social leadership in a new culture with the MMPI. *Journal of Social Psychology, 73*, 219–225.

Association of Directors of Law Enforcement Standards and Training. (2000). *IADLEST. Executive Summary of the Sourcebook: Data compiled from the 50 state Criminal Justice Officer Standards, Training, Certification, and Licensing Programs*. Unpublished manuscript.

Aston, J., & Lavery, J. (1993). The health of women in paid employment: Effects of quality of work role, social support, and cynicism on psychological and physical well-being. *Women & Health, 20*, 1–25.

Atlis, M. M., Butcher, J. N., & Hahn, J. (2002). *MMPI–2 profiles in a large nationwide clinical sample*. Poster presented at the 37th Annual Symposium on Recent Developments in the Use of the MMPI–2 and MMPI–A. Minneapolis, MN, May 18–19, 2002.

Austin, J. S. (1992). The detection of fake good and fake bad on the MMPI–2. *Educational and Psychological Measurement, 52*, 669–674.

Autor, D., & Duggan, M. G. (2002). *The rise in disability recipiency and the decline of unemployment* (Working Paper No. 01-15). Boston: MIT Department of Economics.

Avila-Espada, A., & Jimenez-Gomez, F. (1996). The Castilian version of the MMPI–2 in Spain: Development, adaptation, and psychometric properties. In J. N. Butcher (Ed.), *International adaptation of the MMPI–2* (pp. 305–328). Minneapolis: University of Minnesota Press.

Azan, A. (1989). The MMPI version Hispanic: Standardization and cross-cultural personality study with a population of Cuban refugees (Doctoral dissertation, University of Minnesota, 1988). *Dissertation Abstracts International, 50*, 2144B.

Azen, S. P., Snibbe, H. M., & Montgomery, H. R. (1973). A longitudinal predictive study of success and performance of law enforcement officers. *Journal of Applied Psychology, 57*(2), 190–192.

Babor, T. F., Steinberg, K., & Anton, R. (2000). Talk is cheap: Measuring drinking outcomes in clinical trials. *Journal of Studies on Alcohol, 61*, 55–63.

Bacchiochi, J. R., & Bagby, R. M. (2005). Development and *validation of the Malingering Discriminant Function Index for the MMPI–2*. Submitted for publication.

Baer, R. A., & Miller, J. (2002). Underreporting of psychopathology on the MMPI–2: A meta-analytic review. *Psychological Assessment, 14*(1), 16–26.

Baer, R. A., & Sekirnjak, G. (1997). Detection of underreporting on the MMPI–2 in a clinical population: Effects of information about validity scales. *Journal of Personality Assessment, 69*, 555–567.

Baer, R. A., Wetter, M. W., & Berry, D. T. R. (1992). Detection of underreporting of psychopathology on the MMPI: A meta-analysis. *Clinical Psychology Review, 12*, 509–525.

Baer, R. A., Wetter, M. W., & Berry, D. T. R. (1995). Effects of information about validity scales on underreporting of symptoms on the MMPI–2: An analogue investigation. *Assessment, 2*, 189–200.

Baer, R. A., Wetter, M. W., Nichols, D. S., Greene, R., & Berry, D. T. R. (1995). Sensitivity of MMPI–2 validity scales to underreporting of symptoms. *Psychological Assessment, 7*, 419–423.

Baetens Beardsmore, H. (1986). *Bilingualism: Basic principles* (2nd ed.). San Diego, CA: College Hill.

Bagby, R. M., Basso, M. R., Nicholson, R. A., Bacchiochi, J., & Miller, L. S. (2004). *Distinguishing bipolar depression, major depression, and schizophrenia with the MMPI–2 clinical, content, and PSY–5 scales*. Manuscript submitted for publication.

Bagby, R. M., Buis, T., & Nicholson, R. A. (1995). Relative effectiveness of the standard validity scales in detecting fake-bad and fake-good responding: Replication and extension. *Psychological Assessment, 7*(1), 84–92.

Bagby, R. M., Buis, T., Nicholson, R. A., Parikh, S., & Bacchiochi, J. R. (1999, April). *Distinguishing bipolar depression, major depression, and schizophrenia using the MMPI–2 clinical, content, and PSY–5 scales*. Paper presented at the 34th Annual Symposium on Recent Developments in the Use of the MMPI–2 and MMPI–A, Huntington Beach, CA.

Bagby, R. M., & Marshall, M. B. (2004). Assessing underreporting response bias on the MMPI–2. *Assessment*.

Bagby, R. M., Nicholson, R. A., Bacchiochi, J. R., Ryder, A. G., & Bury, A. S. (2002). The predictive capacity of the MMPI–2 and PAI validity scales and indexes to detect coached and uncoached feigning. *Journal of Personality Assessment, 78*, 69–86.

Bagby, R. M., Nicholson, R. A., & Buis, T. (1998). Utility of the Deceptive–Subtle items in the detection of malingering. *Journal of Personality Assessment, 70*, 405–415.

Bagby, R. M., Nicholson, R. A., Buis, T., & Bacchiochi, J. R. (2000). Can the MMPI–2 validity scales detect depression feigned by experts? *Assessment, 7*(1), 55–62.

Bagby, R. M., Nicholson, R. A., Buis, T., Radovanovic, H., & Fidler, B. J. (1999). Defensive responding on the MMPI–2 in family custody and access evaluations. *Psychological Assessment, 11*(1), 24–28.

Bagby, R. M., Nicholson, R. A., Rogers, R., Buis, T., Seeman, M. V., & Rector, N. A. (1997). Effectiveness of the MMPI–2 validity indicators in the detection of defensive responding in clinical and nonclinical samples. *Psychological Assessment, 9*(4), 406–413.

Bagby, R. M., Rogers, R., & Buis, T. (1994). Detecting malingered and defensive responding on the MMPI–2 in a forensic inpatient sample. *Journal of Personality Assessment, 62*, 191–203.

Bagby, R. M., Rogers, R., Buis, T., & Kalemba, V. (1994). Malingered and defensive response styles on the MMPI–2: An examination of validity scales. *Assessment, 1*, 31–38.

Bagby, R. M., Rogers, R., Buis, T., Nicholson, R. A., Cameron, S. L., Schuller, D. R., & Seeman, M. V. (1997). Detecting feigned depression and schizophrenia on the MMPI–2. *Journal of Personality Assessment, 68,* 650–664.

Bagby, R. M., Rogers, R., Nicholson, R. A., Buis, T., Seeman, M. V., & Rector, N. A. (1997). Effectiveness of the MMPI–2 validity indicators in the detection of defensive responding in clinical and nonclinical samples. *Psychological Assessment,* 9, 406–413.

Bagby, R. M., Ryder, A. G., Ben-Dat, H., Bacchiochi, J., & Parker, J. D. A. (2002). Validation of the dimensional factor structure of the Personality Psychopathology Five in clinical and nonclinical samples. *Journal of Personality Disorders, 16,* 304–316.

Baldrachi, R., Hilsenroth, M., Arsenault, L., Sloan, P., & Walter, C. (1999). MMPI–2 assessment of varying levels of posttraumatic stress in Vietnam combat veterans. *Journal of Psychopathology and Behavioral Assessment, 21,* 109–116.

Banks, S. M., & Kerns, R. D. (1996). Explaining high rates of depression in chronic pain: a diathesis stress framework. *Psychological Bulletin, 119,* 95–110.

Bannatyne, L. A., Gacono, C. B., & Greene, R. L. (1999). Differential patterns of responding among three groups of chronic, psychotic, forensic outpatients. *Journal of Clinical Psychology, 55,* 1553–1565.

Banreti-Fuchs, K. (1975, June). Attitudinal, situational, and mental health correlates of academic achievement at the undergraduate university level. *British Journal of Educational Psychology, 45,* 231.

Barefoot, J. C., Beckham, J. C., Peterson, B. L., Haney, T. L., & Williams, R. B. (1992). Measures of neuroticism and disease status in coronary angiograpy patients. *Journal of Consulting and Clinical Psychology, 60*(1), 127–132.

Barefoot, J. C., Dahlstrom, W. G., & Williams, R. J. (1983). Hostility, CHD incidence, and total mortality: A 25-year follow-up study of 255 physicians. *Psychosomatic Medicine, 45,* 59–63.

Barefoot, J. C., Dodge, K. A., Peterson, B. L., Dahlstrom, W. G., & Williams, R. B. J. (1989). The Cook–Medley Hostility scale: Item content and ability to predict survival. *Psychosomatic Medicine, 51*(1), 46–57.

Barefoot, J. C., Peterson, B. L., Harrell, F. E., Hlatky, M. A., Pryor, D. B., Haney, T. L., et al. (1989). Type A behavior and survival: A follow-up study of 1,467 patients with coronary artery disease. *American Journal of Cardiology,* 64(8), 427–432.

Barefoot, J. C., Smith, R. H., Dahlstrom, W. G., & Williams, R. B. (1989). Personality predictors of smoking behavior in a sample of physicians. *Psychology and Health, 3,* 37–43.

Barrash, J., Rodriguez, E. M., Scott, D. H., Mason, E. E., & Sines, J. O. (1987). The utility of MMPI subtypes for the prediction of weight loss after bariatric surgery. *International Journal of Obesity, 11,* 115–128.

Barrett, P. (1986). Factor comparison: An examination of three methods. *Personality and Individual Differences, 7,* 327–340.

Barrett, P., Putnam, S. H., Axelrod, B. N., & Rapport, L. J. (1998). Some statistical properties of 2 MMPI neurocorrection factors for individuals with closed head injury [Abstract]. *Archives of Clinical Neuropsychology, 13,* 16.

Barrick, M. R., & Mount, M. K. (1996). Effects of impression management and self-deception on the predictive validity of personality constructs. *Journal of Applied Psychology, 81,* 261–272.

Barthlow, D. L., Graham, J. R., Ben-Porath, Y. S., & McNulty, J. L. (1999). Incremental validity of the MMPI–2 content scales in an outpatient mental health setting. *Psychological Assessment, 11*(1), 39–47.

Barthlow, D. L., Graham, J. R., Ben-Porath, Y. S., Tellegen, A., & McNulty, J. L. (2002). The appropriateness of the MMPI–2 K correction. *Assessment,* 9(3), 219–229.

Bartol, C. R. (1991). Predictive validation of the MMPI for small-town police officers who fail. *Professional Psychology: Research and Practice, 22,* 127–132.

Bathurst, K., Gottfried, A. W., & Gottfried, A. E. (1997). Normative data for the MMPI–2 in child custody litigation. *Psychological Assessment, 9,* 205–211.

Batki, S. (1990). Drug abuse, psychiatric disorders, and AIDS: Dual and triple diagnosis. *Western Journal of Medicine, 152,* 547–552.

Beck, A. J., & Maruschak, L. (2001, July). *Mental health treatment in state prisons, 2000* (Bureau of Justice Statistics Special Report). Washington, DC: Office of Justice Programs, Bureau of Justice Statistics, U.S. Department of Justice.

Beck, A. T., Ward, C. H., Mendelson, M., Mock, J., & Erbaugh, J. (1961). An inventory for measuring depression. *Archives of General Psychiatry, 12,* 57–62.

Beckham, J. C., Crawford, A. L., Feldman, M. E., Kirby, A. C., Hertzberg, M. A., Davidson, J. R. T., & Moore, S. D. (1997). Chronic PTSD and chronic pain in Vietnam combat veterans. *Journal of Psychosomatic Research, 43,* 379–389.

Benet, V., & Waller, N. G. (1995). The Big Seven factor model of personality description: Evidence for its cross-cultural generality in a Spanish sample. *Journal of Personality & Social Psychology, 69,* 701–718.

Benotti, P. N., & Forse, R. A. (1995). The role of gastric surgery in the multidisciplinary management of severe obesity. *American Journal of Surgery, 169,* 361–367.

Ben-Porath, Y. S. (1990a). Cross-cultural assessment of personality: The case for replicatory factor analysis. In J. N. Butcher & C. D. Spielberger (Eds.), *Recent advances in personality assessment* (pp. 27–48). Mahwah, NJ: Lawrence Erlbaum Associates.

Ben-Porath, Y. S. (1990b). Using the MMPI–2 to assess coping with stress. *Dissertation Abstracts International, 50,* 4210–4211.

Ben-Porath, Y. S., Butcher, J. N., & Graham, J. R. (1991). Contribution of the MMPI–2 content scales to the differential diagnosis of schizophrenia and major depression. *Psychological Assessment, 3,* 634–640.

Ben-Porath, Y. S., & Forbey, J. D. (2003). *Nongendered norms for the MMPI–2.* Minneapolis: University of Minnesota Press.

Ben-Porath, Y. S., Graham, J. R., Hall, G. C. N., Hirschman, R. D., & Zaragoza, M. S. (Eds.). (1995). *Forensic applications of the MMPI–2*. Thousand Oaks, CA: Sage.

Ben-Porath, Y. S., McCully, E., & Almagor, M. (1993). Incremental validity of the MMPI–2 content scales in the assessment of personality and psychopathology by self-report. *Journal of Personality Assessment, 61*, 557–575.

Ben-Porath, Y. S., & Sherwood, N. E. (1993). *The MMPI–2 content component scales: Development, psychometric characteristics, and clinical application*. Minneapolis: University of Minnesota Press.

Ben-Porath, Y. S., Slutske, W. S., & Butcher, J. N. (1989). A real-data simulation of computerized adaptive administration of the MMPI. *Journal of Consulting and Clinical Psychology, 1*, 18–22.

Ben-Porath, Y. S., & Somwaru, D. (1993, March). *Assessment of personality disorders with the MMPI–2*. Paper presented at the 28th Annual Symposium on Recent Developments in the MMPI–2 and MMPI–A, St. Petersburg Beach, FL.

Ben-Porath, Y. S., & Tellegen, A. (1995). How (not) to evaluate the comparability of MMPI, MMPI–2 profile configurations: A reply to Humphey & Dahlstrom. *Journal of Personality Assessment, 65*(1), 52–58.

Ben-Porath, Y. S., Waller, N. G., Slutske, W. S., & Butcher, J. N. (1988, August). *A comparison of two methods for adaptive administration of MMPI–2 content scales*. Paper presented at the 96th annual meeting of the American Psychological Association, Atlanta, GA.

Berah, E., Butcher, J. N., Miach, P., Bolza, J., Colman, S., & McAsery, P. (1993, October). *Computer-based interpretation of the MMPI–2: An Australian evaluation of the Minnesota Report*. Poster presented at the 28th Annual Conference of the Australian Psychological Association, Gold Coast.

Bernstein, D. N., & Gatchel, R. J. (2000). Biobehavioral predictor variable of treatment outcome in patients with temporomandibular disorders. *Journal of Applied Biobehavioral Research, 5*(2), 101–113.

Berry, D. T. R., Adams, J. J., Clark, C. D., Thacker, S. R., Burger, T. L., Wetter, M. W., et al. (1996). Detection of a cry for help on the MMPI–2: An analog investigation. *Journal of Personality Assessment, 67*, 26–36.

Berry, D. T. R., Baer, R. A., Rinaldo, J. C., & Wetter, M. W. (2002). Assessment of malingering. In J. N. Butcher (Ed.), *Clinical personality assessment: Practical approaches* (pp. 268–302). New York: Oxford University Press.

Berry, D. T. R., & Butcher, J. N. (1998). Detection of feigning of head injury symptoms on the MMPI–2. In C. Reynolds (Ed.), *Detection of malingering during head injury litigation* (pp. 209–238). New York: Plenum Press.

Berry, D. T. R., Cimono, C. R., Chong, N. K., LaVelle, S. H., Ivy, K., Morse, T. L., et al. (2001). MMPI–2 fake-bad scale: An attempted cross-validation of proposed cutting scores for outpatients. *Journal of Personality Assessment, 76*, 296–314.

Berry, D. T. R., Wetter, M. W., & Baer, R. A. (1995). Assessment of malingering. In J. N. Butcher (Ed.), *Clinical personality assessment: Practical approaches* (pp. 236–248). New York: Oxford University Press.

Berry, D. T. R., Wetter, M. W., Baer, R. A., Youngjohn, J. R., Gass, C. S., Lamb, D. G., et al. (1995). Overreporting of closed-head injury symptoms on the MMPI–2. *Psychological Assessment, 76,* 517–523.

Beutler, L. E., & Harwood, T. M. (1995). Prescriptive psychotherapies. *Applied and Preventive Psychology, 4,* 89–100.

Beutler, L. E., Engle, D., Mohr, D., Daldrup, R. J., Bergan, J., Meredith, K., & Merry, W. (1991). Predictors of differential and self-directed psychotherapeutic procedures. *Journal of Consulting and Clinical Psychology, 59,* 333–340.

Beutler, L. E., Goodrich, G., Fisher, D., & Williams, O. B. (1999). Use of psychological tests/instruments for treatment planning. In M. Maruish (Ed.), *The use of psychological testing for treatment planning and outcomes assessment* (2nd ed., pp. 81–113). Mahwah, NJ: Lawrence Erlbaum Associates.

Beutler, L. E., Storm, A., Kirkish, P., Scogin, F., & Gaines, J. (1985). Parameters in the prediction of police officer performance. *Professional Psychology: Research and Practice, 16,* 324–335.

Biaggio, M. K., & Godwin, W. H. (1987). Relation of depression to anger and hostility constructs. *Psychological Reports, 61,* 87–90.

Bieliauskas, L. A. (1980). Life events, 17–OHCS measures, and psychological defensiveness in relation to aid seeking. *Journal of Human Stress, 6,* 28–36.

Bigos, S. J., Battie, M. C., Spengler, D. M., Fisher, L. D., Fordyce, W. E., Hansson, T. H., et al. (1991). A prospective study of work perceptions and psychosocial factors affecting the report of back injury. *Spine, 16,* 1–6.

Binder, J., Mayman, M., & Doehrman, S. (1974). Self-ideal–self-discrepancy as a defensive style. *Comprehensive Psychiatry, 15,* 335–343.

Binder, L. M., & Rohling, M. L. (1996). Money matters: A meta-analytic review of the effects of financial incentives on recovery after closed head injury. *American Journal of Psychiatry, 153,* 7–10.

Biondi, M., Venturi, P., Teodori, A., & Paga, G. (1986). Personality and electrical cortical activation during stress [Italian]. *Medicina Psicosomatica, 31,* 151–166.

Biskin, B. H., & Kolotkin, R. C. (1977). Effects of computerized administration on scores on the Minnesota Multiphasic Personality Inventory. *Applied Psychological Measurement, 1,* 543–549.

Blackburn, R. (1971). MMPI dimensions of sociability and impulse control. *Journal of Consulting & Clinical Psychology, 37,* 166.

Blais, M. A., Hilsenroth, M. J., Castlebury, F., Fowler, J. C., & Baity, M. R. (2001). Predicting *DSM–IV* cluster B personality disorder criteria from MMPI–2 and Rorschach data: A test of incremental validity. *Journal of Personality Assessment, 76*(1), 150–168.

Blake, D. D., Weathers, F. W., Nagy, L. M., Kaloupek, D. G., Gusman, F. F. D., Charney, D. S., & Keane, T. M. (1995). The development of a clinician-administered PTSD scale. *Journal of Traumatic Stress, 8,* 75–90.

Blake, D. D., Weathers, F. W., Nagy, L. M., Kaloupek, D. G., Klauminzer, G., Charney, D. S., & Keane, T. M. (1990). A clinician-rating scale for assessing current and lifetime PTSD: The CAPS–1. *Behavior Therapist, 13*, 187–188.

Blanchard, D. D., McGrath, R. E., Pogge, D. L., & Khadivi, A. (2003). A comparison of the PAI and MMPI–2 as predictors of faking bad in college students. *Journal of Personality Assessment, 80*, 197–205.

Blumenthal, J. A., Barefoot, J. C., Burg, M. M., & Williams, R. B. (1987). Psychological correlates of hostility among patients undergoing coronary angiography. *British Journal of Medical Psychology, 60*, 349–355.

Bohn, M. J., Jr. (1978, July). *Classification of offenders in an institution for young adults*. Paper presented at the 19th International Congress of Applied Psychology, Munich, FDR.

Bohn, M. J., Jr. (1979). Management classification for young adult inmates. *Federal Probation, 43*(4), 53–59.

Bolinskey, P. K., Gottesman, I. I., & Nichols, D. S. (2003). The schizophrenia proneness (*SzP*) scale: An MMPI–2 measure of schizophrenia liability. *Journal of Clinical Psychology, 59*, 1032–1044.

Bolinskey, P. K., Gottesman, I. I., Nichols, D. S., Shapiro, B. M., Roberts, S. A., Adamo, U. H., & Erlenmeyer-Kimling, L. (2001). A new MMPI–derived indicator of liability to develop schizophrenia: Evidence from the New York High-Risk Project. *Assessment, 8*, 127–143.

Bonta, J., & Motiuk, L. L. (1985). Utilization of an interview-based classification instrument: A study of correctional halfway houses. *Criminal Justice and Behavior, 12*, 333–352.

Bootzin, R. R., Manber, R., Loewy, D. H., Kuo, T. F., & Franzen, P. L. (2001). Sleep disorders. In P. B. Sutker & H. E. Adams (Eds.), *Comprehensive handbook of psychopathology* (3rd ed., pp. 671–711). New York: Kluwer Academic/Plenum Publishers.

Bornstein, R. A., & Kozora, E. (1990). Content bias of the MMPI *Sc* scale in neurologic patients. *Neuropsychiatry, Neuropsychology, & Behavioral Neurology, 3*, 200–205.

Bornstein, R. A., Miller, H. B., & van Schoor, T. (1988). Emotional adjustment in compensated head injury patients. *Neurosurgery, 23*, 622–627.

Bowler, R. M., Hartney, C., & Ngo, L. H. (1998). Amnestic disturbance and posttraumatic stress disorder in the aftermath of a chemical release. *Journal of Clinical Neuropsychology, 13*, 455–471.

Bowman, M. (1997). *Individual differences in post-traumatic response: Problems with the adversity–distress connection*. Mahwah, NJ: Lawrence Erlbaum Associates.

Bracken, B. A., & Barona, A. (1991). State of the art procedures for translating, validating, and using psychoeducational tests in cross-cultural assessment. *School Psychology International, 12*, 119–132.

Brady, S., Rierdan, J., Penk, W., Meschede, T., & Losardo, M. (2003). Posttraumatic stress disorder in civilians with serious mental illness. *Journal of Trauma and Dissociation, 4*, 77–90.

Brems, C., & Harris, K. (1996). Faking the MMPI–2: Utility of the subtle–obvious scales. *Journal of Clinical Psychology, 52,* 525–533.

Breslau, N., & Davis, G. C. (1985). Refining *DSM–III* criteria in major depression: An assessment of the descriptive validity of criterion symptoms. *Journal of Affective Disorders,* 9, 199–206.

Bresolin, M. J. (1984). *A comparative study of computer administration of the Minnesota Multiphasic Personality Inventory.* Unpublished doctoral dissertation, Loyola University, Chicago.

Brislin, R. W. (1970). Back translation for cross-cultural research. *Journal of Cross-Cultural Psychology, 1,* 185–216.

Brislin, R. W. (1986). The wording and translation of research instruments. In W. J. Lonner & J. W. Berry (Eds.), *Field methods in cross-cultural research* (pp. 137–164). Beverly Hills, CA: Sage.

Brislin, R. W. (1993). *Understanding culture's influence on behavior.* New York: Harcourt Brace.

Brislin, R. W., Lonner, W. J., & Thorndike, R. M. (1973). *Cross-cultural research methods.* New York: John Wiley & Sons.

Brophy, A. L. (1996). Provisional statistics for MMPI–2 dependency, prejudice, social status, control, and low back pain scales. *Psychological Reports, 78*(3, Pt. 2), 1075–1078.

Brophy, A. L. (2003). MMPI–2 L + K and L + K – F indexes of underreporting: Normative and desirable responding. *Psychological Reports,* 92, 223–227.

Brown, J. M., & Weiss, D. J. (1977). *An adaptive testing strategy for achievement test batteries* (Research Rep. No. 77-6). Minneapolis: University of Minnesota, Department of Psychology, Psychometrics Method Program.

Brulot, M. M., Strauss, E., & Spellacy, F. (1997). Validity of the Minnesota Multiphasic Personality Inventory—2 correction factors for use with patients with suspected head injury. *Clinical Neuropsychologist, 11,* 391–401.

Buchanan, T. (2002). Online assessment: Desirable or dangerous? *Professional Psychology: Research and Practice, 33*(2), 148–154.

Buchanan, T., & Smith, J. L. (1999). Using the Internet for psychological research: Personality testing on the World Wide Web. *British Journal of Psychology,* 90, 125–144.

Bureau of Labor Statistics. (2003). *Annual survey of occupational injury and illness.* Washington, DC: U.S. Department of Labor.

Burish, T. G., & Houston, B. (1976). Construct validity of the Lie scale as a measure of defensiveness. *Journal of Clinical Psychology, 32,* 310–314.

Burns, J. W. (2000). Repression predicts outcome following multidisciplinary treatment of chronic pain. *Health Psychology, 19*(1), 75–84.

Bury, A. S., & Bagby, R. M. (2002). The detection of feigned uncoached and coached post-traumatic stress disorder with the MMPI–2 in a sample of workplace accident victims. *Psychological Assessment, 14*(4), 472–483.

Buss, A. H., & Perry, M. (1992). The aggression questionnaire. *Journal of Personality and Social Psychology, 63*, 452–459.

Butcher, J. N. (Ed.). (1972). *Objective personality assessment: Changing perspectives*. New York: Academic Press.

Butcher, J. N. (1979). Use of the MMPI in personnel selection. In J. N. Butcher (Ed.), *New directions in MMPI research*. Minneapolis: University of Minnesota Press.

Butcher, J. N. (1987). The use of computers in psychological assessment: An overview of practices and issues. In J. N. Butcher (Ed.), *Computerized psychological assessment: A practitioner's guide* (pp. 3–14). New York: Basic Books.

Butcher, J. N. (1988). *Use of the MMPI in personnel screening*. Paper presented at the 22nd Annual Symposium on Recent Developments in the Use of the MMPI, St. Petersburg, FL.

Butcher, J. N. (1990a). *The Minnesota Report: Adult Clinical System*. Minneapolis, MN: National Computer Systems.

Butcher, J. N. (1990b). *The MMPI–2 in psychological treatment*. New York: Oxford University Press.

Butcher, J. N. (1990c). *Use of the MMPI–2 in treatment planning*. New York: Oxford University Press.

Butcher, J. N. (1991). *User's guide for the MMPI–2 Minnesota Report: Alcohol and Drug Abuse System*. Minneapolis, MN: National Computer Systems.

Butcher, J. N. (1994a). Psychological assessment of airline pilot applicants with the MMPI–2. *Journal of Personality Assessment, 62*, 31–44.

Butcher, J. N. (1994b, March). *Use of the MMPI–2 in personnel screening*. Society for Industrial Organizational Psychologists Annual Meeting, Nashville, TN.

Butcher, J. N. (1995). Clinical use of computer-based personality test reports. In J. N. Butcher (Ed.), *Clinical personality assessment: Practical approaches* (pp. 78–94). New York: Oxford University Press.

Butcher, J. N. (Ed.). (1996a). *International adaptations of the MMPI–2: Research and clinical applications*. Minneapolis: University of Minnesota Press.

Butcher, J. N. (1996b). Understanding abnormal behavior across cultures: The use of objective personality assessment methods. In J. N. Butcher (Ed.), *International adaptations of the MMPI–2: Research and clinical applications* (pp. 3–25). Minneapolis: University of Minnesota Press.

Butcher, J. N. (1997a). Base rate information for the forensic samples in the Minnesota Forensic Study. *MMPI–2 News & Profiles*. Minneapolis, MN: MMPI–2 Workshops.

Butcher, J. N. (1997b). Use of computer-based personality test reports in treatment planning. In J. N. Butcher (Ed.), *Personality assessment in managed health care: Using the MMPI–2 in treatment planning* (pp. 153–172). New York: Oxford University Press.

Butcher, J. N. (1998a, March). *Analysis of MMPI–2 S scale subscales to refine interpretation of "good impression."* Paper presented at the 34th Annual Conference of Recent Developments in the Use of the MMPI/MMPI–2, Clearwater, FL.

Butcher, J. N. (1998b). *The Butcher Treatment Planning Inventory (BTPI): Test manual and interpretive guide*. San Antonio, TX: Psychological Corporation.

Butcher, J. N. (1999a). *A beginners guide to the MMPI–2*. Washington, DC: American Psychological Association.

Butcher, J. N. (1999b, May). Points addressed at a hearing of the Committee on Police Selection of the Illinois State Legislature, Springfield, IL.

Butcher, J. N. (Ed.). (2000a). *Basic sources on the MMPI–2*. Minneapolis: University of Minnesota Press.

Butcher, J. N. (2000b). Dynamics of personality test responses: The empiricist's manifesto revisited. *Journal of Clinical Psychology*, *56*(3), 375–386.

Butcher, J. N. (2000c). Use of computer-based personality test reports in treatment planning. In J. N. Butcher (Ed.), *Basic sources on the MMPI–2*. Minneapolis: University of Minnesota Press.

Butcher, J. N. (2001, August). *Assessment with the MMPI–2: Decisions in diverse applications*. Oral presentation, American Psychological Association Convention, San Francisco.

Butcher, J. N. (2002a). Assessing pilots with "the wrong stuff": A call for research on emotional health factors in commercial aviators. *International Journal of Selection and Assessment*, *10*(1), 1–17.

Butcher, J. N. (2002b). How to use computer-based reports. In J. N. Butcher (Ed.), *Clinical personality assessment: Practical approaches* (2nd ed., pp. 109–125). New York: Oxford University Press.

Butcher, J. N. (2002c). Item content in the interpretation of the MMPI–2. In J. N. Butcher (Ed.), *Clinical personality assessment: Practical approaches* (2nd ed., pp. 319–334). New York: Oxford University Press.

Butcher, J. N. (2002d). *User's guide to the Minnesota Report: Revised personnel report* (3rd ed.). Minneapolis, MN: National Computer Systems.

Butcher, J. N. (2003a). Computer-based psychological assessment. In J. R. Graham & J. Naglieri (Eds.), *Comprehensive handbook of psychology, Volume 10: Assessment psychology* (pp. 141–164). New York: John Wiley & Sons.

Butcher, J. N. (2003b). *The Minnesota Report: Adult Clinical System—Revised* (4th ed.). Minneapolis: Regents of the University of Minnesota.

Butcher, J. N. (2003c, June). *Workshop on use of the MMPI–2 in personnel settings*. Presented at the 38th Annual Workshop and Symposium on Recent Developments in the Use of the MMPI–2, Minneapolis, MN.

Butcher, J. N. (2004). Personality assessment without borders: Adaptation of the MMPI–2 across cultures. *Journal of Personality Assessment*, *83*(2), 90–104.

Butcher, J. N. (2005a). *A beginner's guide to the MMPI–2* (2nd ed.). Washington, DC: American Psychological Association.

Butcher, J. N. (2005b). *User's guide for the Minnesota Clinical Report*. Minneapolis, MN: Pearson Assessments.

Butcher, J. N., Aldwin, C., Levenson, M., Ben-Porath, Y. S., Spiro, A., & Bosse, R. (1991). Personality and aging: A study of the MMPI–2 among older men. *Psychology of Aging, 6,* 361–370.

Butcher, J. N., Arbisi, P. A., Atlis, M. M., & McNulty, J. L. (2003). The construct validity of the Lees-Haley Fake-Bad scale (FBS): Does this scale measure malingering and feigned emotional distress? *Archives of Clinical Neuropsychology, 18,* 473–485.

Butcher, J. N., Atlis, M., & Fang, L. (2000). The effects of altered instructions on the MMPI–2 profiles of college students who are not motivated to distort their responses. *Journal of Personality Assessment, 74*(3), 492–501.

Butcher, J. N., Atlis, M., & Hahn, J. (2003). Assessment with the MMPI–2: Research base and future developments. In D. Segal (Ed.), *Comprehensive handbook of psychological assessment* (pp. 30–38). New York: John Wiley & Sons.

Butcher, J. N., Berah, E., Ellertsen, B., Miach, P., Lim, J., Nezami, E., et al. (1998). Objective personality assessment: Computer-based MMPI–2 interpretation in international clinical settings. In C. Belar (Ed.), *Comprehensive clinical psychology: Sociocultural and individual differences* (pp. 277–312). New York: Elsevier.

Butcher, J. N., Cheung, F. M, & Lim, J. (2003). Use of the MMPI–2 with Asian populations. *Psychological Assessment, 15,* 248–256.

Butcher, J. N., & Clark, L. A. (1989). Recent trends in cross-cultural MMPI research and application. In J. N. Butcher (Ed.), *New developments in MMPI research* (pp. 69–112). Minneapolis: University of Minnesota Press.

Butcher, J. N., Dahlstrom, W., Graham, J. R., Tellegen, A., & Kaemmer, B. (1989). *Minnesota Multiphasic Personality Inventory (MMPI–2): Manual for administration and scoring.* Minneapolis: University of Minnesota Press.

Butcher, J. N., Derksen, J., Sloore, H., & Sirigatti, S. (2003). Objective personality assessment of people in diverse cultures: European adaptations of the MMPI–2. *Behavior Research and Therapy, 41,* 819–840.

Butcher, J. N., & Graham, J. R. (1994). The MMPI–2: A new standard for personality assessment and research in counseling settings. *Measurement and Evaluation in Counseling and Development, 27,* 131–150.

Butcher, J. N., Graham, J. R., & Ben-Porath, Y. S. (1995). Methodological problems and issues in MMPI/MMPI–2/MMPI–A research. *Psychological Assessment, 7,* 320–329.

Butcher, J. N., Graham, J. R., Ben-Porath, Y. S., Tellegen, A., Dahlstrom, W. G., & Kaemmer, B. (2001). *Minnesota Multiphasic Personality Inventory—2 (MMPI–2): Manual for administration, scoring, and interpretation* (rev. ed.). Minneapolis: University of Minnesota Press.

Butcher, J. N., Graham, J. R., Williams, C. L., & Ben-Porath, Y. S. (1990). *Development and use of the MMPI–2 content scales.* Minneapolis: University of Minnesota Press.

Butcher, J. N., & Han, K. (1995). Development of an MMPI–2 scale to assess the presentation of self in a superlative manner: The S scale. In J. N. Butcher &

C. D. Spielberger (Eds.), *Advances in personality assessment* (Vol. 10, pp. 25–50). Hillsdale, NJ: Lawrence Erlbaum Associates.

Butcher, J. N., & Han, K. (1996). Methods of establishing cross-cultural equivalence. In J. N. Butcher (Ed.), *International adaptations of the MMPI–2* (pp. 44–66). Minneapolis: University of Minnesota Press.

Butcher, J. N., & Han, K. (2000). Development of an MMPI–2 scale to assess the presentation of self in a superlative manner: The *S* scale. In J. N. Butcher (Ed.), *Basic sources on the MMPI–2* (pp. 177–200). Minneapolis: University of Minnesota Press.

Butcher, J. N., & Hostetler, K. (1990). Abbreviating MMPI item administration: Past problems and prospects for the MMPI–2. *Psychological Assessment: A Journal of Consulting and Clinical Psychology, 2,* 12–22.

Butcher, J. N., Keller, L. S., & Bacon, S. F. (1985). Current developments and future directions in computerized personality assessment. *Journal of Consulting and Clinical Psychology, 53,* 803–815.

Butcher, J. N., Lim, J., & Nezami, E. (1998). Objective study of abnormal personality in cross-cultural settings: The Minnesota Multiphasic Personality Inventory—2 (MMPI–2). *Journal of Cross-Cultural Psychology, 20,* 189–211.

Butcher, J. N., & Miller, K. B. (1998). Personality assessment in personal injury litigation. In A. K. Hess & I. B. Weiner (Eds.), *The handbook of forensic psychology* (2nd ed., pp. 104–126). New York: John Wiley & Sons.

Butcher, J. N., Morfitt, R. C., Rouse, S. V., & Holden, R. R. (1997). Reducing MMPI–2 defensiveness: The effect of specialized instructions on retest validity in a job applicant sample. *Journal of Personality Assessment, 68,* 385–401.

Butcher, J. N., Narikiyo, T., & Bemis-Vitousek, K. (1992). Understanding abnormal behavior in cultural context. In H. Adams & P. Sutker (Eds.), *Comprehensive handbook of psychopathology* (2nd ed., pp. 83–105). New York: Plenum Press.

Butcher, J. N., Nezami, E., & Exner, J. (1998). Psychological assessment of people in diverse cultures. In S. Kazarian & D. R. Evans (Eds.), *Cross-cultural clinical psychology* (pp. 61–105). New York: Oxford University Press.

Butcher, J. N., & Pancheri, P. (1976). *Handbook of cross-national MMPI research.* Minneapolis: University of Minnesota Press.

Butcher, J. N., Perry, J. N., & Atlis, M. M. (2000). Validity and utility of computer-based test interpretation. *Psychological Assessment, 12,* 6–18.

Butcher, J. N., Perry, J., & Hahn, J. (2004). Computers in clinical assessment: Historical developments, present status, and future challenges. *Journal of Clinical Psychology, 60*(3), 331–345.

Butcher, J. N., & Rouse, S. V. (1996). Personality: Individual differences and clinical assessment. *Annual Review of Psychology, 47,* 87–111.

Butcher, J. N., Rouse, S. V., & Perry, J. N. (2000). Empirical description of psychopathology in therapy clients: Correlates of MMPI–2 scales. In J. N. Butcher (Ed.), *Basic sources on the MMPI–2* (pp. 487–500). Minneapolis: University of Minnesota Press.

Butcher, J. N., & Tellegen, A. (1978). MMPI research: Methodological problems and some current issues. *Journal of Consulting and Clinical Psychology, 46*, 620–628.

Butcher, J. N., & Williams, C. L. (1992). *Essentials of MMPI–2 and MMPI–A interpretation*. Minneapolis: University of Minnesota Press.

Butcher, J. N., & Williams, C. L. (2000). *MMPI–2 and MMPI–A: Essentials of clinical interpretation* (2nd ed.). Minneapolis: University of Minnesota Press.

Butcher, J. N., Williams, C. L., Graham, J. R., Tellegen, A., Ben-Porath, Y. S., Archer, R. P., & Kaemmer, B. (1992). *Manual for administration, scoring, and interpretation of the Minnesota Multiphasic Personality Inventory for Adolescents: MMPI–A*. Minneapolis: University of Minnesota Press.

Cabiya, J. J., Lucio, E., Chavira, D. A., Castellanos, J., Gomez, F. C. J., & Velasquez, R. J. (2000). MMPI–2 scores of Puerto Rican, Mexican, and U.S. Latino college students: A research note. *Psychological Reports, 87*(1), 266–268.

Caldwell, A. B. (1970). *Recent advances in automated interpretation of the MMPI*. Paper presented at the 5th Annual Symposium on Recent Developments in the Use of the MMPI, Mexico City, Mexico.

Caldwell, A. B. (1978). Caldwell Report—An MMPI interpretation. In O. K. Buros (Ed.), *The eighth mental measurements yearbook* (Vol. 1). Lincoln: University of Nebraska Press.

Calsyn, D. A., Louks, J. L., & Johnson, J. S. (1982). MMPI correlates of the degree of generalized impairment based on the Halstead–Reitan Battery. *Perceptual and Motor Skills, 55*, 1099–1102.

Camara, W. J., Nathan, J. S., & Puente, A. E. (2000). Psychological test usage: Implications in professional psychology. *Professional Psychology: Research and Practice, 31*, 141–154.

Campos, L. P. (1989). Adverse impact, unfairness, and bias in the psychological screening of Hispanic peace officers. *Hispanic Journal of Behavioral Sciences, 11*, 122–135.

Canul, G. D., & Cross, J. G. (1994). The influence of acculturation and racial identity attitudes on Mexican Americans' MMPI–2 performance. *Journal of Clinical Psychology, 50*, 736–745.

Capwell, D. F. (1945). Personality patterns of adolescent girls, II. Delinquents and nondelinquents. *Journal of Applied Psychology, 29*, 284–297.

Cardwell, S. W. (1982). Why women fail/succeed in ministry: Psychological factors. *Pastoral Psychology, 30*, 153–162.

Carr, A. C., Ghosh, A., & Ancil, R. J. (1983). Can a computer take a psychiatric history? *Psychological Medicine, 13*, 151–158.

Carr, J. L., & Graham, J. R. (1996). Assessing anger with the Minnesota Multiphasic Personality Inventory. In C. D. Spielberger (Ed.), *Stress and emotion: Anxiety, anger, and curiosity* (Vol. 16, pp. 67–82). Washington, DC: Taylor & Francis.

Carragee, E. J. (2001). Psychological screening in the surgical treatment of lumbar disk herniation. *Clinical Journal of Pain, 17*, 215–219.

Carson, G. L. (1966). Leadership and profiles on the MMPI and CPI 177. *Journal of College Student Personnel, 7,* 14–18.

Carter, J. E., & Wilkinson, L. (1984). A latent trait analysis of the MMPI. *Multivariate Behavioral Research, 19,* 385–407.

Cassisi, J. E., & Workman, D. E. (1992). The detection of malingering and deception with a short form of the MMPI–2 based on the L, F, and K scales. *Journal of Clinical Psychology, 48,* 54–58.

Casullo, M. M., & Samartino, L. G. (1996). Studies of the MMPI–2 in Argentina. In J. N. Butcher (Ed.), *International adaptation of the MMPI–2* (pp. 252–264). Minneapolis: University of Minnesota Press.

Centeno, J. G., & Obler, L. K. (2001). Principles of bilingualism. In M. O. Ponton & J. Leon Carrion (Eds.), *Neuropsychology and the Hispanic patient: A clinical handbook* (pp. 75–86). Mahwah, NJ: Lawrence Erlbaum Associates.

Chansky, N. M., & Bregman, M. (1957). Improvement of reading in college. *Journal of Educational Research, 51,* 313–317.

Chase, L. L. (1974). An evaluation of MMPI interpretation systems. *Dissertation Abstracts International, 35,* 6B.

Chavira, D. A., Montemayor, V., Velasquez, R. J., & Villarino, J. (1995). *U.S. Latinos' performance on the Spanish language MMPI–2 and acculturation.* Paper presented at the Annual Symposium on Recent Developments on the Use of MMPI–2, St. Petersburg, FL.

Cheung, F. M., & Song, W. Z. (1989). A review on the clinical applications of the Chinese MMPI. *Psychological Assessment, 1,* 30–37.

Chibnall, J. T., & Tait, R. C. (1999). Social and medical influences on attributions and evaluations of chronic pain. *Psychology and Health, 14,* 719–729.

Childs, R. A., Dahlstrom, W. G., Kemp, S. M., & Panter, A. T. (2000). Item response theory in personality assessment: A demonstration using the MMPI–2 depression scale. *Assessment, 7,* 37–54.

Chisholm, S. M., Crowther, J. H., & Ben-Porath, Y. S. (1997). Selected MMPI–2 scales' ability to predict premature termination and outcome from psychotherapy. *Journal of Personality Assessment, 69,* 127–144.

Chisholm, S. M., Crowther, J. H., & Ben-Porath, Y. S. (2000). Selected MMPI–2 scales' ability to predict premature termination from psychotherapy. In J. N. Butcher (Ed.), *Basic sources on the MMPI–2* (pp. 418–434). Minneapolis: University of Minnesota Press.

Church, A. T., & Katigbak, M. S. (1989). Internal, external, and self-report structure of personality in a non-Western culture: An investigation of cross-language and cross-cultural generalizability. *Journal of Personality & Social Psychology, 57*(5), 857–872.

Cigrang, J. A., & Staal, M. A. (2001). Readministration of the MMPI–2 following defensive invalidation in a military job applicant sample. *Journal of Personality Assessment, 76,* 472–481.

Cimbura, J. A. (2000). An exploration of stress in police officers: A study of the predictive value of preemployment psychological measures in the development of stress reactions in a sample of Ontario police officers. *Dissertation Abstracts International, 60*, 4281.

Ciraulo, D. A., Piechniczek-Buczek, J., & Iscan, E. N. (2003). Outcome predictors in substance use disorders. *Psychiatric Clinics of North America, 26*, 381–409.

Clark, L. A. (1990). Towards a consensual set of symptom clusters for assessment of personality disorders. In J. N. Butcher & C. D. Spielberger (Eds.), *Advances in personality assessment* (Vol. 8, pp. 243–264). Hillsdale, NJ: Lawrence Erlbaum Associates.

Clark, M. E. (1994). Interpretive limitations of the MMPI–2 Anger and Cynicism content scales. *Journal of Personality Assessment, 63*, 89–96.

Clark, M. E. (2000). MMPI–2 negative treatment indicators content and content component scales: Clinical correlates and outcome prediction for men with chronic pain. In J. N. Butcher (Ed.), *Basic sources on the MMPI–2* (pp. 405–417). Minneapolis: University of Minnesota Press.

Cleckley, H. (1982). *The mask of sanity* (5th ed.). St. Louis, MO: Mosby.

Clements, R., & Heintz, J. M. (2002). Diagnostic accuracy and factor structure of the AAS and APS scales of the MMPI–2. *Journal of Personality Assessment, 79*(3), 564–582.

Cofer, C. N., Chance, J., & Judson, A. J. (1949). A study of malingering on the MMPI. *Journal of Psychology, 27*, 491–499.

Cohen, J. (1988). *Statistical power analysis for the behavioral sciences* (2nd ed.). Hillsdale, NJ: Lawrence Erlbaum Associates.

Cole, D. L. (1956). The use of the MMPI and biographical data in predicting practice-teaching performance and subsequent attitudes toward teaching. *American Psychologist, 11*, 367.

Colligan, E. C., Osborne, D., Swenson, W. M., & Offord, K. P. (1983). *The MMPI: A contemporary normative study*. New York: Praeger.

Colotla, V. A., Bowman, M. L., & Shercliffe, R. J. (2001). Test–retest stability of injured workers' MMPI–2 profiles. *Psychological Assessment, 13*(4), 572–576.

Comas-Diaz, L. (2001). Hispanics, Latinos, or Americanos: The evolution of identity. *Cultural diversity and ethnic minority psychology, 7*(2), 115–120.

Comas-Diaz, L., & Jacobsen, F. M. (1987). Ethnocultural identification in psychotherapy. *Psychiatry, 50*, 232–241.

Comas-Diaz, L., & Ramos Grenier, J. (1998). Migration and acculturation. In J. Sandoval, C. L. Frisby, K. F. Geisinger, J. D. Scheuneman, & J. R. Grenier (Eds.), *Test interpretation and diversity: Achieving equity in assessment* (pp. 213–240). Washington, DC: American Psychological Association.

Cook, E. B., & Wherry, R. J. (1950). The urinary 17–ketosteroid output of naval submarine enlisted candidates during two stressful situations. *Human Biology, 22*, 104–124.

Cook, M., Young, A., Taylor, D., & Bedford, A. P. (1996). Personality correlates of psychological distress. *Personality & Individual Differences, 20*, 313–319.

Cook, W. N., & Medley, D. M. (1954). Proposed hostility and pharisaic-virtue scales for the MMPI. *Journal of Applied Psychology, 38*, 414–418.

Costa, P. T., & McCrae, R. R. (1992). *Revised NEO Personality Inventory (NEO PI–R) and NEO Five-Factor Inventory (NEO FFI)*. Odessa, FL: Psychological Assessment Resources.

Costello, R. M., Schneider, S. L., & Schoenfeld, L. S. (1996). Validation of a preemployment MMPI index correlated with disciplinary suspension days of police officers. *Psychology, Crime and Law, 2*, 299–306.

Coyle, F. A., Jr., & Heap, R. F. (1965). Interpreting the MMPI *L* scale. *Psychological Reports, 17*, 722.

Craig, R. J. (1999). *Interpreting personality tests: A clinical manual for the MMPI–2, CPI–R, and 16PF*. New York: John Wiley & Sons.

Craighead, W. E., Hart, A. B., Craighead, L. W., & Ilardi, S. S. (2002). Psychosocial treatments for Major Depressive Disorder. In P. E. Nathan & J. M. Gorman (Eds.), *A guide to treatments that work* (2nd ed., pp. 245–261). New York: Oxford University Press.

Cramer, K. M. (1995). The effects of description clarity and disorder type on the MMPI–2 fake-bad indices. *Journal of Clinical Psychology, 51*, 831–840.

Crespo, G. S., & Gomez, F. J. (2003). The Superlative Scale S of Butcher and Han (1995): The "fake-good" in the Spanish adaptation of the MMPI–2 [Spanish]. *Revista de Psicologia, 21*(1), 5–39.

Crews, W. D., Jefferson, A. L., Broshek, D. K., Rhodes, R. D., Williamson, J., Brazil, A. M., et al. (2003). Neuropsychological dysfunction in patients with end-stage pulmonary disease: Lung transplant evaluation. *Archives of Clinical Neuropsychology, 18*, 353–362.

Cripe, L. I., Maxwell, J. K., & Hill, E. (1995). Multivariate discriminant function analysis of neurologic, pain, and psychiatric patients with the MMPI. *Journal of Clinical Psychology, 51*, 258–268.

Cuellar, I. (1998). Cross-cultural clinical psychological assessment of Hispanic Americans. *Journal of Personality Assessment, 70*, 71–86.

Cullen, M. J., & Ones, D. S. (2003). *Using the MMPI to predict antisocial police behavior*. Unpublished manuscript.

Cullen, M. J., Ones, D. S., Viswesvaran, C., Drees, S., & Langkamp, K. (2003). *A meta-analysis of the MMPI and police officer performance*. Paper presented at the annual conference of the Society for Industrial and Organizational Psychology, Orlando, FL.

Cumella, E. J., Wall, A. D., & Kerr-Almeida, N. (2000). MMPI–2 in inpatient assessment of women with eating disorders. *Journal of Personality Assessment, 75*, 387–403.

Cummins, J. (1984). *Bilingualism and special education: Issues in assessment and pedagogy*. Austin, TX: Pro-Ed.

Dahlstrom, L. E. (1986). MMPI findings on other American minority groups. In W. G. Dahlstrom, D. Lachar, & L. E. Dahlstrom (Eds.), *MMPI patterns of American minorities* (pp. 50–86). Minneapolis: University of Minnesota Press.

Dahlstrom, W. G. (1980). Altered versions of the MMPI. In W. G. Dahlstrom & L. E. Dahlstrom (Eds.), *Basic readings on the MMPI* (pp. 386–393). Minneapolis: University of Minnesota Press.

Dahlstrom, W. G., & Archer, R. P. (2000). A shortened version of the MMPI–2. *Assessment, 7*(2), 131–137.

Dahlstrom, W. G., Lachar, D., & Dahlstrom, L. E. (Eds.). (1986). *MMPI patterns of American minorities*. Minneapolis: University of Minnesota Press.

Dahlstrom, W. G., Welsh, G. S., & Dahlstrom, L. E. (1972). *An MMPI handbook: Clinical interpretation* (Vol. 1, rev. ed.). Minneapolis: University of Minnesota Press.

Dahlstrom, W. G., Welsh, G. S., & Dahlstrom, L. E. (1975). *An MMPI handbook: Vol. II. Research applications* (rev. ed.). Minneapolis: University of Minnesota Press.

Dana, R. H. (1993). *Multicultural assessment perspectives for professional psychology*. Needham Heights, MA: Allyn & Bacon.

Dannenbaum, S. E., & Lanyon, R. I. (1993). The use of subtle items in detecting deception. *Journal of Personality Assessment, 61*, 501–510.

Danziger, K. (1990). *Constructing the subject: Historical origins of psychological research*. New York: Cambridge University Press.

David, K. H. (1968). Ego-strength, sex differences, and description of self, ideal and parents. *Journal of General Psychology, 79*, 79–81.

Davidson, J. R., & Fairbank, J. A. (1993). The epidemiology of post-traumatic stress disorder. In J. R. Davidson & E. B. Foa (Eds.), *Post-traumatic stress disorder:* DSM–IV *and beyond*. Washington, DC: American Psychiatric Press.

Davis, R. N. (1999). Web-based administration of a personality questionnaire: Comparison with traditional methods. *Behavior Research Methods, Instruments, & Computers, 31*, 572–577.

Davis, S. (1991). Violence by psychiatric inpatients: A review. *Hospital and Community Psychiatry, 42*, 585–590.

Dawes, R. M., Faust, D., & Meehl, P. E. (1989). Clinical versus actuarial judgment. *Science, 24*, 1668–1674.

Dearth, C. S., Berry, D., Vickery, C., Vagnini, V., Baser, R., Orey, S., & Cragar, D. (in press). Detection of feigned head injury symptoms on the MMPI–2 in head-injured patients and community controls. *Archives of Clinical Neuropsychology*.

Deinard, A. S., Butcher, J. N., Thao, U. D., Moua Vang, S. H., & Hang, K. (1996). Development of Hmong translation of the MMPI–2. In J. N. Butcher (Ed.), *International adaptation of the MMPI–2* (pp. 194–205). Minnesota: University of Minnesota Press.

Denny, N., Robinowitz, R., & Penk, W. E. (1987). Conducting applied research on Vietnam combat-related post-traumatic stress disorder. *Journal of Clinical Psychology, 43*, 56–66.

Derksen, J. (1995). *Personality disorders: Clinical and social perspectives*. Chichester: John Wiley & Sons.

Derksen, J. (2002). *Descriptieve en structurele psychodiagnostiek* [*Descriptive and structural assessment*] (2nd ed.). Nijmegen, the Netherlands: PEN Tests Publisher.

Derksen, J. (2004). *Psychologische diagnostiek: Enkele structurele en descriptieve aspecten* [Psychological assessment: Some structural and descriptive aspects]. Nijmegen, the Netherlands: PEN Tests Publisher.

Derksen, J., De Mey, H., Sloore, H., & Hellenbosch, G. (1993). *MMPI–2: Handleiding bij afname, scoring en interpretation* [MMPI–2: Manual for administration, scoring and interpretation]. Nijmegen, the Netherlands: PEN Test Publisher.

Derksen, J., De Mey, H., Sloore, H., & Hellenbosch, G. (2004). *MMPI–2: Handleiding voor afname, scoring en interpertatie* [MMPI–2: Manual for test taking, scoring, and interpretation]. Nijmegen, the Netherlands: PEN Tests Publisher.

Derksen, J., Gerits, L., & Verbruggen, A. (2003, June). *MMPI–2 profiles of nurses caring for people with severe behavior problems*. Paper given at the 38th MMPI–2 Conference on Recent Developments in the Use of the MMPI–2 and MMPI–A, Minneapolis, MN.

Derksen, J., Maffei, C., & Groen, H. (1999). *Treatment of personality disorders*. New York: Kluwer Academic/Plenum Publishers.

Derogatis, L. J. (1983). *SCL–90–R administration, scoring, and procedure manual—II*. Towson, MD: Clinical Psychometric Research.

Derry, P. A., Harnadek, M. C. S., McLachlan, R. S., & Sontrop, J. (1997). Influence of seizure content on interpreting psychopathology on the MMPI–2 in patients with epilepsy. *Journal of Clinical and Experimental Neuropsychology, 19*(3), 396–404.

Dersh, J., Polatin, P. B., & Gatchel, R. J. (2002). Chronic pain and psychopathology: Research findings and theoretical considerations. *Psychosomatic Medicine, 64*(5), 773–786.

Detrick, P., Chibnall, J. T., & Rosso, M. (2001). Minnesota Multiphasic Personality Inventory—2 (MMPI–2) in police officer selection: Normative data and relation to the Inwald Personality Inventory. *Professional Psychology: Research and Practice, 32*(5), 484–490.

Dikmen, S., & Reitan, R. M. (1974). Minnesota Multiphasic Personality Inventory correlates of dysphasic language disturbances. *Journal of Abnormal Psychology, 83*, 675–679.

Dikmen, S., & Reitan, R. M. (1977). MMPI correlates of adaptive ability deficits in patients with brain lesions. *Journal of Nervous and Mental Disease, 165*, 247–254.

Ditton, P. J. (1999, July). *Mental health and treatment of inmates and probationers* (Bureau of Justice Statistics Special Report). Washington, DC: Office of Justice Programs, Bureau of Justice Statistics, U.S. Department of Justice.

Dragt, S., & Derksen, J. J. L. (1994). Antwoordpatronen van borderline patiânten op psychologische tests: Een overzicht van de literatuur [Response patterns of borderline patients on psychological tests: An overview of the literature]. In J. J. L. Derksen & H. Groen (Eds.), *Handboek voor de behandeling van borderline patiânten* [Handbook for treatment of borderline patients]. Utrecht, the Netherlands: De Tijdstroom.

Drees, S., Ones, D., Cullen, M., Spilberg, S., & Viswesvaran, C. (2003, April). *Personality and psychopathology assessment in police officer screening and selection: Mandates and practices.* Paper presented at the 18th Annual Conference of the Society for Industrial and Organizational Psychology, Orlando, FL.

Dubno, P. (1961). Group effectiveness in relation to the interaction between decision time characteristics of leaders and task conditions. *Dissertation Abstracts International, 21,* 2390–2391.

Duff, F. L. (1965). Item subtlety in personality inventory scales. *Journal of Consulting Psychology, 29,* 565–570.

Duffy, J. C., & Waterton, J. J. (1984). Underreporting of alcohol consumption in sample surveys: The effect of computer interviewing in fieldwork. *British Journal of Addictions, 79,* 303–308.

Dunn, J. T., & Lees-Haley, P. R. (1995). The MMPI–2 correction factor for closed-head injury: A caveat for forensic cases. *Assessment, 2,* 47–51.

Duthie, B. (1985). *MMPI computerized interpretation manual: Subsection 3.2.* Wakefield, RI: Applied Innovations.

Edwards, A. L. (1957). *The social desirability variable in personality assessment and research.* New York: Dryden.

Edwards, D. W., Holmquist, L., Wanless, R., Wicks, J., & Davis, C. (1998). Comparing three methods of "neuro-correction" for the MMPI–2 [Abstract]. *Journal of the International Neuropsychological Society, 4,* 27–28.

Egger, J. I. M., De Mey, H. R. A., Derksen, J. J. L., & van der Staak, C. P. F. (2003). Cross-cultural replication of the Five-Factor Model and comparison of the NEO–PI–R and MMPI–2 PSY–5 scales in a Dutch psychiatry sample. *Psychological Assessment, 15*(1), 81–88.

Egger, J. I. M., Delsing, P. A. M., & De Mey, H. R. A. (2003). Differential diagnosis using the MMPI–2: Goldberg's index revisited. *European Psychiatry, 18,* 409–411.

Ekman, P. F., Friesen, W. V., & Lutzker, D. R. (1962). Psychological reactions to infantry basic training. *Journal of Consulting Psychology, 26,* 103–104.

Elhai, J. D., Forbes, M. A., Craemer, M., McHugh, T. F., & Frueh, B. C. (2003). Clinical symptomatology of PTSD–diagnosed Australian and United States Vietnam combat veterans: An MMPI–2 comparison. *Journal of Nervous and Mental Disease, 191,* 458–463.

Elhai, J. D., & Frueh, B. C. (2001). Subtypes of clinical presentations in malingerers of post-traumatic stress disorder: An MMPI–2 cluster analysis. *Assessment, 8,* 75–84.

Elhai, J. D., Frueh, B. C., Gold, P. B., Gold, S. N., & Hamner, M. B. (2000). Clinical presentations of post-traumatic stress disorder across trauma populations: A comparison of MMPI–2 profiles of combat veterans and adult survivors of child sexual abuse. *Journal of Nervous and Mental Disease, 188,* 708–713.

Elhai, J. D., Gold, P. B., Frueh, B. C., & Gold, S. N. (2000). Cross-validation of the MMPI–2 in detecting malingered posttraumatic stress disorder. *Journal of Personality Assessment, 75*, 449–463.

Elhai, J. D., Gold, P. B., Sellers, A. H., & Dorfman, W. I. (2001). The detection of malingered posttraumatic stress disorder with MMPI–2 fake-bad indices. *Assessment, 8*, 221–236.

Elhai, J. D., Ruggiero, K. J., Frueh, B. C., Beckham, J. C., Gold, P. B., & Feldman, M. E. (2002). The Infrequency Posttraumatic Stress Disorder scale (Fptsd) for the MMPI–2: Development and initial validation with veterans presenting with combat-related PTSD. *Journal of Personality Assessment, 79*, 531–549.

Ellertsen, B., Havik, O. E., & Skavhellen, R. R. (1996). The Norwegian MMPI–2. In J. N. Butcher (Ed.), *International adaptation of the MMPI–2* (pp. 350–367). Minneapolis: University of Minnesota Press.

Ellingson, J. E., Sackett, P. R., & Hough, L. M. (1999). Social desirability corrections in personality measurement: Issues of applicant comparison and construct validity. *Journal of Applied Psychology, 84*, 155–166.

Emiru, T. (2003). *Translation and adaptation of the MMPI–2 for Ethiopia*. Unpublished doctoral dissertation, University of Minnesota, Minneapolis.

Engdahl, B. E., Eberly, R. E., & Blake, J. D. (1996). Assessment of post-traumatic stress disorder in World War II veterans. *Psychological Assessment, 8*(4), 445–449.

Epker, J., & Gatchel, R. J. (2000). Coping profile differences in the biopsychosocial functioning of patients with temporomandibular disorder. *Psychosomatic Medicine, 62*(1), 69–75.

Ernst, F. A., Francis, R. A., & Enwonwu, C. O. (1990). Manifest hostility may affect habituation of cardiovascular reactivity in Blacks. *Behavioral Medicine, 16*, 119–124.

Everett, J. E., & Entrekin, L. V. (1980). Factor comparability and the advantages of multiple group factor analysis. *Multivariate Behavioral Research, 15*, 165–180.

Eyde, L., Kowal, D. M., & Fishburne, F. J. (1991). The validity of computer-based test interpretations of the MMPI. In T. B. Gutkin & S. L. Wise (Eds.), *The computer and the decision-making process* (pp. 75–123). Hillsdale, NJ: Lawrence Erlbaum Associates.

Falicov, C. J. (1982). Mexican families. In M. McGoldrick, J. K. Pearce, & J. Giordano (Eds.), *Ethnicity and family therapy* (pp. 134–163). New York: Guilford Press.

Falicov, C. J. (1998). *Latino families in therapy: A guide to multicultural practice*. New York: Guilford Press.

Fang, C. Y., & Myers, H. F. (2001). The effects of racial stressors and hostility on cardiovascular reactivity in African American and Caucasian men. *Health Psychology, 20*(1), 64–70.

Fantoni-Salvador, P., & Rogers, R. (1997). Spanish versions of the MMPI–2 and PAI: An integration of concurrent validity with Hispanic patients. *Assessment, 4*, 29–39.

Fawcett, J., Scheftner, W. A., Fogg, L., Clark, D. C., Young, M. A., Hedeker, D., & Gibbons, R. (1990). Time-related predictors of suicide in major affective disorder. *American Journal of Psychiatry, 147,* 1189–1194.

Feyerabend, P. K. (1993). *Against method* (3rd ed.). London: Verso Books.

Fiedler, N., Kipen, H. M., DeLuca, J., Kelly-McNeil, K., & Natelson, B. (1996). A controlled comparison of multiple chemical sensitivities and chronic fatigue syndrome. *Psychosomatic Medicine,* 58(1), 38–49.

Finger, M. S., & Ones, D. S. (1999). Psychometric equivalence of the computer and booklet forms of the MMPI: A meta-analysis. *Psychological Assessment, 11*(1), 58–66.

Fink, A., & Butcher, J. N. (1972). Reducing objections to personality inventories with special instructions. *Educational and Psychological Measurements, 27,* 631–639.

Finn, P. R., Sharkansky, E. J., Brandt, K. M., & Turcotte, N. (2000). The effects of familial risk, personality, and expectancies on alcohol use and abuse. *Journal of Abnormal Psychology, 109,* 122–133.

Finn, S. E. (1996a). Assessing feedback integrating MMPI–2 and Rorschach findings. *Journal of Personality Assessment, 67*(3), 543–557.

Finn, S. E. (1996b). *Manual for using the MMPI–2 as a therapeutic intervention.* Minneapolis: University of Minnesota Press.

Finn, S. E. (1998). Teaching Therapeutic Assessment in a required graduate course. In L. Handler & M. Hilsenroth (Eds.), *Teaching and learning personality assessment* (pp. 359–373). Mahwah, NJ: Lawrence Erlbaum Associates.

Finn, S. E. (1999, March). *Giving clients feedback about "defensive" test protocols: Guidelines from Therapeutic Assessment.* Paper presented at the Society for Personality Assessment annual meeting, New Orleans, LA. (Available from the author)

Finn, S. E. (2000, March). *Therapeutic Assessment: Would Harry approve?* Paper presented at the Society for Personality Assessment annual meeting, Albuquerque, NM, as part of a symposium, "Harry Stack Sullivan and Psychological Assessment," F. B. Evans, III, Chair. (Available from the author)

Finn, S. E. (2002a, March). *Appreciating the power and potential of psychological assessment.* Presidential Address, presented at the Midwinter Meeting of the Society for Personality Assessment, San Antonio, TX. (Available from the author)

Finn, S. E. (2002b, March). *Challenges and lessons of intersubjectivity theory for psychological assessment.* Paper presented at the Society for Personality Assessment annual meeting, San Antonio, TX, as part of a symposium, "Concepts of the Self: Implications for Assessment," M. L. Silverstein, Chair. (Available from the author)

Finn, S. E. (2003). Therapeutic Assessment of a man with "ADD." *Journal of Personality Assessment, 80,* 115–129.

Finn, S. E. (2005). How psychological assessment taught me compassion and firmness. *Journal of Personality Assessment, 84,* 27–30.

Finn, S., & Kamphuis, S. (1995). What a clinician should know about base rates. In J. N. Butcher (Ed.), *Clinical personality assessment: Practical approaches* (pp. 224–235). New York: Oxford University Press.

Finn, S. E., & Martin, H. (1997). Therapeutic assessment with the MMPI–2 in managed care. In J. N. Butcher (Ed.), *Personality assessment in managed care: Using the MMPI–2 in treatment planning* (pp. 131–152). New York: Oxford University Press.

Finn, S. E., Schroeder, D. G., & Tonsager, M. E. (1995). *The Assessment Questionnaire—2 (AQ–2): A measure of clients' experiences with psychological assessment.* Unpublished manuscript. (Available from the first author)

Finn, S. E., & Tonsager, M. (1992). Therapeutic effects of providing MMPI–2 test feedback to college students awaiting therapy. *Psychological Assessment, 4,* 278–287.

Finn, S. E., & Tonsager, M. E. (1997). Information gathering and therapeutic models of assessment: Complementary paradigms. *Psychological Assessment, 9,* 374–385.

Finn, S. E., & Tonsager, M. E. (2002). How Therapeutic Assessment became humanistic. *The Humanistic Psychologist, 30,* 10–22.

Finney, J. C. (1966). Programmed interpretation of MMPI and CPI. *Archives of General Psychiatry, 15*(1), 75–81.

First, M. B., Spitzer, R. L., Gibbson, M., & Williams, J. B. (1995). The Structured Clinical Interview for *DSM–III–R* Personality Disorders (SCID–II): Description. *Journal of Personality Disorders, 9,* 93–91.

Fischer, C. T. (1994). *Individualizing psychological assessment.* Mahwah, NJ: Lawrence Erlbaum Associates. (Original work published 1985)

Fischer, C. T. (2000). Collaborative individualized assessment. *Journal of Personality Assessment, 74,* 2–14.

Fishbain, D. A., Cutler, R., Rosomoff, H. L., & Rosomoff, R. S. (1999). Chronic pain disability exaggeration/malingering and submaximal effort research. *Clinical Journal of Pain, 15,* 244–274.

Fjordbak, T. (1985). Clinical correlates of high Lie scale elevations among forensic patients. *Journal of Personality Assessment, 49,* 252–255.

Flannery, R. B. (1992). *Post-traumatic stress disorder.* New York: Crossroads Press.

Foa, E. B., Keane, T. M., & Friedman, M. J. (Eds.). (2000). *Effective treatments for PTSD: Practice guidelines from the International Society for Traumatic Stress Studies.* New York: Guilford Press.

Follette, W. C., Naugle, A. E., & Follette, V. M. (1997). MMPI–2 profiles of adult women with child sexual abuse histories: Cluster-analytic findings. *Journal of Consulting and Clinical Psychology, 65,* 858–866.

Forbey, J., Ben-Porath, Y., & Tellegen, A. M. (2004, March). *Associations between the relative contributions of the MMPI–2 Restructured Clinical (RC) scales and content scales.* Paper presented at the Annual Meeting of the Society for Personality Assessment, Miami, FL.

Ford, J. D. (1999). Disorders of extreme stress following war-zone military trauma: Associated features of post-traumatic stress disorder or comorbid but distinct symptoms? *Journal of Consulting and Clinical Psychology, 67*, 3–12.

Fordyce, W. E., Bigos, S. J., Batti'e, M. C., & Fisher, L. D. (1992). MMPI Scale 3 as a predictor of back injury report: What does it tell us? *Clinical Journal of Pain, 8*(3), 222–226.

Fow, N. R., Dorris, G., Sittig, M., & Smith-Seemiller, L. (2002). An analysis of the influence of insurance sponsorship on MMPI changes among patients with chronic pain. *Journal of Clinical Psychology, 58*(7), 827–832.

Fowler, R. D. (1966). *The MMPI notebook: A guide to the clinical use of the automated MMPI*. Nutley, NJ: Roche Psychiatric Service Institute.

Fowler, R. D. (1968). MMPI computer interpretation for college counseling. *Journal of Psychology, 69*(2), 201–207.

Fowler, R. D. (1969). Automated interpretation of personality test data. In J. N. Butcher (Ed.), *MMPI: Research developments and clinical applications* (pp. 325–342). New York: McGraw-Hill.

Fowler, R. D. (1987). Developing a computer-based test interpretation system. In J. N. Butcher (Ed.), *Computerized psychological assessment* (pp. 50–63). New York: Basic Books.

Fowler, R. D., & Butcher, J. N. (1987). International applications of computer-based testing and interpretation. *International Journal of Applied Psychology, 36*, 419–429.

Fowler, R. D., & Miller, E. (1969). Computer interpretation of the MMPI: Its use in clinical practice. *Archives of General Psychiatry, 21*, 502–508.

Fox, D. D., Gerson, A., & Lees-Haley, P. R. (1995). Interrelationship of the MMPI–2 validity scales in personal injury claims. *Journal of Clinical Psychology, 51*, 42–47.

Franklin, C. L., Repasky, S. A., Thompson, K. E., Shelton, S. A., & Uddo, M. (2002). Differentiating overreporting and extreme distress: MMPI–2 use with compensation-seeking veterans with PTSD. *Journal of Personality Assessment, 79*, 274–285.

Franklin, C. L., Repasky, S. A., Thompson, K. E., Shelton, S. A., & Uddo, M. (2003). Assessment of response style in combat veterans seeking compensation for posttraumatic stress disorder. *Journal of Traumatic Stress, 16*, 251–255.

Friedman, A. F., Lewak, R., Nichols, D. S., & Webb, J. T. (2001). *Psychological assessment with the MMPI–2* (2nd ed.). Hillsdale, NJ: Lawrence Erlbaum Associates.

Frueh, B. C., Elhai, J. D., Gold, P. B., Monnier, J., Magruder, K. M., Keane, T. M., & Arana, G. W. (2003). Disability compensation seeking among veterans evaluated for posttraumatic stress disorder. *Psychiatric Services, 54*, 84–91.

Frueh, B. C., Smith, D. W., & Barker, S. E. (1996). Compensation seeking status and psychometric assessment of combat veterans seeking treatment for PTSD. *Journal of Traumatic Stress, 9*, 427–439.

Fry, F. D. (1949). A study of the personality traits of college students and of state prison inmates as measured by the MMPI. *Journal of Psychology, 28*, 439–449.

Fulkerson, S. C. (1956). Adaptability screening of flying personnel: Development of a preliminary screening battery. *United States Air Force School of Aviation Medicine Report, 56–84*, 21.

Fulkerson, S. C. (1957). Adaptability screening of flying personnel: Research on the Minnesota Multiphasic Personality Inventory. *United States Air Force School of Aviation Medicine Report, 57–106*, 17.

Fuller, R. K., & Allen, J. P. (2000). Patient to treatment matching. In G. Zerning, A. Saria, M. Kurz, & S. S. O'Malley (Eds.), *Handbook of alcoholism* (pp. 363–368). Boca Raton, FL: CRC Press.

Galea, S., Ahern, J., Resnick, H., Kilpatrick, D., Bucuvalas, M., Gold, J., & Vlahov, D. (2002). Psychological sequelae of the September 11 terrorist attacks in New York City. *New England Journal of Medicine, 346*, 982–987.

Gallagher, J. E., Sweetnam, P. M., Yarnell, J. W. G., Elwood, P. C., & Stansfeld, S. A. (2003). Is Type A behavior really a trigger for coronary heart disease events? *Psychosomatic Medicine, 65*, 339–346.

Gallagher, R. M., Rauh, V., Haugh, L. D., Milhous, R., Callas, P. W., Langelier, R., et al. (1989). Determinants of return-to-work among low back pain patients. *Pain, 39*, 55–67.

Gallagher, R. M., Williams, R. A., Skelly, J., Haugh, L. D., Rauh, V., Milhous, R., & Frymoyer, J. (1995). Workers' compensation and return-to-work in low back pain. *Pain, 61*, 299–307.

Gallagher, R. W., Ben-Porath, Y. S., & Briggs, S. (1997). Inmate views about the purpose of the MMPI–2 at the time of correctional intake. *Criminal Justice and Behavior, 24*, 360–369.

Galton, F. (1885). On the anthropometric laboratory at the late International Health Exhibition. *Journal of the Anthropology Institute, 14*, 205–219.

Gandolfo, R. (1995). MMPI–2 profiles of workers' compensation claimants who present with complaints of harassment. *Journal of Clinical Psychology, 51*(5), 711–715.

Ganellen, R. J. (1994). Attempting to conceal psychological disturbance: MMPI defensive response sets and the Rorschach. *Journal of Personality Assessment, 63*, 423–437.

Gantner, A. B., Graham, J. B., & Archer, R. A. (1992). Usefulness of the MAC scale in differentiating adolescents in normal, psychiatric, and substance abuse settings. *Psychological Assessment, 4*, 133–137.

Garb, H. N. (1998). *Studying the clinician: Judgment research and psychological assessment*. Washington, DC: American Psychological Association.

Garcia, R. E., & Azan-Chaviano, A. A. (1993). *Inventario Multifasico de la Personalidad Minesota—2: Version Hispana* [Minnesota Multiphasic Personality Inventory—2: Spanish version]. Minneapolis: University of Minnesota Press.

Garcia-Preto, N. (1982). Puerto Rican families. In M. McGoldrick, J. K. Pearce, & J. Giordano (Eds.), *Ethnicity and family therapy* (pp. 164–186). New York: Guilford Press.

Garfinkel, P. E., Bagby, R.,Waring, E. M., & Dorian, B. (1997). Boundary violations and personality traits among psychiatrists. *Canadian Journal of Psychiatry, 42*(7), 764–770.

Garrido, M., Gionta, D., Diehl, S., & Boscia, M. (1998, March). *The Megargee MMPI–2 system of inmate classification: A study of its applicability with ethnically diverse inmates*. Paper presented at the Annual Symposium on Recent Developments in the Use of the MMPI–2, Clearwater, FL.

Gass, C. S. (1991a). Emotional variables in neuropsychological test performance. *Journal of Clinical Psychology, 47*, 100–104.

Gass, C. S. (1991b). MMPI–2 interpretation and closed-head injury: A correction factor. *Psychological Assessment, 3*, 27–31.

Gass, C. S. (1992). MMPI–2 interpretation of patients with cerebrovascular disease: A correction factor. *Archives of Clinical Neuropsychology, 7*, 17–27.

Gass, C. S. (1996a). MMPI–2 interpretation and stroke: Cross-validation of a correction factor. *Journal of Clinical Psychology, 52*, 569–572.

Gass, C. S. (1996b). MMPI–2 variables in attention and memory test performance. *Psychological Assessment, 8*, 135–138.

Gass, C. S. (1997, June). *Assessing patients with neurological impairments*. Paper presented at the University of Minnesota MMPI–2 Clinical Workshops and Symposia, Minneapolis, MN.

Gass, C. S. (1999). Assessment of emotional functioning with the MMPI–2. In G. Groth-Marnat (Ed.), *Neuropsychological assessment in clinical practice: A guide to test interpretation and integration* (pp. 457–532). New York: John Wiley & Sons.

Gass, C. S. (2000). Personality evaluation in neuropsychological assessment. In R. D. Vanderploeg (Ed.), *Clinician's guide to neuropsychological assessment* (2nd ed., pp. 155–194). Mahwah, NJ: Lawrence Erlbaum Associates.

Gass, C. S. (2002a). Does test anxiety impede neuropsychological test performance? *Archives of Clinical Neuropsychology, 17*, 860.

Gass, C. S. (2002b). Personality assessment of neurologically impaired patients. In J. N. Butcher (Ed.), *Clinical personality assessment: Practical approaches* (2nd ed., pp. 208–224). New York: Oxford University Press.

Gass, C. S., & Ansley, J. (1994). MMPI correlates of poststroke neurobehavioral deficits. *Archives of Clinical Neuropsychology, 9*, 461–469.

Gass, C. S., Ansley, J., & Boyette, S. (1994). Emotional correlates of fluency test and maze performance. *Journal of Clinical Psychology, 50*, 586–590.

Gass, C. S., & Apple, C. (1997). Cognitive complaints in closed-head injury: Relationship to memory test performance and emotional disturbance. *Journal of Clinical and Experimental Neuropsychology, 19*, 290–299.

Gass, C. S., & Brown, M. C. (1992). Neuropsychological test feedback to patients with brain dysfunction. *Psychological Assessment, 4*, 272–277.

Gass, C. S., & Gonzalez, C. (2003). MMPI–2 short form proposal: CAUTION. *Archives of Clinical Neuropsychology, 18,* 521–527.

Gass, C. S., & Luis, C. A. (2001a). MMPI–2 scale F(p) and symptom feigning: Scale refinement. *Assessment, 8,* 425–429.

Gass, C. S., & Luis, C. A. (2001b). MMPI–2 short form: Psychometric characteristics in a neuropsychological setting. *Assessment, 8,* 213–219.

Gass, C. S., Luis, C. A., Rayls, K., & Mittenberg, W. B. (1999). Psychological status and its influences in acute traumatic brain injury: An MMPI–2 study [Abstract]. *Archives of Clinical Neuropsychology, 14,* 30.

Gass, C. S., & Russell, E. W. (1986). Differential impact of brain damage and depression on memory test performance. *Journal of Consulting & Clinical Psychology, 54,* 261–263.

Gaston, L., Brunet, A., Koszycki, D., & Bradwejn, J. (1996). MMPI profiles of acute and chronic PTSD in a civilian sample. *Journal of Traumatic Stress, 9,* 817–830.

Gatchel, R. J. (2004). Comorbidity of chronic pain and mental health disorders: The biopsychosocial perspective. *American Psychologist, 59*(8), 795–805.

Gatchel, R. J., & Gardea, M. A. (1999). Psychosocial issues: Their importance in predicting disability, response to treatment, and search for compensation. *Neurologic Clinics of North America, 17*(1), 149–166.

Gatchel, R. J., Polatin, P. B., & Kinney, R. K. (1995). Predicting outcome of chronic back pain using clinical predictors. *Health Psychology, 14*(5), 415–420.

Gatchel, R. J., Polatin, P. B., & Mayer, T. G. (1995). The dominant role of psychosocial risk factors in the development of chronic low back pain disability. *Spine, 20*(24), 270–279.

Gatchel, R. J., & Wesiberg, J. N. (Eds.). (2000). *Personality characteristics of clients with pain.* Washington, DC: American Psychological Association.

Gearing, M. I., II. (1981). The new MMPI typology for prisoners: The beginning of a new era in correctional research and (hopefully) practice [Review of *Classifying criminal offenders: A new system based on the MMPI*]. *Journal of Personality Assessment, 45,* 102–107.

Gilberstadt, H., & Duker, J. (1965). *A handbook for clinical and actuarial MMPI interpretation.* Philadelphia: Saunders.

Gilbride, T. V., & Hebert, J. (1981). Psychological adjustment and attitudes toward success and failure. *Journal of Clinical Psychology, 37,* 353–355.

Gillet, I., Simon, M., Guelfi, J. D., Brun-Eberentz, A., Monier, C., Seunevel, F., & Svarna, L. (1996). The MMPI–2 in France. In J. N. Butcher (Ed.), *International adaptation of the MMPI–2* (pp. 395–415). Minneapolis: University of Minnesota Press.

Gilmore, J. D., Lash, S. J., Foster, M. A., & Blosser, S. L. (2001). Adherence to substance abuse treatment: Clinical utility of two MMPI–2 scales. *Journal of Personality Assessment, 77,* 524–540.

Glassmire, D. M., Stolberg, R. A., Greene, R. L., & Bongar, B. (2001). The utility of MMPI–2 suicide items for assessing suicidal potential: Development of a suicidal potential scale. *Assessment, 8*, 281–290.

Glinski, J., Wetzler, S., & Goodman, E. (2001). The psychology of gastric bypass surgery. *Obesity Surgery, 11*, 581–588.

Glover, S., & Lait, M. (2000, January 28). A second rampart officer tells of corruption. *The Los Angeles Times*, p. A–1.

Goldberg, L. R. (1965). Diagnosticians vs. diagnostic signs: The diagnosis of psychosis vs. neurosis from the MMPI. *Psychological Monographs: General & Applied, 79*(9), 29.

Goldberg, L. R. (1970). Man vs. model of man: A rationale, plus some evidence, for a method of improving clinical inferences. *Psychological Bulletin, 73*, 422–432.

Goldberg, L. R. (1972). Man versus mean: The exploitation of group profiles for the construction of diagnostic classification systems. *Journal of Abnormal Psychology, 79*, 121–131.

Goldman, R. S., Robinson, D., Grube, B. S., Hanks, R. A., Putnam, K., Walder, D. J., et al. (2000). General psychiatric symptom measures. In A. J. Rush, H. A. Pincus, & M. B. First (Eds.), *Handbook of psychiatric measures* (pp. 71–92). Washington, DC: American Psychiatric Association.

Goldwater, L., & Duffy, J. (1990). Use of the MMPI to uncover histories of childhood abuse in adult female psychiatric patients. *Journal of Clinical Psychology, 46*, 392–397.

Good, B., & Kleinman, A. (1985). Epilogue: Culture and depression. In A. Kleinman & B. Good (Eds.), *Culture and depression* (pp. 491–506). Berkeley: University of California Press.

Goodwin, R. D., Kroenke, K., Hoven, C. W., & Spitzer, R. L. (2003). Major depression, physical illness, and suicidal ideation in primary care. *Psychosomatic Medicine, 65*(4), 501–505.

Gorsuch, R. L. (1983). *Factor analysis* (2nd ed.). Hillsdale, NJ: Lawrence Erlbaum Associates.

Gottesman, I. I., & Prescott, C. A. (1989). Abuses of the MacAndrew Alcoholism Scale: A critical review. *Clinical Psychology Review, 9*, 223–242.

Gottheil, E., Thornton, C., & Weinstein, S. (2002). Effectiveness of high versus low structure individual counseling for substance abuse. *American Journal on Addiction, 11*, 279–290.

Gough, H. G. (1946). Diagnostic patterns on the Minnesota Multiphasic Personality Inventory. *Journal of Clinical Psychology, 2*, 23–37.

Gough, H. G. (1949). A research note on the MMPI Social I. E. scale. *Journal of Educational Research, 43*, 138–141.

Gough, H. G. (1950). The F minus K dissimulation index for the MMPI. *Journal of Consulting Psychology, 14*, 408–413.

Gough, H. G. (1954). Some common misconceptions about neuroticism. *Journal of Consulting Psychology*, *18*, 287–292.

Gough, H. G., McClosky, H., & Meehl, P. E. (1952). A personality scale for social responsibility. *Journal of Abnormal and Social Psychology*, *47*, 73–80.

Graham, J. R. (1993). *MMPI–2: Assessing personality and psychopathology* (2nd ed.). New York: Oxford University Press.

Graham, J. R. (2000). *MMPI–2: Assessing personality and psychopathology* (3rd ed.). New York: Oxford University Press.

Graham, J. R., Barthlow, D. L., Stein, L. A. R., Ben-Porath, Y. S., & McNulty, J. L. (2002). Assessing general maladjustment with the MMPI–2. *Journal of Personality Assessment*, *78*(2), 334–347.

Graham, J. R., Ben-Porath, Y. S., & McNulty, J. (1999). *MMPI–2 correlates for outpatient community mental health settings*. Minneapolis: University of Minnesota Press.

Graham, J. R., Timbrook, R. E., Ben-Porath, Y. S., & Butcher, J. N. (1991) . Code-type congruence between MMPI and MMPI–2: Separating fact from artifact. *Journal of Personality Assessment*, *57*, 205–215.

Graham, J. R., Watts, D., & Timbrook, R. E. (1991). Detecting fake-good and fake-bad MMPI–2 profiles. *Journal of Personality Assessment*, *57*, 264–277.

Greenblatt, R. L., & Davis, W. E. (1999). Differential diagnosis of PTSD, schizophrenia, and depression with the MMPI–2. *Journal of Clinical Psychology*, *55*(2), 217–223.

Greene, A. F., Coles, C. J., & Johnson, E. H. (1994). Psychopathology and anger in interpersonal violence offenders. *Journal of Clinical Psychology*, *50*, 906–912.

Greene, R. L. (1980). *The MMPI: An interpretive manual*. New York: Grune & Stratton.

Greene, R. L. (1982). Some reflections on "MMPI short forms: A literature review." *Journal of Personality Assessment*, *46*, 486–487.

Greene, R. L. (1987). Ethnicity and MMPI performance: A review. *Journal of Consulting and Clinical Psychology*, *35*(4), 497–512.

Greene, R. L. (1991). *The MMPI–2/MMPI: An interpretive manual*. Boston: Allyn & Bacon.

Greene, R. L. (1994). Relationships among MMPI code type, gender, and setting and the MacAndrew Alcoholism scale. *Assessment*, *1*, 39–46.

Greene, R. L. (2000). *The MMPI–2: An interpretative manual* (2nd ed.). Needham Heights, MA: Allyn & Bacon.

Greene, R. L., & Clopton, J. R. (1999). Minnesota Multiphasic Personality Inventory—2 (MMPI–2). In M. Maruish (Ed.), *The use of psychological testing for treatment planning and outcomes assessment* (2nd ed., pp. 115–151). Mahwah, NJ: Lawrence Erlbaum Associates.

Greene, R. L., & Clopton, J. R. (in press). MMPI–2. In M. Maruish (Ed.), *The use of psychological testing for treatment planning and outcome assessment* (3rd ed.). Hillsdale, NJ: Lawrence Erlbaum Associates.

Greene, R. L., & Garvin, R. D. (1988). Substance abuse/dependence. In R. L. Greene (Ed.), *The MMPI: Use in specific populations* (pp. 159–197). Orlando, FL: Grune & Stratton.

Greene, R. L., Robin, R. W., Albaugh, B., Caldwell, A., & Goldman, D. (2003). Use of the MMPI–2 in American Indians: II. Empirical correlates. *Psychological Assessment, 15*(3), 360–369.

Greene, R. L., Weed, N. C., Butcher, J. N., Arredondo, R., & Davis, H. G. (1992). A cross-validation of MMPI–2 substance abuse scales. *Journal of Personality Assessment, 58*, 405–410.

Greiffenstein, M. F., & Baker, W. J. (2001). Comparison of premorbid and postinjury MMPI–2 profiles in late postconcussion claimants. *Clinical Neuropsychologist, 15*, 162–170.

Greiffenstein, M. F., Baker, W. J., Gola, T., Donders, J., & Miller, L. (2002). The Fake Bad Scale in atypical and severe closed head injury litigants. *Journal of Clinical Psychology, 58*, 1591–1600.

Greiffenstein, M. F., Baker, W. J., & Johnson-Greene, D. (2002). Actual versus self-reported scholastic achievement of litigating postconcussion and severe closed head injury claimants. *Psychological Assessment, 14*, 202–208.

Greiffenstein, M. F., Gola, T., & Baker, W. J. (1995). MMPI–2 validity scales versus domain specific measures in detection of factitious traumatic brain injury. *The Clinical Neuropsychologist, 9*, 230–240.

Gross, K., Keyes, M. D., & Greene, R. L. (2000). Assessing depression with the MMPI and MMPI–2. *Journal of Personality Assessment, 75*(3), 464–477.

Groth-Marnat, G. (2000). Visions of clinical assessment: Then, now, and a brief history of the future. *Journal of Clinical Psychology, 56*(3), 349–365.

Groth-Marnat, G. (2003). *Handbook of psychological assessment* (4th ed.). New York: John Wiley & Sons.

Grove, W. M., & Meehl, P. E. (1996). Comparative efficiency of information (subjective, impressionistic) and formal (mechanical, algorithmic) prediction procedures: The clinical–statistical controversy. *Psychology, Public Policy, and Law, 2*, 293–323.

Grove, W. M., Zald, D. H., Lebow, B. S., Snitz, B. E., & Nelson, C. (2000). Clinical versus mechanical prediction: A meta-analysis. *Psychological Assessment, 12*(1), 19–30.

Gucker, D., & McNulty, J. (2004, May). *The MMPI–2, defensiveness, and an analytic strategy*. Paper presented at the 39th Annual Symposium on Recent Developments in the Use of the MMPI–2, Minneapolis, MN.

Guetrer, J. R. (1994, May). *Assessing interpersonal dominance and warmth with the MMPI–2*. Paper presented at the 29th Annual Symposium on Recent Developments in the Use of the MMPI–2/MMPI–A, Workshop and Symposia, Minneapolis, MN.

Guthrie, G. M. (1949). *A study of the personality characteristics associated with the disorders encountered by an internist*. Unpublished doctoral dissertation, University of Minnesota.

Guthrie, P. C., & Mobley, B. D. (1994). A comparison of the differential diagnostic efficiency of three personality disorder inventories. *Journal of Clinical Psychology, 50,* 656–665.

Halcón, L. L., Robertson, C. L., Savik, K., Johnson, D. R., Spring, M. A., Butcher, J. N., et al. (2004). Trauma and coping in Somali and Oromo refugee youth. *Journal of Adolescent Health, 35,* 17–25.

Hall, G. C. N., Bansal, A., & Lopez, I. R. (1999). Ethnicity and psychopathology: A meta-analytic review of 31 years of comparative MMPI/MMPI–2 research. *Psychological Assessment, 11,* 186–197.

Han, K. (1996). The Korean MMPI–2. In J. N. Butcher (Ed.), *International adaptation of the MMPI–2* (pp. 88–136). Minneapolis: University of Minnesota Press.

Han, K., Weed, N. C., Calhoun, R. F., & Butcher, J. N. (1995). Psychometric characteristics of the MMPI–2 Cook–Medley Hostility scale. *Journal of Personality Assessment, 65,* 567–585.

Handel, R. W., & Ben-Porath, Y. S. (2000). Multicultural assessment with the MMPI–2: Issues for research and practice. In R. H. Dana (Ed.), *Handbook of cross-cultural and multicultural personality assessment.* Mahwah, NJ: Lawrence Erlbaum Associates.

Handel, R. W., Ben-Porath, Y. S., & Watt, M. (1999). Computerized adaptive assessment with the MMPI–2 in a clinical setting. *Psychological Assessment, 11,* 369–380.

Handler, L. (1995). The clinical use of figure drawings. In C. Newmark (Ed.), *Major psychological assessment instruments* (pp. 206–293). Boston: Allyn & Bacon.

Hanley, C. (1957). Deriving a measure of test-taking defensiveness. *Journal of Consulting Psychology, 21,* 391–397.

Hansen, F. R., Biering-Sorensen, F., & Schroll, M. (1995). Minnesota Multiphasic Personality Inventory profiles in persons with or without low back pain. *Spine, 20*(24), 2716–2720.

Hanson, W. E., Claiborn, C. D., & Kerr, B. (1997). Differential effects of two test-interpretation styles in counseling: A field study. *Journal of Counseling Psychology, 44,* 400–405.

Hanvik, L. J. (1951). MMPI profiles in patients with low-back pain. *Journal of Consulting Psychology, 15,* 350–353.

Hare, R. D. (1991). *Manual for the Hare Psychopathy Checklist—Revised.* Toronto, Ontario, Canada: Multi-Health Systems.

Hargrave, G. E., Hiatt, D., & Gaffney, T. W. (1986). A comparison of MMPI and CPI test profiles for traffic officers and deputy sheriffs. *Journal of Police Science & Administration, 14,* 250–258.

Harkness, A. R. (1990). Phenotypic dimensions of the personality disorders (Doctoral dissertation, University of Minnesota, 1989). *Dissertation Abstracts International, 50,* 5880b (12b).

Harkness, A. R. (1992). Fundamental topics in the personality disorders: Candidate trait dimensions from lower regions of the hierarchy. *Psychological Assessment, 4*, 251–259.

Harkness, A. R. (2002). Theory and measurement of personality traits. In J. N. Butcher (Ed.), *Clinical personality assessment: Practical approaches* (2nd ed., pp. 24–39). New York: Oxford University Press.

Harkness, A. R., & Lilienfeld, S. O. (1997). Individual differences science for treatment planning: Personality traits. *Psychological Assessment, 9*, 349–360.

Harkness, A. R., & McNulty, J. L. (1994). The Personality Psychopathology Five (PSY–5): Issue from the pages of a diagnostic manual instead of a dictionary. In S. Strack & M. Lorr (Eds.), *Differentiating normal and abnormal personality* (pp. 291–315). New York: Springer.

Harkness, A. R., McNulty, J. L., & Ben-Porath, Y. S. (1995). The Personality Psychopathology Five (PSY–5): Constructs and MMPI–2 scales. *Psychological Assessment, 7*, 104–114.

Harkness, A. R., McNulty, J. L., Ben-Porath, Y. S., & Graham, J. R. (2002). *MMPI–2 Personality Psychopathology Five (PSY–5) scales: Gaining an overview for case conceptualization and treatment planning*. Minneapolis: University of Minnesota Press.

Harkness, A. R., McNulty, J. L., Ben-Porath, Y. S., & Graham, J. R. (1999). *MMPI–2 Personality Psychopathology 5 (PSY–5) scales: MMPI–2 test reports*. Minneapolis: University of Minnesota Press.

Harkness, A. R., McNulty, J. L., Finger, M. S., Arbisi, P. A., & Ben-Porath, Y. S. (1999, April). *The pleiometric nature of psychoticism items, or why the Big-5 does not measure psychoticism*. Paper presented at the 34th Annual MMPI–2 Symposium, Huntington Beach, CA.

Harkness, A. R., Royer, M. J., & Gill, T. P. (1996, June). *Organizing MMPI–2 feedback with psychological constructs: PSY–5 scales and self-adaption*. Paper presented at the 31st Annual Symposium on Recent Developments in the Use of the MMPI–2/MMPI–A, Workshop and Symposia, Minneapolis, MN.

Harkness, A. R., Spiro, A. III, Butcher, J. N., & Ben-Porath, Y. S. (1995, August). *Personality Psychopathology Five (PSY–5) in the Boston VA Normative Aging Study*. Paper presented at the 103rd Annual Convention of the American Psychological Association, New York, NY.

Harrell, T. W., & Harrell, M. S. (1973). The personality of MBAs who reach general management early. *Personnel Psychology, 26*, 127–134.

Harris, G. T., Rice, M. E., & Quinsey, V. L. (1993). Violent recidivism of mentally disordered offenders: The development of a statistical prediction instrument. *Criminal Justice and Behavior, 20*, 315–335.

Harris, R. E., & Lingoes, J. C. (1955). *Subscales for the MMPI: An aid to profile interpretation*. Unpublished manuscript, Department of Psychiatry, University of California at San Francisco.

Harris, R. E., & Lingoes, J. C. (1968). *Subscales for the MMPI: An aid to profile interpretation* (Revised). Unpublished manuscript, Department of Psychiatry, University of California at San Francisco.

Harrison, P. A., & Hoffmann, N. G. (1989). *SUDDS: Substance Use Disorders Diagnostic Schedule manual*. St. Paul, MN: New Standards.

Harrison, P. M., & Beck, A. J. (2003, July). *Prisoners in 2002* (Bureau of Justice Statistics Bulletin, NCJ 200248). Washington, DC: U.S. Department of Justice, Bureau of Justice Statistics.

Harrison, P. M., & Karberg, J. C. (2003, April). *Prison and jail inmates at midyear 2002* (Bureau of Justice Statistics Bulletin, NCJ 198877). Washington, DC: U.S. Department of Justice, Bureau of Justice Statistics.

Hartshorne, E. (1956). A comparison of certain aspects of student leadership and nonleadership: Significant differences on four psychometric tests. *Journal of Educational Research, 49*, 515–522.

Hathaway, S. R. (2000). Scales 5 (Masculinity–Femininity), 6 (Paranoia), and 8 (Schizophrenia). In J. N. Butcher (Ed.), *Basic sources on the MMPI–2* (pp. 49–56). Minneapolis: University of Minnesota Press. (Original work published 1956)

Hathaway, S. R., & McKinley, J. C. (1940). A multiphasic personality schedule (Minnesota): I. Construction of the schedule. *Journal of Psychology, 10*, 249–254.

Hathaway, S. R., & McKinley, J. C. (1943). *The Minnesota Multiphasic Personality Schedule*. Minneapolis: University of Minnesota Press.

Hathaway, S. R., & Meehl, P. E. (1951a). *An atlas for the clinical use of the MMPI*. Minneapolis: University of Minnesota Press.

Hathaway, S. R., & Meehl, P. E. (1951b). The MMPI. In *Military Clinical Psychology*, Department of the Army, Technical Manual, TM 8-242; Department of the Air Force Manual, AFM 160-45.

Hathaway, S. R., & Monachesi, E. D. (1963). *Adolescent personality and behavior*. Minneapolis: University of Minnesota Press.

Heaton, R. K., & Crowley, T. J. (1981). Effects of psychiatric disorders and their somatic treatments on neuropsychological test results. In S. B. Filskov & T. J. Boll (Eds.), *Handbook of clinical neuropsychology* (pp. 481–525). New York: John Wiley & Sons.

Heaton, R. K., Smith, H. H., Lehman, R. A., & Vogt, A. J. (1978). Prospects for feigning believable deficits on neuropsychological testing. *Journal of Consulting and Clinical Psychology, 46*, 892–900.

Heilbrun, A. B. (1984). Cognitive defenses and life stress: An information-processing analysis. *Psychological Reports, 54*, 3–17.

Heilbrun, K., & Heilbrun, A. (1995). Risk assessment with MMPI–2 in forensic evaluations. In Y. S. Ben-Porath, J. R. Graham, G. C. N. Hall, R. D. Hirschman, & M. S. Zaragoza (Eds.), *Forensic applications of MMPI–2* (pp. 160–178). Thousand Oaks, CA: Sage.

Heilman, K. M., Bowers, D., & Valenstein, E. (1993). Emotional disorders associated with neurological diseases. In K. M. Heilman & E. Valenstein (Eds.), *Clinical neuropsychology* (3rd ed., pp. 461–497). New York: Oxford University Press.

Heinze, M. C., & Purisch, A. D. (2001). Beneath the mask: Use of psychological tests to detect and subtype malingering in criminal defendants. *Journal of Forensic Psychology Practice, 1*, 23–52.

Helms, J. E. (1992). Why is there no study of cultural equivalence in standardized cognitive ability testing? *American Psychologist, 47*, 1083–1101.

Henrichs, T. F. (1981). Using the MMPI in medical consultations. In J. N. Butcher, W. G. Dahlstrom, M. Gynther, & W. Schofield (Eds.), *Clinical notes on the MMPI* (Vol. 6). Minneapolis, MN: National Computer Systems.

Herman, J. (1992). Complex PTSD. *Journal of Traumatic Stress, 5*, 377–391.

Hernandez, J. (1994). *MMPI–2 performance as a function of acculturation*. Unpublished master's thesis, Sam Houston State University, Huntsville, TX.

Hersch, P. D., & Alexander, R. W. (1990). MMPI profile patterns of emotional disability claimants. *Journal of Clinical Psychology, 46*(6), 795–799.

Hiatt, D., & Hargrave, G. E. (1988a). MMPI profiles of problem peace officers. *Journal of Personality Assessment, 52*, 722–731.

Hiatt, D., & Hargrave, G. E. (1988b). Predicting job performance problems with psychological screening. *Journal of Police Science & Administration, 16*, 122–135.

Hilakivi, I., Alihanka, J., Airikkala, P., & Laitinen, L. (1992). Alertness and sleep in young men during military service. *Acta Neurologica Scandinavica, 86*, 616–621.

Hills, H. A. (1995). Diagnosing personality disorders: An examination of the MMPI–2 and MCMI–II. *Journal of Personality Assessment, 65*, 21–34.

Hjemboe, S., & Butcher, J. N. (1991). Couples in marital distress: A study of demographic and personality factors as measured by the MMPI–2. *Journal of Personality Assessment, 57*, 216–237.

Hjemboe, S., Butcher, J. N., & Almagor, M. (1992). Empirical assessment of marital distress: The Marital Distress scale for the MMPI–2. In C. D. Spielberger & J. N. Butcher (Eds.), *Advances in personality assessment* (Vol. 9, pp. 141–152). Hillsdale, NJ: Lawrence Erlbaum Associates.

Hoffman, R. G., Scott, J. G., Emick, M. A., & Adams, R. L. (1999). The MMPI–2 and closed-head injury: Effects of litigation and head injury severity. *Journal of Forensic Neuropsychology, 1*, 3–13.

Hoffmann, H. E. (1970). Use of avoidance and vigilance by repressors and sensitizers. *Journal of Consulting and Clinical Psychology, 34*, 91–96.

Holden, R. R., & Jackson, D. N. (1979). Item subtlety and face validity in personality assessment. *Journal of Consulting and Clinical Psychology, 47*, 459–468.

Holroyd, R. G. (1964). Prediction of defensive paranoid schizophrenics using the MMPI. *Dissertation Abstracts, 25*, 2048–2049.

Hostetler, K., Ben-Porath, Y., Butcher, J. N., & Graham, J. R. (1989). *New subscales for the MMPI–2 Social Introversion (Si) scale*. Paper presented at the Society of Personality Assessment meetings, New York, NY.

Hough, L. M. (1998). Effects of intentional distortion in personality measurement and evaluation of suggested palliatives. *Human Performance, 11*, 209–244.

Hough, L. M., Eaton, N. K., Dunnette, M. D., Kamp, J. D., & McCloy, R. A. (1990). Criterion-related validities of personality constructs and the effect of response distortion on those validities. *Journal of Applied Psychology, 75,* 581–595.

Hough, L. M., & Schneider, R. J. (1996). Personality traits, taxonomies, and applications in organizations. In K. R. Murphy (Ed.), *Individual differences and behavior in organizations* (pp. 31–88). San Francisco: Jossey-Bass.

Houts, A. (2002). Discovery, invention, and the expansion of the modern *Diagnostic and Statistical Manual of Mental Disorders.* In L. Beutler & M. Malik (Eds.), *Rethinking the* DSM: *A psychological perspective* (pp. 17–65). Washington DC: American Psychological Association.

Hui, C. H., & Triandis, H. C. (1985). Measurement in cross-cultural psychology: A review and comparison of strategies. *Journal of Cross-Cultural Psychology, 16,* 131–152.

Hui, C. H., & Triandis, H. C. (1989). Effects of culture and response format on extreme response style. *Journal of Cross-Cultural Psychology, 20,* 296–309.

Hulin, C. L. (1987). A psychometric theory of evaluations of item and scale translations: Fidelity across languages. *Journal of Cross-Cultural Psychology, 18*(2), 115–142.

Hulin, C. L., Drasgow, F., & Parsons, C. K. (1983). *Item response theory: Applications to psychological measurement.* Homewood, IL: Dow Jones Irwin.

Hurtado, A. (1995). Variations, combinations, and evolutions: Latino families in the United States. In R. E. Zambrana (Ed.), *Understanding Latino families: Scholarship, policy, and practice* (pp. 40–61). Thousand Oaks, CA: Sage.

Ide, N., & Paez, A. (2000). Complex PTSD: A review of recent issues. *International Journal of Emergency Mental Health, 2,* 43–51.

Imboden, J. B., Canter, A., & Cluff, L. E. (1961). Convalescence from influenza: A study of the psychological and clinical determinants. *Archives of Internal Medicine, 108,* 115–121.

Inman Hanlon, T., Esther, J. K., Robertson, W. T., Hall, C. D., & Robertson, K. R. (2002). The Minnesota Multiphasic Personality Inventory—2 across the human immunodeficiency virus spectrum. *Assessment,* 9(1), 24–30.

Irvine, S. H. (1979). The place of factor analysis in cross-cultural methodology and its contribution to cognitive theory. In L. H. Eckensberger, W. L. Lonner, & Y. H. Poortinga (Eds.), *Cross-cultural contributions to psychology: Vol. 2* (pp. 300–341). Amsterdam: Swets & Zeitlinger.

Isenhart, C. E., & Silversmith, D. J. (1997). MMPI–2 response styles: Generalization to alcoholism assessment. In G. A. Marlatt & G. R. VandenBos (Eds.), *Addictive behaviors* (pp. 340–354). Washington, DC: American Psychological Association.

Iverson, G. L., & Barton, E. (1999). Interscorer reliability of the MMPI–2: Should TRIN and VRIN be computer scored? *Journal of Clinical Psychology,* 55(1), 65–69.

Iverson, G. L., Franzen, M. D., & Hammond, J. A. (1995). Examination of inmates' ability to malinger on MMPI–2. *Psychological Assessment, 4,* 111–117.

Jackson, J. L., Houston, J. S., Hanling, S. R., Terhaar, K. A., & Yun, J. S. (2001). Clinical predictors of mental disorders among medical outpatients. *Archives of Internal Medicine, 161*(6), 875–879.

Jaranson, J., Butcher, J. N., Halcón, L., Johnson, D. R., Robertson, C., Savik, K., et al. (2004). Somali and Oromo refugees: Correlates of torture and trauma. *American Journal of Public Health,* 94, 591–597.

Jemelka, R. P., Wiegand, G. A., Walker, E. A., & Trupin, E. W. (1992). Computerized offender assessment: Validation study. *Psychological Assessment, 4,* 138–144.

Jensen, A. R. (1957). Authoritarian attitudes and personality maladjustment. *Journal of Abnormal & Social Psychology, 54,* 303–311.

Jiang, W., Alexander, J., Christopher, E., Kuchibhatla, M., Gaulden, L. H., Cuffe, M. S., et al. (2001). Relationship of depression to increased risk of mortality and rehospitalization in patients with congestive heart failure. *Archives of Internal Medicine, 161*(15), 1849–1856.

Joreskog, K. G. (1971). Simultaneous factor analysis in several populations. *Psychometrika, 36,* 409–426.

Kadden, R. M., Longabaugh, R., & Wirtz, P. W. (2003). The matching hypothesis: Rationale and predictions. In T. Babor & F. K. DelBoca (Eds.), *Treatment matching in alcoholism* (pp. 81–102). New York: Cambridge University Press.

Kamphuis, J., & Finn, S. E. (2002). Incorporating base rate information in daily clinical decision making. In J. N. Butcher (Ed.), *Clinical personality assessment: Practical approaches* (2nd ed., pp. 257–268). New York: Oxford University Press.

Kamphuis, J. H., & Nabarro, G. (1999, July). *Time efficient therapeutic assessment in a day-treatment clinic for affective disorders in the Netherlands.* Paper presented at the XVI Congress of Rorschach and Projective Methods, Amsterdam, the Netherlands, as part of a symposium, "Therapeutic Assessment around the World," S. E. Finn, chair. (Available from the first author)

Kasapis, C., Amador, X. F., Yale, S. A., Strauss, D., & Gorman, J. M. (1996). Poor insight in schizophrenia: Neuropsychological and defensive aspects. *Schizophrenia Research, 20,* 123.

Kasl, S. V. (1970). Blood pressure changes in men undergoing job loss: A preliminary report. *Psychosomatic Medicine, 32,* 19–38.

Katon, W. J., Lin, E., Russo, J., & Unutzer, J. (2003). Increased medical costs of a population-based sample of depressed elderly patients. *Archives of General Psychiatry,* 60(9), 897–903.

Kawachi, I., Sparrow, D., Kubzansky, L. D., Laura, D., Spiro, A., Vokonas, P., et al. (1998). Prospective study of a self-report Type A scale and risk of coronary heart disease: Test of the MMPI–2 Type A scale. *Circulation,* 98(5), 405–412.

Kawachi, I., Sparrow, D., Spiro, A., Vokonas, P., Pantel, S., & Weiss, S. T. (1996). Mycoardial ischemia/coronary artery vasoconstriction/thrombosis/myocardial infarction: A prospective study of anger and coronary heart disease: The normative aging study. *Circulation,* 94(9), 2090–2095.

Keane, T. M., Caddell, J. M., & Taylor, K. L. (1988). Mississippi scale for combat-related PTSD validity. *Journal of Consulting and Clinical Psychology, 36,* 85–90.

Keane, T. M., & Kaloupek, D. G. (1997). Comorbid psychiatric disorders in PTSD: Implications for research. In R. Yehuda & A. MacFarlane (Eds.), *Psychobiology of post-traumatic stress disorder.* New York: Annals of the New York Academy of Science.

Keane, T. M., Malloy, P. F., & Fairbank, J. A. (1984). Empirical development of an MMPI subscale for the assessment of post-traumatic stress disorder. *Journal of Consulting and Clinical Psychology, 52,* 888–891.

Keane, T. M., Weathers, F. W., & Foa, E. B. (2000). Diagnosis and assessment. In E. B. Foa, T. M. Keane, & M. J. Friedman (Eds.), *Effective treatments for PTSD* (pp. 18–38). New York: Guilford Press.

Keane, T. M., Weathers, F. W., & Kaloupek, D. G. (1992). Psychological assessment of post-traumatic stress disorder. *PRQ, 3,* 1–3.

Keane, T. M., Wolfe, J., & Taylor, K. L. (1987). Post-traumatic stress disorder: Evidence for diagnostic validity. *Journal of Clinical Psychology, 43,* 32–43.

Keller, L. S., & Butcher, J. N. (1991). *Assessment of chronic pain patients with the MMPI–2* (Vol. 2). Minneapolis: University of Minnesota Press.

Kelly, W. L. (1974). Psychological prediction of leadership in nursing. *Nursing Research, 23,* 38–42.

Kendall, P. C., Edinger, J., & Eberly, C. (1978). Taylor's MMPI correction for spinal cord injury: Empirical endorsement. *Journal of Consulting and Clinical Psychology, 46,* 370–371.

Kennedy, W. A., Nielson, W., Lindner, R., Turner, J., & Moon, H. (1960). Psychological measurements of future scientists. *Psychological Reports, 7,* 515–517.

Kent, M. P., Busby, K., Johnston, M., Wood, J., & Docherty, C. (2000). Predictors of outcome in a short-term psychiatric day hospital program. *General Hospital Psychiatry, 22,* 184–194.

Kerns, R. D., Turk, D. C., & Rudy, T. E. (1985). The West Haven–Yale Multidimensional Pain Inventory (WHYMPI). *Pain, 23,* 345–356.

Kessler, R. C., Sonnega, A., Bromet, E., Hughes, M., & Nelson, C. B. (1995). Post-traumatic stress disorder in the National Comorbidity Survey. *Archives of General Psychiatry, 52,* 1048–1060.

Kiely, G. L., Zara, A. R., & Weiss, D. J. (1983, January). *Alternate forms reliability and concurrent validity of adaptive and convergent tests with military recruits.* Draft report submitted to Navy Personnel Research and Development Center, San Diego, CA.

Kinder, B. N., Curtiss, G., & Kalichman, S. (1986). Anxiety and anger as predictors of MMPI elevations in chronic pain patients. *Journal of Personality Assessment, 50,* 651–661.

Kirz, J. L., Drescher, K. D., Klein, J. L., Gusman, F. D., & Schwartz, M. F. (2001). MMPI–2 assessment of differential post-traumatic stress disorder patterns in combat veterans and sexual assault victims. *Journal of Interpersonal Violence, 16*, 619–639.

Kleinke, C. L., & Spangler, A. S. (1988). Predicting treatment outcome of chronic back pain patients in a multidisciplinary pain clinic: Methodological issues and treatment implications. *Pain, 33*, 41–48.

Kleinman, A. (1986). *Social origins of distress and disease: Depression, neuroasthenia, and pain in modern China*. New Haven, CT: Yale University Press.

Kleinmuntz, B. (1964). MMPI decision rules for the identification of college maladjustment: A digital computer approach. *Psychological Monographs: General & Applied, 77*(4), 1–22.

Kleinmuntz, B. (1975). The computer as clinician. *American Psychologist, 30*, 379–387.

Klonsky, E. D., & Bertelson, A. D. (2000). MMPI–2 clinical scale difference between dysthymia and major depression. *Assessment, 7*, 143–149.

Knapen, S. (2002). *Typerende antwoordpatronen van borderline patiânten op de MMPI–2* [Typical response patterns of borderline patients on the MMPI–2]. Brussels, Belgium: Vrije Universiteit, Afdeling Klinische Psychologie.

Knisely, J. S., Barker, S. B., Ingersoll, K. S., & Dawson, K. S. (2000). Psychopathology in substance-abusing women reporting childhood sexual abuse. *Journal of Addictive Diseases, 19*(1), 31–44.

Kokkevi, A. (1996). The Greek MMPI–2: A progress note. In J. N. Butcher (Ed.), *International adaptation of the MMPI–2* (pp. 442–448). Minneapolis: University of Minnesota Press.

Korestzky, M. B., & Peck, A. H. (1990). Validation and cross-validation of the PTSD subscale for the MMPI with civilian trauma victims. *Journal of Clinical Psychology, 46*(3), 296–299.

Koson, D., Kitchen, C., Kochen, M., & Stodolsky, S. (1970). Psychological testing by computer: Effect on response bias. *Educational and Psychological Measurement, 30*, 803–810.

Krinsley, K. (1996). Psychometric review of the Evaluation of Lifetime Stressors (ELS) questionnaire and interview. In B. H. Stamm (Ed.), *Measurement of stress, trauma, and adaptation*. Lutherville, MD: Sidran Press.

Kubzansky, L. D., Sparrow, D., Vokonas, P., & Kawachi, I. (2001). Is the glass half empty or half full? A prospective study of optimism and coronary heart disease in the normative aging study. *Psychosomatic Medicine, 63*, 910–916.

Kuhn, T. S. (1970). *Structure of scientific revolutions* (2nd ed., enlarged). Chicago: University of Chicago Press.

Kulka, R. A., & Schlenger, W. E. (1986). *The National Vietnam Veterans Readjustment Study: Report of a validation pre-test to the Office of Technology Assessment*. (Available from the authors at the Division of Social Policy Research, Box 12191, Research Triangle Institute, Research Triangle Park, NC 22709)

Kulka, R. A., Schlenger, W. E., Fairbank, J. A., Hough, R. L., Jordan, B. K., Marmar, C. R., & Weiss, D. S. (1990). *Trauma and the Vietnam War generation*. New York: Brunner/Mazel.

Kulka, R. A., Schlenger, W. E., Fairbank, J. A., Hough, R. L., Jordan, B. K., Marmar, C. R., & Weiss, D. S. (1991). Assessment of post-traumatic stress disorder in the community: Prospects and pitfalls from recent studies of Vietnam veterans. *Psychological Assessment, 3*, 547–560.

Lachar, D. (1974). *The MMPI: Clinical assessment and automated interpretation*. Los Angeles: Western Psychological Services.

Lachar, D. (1979). How much of a good thing is enough?: A review of T. A. Fashingbauer and C. A. Newmark, Short forms of the MMPI. *Contemporary Psychology, 24*, 116–117.

Ladd, J. S. (1998). The F(P) Infrequency–Psychopathology scale with chemically dependent inpatients. *Journal of Clinical Psychology, 54*, 665–671.

Lally, S. J. (2003). What tests are acceptable for use in forensic evaluations? A survey of experts. *Professional Psychology: Research and Practice, 34*(5), 491–498.

Lamb, D. G., Berry, D. T. R., Wetter, M. W., & Baer, R. A. (1994). Effects of two types of information on malingering of closed head injury on the MMPI–2: An analog investigation. *Psychological Assessment*, 6, 8–13.

Lambert, M. E., Andrews, R. H., Rylee, K., & Skinner, J. (1987). Equivalence of computerized and traditional MMPI administration with substance abusers. *Computers in Human Behavior, 3*, 139–143.

Lambert, M. J., & Lambert, J. M. (1999). Use of psychological tests for assessing treatment outcome. In M. Maruish (Ed.), *The use of psychological testing for treatment planning and outcomes assessment* (2nd ed., pp. 115–151). Mahwah, NJ: Lawrence Erlbaum Associates.

Lance, B. R., & Krishnamurthy, R. (2003, March). *A comparison of three modes of MMPI–2 test feedback*. Paper presented at the Midwinter Meeting of the Society for Personality Assessment, San Francisco, CA. (Available from , Florida Tech, School of Psychology, 150 West University Blvd., Melbourne, FL 32901)

Lanyon, R. I., & Almer, E. R. (2002). Characteristics of compensable disability patients who choose to litigate. *Journal of American Academy of Psychaitry Law, 30*(3), 400–404.

Lanyon, R. I., & Lutz, R. W. (1984). MMPI discrimination of defensive and nondefensive felony sex offenders. *Journal of Consulting and Clinical Psychology, 52*, 841–843.

Larrabee, G. J. (1998). Somatic malingering on the MMPI and MMPI–2 in personal injury litigants. *Clinical Neuropsychologist, 12*(2), 179–188.

Larrabee, G. J. (2000). Forensic neuropsychological assessment. In R. D. Vanderploeg (Ed.), *Clinician's guide to neuropsychological assessment* (2nd ed., pp. 301–336). Mahwah, NJ: Lawrence Erlbaum Associates.

Larrabee, G. J. (2003a). Detection of malingering using atypical performance patterns on standard neuropsychological tests. *The Clinical Neuropsychologist, 17*, 410–425.

Larrabee, G. J. (2003b). Detection of symptom exaggeration with the MMPI–2 in litigants with malingered neurocognitive dysfunction. *The Clinical Neuropsychologist, 17*, 54–68.

Larrabee, G. J. (in press). Detection of symptom exaggeration with the MMPI–2 in litigants with malingered neurocognitive deficit. *Clinical Neuropsychologist.*

Lauer, J. B., Wampler, R., & Lantz, J. B. (1996). MMPI profiles of female candidates for obesity surgery: A cluster analytic approach. *Obesity Surgery*, 6, 28–37.

Lazarus, A. A. (1981). *The practice of multimodal therapy*. New York: McGraw-Hill.

Lazarus, A. A. (1989). *The practice of multimodal therapy: Systematic, comprehensive, and effective psychotherapy*. Baltimore: Johns Hopkins University Press.

Leary, T. (1956). *Multilevel measurement of interpersonal behavior*. Berkeley, CA: Psychological Consultation Service.

Leary, T. (1957). *Interpersonal diagnosis of personality: A functional theory and methodology for personality evaluation*. New York: Ronald Press.

Lees-Haley, P. R. (1991). Ego strength denial on the MMPI–2 as a clue to simulation of personal injury in vocational neuropsychological and emotional distress evaluations. *Perceptual and Motor Skills, 72*, 815–819.

Lees-Haley, P. R. (1992). Efficacy of MMPI–2 validity scale and MCMI–II modifier scales for detecting spurious PTSD claims: *F*, *F* – *K*, Fake-Bad Scale, Ego Strength, Subtle–Obvious subscales, DIS, and DEB. *Journal of Clinical Psychology, 48*(5), 681–689.

Lees-Haley, P. R. (1997). MMPI–2 base rates for 492 personal injury plaintiffs: Implications and challenges for forensic assessment. *Journal of Clinical Psychology, 53*, 745–755.

Lees-Haley, P. R., English, L. T., & Glenn, W. J. (1991). A fake-bad scale on the MMPI–2 for personal injury claimants. *Psychological Reports, 68*, 203–210.

Lees-Haley, P. R., Smith, H. H., Williams, C. W., & Dunn, J. T. (1996). Forensic neuropsychological test usage: An empirical survey. *Archives of Clinical Neuropsychology, 11*, 45–52.

Leiker, M., & Hailey, B. (1988). A link between hostility and disease: Poor health habits? *Behavioral Medicine, 14*, 129–133.

LePage, J. P., & Mogge, N. L. (2001). Validity rates of the MMPI–2 and PAI in a rural inpatient psychiatric facility. *Assessment, 8*, 67–74.

Lerner, F. (1996). *PILOTS database: User's guide* (2nd ed.). Veterans Administration Medical Center, White River Junction, VT: National Center for Post-Traumatic Stress Disorder.

Lessenger, L. H. (1997). Acculturation and MMPI–2 scale scores of Mexican American substance abuse patients. *Psychological Reports, 80*, 1181–1182.

Levenson, H., Glenn, N., & Hirschfeld, M. L. (1988). Duration of chronic pain and the Minnesota Multiphasic Personality Inventory: Profiles of industrially injured workers. *Journal of Occupation Medicine, 30*(10), 809–812.

Levenson, M. R., Aldwin, C. M., Butcher, J. N., De Labry, L., Workman-Daniels, K., & Bossé, R. (1990). The MAC scale in a normal population: The meaning of "false positives." *Journal of Studies on Alcohol, 51*, 457–462.

Levine, E. S., & Padilla, A. M. (1980). *Crossing cultures in psychotherapy: Pluralistic counseling for the Hispanic*. Belmont, CA: Wadsworth.

Levinson, R. (1988). Developments in the classification process: Quay's AIMS approach. *Criminal Justice and Behavior, 15*, 24–38.

Levitt, E. E., & Gotts, E. E. (1995). *The clinical application of MMPI special scales* (2nd ed.). Hillsdale, NJ: Lawrence Erlbaum Associates.

Lewak, R. W., Marks, P. A., & Nelson, G. E. (1990). *Therapist guide to the MMPI and MMPI–2: Providing feedback and treatment*. Muncie, IN: Accelerated Development.

Lewis, J. L. Simcox, A. M., & Berry, D. T. R. (2002). Screening for feigned psychiatric symptoms in a forensic sample by using the MMPI–2 and the Structured Inventory of Malingered Symptomatology. *Psychological Assessment, 14*, 170–176.

Leys, R. (2000). *Trauma: A genealogy*. Chicago: University of Chicago Press.

Libet, J. M., & Lewinsohn, P. M. (1973). Concept of social skill with special reference to the behavior of depressed persons. *Journal of Consulting and Clinical Psychology, 40*, 304–312.

Lilienfeld, S. O. (1999). The relation of the MMPI–2 Pd Harris–Lingoes subscales to psychopathy, psychopathy facets, and antisocial behavior: Implications for clinical practice. *Journal of Clinical Psychology, 55*(2), 241–255.

Lim, J., & Butcher, J. N. (1996). Detection of faking on the MMPI–2: Differentiation among faking-bad, denial, and claiming extreme virtue. *Journal of Personality Assessment, 67*(1), 1–25.

Linbald, A. D. (1994). Detection of malingered mental illness within a forensic population: An analogue study. *Dissertation Abstract International, 54-B*, 4395.

Linehan, M. M. (1993). *Cognitive–behavioral treatment of borderline personality disorder*. New York: Guilford Press.

Linehan, M. M. (1997). Validation and psychotherapy. In A. C. Bohart & L. S. Greenberg (Eds.), *Empathy reconsidered: New directions in psychotherapy* (pp. 353–392). Washington, DC: American Psychological Association.

Lipkus, I. M., Barefoot, J. C., Williams, R. B., & Siegler, I. C. (1994). Personality measures as predictors of smoking initiation and cessation in the UNC alumni heart study. *Health Psychology, 13*(2), 149–155.

Litz, B. (Ed.). (2004). *Early intervention for trauma and traumatic loss*. New York: Guilford Press.

Litz, B. T., Penk, W., Walsh, S., Hyer, L., Blake, D. D., Marx, B., et al. (1991). Similarities and differences between Minnesota Multiphasic Personality Inventory (MMPI) and MMPI–2 applications to the assessment of posttraumatic stress disorder. *Journal of Personality Assessment, 57*, 238–254.

Livesley, W. J., Jackson, D. N., & Schroeder, M. L. (1989). A study of the factorial structure of personality disorder. *Journal of Personality Disorders, 3*, 292–306.

Lopez, S. R., & Weisman, A. (2004). Integrating a cultural perspective in psychological test development. In R. J. Velasquez, L. M. Arellano, & B. W. McNeill (Eds.), *The handbook of Chicana/o psychology and mental health* (pp. 129–152). Mahwah, NJ: Lawrence Erlbaum Associates.

Lopez-Baez, S. (1999). Marianismo. In J. S. Mio, J. E. Trimble, P. Arredondo, H. E. Cheatham, & D. Sue (Eds.), *Key words in multicultural interventions: A dictionary* (p. 183). Westport, CT: Greenwood Press.

Love, A. W., & Peck, C. L. (1987). The MMPI and psychological factors in chronic low back pain: A review. *Pain, 28*, 1–12.

Lucio, E. M., Ampudia, A., Duran, C., Leon, I., & Butcher, J. N. (2001). Comparisons of Mexican and American norms of the MMPI–2. *Journal of Clinical Psychology, 57*, 1459–1468.

Lucio, E. M., Palacios, H., Duran, C., & Butcher, J. N. (1999). MMPI–2 with Mexican psychiatric inpatients. *Journal of Clinical Psychology, 55*, 1541–1552.

Lucio, E. M., Reyes-Lagunes, I., & Scott, R. L. (1994). MMPI–2 for Mexico: Translation and adaptation. *Journal of Personality Assessment, 63*, 105–116.

Lucio, E. M., & Reyes-Lagunes, I. (1996). The Mexican version of the MMPI–2 in Mexico and Nicaragua: Translation, adaptation, and demonstrated equivalency. In J. N. Butcher (Ed.), *International adaptation of the MMPI–2* (pp. 265–284). Minneapolis: University of Minnesota Press.

Lumry, A. E., Gottesman, I. I., & Tuason, V. B. (1982). MMPI state dependency during the course of bipolar psychosis. *Psychiatry Research, 7*, 59–67.

Lushene, R. E., O'Neil, H. H., & Dunn, T. (1974). Equivalent validity of a completely computerized MMPI. *Journal of Personality Assessment, 38*, 353–361.

Lyons, J. A., & Keane, T. M. (1992). Keane PTSD scale: MMPI and MMPI–2 update. *Journal of Traumatic Stress, 5*, 111–117.

Lyons, J. A., & Wheeler-Cox, T. (1999). MMPI, MMPI–2 and PTSD: Overview of scores, scales and profiles. *Journal of Traumatic Stress, 12*(1), 175–183.

MacAndrew, C. (1965). The differentiation of male alcoholic outpatients from nonalcoholic psychiatric outpatients by means of the MMPI. *Quarterly Journal of Studies on Alcohol, 26*, 238–246.

MacAndrew, C. (1979). MAC scale scores of three samples of men under conditions of conventional versus independent scale administration. *Journal of Studies on Alcohol, 40*, 138–141.

MacAndrew, C. (1981). What the MAC scale tells us about men alcoholics: An interpretive review. *Journal of Studies on Alcohol, 42*, 604–625.

MacPherson, G., & Jones, L. (Eds.). (2004). Risk assessment and management. *Issues in Forensic Psychology, 5*. Leicester, UK: Division of Forensic Psychology, British Psychological Society.

Maddi, S. R., Fox, S. R., Khoshaba, D. M., Harvey, R. H., Lu, J. L., & Persico, M. (2001). Reduction in psychopathology following bariatric surgery for morbid obesity. *Obesity Surgery, 11*, 680–685.

Maddi, S. R., Khoshaba, D. M., Persico, M., Bleecker, F., & VanArsdall, G. (1997). Psychosocial correlates of psychopathology in a national sample of the morbidly obese. *Obesity Surgery, 7*, 397–404.

Makover, R. B. (1992). Training psychotherapists in hierarchical treatment planning. *Journal of Psychotherapy Practice and Research, 1*, 337–350.

Marin, G., & Triandis, H. C. (1985). Allocentrism as an important characteristic of the behavior of Latin Americans and Hispanics. In R. Diaz-Guerrero (Ed.), *Cross-cultural and national studies in social psychology* (pp. 85–104). Amsterdam: Elsevier Science.

Marin, G., & VanOss-Marin, B. (1991). *Research with Hispanic populations*. Newbury Park, CA: Sage.

Marks, P. A., & Seeman, W. (1963). *The actuarial description of abnormal personality: An atlas for use with the* MMPI. Baltimore: Williams & Wilkins.

Marks, P. A., Seeman, W., & Haller, D. L. (1975). *The actuarial use of the* MMPI *with adolescents and adults*. Baltimore: Williams & Wilkins.

Marsh, S. H. (1962). Validating the selection of deputy sheriffs. *Public Personnel Review, 23*, 41–44.

Maruta, T., Colligan, R. C., Malinchoc, M., & Offord, K. P. (2000). Optimists versus pessimists: Survival rate among medical patients over a 30-year period. *Mayo Clinic Proceedings, 75*, 140–143.

Matarazzo, J. D. (1986). Computerized clinical psychological interpretations: Unvalidated plus all mean and no sigma. *American Psychologist, 41*, 14–24.

Mathews, B., Gassen, M., & Pietz, C. (2004, May). *Validation of Megargee's* Fc *scale for the MMPI–2*. Paper presented at the 39th Annual Symposium on Recent Developments on the MMPI–2/MMPI–A, Minneapolis, MN.

Mattson, M. E., Babor, T., Cooney, T., & Conners, G. (1998). Matching patients with alcohol disorders to treatments: Clinical implications from Project MATCH. *Journal of Mental Health, 7*, 589–602.

McBride, J. R., & Martin, J. T. (1983). Reliability and validity of adaptive ability tests in a military setting. In D. J. Weiss (Ed.), *New horizons in testing: Latent trait test theory and computerized adaptive testing* (pp. 223–236). New York: Academic Press.

McCaffrey, R. J., & Lynch, J. K. (1996). Survey of the educational backgrounds and specialty training of instructors in clinical neuropsychology in APA–approved graduate training programs: A 10-year follow-up. *Archives of Clinical Neuropsychology, 11*, 11–19.

McConnaughy, E. A., DiClemente, C. C., Prochaska, J. O., & Velicer, W. F. (1993). Stages of change in psychotherapy: A follow-up report. *Psychotherapy, 26*, 494–503.

McCrae, R. R. (1993). Moderated analyses of longitudinal personality stability. *Journal of Personality and Social Psychology, 65*, 577–585.

McCreary, C. (1985). Empirically derived MMPI profile clusters and characteristics of low back pain patients. *Journal of Consulting and Clinical Psychology, 53*(4), 558–560.

McFall, M. E., Moore, J. E., Kivlahan, D. R., & Capestany, F. (1988). Differences between psychotic and nonpsychotic patients on content dimensions of the MMPI *Sc* scale. *Journal of Nervous and Mental Disease, 176*, 732–736.

McGrath, R. E., & Ingersoll, J. (1999). Writing a good cookbook. I. A review of MMPI high-point studies. *Journal of Personality Assessment, 73*, 149–178.

McKenna, T. & Butcher, J. N. (1987, March). *Use of the revised MMPI in the assessment of chemical dependency*. Paper presented at the 22nd Annual Symposium on Recent Developments in the Use of the MMPI, Seattle, WA.

McKinley, J. C., & Hathaway, S. R. (1980a). Scale 1 Hypochondriasis. In W. G. Dahlstrom & L. Dahlstrom (Eds.), *Basic readings on the MMPI* (pp. 12–23). Minneapolis: University of Minnesota Press.

McKinley, J. C., & Hathaway, S. R. (1980b). Scales 3 (Hysteria), 9 (Hypomania), and 4 (Psychopathic Deviate). In W. G. Dahlstrom & L. Dahlstrom (Eds.), *Basic readings on the MMPI* (pp. 42–63). Minneapolis: University of Minnesota Press.

McLellan, A. T., Kushner, H., Metzger, D., & Peters, R. (1992). The fifth edition of the Addiction Severity Index. *Journal of Substance Abuse Treatment*, 9, 199–213.

McNally, R. J. (2003). *Remembering trauma*. Cambridge, MA: Belknap Press/Harvard University Press.

McNally, R. J., Bryant, R. A., & Ehlers, A. (2003). Does early psychological intervention promote recovery from post-traumatic stress? *Psychological Science in the Public Interest, 4*, 45–79.

McNulty, J. L., Ben-Porath, Y. S., & Graham, J. R. (1998). An empirical examination of the correlates of well-defined and not defined MMPI–2 code types. *Journal of Personality Assessment, 71*, 393–410.

McNulty, J. L., Ben-Porath, Y. S., & Watt, M. (1997, June). *Predicting SCID–II personality disorder symptomatology: A comparison of the PSY–5 and Big Five models*. Paper presented at the 31st Annual MMPI–2 and MMPI–A Symposium, Minneapolis, MN.

McNulty, J. L., Graham, J. R., Ben-Porath, Y. S., & Stein, L. A. R. (1997). Comparative validity of MMPI–2 scores of African American and Caucasian mental health center clients. *Psychological Assessment*, 9, 464–470.

McNulty, J. L., Harkness, A. R., & Ben-Porath, Y. S. (1998, March). *Theoretical assertions and empirical evidence: How MMPI–2 PSY–5 scales are linked with the MPQ, ZKPQ–III, and NEO–PI–R*. Paper presented at the 33rd Annual MMPI–2 Symposium, Clearwater, FL.

McNulty, J. L., Harkness, A. R., & Wright, C. L. (1994, April). *Chart diagnoses and the validity of MMPI–2–based PSY–5 scales*. Paper presented at the 40th Annual Convention of the Southwestern Psychological Association, Tulsa, OK.

Meehl, P. E. (1945). The dynamics of "structured" personality tests. *Journal of Clinical Psychology, 1*, 296–303.

Meehl, P. E. (1954). *Clinical versus statistical prediction: A theoretical analysis and a review of the evidence*. Minneapolis: University of Minnesota Press.

Meehl, P. E. (1956). Wanted—a good cookbook. *American Psychologist, 11*, 262–272.

Meehl, P. E. (1962). Schizotaxia, schizotypy, schizophrenia. *American Psychologist, 17*, 827–838.

Meehl, P. E. (1972). Reactions, reflections, projections. In J. N. Butcher (Ed.), *Objective personality assessment: Changing perspectives* (pp. 131–189). New York: Academic Press.

Meehl, P. E. (1975). Hedonic capacity: Some conjectures. *Bulletin of the Menninger Clinic, 39*, 295–307.

Meehl, P. E. (1987). "Hedonic capacity" ten years later: Some clarifications. In D. C. Clark & J. Fawcett (Eds.), *Anhedonia and affect deficit states* (pp. 47–50). New York: PMA.

Meehl, P. E., & Hathaway, S. R. (1946). The K factor as a suppressor variable in the Minnesota Multiphasic Personality Inventory. *Journal of Applied Psychology, 30*, 525–564.

Meehl, P. E., & Rosen, A. (1955). Antecedent probability and the efficiency of psychometric signs, patterns, and cutting scores. *Psychological Bulletin, 52*, 194–216.

Megargee, E. I. (Ed.). (1977). A new classification system for criminal offenders [Special issue]. *Criminal Justice and Behavior, 4*(2).

Megargee, E. I. (1979). *How to do publishable research with the MMPI. Clinical notes on the MMPI*. Minneapolis, MN: National Computer Systems.

Megargee, E. I. (1994). Using the Megargee MMPI–based classification system with the MMPI–2s of male prison inmates. *Psychological Assessment, 6*, 337–344.

Megargee, E. I. (1995). Use of the MMPI–2 in correctional settings. In Y. S. Ben-Porath, J. R. Graham, G. C. N. Hall, R. D. Hirschman, & M. S. Zaragoza (Eds.), *Forensic applications of the MMPI–2* (pp. 127–159). Thousand Oaks, CA: Sage.

Megargee, E. I. (1997). Using the Megargee MMPI–based classification system with MMPI–2s of female prison inmates. *Psychological Assessment, 9*, 75–82.

Megargee, E. I. (2000). *User's guide: MMPI–2 Criminal Justice and Correctional Report for Men*. Minneapolis, MN: NCS Assessments.

Megargee, E. I. (2002). Assessing the risk of aggression and violence. In J. N. Butcher (Ed.), *Clinical personality assessment: Practical approaches* (2nd ed., pp. 435–451). New York: Oxford University Press.

Megargee, E. I. (2003). Psychological assessment in correctional settings. In J. R. Graham & J. A. Naglieri (Eds.), *Handbook of psychology. Vol. 10: Assessment psychology* (pp. 365–388). Hoboken, NJ: John Wiley & Sons.

Megargee, E. I. (2004, May). *Development and validation of an MMPI–2 Infrequency Scale* (Fc) *for use with criminal offenders*. Paper presented at the 39th Annual Symposium on Recent Developments of the MMPI–2/MMPI–A, Minneapolis, MN.

Megargee, E. I. (in press). *Using MMPI–2 in criminal justice and correctional settings: An empirical approach*. Minneapolis: University of Minnesota Press.

Megargee, E. I., & Bohn, M. J., Jr. (with Meyer, J., & Sink, F.). (1979). *Classifying criminal offenders: A new system based on the MMPI*. Beverly Hills, CA: Sage.

Megargee, E. I., & Carbonell, J. L. (1995). Use of the MMPI–2 in correctional settings. In Y. S. Ben-Porath, J. R. Graham, G. C. N. Hirschman, & M. S. Zaragoza (Eds.), *Forensic applications of the MMPI–2* (pp. 127–159). Thousand Oaks, CA: Sage.

Megargee, E. I., Carbonell, J. L., Bohn, M. B., Jr., & Sliger, G. L. (2001) *Classifying criminal offenders with MMPI–2: The Megargee system.* Minneapolis: University of Minnesota Press.

Megargee, E. I., Cook, P. E., & Mendelsohn, G. A. (1967). Development and validation of an MMPI scale of assaultiveness in overcontrolled individuals. *Journal of Abnormal Psychology, 72,* 519–528.

Megargee, E. I., Mercer, S. J., & Carbonell, J. L. (1999). MMPI–2 with male and female state and federal prison inmates. *Psychological Assessment, 11,* 177–185.

Mendez-Quevado, K. M., & Butcher, J. N. (in press). The use of the MMPI and MMPI–2 in Cuba: A historical overview from 1950 to the present. *International Journal of Clinical and Health Psychology.*

Mendoza-Newman, M. C. (1999). *Level of acculturation, socioeconomic status, and the MMPI–A performance of a nonclinical Hispanic adolescent sample.* Unpublished doctoral dissertation, Pacific Graduate School of Psychology, Palo Alto, CA.

Merbaum, M. (1977). Some personality characteristics of soldiers exposed to extreme war stress: A follow-up study of post-hospital adjustment. *Journal of Clinical Psychology, 33,* 558–562.

Meyers, J. E., Millis, S. R., & Volkert, K. (2002). A validity index for the MMPI–2. *Archives of Clinical Neuropsychology, 17,* 157–169.

Michel, D. M. (2002). Psychological assessment as a therapeutic intervention in patients hospitalized with eating disorders. *Professional Psychology: Research and Practice, 33*(5), 470–477.

Milhous, R. L., Haugh, L. D., Frymoyer, J. W., Ruess, J. M., Gallagher, R. M., Wilder, D. G., & Callas, P. W. (1989). Determinants of vocational disability in patients with low back pain. *Archives of Physical Medicine and Rehabilitation, 70,* 589–593.

Millard, R. W., & Jones, R. H. (1991). Construct validity of practical questionnaires for assessing disability of low-back pain. *Spine, 16*(7), 835–838.

Miller, D. A., Johnson, J. H., Klingler, D. E., Williams, T. A., & Giannetti, R. A. (1977). Design for an online computerized system for MMPI interpretation. *Behavior Research Methods and Instrumentation,* 9, 117–122.

Miller, H. R., Goldberg, J. O., & Streiner, D. L. (1995). What's in a name? The MMPI–2 PTSD scales. *Journal of Clinical Psychology, 51*(5), 626–631.

Miller, M. W., Grief, J. L., & Smith, A. A. (2003). Multidimensional personality questionnaire profiles of veterans with traumatic combat exposure: Externalizing and internalizing subtypes. *Psychological Assessment, 15*(2), 216–222.

Miller, T. R. (1991). The psychotherapeutic utility of the five-factor model: A clinician's experience. *Journal of Personality Assessment, 57,* 415–433.

Miller, W. R., & Tonigan, J. S. (1997). Assessing drinkers' motivation for change: The Stages of Change Readiness and Treatment Eagerness scale (SOCRATES). In G. A. Marlatt & G. R. VandenBos (Eds.), *Addictive behaviors* (pp. 355–369). Washington, DC: American Psychological Association.

Millon, T., Davis, R. D., & Millon, C. (1997). *Manual for the Millon Clinical Multiaxial Inventory—III (MCMI–III)* (2nd ed.). Minneapolis, MN: National Computer Systems.

Mitchell, J. E., Lancaster, K. L., Burgard, M. A., Howell, L. M., Krahn, D. D., Crosby, R. D., et al. (2001). Long-term follow-up of patients' status after gastric bypass. *Obesity Surgery, 11*(4), 464–468.

Mittenberg, W., Tremont, G., & Rayls, K. R. (1996). Impact of cognitive function on MMPI–2 validity in neurologically impaired patients. *Assessment, 3*, 157–163.

Mollen, M., Baer, H., Evans, H., Lankler, R. C., & Tyler, H. R. (1994). *Commission to Investigate Allegations of Police Corruption and the Anti-Corruption Procedures of the Police Department: Commission report*. New York: Braziller.

Montgomery, G. T., & Orozco, S. (1985). Mexican Americans' performance on the MMPI as a function of level of acculturation. *Journal of Clinical Psychology, 41*, 203–212.

Morales, E. (1996). Gender roles among Latino gay and bisexual men: Implications for family and couple relationships. In J. Laird & R. J. Green (Eds.), *Lesbians and gays in couples and families: A handbook for therapists* (pp. 272–297). San Francisco: Jossey-Bass.

Moreland, K. L. (1985a). Landmarks in computer-assisted psychological assessment. *Journal of Consulting and Clinical Psychology, 53*, 748–759.

Moreland, K. L. (1985b). Validation of computer-based interpretations: Problems and prospects. *Journal of Consulting and Clinical Psychology, 53*, 816–825.

Moreland, K. L. (1987). Computerized psychological assessment: What's available. In J. N. Butcher (Ed.), *Computerized psychological assessment: A practitioner's guide* (pp. 64–86). New York: Basic Books.

Moreno, K. E., Wetzel, C. D., McBride, J. R., & Weiss, D. J. (1984). Relationship between corresponding Armed Services Vocational Aptitude Battery (ASVAB) and Computerized Adaptive Testing (CA) subtests. *Applied Psychological Measurement*, 8(2), 155–163.

Morey, L. C. (1991). *Personality Assessment Inventory: Professional manual*. Odessa, FL: Psychological Assessment Resources.

Morey, L. C., & Smith, M. R. (1988). Personality disorders. In R. L. Greene (Ed.), *The MMPI: Use in specific populations* (pp. 110–158). Orlando, FL: Grune & Stratton.

Morey, L. C., Waugh, M. H., & Blashfield, R. K. (1985). MMPI scales for *DSM–III* personality disorders: Their derivation and correlates. *Journal of Personality Assessment, 49*, 245–251.

Morin, C. M., & Edinger, J. D. (1999). Sleep/wake disorders. In T. Millon, P. H. Blaney, & R. D. Davis (Eds.), *Oxford textbook of psychopathology* (pp. 390–409). London: Oxford University Press.

Morrell, J. S., & Rubin, L. J. (2001). The Minnesota Multiphasic Personality Inventory—2, posttraumatic stress disorder, and women domestic violence survivors. *Professional Psychology: Research and Practice, 32*, 151–156.

Mumola, C. J. (1999, January). *Substance abuse and treatment, state and federal prisoners, 1997* (Bureau of Justice Statistics Special Report). Washington, DC: Office of Justice Programs, Bureau of Justice Statistics, U.S. Department of Justice.

Munley, P. H., Bains, D. S., Bloem, W. D., & Busby, R. M. (1995). Post-traumatic stress disorder and the MMPI–2. *Journal of Traumatic Stress, 8*, 171–178.

Murphy, J. R. (1978). Mexican-Americans' performance on the MMPI: As compared with Anglo Americans (Doctoral dissertation, U.S. International University, San Diego, CA, 1978). *Dissertation Abstracts International* (1981), 41B, 3582.

Myer, G. J., Finn, S. E., Eyde, L. D., Kay, G. G., Moreland, K. L., Dies, R. R., et al. (2001). Psychological testing and psychological assessment: A review of evidence and issues. *American Psychologist, 56*(2), 128–165.

Nair, T. (1974). Social skills and attitudes of managers: A comparative study of engineer and non-engineer managers with and without management education. *Indian Manager, 5*, 139–153.

Naliboff, B. D., McCreary, C. P., McArthur, D. L., Cohen, M. J., & Gottlieb, H. J. (1988). MMPI changes following behavioral treatment of chronic low back pain. *Pain, 35*, 271–277.

Narayanan, L., Menon, S., & Levine, E. L. (1995). Personality structure: A culture-specific examination of the five-factor model. *Journal of Personality Assessment, 64*(1), 51–62.

National Center for Veterans Analysis and Statistics. (1995). *National Survey of Veterans* (NSV9503). Washington, DC: U.S. Government Printing Office.

National Commission on Correctional Health Care. (2003a). *Standards for health services in jails*. Chicago: Author.

National Commission on Correctional Health Care. (2003b). *Standards for health services in prisons*. Chicago: Author.

National Computer Systems. (1982). Minnesota Multiphasic Personality Inventory: User's guide for the Minnesota Report. Minneapolis, MN: National Computer Systems.

Nelson, L. (1995). Use of the MMPI and MMPI–2 in forensic neurological evaluations. In Y. S. Ben-Porath, J. R. Graham, G. C. N. Hall, R. D. Hirschman, & M. S. Zaragoza (Eds.), *Forensic applications of the MMPI–2* (pp. 202–221). Thousand Oaks, CA: Sage.

Nelson, L. D., Elder, J. T., Tehrani, P., & Groot, J. (2003). Measuring personality and emotional functioning in multiple sclerosis: A cautionary note. *Archives of Clinical Neuropsychology, 18*, 419–429.

Newberry, L. A. (1967). Defensiveness and need for approval. *Journal of Consulting Psychology, 31*, 396–400.

Newman, F. L., Ciarlo, J. A., & Carpenter, D. (1999). Guidelines for selecting psychological instruments for treatment planning and outcome assessment. In M. Maruish (Ed.), *The use of psychological testing for treatment planning and outcomes assessment* (2nd ed., pp. 153–170). Mahwah, NJ: Lawrence Erlbaum Associates.

Newman, F. L., & Dakof, G. A. (1999). Progress and outcome assessment of individual patient data: Selecting single-subject design and statistical procedures. In M. Maruish (Ed.), *The use of psychological testing for treatment planning and outcomes assessment* (2nd ed., pp. 211–223). Mahwah, NJ: Lawrence Erlbaum Associates.

Newman, F. L., & Tejeda, M. J. (1999). Selecting statistical procedures for progress and outcome assessment: The analysis of group data. In M. Maruish (Ed.), *The use of psychological testing for treatment planning and outcomes assessment* (2nd ed., pp. 225–266). Mahwah, NJ: Lawrence Erlbaum Associates.

Newman, M. L., & Greenway, P. (1997). Therapeutic effects of providing MMPI–2 feedback to clients at a university counseling service: A collaborative approach. *Psychological Assessment, 9*, 122–131.

Nezami, E., & Zamani, R. (1996). The Persian MMPI–2. In J. N. Butcher (Ed.), *International adaptation of the MMPI–2* (pp. 506–522). Minneapolis: University of Minnesota Press.

Niaura, R., Banks, S. M., Ward, K. D., Stoney, C. M., Spiro, A., Aldwin, C. M., et al. (2000). Hostility and the metabolic syndrome in older males: The Normative Aging Study. *Psychosomatic Medicine, 62*, 7–16.

Nichols, D. S. (1988). Mood disorders. In R. L. Greene (Ed.), *The MMPI: Use in specific populations* (pp. 74–109). Orlando, FL: Grune & Stratton.

Nichols, D. S. (1991). *Development of a global measure for positive mental health.* Unpublished manuscript.

Nichols, D. S. (2001). *Essentials of MMPI–2 assessment.* New York: John Wiley & Sons.

Nichols, D. S. (in press). Old wine in new bottles? MMPI–2 Restructured Clinical (RC) scales: Development, validation, and interpretation. *Journal of Personality Assessment.*

Nichols, D. S., & Greene, R. L. (1991, March). *New Measures for Dissimulation on the MMPI/MMPI–2.* Paper presented at the 26th annual symposium on Recent Developments in the Use of the MMPI, St. Petersburg Beach, FL.

Nichols, D. S., & Greene, R. L. (1997). Dimensions of deception in personality assessment: The example of the MMPI–2. *Journal of Personality Assessment, 68*(2), 251–266.

Nichols, D. S., & Greene, R. L. (2004a). *A factor analysis of the items of Pa1, RC6, and related manifest paranoid item content.* Unpublished analyses.

Nichols, D. S. & Greene, R. L. (2004b). *MMPI–2 Psychopathy (PSP) scale.* Unpublished paper. (Paper available from D. S. Nichols, Portland, OR.)

Nichols, D. S., Greene, R., & Schmolck, P. (1989). Criteria for assessing inconsistent patterns of item endorsement on the MMPI: Rationale, development, and empirical trials. *Journal of Clinical Psychology, 45*, 239–250.

Nicholson, R. A., Mouton, G. J., Bagby, R. M., Buis, T., Peterson, S. A., & Buigas, R. A. (1997). Utility of MMPI–2 indicators of response distortion: Receiver operating characteristic analysis. *Psychological Assessment, 9*, 471–479.

Norcross, J. C., & Beutler, L. E. (1997). Determining the therapeutic relationship of choice in brief therapy. In J. N. Butcher (Ed.), *Objective psychological assessment in managed health care: A practitioner's guide* (pp. 42–60). New York: Oxford University Press.

Norris, F. H., & Riad, J. K. (1997). Standardized self-report measures of civilian trauma and post-traumatic stress disorder. In J. P. Wilson & T. M. Keane (Eds.), *Assessing psychological trauma and PTSD* (pp. 7–42). New York: Guilford Press.

Nunnally, J. C. (1978). *Psychometric theory* (2nd ed.). New York: McGraw-Hill.

O'Dell, J. (1972). P. T. Barnum explores the computer. *Journal of Consulting and Clinical Psychology, 38*, 270–273.

Oetting, E. (1966). Examination anxiety: Prediction, physiological response, and relation to scholastic performance. *Journal of Counseling Psychology, 13*, 224–227.

Oetting, E. R., & Deffenbacher, J. L. (1980). *The Test Anxiety Profile (TAP) manual*. Fort Collins, CO: Rocky Mountain Behavioral Sciences Institute.

Okazaki, S., & Sue, S. (1995). Methodological issues in assessment research with ethnic minorities. *Psychological Assessment, 7*, 367–375.

Okazaki, S., & Sue, S. (2000). Implications of test revisions for assessment with Asian Americans. *Psychological Assessment, 12*, 272–280.

O'Laughlin, M. S. (1994). The prediction of aggressive acting-out: A validity comparison of the MMPI–2 *F*, 4, 9 index with several short anger scales. *Dissertation Abstracts International, 54*, 4929.

Oleske, D. M., Anderson, G. B. J., Lavender, S. A., & Hahn, J. J. (2000). Association between recover outcomes for work-related low back disorders and personal, family, and work factors. *Spine, 25*(10), 1259–1265.

Olfson, M., Lewis-Rernandex, R., Weissman, M. M., Feder, A., Gameroff, M. J., Pilowsky, D., & Fuentes, M. (2002). Psychotic symptoms in an urban general medicine practice. *American Journal of Psychiatry, 159*(8), 1412–1419.

Omdal, R., Waterloo, K., Koldingsnes, W., Husby, G., & Mellgren, S. I. (2003). Fatigue in patients with systemic lupus erythematosis: The psychosocial aspects. *Journal of Rheumatology, 30*(2), 283–287.

Ones, D. S., & Viswesvaran, C. (1998). Integrity testing in organizations. In R.W. Griffin & A. O'Leary-Kelly (Eds.), *Dysfunctional behavior in organizations: Violent and deviant behavior. Monographs in organizational behavior and industrial relations* (Vol. 23, Parts A & B; pp. 243–276). Stamford, CT: Jai Press.

Ones, D. S., Viswesvaran, C., & Schmidt, F. L. (1993). Comprehensive meta-analysis of integrity test validities: Findings and implications for personnel selection and theories of job performance. *Journal of Applied Psychology, 78*, 679–703.

Oquendo, H., Horwath, E., & Martinez, A. (1992). Ataques de nervios: Proposed diagnostic criteria for a culture-specific syndrome. *Culture, Medicine, and Psychiatry, 16*, 367–376.

Osburn, H. G. (2000). Coefficient alpha and related internal consistency reliability coefficients. *Psychological Methods, 5*(3), 343–355.

O'Sullivan, M. J., Peterson, P. D., Cox, G. B., & Kirkeby, J. (1989). Ethnic populations: Community mental health services, ten years later. *American Journal of Community Psychology, 17*, 17–30.

Otis, J. D., Keane, T. M., & Kerns, R. D. (2003). An examination of the relationship between chronic pain and PTSD. *Journal of Rehabilitation Research and Development, 40*, 397–406.

Otto, R. (2002). Use of the MMPI–2 in forensic settings. *Journal of Forensic Psychology Practice, 2*(3), 71–92.

Otto, R., & Butcher, J. N. (1995). Computer-assisted psychological assessment in child custody evaluations. *Family Law Quarterly, 29*, 7996.

Otto, R., & Collins, R. P. (1995). Use of the MMPI–2/MMPI–A in child custody evaluations. In Y. S. Ben-Porath, J. R. Graham, G. C. N. Hall, R. D. Hirschman, & M. S. Zaragoza (Eds.), *Forensic applications of the MMPI–2* (pp. 222–252). Thousand Oaks, CA: Sage.

Padilla, A. M. (1992). Reflections on testing: Emerging trends and new possibilities. In K. F. Geisinger (Ed.), *Psychological testing of Hispanics* (pp. 271–284). Washington, DC: American Psychological Association.

Padilla, A. M., & Ruiz, R. A. (1973). Latino mental health: A review of the literature (DHEW Publication No. ADM 74-113). Washington, DC: U.S. Government Printing Office.

Padilla, A. M., & Ruiz, R. A. (1975). Personality assessment and test interpretation of Mexican Americans: A critique. *Journal of Personality Assessment, 39*, 103–109.

Padilla, E. R., Olmedo, E. L., & Loya, F. (1982). Acculturation and the MMPI performance of Chicano and Anglo college students. *Hispanic Journal of Behavioral Sciences, 4*, 451–466.

Pancheri, P., & Biondi, M. (1987). Computerized psychological assessment in Italy: State of the art. In J. N. Butcher (Ed.), *Computerized psychological assessment* (pp. 236–260). New York: Basic Books.

Pancheri, P., Sirigatti, S., & Biondi, M. (1996). Adaptation of the MMPI–2 in Italy. In J. N. Butcher (Ed.), *International adaptation of the MMPI–2* (pp. 416–421). Minneapolis: University of Minnesota Press.

Paniagua, F. A. (1998). *Assessing and treating culturally diverse clients: A practical guide*. Thousand Oaks, CA: Sage.

Park, C., Cohen, G., & Murch, R. (1996). Assessment and prediction of stress-related growth. *Journal of Personality, 64*, 71–105.

Pasveer, K. A., & Ellard, J. H. (1998). The making of a personality inventory: Help from the WWW. *Behavior Research Methods, Instruments, & Computers, 30*, 309–313.

Patrick, J. (1988). Personality characteristics of work-ready workers' compensation clients. *Journal of Clinical Psychology, 44*(6), 1009–1012.

Paulhus, D. L. (1984). Two-component models of socially desirable responding. *Personality and Individual Differences, 46*, 598–609.

Paulhus, D. L. (1986). Self-deception and impression management in test responses. In A. Angleitner & J. S. Wiggins (Eds.), *Personality assessment via questionnaires: Current issues in theory and measurement* (pp. 143–165). Berlin, Germany: Springer-Verlag.

Paulhus, D. L. (2002). Socially desirable responding: The evolution of a construct. In H. I. Braun, D. N. Jackson, & D. E. Wiley (Eds.), *The role of constructs in psychological and educational measurement* (pp. 49–69). Mahwah, NJ: Lawrence Erlbaum Associates.

Payne, F. D., & Wiggins, J. S. (1972). MMPI profile types and the self-report of psychiatric patients. *Journal of Abnormal Psychology, 79*, 1–8.

Pearson, J. S., Rome, H. P., Swenson, W. M., Mataya, P., & Brannick, T. L. (1965). Development of computer system for scoring and interpretation of MMPI in a medical clinic. *Annals of New York Academy of Sciences, 126*, 684–692.

Pearson, J. S., & Swenson, W. M. (1967). *A user's guide to the Mayo Clinic automated MMPI program*. New York: Psychological Corporation.

Pelcovitz, D., van der Kolk, B., Roth, S., Mandel, F., Kaplan, S., & Resick, P. (1997). Development of a criteria set and a Structured Interview for Disorders of Extreme Stress (SIDES). *Journal of Traumatic Stress, 10*, 3–16.

Penk, W. E. (1981). Assessing substance abusers with the MMPI. In W. Grant, J. Butcher, M. Gynther, & W. Schofield (Eds.), *Clinical notes on the MMPI* (pp. 1–10). Nutley, NJ: Roche.

Penk, W. E., Drebing, C., & Schutt, R. (2002). PTSD in the workplace. In J. C. Thomas & M. Hersen (Eds.), *Handbook of mental health in the workplace* (pp. 215–249). Thousand Oaks, CA: Sage.

Penk, W. E., Peck, R. F., Robinowitz, R., Bell, W., & Little, D. (1988). Coping and defending styles among Vietnam combat veterans seeking treatment for PTSD and substance use disorder. In M. Galanter (Ed.), *Recent developments in alcoholism: Vol. 6* (pp. 69–88). New York: Plenum Press.

Penk, W. E., Robinowitz, R., Black, J., Dolan, M., Bell, W., Roberts, W., & Skinner, J. (1989). Comorbidity: Lessons learned about post-traumatic stress disorder from developing scales for the MMPI. *Journal of Clinical Psychology, 45*, 24–32.

Pensa, R., Dorfman, W. I., Gold, S. N., & Schneider, B. (1996). Detection of malingered psychosis with the MMPI–2. *Psychotherapy in Private Practice, 14*, 47–63.

Perez-Foster, R. (1998). *The power of language in the clinical process: Assessing and treating the bilingual person*. Northvale, NJ: Jason Aronson.

Perrin, S., Van Hasselt, V. B., Basilio, I., & Hersen, M. (1996). Assessing the effects of violence on women in battering relationships with the Keane MMPI–PTSD scale. *Journal of Traumatic Stress, 9*, 805–816.

Perrin, S., Van Hasselt, V. B., & Hersen, M. (1997). Validation of the Keane MMPI–PTSD scale against *DSM–III–R* criteria in a sample of battered women. *Violence & Victims, 12*(1), 99–104.

Perry, J. N. (2002). Assessment of treatment resistance via questionnaire. In J. N. Butcher (Ed.), *Clinical personality assessment: Practical approaches* (2nd ed., pp. 96–108). New York: Oxford University Press.

Peters, J. M. (2000). *The effect of Therapeutic Assessment on women with eating disorders*. Unpublished doctoral dissertation, University of Texas, Austin.

Petroskey, L. J., Ben-Porath, Y. S., & Stafford, K. P. (2003). Correlates of the Minnesota Multiphasic Personality Inventory–2 (MMPI–2) Personality Psychopathology Five (PSY–5) scales in a forensic assessment setting. *Assessment, 10*, 393–399.

Pinsoneault, T. B. (1996). Equivalency of computer-assisted and paper-and-pencil administered versions of the Minnesota Multiphasic Personality Inventory—2. *Computers in Human Behavior, 12*, 291–300.

Piotrowski, C., & Lubin, B. (1990). Assessment practices of health psychologists: Survey of APA division 38 clinicians. *Professional Psychology: Research and Practice, 21*(2), 99–106.

Pollack, D. R., & Grainey, T. F. (1984). A comparison of MMPI profiles for state and private disability insurance applicants. *Journal of Personality Assessment, 48*(2), 121–125.

Pongpanich, L. (1996). Use of the MMPI–2 in Thailand. In J. N. Butcher (Ed.), *International adaptation of the MMPI–2* (pp. 162–174). Minneapolis: University of Minnesota Press.

Poortinga, Y. H. (1989). Equivalence of cross-cultural data: An overview of basic issues. *International Journal of Psychology, 24*, 737–756.

Pope, K. S., Butcher, J. N., & Seelen, J. (1993). *The MMPI, MMPI–2, and MMPI–A in court: A practical guide for expert witnesses and attorneys*. Washington, DC: American Psychological Association.

Pope, K. S., Butcher, J. N., & Seelen, J. (2000). *The MMPI, MMPI–2 and MMPI–A in court: A practical guide for expert witnesses and attorneys* (2nd ed.). Washington, DC: American Psychological Association.

Posthuma, A. B., & Harper, J. F. (1998). Comparison of MMPI–2 responses of child custody and personal injury litigants. *Professional Psychology: Research and Practice, 29*, 437–443.

Prenger, J. H. (2000). *Neurological content and impact on personality assessment scale elevations*. Unpublished master's thesis, Lakehead University, Thunder Bay, Ontario, Canada.

Prince, R. H. (1983). Is anorexia nervosa a culture-bound syndrome? *Transcultural Psychiatric Research Review, 20*, 299–300.

Pritchard, D. A., & Rosenblatt, A. (1980). Racial bias in the MMPI: A methodological review. *Journal of Consulting and Clinical Psychology, 48*, 263–267.

Prochaska, J. O., & DiClemente, C. C. (1982). Transtheoretical therapy: Toward a more integrative model of change. *Psychotherapy: Theory, Research and Practice, 19*, 276–288.

Prochaska, J. O., & DiClemente, C. C. (1986). Toward a comprehensive model of change. In W. R. Miller & N. Heather (Eds.), *Treating addictive behaviors: Processes of change* (pp. 3–27). New York: Plenum Press.

Prochaska, J. O., Velicer, W. F., Rossi, J. S., Goldstein, M. G., Marcus, B. H., Rakowski, W., et al. (1994). Stages of change and decisional balance for 12 problem behaviors. *Health Psychology, 13*, 39–46.

Purves, C. (2002). Collaborative assessment with involuntary populations: Foster children and their mothers. *The Humanistic Psychologist, 30*, 164–174.

Rayls, K. R., Mittenberg, W., Burns, W. J., & Theroux, S. (2000). Prospective study of the MMPI–2 correction factor after mild head injury. *Clinical Neuropsychologist, 14*, 546–550.

Reda, G. (1948). *Translation of the MMPI*. Unpublished manuscript.

Regier, D. A., Farmer, M. E., Rae, D. S., Locke, B. Z., Keith, S. J., Judd, L. L., & Goodwin, F. K. (1990). Comorbidity of mental disorders with alcohol and other drug abuse. Results from the Epidemiologic Catchment Area (ECA) Study. *Journal of the American Medical Association, 264*, 2511–2518.

Regier, D. A., Myers, J. K., Kramer, M., Robins L. N., Blazer, D. G., Hough, R. L., et al. (1984). The NIMH Epidemiologic Catchment Area program. Historical context, major objectives, and study population characteristics. *Archives of General Psychiatry, 41*(10), 934–941.

Reichenback, H. (1957). *Experience and prediction*. Chicago: University of Chicago Press. (Original work published 1938)

Reitan, R. M., & Wolfson, D. (1993). *The Halstead–Reitan Neuropsychological Test Battery: Theory and clinical interpretation* (2nd ed.). Tucson, AZ: Neuropsychology Press.

Reitan, R. M., & Wolfson, D. (1997). Emotional disturbances and their interaction with neuropsychological deficits. *Neuropsychology Review, 7*, 3–19.

Repko, G. R., & Cooper, R. (1983). A study of the average workers' compensation case. *Journal of Clinical Psychology, 39*, 287–295.

Repko, G. R., & Cooper, R. (1985). The diagnosis of personality disorder: A comparison of MMPI profile, Millon inventory and clinical judgment in a workers' compensation population. *Journal of Clinical Psychology, 41*(6), 867–881.

Riley, J. L., Robinson, M. E., Geisser, M. E., Wittmer, V. T., & Smith, A. G. (1995). Relationship between MMPI–2 cluster profiles and surgical outcome in low-back pain patients. *Journal of Spinal Disorders, 8*(3), 213–219.

Rissetti, F. J., Himmel, E., & Gonzalez-Moreno, J. A. (1996). Use of the MMPI–2 in Chile: Translation and adaptation. In J. N. Butcher (Ed.), *International adaptation of the MMPI–2* (pp. 221–251). Minneapolis: University of Minnesota Press.

Robin, R. W., Greene, R. L., Albaugh, B., Caldwell, A., & Goldman, D. (2003). Use of the MMPI–2 in American Indians: I. Comparability of the MMPI–2 between two tribes and with the MMPI–2 normative group. *Psychological Assessment, 15*, 351–359.

Roeloffs, C. A., Fink, A., Unutzer, J., Tang, L., & Wells, K. B. (2001). Problematic substance use, depressive symptoms, and gender in primary care. *Psychiatric Services, 52*(9), 1251–1253.

Rogers, R. (2001). *Handbook of diagnostic and structured interviewing*. New York: Guilford Press.

Rogers, R., Bagby, R. M., & Chakraborty, D. (1993). Feigning schizophrenic disorder on the MMPI–2: Detection of coached simulators. *Journal of Personality Assessment, 60*, 215–226.

Rogers, R., Bagby, R. M., & Dickens, S. E. (1992). *Structured interview of reported symptoms: Professional manual*. Odessa, FL: Psychological Assessment Resources.

Rogers, R., Sewell, K. W., Martin, M. A., & Vitacco, M. J. (2003). Detection of feigned mental disorders: A meta-analysis of the MMPI–2 and malingering. *Assessment, 10*(2), 160–177.

Rogers, R., Sewell, K. W., Morey, L. C., & Ustad, K. L. (1996). Detection of feigned mental disorders on the Personality Assessment Inventory: A discriminant analysis. *Journal of Personality Assessment, 60*, 554–560.

Rogers, R., Sewell, K. W., & Salekin, R. (1994). A meta-analysis of malingering on the MMPI–2. *Assessment, 1*, 227–237.

Rogers, R., Sewell, K. W., & Ustad, K. L. (1995). Feigning among chronic outpatients on the MMPI–2: A systematic examination of fake-bad indicators. *Assessment, 2*, 81–89.

Rogler, L. H. (1999). Methodological sources of cultural insensitivity in mental health research. *American Psychologist, 54*(6), 424–433.

Rohling, M. L., Binder, L. M., & Langhinrichsen-Rohling, J. (1995). Money matters: A meta-analytic review of the association between financial compensation and the experience and treatment of chronic pain. *Health Psychology, 14*(6), 537–547.

Rome, H. P., Swenson, W. M., Mataya, P., McCarthy, C. E., Pearson, J. S., Keating, F. R., & Hathaway, S. R. (1962). Symposium on automation techniques in personality assessment. *Proceedings of the Staff Meetings of the Mayo Clinic, 37*, 61–82.

Roper, B. L., Ben-Porath, Y. S., & Butcher, J. N. (1995). Comparability and validity of computerized adaptive testing with the MMPI–2. *Journal of Personality Assessment, 65*, 358–371.

Rosen, E. (1958). *Translation and adaptation of personality tests for use in other cultures*. Unpublished manuscript, University of Minnesota, Minneapolis.

Rosenblum, A., Joseph, H., Fong, C., Kipnis, S., Cleland, C., & Portenoy, R. K. (2003). Prevalence and characteristics of chronic pain among chemically dependent patients in methadone maintenance and residential treatment facilities. *Journal of the American Medical Association, 289*(18), 2370–2378.

Rosenthal, R., Rosnow, R. L., & Rubin, D. B. (2000). *Contrasts and effect sizes in behavioral research: A correlational approach*. New York: Cambridge University Press.

Ross, S. R., Millis, S. R., Krukowski, R. A., Putnam, S. H., & Adams, K. M. (in press). Detecting incomplete effort on the MMPI–2: An examination of the Fake-Bad scale in mild head injury. *Journal of Clinical and Experimental Neuropsychology*.

Ross, S. R., Putnam, S. H., Gass, C. S., Bailey, D. E., & Adams, K. M. (2003). MMPI–2 indices of psychological disturbance and attention and memory test performance in head injury. *Archives of Clinical Neuropsychology, 18*, 905–916.

Rothke, S. E., Friedman, A. F., Jaffe, A. M., Greene, R. L., Wetter, M. W., Cole, P., & Baker, K. (2000). Normative data for the *F(p)* scale of the MMPI–2: Implications for clinical and forensic assessment of malingering. *Psychological Assessment, 12*(3), 335–340.

Rouse, S. V., & Butcher, J. N. (1995). *Annotated bibliography on the use of the MMPI/MMPI–2 in personnel and educational selection*. Minneapolis: University of Minnesota Press.

Rouse, S. V., Butcher, J. N., & Miller, K. B. (1999). Assessment of substance abuse in psychotherapy clients: The effectiveness of the MMPI–2 substance abuse scales. *Psychological Assessment, 11*(1), 101–107.

Ruchinskas, R. A., Broschek, D. K., Crews, W. D., Barth, J. T., Francis, J. P., & Robbins, M. K. (2000). A neuropsychological normative database for lung transplant candidates. *Journal of Clinical Psychology in Medical Settings, 7*(2), 107–112.

Russell, G. L., Fujino, D. C., Sue, S., & Cheung, M. (1996). The effects of therapist–client ethnic match in the assessment of mental health functioning. *Journal of Cross-Cultural Psychology, 27*(5), 598–615.

Sackeim, H. A., & Gur, R. C. (1978). Self-deception, confrontation and consciousness. In G. E. Schwartz & D. Shapiro (Eds.), *Consciousness and self-regulation: Advances in research* (pp. 139–197). New York: Plenum Press.

Safran, J. D., & Muran, J. C. (2000). *Negotiating the therapeutic alliance: A relational treatment guide*. New York: Guilford Press.

Salgado, J. F., & Moscoso, S. (2003). Internet-based personality testing: Equivalence of measures and assessors' perceptions and reactions. *International Journal of Selection and Assessment, 11*(2/3), 194–205.

Santiago-Rivera, A., Arredondo, P., & Gallardo-Cooper, M. (2002). *Counseling Latinos and la familia: A practical guide*. Thousand Oaks, CA: Sage.

Sapp, M., Farrell, W. C., Johnson, J. H., & Ioannidis, G. (1997). Utilizing the PK scale of the MMPI–2 to detect post-traumatic stress disorder in college students. *Journal of Clinical Psychology, 53*(8), 841–846.

Scheibe, S., Bagby, R. M., Miller, L. S., & Dorian, B. J. (2001). Assessing posttraumatic disorder with the MMPI–2 in a sample of workplace accident victims. *Psychological Assessment, 13*, 369–374.

Schiele, B. C., & Brozek, J. (1948). "Experimental neurosis" resulting from semistarvation in man. *Psychosomatic Medicine, 10*, 31–50.

Schiele, B. C., Baker, A. B., & Hathaway, S. R. (1943). The Minnesota Multiphasic Personality Inventory. *Lancet, 63*, 292–297.

Schill, T., & Wang, S. (1990). Correlates of the MMPI–2 Anger content scale. *Psychological Reports, 67*, 800–802.

Schlenger, W. E., & Kulka, R. A. (1989). *PTSD scale development for the MMPI–2*. Research Triangle Park, NC: Research Triangle Institute.

Schlenger, W. E., Kulka, R. A., Fairbank, J. A., Hough, R. L., Jordan, A. K., Marmer, C. R., & Weiss, D. S. (1992). The prevalence of post-traumatic stress disorder in the Vietnam generation: A multimodal, multisource assessment of psychiatric disorder. *Journal of Traumatic Stress, 5*, 333–363.

Schmaling, K. B., & Jones, J. F. (1996). MMPI profiles of patients with chronic fatigue syndrome. *Journal of Psychosomatic Research, 40*(1), 67–74.

Schneider, K. (1959). *Clinical psychopathology*. New York: Grune & Stratton.

Schnoll, S., & Weaver, M. (2003). Addiction and pain. *American Journal of Addiction, 12*(Suppl. 2), S27–S35.

Schnurr, P. P., Rosenberg, S. D., & Friedman, M. J. (1993). Change in MMPI scores from college to adulthood as a function of military service. *Journal of Abnormal Psychology, 102*, 288–296.

Schofield, W. (1953). A study of medical students with the MMPI: II. Group and individual changes after 2 years. *Journal of Psychology, 36*, 137–141.

Schretlen, D. (1988). The use of psychological tests to identify malingered symptoms of mental disorder. *Clinical Psychology Review, 8*, 451–476.

Schroeder, D. G., Hahn, E. D., Finn, S. E., & Swann, W. B., Jr. (1993, June). *Personality feedback has more impact when mildly discrepant from self views*. Paper presented at the fifth annual convention of the American Psychological Society, Chicago, IL.

Schuldberg, D. (1988). The MMPI is less sensitive to the automated testing format than it is to repeated testing: Item and scale effects. *Computers in Human Behaviors, 4*, 285–298.

Schwartz, M. F., & Graham, J. R. (1979). Construct validity of the MacAndrew Alcoholism scale. *Journal of Consulting and Clinical Psychology, 47*, 1090–1095.

Scogin, F., Schumacher, J., Gardner, J., & Chaplin, W. (1995). Predictive validity of psychological testing in law enforcement settings. *Professional Psychology: Research and Practice, 26*, 68–71.

Scotti, J. R., Sturges, L. V., & Lyons, J. A. (1996). The Keane PTSD scale extracted from the MMPI: Sensitivity and specificity with Vietnam veterans. *Journal of Traumatic Stress, 9*, 643–650.

Sechrest, L., Fay, T., & Zaida, S. (1972). Problems of translation in cross-cultural research. *Journal of Cross-Cultural Psychology, 1*, 41–56.

Selzer, M. L. (1971). The Michigan Alcoholism Screening Test: The quest for a new diagnostic instrument. *American Journal of Psychiatry, 127*, 1653–1658.

Senior, G., & Douglas, L. (2001a, October/November). *Challenging the validity of the MMPI–2 Infrequency scales*. Poster presented at the 21st Annual Conference of the National Academy of Neuropsychology, San Francisco, CA.

Senior, G., & Douglas, L. (2001b). Misconceptions and misuse of the MMPI–2 in assessing personal injury claimants. *NeuroRehabilitation, 16*, 203–213.

Sesso, H. D., Kawachi, I., Vokonas, P., & Sparrow, D. (1998). Depression and the risk of coronary heart disease in the normative aging study. *American Journal of Cardiology, 82*, 851–856.

Shaffer, J. W., Nusbaum, K., & Little, J. M. (1972). MMPI profiles of disability insurance claimants. *American Journal of Psychiatry, 129*, 403–407.

Sharpe, J. E., & Desai, S. (2001). The revised NEO Personality Inventory and the MMPI–2 Psychopathology Five in the prediction of aggression. *Personality and Individual Differences, 31*, 505–518.

Shekele, R. B., Vernon, S. W., & Ostfeld, A. M. (1991). Personality and coronary heart disease. *Psychosomatic Medicine, 53*(2), 176–184.

Sherman, R. A., Camfield, M. R., & Arena, J. G. (1995). The effect of presence or absence of low back pain on the MMPI's conversion V. *Military Psychology, 7*(1), 29–38.

Shores, E. A., & Carstairs, J. R. (1998). Accuracy of the MMPI–2 computerized Minnesota report in identifying fake-good and fake-bad response sets. *Clinical Neuropsychologist, 12*(1), 101–106.

Shusman, E. J., Inwald, R. E., & Landa, B. (1984). Correction officer job performance as predicted by the IPI and the MMPI: A validation and cross-validation study. *Criminal Justice & Behavior, 11*, 309–329.

Siegel, J. C. (1996). Traditional MMPI–2 validity indicators and initial presentation in custody evaluations. *American Journal of Forensic Psychology, 14*, 55–63.

Siegel, W. C., Hlatky, M. A., Mark, D. B., Barefoot, J. C., Harrell, F. E., Pryor, D. B., & Williams, R. B. (1990). Effect of Type A behavior on exercise test outcome in coronary artery disease. *American Journal of Cardiology, 66*(2), 179–182.

Siegel, W. C., Mark, D. B., Hlatky, M. A., Harrell, F. E., Pryor, D. B., Barefoot, J. C., & Williams, R. B. (1989). Clinical correlates and prognostic significance of Type A behavior and silent myocardial ischemia on the treadmill. *American Journal of Cardiology, 64*(19), 1280–1283.

Siegler, I. C., Costa, P. T., Brummett, B. H., Helms, M. J., Barefoot, J. C., Williams, R. B., et al. (2003). Patterns of change in hostility from college to midlife in the UNC alumni heart study predict high-risk status. *Psychosomatic Medicine, 65*, 738–745.

Siegler, I. C., Peterson, B. L., Barefoot, J. C., & Williams, R. B. (1992). Hostility during late adolescence predicts coronary risk factors at midlife. *American Journal of Epidemiology, 136*(2), 146–154.

Siegler, I. C., Zonderman, A. B., Barefoot, J. C., Williams, R. B., Costa, P. T., & McCrae, R. R. (1990). Predicting personality in adulthood from college

MMPI scores: Implications for follow-up studies in psychosomatic medicine. *Psychosomatic Medicine, 52*(6), 644–652.

Siegman, A. W., Kubzansky, L. D., Kawachi, I., Boyle, S., Vokonas, P., & Sparrow, D. (2000). A prospective study of dominance and coronary heart disease in the normative aging study. *American Journal of Cardiology, 86*, 145–149.

Sillanpaa, M. C., Agar, L. M., & Axelrod, B. N. (1999). Minnesota Multiphasic Personality Inventory—2 validity patterns: An elucidation of Gulf War syndrome. *Military Medicine, 164*(4), 261–263.

Sines, J. O. (1966). Actuarial methods in personality assessment. In B. A. Maher (Ed.), *Progress in experimental personality research* (Vol. 3, pp. 133–193). New York: Academic Press.

Sines, L. K., Baucom, D. H., & Gruba, G. H. (1979). A validity scale sign calling for caution in the interpretation of MMPIs among psychiatric inpatients. *Journal of Personality Assessment, 43*, 604–607.

Singer, H. K., Ruchinskas, R. A., Riley, K., Broschek, D. K., & Barth, J. T. (2001). The psychological impact of end-stage lung disease. *Chest, 120*, 1246–1252.

Sivec, H. J., Hilsenroth, M. J., & Lynn, S. J. (1995). Impact of simulating borderline personality disorder on the MMPI–2: A costs-benefits analysis. *Journal of Personality Assessment, 64*, 295–311.

Sivec, H. J., Lynn, S. J., & Garske, J. P. (1994). The effect of somatoform disorder and paranoid psychotic role-related dissimulations as a response set on the MMPI–2. *Assessment, 1*, 69–81.

Slesinger, D., Archer, R. P., & Duane, D. (2002). MMPI–2 characteristics in a chronic pain population. *Assessment,* 9(4), 406–414.

Sloore, H., Derksen, J., De Mey, H., & Hellenbosch, G. (1996). The Flemish/Dutch version of the MMPI–2: Development and adaptation of the inventory for Belgium and the Netherlands. In J. N. Butcher (Ed.), *International adaptations of the MMPI–2: Research and clinical application.* (pp. 329–460). Minneapolis: University of Minnesota Press.

Smith, M. B., Hoffman, N. G., & Nederhoed, R. (1995). The development and reliability of the Recovery Attitude and Treatment Evaluator—Questionnaire I (RAATE–QI). *International Journal of the Addictions, 30*, 147–160.

Sobchik, L. (1989). Psychodiagnostic criteria for managerial personnel. *Soviet Journal of Psychology, 10*, 29–35.

Sobell, L. C., & Sobell, M. B. (1990). Self-report issues in alcohol abuse: State of the art and future directions. *Behavioral Assessment, 12*, 91–106.

Soliman, A. M. (1996). Development of an Arabic translation of the MMPI–2: With clinical application. In J. N. Butcher (Ed.), *International adaptation of the MMPI–2* (pp. 463–486). Minneapolis: University of Minnesota Press.

Sommer, D., & Lasry, J. C. (1984). Personality and reactions to stressful life events. *Canada's Mental Health, 32*, 19–20.

Somwaru, D. P., & Ben-Porath, Y. S. (1995a). *Assessment of personality disorders with the MMPI–2.* Clinical workshops on the MMPI–2 and MMPI–A at the

30th Annual Symposium on Recent Developments in the Use of the MMPI, MMPI–2, and MMPI–A, St. Petersburg, FL.

Somwaru, D. P., & Ben-Porath, Y. S. (1995b, March). *Development and reliability of MMPI–2–based personality disorder scales*. Paper presented at the 30th Annual Symposium on Recent Developments in the MMPI–2 and MMPI–A, St. Petersburg Beach, FL.

Sperber, A. D., Devellis, R. F., & Boehlecke, B. (1994). Cross-cultural translation: Methodology and validation. *Journal of Cross-Cultural Psychology, 25*, 501–524.

Spielberger, C. D. (1979). *Preliminary manual for the State–Trait Personality Inventory (STPI)*. Tampa: University of South Florida.

Spitzer, R. L., Gibbon, M., Skodol, A. E., Williams, J. B. W., & First, M. B. (1994). DSM–IV *casebook: A learning companion to the* Diagnostic and Statistical Manual of Mental Disorders, Fourth Edition. Washington, DC: American Psychiatric Press.

Spitzer, R. L., Williams, J. B. W., Gibbon, M., & First, M. B. (1990). *Structured Clinical Interview for* DSM–IIIR. Washington, DC: American Psychiatric Press.

Spring, M., Westermeyer, J., Halc¢n, L., Savik, K., Jaranson, J., Robertson, C., et al. (2003). Sampling in difficult-to-access refugee and immigrant communities. *Journal of Nervous and Mental Disease, 191*(12), 813–819.

Stanovich, K. E. (2004). *How to think straight about psychology* (7th ed.). Boston: Allyn & Bacon.

Steffan, J. S., Clopton, J. R., & Morgan, R. D. (2003). An MMPI–2 scale to detect malingered depression (Md). *Assessment, 10*, 382–392.

Stein, L. A. R., Graham, J. R., Ben-Porath, Y. S., & McNulty, J. R. (1999). Using the MMPI–2 to detect substance abuse in an outpatient mental health setting. *Psychological Assessment, 11*(1), 94–100.

Stilley, C. S., Miller, D. J., Gayowski, T., & Marino, I. R. (1998). Psychological characteristics of candidates for liver transplantation. *Clinical Transplantation, 12*, 416–424.

Storm, J., & Graham, J. R. (2000). Detection of coached general malingering on the MMPI–2. *Psychological Assessment, 12*(2), 158–165.

Strassberg, D. S. (1997). A cross-national validity study of four MMPI–2 content scales. *Journal of Personality Assessment, 69*, 596–606.

Strassberg, D. S., Tilley, D., Bristone, S., & Oei, T. P. S. (1992). The MMPI and chronic pain: A cross-cultural view. *Psychological Assessment, 4*(4), 493–497.

Strauss, M. E., Brandt, J., & McSorley, P. (1986). Visual vigilance and psychopathology. *Psychiatry Research, 18*, 285–287.

Streiner, D. L. (2003). Diagnostic tests: Using and misusing diagnostic and screening tests. *Journal of Personality Assessment, 81*, 209–219.

Strong, D. R., Greene, R. L., Hoppe, C., Johnston, T., & Olesen, N. (1999). Taxometric analysis of impression management and self-deception on the MMPI–2 in child custody litigants. *Journal of Personality Assessment, 73*, 1–18.

Strong, D. R., Greene, R. L., & Kordinak, S. T. (2002). Taxometric analysis of impression management and self-deception in college student and personnel evaluation settings. *Journal of Personality Assessment, 78*, 161–175.

Strong, D. R., Greene, R. L., & Schinka, J. A. (2000). A taxometric analysis of MMPI–2 infrequency scales [*F* and *F(p)*] in clinical settings. *Psychological Assessment, 12*, 166–173.

Stukenberg, K., Brady, C., & Klinetob, N. (2000). Use of the MMPI–2's VRIN scale with severely disturbed populations: Consistent responding may be more problematic than inconsistent responding. *Psychological Reports*, 86, 3–14.

Suarez, E. C. (2003). Joint effect of hostility and severity of depressive symptoms on plasma interleukin-6 concentration. *Psychosomatic Medicine*, 65, 523–527.

Suarez, E. C., Kuhn, C. M., Schanberg, S. M., Williams, R. B., & Zimmermann, E. A. (1998). Neuroendocrine, cardiovascular, and emotional responses of hostile men: The role of interpersonal challenge. *Psychosomatic Medicine*, 60(1), 78–88.

Substance Abuse and Mental Health Services Administration (SAMHSA). (2002). *Results from the 2001 National Household Survey on Drug Abuse: Volume II. Technical appendices and selected data tables* (Office of Applied Studies, NHSDA Series H-18, DHHS Publication No. SMA 02-3759). Rockville, MD: NHSDA.

Sue, D. W., & Sue, D. (1990). *Counseling the culturally different: Theory and practice* (2nd ed.). New York: John Wiley & Sons.

Sue, S., Fujino, D. C., Hu, L., Takeuchi, D. T., & Zane, N. (1991). Community mental health services for ethnic minority groups: A test of the cultural responsiveness hypothesis. *Journal of Consulting & Clinical Psychology*, 59, 533–540.

Sue, S., Keefe, K., Enomoto, K., Durvasula, R. S., & Chao, R. (1996). Asian American and White college students' performance on the MMPI–2. In J. N. Butcher (Ed.), *International adaptations of the MMPI–2: Research and clinical applications* (pp. 206–220). Minneapolis: University of Minnesota Press.

Sundberg, N. (1954). Eine ubersettzung der Minnesota Multiphasic Personality Inventory [A translation of the MMPI]. Minneapolis: University of Minnesota Press.

Sundberg, N. D. (1985). Review of the Minnesota Multiphasic Personality Inventory. Behaviordyne Psychodiagnostic Laboratory Service. In J. V. Mitchell Jr. (Ed.), *The ninth mental measurements yearbook* (p. 1003–1005). Lincoln, NE: Buros Institute of Mental Measurements.

Sutker, P. B., & Allain, A. N. (1996). Assessment of PTSD and other mental disorders in World War II and Korean conflict POW survivors and combat veterans. *Psychological Assessment*, 8(1), 18–25.

Sutker, P. B., Allain, A. N., & Motsinger, P. A. (1988). MMPI–derived psychopathology subtypes among former prisoners of war (POWs): Replication and extension. *Journal of Psychopathology and Behavioral Assessment, 10*, 129–139.

Swartz, L. (1985). Anorexia nervosa as a culture-bound syndrome. *Social Science and Medicine, 20*, 725–730.

Sweet, J. J., Tovian, S. M., & Suchy, Y. (2002). Psychological assessment in medical settings. In J. Graham & J. Naglieri (Eds.), *Handbook of psychology: Vol. 10. Assessment psychology* (pp. 291–315). Hoboken, NJ: John Wiley & Sons.

Swenson, W. M., Rome, H. P., Pearson, J. S., & Brannick, T. L. (1965). A totally automated psychological test experience in a medical center. *Journal of the American Medical Association, 191*, 925–927.

Talbert, F. Z., Albrecht, N. N., Albrecht, J. W., Boudewyns, P. A., Hyer, L. A., Touze, J. H., & Lemmon, C. R. (1994). MMPI Profiles in PTSD as a function of comorbidity. *Journal of Clinical Psychology, 50*, 529–537.

Taylor, J. A. (1958). The effects of anxiety level and psychological stress. *Journal of Abnormal & Social Psychology, 57*, 55–60.

Tedeschi, R. G., & Calhoun, L. G. (1996). The Post-Traumatic Growth Inventory: Measuring the positive adaptation of trauma. *Journal of Traumatic Stress, 9*, 455–471.

Tedeschi, R. G., Park, C. L., & Calhoun, L. G. (Eds.). (1998). *Post-traumatic growth: Positive changes in the aftermath of crisis*. Mahwah, NJ: Lawrence Erlbaum Associates.

Tellegen, A. (1964). The Minnesota Multiphasic Personality Inventory. In L. E. Abt (Ed.), *Progress in clinical psychology* (Vol. 6, pp. 30–48). New York: Grune & Stratton.

Tellegen, A. (1982). *Brief manual for the Differential Personality Questionnaire*. Unpublished manuscript, University of Minnesota, Twin Cities Campus (Minneapolis). [Since renamed *Multidimensional Personality Questionnaire*]

Tellegen, A. (1985). Structures of mood and personality and their relevance to assessing anxiety, with an emphasis on self-report. In A. H. Tuma & J. D. Maser (Eds.), *Anxiety and the anxiety disorders* (pp. 681–706). Hillsdale, NJ: Lawrence Erlbaum Associates.

Tellegen, A., & Atkinson, G. (1974). Openness to absorbing and self-altering experiences ("absorption"), a trait related to hypnotic susceptibility. *Journal of Abnormal Psychology, 83*, 268–277.

Tellegen, A., & Ben-Porath, Y. S. (1993). Code-type comparability of the MMPI and MMPI–2: Analysis of recent findings and criticisms. *Journal of Personality Assessment, 61*, 489–500.

Tellegen, A., & Ben-Porath, Y. S. (2000). The new uniform T scores for MMPI–2: Rationale, derivation, and appraisal. In J. N. Butcher (Ed.), *Basic sources on the MMPI–2* (pp. 111–127). Minneapolis: The University of Minnesota Press.

Tellegen, A., Ben-Porath, Y. S., McNulty, J. L., Arbisi, P. A., Graham, J. R., & Kaemmer, B. (2003). *The MMPI–2 Restructured Clinical (RC) scales: Development, validation, and interpretation*. Minneapolis: University of Minnesota Press.

Tellegen, A., Butcher, J. N., & Hoegland, T. (1993). Are unisex norms for the MMPI–2 needed? Would they work? *MMPI–2 News & Profiles, 4*(1), 1–2.

Thomas-Riddle, F. (2000). The relationship between life stress, work stress, and traumatic stress and burnout and cynicism in police officers. *Dissertation Abstracts International, 60,* 9B, 4914.

Timbrook, R. E., & Graham, J. R. (1994). Ethnic differences on the MMPI–2? *Psychological Assessment, 6,* 212–217.

Timbrook, R. E., Graham, J. R., Keiller, S. W., & Watts, D. (1993). Comparison of the Weiner–Harmon subtle–obvious scales and the standard validity scales in detecting valid and invalid MMPI–2 profiles. *Psychological Assessment, 5,* 53–61.

Torki, M. A. (2000). Ego strength and stress reaction in Kuwaiti students after the Iraqi invasion. *Psychological Reports, 87,* 188–192.

Tran, B. N. (1996). Vietnamese translation and adaptation of the MMPI–2. In J. N. Butcher (Ed.), *International adaptation of the MMPI–2* (pp. 175–193). Minneapolis: University of Minnesota Press.

Triandis, H. C. (1994). *Culture and social behavior.* New York: McGraw-Hill.

Trull, T. J. (1991). Discriminant validity of the MMPI borderline personality disorder scale. *Psychological Assessment, 3,* 323–238.

Trull, T. J., Useda, J. D., Costa, P. T., & McCrae, R. R. (1995). Comparison of the MMPI–2 Personality Psychopathology Five (PSY–5), the NEO–PI, and NEO–PI–R. *Psychological Assessment, 7,* 508–516.

Trunzo, J. J., Petrucci, R. J., Carter, A., & Donofrio, N. (1999). Use of the MMPI and MMPI–2 in patients being evaluated for cardiac transplant. *Psychological Reports, 85,* 1105–1110.

Tsushima, W. T., & Tsushima, V. G. (2001). Comparison of the Fake Bad Scale and other MMPI–2 validity scales with personal injury litigants. *Assessment, 8,* 205–212.

Tucker, L. R. (1951). *A method for synthesis of factor analysis studies* (Personal Research Section Report No. 984). Washington, DC: Department of the U.S. Army.

U.S. Bureau of the Census. (1992). *Population projections of the United States, by age, sex, race, and Hispanic origin: 1992 to 2050* (Current Population Reports, pp. 25–1092). Washington, DC: U.S. Government Printing Office.

Ursano, R. J., Bell, C., Spencer, E., Friedman, M., Norwood, A., Pfefferbaum, B., et al. (2004). Practice guidelines for the treatment of patients with acute stress disorder and post-traumatic stress disorder. *American Journal of Psychiatry, 161*(Suppl.), 4–23.

Vale, C. D., & Keller, L. S. (1987). Developing expert computer systems to interpret psychological tests. In J. N. Butcher (Ed.), *Computerized psychological assessment: A practitioner's guide* (pp. 64–83). New York: Basic Books.

Van der Kolk, B., Pelcovitz, D., Roth, S., Mandel, F., McFarlane, A., & Herman, J. (1996). Dissociation, somatization, and affect dysregulation: The complexity of adaptation to trauma. *American Journal of Psychiatry, 153*(Suppl. 7), 83–93.

Van Valkenburg, C., Lowry, M., Winokur, G., & Cadoret, R. (1977). Depression spectrum disease versus pure depressive disease. *Journal of Nervous & Mental Disease, 165*, 341–347.

VandenBos, G. R., & Williams, S. (2000). The Internet versus the telephone: What is telehealth anyway? *Professional Psychology: Research and Practice, 31*, 480–492.

Vanderploeg, R. D., Sison, G. F. P., & Hickling, E. J. (1987). A reevaluation of the use of the MMPI in the assessment of combat-related PTSD. *Journal of Personality Assessment, 51*, 140–150.

Vega, W. A. (1995). The study of Latino families: A point of departure. In R. E. Zambrana (Ed.), *Understanding Latino families: Scholarship, policy, and practice* (pp. 3–17). Thousand Oaks, CA: Sage.

Velasquez, R. J., Ayala, G. X., & Mendoza, S. A. (1998). *Psychodiagnostic assessment of U.S. Latinos: MMPI, MMPI–2, and MMPI–A results*. East Lansing, MI: Julian Samora Research Institute.

Velasquez, R. J., Ayala, G. X., Mendoza, S., Nezami, E., Castillo-Canez, I., Pace, T., et al. (2000). Culturally competent use of the Minnesota Multiphasic Personality Inventory–2. In I. Cuellar & F. Paniagua (Eds.), *Handbook of multicultural mental health: Assessment and treatment of diverse populations*. San Diego, CA: Academic Press.

Velasquez, R. J., & Burton, M. P. (2004). Psychotherapy of Chicano men. In R. J. Velasquez, L. M. Arellano, & B. W. McNeill (Eds.), *The handbook of Chicano/a psychology and mental health* (pp. 177–192). Mahwah, NJ: Lawrence Erlbaum Associates.

Velasquez, R. J., & Callahan, W. J. (1992). Psychological testing of Hispanic Americans in clinical settings: Overview and issues. In K. F. Geisinger (Ed.), *Psychological testing of Hispanics* (pp. 253–266). Washington, DC: American Psychological Association.

Velasquez, R. J., Chavira, D. A., Karle, H. R., Callahan, W. J., Garcia, J. A., & Castellanos, J. (2000). Assessing bilingual and monolingual Latino students with translations of the MMPI–2: Initial data. *Cultural Diversity and Ethnic Minority Psychology*, 6, 65–72.

Velasquez, R. J., Garrido, M., Castellanos, J., & Burton, M. P. (2004). Culturally competent assessment of Chicana/os with the Minnesota Multiphasic Personality Inventory—2. In R. J. Velasquez, L. M. Arellano, & B. W. McNeill (Eds.), *The handbook of Chicana/o psychology and mental health* (pp. 153–174). Mahwah, NJ: Lawrence Erlbaum Associates.

Velasquez, R. J., Gonzales, M., Butcher, J. N., Castillo-Canez, I., Apodaca J. X., & Chavira, D. (1997). Use of the MMPI–2 with Chicanos: Strategies for counselors. *Journal of Multicultural Counseling and Development, 25*, 107–120.

Velasquez, R., Maness, P. J., & Anderson, U. (2002). Culturally competent assessment of Latino clients. In J. N. Butcher (Ed.), *Clinical personality assessment* (2nd ed., pp. 154–170). New York: Oxford University Press.

Vendrig, A. A. (1999). Prognostic factors and treatment-related changes associated with return to work in the multimodal treatment of chronic back pain. *Journal of Behavioral Medicine, 22*(3), 217–232.

Vendrig, A. A. (2000). The Minnesota Multiphasic Personality Inventory and chronic pain: A conceptual analysis of a long-standing but complicated relationship. *Clinical Psychology Review, 20*(5), 533–559.

Vendrig, A. A., Derksen, J. J. L., & De Mey, H. R. (2000). MMPI–2 Personality Psychopathology Five (PSY–5) and prediction of treatment outcome for patients with chronic back pain. *Journal of Personality Assessment, 74*(30), 423–438.

Viglione, D. J., Wright, D. M., Dixon, N. T., Moynihan, J. E., DuPuis, S., & Pizitz, T. D. (2001). Evading detection on the MMPI–2: Does caution produce more realistic patterns of responding? *Assessment, 8*(3), 237–250.

Walkey, F. H., & Green, D. E. (1990). The factor structure of the Eysenck Personality Inventory revealed in the responses of Australian and New Zealand subjects. *Personality and Individual Differences, 11*, 571–576.

Wallace, P. (1999). *The psychology of the Internet*. Cambridge, England: Cambridge University Press.

Waller, N. G., & Reise, S. P. (1989). Computerized adaptive personality assessment: An illustration with the Absorption scale. *Journal of Personality and Social Psychology, 57*, 1051–1058.

Walters, G. D. (1988). Schizophrenia. In R. L. Greene (Ed.), *The MMPI: Use in specific populations* (pp. 50–73). Orlando, FL: Grune & Stratton.

Walters, G. L., & Clopton, J. R. (2000). Effect of symptom information and validity scale information on the malingering of depression on the MMPI–2. *Journal of Personality Assessment, 75*, 183–199.

Watkins, D. (1989). The role of confirmatory factor analysis in cross-cultural research. *Journal of Psychology, 24*, 685–701.

Watkins, M. W., & McDermott, P. A. (1991). Psychodiagnostic computing: From interpretive programs to expert systems. In T. R. Gutkin & S. L. Wise (Eds.), *The computer and the decision-making process* (pp. 11–42). Hillsdale, NJ: Lawrence Erlbaum Associates.

Watson, C. G., Juba, M., Anderson, P. E., & Manifold, V. (1990). What does the Keane et al. PTSD scale for the MMPI measure? *Journal of Clinical Psychology, 46*, 600–606.

Watson, D., & Clark, L. A. (1984). Negative affectivity: The disposition to experience aversive emotional states. *Psychological Bulletin, 96*, 465–490.

Watson, D., & Clark, L. A. (1993). Behavioral disinhibition versus constraint: A dispositional perspective. In D. M. Wegner & J. W. Pennebaker (Eds.), *Handbook of mental control* (pp. 506–527). New York: Prentice Hall.

Watson, D., & Clark, L. A. (1997). Extraversion and its positive emotional core. In R. Hogan, J. Johnson, & S. Briggs (Eds.), *Handbook of personality psychology* (pp. 767–793). San Diego, CA: Academic Press.

Watson, D., Clark, L. A., & Tellegen, A. (1984). Cross-cultural convergence in the structure of mood: A Japanese replication and a comparison with U.S. findings. *Journal of Personality and Social Psychology, 47,* 127–144.

Weathers, F. W., & Keane, T. M. (1999). Psychological assessment of traumatized adults. In P. A. Saigh & J. D. Bremer (Eds.), *Post-traumatic stress disorder: A comprehensive review* (pp. 219–247). Boston: Allyn & Bacon.

Webster, C. D., Douglas, K. S., Eaves, D., & Hart, S. D. (1997). *HCR–20: Assessing risk for violence* (Version 2). Vancouver, BC: Mental Health, Law, and Policy Institute, Simon Fraser University.

Weed, N. C. (1993). An evaluation of the efficacy of MMPI–2 indicators of validity. *Dissertation Abstracts International, 53,* 3800.

Weed, N. C., Butcher, J. N., & Ben-Porath, Y. S. (1995). MMPI–2 measures of substance abuse. In J. N. Butcher & C. D. Spielberger (Eds.), *Advances in personality assessment* (Vol. 10, pp. 121–145). Hillsdale, NJ: Lawrence Erlbaum Associates.

Weed, N. C., Butcher, J. N., McKenna, T., & Ben-Porath, Y. S. (1992). New measures for assessing alcohol and drug abuse with the MMPI–2: The APS and AAS. *Journal of Personality Assessment, 58,* 389–404.

Weiss, D. J. (1985). Adaptive testing by computer. *Journal of Consulting and Clinical Psychology, 53,* 774–789.

Weiss, D. J., & Suhdolnik, D. (1985). Robustness of adaptive testing to multidimensionality. In D. J. Weiss (Ed.), *Proceedings of the 1982 Item Response Theory and Computerized Adaptive Testing Conference* (pp. 248–280). Minneapolis: University of Minnesota, Department of Psychology, Computerized Adaptive Testing Laboratory.

Weiss, D. J., & Vale, C. D. (1987). Computerized adaptive testing for measuring ability and other psychological variables. In J. N. Butcher (Ed.), *Computerized psychological assessment* (pp. 325–343). New York: Basic Books.

Weiss, D., & Yoes, M. (1990). Item response theory (chap. 3). In R. Hambleton & J. Zaal (Eds.), *Advances in educational and psychological testing: Theory and applications*. Boston: Kluwer Academic Publishers.

Welburn, K. R., Fraser, G. A., Jordan, S. A., Cameron, C., Webb, L. M., & Raine, D. (2003). Discriminating dissociative identity disorder from schizophrenia and feigned dissociation on psychological tests and structured interview. *Journal of Trauma & Dissociation, 4,* 109–130.

Werner, O., & Campbell, D. (1970). Translating, working through interpreters, and the problem of decentering. In R. Naroll & R. Cohen (Eds.), *A handbook of methods in cultural anthropology*. New York: American Museum of Natural History.

Wetter, M. W., Baer, R. A., Berry, D. T. R., Smith, G. T., & Larsen, L. H. (1992). Sensitivity of MMPI validity scales to random responding and malingering. *Psychological Assessment, 4,* 369–374.

Wetter, M. W., Baer, R. A., Berry, D. T., Robinson, L. H., & Sumpter, J. (1993). MMPI–2 profiles of motivated fakers given specific symptom information: A comparison to matched patients. *Psychological Assessment, 5,* 313–323.

Wetter, M., Baer, R., Berry, D., & Reynolds, S. (1994). The effect of symptom information on faking on the MMPI–2. *Assessment, 1*, 199–207.

Wetter, M. W., & Corrigan, S. K. (1995). Providing information to clients about psychological tests: A survey of attorneys' and law students' attitudes. *Professional Psychology: Research and Practice, 26*, 1–4.

Wetter, M. W., & Deitsch, S. E. (1996). Faking specific disorders and temporal response consistency on the MMPI–2. *Psychological Assessment, 8*, 39–47.

Wetzel, R. D., Guze, S. B., Cloninger, C. L., Martin, R. L., & Clayton, P. J. (1994). Briquet's syndrome (hysteria) is both a somatoform and a "psychoform" illness: A Minnesota Multiphasic Personality Inventory study. *Psychosomatic Medicine, 56*(6), 564–569.

Weyermann, A. G., Norris, F. H., & Hyer, L. A. (1996). Examining comorbidity and post-traumatic stress disorder in a Vietnam veteran population using the MMPI–2. *Journal of Traumatic Stress, 9*(2), 353–360.

Whitworth, R. H., & McBlaine, D. D. (1993). Comparison of the MMPI and MMPI–2 administered to Anglo- and Hispanic-American university students. *Journal of Personality Assessment, 61*(1), 19–27.

Wiener, D. N. (1948). Subtle and obvious keys for the MMPI. *Journal of Consulting Psychology, 11*, 104–106.

Wiggins, J. S. (1959). Interrelationships among the MMPI measures of dissimulation under standard and social desirability instructions. *Journal of Consulting Psychology, 23*, 419–427.

Wiggins, J. S. (1964). Convergences among stylistic response measures from objective personality tests. *Educational and Psychological Measurement, 24*, 551–562.

Wiggins, J. S. (1966). Substantive dimensions of self-report in the MMPI item pool. *Psychological Monographs, 80* (Whole No. 630).

Wiggins, J. S. (1969). Content dimensions in the MMPI. In J. N. Butcher (Ed.), *MMPI: Research developments and clinical applications* (pp. 127–180). New York: McGraw-Hill.

Wilkinson, L., & The Task Force on Statistical Inference. (1999). Statistical methods in psychology journals: Guidelines and explanations. *American Psychologist, 54*, 594–604.

Williams, C. L. (1980a). A comparison of a behavioral role play and an Empirical Self-Report Inventory in assessing social behavior. *Dissertation Abstracts International, 40*, 3429.

Williams, C. L. (1980b). Type A behavior, hostility, and coronary atherosclerosis. *Psychosomatic Medicine, 42*, 539–549.

Williams, J. E., & Weed, N. C. (2004). Relative user ratings of MMPI–2 computer-based test interpretations. *Assessment, 11*, 316–329.

Williams, R. B., Jr., Barefoot, J. C., Haney, T. L., Harrell, F. E., Blumentahl, J. A., Pryor, D. B., & Peterson, B. (1988). Type A behavior and angiographically documented coronary artherosclerosis in a sample of 2,289 patients. *Psychosomatic Medicine, 50*(2), 139–152.

Williams, R. B., Jr., Haney, T. L., Lee, K. L., Kong, Y. H., Blumenthal, J. A., & Whalen, R. E. (1980). Type A behavior, hostility, and coronary artherosclerosis. *Psychosomatic Medicine, 42*, 539–549.

Williamson, E. G., & Hoyt, D. (1952). Measured personality characteristics of student leaders. *Educational & Psychological Measurement, 12*, 65–78.

Wilson, J. P., & Keane, T. M. (Eds.). (1997). *Assessing psychological trauma and PTSD*. New York: Guilford Press.

Wilson, J. W., & Walker, A. J. (1990). Toward an MMPI trauma profile. *Journal of Traumatic Stress, 3*, 151–167.

Wingard, D. L., & Berkman, L. F. (1983). Mortality risk associated with sleeping patterns among adults. *Sleep, 6*, 102–107.

Wink, P., & Donahue, K. (1997). The relation between two types of narcissism and boredom. *Journal of Research in Personality, 31*, 136–140.

Winokur, G. (1979a). Familial (genetic) subtypes of pure depressive disease. *American Journal of Psychiatry, 136*, 911–913.

Winokur, G. (1979b). Unipolar depression: Is it divisible into autonomous subtypes? *Archives of General Psychiatry, 36*, 47–52.

Winokur, G., Behar, D., Van Valkenburg, C., & Lowry, M. (1978). Is a familial definition of depression both feasible and valid? *Journal of Nervous & Mental Disease, 166*, 764–768.

Winokur, G., & Coryell, W. (1992). Familial subtypes of unipolar depression: A prospective study of familial pure depressive disease compared to depression spectrum disease. *Biological Psychiatry, 32*, 1012–1018.

Wise, E. A. (1996). Diagnosing post-traumatic stress disorder with the MMPI clinical scales: A review of the literature. *Journal of Psychopathology and Behavioral Assessment, 18*, 71–81.

Woessner, R., & Caplan, B. (1995). Affective disorders following mild to moderate brain injury: Interpretive hazards of the SCL–90–R. *Journal of Head Trauma Rehabilitation, 10*, 78–89.

Woessner, R., & Caplan, B. (1996). Emotional distress following stroke: Interpretive limitations of the SCL–90–R. *Assessment, 3*, 291–306.

Wong, J. L., Lerner-Poppen, L., & Durham, J. (1998). Does warning reduce obvious malingering on memory and motor tasks in college samples? *International Journal of Rehabilitation and Health, 4*, 153–165.

Woodworth, R. W. (1920). *The personal data sheet*. Chicago: Stoelting.

Wooten, A. J. (1983). MMPI profiles among neuropsychology patients. *Journal of Clinical Psychology, 39*, 392–406.

Wooten, A. J. (1984). Effectiveness of the K correction in the detection of psychopathology and its impact on profile height and configuration among young adult men. *Journal of Consulting and Clinical Psychology, 52*, 468–473.

World Health Organization (WHO). (1973). *The international pilot study of schizophrenia*. Geneva, Switzerland: Author.

Yamaguchi, S., Kuhlman, D. M., & Sugimori, S. (1995). Personality correlates of allocentric tendencies in individualist and collectivist cultures (Special section: Culture and self). *Journal of Cross-Cultural Psychology*, *26*(6), 658–672.

Yan, L. L., Liu, K., Matthews, K. A., Daviglus, M. L., Ferguson, T. F., & Kiefe, C. I. (2003). Psychosocial factors and risk of hypertension: The coronary artery risk development in young adults (CARDIA) study. *Journal of the American Medical Association*, *290*(16), 2138–2148.

Young, A. (1995). *The harmony of illusions: Inventing post-traumatic stress disorder*. Princeton, NJ: Princeton University Press.

Youngjohn, J. R. (1995). Confirmed attorney coaching prior to neuropsychological evaluation. *Assessment*, *2*, 279–283.

Youngjohn, J. R., Burrows, L., & Erdal, K. (1995). Brain damage or compensation neurosis? The controversial post-concussive syndrome. *Clinical Neuropsychologist*, *9*, 595–598.

Youngjohn, J. R., Davis, D., & Wolf, L. (1997). Head injury and the MMPI–2: Paradoxical effects and the influence of litigation. *Psychological Assessment*, *9*, 177–184.

Youngjohn, J. R., Lees-Haley, P. R., & Binder, L. M. (1999). Comment: Warning malingerers produces more sophisticated malingering. *Archives of Clinical Neuropsychology*, *14*, 511–515.

Zeigler, D. K., & Paolo, A. M. (1995). Headache symptoms and psychological profile of headache-prone individuals: A comparison of clinic patients and controls. *Archives of Neurology*, *52*, 602–606.

Zeigler, D. K., & Paolo, A. M. (1996). Self-reported disability due to headache: A comparison of clinic patients and controls. *Headache*, *36*, 476–480.

Zickar, M. J., Rosse, J. G., Levin, R. A., & Hulin, C. L. (1997). *Modeling the effects of faking on personality instruments*. Manuscript submitted for publication.

Zillmer, E. A., & Perry, W. (1996). Cognitive-neuropsychological abilities and related psychological disturbance: A factor model of neuropsychological, Rorschach, and MMPI indices. *Assessment*, *3*, 209–224.

Zuckerman, M. (1972). What is the sensation seeker? Personality trait and experience correlates of the Sensation-Seeking scales. *Journal of Consulting and Clinical Psychology*, *39*, 308–321.

Zuckerman, M. (1994). *Behavioral expressions and biosocial bases of sensation seeking*. New York: Cambridge University Press.

Zuckerman, M., & Link, K. (1968). Construct validity for the Sensation-Seeking scale. *Journal of Consulting & Clinical Psychology*, *32*, 420–426.

INDEX

ABOUT THE EDITOR

James N. Butcher, PhD, was born in West Virginia. He enlisted in the Army when he was 17 years old and served in the airborne infantry for 3 years, including a 1-year tour in Korea during the Korean War. After military service, he attended Guilford College, graduating in 1960 with a BA in psychology. He received an MA in experimental psychology in 1962 and a PhD in clinical psychology from the University of North Carolina at Chapel Hill. He was awarded Doctor Honoris Causa from the Free University of Brussels, Belgium, in 1990. In 2005, he was also awarded an honorary doctorate (Laurea Honoris Causa in Psicologia) from the University of Florence, Italy.

He is currently professor emeritus of psychology in the Department of Psychology at the University of Minnesota and was associate director and director of the clinical psychology program at the university for 19 years. He was a member of the University of Minnesota Press's MMPI Consultative Committee, which undertook the revision of the MMPI in 1989. He was formerly the editor of *Psychological Assessment*, a journal of the American Psychological Association (APA), and serves as consulting editor or reviewer for numerous other journals in psychology and psychiatry. Throughout most of his career, he maintained a private clinical practice specializing in psychological assessment and psychotherapy.

In 1969, he was a cofounder of a free clinic in Minneapolis (The Walk-In-Counseling Center) that provided free brief psychological treatment to persons seeking help. Dr. Butcher has also been actively involved in developing and organizing disaster response programs for dealing with human problems following airline disasters. He organized a model crisis intervention disaster response for the Minneapolis–St. Paul Airport and organized and supervised the psychological services offered following two major airline disasters: Northwest Flight 255 in Detroit, Michigan, and Aloha Airlines on Maui. He is a fellow of the American Psychological Association and the Society for Personality Assessment. He has published more than 50 books and more than 175 articles in the fields of abnormal psychology, cross-cultural psychology, and personality assessment.